The Psychoanalytic Study
of the Child

VOLUME XXIV

The Psychoanalytic Study

of the Child

VOLUME XXIV

INTERNATIONAL UNIVERSITIES PRESS, INC.
New York   New York

Manufactured in the United States of America

CONTENTS

Contributions to Psychoanalytic Theory

Aspects of Normal and Pathological Development

Clinical Contributions

Applications of Analysis

CONTRIBUTIONS TO PSYCHOANALYTIC THEORY

LIBIDINAL OBJECT CONSTANCY AND MENTAL REPRESENTATION

SELMA FRAIBERG (Ann Arbor, Michigan)

This essay attempts to examine the concept of "object constancy" in psychoanalytic usage, as a term that embraces libidinal and cognitive aspects of human attachment in infancy. Our literature shows considerable range and variations in usage of the term "object constancy," which reflect its mixed origins in general psychology and psychoanalysis, and semantic changes in the word "constancy" as it came into the literature of psychoanalysis. In this essay, I shall take up these aspects of the problem:

1. Historical roots of the term "object constancy" in psychoanalysis and general psychology;

2. Variations in usage, definitions, and criteria for the attainment of libidinal object constancy as derived from the psychoanalytic literature;

3. Mental representation and object constancy;

4. The problem of infantile hallucinatory experience as postulated in psychoanalysis and an attempt to infer from existing models of cognitive development the possible links between the negative hallucination and objective tests of the capacity to evoke the image of an object that is not present in reality;

Supported by National Institutes of Child Health & Development, Grant #HD-01-444-02.

Professor of Child Psychoanalysis, Department of Psychiatry, University of Michigan Medical School, Ann Arbor, Michigan.

An early draft of this paper was presented to Dr. Humberto Nagera's Psychoanalytic Concepts Seminar. I am deeply indebted to Dr. Nagera and to seminar colleagues for a close examination of the problems, for lively argument, and for expertise in a number of areas related to this topic. I wish to express my appreciation to Morton Chethik for assistance in surveying the literature, to Edna Adelson and Martin Mayman for reading and criticizing the revised version.

5. A proposal for a definition of mental representation which is consistent with the objective findings of genetic psychology and the inferences from the dream work derived from psychoanalytic study.

Historical Roots of the Term Object Constancy in Psychoanalysis and General Psychology

The term "object constancy" was first used in psychoanalytic literature by Heinz Hartmann (1952), who referred to it in this context:

Also there is a long way from the object that exists only as long as it is need satisfying to that form of satisfactory object relations that includes object constancy. . . . This constancy probably presupposes on the side of the ego a certain degree of neutralization of aggressive as well as libidinal energy . . . ; and on the other hand it might well be that it promotes neutralization [p. 163].

In his 1953 essay on the metapsychology of schizophrenia, Hartmann links his use of the term "constancy" to Piaget's "object concept":

Here I want to say a few words about another aspect of the separation of self and object, which also is a step toward the *constancy* of the latter. First the infant does not distinguish between the objects and his activities vis-à-vis the objects. In the words of Piaget (1937), the object is still nothing but a prolongation of the child's activity. Later, in the course of those processes that lead to a distinction of object and self, the child also learns to make a distinction between his activity and the object toward which this activity is directed. The earlier stage may be correlated with magic action and probably represents a transitory step in ego (or, rather, pre-ego) development, interposed between simple discharge and true ego-directed and organized action. The later stage represents one aspect of "objectivation" which is an ego contribution to the development of object relations and an essential element in the institution of the reality principle. Piaget's finding agrees rather well with the findings of analysis, and it means, metapsychologically speaking, that from then on there is a difference between the cathexis of an object-directed ego function and the cathexis of an object representation [p. 187f.; my italics].

In the 1956 essay on the reality principle, Hartmann says,

> Both the development of ego functions and the *constitution of constant objects* represent a moving away from what Freud calls primary narcissism, and are closely interrelated. . . . In contact and communication with the object, the child learns to demarcate his "self" and to realize the first vestiges of objectivity [p. 255; my italics].

From these references it appears that the introduction of the term "object constancy" was linked originally with Piaget's object concept and, while the dimension of "human object relations" was brought in from the psychoanalytic side, Hartmann was clearly seeking a formulation that would embrace both the cathexis of the human object and the constitution of its objectivity.

Yet, the term "constancy" is not Piaget's in designating the achievement of "objectivity." Piaget (1937) employs the term "permanence" for the achievement of an object concept (Stage VI in sensorimotor development, sixteen to eighteen months) and refers to "constancy" as an attribute of permanence; thus constancy is not identical with permanence. The term "constancy," however, appears in general psychological usage, and Hartmann, who was of course familiar with the term, employed it consistently in a number of his writings in contexts that clearly showed its reference to psychological usage. (In a letter to me, Hartmann, replying to my questions, attributes one source of this term to general psychology.)

In general psychology, "constancy" is employed with the specific meaning of an object that "preserves its essential character despite variations introduced into the situation surrounding it" (Werner, 1957, p. 108). "Constancy," then, refers to the stable, "objective," permanent attributes of things, which implies autonomy from the subject and his perception or his actions. Until this level of conceptual development is achieved by the infant the psychoanalyst is in agreement with Werner that we can only speak of "things of action," phenomena which are experienced by the infant as a consequence of his actions or attitudes.

Hartmann's introduction of the term "object constancy" appeared in a paper presented at the Symposium on "The Mutual Influences in the Development of Ego and Id," to which Anna Freud and Willie Hoffer also made far-reaching contributions. If we examine their papers along with Hartmann's essay, we can see the central tendencies in psychoanalytic thought that led to a later elaboration of the concept "object constancy" in psychoanalytic literature.

Hoffer (1952) differentiates two major phases in the first year of life, the first corresponding to the period of primary narcissism in which the relations with the mother are governed by body needs and their satisfaction and the mother is indistinguishable from the infant's own body. The transition to "the psychological object" (Hoffer's term) is seen by him as "a drawing away of cathexis" from the body to the mother as the consequence of her ministrations to need, a shift, then, from narcissistic libido to object libido.

Anna Freud (1952), working within the same framework as Hoffer—from the need-satisfying object to the psychological object —offered the hypothesis that the step from the first stage to the second stage is determined by a decrease in the drives themselves. She says:

> While the infant is under the full impact of his needs—in terms of mental functioning; completely dominated by the pleasure principle—he demands from the object one thing only, that is immediate satisfaction. An object which fails to fulfill this purpose at a given moment cannot be maintained as such and is exchanged for a more satisfying one. The needs have to lessen in strength, or have to be brought under ego control, before nonsatisfying (for instance, absent) objects can retain their cathexis. . . .
>
> [She cites her own observations:] In the earliest months of life it seems possible to exchange the object, provided the form of need satisfaction given to the infant remains unaltered. Later (appr. after five months) the personal attachment to the object increases in importance; it becomes possible then to vary the satisfactions, provided the object remains the same. At that stage (appr. five to twenty-four months) separation from the object causes extreme distress, but the infant is so exclusively dominated by his needs that he cannot maintain his attachment to a nonsatisfying object for more than a given period (varying from several hours to several days). After this interval, which is most upsetting for the child, need satisfaction is accepted from and attachment (cathexis) is transferred to a substitute. As the ego

matures and the pleasure principle yields to the reality principle, children gradually develop the ability to retain libidinal cathexis to absent love objects during separations of increasing lengths [p. 44f.].

We should note that while the Amsterdam symposium gave birth to the concept of libidinal object constancy, the term "constancy" was not yet used by Anna Freud or Willie Hoffer to represent the establishment of the libidinal tie to the mother.

Anna Freud uses the term "object constancy" for the first time, I believe, in 1960 in her discussion of John Bowlby's paper, "Grief and Mourning in Infancy and Early Childhood." The term appears in this context:

> Any assessment of the eventual pathological consequences of a separation trauma is inseparable, in our belief, from the assessment of the level of libido development at the time of its occurrence. Results vary according to the fact whether at the moment of separation the tie to the mother was still of a narcissistic nature, dominated by the search for instinctual satisfactions; or whether in the relationship to the mother the personal and affectionate elements had begun to predominate, transforming the attachment into object love; or whether the child had attained *the level of so-called object constancy. In this last instance the image of a cathected person can be maintained internally* for longer periods of time, irrespective of the real object's presence or absence in the external world, and much internal effort will be needed before the libido is withdrawn. Such withdrawal happens gradually by means of the painful disengagement process known to us as mourning [p. 61f.; my italics].

In this and a number of later essays, Anna Freud employs the term "object constancy" to represent the libidinal attachment to the mother, but she does not use the word "constancy" in its cognitive sense. She is explicit in her statement at the Panel Discussion (1968).

> It is evidently a concept which has caused a good deal of confusion recently in analytic thinking, introduced by people who approached it not from the analytical but from the psychological side. They define object constancy as the child's capacity to keep an inner image of the object in the absence of the object in the external world. I have never used the concept in that sense and in our Clinic some people have followed my example.

What we mean by object constancy is the child's capacity to keep up object cathexis irrespective of frustration or satisfaction. At the time before object constancy the child withdraws cathexis from the unsatisfactory or unsatisfying object. Also in times when no need or libidinal wish is present in the child, the object is considered as non-existent, unnecessary. The turning towards the object takes place again when the wish or need arises. After object constancy has been established the person representing the objects keeps this place for the child whether he satisfies or frustrates. If you use the concept this way it is related closely to the overcoming of what we call the need-satisfying phase. The need-satisfying phase is pre-object constancy; when it has been passed and the next step has been taken, object constancy comes into being. The object keeps its place. That is at least how I use it; other people may use it differently [p. 506].

Anna Freud's use of the term "constancy" connotes stability of the object cathexis in infancy and is in her view not related to "constancy" in general psychology. In Anna Freud's words, "the object keeps its place," has relative autonomy from the fluctuations of need states, in which case "constancy" means stability of the libidinal cathexis to mother and not stability of the object *qua* object in general psychological usage.

At the same Panel Discussion (1968), David Beres raised the question as to whether object cathexis on this level (libidinal object constancy) did not presuppose the existence of mental representation of the mother. I shall return to this very interesting discussion later, since it has bearing upon the relationship of "libidinal object constancy" and "object constancy" in general psychology.

VARIATIONS IN USAGE, DEFINITIONS, AND CRITERIA

As the term "object constancy" came into general usage among psychoanalysts, some writers retained its original meaning in general psychology; with others it acquired a meaning specific for psychoanalysis, that is, the establishment of the libidinal tie to the mother.

In context, among a number of psychoanalytic references, the term "constancy" is often used in its familiar, colloquial sense without reference to psychological constancy.

. . . the establishment of lasting emotional relations with the mother, i.e., of object constancy . . . [Jacobson, 1964, p. 63].

. . . institutions need not be pathogenic if object constancy is safeguarded in the ratio and schedules of nurses . . . [Alpert, 1965, p. 166].

. . . a mothering person who could give the child an unwavering sense of object constancy . . . [Alpert, 1965, p. 275].

Here usage closely follows one of the dictionary definitions of "constancy": "Steadfastness of attachment to a person or cause; faithfulness, fidelity" (Oxford English Dictionary). In this context, "constancy" is a qualitative term connoting a durable, permanent attachment. Since constancy in its colloquial sense exactly describes the qualitative aspect of the infant's tie to the mother, the formation of the permanent love bond, it has gained some currency in psychoanalytic usage in this sense without any of its connotations in general psychology. It is, of course, perfectly valid for us to employ "constancy" in the sense of "steadfastness of attachment"—but the term has been pre-empted by general psychology. This is where the semantic differences arise.

To augment the semantic problem, some writers do introduce into the concept of libidinal object constancy (i.e., the "steadfastness of attachment") a "quality of being invariable" which has specific psychoanalytic connotations, yet is relative to psychological "constancy." The libidinal cathexis of mother, which remains stable regardless of fluctuations in need states or externally imposed frustrations, has the quality of being invariable; this presupposes a mother who retains her identity for the child regardless of variations in satisfaction or nonsatisfaction.

The factor of "invariability" is also introduced in the psychoanalytic concept of love object constancy by those writers who link the libidinal bond to mother with mental representation. The following sample is taken from John Frosch (1966):

. . . consistency in the behavior of the primary love object is necessary; it facilitates the formation of an object representation which can remain constant in time and space and consistent with itself in spite of subsequent alterations and changes in the object relations of the developing individual (Spitz and Wolf, 1949, p. 110). When these features characterize object representation, we have object constancy. Its establishment facilitates the tolerance of temporary separation from the love object as well as the ability to tolerate ambivalence toward the love object [p. 350].

Frosch specifically states that the psychoanalytic concept of object constancy "is not to be confused with the concept of the 'stable object' in academic psychology." This presents a puzzle to my mind, since Frosch's phrasing "an object representation which can remain constant in time and space" exactly defines "constancy" for Werner and Piaget. It is not inconsistent with psychoanalytic theory that the drive "object" can also be an "object" in the psychological sense, that is, "have objectivity" and autonomy from the subject's perception. This is apparently what Hartmann had in mind when he first introduced the term object constancy from general psychology and was seeking correlates in cognition for the libidinal investment of mother.

René Spitz makes his most explicit statement regarding the drive and conceptual attributes of "object constancy" in "Metapsychology and Infant Observation" (1966):

> These developments [referring to gratification and learning] combine with the growing memory, while apperception of mnemonic traces becomes more and more efficient. Both are instrumental in helping the baby to achieve a stable, consistent memory image of his mother. Hartmann (1952) refers to this as the establishment of object constancy.
> Up to this point, one and the same person, the mother, was alternatively a good or a bad object. She became a bad object when she refused to gratify the desire of the baby, for this refusal triggered his aggressive drive; when shortly thereafter she gratified his wish, or rather his need, she became the good mother, toward whom libidinal drives were directed [p. 137].

Spitz then links "object constancy" with "a stable, consistent memory image" (i.e., mental representation) of the mother. The achievement of mental representation is seen both in terms of drive organization (fusion of libidinal and aggressive drives) and cathexis of the memory image of the mother. The identity of mother is established through unification of "good" and "bad" memory traces.

Spitz places the establishment of object constancy at eight months, using the criterion of stranger anxiety (1957).

The eight-months anxiety is a much simpler performance; the sequence is as follows. The child produces first a scanning behavior, namely the seeking for the lost love object, the mother. A decision is now made by the function of judgment "whether something which is present in the ego as an image, can also be re-discovered in perception" (Freud, 1925). The realization that it cannot be rediscovered in the given instance provokes a response of unpleasure. In terms of the eight-months anxiety, what we observe can be understood as follows: the stranger's face is compared to the memory traces of the mother's face and found wanting. This is not mother, she is still lost. Unpleasure is experienced and manifested [p. 54].

In a letter, I asked Dr. Spitz whether I was correct in interpreting his statements on the significance of the eight-months anxiety as an indicator of the achievement of object constancy, and as a demonstration of the infant's capacity to evoke the image of the mother in her absence. He replied:

You are quite correct in assuming my interpretation of the eight-months anxiety as an indicator of the child's capacity to evoke the image of the absent object. . . . However, this observation refers to a special stress situation. . . . I have . . . no sufficient systematic work on the subject to venture the statement that the mother's image can be evoked by the child at all times and under less stressful circumstances than at the stage of the eight-months anxiety, though I consider it highly probable.
. . . In other words, I consider the eight-months anxiety a proof of the establishment of object constancy in regard to the libidinal object.

Spitz, too, has sought links between the psychoanalytic theory of object constancy and the genetic psychology of Piaget. He has seen that where mental representation and objectivation are concerned, there is common ground between the psychoanalytic investigator of early mental processes and Piaget. In the appendix to *The First Year of Life* (1965), Spitz's collaborator, W. Godfrey Cobliner, attempts to work out parallels and stage-specific criteria uniting Spitz's findings in human object relations with those of Piaget in the development of the object concept. In a later section of this essay I shall return to this topic.

Humberto Nagera (1966) has used the term "object constancy" to connote the exclusive bond to the mother with emphasis on the developmental process which leads to the establishment of the stable attachment. He said:

> Obviously, the transition from the phase of need satisfaction to object constancy is a very slow and gradual process which starts in the third or fourth month, gains further impetus during the second half of the first year, and reaches its full development during the second year of life. In most cases it is already well established toward the end of the first half of the second year [p. 415].

In placing the *attainment* of object constancy in the second half of the second year, Nagera provides clarification in usage which, I believe, successfully mediates the differences among a number of authors. Some of the differences which have appeared among psychoanalytic writers have arisen through usage in which "object constancy" connotes a developmental stage, and whether the term implies the emergence of that stage, or the attainment of a point on a scale with specific criteria, is often not clear or must be inferred from context.

Margaret Mahler follows Hartmann in usage of the term "object constancy." In her essay, "On the Significance of the Normal Separation-Individuation Phase" (1965), Mahler uses "object constancy" in this context:

> *The fourth subphase* of separation-individuation is the period during which an increasing degree of object constancy (in Hartmann's sense) is attained (twenty-five to thirty-six months). At the beginning of this subphase, the child still remains in the original playroom setting, with the mother readily available in the mothers' sitting section. We have found that, as this phase proceeds, the child is able gradually to accept once again separation from the mother (as he did in the "practicing" period); in fact, he seems to prefer staying in the familiar playroom without the mother, to going out of this room with her. We regard this as a sign of the *achievement of beginning object constancy* [p. 167; my italics].
>
> [Again, in 1966, she speaks of] the fourth subphase of separation-individuation in which a certain degree of *object constancy*

will be attained: i.e., mental representations of the mother become intrapsychically available (Hartmann, 1952). The memory traces of the love object enable the child to remain away from the mother for some length of time and still function with emotional poise, provided he is in a fairly familiar environment. Presumably this is so because inner representations of the mother are available to him [p. 156].

Mahler, then, specifically links the attainment of object constancy with the emergence of a stable mental representation which enables the child to tolerate separation from the mother.

Since the term "object constancy" has acquired diverse meanings in our literature, its stage-specific attributes are variously described and cannot be understood unless we can infer from context which usage the author follows. In this way, too, we can understand a puzzle in the range of age norms which appear in our literature for the attainment of object constancy. This range among eleven writers consulted extended from six months of age to twenty-five months. The apparent discrepancy seems to be the result of differences in definition. The writers who ascribe the beginnings of object constancy to the middle of the first year are using "constancy" only in the sense of attachment to the love object. The writers who give a range from eight months to eighteen months of age are adding some form of mental representation to the criteria for libidinal cathexis of the object; those who place object constancy at eighteen months appear to be following Piaget's criteria for mental representation and object concept. The one writer (Mahler) who placed object constancy at twenty-five months was using still more restrictive criteria on the libidinal-cognitive scale, in which mental representation of the mother had attained a high level of stability.

As we shall see further, it is *not* in the evidence for the libidinal attachment that the disparate views on libidinal object constancy appear, but in the evidence for "mental representation" of the mother and "objectivation" of the mother, the cognitive aspects of the exclusive, binding tie to mother.

The problem can be summarized in this way: If we can demonstrate that between six months and twelve months of age the infant's attachment to the mother becomes increasingly selective, exclusive, and relatively independent of need and the satisfaction of need, if we can demonstrate anxiety at separation from the mother during this period, what concomitant processes in cognition are at work in these increasingly selective responses? Do the highly differentiated responses require a particular form of mental representation of the mother? Does the reaction to loss indicate a capacity to evoke the image of the absent mother? Do the qualitative changes in the libidinal attachment to mother represent an achievement in "objectivation" of mother, that is, is mother seen as separate and autonomous from the infant self?

While all writers consulted take into account perceptual and cognitive aspects of the libidinal tie to the mother, there are wide differences among them in the attribution of (1) objectivation of the mother and (2) mental representation of the mother as conditions for the emergence of the stable, exclusive, permanent investment of the mother. I think these differences can be explained on this basis:

We are on firm analytic ground in a well-researched area when we speak of the investment of the mother and the primacy of the mother as love object in the period of six months to one year. Here, our data are derived from studies of normal infants and from the pathological sequelae in development, that is, absence of the bond to mother or temporary or permanent rupture of these bonds. Here, too, our data are largely confirmed by studies outside of the field of psychoanalysis.

We are on less certain ground—a circumstance that we share with other psychologies—in our investigation of the genetic aspects of memory and the stage-specific characteristics of "objectivation." Here, too, we have semantic disharmony in our use of the term "mental representation" and "object." In psychoanalysis we employ the term "mental representation" to cover a wide variety of mental phenomena, from simple registrations to evocative memory. We use the term "object" most familiarly as "object of drives" and also to represent a person, or thing, or universe of things which are perceived as external to the self and have autonomy from the self.

MENTAL REPRESENTATION AND OBJECT CONSTANCY

Nearly all writers consulted link the achievement of libidinal object constancy with some form of mental representation of the mother. Where differences occur among these writers, I think we can find the differences through usage:

1. The term "mental representation" is used to cover a broad spectrum of cognitive acts in psychoanalysis ranging from simple registrations and primitive hallucinatory phenomena to mental operations which involve a high degree of complexity in symbolic thought. Since our vocabulary does not designate gradients in this series, the kind of mental representation referred to in explanatory texts must be inferred from contexts.

2. There is not yet agreement among psychoanalytic writers regarding the level of complexity in mental representation of the mother which must be assumed as a correlate for libidinal attachment.

3. Some of the criteria for mental representation of the mother assume a higher level of complexity in symbolic memory than can be demonstrated through objective infant studies.

Some aspects of the problem of usage emerge in the following exchange at the Panel Discussion (1968) between David Beres and Anna Freud:

Dr. David Beres: The point I would like to make on the subject of object constancy is that I agree entirely with Miss Freud's and Dr. Lampl-de Groot's definitions of it. But I see no reason not to include, as part of the problem of object constancy, the psychological problem of mental representation. I would say that without the development of the child to the point where it has the capacity to form a mental representation of the object which remains in the psychic apparatus (and I am using a very crude metaphor here), in the absence of the object, object constancy in Miss Freud's sense would not be something of which the child would be capable. I think that there is no reason to eliminate the psychological aspect, I am not sure that Miss Freud meant to do so. . . .

Miss Freud: I certainly did not mean to neglect the psychological side altogether, namely the establishment of an independent inner image. I only think that the two processes are different from each other. The capacity to retain an inner image comes before object constancy. To my mind it is characteristic and relevant for another advance in the child's life as shown in Spitz's book, *The First Year of Life.* With this capacity the child takes the step from the object being an object for the id, to being an object for the ego. But that is not the same as object constancy. Object constancy means, on top of that, to retain attachment even when the person is unsatisfactory [p. 507].

David Beres, then, is using "mental representation" as the capacity to evoke the image of the mother in the absence of the mother in perception. Here, mental representation means "evocative memory." On a scale of cognitive development, evocative memory requires a capacity for symbolic operations which many writers place at approximately eighteen months of age.

Anna Freud in her statement places "the capacity to retain an inner image" before object constancy. Since in her definition object constancy begins around the middle of the first year, she is undoubtedly speaking of a form of mental representation which is available to the infant at six to eight months of age, one of course which is far removed in complexity from the evocative memory of the second year. We do not have a descriptive term in psychoanalysis which differentiates this form of mental representation from evocative memory.

Some of the ambiguities in usage might be clarified if we distinguished between "recognition memory" and "evocative memory," following Piaget. Thus, a memory trace or a mental image of the mother does not in itself imply the capacity to evoke the image of mother independent of the presenting stimulus of her face or voice. *Recognition* can take place when the person or "thing" perceived has characteristics or signs which revive mnemonic traces laid down through previous experience. The test for *evocative memory* is the demonstrated capacity to evoke the image without the presenting stimulus. (Later, I would like to expand this definition to take into account the hallucinatory phenomena which we in psychoanalysis associate with the beginnings of mental life.)

The differences between recognition memory and evocative memory are acknowledged in everyday human experience. For example, if I should set myself the task of trying to remember the students in a class that I taught twenty years ago, I may be able to produce a picture of only three or four of twenty-five students. But if I should meet one of the students whose memory I cannot evoke, I may recognize his face immediately, and may even be able to remember which seat he occupied and a number of other details. This means that the presentation of that forgotten face revived the picture stored in memory; the face provided signs, the picture was "compared" by means of these signs, and recognition took place.

This matching of pictures by means of signs is "recognition" memory. We can only speak of "evocative memory" in the true sense, in the first example, when I can produce the picture without the presence of the student in reality. In infant development it is useful to discriminate between recognition memory, which can only be elicited by signs, and evocative memory, which has autonomy from objective signs.

It is "evocative memory" that Freud had in mind when he said, in the essay, "Negation" (1935): "thinking possesses the capacity to bring before the mind once more something that has once been perceived, by reproducing it as a presentation without the external object having still to be there" (p. 237).

David Beres (1968) carefully discriminates between "mental registrations" and "mental representation" and employs "mental representation" restrictively to connote "evocative memory."

At what point in development is the infant capable of evoking the image of the mother when she is not present in reality?

When the baby of six months begins to demonstrate his preference for his mother, through selective smiling and vocalization, when the baby demonstrates that his attachment to the mother has relative independence from need satisfaction, does this behavior toward the mother indicate a capacity to evoke the mother's image in her absence? Or can we explain these selective responses to the mother on the basis of recognition memory for a highly cathected object?

When the baby at seven to ten months displays anxiety in response to the stranger, is this a demonstration of evocative memory for the mother? Or can we explain this phenomenon on the basis of an advance in recognition memory? If the baby sobers or cries at the sight of the stranger's face, he certainly demonstrates the ability to make the perceptual discriminations between familiar faces and unfamiliar faces, cathected objects and noncathected objects, but the act of nonrecognition may only tell us that recognition memory has progressed to a certain level of complexity.

The anxiety which is manifest in this experience of nonrecognition can be interpreted without the attribution of evocative memory. While it has been suggested by Spitz that the anxiety is a reaction to "not finding" the mother in reality, even this hypothesis does not require the capacity to evoke the image of the "lost" mother. On the contrary, if a mother is "lost" when she is not perceived, this may be taken as evidence that the mental image of the mother is still unstable, is not independent of perception, and requires affirmation from visual experience.

If, as Spitz suggests, stranger anxiety is related to "not finding" the mother in reality, can we accommodate this interpretation within the framework of recognition memory? Recognition memory stabilizes itself through repetition. The appearance in the perceptual field of mother's face elicits the joy of recognition, the revival of highly cathected memory traces. In this transitional period for the baby, when mental operations begin to take into account the objective attributes of persons and things, we may suppose a kind of expectation in the baby that the people and things of his world should have resonance in memory. On the eight-month level of cognitive development, is it possible that the face that cannot be affirmed, "placed" through memory, is momentarily disruptive to the child's sense of the "real," that expectations are not confirmed? Is it perhaps a "spooky" experience, like the dream in which one enters the familiar kitchen of childhood, with mother at the stove, her back to the dreamer, and mother turns around . . . and suddenly one confronts the face of a stranger!

What I am suggesting is that an "expectation" that a familiar and beloved face should manifest itself in a familiar surround does not require the intervention of evocative memory. The child who is capable of evocative memory can sustain the image of the mother *not* present in perception which should theoretically diminish the disturbing effect of a strange face. Following this line of thought one might venture the hypothesis that the *waning* of stranger anxiety at twelve to thirteen months should have correlates in cognitive development, another step toward autonomy of the image from perceptual experience. (There is, I believe, some support for this hypothesis in Piaget's work.)

When the child demonstrates anxiety during brief separations from the mother, does this constitute evidence for evocative memory? Benjamin's studies show that the peak of separation anxiety appears around one year of age. Anxiety at loss of the mother certainly testifies to the strength of the libidinal tie to mother and of her valuation above all other persons. Does the anxiety constitute evidence that the child sustains a mental image of the mother in her absence? One could argue the other way, also—that separation anxiety is greater during the period eight to thirteen months because the libidinal bond has been forged, the mother is *recognized* as the all-important, indispensable person, but there is not yet a stable mental representation of the mother that can sustain the child during brief separations. All psychoanalytic writers consulted on this problem seem to agree that the stabilization of mental representations of the mother takes place gradually over a period of years. Our question is: When can we say the capacity to evoke the image of the absent object *begins?* What are the criteria? The criterion of separation anxiety remains arguable as long as we need the criterion "tolerance of separation" at the other end of the scale. That is, if we regard tolerance for brief separations at twenty to twenty-six months as an indicator of the stability of the mental representation, intolerance, bordering on severe anxiety states between the ages of eight to thirteen months, must testify to the instability of mental representations. Such an unstable representation, one that is still dependent upon "signs," cannot yet qualify as evocative memory in a strict definition of the term.

Contributions of Piaget

Piaget's empirical studies of cognitive development in the sensorimotor period provide us with valuable criteria for the evolution of evocative memory during the first eighteen months of life. Piaget supports his findings with rich and detailed infant protocols which permit the psychoanalytic student of child development to follow the data and his inferences. These findings have made welcome additions to our literature, and, as we have seen, contributed in some measure to Hartmann's thinking on the subject of object constancy and to Spitz and Cobliner's studies of the cognitive aspects of libidinal development. Piaget has sometimes been criticized by psychoanalysts because he has not concerned himself with the affective components of cognition (although he does tangentially), and this, of course, is a central problem for the psychoanalyst in studying the mental development of infants. Further, his empirical work on the child's construction of an object world was based largely on the child's behavior toward inanimate objects, toys, and the problem of relevance to the human object comes into the psychoanalytic assessment. Finally, since Piaget's work on infant memory concerned itself with the percept and the withdrawal of the percept from the visual field, the whole large question of the hallucination in infant need states is left unanswered for the psychoanalyst who needs empirical data from infancy. This was not an area of interest to Piaget. In any case, the problem of setting up experimental conditions for the study of hallucinations in infancy is so formidable that we can only congratulate those who have left the field to us.

Yet, I think it can be demonstrated that Piaget's data have great importance for the psychoanalytic student of memory in infancy. We have from Piaget a set of stage-specific criteria for the development of memory based upon exteroceptive experience in infancy. Piaget's original work has since been validated by two independent studies, testing large infant populations (Décarie, 1965; Escalona, 1968). If the data for mental representation of exteroceptive experience are known, we can formulate certain hypotheses regarding the capacity of the infant to hallucinate during need states.

If we assume that the image of exteroceptive experience and the image of gratification in need states are united through a mutual feedback system, the infant's memory of an "object" that has been withdrawn from his visual field must have correlates in the infant's capacity to produce an image in need states. Since the picture must first be present as a visual percept, there is a given primacy in exteroceptive experience for the registration of the early mental traces. The most conservative inference that can be drawn is that no memory can be evoked through a need stimulus that is organized on a level of greater complexity than that present in the behavior toward the external stimulus. That is, if an infant cannot sustain the memory of an object hidden before his eyes under a screen, it is unlikely that the same infant can produce or sustain the memory of an object independent of a stimulus arising in a need state.

If this is true, the empirical data from Piaget's studies of the "object concept" and evocative memory can provide us with much needed baseline information for the study of the hallucinatory phenomena which we postulate in early mental life. To me, as for all psychoanalysts, the dream provides incontrovertible evidence that need gives rise to the image of its satisfaction. At what point in development is the infant capable of producing an image through need? At what point is he capable of producing a picture independent of need *and* the percept?

The dream can tell us that there was a time in mental development when sensory pictures emerged without unity and coherence and without taking into account time, causality, or the permanence of things not perceived. The dream has informed us of the phenomena of early mental life, but it cannot, of course, tell us how and when these disordered elements were bound together and how intelligence became free from the bond of the stimulus.

Does it matter? If reconstruction in the analysis of an adult or a child cannot tell us exactly when certain crucial events took place, it may not matter for the conduct of the analysis or for the patient's prognosis. It only matters that the memory can be revived. But for the psychoanalytic student of child development and for psychoanalytic theory itself, there must be something like a chronology and stage-specific criteria for the organization of memory in infancy or we are handicapped in the study of ego development. Such questions as: What is the relationship between libidinal object constancy and "the stable object" in general psychological terms? or: What do we mean by mental representation? are of central interest to us. In this way the objective findings of other psychologists can enrich our understanding of mental processes in infancy and can help us clarify a number of difficult problems in the area of libidinal object relations and the construction of an objective world.

For us, as well as other psychologists, the study of the genetic aspects of memory and its stage-specific characteristics must be inferred from behavior signs. The key to the dream was Freud's great gift to the psychology of thinking, and what is unknown and not yet fathomed in the genetic aspects of memory is really the fault of our subject, who is slow at picking up language before eighteen months. But if we have the key to the dream and data from a growing number of developmental studies in psychoanalysis, we can begin to chart the territory. Piaget's work gives us another key, a stratification of cognitive development during the first eighteen months of life with impeccable data for the study of memory when the percept is withdrawn.

In the final section of this paper, I shall attempt to bring together Piaget's thinking and our psychoanalytic views on the subject of evocative memory and suggest a formulation for evocative memory that is consistent with psychoanalytic data and the findings of Piaget.

At this point it might be useful to begin with a short summary of Piaget's experimental procedures and the findings which led him to deduce the presence of evocative memory in the infant eighteen months of age. The summary is my own;[1] since it was necessary to present this material in a highly condensed form in this essay, I worked out an abbreviated version which emphasizes for the psychoanalytic reader the progressive autonomy of memory from the presenting stimulus.

Piaget's Case

Piaget deals most extensively with the problem of mental representation in his work *The Child's Construction of Reality* (1937). Evocative memory in Piaget's view is linked indissolubly with the development of the object concept, that is, the concept of an object as external to the self, having autonomy from the self and the subject's perception of it. There can be no "object concept" without "mental representation," no "mental representation" without an "object concept," both achievements involve mental operations on a symbolic level, both achievements must take into account the permanence of an object that is not present in perception. The experimental procedures which I shall summarize are well known—a sequence of screened-object tests presented to the infant during the first eighteen months of life. Piaget's sequence has been confirmed in the studies by Décarie and Escalona. Both authors have worked out object concept scales and age ranges. The larger samples employed by both investigators have resulted in slightly different

---

[1] Excellent and detailed summaries are available in the writings of Peter H. Wolff (1960) and Thérèse Gouin Décarie (1965).

age distributions from those obtained by Piaget. In referring to age ranges, I shall cite the ranges established in Décarie's testing.[2]

There are six clearly defined stages in the development of the object concept which correspond to six stages of mental operations which Piaget has adduced from his studies of infant intelligence. For purposes of our psychoanalytic examination of the problem I shall summarize Piaget's findings for Stages III through VI (roughly five months to eighteen months of age).

Stage III—Five to Eight Months of Age

Until eight months of age, the baby will make no attempt to recover a favorite toy or a test toy that has been moved before his eyes and placed under a simple screen (e.g., a cloth or a pillow).

Inferences: *Object Concept.* The toy has no existence for the baby when it disappears from his perceptual field. The baby attributes no substantiality to an object not perceived; it has no objective stability. *Memory.* The baby cannot sustain the image of the object in memory when barriers to his perception are presented.

Stage IV—Eight to Thirteen Months

Between eight months and thirteen months of age the infant will search for an object hidden before his eyes under a single screen. He will remove the barrier and recover the object. If the examiner introduces two screens (and another level of complexity) and hides the object first under screen A and then under screen B, the baby, even though witness to the successive displacements, will search for the object only under screen A where he had first recovered it. When he does not recover the object, he gives up the search.

Inferences: *Object Concept.* The baby is now *beginning* to attribute some kind of objectivity to things screened from his perception, but he has no notion of objective permanence; the object can be found only in one place, the place where he first recovered it. *Memory.* The baby can sustain the mental image of the vanished object for the few seconds that elapse between his perception of it and the screening, which enables him to conduct his simple search. When another event intervenes (screen B), there is no evidence

---

2 Escalona's ranges were not available to me at the time of this writing.

from the infant's behavior that after his failure to recover the object under screen A, memory of the object has been sustained.

Stage V—Thirteen to Eighteen Months

Between the ages of thirteen months and eighteen months the baby will search for an object under two or more screens, provided he has *seen* the object disappear under successive screens. If a single *invisible* displacement takes place (a sleight-of-hand maneuver in the examiner's hiding game), the baby will not be able to deduce the probable hiding place of the object and will give up his search.

Inferences: *Object Concept.* The baby has acquired the notion that an object can follow its own itinerary, so to speak, and is not bound to a single point in space (as in Stage IV), but this idea is *still linked to his own perception,* he must follow its displacements with his eyes. *Memory.* The baby can sustain the mental image of the vanished object through successive displacements but must still rely upon the object's continuous manifestations of itself to his eyes (each displacement is accompanied by discovery and verification). The failure of the object to manifest itself to him in the invisible displacement appears to have the effect of erasing the mental image; the baby does not continue his search and gives no sign that a cathected image persists.

Stage VI—Eighteen Months

At approximately eighteen months of age, the baby begins to take into account invisible displacements. In the experimental procedures the object is subjected to at least one displacement which the baby cannot see. The baby conducts a search which for the first time makes use of deduction. He deduces the probable hiding place of the object from information and clues available to him and sustains his search until he finds the object.

Inferences: *Object Concept.* The baby demonstrates belief that the object exists independent of his perception of it; his sustained search in spite of the invisible displacement has the meaning: "It must be someplace." The object has "permanence" in Piaget's terms; it has autonomy from the infant self, from his actions, his perceptions. Its displacements in space follow independent laws. *Memory.* The baby can sustain the mental image of the absent object in spite of all experimental barriers to perception. In the absence of perceptual cues or *any sign,* he can *evoke the image of the absent object* and pursue it; his deduction regarding the probable hiding place involves mental operations in which the entire sequence of actions must be recalled, "played back" in the memory record, which constitutes a further extension of the capacity for evocative memory.

Summary of Piaget's Position

1. For Piaget true mental representation is evocative memory. The capacity to evoke the image of the absent object is not demonstrated in his infant studies until eighteen months of age. Piaget reminds us that these findings correlate with other cognitive achievements at the middle of the second year. It is at this time that symbolic thought is manifest in speech through naming with correct referents. It is at this time, too, that the young child begins to demonstrate his capacity for "deferred imitation" in Piaget's terms, that is the ability to imitate in the absence of the mode! and without signs from the model, the period of the beginning of play, of imagining.

2. Until the middle of the second year when the child gives his first demonstrations of evocative memory (following the strict criteria described in the preceding section), the child is capable of increasingly fine perceptual discriminations and inferences which Piaget places in the category of "recognition memory." Thus, in the experimental demonstrations of the baby through Stage V, the child conducts his search only as long as "signs" are available to him, the sign given directly by perception before the object disappears, or the sign given by the screen itself as "a hiding place." No examples appear until Stage VI of the child's ability to evoke the image of the absent object independent of a sign.

The Psychoanalytic Case

The applicability of Piaget's findings to psychoanalytic investigations in the mental representation of the libidinal object and the objectivation of the mother can raise questions among analysts. It can be argued, for example, that the libidinal object has primacy as a perceptual object and that tests involving inanimate objects do not fairly represent the cognitive aspects of the most highly invested human object relationships. It can be argued that tests involving barriers to visual perception in affectively neutral circumstances do not tap the heart of the problem for psychoanalysis, which is the hallucinatory image arising from need states as hypothesized in psychoanalytic theory. These are valid objections in my views, too, but these are problems for the psychoanalytic investigator, and the answers must come from our own research.

Such differences do not diminish the value of Piaget's findings for psychoanalysts. Piaget's meticulous work on the infant's construction of an object world and the mental operations that lead to evocative memory provide valuable baseline information for the psychoanalytic investigator. If we are correct in our assumptions in psychoanalysis that the human object has a nuclear primacy in cognition, then we can assume a relationship between the cognition of persons and things (which, in fact, we do), but this would affect only the temporal sequence by giving a kind of human priority to cognitive events. It does not change the structure of the cognitive act. Perception, recognition, evocative memory follow the same structural and maturational laws for human objects and inanimate objects; the differences that we discern in psychoanalysis are affective and are defined in energic terms; we can speak of degrees of cathexis but not of a different kind of mental representation. Similarly, we do not need a different set of criteria for objectivation of the human object and objectivation of the inanimate object. The human object may take temporal precedence, but the mental operations that lead to the construction of an object world are probably identical in each instance.

If we can accept these conditions, we can use Piaget's findings to construct certain hypotheses regarding mental representation of the mother (evocative memory) and objectivation of the mother. The hypotheses need to be tested through direct observation of infants by psychoanalytic investigators. Some of the work has been done in this area: some remains for further investigation.

Some Hypotheses Regarding Evocative Memory for the Mother

1. The capacity of the infant to evoke the image of the absent mother may precede the capacity to evoke the image of an absent "thing," but should appear in close temporal contiguity to "thing"

representation. This gives us a baseline of eighteen months for "evocation of the thing" (Piaget) and the expectation that "evocation of the image of the absent mother" appears shortly before the eighteen-month period.

2. The capacity to "hallucinate" the mother, or another image of gratification, during need states is unresearched, and we have no stage-specific criteria. Since the hallucinated image at any point in the developmental scale can never represent a higher level of differentiation or complexity than the image produced through exteroceptive experience, the data available to us through objective tests of the infant's perceptual development should give us points of reference for inferring the characteristics of hallucinatory experience. Thus, (a) if need gives rise to the image of satisfaction, the picture produced through a rise in need tensions cannot be a better copy of the real object than one that registers through direct perception. And, (b) the capacity to evoke the image of an object withdrawn from perception must have correlates in the capacity to evoke the image of an object in need states.

3. The mental processes that lead to "objectivation" of the mother, the concept of mother as having autonomy from the self and a substantial existence when she is not perceived, can be presumed to follow the same sequential development as the construction of objective permanence of "things," although the time order may be altered on the basis of cathexis and valuation of the mother over "things." Since objectivation in this sense must be linked to the capacity for evocative memory, the location on a developmental timetable of evocative memory for the mother should establish the age of attainment of objectivation of mother.

The Problem of Reconciling These Data from Two Psychologies

Both Thérèse Gouin Décarie and W. Godfrey Cobliner (with Spitz) have attempted to reconcile the psychoanalytic criteria for mental representation (evocative memory) and objectivation of the mother with Piaget's criteria. Since 1960 I have been at work in the same area, seeking comparative data on blind and sighted infants.

Using psychoanalytic criteria for libidinal object relations and mental representation, and Piaget's criteria for the development of object permanence and mental representation, Décarie constructed

two scales, an Objectal Scale for libidinal object relations and an
Object Concept Scale, using Piaget's criteria. The psychoanalytic
criteria were taken from authoritative sources in our literature and
were employed with fastidious attention to nuances in psychoanalytic usage. Since nearly all of these criteria appear in one or another
form on standard developmental tests for infants, it was possible
to obtain age norms for each of these items and rank them on a
scale. The Object Concept criteria were, of course, explicit in
Piaget's work. Both scales were administered to a group of ninety
infants. The sequence obtained through the administration of the
Piaget scales was invariant, though the normative age groupings
were corrected in this large sample. The sequence obtained through
the administration of the Objectal Scale was variable in more than
one half the subjects. Décarie herself offers a number of sound
reasons for the heterogeneous protocols she obtained. They do not
invalidate the psychoanalytic criteria as "indicators" of libidinal
attachment, but they do suggest that the order of the appearance of
signs has variability for at least some items. This will need to be in-
vestigated in future psychoanalytic research.

In Décarie's work, the most serious obstacle in seeking correlates
between mental representation of the human object and mental
representation of the "thing" was the absence of consensus among
psychoanalytic writers in usage of the term "mental representation"
and in identifying the characteristics of "evocative memory." Some
of the behaviors which we in analysis interpret as manifestations of
evocative memory were, in Décarie's view, uncertain signs; that is,
while the behavior itself was manifestly a sign of libidinal cathexis
of the human object, it did not require the intervention of evocative
memory for its performance.

Analysis of the homogeneous protocols permitted the ranking of
stage-specific characteristics in libidinal object relations and a comparison of these ranks with the Piaget scale ranks. Here the correspondence between stage-specific characteristics of libidinal object
relations and the construction of the object concept showed closer
correspondence. There remained, however, a gap in age intervals
within the two scales. The gap appeared at the point on each scale
where "evocative memory" is presumed to intervene. Décarie attempted to bridge the gap by advancing Piaget's criteria for evoca-

tive memory (from eighteen to fifteen months) and by placing evocative memory for the mother at one year of age, which left a three-month interval between the two scales which could be postulated as the difference represented between evocation of the human object and the inanimate object. Piaget, in an otherwise commendatory preface to Décarie's book, took exception to this revision of his criteria for evocative memory and affirmed his position on the eighteen-month criteria, citing corroboration from other studies.

W. Godfrey Cobliner, in his appendix to Spitz's *The First Year of Life,* also addresses himself to the problem of reconciling Piaget's data with psychoanalytic data, specifically Spitz's interpretation of the eight-months anxiety as an indicator of mental representation of the mother. The problem for Cobliner was to bring Spitz's eight-month criteria for evocative memory into harmony with Piaget's criteria. In order to do this, he had to give another value to Piaget's Stage V criteria and to place evocative memory for the inanimate object at approximately eleven months of age, where Piaget explicitly places it at Stage VI, eighteen months.

These efforts to conciliate the positions of Piaget and psychoanalysis on the appearance of evocative memory require us to stretch the evidence in ways that are uncongenial to both psychoanalysis and Piaget. If we accept Cobliner's criteria for mental representation of the mother at eight months (stranger anxiety), we have a ten-months gap between evocative memory for the human object and evocative memory for the toy, which is not demonstrated until eighteen months on Piaget's scale or the standardized scales of Décarie and Escalona. Even postulating a priority for the highly invested human object, we cannot account for this ten-months gap. If, in fact, there is a generalization in memory from the person to the thing, as Hartmann has proposed on a cathectic basis, such a generalization should take place without marked delay. It is difficult to imagine that once the capacity for evocative memory is achieved, it is isolated from all other experience. Generalization is the very nature of intelligence. (To illustrate, in the same eighth-month period that is under discussion, the attribution of qualities to the mother, the valuation of mother, has a counterpart in the child's new valuation and preferential treatment of toys and other "things." One could construct other parallels, stage by stage, but the case

would be much strengthened by detailed day-by-day observations of
infants by psychoanalysts who are interested in the problem.)

The problem of reconciling data really centers around criteria
for evocative memory in psychoanalysis. As we have seen, such
criteria as valuation of the mother, stranger anxiety, and separation
anxiety, which come in during the second half of the first year,
do not require more than a highly selective and differentiated
"recognition memory" in the infant. I have been led in this direction not only by my interest in the theoretical problem but by the
findings in my research on infants totally blind from birth.

Some Data from Our Research on Blind Infants

To study the development of libidinal object relations in blind
infants we used criteria for each developmental stage for which
there is agreement among psychoanalysts. In each of our observational sessions we made detailed narrative records of the baby's
behavior in relation to the mother. As another aspect of our research, we studied the development of the object concept using
highly cathected toys as well as test objects, following a modified
Piaget scale.

The results for ten otherwise intact infants, totally blind from
birth, can be summarized: Each of these babies met the criteria for
human object relations that we accept for sighted children under
one year of age. In the second half of the first year, the kind of
exclusive love for the mother, the highly differentiated responses
to mother, the discrimination of mother and stranger, negative reactions to the stranger, and the inability to accept substitutes for
mother, were all demonstrated by these blind babies.

At the same time the results of our "object concept test," which
is, of course, a test of mental representation, showed a stage-by-stage
lag of three to six months in the ability to sustain the memory of
an object after it had left the tactile or auditory sphere. The Stage
VI demonstration, the ability to evoke the memory of the object
independent of perceptual cues, was the most difficult task of all
for our blind children.

We are then left with evidence that further complicates the relationship between libidinal object relations and the capacity for
evocative memory. If we use the eight- to ten-months period as a

point of reference, we have all the criteria for libidinal object relations including stranger reactions among the blind babies. But at eight to ten months, the sighted baby has attained Stage IV on Piaget's scale, which tests the capacity to sustain the memory of an object for a few seconds after it has disappeared from the perceptual field. Our babies are still in Stage III (no memory for an object that has left the immediate perceptual field). This means, of course, that a child who is retarded (by sighted child standards) in memory function need not be retarded in his libidinal object relations.

The Problem of the Hallucinatory Image

At the center of all these problems of definition and criteria for evocative memory is the problem of the hallucinatory image which we, in psychoanalysis, regard as "the primary model of thought" (Rapaport, 1960). The dream provides us with compelling evidence that there are genetic links between drives and memory; need gives rise to the image of gratification. We can assume with Rapaport that the earliest forms of this imagery are diffuse and undifferentiated, and only gradually in the course of infant development do these images differentiate into discrete objects. It is further assumed in psychoanalytic thinking that memory gradually achieves some degree of autonomy from drive stimuli, and many psychoanalytic writers believe that the infant's capacity to retain the cathexis to the mother independent of fluctuations of need states is an indicator of the emerging autonomy of memory from drive stimuli. In the previous section I have raised some questions regarding the criteria which are employed for the demonstration of the infant's capacity to evoke the image of the mother independent of need and independent of her presence in reality.

Yet, the problem of the hallucinatory image and its relationship to evocative memory remains, and is most compelling for the psychoanalyst engaged in child development study. It is a vital link in the story of cognition, yet it can only be known by inference.

Our case is a difficult one because we cannot easily set up the experimental conditions for studying the infant's capacity to hallucinate. In the absence of language we must infer from behavioral signs, yet the signs can be ambiguous and cannot tell us the content of imagery if it is present. If the infant of eight months is hungry and begins mouthing or sucking movements, is this simply the activation of a sensorimotor schema to the stimulus of visceral sensations, is it an undifferentiated state of "expectedness" stimulated by visceral sensations, as Décarie suggests, or is there a picture of the mother or food stimulated by need?

A Digression and a Possible Solution

To answer some of these questions for myself, I took a long detour which I shall now describe. The detour involves some animal observations. Here, I feel apologetic. I would have much preferred infant observations, but the elderly Beagle who is the subject of these investigations offered certain advantages for study. I can provide experimental evidence that his sensorimotor intelligence placed him not higher than Stage IV on a scale of mental representation. He was also capable of expressing a limited number of wants during need states. As a subject for the study of the negative hallucination he afforded one great advantage over the human infant. His range of mobility exceeded the possibilities of a human child at Stage IV, and, like most dogs, he translated his wants into specific motor actions which were sometimes very clear.

Late in the evening, usually around ten o'clock, Brandy would rouse himself from a doze, shake himself, and march over to my chair. He would stand before me, wag his tail in greeting, and bark in a peremptory fashion. I would then say, "What do you want, Brandy?" and stand up, waiting for a signal from him. He would then lead the way to the kitchen, and to one of two places in the kitchen. If he wanted a biscuit, he would stand before the packaged food cupboard and bark. I would then get the biscuits and feed him a snack. If he wanted something more substantial, like meat, he would stand before the refrigerator door and bark in the same commanding way.

Up to the time that the door to the cupboard was opened, or the refrigerator door opened, Brandy's behavior clearly indicated that he wanted "something" and his choice of two doors leading to (1) biscuits and (2) meat indicates that some kind of sensory image was evoked without the presentation of the stimulus in reality.

Is this evocative memory? I think not. Yet it satisfies the definition, "the evocation of absent realities!" Yes, but then something needs to be qualified in the definition. We are willing to credit Brandy with at least two sensory images without the presenting external stimulus, but both images are produced by an inner stimulus of need, and, I believe, *only by the stimulus of need.*

If we construct another test and qualify the definition we should ask: If there is no organic stimulus, can Brandy evoke the image of a biscuit or a piece of meat, even in the most diffuse form? I think this is highly unlikely on theoretical grounds. On this level of sensorimotor intelligence, "wanting" is united with an action schema; the registration of need, raised to a certain intensity, activates a motor pattern. We can be reasonably sure that if some form of motor expression is not manifest, no "image of satisfaction" is available to the dog. Brandy would probably not be able to keep to himself a lonely vision of delights in the refrigerator. If, then, the action schemas can provide signs of a sensory image of need satisfaction, they also tell us that *the image is entirely at the disposal of the stimulus.*

There is some correspondence, then, between the sensory image evoked through need states in Brandy and the hallucinatory image which we postulate in the development of human intelligence. But intelligence in human infancy becomes free of the bonds of the stimulus; there will be a point in the development of human intelligence when an image can be evoked with relative autonomy from need states *and* the presenting stimulus in exteroceptive experience. This leads us back to one of the recurrent questions in this investigation: Is there a correlation between the level of mental operations demonstrated for exteroceptive data (the object not present in reality) and the level of mental operations required for the hallucination of a drive object during need states?

What were the limits of Brandy's sensorimotor intelligence when presented with the problem of a desirable object that is withdrawn from his perceptual field?

Now I shall describe another set of observations on the same dog which derive from certain informal tests. Our daughter, Lisa, then nine, had been following some of my baby work with interest. She

was intrigued with the baby's reactions to screened objects and began a series of tests with Brandy. When Lisa reported her first test
results, she was visibly shocked and her confidence in our dog's intelligence was shaken for the first time. I then observed these tests,
observed them many times, in fact, and this is what I saw:

Lisa showed Brandy a biscuit. Then slowly, so that he could
follow the biscuit with his eyes, she concealed it in the rolled-up
cuff of her jeans. Brandy recovered the biscuit. (This part of the
procedure was part of a game with Brandy, and he could always
recover the biscuit in the cuff of the jeans.) In the second part of the
procedure, Lisa again placed the biscuit in her jean cuffs while
Brandy followed the action with his eyes. Then Lisa removed the
biscuit and did not give it to Brandy, but moved it slowly *in his
visual range* to her *pocket,* and left it there. Brandy searched for
the biscuit in the first hiding place, the jeans cuff! He then stared
at the cuff of the jeans, waited for a decent interval, then whined
piteously, begging Lisa with his eyes, and gave up the search.

In repeated experiments, the results were invariable. Brandy
always searched for the biscuit in the first hiding place. This is all
the more remarkable when we consider that Brandy was a scent
hound and should have easily tracked the displacements of the biscuit on scent alone. He behaved in this test as if the data of vision
had no connection with the data of smell and when the biscuit disappeared from vision behind the second screen, he could not account
for its displacement and searched for it under the first screen. This
was *the* place where a vanished biscuit must be found. Clearly, then,
the biscuit had no "permanence" as an object in Piaget's terms, but
was conceived as belonging to "a place."

I should say that when I reported these informal test results to
my psychologist friends, they sneered. As one of them said bluntly,
"Why use Brandy for these experiments? Everyone knows he's a
dumb dog!" I will not debate the question of Brandy's intelligence.
There may, in fact, be dogs who can do slightly better than Brandy
on such a test, but no dog has yet presented evidence that he is
capable of true evocative memory.[3]

3 See also David Beres (1968).

Correspondence between the Two Sets of Data

I think it can be shown that the "hallucinated" biscuit of need states and the biscuit that is screened from vision are organized on the same level of complexity and are mediated by "signs." *Both sets of mental operations are "stimulus bound."*

The level of sensorimotor intelligence demonstrated by Brandy on Lisa's biscuit test can be equated with Stage IV on the Piaget scale (eight to twelve months on a standardized scale for infants). Brandy can recover a biscuit behind one screen when he has seen it disappear before his eyes. That is, the mental image is still linked with the visual stimulus and its stability is conceived as "belonging to one place." Once the hiding place is moved, Brandy cannot "move" his picture to a second place and he pursues the biscuit at the place where he had first seen it disappear. The link between vision and the biscuit is the screen (the cuff of Lisa's jeans), where he had first seen the hiding of the object. Every time his gaze returns to the cuff of the jeans, he behaves as if the biscuit should materialize from the seams. When it does not, the screen loses its sign value, the cathexis of the mental image of "biscuit" wanes, and he gives up the hunt. Apparently he does not brood about the problem.

The child of eight months behaves in much the same way toward an object when more than one barrier to perception is introduced. And I can do the same thing myself when a series of distractions interpose themselves between a task set up in memory and the execution of that task! Given an hour or two of successive barriers to memory, I may forget where I left the grocery list when the phone began to ring. However, both I and a reasonably intelligent eighteen-month-old child can uncover a series of barriers to memory by mentally reconstructing the sequence, running the sequence over again in memory or running it backward. Unless my grocery list is caught up in intrapsychic conflict, I can employ evocative memory to reconstruct its displacements. I can recover a grocery list that has left my perceptual field two hours ago.

This grocery list (which now appears overdetermined in my argument!) can be turned another way for our purposes. No one will be surprised to learn that I can prepare a grocery list and produce a mental image of every item on that list without being hungry, and without any visceral signs or promptings. Somewhere around the middle of the second year of life, the child's vocabulary will tell us that he, too, can evoke the image of a small range of objects having relative autonomy from need states as well as exteroceptive experience. This dating through speech gives us the age eighteen months as a point of reference for the establishment of an image that has autonomy from exteroceptive experience.

Is it possible, however, that an image of the need-satisfying person or object can be evoked independent of the need stimulus or the presentation in reality at an earlier stage of development? There is really no way of proving or disproving this possibility, but if I can borrow our overworked Beagle once again for illustration, I think he can help us construct a useful hypothesis.

Brandy's performance on a sensorimotor scale places him at Stage IV for exteroceptive data. He has extended "recognition memory" to a point where he can sustain the image of an object as long as objective signs are available to him (i.e., seeing the object disappear, seeing the screen behind which it disappeared). Brandy's behavior during "need states" ("wanting" a biscuit or meat, signaling to me, walking to the kitchen) is also dependent upon a stimulus, this time we suppose an organic stimulus. In each set of observations we assume a kind of mental representation; in each set (inner and outer) we have evidence that the sensory image is at the disposal of a stimulus or sign. In both the image of need states and the image of exteroceptive experience there is no evidence that the image can be produced without a specific stimulus. If the stimulus biscuit is withdrawn from exteroceptive experience, Brandy can sustain some kind of diffuse image of the biscuit for a few seconds on the basis of a sign (the screen). Then the image dissolves, as we infer from his behavior. If somatic longings are stirred, Brandy can produce some kind of sensory image that leads him to seek one of two kinds of need-satisfying objects. He can apparently sustain such an image for the duration of the stimulus. If no organic stimulus is present to give rise to a sensory image, we have reason to believe that no image appears. (We infer this through the absence of motor expression.) *If all these observations have been fairly made, the hallucinatory experience of need is organized on the same level of sensorimotor intelligence as the image of the real object withdrawn from perception.* Both images are stimulus bound; i.e., the image of ex-teroceptive experience cannot be produced without a stimulus or sign and cannot be sustained for more than a few seconds after the real object has left the perceptual field; the hallucinatory image on this level of cognition cannot be produced without a need stimulus and it can be sustained only for the duration of that stimulus raised to a certain intensity. If memory for the real biscuit behind the screen is placed at Stage IV on the sensorimotor scale, then memory for the hallucinated biscuit of need states has excellent correspond-ence with Stage IV criteria; the level of mental operations for the hallucinated image is also Stage IV.

This is all that Brandy can tell us, however, since he never got any smarter, but the baby at Stage IV is moving toward complex mental operations which will obtain a high degree of autonomy from the stimulus in the next year. Yet, I think these animal ob-servations can provide us with some useful hypotheses for the con-struction of the intervening stages.

I would propose that images produced through need states and mental images produced through exteroceptive experience may be organized on a scale of coordinates. Given the data for exteroceptive experience in the screened toy experiments, the grades of progres-sive autonomy from the stimulus will be the same for the image of exteroception as for the image of need. Thus, the capacity to sustain the image of an object independent of perception which is meas-ured on the objective scale of Piaget has short duration at Stage IV (eight to twelve months) but gains relative autonomy from the presenting stimulus at Stage VI (eighteen months). The capacity to sustain the image of need independent of the need stimulus may be presumed to have correlates stage by stage in which "distance from the stimulus" (drives, organic need) follows a progressive course toward autonomy, and the lengthening intervals may themselves have close correspondence with those on the exteroceptive scale, i.e., from stimulus, to sign (recognition), to evocation without a sign.

At the present time we have no experimental data to support this hypothesis on cognitive levels below the acquisition of speech. But this hypothesis is consistent with what we know of conceptual intelligence. Conceptual development is coherent; it synthesizes and organizes data from all perceptual experience ("inner and outer," as we would say in psychoanalysis); it generalizes and abstracts.

For these reasons it is difficult to imagine that the baby at eight months can employ mental operations on one level for exteroceptive data and another level, one of higher complexity, for the stimuli of need states. Where cathexis of the object, particularly the libidinal object, provides another variable, we may find a priority in the time-table, but we must suppose that the priority will appear close to the beginning of each new phase of mental operations; we cannot posit a gap of two stages, or ten months, on the cognitive scale.

If this argument has merit, the capacity to evoke the image of the mother with relative autonomy from need states and from the presenting stimulus of the mother will appear close to the time on the age scale that has been experimentally verified for evocative memory of the "thing." Piaget's empirical work gives us the age eighteen months for evocation of the inanimate object; we may postulate a period close to eighteen months for evocation of the image of the human object.

An Expanded Definition of Mental Representation?

Finally, I would like to propose a reformulation to cover one form of mental representation (evocative memory) which may satisfy our requirements in psychoanalytic theory and which takes into account the sequences established by Piaget during the sensorimotor period of development (i.e., recognition memory to true evocative memory). If the objective criteria for evocative memory are based upon "autonomy of the image from stimulus or sign," there must be corresponding criteria for the image of need satisfaction, stated as "the image that has autonomy from the stimulus of need." In this formulation the hallucinatory image of need is not "evocative memory" as long as it is bound to a specific stimulus. And while the hallucination of need states is, in fact, a kind of "evocation of absent realities" and, we think, may be the vital link in the sequence of mental operations that lead to true evocative memory, it does not qualify as "evocative memory" in strict usage, as long as it is bound to a specific need stimulus or sign.

I would then suggest this formulation which brings the hallucination of need states into harmony with the scale of mental operations deduced from objective data: *Evocative memory is the production of a mental image that has relative autonomy from the stimuli of exteroceptive experience and the stimuli of drives and need states.*

Summary

The concept of object constancy in psychoanalytic usage has been reviewed in its libidinal and cognitive aspects. There is agreement among psychoanalytic writers that the libidinal tie to the mother is formed during the first year of life and the term "object constancy" is employed by many psychoanalytic writers to designate the achievement of the libidinal bond. Where differences occur among psychoanalytic writers in defining the term "object constancy," these differences appear in the cognitive aspects of libidinal object relations. The mental representation of the mother is variously attributed to early and later phases of libidinal attachment, which suggests differences in definition of the term "mental representation." This essay suggests, following Piaget, that a distinction between "recognition memory" and "evocative memory" may clarify usage in psychoanalytic studies.

The problem of the hallucinatory experience of infancy was examined and an attempt was made to find correlates in the mental image of need states and the mental image of an object withdrawn from exteroceptive experience. A hypothesis was presented in which both sets of images are organized on a scale of coordinates with progressive autonomy from the stimulus or sign.

BIBLIOGRAPHY

Alpert, A. (1965), Introductory and Closing Remarks: Institute on Programs for Children Without Families. *J. Amer. Acad. Child Psychiat.*, 4:163-167; 272-278.
Benjamin, J. D. (1959), Prediction and Psychopathologic Theory. In: *Dynamic Psychopathology in Childhood*, ed. L. Jessner & E. Pavenstedt. New York: Grune & Stratton, pp. 6-77.
—— (1961a), Some Developmental Observations Relating to Theory of Anxiety. *J. Amer. Psa. Assn.*, 9:652-668.
—— (1961b), The Innate and the Experiential in Development. In: *Lectures in Experimental Psychiatry*, ed. H. W. Brosin. Pittsburgh: University of Pittsburgh Press, pp. 19-42.
—— (1963), Further Comments on Some Developmental Aspects of Anxiety. In: *Counterpoint: Libidinal Object and Subject*, ed. H. S. Gaskill. New York: International Universities Press, pp. 121-153.

Beres, D. (1968), The Humanness of Human Beings: Psychoanalytic Considerations. *Psa. Quart.*, 37:487-522.

Cobliner, W. G. (1965), Appendix: The Geneva School of Genetic Psychology and Psychoanalysis: Parallels and Counterparts. In R. A. Spitz: *The First Year of Life*. New York: International Universities Press, pp. 301-356.

Décarie, T. G. (1965), *Intelligence and Affectivity in Early Childhood*. New York: International Universities Press.

Escalona, S. K. (1968), *The Roots of Individuality*. Chicago: Aldine.

Freud, A. (1952), The Mutual Influences in the Development of Ego and Id. *This Annual*, 7:42-50.

—— (1960), Discussion of Dr. John Bowlby's Paper. *This Annual*, 15:53-62.

—— (1963), The Concept of Developmental Lines. *This Annual*, 18:245-265.

—— (1965), *Normality and Pathology in Childhood*. New York: International Universities Press.

Freud, S. (1925), Negation. *Standard Edition*, 19:235-239. London: Hogarth Press, 1961.

Frosch, J. (1966), A Note on Reality Constancy. In: *Psychoanalysis—A General Psychology*, ed. R. M. Loewenstein, L. M. Newman, M. Schur, & A. J. Solnit. New York: International Universities Press, pp. 349-376.

Hartmann, H. (1952), The Mutual Influences in the Development of Ego and Id. *Essays on Ego Psychology*. New York: International Universities Press, 1964, pp. 155-182.

—— (1953), Contribution to the Metapsychology of Schizophrenia. *Essays on Ego Psychology*. New York: International Universities Press, 1964, pp. 182-206.

—— (1956), Notes on the Reality Principle. *Essays on Ego Psychology*. New York: International Universities Press, 1964, pp. 241-267.

—— Kris, E., & Loewenstein, R. M. (1946), Comments on the Formation of Psychic Structure. *This Annual*, 2:11-38.

Hoffer, W. (1950), Development of the Body Ego. *This Annual*, 5:18-24.

—— (1952), The Mutual Influences in the Development of Ego and Id: Earliest Stages. *This Annual*, 7:31-41.

—— (1955), *Psychoanalysis: Practical and Research Aspects*. Baltimore: Williams & Wilkins.

Jacobson, E. (1964), *The Self and the Object World*. New York: International Universities Press.

Mahler, M. S. (1963), Thoughts about Development and Individuation. *This Annual*, 18:307-324.

—— (1965), On the Significance of the Normal Separation-Individuation Phase. In: *Drives, Affects, Behavior*, Vol. 2, ed. M. Schur. New York: International Universities Press, pp. 161-169.

—— & Furer, M. (1963), Certain Aspects of the Separation-Individuation Phase. *Psa. Quart.*, 32:1-14.

—— & Gosliner, B. J. (1955), On Symbiotic Child Psychosis. *This Annual*, 10:195-212.

—— & La Perriere, K. (1965), Mother-Child Interaction during Separation-Individuation. *Psa. Quart.*, 34:483-498.

Nagera, H. (1966), Sleep and Its Disturbances Approached Developmentally. *This Annual*, 21:393-447.

Panel Discussion (1968), held at the 25th Congress of the International Psychoanalytical Association, Copenhagen, July, 1967. *Int. J. Psa.*, 49:506-512.

Piaget, J. (1937), *The Construction of Reality in the Child*. New York: Basic Books, 1954.

—— (1945), *Play, Dreams, and Imitation in Childhood*. New York: Norton, 1951.

Rapaport, D. (1960), *The Structure of Psychoanalytic Theory* [*Psychological Issues*, Monogr. 6]. New York: International Universities Press.

Spitz, R. A. (1957), *No and Yes: On the Genesis of Human Communication*. New York: International Universities Press.

—— (1959), *A Genetic Field Theory of Ego Formation*. New York: International Universities Press.

—— (1965), *The First Year of Life*. New York: International Universities Press.

—— (1966), Metapsychology and Infant Observation. In: *Psychoanalysis—A General Psychology*, ed. R. M. Loewenstein, L. M. Newman, M. Schur, & A. J. Solnit. New York: International Universities Press, pp. 123-151.

—— & Wolf, K. M. (1946), Anaclitic Depression: An Inquiry into the Genesis of Psychiatric Conditions in Early Childhood. *This Annual*, 2:313-342.

—— —— (1949), Autoerotism: Some Empirical Findings and Hypotheses on Three of Its Manifestations in the First Year of Life. *This Annual*, 3/4:85-120.

Werner, H. (1957), *Comparative Psychology of Mental Development*. New York: International Universities Press.

Wolff, P. H. (1960), *The Developmental Psychologies of Jean Piaget and Psychoanalysis* [*Psychological Issues*, Monogr. 5]. New York: International Universities Press.

THE UNREMEMBERABLE AND THE UNFORGETTABLE

Passive Primal Repression

ALVIN FRANK, M.D. (St. Louis)

The relationship between past and present—between what is forgotten in childhood and what endures and reappears in the adult in the guise of character, symptoms, screen memories, and transferences—continues to occupy a central position in psychoanalytic interest. However, the application of the concept of childhood primal repression is often derived more from the spirit of Freud's writings than from his incomplete, infrequent, explicit expositions. In addition, the theory of childhood repression and amnesia lags in contrast to impressive advances in other areas. This paper is an attempt to explore certain clinical and theoretical aspects of primal repression in a way consistent with current psychoanalytic clinical practice and psychology.

PRIMAL REPRESSION IN FREUD'S WRITINGS

In reviewing the development of the concept of primal repression in Freud's writings, Frank and Muslin (1967) observed three distinct phases. The first, from about 1895 to 1898, we regarded as *prototypical*. Trauma could affect later mental life through deferred unconscious activity resulting in specific neuroses. The trauma was overt (e.g., sexual seduction) and the result specific (e.g., hysteria).

The second phase was from 1900 to 1915. Repression, explicitly defined as the exclusion of ideational content from consciousness,

---

The author is particularly indebted to Drs. Heinz Kohut and Gene Borowitz for their criticism and suggestions.

was now described as a universal phenomenon in normal development. As a result of the deferred development of the secondary
processes in childhood, certain early impressions and their wishful
forces are "primarily repressed"; Freud also described the process
as "a passive lagging behind," i.e., subject to "fixation." In line
with this characterization, we called this phase a theory of *passive
primal repression*. The forces involved continue to exert an indirect, and at times profound, effect on mental life. However, their
ideational representatives, because of their lack of preconscious
representation (at this stage in the development of the theory, still
intimately associated with verbal mnemic symbols), are inaccessible
to consciousness. Furthermore, the later fulfillment of these wishful
impulses results in unpleasure (as well as the pleasure of discharge)
because of the discrepancies between the primary and secondary
processes and, inferentially, the latter's implicit standards and prohibitions. Later associatively related impulses are subject to the
same repressive forces; hence primal repression (alternatively desig-
nated as "fixation") is a necessary precondition for later repression
(repression proper, or secondary repression). The primal repression
in this formulation is maintained by system Preconscious anticathexes.

In the third phase, consonant with revolutionary changes in the
theory of anxiety in *Inhibition, Symptoms and Anxiety,* Freud presented a new formulation. Primal repression was regarded, from the
first, as an active defensive process. Previously he had proposed no
motive for primal repressions; only after the establishment of the
secondary processes and the primally repressed could once pleasurable fulfillment lead to unpleasure. Now a motive—a specific stimulus for production of the unpleasure responsible for the primal
repression—was explicitly defined. *Active defensive primal repression* occurs as a result of unpleasure associated with overstimulation
of the immature mental apparatus. Thus the process of primal repression, as redefined in 1926, was initiated in response to the unpleasure associated with an economic factor.

While Freud repeatedly associated the earliest outbreaks of anxiety (i.e., anxiety resulting from overstimulation of the mental apparatus rather than signal anxiety) with the earliest repressions, he
also associated this defense with a certain degree of ego organization,

specifically with the preconscious state. Hence we inferred that active defensive primal repression was not present in the first days or weeks of life, but began with the development of the preconscious state. In addition, in contrast to the 1900-1915 concept, the ideational representatives of active defensive primal repression may once have possessed, and subsequently lost, preconscious representation. In the absence of further comment by Freud, we felt justified in considering two dividing lines between active defensive primal repression (i.e., as defined in 1926) and repression proper in normal development. The first is associated with the stable establishment of the danger situation-signal anxiety sequence for any given situation of instinctual overstimulation. The second dividing line is the end of the usual developmental series of such situations, which is in turn associated with the formation of the superego.

In contrast to Brenner (1957), we considered that Freud's changing use of the designation *primal repression* did not connote his abandonment of the earlier (1900-1915) formulation; an examination of his later writings demonstrated to our satisfaction that he now presupposed the existence of this phenomenon, although he used the phrase, *primal repression,* in another context (1939, p. 96f.; and 1940, p. 163). Therefore, the newer theory represented an addition rather than a correction. It seemed likely that these two processes continue side by side in the developing mental apparatus.

In addition, using Freud's later diagrammatic models of the mature mental apparatus, we speculated on the topographic and structural characteristics of unconscious contents subject to each type of primal repression. *Passive primal repression* corresponds to a portion of the area where ego and id are not sharply separated, but gradually merge. In contrast, that which is termed *actively primally repressed* is quite sharply separated from the preconscious ego by the repression barrier.

My purpose here is to explore and clarify further the phenomena and concepts corresponding to the theory of *passive primal repression.* No one can be certain whether or not Freud's use of primal repression in another sense connoted his abandonment of this theory per se. However, there can be no doubt that he continued to consider the relative immaturity of the preconscious system (and after 1923 in *The Ego and the Id,* of certain higher level ego functions) associated with secondary process organization as an important factor in the inaccessibility and form of the memories of early childhood. Subsequent psychoanalytic experience has confirmed this view. An indication of the importance of these considerations is that they led, for example, to some of the most telling criticisms of Melanie Klein's theoretical constructs (Glover, 1945).

The use of the term, *passive primal repression,* in other than a historical sense may well be objected to as misleading and self-contradictory. In every other psychoanalytic context, *repression* connotes a defense, yet it is used here to describe a developmental rather than defensive vicissitude. The very imagery evoked by this word is one of active exclusion. Furthermore, prefacing the word *repression* (with its connotation of action) with the word *passive* introduces an apparent contradiction and confusion. Also, the process involved—the laying down and organization of memory traces in the infantile mental apparatus (regardless of the presence or absence of preconscious representation)—can hardly be characterized as "passive." Finally Freud's last theory of primal repression is more specifically and accurately characterized by this term. Why not let its earlier use die a natural death, and in the process avoid overlapping terminology and continued muddying of the waters?

However, the advantages of continued use of *passive primal repression* are also compelling. Freud's use of the term *primal repression* constitutes more than historical precedent. Unless the two processes—passive and active primal repression—are clearly and explicitly distinguished when using the term *primal repression,* the attributes and characteristics of one are bound to be confused with those of the other (e.g., Purves, 1966, p. 78). Furthermore, a number of analysts continue to use *primal repression* primarily or exclusively in this earlier sense *(vide infra).*

The overlapping of terms also has other justification. Although distinct models and examples of passive or active primal repression can be provided, the two phenomena are probably often simultaneously or alternately involved. Furthermore, the absence of preconscious representation (whether determined by developmental vicissitudes, overstimulation of the mental apparatus, or an anxiety signal) is the common feature of passive primal repression, active primal repression, and repression proper. In each case, it leads to the identical result: the higher segments of the mind are not in communication with the lower. It is this common result, expressed clinically, which confronts the analyst in his work and research. The use of the same noun, *repression,* to characterize the identical feature (absence of preconscious representation associated with the identical result common to these processes) has merit. Hence, despite the serious disadvantages of this term, its advantages, in my opinion, justify its continued and expanded use.

In this paper, the continued use of the term *primal repression* in the sense of *passive primal repression* will first be reviewed. Secondly, clinical, experimental, and theoretical work having relevance to the nature, form, recording, and reproduction of the experiences of early childhood can only be sampled. Finally, after considering the concept of *passive primal repression* from the standpoint of contemporary psychoanalytic theory, illustrations of its applicability to clinical material will be provided.

Passive Primal Repression in the Psychoanalytic Literature

As previously stated, a number of analysts continue to use *primal repression* in the sense of *passive primal repression.* They include Charny et al. (1966, pp. 388-398) and Lantos (1955, p. 282f.), both of whom cite the 1915 "Repression" paper in reference to the primal repression of early childhood impressions. Similarly, Rapaport (1951, pp. 322, 694-696) uses a model of cathectic dynamics for primal repression, which is derived from the 1915 "Unconscious" paper.

The even more specific association of primal repression with the preverbal period (reminiscent of Freud's original emphasis on the mnemic residues of speech) is made by several analysts, including Glover (1939, Ch. 5) and Anna Freud. The latter describes "elements under primary repression, which are preverbal, have never formed part of the organized ego, and cannot be 'remembered,' only relived within the transference." She also refers to the primary repression of "early cannibalistic fantasies" as dealt with "before an effective ego or superego are formed" (1965, pp. 31-32, 175). Whitman and K. Eissler apply the concept in its most concrete form, i.e., primal repression refers to that within the mental apparatus which has never been conscious. Accordingly, Whitman (1963) extends primal repression to include "never conscious" *adult* phenomena, specifically certain dreams in adults which cannot be recovered in an experimental setting.[1] Eissler (1962, pp. 36-39), using the association between what "never was conscious" and the primally repressed, compares primal repression with certain sensory experiences in adult life. He bases this analogy on Fisher's study of subliminally tachistoscopically exposed images.[2]

THE NATURE, FORM, RECORDING, AND REPRODUCTION OF THE EXPERIENCES OF EARLY CHILDHOOD

Since 1893, when Breuer and Freud made their revolutionary statement that "hysterics suffer from reminiscences" (p. 7), the relationships between the form of remembering, the initiating event of the memory, and the specific mode of recovery have been important in the technique of clinical psychoanalysis. As early as 1900, in *The Interpretation of Dreams,* Freud quoted himself as telling a patient that "the earliest experiences of childhood were 'not obtainable any longer* as such,' but were replaced in analysis by 'transferences' and dreams" (p. 184). In "Remembering, Repeating, and Working-Through" he referred to a group of "purely internal acts" as processes in which "it particularly often happens that something is 'remembered' which could never have been 'forgotten' because it was never at any time noticed—was never conscious" (1914, p. 149).

[1] This proposition is untenable if one acknowledges the infantile wish origin of dreaming. It is the primally repressed childhood wish which initiates the dream; repression proper is responsible for its loss. Rather than the dream having been primally repressed, the dream itself is the product of primal repression.

[2] Somewhat surprisingly, comparatively few authors explicitly use the term *primal repression* as redefined by Freud in *Inhibitions, Symptoms and Anxiety.* Pearson (1953) implies this usage and Madison uses the term to encompass "all the traumas up to the development of the superego" (1961, Ch. 6). Purves notes the 1926 change in Freud's theoretical position and attempts to reconcile the change with the earlier concept, which Purves still considers valid (1966, p. 78). Brenner (1957) clearly distinguishes between the earlier and later concepts; he understands Freud to have completely replaced the former concept with the latter.

Other work involving the term or concept of primal repression cannot be neatly categorized as corresponding to either of the stages in Freud's development of the theory. Here the two noteworthy trends are toward primitivization of the concept (Nunberg, 1932, pp. 223, 226, 234-236; K. Eissler, 1953, pp. 220-224; M. Klein, 1932, p. 183f.) and open disagreement and/or departure from Freud's basic theses (Johnson, 1951; Hambidge, 1956).

Here, "conviction" regarding the memory is crucial. In the same paper Freud included in the unrememberable category external experiences occurring in very early childhood and not understood at the time, though later understood and revealed through dreams; this probably is a reference to the Wolf Man case (1918).[3]

In 1938, Isakower published a description of an alteration of ego state (usually hypnagogic) characterized by the blurring of distinctions between the self and external percepts:

> The principal bodily regions concerned are the mouth, the skin and the hand. In many cases there are, as well, distinct sensations of floating, sinking and giddiness. . . . Most striking of all is the blurring of the distinction between quite different regions of the body, e.g., between mouth and skin, and also between what is internal and what is external, the body and the outside world. We note too the amorphous character of the impressions conveyed by the sense-organs. The visual impression is that of something shadowy and indefinite, generally felt to be 'round,' which comes nearer and nearer, swells to a gigantic size and threatens to crush the subject. It then gradually becomes smaller and shrinks up to nothing. Sometimes there is fire somewhere in the room. The auditory impression is of a humming, rustling, babbling, murmuring, or of an unintelligible monotonous speech. The tactile sensation is of something crumpled, jagged, sandy or dry, and is experienced in the mouth and at the same time on the skin of the whole body. Or else the subject feels enveloped by it or knows that it is close at hand. Sometimes it feels as if there were a soft yielding mass in his mouth, but at the same time he knows it is outside him [p. 332f.].
>
> [Isakower proposed that these phenomena were] a revival of very early ego-attitudes, . . . they are mental images of sucking at the mother's breast and of falling asleep there when satisfied. The large object which approaches probably represents the breast, with its promise of food. When satisfied, the infant loses interest in the breast, which appears smaller and smaller and finally vanishes away. The mother's breast is the sole representative of the objects in the external world; at this stage it is not the mother as a person but only her breast which is the object [p. 341f.].

---

[3] Freud repeated essentially these same considerations in his Wolf Man paper (1918, pp. 48-60) and the *Introductory Lectures on Psycho-Analysis* (1916-1917, lectures XXIII, XXVII, XXVIII). The therapeutic adequacy of "conviction" as equivalent to recollection was maintained as late as his last technical paper (1937).

Subsequently, others have explored implications of various features of this ego state (e.g., Bonnard, 1960; Lewin, 1953; Spitz, 1955), as well as its regressive defensive use (e.g., Fenichel, 1945; Fink, 1967; Gill, 1963; Heilbrunn, 1953). The Isakower phenomenon remains for most analysts the example *par excellence* of the adult reproduction of an early childhood experience.

Anthony (1961) has described similar "screen sensations," observed in the analysis of a schizoid adolescent girl. For example:

> . . . she said, "I feel giddy," and curled up on her side. She began to shiver and put her arms round the cushion with her face almost buried in it. She began to mumble not very clearly: "So happy, so very happy . . . so kind . . . everyone kind and happy and good . . . lovely feeling . . . all colors . . . such nice taste . . . good taste . . . I'm flying . . . the blue's coming near . . . it's going away . . . it's gone. . . . It was like having a dream when I was awake" [p. 218].

Anthony compared his patient's screen sensations (involving the reliving of an experience at nine months while still on the breast) with those described by Marcel Proust in his *Remembrance of Things Past*. In both cases, the original sensory impressions dated from the first months of life, the same period as the Isakower phenomenon. During this time, the world of the infant is predominantly the breast and is characterized by feelings of magical omnipotence, hallucinatory wish fulfillment, absence of ego boundaries, and primitive, ill-defined, syncretic, synesthetic perceptions. Borderline, schizoid, and isolated people manifesting a high degree of orality, with fixation points at an early sucking level, are prone to these experiences.

Others have also considered the relevance of early ego capacities and states to the later reproduction of associated experiences and affects. Among them, Woodbury's (1966) interest is in "altered body ego experiences," "sensations of a change in the organization (size, configuration, and spatial orientation) and sense of unity of the body ego with effects . . . upon object and self representation and the relationship between the two" (p. 273). Such experiences include most of the phenomena described above. He also considers them a "formal" regression to earlier perceptual modes, later available for use as defense.

Niederland (1965) emphasized in the recovery of repressed memories the importance of "the specific state of the ego, especially in relation to its perceptual and sensory functioning at the time of the original experience—as well as . . . its functioning at the time of the recovery of the memory in analysis." In a case illustration, a presumably schizophrenic young man habitually dressed in layer upon layer of garments, regardless of the weather. A dream depicted him near or at the North Pole, his bed a block of ice or a refrigerator, surrounded by the ice, cold and darkness of a seemingly endless night. When dawn finally came, some people walked in and out of the room where he was lying. Reconstruction proposing that there had been a corresponding concrete experience in childhood led to confirmation by the parents. When he was "less than a year old, they indeed had had to 'thaw him out' of his urine, feces, and vomitus because 'by mistake' they had left the window of his room half-open throughout a very cold winter night." There was no recall on the patient's part, but his "excitement" on confirmation of the reconstruction is suggestive of solid conviction. The dream was "a turning point in the treatment and in his life" (p. 566ff.).

It is likely that this is also an example of relatively uncomplicated passive primal repression, falling into Freud's category of external experiences not understood at the time but subsequently understood and revealed through a dream. This patient could not forget his terrible childhood experience. As a matter of fact, without remembering it, he continued to "dress for the occasion." Not until a memory was provided through Niederland's reconstruction could the patient realize that he was reacting to the past rather than the present. At this point he could leave the past and its awful consequences.

Niederland drew on his clinical experience to propose that fragmentary and disconnected remembering is derived from early visual experiences. In contrast, still earlier experiences lead to a more global type of perception including kinesthetic, olfactory, and auditory modalities. The re-experiencing, understanding, and translation of these primitive ego states by the more developed apparatuses of the adult ego are of particular therapeutic value. Loewald (1955), with particular emphasis on economic considerations, has also cited the therapeutic importance of such synthesis and integration.

Kris (1956) has discussed the difficulties inherent in the interpretation of archaic impulses. Such interpretation should not provide patients with an "id vernacular" which can be used in the service of resistance. The more archaic the material, the more pervasive its derivatives. Accordingly, the broader the base from which a reconstruction is reached, the greater the chance of impact.

> The area where the most effective link between reconstruction and experience can be established is subject to great variations according to factors in the patient's personality and illness which I am at a loss to specify. To mention contrasting examples: I remember one instance in which the aggressive and teasing interplay between mother and child during early feeding was mainly reconstructed from the consistency and gradual sharpening of verbalizations in the transference situation—a reconstruction accidentally and spontaneously confirmed by an early observer, who had been in the house when the mother breast fed the patient. In another instance, the discussion of the long-suppressed dissatisfaction in life was during later stages of analysis accompanied by burning sensations in the oral cavity and the palate. Interpretations of the traumatic experience in the suppression of rage, focused in earlier remembered instances from the period of toilet training, could thus plausibly be extended into the nursing situation. In both these instances, however, the patient's conviction could only arise by the felt or experienced link between past and present [p. 72].

In addition, Kris demonstrated how later events play an important part in determining the meaning, effect, and form of representation of earlier traumatic experiences. Such factors obviously complicate later reconstruction. Fortunately, the meaning of these events and the anticathectic investment opposing the re-emergence of associated instinctual derivatives and affects are much more important than accurate reproduction of the actual events.

The work of these authors confirms common-sense expectations regarding the traumatic experiences of early childhood. The events are recorded in the mental apparatus as originally perceived, i.e., in keeping with the capacities of the infant or overwhelmed child.

The same is true of the organization of events.[4] However, what of the mass of relatively optimal early childhood experiences? They too must be initially recorded in the same manner. They are rarely revived in analysis except in reference to conflict. When they do reappear, as in screen memories, we are justifiably suspicious. We repeatedly find that they owe their continued existence and revival to associated traumatic experiences or patterns. Is it enough to cite the economic considerations at the time these optimal memories were laid down, i.e., that the memories were never hypercathected as the result of excessive frustration or overstimulation? This cannot be an adequate explanation, inasmuch as it ignores the possibility of later condensation in the unconscious ego. The probability that early optimal memories are involved in some process of structural change or reorganization is inescapable.

We generally find evidence of such optimal experiences in the form of ego strengths. Examples include Erikson's (1950) "ego qualities" of "trust," "autonomy," etc., and Benedek's (1938) "confidence." In addition, what Winnicott has termed "capacities," such as "to be alone" (1958) or "for concern" (1963), fall into this category. Such studies as Spitz's hospitalism (1945) and Provence and Lipton's *Infants in Institutions* (1962) confirm the crucial importance of such positive experiences and the corresponding memory traces in the development of the child. Children deprived of such optimal experiences show profound deficiences in ego development in many areas, including, at times, qualities necessary for life itself.

The premise that early nontraumatic memory traces later became, at least in part, "capacities," "ego qualities," or "strengths" presupposes an intervening process responsible for this transformation. It would consist of the progressive and oft-repeated reordering

[4] Rarely one encounters an objection to this point of view. For an example, see Bernstein and Blacher (1967).

Many observational data also contribute to these conclusions, such as the observations and interpretations (although not necessarily the theoretical systems) of Piaget (Wolff, 1960) pertaining to the development of the autonomous sphere of the ego. The psychoanalytic theory for the development of the secondary processes has kept pace. Beginning with Chapter VII of *The Interpretation of Dreams* (1900) and "Formulations on the Two Principles of Mental Functioning" (1911), it includes such landmark contributions as Ferenczi's "Stages in the Development of Reality" (1913) and Rapaport's "On the Psycho-Analytic Theory of Thinking" (1950). And, of course, the contributions of child analysis are so extensive that they cannot be listed separately.

of these memories in response to internal and external stimuli and experiences; each reorganization widens the gap between the form of the original memory traces and its later reorganized representation. Changes in the libidinal and aggressive cathexes of the memory traces would be inevitable. The degree of fusion and neutralization occurring may generally determine the stability and resistance to regression of the later structures. In the first five or six years of life, the ego is notoriously unstable and prone to regression. Latency offers an opportunity for substantial consolidation and stabilization.

The concept of *change of function*, implicit in this transformation of early memory traces into ego capacities, is well established in psychoanalytic psychology. As described by Hartmann (1939), it involves early behavior forms and defensive attitudes which evolve as relatively independent structures and come to serve other functions (pp. 25-26, 49-50). In addition, Hartmann mentions specifically the *change of function* implicit in the transformation of what were once *magic images* into forms of artistic representation (p. 77). Hence, little, if any, expansion of this concept is required to account for change in the memory traces of early childhood.

To summarize, most memory traces of the relatively optimal experiences of early childhood undergo a *change of function* eventuating in ego strengths, capacities, and qualities. The underlying processes of reorganization, fusion, and neutralization of energy result in an estrangement of the later structures from the original experiences. This, in turn, is another factor in the normal amnesia of childhood.[5]

THE METAPSYCHOLOGY OF PASSIVE PRIMAL REPRESSION

Freud began with observable clinical phenomena, the influences of childhood experiences on the adult mental apparatus. He periodically attempted to conceptualize and explain them at higher levels of abstraction, each time in the context of, and limited by,

---

[5] According to Mahler and Elkish (1953), the parents of psychotic children frequently stress their children's "fabulous memory." This phenomenon is usually ascribed to a "failure of repression" as the result of grave ego defects. It must, however, be partially a result of the absence of processes leading to the change of function described above.

the theoretical concepts then formulated. Yet, even in his first expositions of the (as yet unnamed) concept of primal repression are
condensed the anlagen of his later theories. Our concept of *passive
primal repression* has been largely based on Freud's writings, 1900-
1915. This paper attempts to characterize the process in terms of
current psychoanalytic theory; it covers changes based on Freud's
explicit additions and corrections, and also changes corresponding
to advances by Freud's co-workers and heirs, many of which have
been reviewed here. In addition, it separates out those aspects which
were originally included as the result of Freud's intuitive condensation. Those features which we can now see as appropriate to the
later, necessary, yet still unformulated theory of *active defensive
primal repression* have been eliminated.

Approached in this way, a current theory of *passive primal repression* would be:[6]

1. Maturational and Developmental: As the result of the gradual
development (in normal maturation) of the ego apparatuses involving the organization of perception and thought according to laws of
the secondary processes, a large store of infantile wishful impulses
and memories are incomprehensible and inaccessible to ordinary
consciousness. They lack the formal characteristics necessary for
translation into coherent thought and memory. Their form and
organization are determined by the capacities and characteristics
of the immature mental apparatus then existent.

2. Structural: In their original condition, these more or less
highly cathected memories reside in the area where unconscious id
and ego gradually merge (Freud, 1933, p. 78). However, they are
subject to various vicissitudes as described below.

3. Dynamic and Economic: To the degree that these impressions represent experiences in a range of optimum frustrations, they
participate in the progressive neutralization described by Kohut and
Seitz (1963). To the degree that they represent highly cathected
memories of traumatic intensity, they are *fixations,* exerting a potentially pathological affect on the developing mental apparatus. In
the latter situation, they may from the time of inception evoke
primitive defenses then available to the mental apparatus (e.g., re-

---

[6] For purposes of comparison see Frank and Muslin (1967, p. 64f.).

versal, turning upon the self, etc.). After the establishment of the reality principle through the evolution of the secondary processes, their revival may in addition evoke *active defensive primal repression* with its preconscious anticathexes. In this case, later associatively linked experiences will be subject to repression proper, just as in active defensive primal repression. This situation corresponds to Jacobson's description of resolving infantile repressions to find more primitive defenses beneath (1957, pp. 78, 82ff.).

Refinements of the structural hypotheses and assumptions regarding the two forms of primal repression lead to greater discrimination and specificity when considering passive primal repression from the structural, dynamic, and economic viewpoints. The important change here is in the consideration of Freud's formulations regarding preconscious anticathexes as foreshadowing his later (1926) theory of *active primal repression*. Hence they are only secondarily pertinent to passive primal repression, as described above.[7]

4. Adaptive: Even inaccessible memory traces of optimal frustration facilitate development and maturation of the mental apparatus in a realistically oriented, effective, and fulfilling manner. This is the result of a change of function occurring as a consequence of the progressive and repeated reorganization of memory traces (in response to continued nontraumatic internal and extenal stimuli and experiences). It is associated with the progressive fusion and neutralization of the involved energies. These processes culminate in ego strengths, capacities, and qualities. They are, in turn, an additional factor in the normal amnesia of childhood.

On the other hand, highly cathected inaccessible memory traces of traumatic intensity facilitate maladaptation through their direct fixative effects and influence on subsequent development stages and tasks.

Thus characterized, *passive primal repression* does not initially serve a defensive purpose but is more accurately termed a *mental event* or, at times, a *fixation*. Hence, it conforms more precisely to

[7] This adjustment preserves the internal consistency of both theories. It corresponds to hints, at the time of the 1915 papers, that Freud was already being inconsistent in treating primal repression as an *active* process while explicitly describing it as a *passive* process (Frank and Muslin, p. 63n.). In addition, he stated a year earlier that the Wolf Man's childhood homosexual attitude was repressed because of its "overwhelming intensity" (1918, p. 110f.).

Freud's original *explicit* proposition. Passive primal repression refers in this sense to the unrememberable "memories" of childhood, which at times can be inferred through: deductions based on alterations of ego states and certain characteristics or contents of these states; certain "screen" phenomena; certain symptoms; symptomatic behavior and character alterations; and the reproduction of early impressions by reliving them in the psychoanalytic situation. Paradoxically, some of these same "memories" could as aptly be titled *unforgettable* as *unrememberable,* so profound is their effect.

Previously it was proposed that what was recorded in the mental apparatus prior to its ability to respond with *active primal repression* (i.e., *the passively primally repressed*) could, in the event of its revival, later be *actively primally repressed.* Another possibility exists for the association of these phenomena. Any traumatic (in the economic sense) event evoking *active primal repression* might, in a given instance, be sufficiently powerful to overwhelm the immature ego apparatuses involving secondary process mentation and organization. In this event, a state operationally equivalent to that consistent with *passive primal repression* would prevail. Although the mental apparatus optimally possesses the ego apparatuses of secondary process mentation, such apparatuses would be rendered functionally inoperative. A similar situation may occur under the impact of physiological trauma. This variable involves not only the strength of the instinctual drive but also: the extent of ego development and degree of consolidation; the presence or absence of concurrent trauma or ego vulnerability; and the state of the ego at the actual moments of trauma.[8] It seems reasonable to infer a sort of rough reciprocity between passive and active primal repression as each undergoes its vicissitudes, the balance tipping more and more toward the latter with age. With the eventual consolidation in adult life of the ego apparatuses involved, overwhelming trauma in time leads to the familiar *traumatic neurosis* (Freud, 1920, pp. 12-14, 31-35).

---

[8] Niederland's first case, in the paper discussed above (1965), is very probably an example. See also Stein (1965).

THE DATA OF OBSERVATION: CLINICAL ILLUSTRATIONS

In the preceding section, I have discussed *passive primal repression* according to Waelder's *level of clinical theory* (1962, p. 620f.); now, specific examples of analytic material will be given—including primarily data at the *level of observation* (i.e., what the patient said and did), and the relationship of such data to "other behavior or conscious content" at the *level of clinical interpretation.* In addition, generalizations will be made or implied about related phenomena such as symptoms, character, and behavior patterns at the *level of clinical generalization.*[9]

In considering this material, the reader should keep some qualifying factors in mind. First, that the tendency to exaggerate the impact of a single experience on the infant or child is reinforced by what Anna Freud (1951) so aptly called "the telescoping of events" in memory:

> An action which we see the infant repeat a hundred times may in later life be represented as one traumatic happening. . . . One traumatic prohibition or punishment, remembered or reconstructed, becomes the representative of hundreds of frustrations which had been imposed on the child; one longer separation from the mother takes over the combined effect of innumerable times when the infant has been left alone in his cot, his room, at bedtime, etc. [p. 26f.].

Similarly, the editing of clinical material to demonstrate one particular aspect inevitably introduces a false impression of simplicity. While overdetermining factors are cited or implied here, their exposition is made impossible by limitations of space. These illustrations are meant to demonstrate only one aspect of multifaceted and multi-determined patterns of behavior, feeling, and personality, i.e., that aspect corresponding to *passive primal repression.*

Illustration 1

At the age of twenty-two, an unmarried male graduate student began analysis. The first three and a half years of his analysis were

---

[9] From these generalizations are derived concepts at *the level of clinical theory;* even more abstract is the level of metapsychology.

characterized by intense and stubborn resistances. Progress was made, but slowly and sporadically. Nevertheless, important themes emerged and were analyzed during this time. The patient's feminine identification—including what he saw as the narcissistic advantages in the passivity of the feminine role—became clear; his wish to be a woman expressed, yet simultaneously guarded against, his rage and fantasied omnipotent aggressiveness. The absence of stable masculine figures in the patient's life, his mother's exhibiting herself repeatedly to him, and "accidental" primal scene exposure on several occasions were some of the major early influences upon the patient. Further, his experiences with his mother seemed most often characterized by overgratification and excessive stimulation, followed by sudden frustration, rejection, or punishment.

The insights associated with this work seemed solid and well integrated, yet despite some clinical improvement the patient was mired in transference resistance. Indeed, it seemed that the more he learned about his feminine aspirations, the freer he became in their expression during analytic hours and in his sexual relationships with women. I was also impressed by the ease with which he seemed to ignore the fact that he was, indeed, a man and his partner a woman, and particularly that each was a separate person. It seemed an important factor, and I reflected occasionally on the ego defects which might explain such a pattern, without reaching any definite conclusions.

Under stress, the patient periodically demonstrated a certain pattern of behavior, first seen by the analyst as an extreme plasticity during analytic hours. The patient seemed to be acting, as on a stage.[10] In the latter part of the fourth year of analysis, this state recurred. During the same period he began to sing to himself. He experienced the room as growing smaller, himself as growing in size to meet it. He reported wanting to bite and swallow his girlfriend's nipples and breasts. At the same time he was surprised when her feelings differed from his own. Masturbation increased in frequency. He became sexually excited when looking at himself in the mirror. He reported experiencing masculine and feminine sensations and

---

[10] If this state had pervaded his everyday behavior, it would have corresponded to that of the "as if" character, as described by H. Deutsch (1942).

excitement simultaneously. He recognized that when his girlfriend performed fellatio he always had a simultaneous feeling that he was doing it to himself. When she suckled at his nipple, he had a simultaneous feeling of suckling and being suckled. "Half of sex for me is being both things at one time." He was attracted and excited by teen-age boys who reminded him of himself at that age. He had fantasies of kissing himself during the analytic hours. He acknowledged a reservoir within himself of wishes to be touched, fondled, kissed, caressed, loved, and admired. He explained what was happening as related to his wish to be a woman during lovemaking. The analyst stated it was also like being a baby. The patient said it made no difference, he couldn't remember back then anyway.

My statement was as follows: "I think that we see in you a tremendous reservoir of very powerful needs to be touched, to be caressed, to be kissed, to be fondled, to be admired and that in this state you don't feel other people as different from yourself; this tells us as much as any memory could—that somewhere along the line you didn't get all that you wanted or needed, or that you got a lot and were then sharply deprived. It adds up to the same thing —that there is this tremendous reservoir."

The patient's response was skeptical. What could he do about it? Nothing at all. This was the time for "operation bootstrap," to pull himself up, to try and compensate for these things. At this point I announced the end of the hour. The patient very spontaneously said that he did not want to leave. He then remained on the couch, silent, for a minute before rising and leaving (the first time this had happened).

The patient looked exhilarated at the beginning of the next hour. He spoke rapidly and in an excited way. "I thought you would never get here. I have been waiting for you so eagerly. What you said yesterday—it had such a profound effect on me. I nearly called you last night. I wanted to. It's funny. It didn't seem to make that much difference when you said it yesterday. I didn't want to leave yesterday though. My feelings were so exhilarated. I felt so full of energy I didn't know what to do with it all. I didn't go to sleep until 4 o'clock. I worked and I worked efficiently until 3:30, then went out for a snack, then came back and went to sleep. All of this energy. I don't know what it was. Things seem to make sense to me . . . like wanting to be a woman and get all of those things. Also my work, when it involves taking care of people. It is like I hated doing it and then had to be very intellectual because I hated it so. It is very hard to put into words. I don't think I can. I wanted to call you up . . . I feel differently about myself. I feel more like other people, really me. . . . The feeling I have had, it is so different. It is so hard to describe. Like I am a real human being. I don't know." At the end of the hour there was a repetition of the feeling of fusing with the room.

In this case, I understood the phenomena described as manifestations of highly cathected *passively primally repressed* memories, appropriate to a period when the distinction between self and object was not yet firmly established. The patient experienced his surroundings, including my office (as an extension of myself), as part of himself in the transference relationship. The recognition and reconstruction of these infantile experiences as related to the current situation could be brushed aside, probably through isolation and denial, until the end of the hour; at that time, departure from the analyst and the office must have reinforced the reality of his separateness and swung the balance in favor of his observing ego.

These hypotheses were confirmed by the patient's later reactions, particularly by evidence of intrapsychic energy shifts. The hypomanic manifestations were the result of newly available energies, freed from primitive defensive and other structures, which were now disintegrating. An analogous feeling of "Joy stemming from the sudden availability of energy previously expended in maintaining repressive processes, and from a diminution of anxiety" was associated with "screen sensations" (Anthony, 1961, p. 234). The patient continued to be exhilarated and overstimulated for about two weeks, and there was a more enduring increase in his energy level after this time. Previously, he had felt that he lacked energy for his work, had to drag himself out of bed in the morning, and needed midday naps in order to refresh himself. This was no longer the case. His analytic work continued at a faster pace and led to a successful conclusion. The regressive phenomena described recurred occasionally for several months, but even then in attenuated form.

Illustration 2

Danny began analysis at the age of five.[11] A battery of psychological tests, given after his private school had retained him in kindergarten, indicated that he might have some emotional disturbance. The tests also were indicative of mild mental retardation. His parents had noted his "extreme unhappiness." He had no friends, always appeared tense, and was easily frustrated. The analyst noted very poor muscular coordination and extreme constriction in every movement.

At the time of the diagnostic interviews, the child's mother stated that she had been depressed for approximately a month when he was eight months old; after this, both parents felt that Danny had changed. He gradually seemed to lose his enthusiasm, which was replaced by a look of sadness. At this time, they first noticed his poor muscular coordination.

The early part of Danny's analysis was characterized by frequent attacks on the analyst, and loss of bowel control with smearing; much of his behavior was accompanied by wild and maniacal laughter. With this profound regression, his lack of coordination disappeared, and he demonstrated that his basic physical endowment in this area was really superior. The analyst felt that release from internal controls, resulting from the regression, was responsible for the muscular improvement. The skeletomuscular inhibition was seen as an attempt both to express through constant tension and to control overwhelming aggressive impulses.

Separation from the analyst began to provoke extreme anxiety to the point of panic; yet the child was only very gradually and occasionally able to react to the analyst as well-meaning and potentially helpful. During these months, a specific theme was frequently repeated—that of someone or something being tied up. For example, Danny fantasied that he was in a boat, pursued by hundreds of bigger people intent on subduing him and tying him up in retaliation for a theft. Since the age of four, he had been afraid of robbers entering his room at night and tying him up. There were innumerable fantasies of his tremendous power and strength, all involving break-

[11] I am indebted to Dr. Roy Mendelsohn for this case.

ing loose from bonds. Or, again repeatedly, a burglar climbed on him and pinned him down. His gun went off and shot the burglar, who then left to repeat the same act with his sister; the fantasy ended with the burglar capturing his sister and tying *her* up. Similarly, he was the world's greatest "wild horse catcher." He chased and pursued wild horses and bulls, and then tied them up as they tried to escape. Or he was going to have lots of girls and make babies with them. His boyfriend was jealous, so Danny attacked him in order to protect the girls, then tied him up and destroyed him.

Toward the end of the second year of analysis, the theme of being tied up began to be lived in the analysis, apparently in response to feelings about separation. Previously the patient had generally indicated gratitude, despite his protests, when he had been out of control and been physically restrained by the analyst. Now even accidental contact precipitated intense hatred: "You hurt me and won't let me go. I hate you, I can't stand it. I am leaving, I have got to get out of here, you are trying to tie me down." Fantasies began to be "lived in" in the analytic situation—so real that he completely ignored reality. When he sat, he felt himself completely immobilized and screamed that he was tied up and could not move. Alternately, he collected large bundles of string in order to surround completely his analyst's office with "ropes." He wove the bushes outside the analyst's first floor window so that they too enclosed the office and "tied up" the analyst.

It was at this point that the analyst, seeking some explanation for the specific details of the relived fantasy, recalled the mother's depression. He met with the parents and described the patient's reactions to separation. The mother then recalled the details of her depression. An extremely close relative had been killed in an accident, and she had spent the next month at the home of the relative's mother. During this time, she was annoyed by her child's demands. She strapped him into a baby chair and left him each day, and returned only to meet his physical needs, usually feeding him while he remained strapped in the chair. Later, she had felt extreme guilt, and had "forgotten" her treatment of Danny—until reminded by the analyst's description of his behavior.

When the analyst tried to tell the child what he had learned, he was interrupted as soon as he connected the patient's behavior with his mother. The patient insisted on hearing about this directly from her. Afterward, Danny's analytic work continued at an accelerated pace, and his ability to differentiate present reality from past improved markedly. While he could never remember the traumatic events, he recognized their influence on his reactions.

The themes of "tying" and "being tied" recurred in the subsequent analysis of each psychosexual stage; they were incorporated into the patient's perceptions, fantasies, and reactions in a manner characteristic of each stage. Following this period of analysis and working through, the theme of tying disappeared from his fantasies and transference reactions until it reappeared, much less intensely, as part of the termination process.

Illustration 3

In the preceding cases, *passively primally repressed* memories which were associated with early ego states were reproduced and relived in the analytic situation. Understanding and communicating the nature of the experience, reconstructing the nature of the trauma, and supplying the missing events were measures employed. In both cases, crucial change soon occurred as the result of these interventions. But the concept of passive primal repression is not limited in its application to definitive reconstruction of the infantile trauma. In the present case, the concept of passive primal repression was useful in forming a therapeutic alliance with a person whose character was necessarily structured to maintain an attitude of extreme self-sufficiency and aloofness.

The patient was a twenty-five-year-old unmarried woman who had been epileptic since the age of eleven; she began analysis after a six-month period of psychotherapy. At the start, she described analysis as a game, the object of which was to anticipate, outwit, and control the analyst. However, she gradually began to reveal a great fear of her inner life. Not only did she live in a world of fragile, precious, irreplaceable, private fantasy, but she also equated her feelings with the uncontrollable, overwhelming, terrifying outbursts of the epileptic seizures. Her few reported dreams (e.g., one was of a herd of wild horses descending upon her) and reports of her feeling states confirmed that her balance was precarious.

In the tenth month of analysis, she introduced a few remarks about the inadequacy of verbal communication. Words simply didn't work for her; she felt limited in her ability to describe her feelings in words, and she was never sure whether the other person really understood. In reality, her vocabulary was excellent and her ability to express herself verbally at all levels of abstraction was quite good.

In the fourteenth month of analysis, she took a short vacation to the northeastern United States. She had previously spoken of her great love for the mountains of Vermont and New Hampshire during her college years. She had emphasized particularly the pleasure associated with "rock climbing," trips of exploration, and the mastery of the unfamiliar terrain of this area. On these occasions, I had reflected, privately, that the pleasure she described seemed identical to the experience of the toddler in his efforts to explore and master the inanimate world.[12] Following her vacation, she was nine minutes late for her first appointment, then silent for another six minutes. I asked her whether anything kept her from talking, and she answered that she just didn't want to talk. She had had a very good time, and she feared that telling me about it would somehow spoil it. In talking to her parents about the vacation, she had related everything she had done exactly as she had done it, but had not mentioned her feelings. In fact, her father had had to ask specifically whether she had enjoyed herself. I asked the patient if her explanation meant that she simply didn't feel like sharing her feelings with me—or whether somehow, in the very translation into words, they would be lost. She answered that both were true, but mostly the latter. She could only refer to her vacation experiences with certain people who had shared them and who had the same feelings about them. With these people there was no need to describe her feelings or put them into words. Instead, mere references to the experience were adequate. The feelings involved were, nevertheless, very basic;

[12] More specifically, these experiences correspond to Mahler's second phase of separation-individuation—"the practicing period" at ten to fifteen months: "The child now steadily increases his practicing of motor skills and exploration of his expanding environment, both human and inanimate. This is true whether the infant has started to toddle or is in the process of becoming proficient in ordinary crawling, righting himself, or paddling around rapidly, using his entire body in a belly crawl. The main characteristic of this subphase is the great narcissistic investment of the child in his own functions and his own body, as well as in the objects and objectives of his expanding investigation of reality" (Mahler and La Perriere, 1965, p. 484f.).

when enjoying them, she had felt alive, and when away from the
scenes that stimulated these feelings, she felt dead.

My reasoning during the hour was as follows. The patient had
indicated previously her preoccupation with total control of terrifying and overwhelming internal processes. In addition, she had made
it clear that she felt my understanding a disruptive intrusion. I em-
pathetically and intellectually understood that the pleasure described
in the first part of the hour involved the reliving of certain passively
primally repressed experiences. While specific interpretation was
deemed premature and potentially overwhelming, I felt it important
to share my understanding of the primitive, unverbalizable, nature
of her experiences—thus hoping to strengthen the tenuous but developing therapeutic alliance, and continue the process of gradual
ego expansion through empathy. I specifically wanted the patient to
know that I understood her superficial defiance as designed to conceal her inability to verbalize. I felt also that the patient would
have to experience me as empathetic to her pleasurable primitive
feelings before she could take the risk of facing and sharing her more
terrifying inner perceptions. This intervention was one of the first
steps in the translation of her primitive feeling states into understandable verbal concepts. With time and continued analytic work,
she was able to describe and understand a variety of her primitive
feeling states including many directly associated with her epilepsy.
Of particular value was the analysis and reconstruction of how such
states influenced her interaction with important childhood figures to
produce characteristic patterns of object relations.

Over a period of time, very early experiences were frequently
superimposed on her current life. The following, from the third
year of analysis, shows the influence of *passively primally repressed*
nursing experiences where tension relief is intimately associated with
oral satisfaction:

> Last night was the first time that we all had dinner together—
> all of us—mother, father, guests with their children, and me. It
> was really very disorganized. Ordinarily, I use dinner to settle
> down. For example, if something's bothering me, I'll gripe about
> it. Last night, of course, I couldn't do that. The funny thing
> is that I had a reaction later, not then. The reaction was I felt as
> if I hadn't eaten at all. I can't explain it, that's how I felt. I

went ahead and did some work, but without any enthusiasm. Then after a while I began to get very depressed. It was associated with this feeling that I hadn't eaten as if I didn't expect this to ever end. I tried to explain this to myself, and that's what I kept coming back to.

Here, eating was intimately associated with tension relief just as in the first months of life. When the patient's usual auxiliary methods of relieving tension during dinner were compromised, she later felt that she had not eaten at all. Tension relief and oral satiation were as one. She knew that she could eat at any time; yet her reaction was that of a very young infant, hungry and distraught, unable to grasp that mother would feed her in time. The lack of time perspective inherent in the inability to anticipate characterizes the very primitive ego. The fusion of tension relief and eating, along with the inability to anticipate, indicates that the patient was reliving *passively primally repressed* experiences of early infancy.

Illustration 4: A Qualifying Case

The following illustration is *not* a case of passive primal repression, but is, rather, a case involving a screen memory derived from a later period. Here, a patient attempted to "blame" her difficulties with men on a traumatic separation from her father in the eighth or ninth month of life, instead of facing feelings and conflicts corresponding to the later phallic and oedipal stages.

One must proceed with caution in evaluating what patients present as preverbal trauma. The formal characteristics of the transference manifestations and the presence of ego deficits are the most reliable indications of early trauma. Reports of early experiences, even when apparently confirmed by corroborative witnesses, are most often screen memories. In fact, Freud's original example in "Screen Memories" (1899) involves a memory of the third year used as a screen for a later event at age seventeen. In the The Psychopathology of Everyday Life (1901), he places such "retro-active" memories with those that have been "pushed ahead" or involve contemporary events (p. 44). Furthermore, a screen memory may serve more than one master; for example, the function of a screen memory as part of a mutually accepted "family legend" is not uncommon.

The need for caution in this regard was shown clearly by the following material, taken from my records of the analysis of a twenty-four-year-old unmarried woman. In the course of the patient's diagnostic interview, she stated that her father had been drafted when she was seven or eight months old. Her mother had often repeated that her father's departure had greatly upset the patient; she reportedly had become physically ill immediately afterward, and the mother attributed the illness to this separation. During the analysis, it became clear that the patient was using this memory as a rationalization, to explain and dismiss her difficulties with men.

In the first months of analysis, transference manifestations soon paralleled the relationship that had existed with her father since she was eight or nine years of age. The patient "regretted" her open contempt for the analyst which, if freely expressed, would "destroy" him. As in her reactions to her father, she considered the analyst insensitive, unable to fulfill her needs, inferior, provocative and infuriating. At this time, the patient was constantly on the verge of leaving analysis.

About a year later, the patient's transference resistance became increasingly untenable. She then related a dream in which her boyfriend, an army officer, was about to leave the city; this much corresponded to reality. In the dream, there was reproduced a scene from a home movie. While vague, the picture in her mind's eye was of her father, perhaps already in uniform, at a going-away party given at the time of his induction. She was not as sure of her age at that time as she had been previously, but said that it surely must have been before she was a year old. Her father had repeatedly stated that she couldn't walk or talk when he had left home, but that she could do both on his return.[13]

At this point, I privately considered whether or not the patient was currently reliving her reactions to passively primally repressed memories of the father's departure. However, the lack of formal

[13] The fact that the patient presented this scene as remembered and dated it to the latter part of the first year is taken here as *prima facie* evidence of its status as a screen memory. The use of a home movie as a device to add credence to the memory is regarded as incidental. In any event, since the memory was not of the event itself, but of a movie of the event, it is possible that there will be some objection to its categorization as a screen memory. This, however, would not affect any of the essentials of the phenomena involved.

characteristics specific to the first year of life was one of many de-
terrents to this reconstruction, and it soon was confirmed that the
patient had presented a screen memory.

During the next analytic hour the patient said that she had
talked to her mother about the movie and it did not exist. There
had been no such going-away party and no such movie. In fact, independent events had convinced her that her father could not have
been drafted before she was well over a year old. She hated to admit
this because she didn't want to admit that she wasn't walking at
twelve or thirteen months. It was important for her to believe that
she had been precocious, and her family had encouraged her in this
fantasy. With her next associations, the patient then began to explore new material, from which conflicts at the phallic and oedipal
stages were ultimately analyzed.

DISCUSSION AND SUMMARY

In line with Freud's development of the concept of primal repression, an attempt has been made here to categorize the unrememberable memories of childhood. This paper explores some aspects of memories which as such are not directly recoverable because
of the immaturity of the mental apparatus at the time when the
significant impressions occurred. The process has been characterized
and described and its relationship to certain unconscious defenses
defined.

Passive primal repression is one possible vicissitude of the period
when primary processes dominate the behavior and thinking of the
child. Up to eighteen months of age, primary processes are in the
foreground; only intermittently is there evidence of higher ego functions strong enough to curb the child's free impulsive and instinctive
expressions (A. Freud, 1951). As stressed by Freud, the importance
of speech at this age in the transition from primary to secondary
process mentation has been repeatedly confirmed. Even after this
stage, however, physiological, environmental, and emotional trauma
may overwhelm the higher ego functions, and create conditions suitable for *passive primal repression*.

In addition, another factor responsible for the amnesia of early
childhood has been discussed—the transformation through reor-

ganization of many optimal infantile memories into ego qualities, strengths, and capacities. Because of this change of function, these experiences are no longer recoverable, usually not even in analysis. Finally, cases illustrating the application of the concept of *passive primal repression* have been presented at the clinical level.

BIBLIOGRAPHY

Anthony, E. J. (1961), A Study of "Screen Sensations." *This Annual*, 16:211-245.
Benedek, T. (1938), Adaptation to Reality in Early Infancy. *Psa. Quart.*, 7:200-215.
Bernstein, A. E. H. & Blacher, R. S. (1967), The Recovery of a Memory from Three Months of Age. *This Annual*, 22:156-161.
Bonnard, A. (1960), The Primal Significance of the Tongue. *Int. J. Psa.*, 41:301-307.
Brenner, C. (1957), The Nature and Development of the Concept of Repression in Freud's Writings. *This Annual*, 12:19-46.
Breuer, J. & Freud, S. (1893-1895), Studies on Hysteria. *Standard Edition*, 2. London: Hogarth Press, 1955.
Charny, E. J., Carroll, E. J., & Loeb, F. F. (1966), General Systems Theory and Psychoanalysis: I & II. *Psa. Quart.*, 35:377-398.
Deutsch, H. (1942), Some Forms of Emotional Disturbance and Their Relationship to Schizophrenia. *Psa. Quart.*, 11:301-321.
Eissler, K. R. (1953), Notes upon the Emotionality of a Schizophrenic Patient and Its Relation to Problems of Technique. *This Annual*, 8:199-251.
—— (1962), On the Metapsychology of the Preconscious: A Tentative Contribution to Psychoanalytic Morphology. *This Annual*, 17:9-41.
Erikson, E. H. (1950), *Childhood and Society*. New York: Norton.
Fenichel, O. (1945), *The Psychoanalytic Theory of Neurosis*. New York: Norton.
Ferenczi, S. (1913), Stages in the Development of Reality. In: *Sex in Psychoanalysis*. Boston: Badger, 1950. pp. 213-239.
Fink, G. (1967), Analysis of the Isakower Phenomenon. *J. Amer. Psa. Assn.*, 15:281-293.
Frank, A. & Muslin, H. (1967), The Development of Freud's Concept of Primal Repression. *This Annual*, 22:55-76.
Freud, A. (1951), Observations on Child Development. *This Annual*, 6:18-30.
—— (1965), *Normality and Pathology in Childhood*. New York: International Universities Press.
Freud, S. (1899), Screen Memories. *Standard Edition*, 3:301-322. London: Hogarth Press, 1962.
—— (1900), The Interpretation of Dreams. *Standard Edition*, 4 & 5. London: Hogarth Press, 1953.
—— (1901), The Psychopathology of Everyday Life. *Standard Edition*, 6. London: Hogarth Press, 1960.
—— (1911), Formulations on the Two Principles of Mental Functioning. *Standard Edition*, 12:213-226. London: Hogarth Press, 1958.
—— (1914), Remembering, Repeating, and Working-through. *Standard Edition*, 12:145-156. London: Hogarth Press, 1958.
—— (1915a), Repression. *Standard Edition*, 14:141-158. London: Hogarth Press, 1957.
—— (1915b), The Unconscious. *Standard Edition*, 14:159-215. London: Hogarth Press, 1957.
—— (1916-1917), Introductory Lectures on Psycho-Analysis. *Standard Edition*, 15 & 16. London: Hogarth Press, 1963.

—— (1918 [1914]), From the History of an Infantile Neurosis. *Standard Edition*, 17:3-123. London: Hogarth Press, 1955.

—— (1920), Beyond the Pleasure Principle. *Standard Edition*, 18:7-64. London: Hogarth Press, 1955.

—— (1923), The Ego and the Id. *Standard Edition*, 19:3-66. London: Hogarth Press, 1961.

—— (1933), New Introductory Lectures on Psycho-Analysis. *Standard Edition*, 22:3-182. London: Hogarth Press, 1964.

—— (1937), Constructions in Analysis. *Standard Edition*, 23:255-269. London: Hogarth Press, 1964.

—— (1939 [1934-1938]), Moses and Monotheism: Three Essays. *Standard Edition*, 23:3-137. London: Hogarth Press, 1964.

—— (1940 [1938]), An Outline of Psycho-Analysis. *Standard Edition*, 23:141-207. London: Hogarth Press, 1964.

Gill, M. M. (1963), *Topography and Systems in Psychoanalytic Theory* [*Psychological Issues*, Monogr. 10]. New York: International Universities Press.

Glover, E. (1939), *Psycho-Analysis*. London & New York: Staples Press.

—— (1945), Examination of the Klein System of Child Psychology. *This Annual*, 1:75-118.

Hambidge, G. (1956), On the Ontogenesis of Repression. *Psa. Rev.*, 43:195-203.

Hartmann, H. (1939), *Ego Psychology and the Problem of Adaptation*. New York: International Universities Press, 1958.

Heilbrunn, G. (1953), Fusion of the Isakower Phenomenon with the Dream Screen. *Psa. Quart.*, 22:200-204.

Isakower, O. (1938), A Contribution to the Pathopsychology of Phenomena Associated with Falling Asleep. *Int. J. Psa.*, 19:331-345.

Jacobson, E. (1957), Denial and Repression. *J. Amer. Psa. Assn.*, 5:61-92.

Johnson, A. M. (1951), Some Etiological Aspects of Repression, Guilt and Hostility. *Psa. Quart.*, 20:511-527.

Klein, M. (1932), *The Psycho-Analysis of Children*. London: Hogarth Press.

Kohut, H. & Seitz, P. F. D. (1963), Concepts and Theories of Psychoanalysis. In: *Concepts of Personality*, ed. J. M. Wepman & R. W. Heine. Chicago: Aldine Publishing Co., pp. 113-141.

Kris, E. (1956), The Recovery of Childhood Memories. *This Annual*, 11:54-88.

Lantos, B. (1955), On the Motivation of Human Relationships: A Preliminary Study Based on the Concept of Sublimation. *Int. J. Psa.*, 36:267-288.

Lewin, B. D. (1953), Reconsideration of the Dream Screen. *Psa. Quart.*, 22:174-199.

Loewald, H. W. (1955), Hypnoid State, Repression, Abreaction and Recollection. *J. Amer. Psa. Assn.*, 3:201-210.

Madison, P. (1961), *Freud's Concept of Repression and Defense: Its Theoretical and Observational Language*. Minneapolis: University of Minnesota Press.

Mahler, M. S. & Elkisch, P. (1953), Some Observations on Disturbances of the Ego in a Case of Infantile Psychosis. *This Annual*, 8:252-261.

—— & La Perriere, K. (1965), Mother-Child Interaction during Separation-Individuation. *Psa. Quart.*, 34:483-498.

Niederland, W. G. (1965), The Role of the Ego in the Recovery of Early Memories. *Psa. Quart.*, 34:564-571.

Nunberg, H. (1932), *Principles of Psychoanalysis*. New York: International Universities Press, 1955.

Pearson, G. H. J., rep. (1953), A Note on Primal Repression. *Bull. Phila. Assn. Psa.*, 3:42.

Provence, S. & Lipton, R. (1962), *Infants in Institutions*. New York: International Universities Press.

Purves, W. (1966), The Problem of Anxiety Revisited. *Bull. Phila. Assn. Psa.*, 16:71-81.

Rapaport, D. (1950), On the Psycho-Analytic Theory of Thinking. *Int. J. Psa.*, 31:161-170.
—— (1951), *Organization and Pathology of Thought.* New York: Columbia University Press.
Spitz, R. A. (1945), Hospitalism. *This Annual*, 1:53-74.
—— (1955), The Primal Cavity. *This Annual*, 10:215-240.
Stein, M. (1965), States of Consciousness in the Analytic Situation: Including a Note on the Traumatic Dream. In: *Drives, Affects, Behavior*, Vol. II, ed. M. Schur. New York: International Universities Press, pp. 60-86.
Waelder, R. (1962), Book Review: Psychoanalysis, Scientific Method, and Philosophy. *J. Amer. Psa. Assn.*, 10:617-637.
Whitman, R. M. (1963), Remembering and Forgetting Dreams in Psychoanalysis. *J. Amer. Psa. Assn.*, 11:752-774.
Winnicott, D. W. (1958), The Capacity to Be Alone. *Int. J. Psa.*, 39:416-420.
—— (1963), The Development of the Capacity for Concern. *Bull. Menninger Clin.*, 27:167-176.
Wolff, P. H. (1960), *The Developmental Psychologies of Jean Piaget and Psychoanalysis* [*Psychological Issues*, Monogr. 5]. New York: International Universities Press.
Woodbury, M. A. (1966), Altered Body-Ego Experiences: A Contribution to the Study of Regression, Perception, and Early Development. *J. Amer. Psa. Assn.*, 14:273-303.

ANTHROPOMORPHISM

Motive, Meaning, and Causality in Psychoanalytic Theory

WILLIAM I. GROSSMAN, M.D. and
BENNETT SIMON, M.D. (New York)

> There are two kinds of vanity: public
> vanity and private vanity which is
> called good conscience, human re-
> spect, self-esteem, so true it is that
> there are in each man two men, he
> who acts and he who criticizes. Inner
> life is the perpetual wheedling, by the
> man who acts, of the man who criti-
> cizes.
>
> GUSTAVE FLAUBERT,
> *Intimate Notebook* (p. 17)

IS ANTHROPOMORPHISM A PROBLEM IN PSYCHOANALYTIC THEORY?

At a meeting of the Vienna Psychoanalytic Society in 1906, there
was a discussion of the merits and dangers of anthropomorphism in
psychology. At the end of the discussion, Freud observed that "it is
not at all necessary to outgrow it [anthropomorphism]. Our understanding reaches as far as our anthropomorphism" (see Nunberg and
Federn, p. 136). This statement implies that there is an essential
relationship between anthropomorphic formulation and psychoanalytic understanding. For some time, the necessity of anthropomorphism in psychoanalytic theory has been questioned. Attempts have

From the Division of Psychiatry, Montefiore Hospital and Medical Center and
Albert Einstein College of Medicine.

We would like to express our appreciation to our colleagues who read this work
in various stages of completion. To Drs. Leo Spiegel and Alan Tyson we owe special
thanks for their detailed and searching critical reading.

been made to purge the theory of its presence, and opinion is evenly divided on the extent to which it is present at all. These issues are sharply drawn with respect to the structural theory. In the *Vocabulaire de la Psychanalyse* (Laplanche and Pontalis, 1967, p. 488), we find the following statement:

> Even in the choice of terms to designate the agencies, one sees that the model here is no longer one borrowed from the physical sciences, but is thoroughly marked by anthropomorphism. The intrasubjective field tends to be conceived on the model of inter-subjective relationships. The systems are represented as relatively autonomous people within the person (one may say, for example, that the superego behaves sadistically toward the ego). To this extent, the scientific theory of the psychic apparatus tends to approach the manner in which the subject sees himself in fantasy and, perhaps, even has constructed himself [our translation].

By contrast, the American *Encyclopedia of Psychoanalysis* (p. 418) quotes Hartmann (1959, p. 344) on this subject:

> Still, some of these constructs seem particularly suspect to many critics of analysis. An occasional lack of caution in the formulation of its propositions, or Freud's liking for occasional striking metaphors, has led to the accusation against analysis of an anthropomorphization of its concepts. But in all those cases a more careful formulation can be substituted which will dispel this impression.

In general, modern sentiment, in accord with prevailing scientific values, accepts without hesitation the view that anthropomorphism is an impediment to the development of scientific psychology. An exception is Masserman (1946, p. 169) who states, "the allegation of 'anthropomorphism' is itself a tautology, since all data are derived from the personal experience and interpretations of the individual and all conceptual terms have reference to essentially human forms and meanings. In effect, then, all 'systems of thought' in all languages, whether applied to the conduct of electrons, cats, or theorists is basically 'anthropomorphic'—and the term itself becomes particularly redundant when applied to any theory of behavior whatsoever." Nash (1962) accepts anthropomorphic metaphor as a temporary necessity (ultimately to be abandoned):

Abandonment of the metaphor of intrapersonal persons in favor of a language of "tensions between [intrapersonal] organizations," suggested by Hartmann, Kris, and Loewenstein in order to clarify the confusion in Freud's formulation, becomes unnecessary once the relations between ego and self are disentangled. The correct relations between ego and self are indeed seen more clearly in terms of the play-within-a-play metaphor. Although primitive metaphors ought *ultimately* to be supplanted (or at least supplemented) by more accurate statements of relationship between observed phenomena, the present replacement of the vivid and fertile metaphor of intrapersonal persons by a technical language which is neither as vivid as the frank metaphor, nor firmly grounded in psychological experience by well-defined operations, would be premature [p. 28].

In their now classic paper on the formation of psychic structure, Hartmann, Kris, and Loewenstein (1946) briefly discussed the place of anthropomorphism in concept formation in psychoanalysis. These authors begin the relevant portion of their discussion by noting that Freud's subject matter was the study of psychic conflict. They point out that:

The concept of a psychic conflict is integral to many religious systems and many philosophical doctrines. Ever more frequently since the days of enlightenment had the great masters of intuitive psychology, had writers, poets, and philosophers described the life of man as torn between conflicting forces. Freud's contribution conquered this area for the rule of science. The study of psychic conflict in general, and more specifically that of the pathognomic nature of certain conflicts, suggested that the forces opposing each other in typical conflict situations were not grouped at random; rather that the groups of opposing forces possessed an inner cohesion or organization [p. 13].

They further elaborate by noting that the interest of French psychiatry in multiple personalities during the latter part of the nineteenth century "supported the idea that other less dramatic manifestations of mental illness could be understood in terms of 'man divided against himself' " (p. 13). They then discuss the development of the tripartite model, noting that:

These three psychic substructures or systems are not conceived of as independent parts of personality that invariably oppose each other, but as three centers of psychic functioning that can be characterized according to their developmental level, to the amount of energy vested in them, and to their demarcation and interdependence at a given time [p. 14].

Furthermore, they remark that the psychic systems are defined by the functions attributed to them, observing that "In adopting the *functions* exercised in mental processes as the decisive criterion for defining the psychic systems Freud used physiology as his model in concept formation" (p. 15).

In our opinion, this statement gives too much weight to the role of physiological models in Freud's thinking. What it neglects is the pervasive role of interpersonal and social analogies in providing process terms for theoretical formulations (e.g., the term *Instanz* in *The Interpretation of Dreams,* translated as "agency," is drawn from the legal sphere, certainly not from physiology). The importance of the interpersonal source of analogies will be developed over the course of the paper.

Having thus introduced the structural concepts for discussion, these authors proceed to consider the frequently raised objections that the structural terms are "dramatic in an anthropomorphic sense." They continue:

Clearly, whenever dramatization is encountered, metaphorical language has crept into scientific discourse and that there is danger in the use of metaphor in science hardly needs to be demonstrated; danger, it should be added, to which Freud (1933) himself drew our attention. However, it remains a problem worth some further discussion, under what conditions the danger outweighs the advantage. The danger obviously begins if and when metaphor infringes upon meaning: in the case in point, when the structural concepts are anthropomorphized. Then the functional connotations may be lost and one of the psychic systems may be substituted for the total personality [p. 16].

They offer an illustration of how an anthropomorphic Freudian sentence may be reformulated in an effort to eliminate its anthropomorphic implications. In brief, they substitute "degrees of tension" between psychic agencies for terms of those agencies "loving" or "hating" each other. To that example, we shall return later to see whether or not such reformulations are, in fact, able to perform the function for which they are designed.

For the moment, however, the other portion of their discussion is of more interest. They point out that there is an impoverishment of the "plasticity of language" whenever such a reformulation is attempted.

> Thus the metaphorical expression comes closer to our immediate understanding, since the anthropomorphism it introduces corresponds to human experience. Our reformulation shows that not the concepts which Freud introduced are anthropomorphic, but that the clinical facts he studied and described led us to understand what part anthropomorphism plays in introspective thinking.
>
> [However, while offering their appreciation of the descriptions of the nineteenth century French psychiatrists, they remark:] But the metaphorical language of descriptive psychiatry did not permit in the nineteenth century, and no reformulations in terms of existential psychology will permit in the twentieth century, the step from empathy to causal explanation. This step became possible only after conceptual tools had been adopted which permitted a more generalized penetration of the phenomena; a penetration that becomes possible only at some distance from immediate experience. This was the function of Freud's structural concepts. If we use these concepts in a strict sense, the distance from experience grows. Freud's metaphorical usage of his own terms was clearly intended to bridge this gap. It might thus be said that Freud's usage bears the imprint of the clinical source from which the concepts were originally derived, the imprint of the communication with the patients. Requirements of communication may ever again suggest richness of metaphor, but metaphors should not obscure the nature of the concepts and their function in psychoanalysis as a science. That function is to facilitate explanatory constructs. Briefly, the structural concepts are amongst our most valuable tools, since they stand in a genetic context [p. 17].

In summary, then, we might say that the argument is as follows: first, that the structural concepts are derived from the study of conflict and the grouping of the forces in conflict; second, function defines the structural agencies and these agencies are readily anthropomorphized; and third, this tendency is dangerous for theory. Fourth, they feel that it is not necessary to anthropomorphize these concepts and that appropriate formulation alone may avoid the dangers of anthropomorphism. Anthropomorphism is not without some value, however, since it is close to immediate experience, and we have been led through Freud's study of clinical facts to an understanding of the part played by anthropomorphism in introspective thinking. The fifth point is that "Freud's metaphorical usage of his own terms" was intended to bridge that gap from empathy to causal explanation, that this was the function of Freud's structural concepts, and that their strict use enables us to remove ourselves further from immediate experience in developing our concepts.

The preceding quotations appear to imply that the problem of anthropomorphism in theory is related to the anthropomorphism of introspective thinking, the core of our clinical data. The additional claim seems to be made that the anthropomorphic coloring of theoretical propositions is due to an excessively great closeness between theoretical propositions and clinical observations. It would be useful to consider the kinds of theoretical propositions which are most often rendered in anthropomorphic terms. These are by no means limited to clinical propositions.

The relevant questions at issue in this discussion are: (1) How is the anthropomorphism of introspective thinking related to the anthropomorphism of clinical propositions? (2) Does more careful formulation dispel the anthropomorphism? That is, is it really less anthropomorphic to speak of "tension" between ego and superego than to speak of love and hate? (3) Have the more abstract aspects of psychoanalytic theory succeeded in taking "the step from empathy to causal explanation?" The metaphors, as Freud implies (see above), may not simply "infringe on meaning" (Hartmann, Kris, and Loewenstein, quoted above) but perhaps supply it. To explore these possibilities, we shall examine the ways in which anthropomorphic metaphors (direct and implied) have served psychoanalytic theory.

THE ANTHROPOMORPHISM OF INTROSPECTION

The anthropomorphism of introspection refers to our tendency to talk about ourselves in terms of inner people. For example, we commonly speak of ourselves as having an "inner voice of conscience," or of our "struggles with ourselves." We also speak in terms such as "the idea came to me," "self-control," "be overcome with emotion," etc. In these latter expressions, the anthropomorphism is less explicit, but nevertheless evident. For example, the phrase, "an idea came to me," involves reification or personification of a psychological process.

The phrase, "a struggle with oneself," highlights how the experience of inner turmoil is converted by anthropomorphism to the language of warring parties within the person, i.e., language of conflict. Such popular expressions already imply divisions within the mind and conflicts of motives and interests. Expressions such as "the better part of me" not only imply a division, but begin to group motives and interests within the mind. These groupings tend to be modeled on the conflicting demands made by the parents, and other people, on the individual throughout his development.

In its most general definition, "anthropomorphism" means ascribing any human attribute to something other than man. These attributes include feelings, appetites, actions, physical structure, and biological properties, as well as motives and intentions. Anthropomorphism often implies the notion of "animism," the attributing of life, or a living soul, to inanimate structures or forces. In general, animism is a variant of anthropomorphism since the "anima" or "soul" turns out to be a human soul. We use the term "sociomorphism" to refer to social process and structures as analogies or metaphors. The term "theriomorphism," rendering something in the form of an animal, belongs here, too. This usage can also be seen as closely related to anthropomorphism. One could speak of the experience of a sexual urge as "as if I'm chained to a madman" or as if "there is a wild animal inside me." The addict's phrase, "a monkey on my back," personifies, so to speak, the inner compulsion to continue taking the drug. "Animal passion" is a still more familiar phrase of this type.

Such rich language also illustrates what should come as no surprise: that the language of inner experience is first and foremost metaphorical. The metaphors are drawn primarily, perhaps even exclusively, from social interaction and from the person experiencing certain physical events and situations. C. S. Lewis's (1967) study of the word "conscience" illustrates several points about the metaphorical description of inner life. He demonstrates that the term originally referred to a shared knowledge of a guilty secret. Changing usage gradually internalized the secret and those who shared it. Thus, the term describing the inner function is already, historically speaking, a sociomorphic metaphor. What this example further illustrates is that even a term which we would think of as denoting a particular inner function, "conscience," is one that is already richly metaphorical. Even terms which appear solely denotative of inner experience have their origin in interpersonal situations and experiences. We may mention, in passing, the other major source of the metaphors for describing mental life, i.e., certain bodily sensations. In particular, terms denoting affective states, such as anxiety, elation, and depression, are in part concretizations of a bodily experience or the experiences a person might have in a particular physical situation (cf. Sarbin, 1964, 1968).

The capacity for introspection develops in the child *pari passu* with the acquisition of the vocabulary for the conceptualization and description of inner life. It is the adult world which provides the child, in a variety of situations, with the tools for labeling his inner states. Prominent are terms by which we help the child establish the distinction between the inner and outer world. The labeling of affective states is also very prominent in our "instruction" to children. The language that we have to offer the child to denote his inner experience is of necessity anthropomorphic. The child's view of all reality, both outer and inner, certainly inclines toward the anthropomorphic. When we speak to him about his inner experience and use anthropomorphic language, we are using terminology which is quite suited to the level of development of cognition in the child, as well as using the language which we adults have to describe these states.

This point of view is by no means only a recent one and is already sketched out in the *Minutes of the Vienna Psychoanalytic Society* (Vol. I, p. 122). There Moebius says, and Freud agrees, that our sense organs are equipped only for the perception of the external world, and not for self-observation. "It is only late and by means of a trick [*Kunstgriff*], as it were, that we learn to direct our attention to certain inner processes. These enter our consciousness by associating themselves with verbal representations. The perception of our thought processes occurs only with the help of words."

We have spoken of the anthropomorphisms of introspection that appear in common speech and that are imbedded in common language, as well as the learning of these terms by the developing child.

In clinical work, certain conditions are prominently associated with the anthropomorphism of introspection. Thus, an obsessional patient with complaints of depression, work inhibition, and some sexual difficulties speaks habitually of one part of himself mistreating the other part, or how he uses his "neurosis" to punish himself, or of his endless arguments with himself. He then has a sequence of dreams, which in the manifest content represent thugs, criminals, and police in conflict, with each treating the other brutally. In associating to the dream, the patient was now in the role of policeman, and now in the role of the criminal, as in acts of petty thievery. The manifest content, then, is in fact an even more anthropomorphic rendering of his conscious experience of inner conflict. For this man, to paraphrase Flaubert, his inner life is the perpetual wheedling of the man who acts by the man who criticizes. States of heightened self-observation, such as depersonalization, of course, present an extreme case of the experienced split between the observer and the observed, both parts of the self. Here, however, defenses have blotted out the experience of conflict.

In paranoid states, although there is no explicit experience of *inner* conflict, we can recognize that the patient's thoughts and feelings are divided between those ascribed to him and those ascribed to outside agents.

In all of these states, then, the person either experiences an inner division, or split, or this split is revealed by low-level inference from the associations. Both kinds of splits may be seen in dreams. In some dreams, "we" are observing what is going on, even in scenes in which "we" are participating in the ongoing activity. Along another plane of cleavage, we can, with the aid of associations, see another split, i.e., the characters in the dream may represent parts of one's self.

It was in close relationship to these states, obsessions, delusions of observation, dream life, and depressions, that Freud developed the notion of the superego. The activities of this agency, as has often been noted (e.g., Spiegel, 1966), are most frequently experienced anthropomorphically, and given theoretical statement in anthropomorphic language. Consideration of these clinical conditions also led Freud to take up the relationship between self-observation, self-criticism, self-reproach, and the capacity for theoretical speculation. The notion of splits within the mind, typically rendered anthropomorphically, is also intimately related to the activity of introspection (Grossman, 1967).

To summarize: The clinical data are anthropomorphic to the extent that introspectable mental life is anthropomorphic. Inner mental life is commonly, though not exclusively, reflected on and reported in anthropomorphic and sociomorphic terms. Inner experience must be described metaphorically, and these are the metaphors most readily at hand. Anthropomorphic terms import into the description of mental life the notion of conflicting motives and interests within the person, and in some instances, conflicting persons within the person. At times, these metaphors also group and organize the warring interests and wishes. In certain clinical states, anthropomorphisms are more in evidence and more pervasive. Undoubtedly there is marked interindividual variation in this respect. Common language provides the developing child with the terms, including the anthropomorphic terms, which allow him to label inner states, and these anthropomorphisms are eminently well suited to the thinking of the developing child. The animism of childhood thinking may be the matrix out of which the anthropomorphism of introspection arises.

Anthropomorphism in Theory

In attempting to explain the puzzling data that emerged in the course of his therapeutic work with patients, Freud evolved a variety of theories. In his early papers, we find an admixture of different types of explanation. Some of these are etiological theories, which account for the symptoms of an illness in terms of specific constitutional elements. For instance, syphilis in a parent was suggested as a predisposition to hysteria. Other etiological factors were specific early sexual seduction or harmful current practices such as coitus interruptus and masturbation. The efforts further to define the ways in which these agents were effective led to a consideration of their influences on the mind. One kind of postulated effect was either a depletion of energy, or an undischarged painful excess. In these cases, the mind was affected by some sort of toxic process, and the complaints of the patient that he was nervous, weak and so on, could be so understood.

The hypnoid state concept, which Freud disavowed after his break with Breuer, was an attempt to account for the impact of experience by means of a concept of a susceptible state. With the concepts of defense hysteria and counterwill, he began to deal with splits within the mind itself. In his paper on "The Neuro-psychoses of Defence" (1894), the idea that one part of the mind is unacceptable to the other is further developed in relation to obsessions and paranoid ideas.

As Stewart (1967) has observed, Freud did not first propose organic or somatic theories and then replace them by psychological ones. Quite the contrary, he was often at pains to combine the two. Here we should like to distinguish between three kinds of theories. One type attributes psychic illness or phenomena to the effects of somatic substances on the mind and brain. The second is a "state of mind or brain" theory. The third is the conflict model. In his early papers, drafts, and the "Project," Freud tried to integrate these approaches. In the "Project" (1895), he attempted to design a brain which would accommodate all of them and explain their interdependencies. He was well aware of the different kinds of mental-somatic relations implied by these different models. The actual neuroses were directly due to somatic effects and no conflict could be found which could be said to be expressed by the symptoms. When intrapsychic conflict was a cause of symptoms, the organic was just as surely present, but, as it were, behind the scenes. Therefore, the state of fatigue could account only for the *conditions favoring* a slip of the tongue. It was the psychic steps interposed between the organic substrate and the symptomatic act which provided the *explanation* (1916-1917, p. 60f.).

For the purposes of this discussion, an especially interesting feature of the "Project" is Freud's attempt to grapple with consciousness and brain. Even earlier (1891, pp. 54-57) he had proposed an explicitly parallelistic relationship between mind and brain. In the "Project," he attempted to account for the *qualities* and conflicts of experience in terms of *quantities* of excitation and *organization* of neurones. Thus, the elements and properties of the explanatory model were different from the elements and properties of that which was to be explained. Although a certain parallelism was retained (1895, p. 311), it was invested in a particular set of neurones.

The abandonment of the "Project" was the abandonment of an attempt at explanation in terms of postulated elements having special quantitative properties. The subsequent models relied on a particular type of parallelism between the form of the mental apparatus and the "elements" of experience. In part, this was accomplished through "bridge concepts" and analogies between somatic and mental functions; in part, by the "person-within-the-person" model.

Of the "bridge concepts" we shall say more later. At this point, we wish to show their role in parallelistic or isomorphic theory construction. Thus, "damming up of affect" and consequent failure to "discharge" are *analogous* to somatic sexual processes as Freud conceived them. At the same time, "damming up of affect" is a theoretical metaphor for "not expressing feelings." The choice of these terms places in the mental model a construction having the same form as the experience. Stated crudely, something dammed up in experience has its counterpart in something dammed up in the model. Another example would be Freud's efforts to represent pleasure and unpleasure in experience (at whatever level) as a direct function of a level of excitation in the model.

While the anthropomorphic and parallelistic aspects of the model may be covert in the foregoing instances, they are readily evident in the "person-within-the-person" formulations. This type of theory subdivides human experience into larger segments, and in psychoanalysis, at least, has focused on the grouping and vicissitudes of motives. To subdivide experience and to construct a model of mind in this way has certain immediate consequences. First, where it is a question of subdivision into the person's motives and other functions, the theory has a functional character. Second, the categories and functions are usually observer-oriented and often *adult*-oriented. Third, if each separate group of functions and motives is assigned to its own part of the mind, each part of the mind has become a homunculus. These three factors make this type of mental model anthropomorphic. This model is fundamentally different from one which starts from some basic property of organisms, or of systems, or of nervous tissue, and so on, and proceeds to elaborate the complex behavior from the simpler elements and their properties. In the latter, as in Freud's neuronal model or in reflex models, the properties of the elements are intrinsically different from the results of their organization. In the "person-within-the-person" model of psychoanalysis, both the integrated person and the parts of his mind have motives, interests, and so on. Consequently, it is the meanings and values dominating integrated behavior which dominate the interrelationships of the parts of the mind. In its pure form, such a model then studies the interrelationships and organizations of the multiple meanings of behavior and experience. It will be readily appreciated that what we have been summarizing here is a set of models ranging from those dominated by some sort of biophysical causality to those dealing with the organization of meaning in experience. Freud began his career with a mixture of such theories, and modern psychoanalysis continues in this tradition.

These different aspects of Freud's theory-making are well exemplified in *The Interpretation of Dreams*. In dealing with the problem of interpreting dreams, he deals mainly with the person in conflict. There are wishes that cannot be gratified and motives that must be disguised or deflected. The model of mind that emerges from this view of things is one in which the mind is split or is divided between a part that wishes to discharge and gratify impulses and a part that forbids, controls, and censors. Dream life allows us to get a clearer picture of, or to infer, this conflict and this split, but of course many waking behaviors and even conscious mental experience provide examples of the mind as divided. Needless to say, this is a paradigmatic summary of what is involved both in the interpretation of dreams and the construction of theory. It does not represent a historical or actual clinical statement as to the relationship between the data of dream life, the process of interpretation, and the model of mind that emerges. In brief, it is well recognized that these three, namely, the dream itself, the theory of interpretation, and the theory or the model of mind, are intimately connected.

We can then see the mind as divided. One part is taken to be the mental representative of the claims of the "animal" or "the bodily parts" within us, or the child who is driven by organic demands; the other is the representative of the claims of reality, of the social world, of reason and of morality. Such a division is already implicit in *The Interpretation of Dreams* in the separation between the Conscious and the Unconscious, controlled by censorship and the mechanism of repression. It comes to fruition and is made explicit in *The Ego and the Id* (1923).

What we can see at this point is that the model has posited corresponding portions of the mental apparatus for each of the terms of the conflict. The divisions of the mind that are posited, namely, an impulsive, wish-dominated portion versus a morally and socially responsible portion of the mind, correspond to a number of popular and widely held views as to the nature of human behavior and the nature of the human mind. It should be pointed out that at one level what is described in this model of mind is that man has several different functions, such as the function of gratifying bodily wishes and impulses, and the function of fulfilling the demands of the social and moral realm. These different functions *of the man* in action are then carried over to a theory of mind that says that the mind has two different kinds of functions that frequently are in conflict with each other. Or, the clinical data show that the person is in conflict; the "model" says the parts or functions of the mind are in conflict.

We can see then that the model has become anthropomorphic by virtue of introducing into the mind different parts that have different interests, claims, and wishes, just as does the person himself. We have been tending to stress those divisions which became most important in the structural theory. One should not, however, overlook the anthropomorphism in the topographical theory. Freud seems to allude to this in his justification of the concept *Ucs*. In writing of the nature of unconscious mental processes, he compares them with conscious ones: "all the categories which we employ to describe conscious mental acts, such as ideas, purposes, resolutions and so on, can be applied to them" (1915, p. 168). In the same paper, Freud compares the assumption of unconscious mental processes with the inference that other people possess consciousness. He suggests that the manifestations of the unconscious are to be explained as though they belonged to the mental life of another person. Finally, he states that the "assumption of unconscious mental activity appears to us

. . . as a further expansion of the primitive animism which caused us to see copies of our own consciousness all around us" (p. 171).

The anthropomorphism of the model is further highlighted by the various anthropomorphic and sociomorphic analogies that Freud uses in *The Interpretation of Dreams*. For example, Freud cited the story of the poor married couple who were granted three wishes to describe the dreamer in his relation to his dream wishes. He says, "a dreamer in his relation to his dream-wishes can only be compared to an amalgamation of two separate people who are linked by some important common element" (p. 581n.). It is clear that this is not only an analogy but is another statement of the idea that the different parts of the mind or the different agencies represent different and often conflicting interests, claims, and wishes. This analogy of the three wishes and others, such as the entrepreneur, and analogies of electorate and political divisions within the state and numerous others, are not merely analogies or ways of speaking. It should be recognized that they not only carry with them the ideas of conflicting intentions, but are a way of describing the *process* of conflicting intentions.

Perhaps a word of clarification would be useful at this point. In referring to these metaphors, we are not assuming that individual metaphors are to be taken in some concrete or literal sense as explanations of conflict in themselves. We believe that the aggregate of such anthropomorphic metaphors, which appear in profusion in Freud's writing, implies a fundamentally anthropomorphic model of mind. These anthropomorphic metaphors thus reveal the actual use that anthropomorphism has in the theory. This use is that it imports process terms, terms of conflict and motive, into a model of mind. Furthermore, we can also see in these anthropomorphic metaphors, as well as in sociomorphic metaphors, the way in which ordinary usage is served by the same sorts of process terms. Thus, we commonly refer to motives and conflict in both the inner life and the social life.

Another important feature of these analogies is that they cast the form of the mind into the form of social interaction. We shall return to this point later when we discuss how Freud discovers once more in the forms of social life the forms of the mind and mental life. We shall argue that what appears to be a finding of mental process in social process is in a sense only a refinding. Moreover, the ultimate fate of these anthropomorphisms in the model of mind depends on how else the systems or agencies or parts of the mind can be characterized and defined. If they can be analyzed into terms and propositions that are not anthropomorphic, then it would be fair to say that the anthropomorphisms are introduced only by way of first approximation. However, it is our impression that the attempts to date to resolve these systems into constituent parts have, by and large, only further subdivided these systems of intention and wishing and have not necessarily contributed a new level of analysis. Abstract terms which have been substituted for language of intention have, it emerges, no other definition than the terms of intentionality for which they are supposed to substitute.

We have now seen how a particular early model of mind, the topographic model, is constructed in large measure by making the parts of the mind congruent with grouping of motives in experience. The form of the mental apparatus corresponds with the alignment of conflicting interests and wishes. The model appears to retain this basic form, even though psychoanalytic theory recognizes multiple conflicts and multiple levels of conflict of which we see only derivatives in awareness. The principle of congruence, or parallelism, is retained in the structural formulations, as well as in topographic models. In addition, this principle of congruence between the products of mind, or the form of experience, and the "actual structure" of mind finds its expression in certain concepts in psychoanalytic theory that have not ordinarily been looked at in this manner.

A. The concept of endopsychic perception[1] is found in Freud's early writings and soon disappears without any special notice of re-

---

[1] The following is a list of all the references to endopsychic perception that we have located. The earliest is 1897 and the latest is 1913.

1897 Letter 78, p. 237 (in *The Origins of Psychoanalysis*).
1900 *The Interpretation of Dreams*, p. 506.
1901 *The Psychopathology of Everyday Life*, p. 258.
1906 *Minutes of the Vienna Psychoanalytic Society*, Vol. I, pp. 146-148.
1907 "Delusions and Dreams in Jensen's *Gradiva*," p. 51.
1909 "Notes upon a Case of Obsessional Neurosis," p. 163.
1911 "Psycho-Analytic Notes on an Autobiographical Account of a Case of Paranoia." *Standard Edition*, 12:3-82.
1912 Letter to C. G. Jung (in Jones, Vol. II, p. 450).
1913 *Totem and Taboo*, pp. 92-94.
     A related passage is in "The Uncanny" (1919), pp. 234-236.

jection. This concept supposes that the working and contents of the mind are somehow perceived, but not recognized as such. Instead, they are found again projected into the external world as animistic or delusional explanations of natural events and social experience. In this conception, the assumption of parallelism takes the form of a finding of the structure, processes, and contents of the mind, displaced into a new location, accounting for the structure of experience. Thus, in one of the passages in which Freud spells out his conception of endopsychic perception, we find (1913, p. 92):

> Spirits and demons . . . are only projections of man's own emotional impulses. He turns his emotional cathexes into persons, he peoples the world with them and meets his internal mental processes again outside himself.

That the study of man's perceptions of the external world is, in fact, a direct route to learning about the actual structure of mind, is stated quite explicitly by Freud. He states that it is the task of scientific psychology to translate back into intrapsychic terms the language of events found in myths, delusions, and religions, and "to transform *metaphysics* into *metapsychology*" (1901, p. 259).

B. A counterpart conception embodying this assumption of parallelism is that of internalization in the development of the mind. According to one meaning of this conception, the "actual structure of mind" is built up of replicas of experiences of object relations and their attendant impulses and conflicts. This genetic concept already reflects the assumption that the mental apparatus, as it develops, shall resemble its experiences. This assumption, it should be noted, is the basis for a psychoanalytic approach to explaining the fact of the anthropomorphism of introspection.

C. The "picket-fence" model of the mind that Freud develops in *The Interpretation of Dreams* embodies the assumption of a correspondence or congruence between the form and structure of experience and the form of the mental apparatus. The model states that the direction of impulses in the mental apparatus is tied to the sequence of structures. Memories are laid down in the sequence in which they were experienced. This means that the earliest memories are registered in primarily the visual mode, and the visual mode, by definition in this framework, corresponds to the more impulsive bodily-need-driven parts of the mind. The other end of the apparatus represents the executive, controlling, verbal portion of the mind, which is late in developing. It should be noted that even though the censor is not explicitly localized within the structures, the model, nevertheless, presents the mind as split or divided into parts which function in terms of conflicts of wishes or conflicts of interests. In this light, we can further understand Freud's statement that at the bottom, the three types of regression, namely, temporal, topographical, and formal, are identical (1900, p. 548). This discovery is, in fact, a making explicit of an assumption built into the model.

D. Freud's interest in history, society, and biology was oriented primarily toward an understanding of how these forces mold and influence the mental apparatus and how they are registered and represented in the mind. He did not seek to understand these areas in their own terms. In *Moses and Monotheism* (1939), he explained that he was "not an ethnographer but a psycho-analyst." It appears to us that, in order to discuss these questions, Freud constructed a system of equivalent structures and forces unifying the study of history, society, biology, and the mind of the individual. In some instances, this series of equations, which we term constructing an isomorphism, is stated rather explicitly. In other instances, particularly in his statements about biology, the equations are more implicit. For example, in speaking of the history of the human race, or the history of the Jews, he can speak of the "infancy" of a group or of its "latency period" and quite explicitly compare them to developmental stages of the individual. In his treatment of society, as in *Group Psychology and the Analysis of the Ego* (1921), he uses a preformed model of the mob, that provided by Le Bon, which treats the mob as an organization, or an organism, with purposes, intentions, motives, and a particular psychology of its own. The mob is equated with an individual, and the properties and functions of an individual person are ascribed to the mob.

His treatment of biology has two aspects. The first, in the earliest writings on instincts, is the effort to utilize certain forms of biological thinking to help formulate the notion of instincts. The second treatment of biology, in *Beyond the Pleasure Principle* (1920), is somewhat more formidable. There he states explicitly that the universe as a whole is dominated by the same two principles that dominate and regulate the mental life of the individual person (life and death instincts). However, even in his discussion of the division of instincts for the purposes of clarifying instinct theory, we find that he subtly equates instincts with intentions or motives.

> However jealously we usually defend the independence of psychology from every other science, here we stood in the shadow of the unshakable biological fact that the living individual organism is at the command of two intentions, self-preservation and the preservation of the species, which seem to be independent of each other, which, so far as we know at present, have no common origin and whose interests are often in conflict in animal life [1933, p. 95].

Note that these two terms, *intentions* and *interests,* are applied to instincts, thus ascribing human purposes to biological forces. Another example of this kind of isomorphic reduction of the world of nature and of the mind can be seen in one of his last statements about instincts in "Analysis Terminable and Interminable" (1937). There he cites the early Greek philosopher, Empedocles, who developed a viewpoint about the role of strife versus love as a major cosmic conflict. Freud compares the similarities and differences between this notion and his own theory of life and death instincts:

> But the theory of Empedocles which especially deserves our interest is one which approximates so closely to the psycho-analytic theory of the instincts that we should be tempted to maintain that the two are identical, if it were not for the difference that the Greek philosopher's theory is a cosmic phantasy while *ours* is content to claim biological validity. *At the same time, the fact that Empedocles ascribes to the universe the same animate nature as to individual organisms robs this difference of much of its importance* [p. 245f.; our italics].

We take this to mean that Freud sees in the writings of the philosopher that he is talking about mind or the individual even though he uses the terminology of the cosmos and of cosmic principles. In this same passage, we also see that Freud utilizes as a buttress for his own theory a viewpoint which makes biology, the cosmos, and the mind isomorphic and anthropomorphic.

These four examples of isomorphism (A, B, C, D) demonstrate how the mind and the world at large are anthropomorphized and considered to be organized in the same formal pattern. Such an equation of these different structures permits the same process terms of conflict, motive, and intention to be used in describing processes in each of the domains. Effectively then, each of these areas is modeled on conscious, anthropomorphized experience and the models that are derived are empathically meaningful.

To return then to the focal questions: how does anthropomorphism get into psychoanalytic models of mind, and what functions does it serve there?

1. Introspectable experience is rendered anthropomorphically and sociomorphically. The anthropomorphic language portrays conflicts and groups the terms of the conflicts.
2. The experience of conflicting intentions is rendered in anthropomorphic language and is intimately connected with certain commonly accepted and popularly held views about the division of the mind, such as the division of the mind into a moral part, a reality-oriented part, and an animal-impulsive or a childish part.
3. Psychoanalytic theory, then, does in fact what various common and popular divisions of mind do. The psychoanalytic models of the mental apparatus posit an apparatus that has a part corresponding to each of the terms of the conflict. The language of the relationships among these parts and of the functions ascribed to these parts is primarily anthropomorphic and sociomorphic.
4. The individual functions of parts of the mind are described along the model of conscious introspectable experience.

What we are here describing, then, is a basic approach to, or a certain style of, building a model of the mind and its relations to the environment. What we term the assumption of isomorphism is, in effect, Freud's working hypothesis about how the forces of culture and biology are registered and represented in the mental life of the individual. With this hypothesis, Freud claims that we can "read out" from the products of mental life, both introspectable and unconscious, the experience of the individual of the past life of his race, of his own past life, and of the structure of his own mind (endopsychic perception). Of course, proper *translation* (e.g., 1915, p. 167) is indispensable. One must learn the mode of translating the manifest content into latent content. Thus, from the data provided by an individual patient, or a few patients, Freud attempted to make statements about past and present events or forces in the inner and outer world of the person.

What emerges as of crucial importance in Freud's approach to the study of biology, history, and society in their relation to the mind is the notion of *experience,* though Freud does not emphasize this particular term. What the psychoanalyst sees is that which the mind, or the person, has *experienced* of the structure and forces of these different realms, i.e., the meaning of the events to the person. For Freud, in certain respects, it is indeed of secondary interest whether the patient was actually seduced or experienced (i.e., fantasied) a particular relationship as a seduction. In dealing with reconstructions, particularly on the part of the individual, but even for the past of the race, or the ethnic group, the data with which analyst and patient deal concern the past event as experienced. As for other purposes, however, it is more important to know the "actuality," as well as the way in which it was experienced.

We should like to add that the utility or lack of utility of the isomorphic assumption, and the entailed anthropomorphism, for the understanding of history, anthropology, biology, etc., cannot be ascertained by psychoanalysis. It must be decided by the methodologies appropriate to those several disciplines. However, within psychoanalysis, one must recognize that there is another approach to the study of these realms, in relation to the mind. Thus, we speak, for example, as Erikson (1964) and Hartmann (1947) have, of the different *possibilities* that historical process and historical change may provide for the mental life of a particular individual. Or one could consider the range of potentialities, capacities, and limitations that biological processes provide for human mental life. It is our conviction that this kind of model is not to be taken either as contradictory or as supplementary to the isomorphic model, but rather that the two models are addressed to different issues.

The isomorphic approach, as seen in Freud, seems to imply causal connections between these other forces, e.g., those of biology and the forces of the mind, via the transferring of similar forms. Thus, the duality of life and death as biological forces "brings about" the duality of instinct in the mental life. It is not the criticism that this approach is teleological that we wish to stress. Rather, we point to its underlying assumption; namely, that these forces have meaning. They exert their influence through their meaning, just as the events of childhood exert their influence through their meaning, that is, as they are experienced by the child.

This model does not account for the mechanism by which actuality acquires meaning. It assumes the equation of repeating and remembering. The model ignores the possibility that the finding of similar forms is a function of the synthetic and creative capacities of the subject or of the observer, who can find personal meanings writ large in the world around him.

In contrast, the kinds of evolutionary and adaptive models proposed by Hartmann and Erikson aim at a causal framework. There one can begin to examine how actuality and impersonal forces enter into the development of the capacities for constructing personal meanings. The assumption of primary autonomous functions as independent variables in experience is one example. These functions account for the way in which the limits of innate psychological capacity may help shape the nature of psychological experience, without their being represented in the content of that experience. Similarly, Erikson's conception of the role of culture stresses the ways in which cultures promote conflicts and offer paths of resolution. This is in contrast to those views emphasizing the transmission of forms and contents from culture to individual.

Meaning and Causality

We have now examined something of the role of anthropomorphism in theory and indicated, in broad outline, the way in which anthropomorphism comes into a theoretical model of mind. The question then becomes: can we remove the anthropomorphism from psychoanalytic theory either by more careful formulation of psychoanalytic propositions or by a change in terminology? We must be certain that what looks like a more careful formulation is not merely a thinly disguised change of terminology. The most prominent examples in psychoanalytic theory, in fact dating from Freud's earliest writings, of efforts at systematization have invoked physical models. These are couched mainly in hydraulic or electrical or magnetic terminology.

The physical metaphor implies a physical model. It is not empathically evocative in its main intent, so that this lends an impersonal quality to the formulation. The abstractness and utility of formulations will only be illusory, however, unless these formulations can be systematically interrelated and shown to have referents other than the observation metaphorically represented. One such referent, for instance, might be hypotheses regarding the correlation of mental events with neurophysiological organizations. Rubinstein (1965, 1967) discusses in detail the possible referents of psychoanalytic theoretical terms, speaking, however, not of neurophysiological terms, but of "protoneurophysiological" terms. The referents of theoretical concepts need not be only neurophysiological, however. Our search for more basic mechanisms might lead us instead to psychological concepts derivable from psychological research other than psychoanalytic observation, but nonetheless useful in an explanatory way. In addition, other biological and developmental concepts would be very likely necessary to enlarge our view of how meanings are established, elaborated, and maintained.

If a physical model is indeed to be a vehicle for a systematic exploration and exposition in an enlarging of the theory, then it must be more than another evocative metaphor. In discussions of the use of physical models in psychoanalysis the point is often missed that renditions of physical theories in ordinary language represent a rather limited sense of the full force of the physical conception, which is of course to be found in one or more mathematically formulated relationships. It is possible to speak of energy as the "ability to do work." It would then appear that physical energy and psychic energy would have a great deal in common, or be strictly analogous. However, to speak of energy in this sense as "ability" to do work represents an anthropomorphization of the physical concepts, or an attempt to give a simplified and empathically meaningful exposition of a physical notion. The full weight of the physical proposition is carried in mathematical statement. Still another problem, too often neglected, is that any model entails logical consequences in the relationships of its components. In the case of physical models of psychoanalysis, e.g., energy, they do not lead to resolvable or testable hypotheses. In fact, efforts to define further the logical consequences of the acknowledged properties of energy are usually dismissed as taking the model too literally.

Let us now examine the example offered by Hartmann, Kris, and Loewenstein (1946, p. 16) as a kind of reformulation that removes the impression of anthropomorphism in the theory.

> In order to illustrate the vicissitudes of meaning in this area, we select as an example the Freudian sentence: "The Ego presents itself to the Superego as love object." The metaphor expresses the relations of two psychic organizations by comparing it to a love relation between individuals, in which the one is the lover and the other the beloved. However, the sentence expresses an important clinical finding: self-love can easily and does, under certain conditions, substitute for love of another person. Self-love in this formulation indicates that approval of the self by the superego concerns the self in lieu of another person.
>
> We replace the word "ego" in Freud's text by the word "self." We do so since the ego is defined as part of the personality, and since Freud's use of the word is ambiguous. He uses "ego" in reference to a psychic organization and to the whole person. Before we can attempt to reformulate Freud's proposition, it is essential to go one step further. In a more rigorous sense, we find it advisable not to speak of "approval" or "disapproval" by the superego, but simply to speak of different kinds and degrees of tension between the two psychic organizations, according to the presence or absence of conflict between their functions. Approval would be characterized by a diminution of tension; disapproval by its increase.

This reformulation consists of translating the notion of self-approval and self-love, one part of the self approving or loving another part, into the language of degrees of tension between two psychic systems, ego and superego. In a later revision of the paper (1964) the authors substituted a different sentence from Freud for their reformulation in which the ego offers itself to the *id* as a libidinal object. We have not used that latter version because the sentence marking the transition from self-approval to "tension" has been there omitted. That omission makes their argument somewhat less clear.

The advantage of the "tension" formulation is that a proposition of this form can refer to a conflict between two agencies without that conflict necessarily being introspectable. "Tension" becomes a useful low-order explanatory term for phenomena such as self-destructive behavior, where neither conflict nor painful affects (e.g., guilt) are experienced consciously. The language of "tension" provides some "distance" from the data of observation. "Tension" is not simply equated with the affective experience of self-approval or disapproval or any particular affect such as guilt or shame. "Tension" might be equated with a term such as unconscious guilt.

However, the substitution of tension for the clearly anthropomorphic terms of self-love, self-approval, and of the ego being love object of the superego does not seem to be entirely successful. "Tension" in this setting appears to be evocative and not strictly denotative. It is a subtle form of evocation, however, since its use depends on the fact that it refers both to the *experience* of psychological tension and to tension as a physical concept. Note that tension as a physical concept is defined mathematically and that its use otherwise is to a great extent anthropomorphic. Hence, "tension" serves merely as a restatement of the proposition that there is a conflict between two psychic agencies. As such, it is no more or no less metaphorical than the term "conflict." The criteria for "tension" are, as far as can be seen, the same as the criteria for conflict; "degree of tension" cannot be described in terms different from "intensity of conflict." Furthermore, in what terms other than in reference to certain specific clinical observations can we speak of "different kinds and degress of tension" between the two psychic organizations?

"Tension" along with terms such as "unconscious affects" have their value in organizing the clinical data. Yet they introduce a certain ambiguity. That ambiguity resides in the fact that the theoretical term is modeled upon the conscious experience. Thus, when we refer to "conscious guilt" we make a descriptive statement. "Unconscious guilt" postulates a theoretical entity whose precise relationship to its model in consciousness is not entirely specified. Furthermore, the "tension" formulation does not sufficiently characterize either conscious or unconscious guilt, or differentiate them from one another.

Perhaps another statement of this point of view will be of help. When we substitute terms of superego and ego tensions for terms of love, hate, and guilt, we have specified agents and their interactions. The question now is: can we specify either the nature of the actions or of the agents? When we say that the superego loves the ego, we cannot specify the nature of the love which gives it force as an agent, nor can we specify the nature of that force or tension. We cannot specify the nature of the agents except by their definition in the behavior from which they are inferred in the first place. In contrast, let us take an example of an anthropomorphic expression in chemistry. One commonly says that "acids attack bases" or "acids and bases react with each other and neutralize each other." In these instances, the anthropomorphic expression is a colloquial way of referring to processes which can be specified and characterized at several different levels. The reaction results in a change in readily observable physical properties, by which one could, in fact, define such a term as neutralization. The final mixture is neither sour nor soapy, but may in fact taste salty. In short, it has none of the outstanding physical properties of its antecedents. More important, from the point of view of building a theory of chemistry, is the fact that we have mathematical expressions to describe the reaction in a conceptual framework of terms such as ions and electrical charges into which this concept of neutralization fits. The quantitative expressions and the concepts of ions are derived from a number of sources other than this one experiment. Further, the "ionic hypothesis" is testable and has implications which lead to entirely new areas of observation beyond the simple class of reactions we have described, namely, neutralization. It is abundantly clear that psychoanalytic theoretical terms such as "neutralization" or "energy" or "cathexis" serve the function of bringing together seemingly diverse clinical phenomena. It is also clear, however, that their function ends when this grouping and classification is complete.[2] One use of these economic terms, as we have suggested, resides in their bridging

[2] To this extent we are in agreement with Rycroft (1968, p. 43) in his characterization of the theoretical status of psychic energy. "It is hard to avoid the conclusion that Freud's theory of bound and mobile energy has little to do with the concept of energy as used by the 'other natural sciences,' but that it is really a theory of MEANING in disguise."

the gap from experienced intensities of thought and feeling to system language, but one can go no further. This use of terms in both descriptive and theoretical senses has been discussed by Rubinstein (1965). Schafer (1967), in a similar vein, points to the difficulty in distinguishing between the use of terms in a phenomenological versus a systematic sense, e.g., in discussions of the superego. Our discussion would seem to illustrate the way in which theoretical usage may carry over the anthropomorphism in descriptions of experienced conflict by treating the unconscious conflict in the same terms, without giving these terms any other theoretical referent.

The double usage of analytic terms, a usage in fact to which Freud himself pointed in speaking of the descriptive and systemic and dynamic senses of the term "unconscious," corresponds to a number of similar, though not identical, pairs of dichotomous concepts, i.e.,

(1) intention and causality
(2) phenomenologic and systemic
(3) empathy and causality
(4) subjective language and objective language
(5) person and organism
(6) wish and biological need.[3]

In all of these pairs, the left-hand term corresponds to the view from within, i.e., the subjective experience of an agent. The right-hand terms correspond to the objective orientation of an observer (cf. Grossman, 1967).

A formulation in phenomenological or subjective terms orders subjective experience, but is logically independent of formulations in which subjective experience is treated objectively. The use of subjective terms in an objective way creates a bridge between two logically independent orders. It then uses the language of subjective experience in two ways. It allows the observer to speak about the subjective experience of the subject *as though* it were observable. It is a verbal link which attempts to remove the logical separation by *definition*. The use of the same term in both ways makes this

---

[3] One is tempted to include in this list "understanding and explanation" because discussions of these terms, by Eissler (1968) and Hartmann (1927), trench heavily on these same issues. However, this particular pair also involves problems which are of a different order.

effort an implicit one rather than an explicit one. Furthermore, substituting abstract terms does not accomplish the leap across this logical gap. The only way the abstraction process works is via such bridge concepts which link causal and empathic by definition, and by means of parallelistic assumptions about the nature of the apparatus and the nature of experience, such as we have described in the earlier portion of this paper.

There are several varieties of concepts which speak of subjective experience in objective terms. One group gives a theoretical, or systematic, status to the terms of commonplace experience. "Tension" (see above) is one such example. Others are: libidinal investment, the wish, the system Conscious, narcissism, and the self. Another group of terms such as "depression" and "anxiety" are commonly used both to denote clinical states and subjective experience. These terms create entities by reifying the terms designating the subjective states and their *observable concomitants* (Sarbin, 1964, 1968). The third type is seen in the concept of "drive," which brings together a quality of subjective experience and a concept of biological functioning. It is clear that the use of any of these bridge terms always requires further specification of the sense in which it is being used. In all of these cases, diverse models of observation, experience, and conceptualization are amalgamated by means of a linguistic device.

Using different terminologies, the issue of these two logically independent realms has been discussed by a number of authors, including Brierley (1951), Grossman (1967), G. S. Klein (1966, 1968), Kohut (1959), Mischel (1964), Meissner (1966), Rycroft (1968), and Sutherland (1963). With still a somewhat different focus, but quite germane to the present issues, Schafer (1968) outlined what he considers two types of theory within psychoanalysis, which he calls the "adaptational" and "dynamic" types of conceptualization. He states that Freud attempted both types of conceptualization, but did not always differentiate and coordinate the two approaches: "Roughly speaking, his evolutionary, adaptational formulations of the psychic apparatus are the ones that tend to be quasi-neuro-physiological and mechanistic, and it is his dynamic psychological formulations that tend to be anthropomorphic." Schafer does not necessarily hold to their being logically incompatible, and in fact he argues that each has its value, but "distinguishing one from the other helps one to understand what these authors [Hartmann and Rapaport] and Freud are doing in one context or another" (p. 51). We speak with Schafer of *coordinating* two types of approach in dealing with two logically independent models of explanation. The only way to use them simultaneously is by coordinating them in their application to the empirical unity of the phenomena under study. For example, in psychophysiological research we work with a notion of covariants, such as the physiological concomitants of a reported experience. The coordination is an *empirical* activity, which is not equivalent to providing a unitary explanation for experience and physiology. We may try to establish a concordance, or parallelism, which will tell something about correlations. Only some superordinate framework, yet to be discovered, could provide one logical system in which both aspects could be encompassed (cf. Langer, 1967). In current dream research, for example, there is a high correlation between dreaming and rapid eye movement sleep (REMS). However, no greater understanding of the *meaning* of dreams is derived from the clarification of the REM mechanism. Even the question of the precise nature of the correlation between dreaming and REM sleep remains a matter of controversy. In the psychophysiology of affect, too, perfect correlations are not found between an affective state, as defined physiologically, and the same state as defined experientially.

The question of how to deal with these various contrasting pairs of terms is one which was taken up in the very earliest of Freud's psychoanalytic writings, and even in his neurological writings (1891). In the "Project" (1895), he attempted to conceptualize the transformation of qualities into quantities. In *The Interpretation of Dreams* he took up the same issue again in relation to the question of how the wish or the intention (psychological functions) arises from the basic biological organization of the infant. In *Studies on Hysteria* (1893-1895) one can see throughout the work, particularly in the contrast between Breuer's section and Freud's section, the attempt to conceptualize clinical phenomena in both causal and motivational terms. Freud's discussion of the organization of memories and their role in pathogenesis, for example, represents an early formulation of the relationship between causal factors and motivational factors in pathogenesis. In general, in these early writings, one finds a constant interplay between dynamic, i.e., conflict-defense, formulations of psychological states and physiological, mechanical, and neurological expositions of these conditions.

The problem of the distinction between the two types of formulation, one in causal terms and the other in intentional terms, permeates virtually every level of the theory, in every stage of its development. It goes beyond questions of whether or not experience can be reduced to neurophysiological terms. We encounter this difficulty whenever we try to distinguish descriptive from systematic usage of terms, or experiential usage from systematic. For example, in 1912, Freud said (p. 264):

> It is by no means impossible for the product of unconscious activity to pierce into consciousness, but a certain amount of exertion is needed for this task. When we try to do it in ourselves, we become aware of a distinct feeling of *repulsion* which must be overcome, and when we produce it in a patient we get the most unquestionable signs of what we call his *resistance* to it.

Thus, there is an *experienced feeling* of the resistance to making the unconscious conscious. Resistance has an introspectable referent and a theoretical sense as well. This statement quite clearly also implies an introspectable aspect to energy. In fact, the systematic and experiential uses of "energy" and "libido" are not consistently distinguished in Freud's writings. He may speak of "libido" or "cathexis" as equivalent to investment or interest (e.g., 1911, p. 70; 1917, p. 224).

Summary and Conclusions

Thus, we have come full circle in our investigation of the role of anthropomorphism in psychoanalytic theory. We began with Freud's assertion that our understanding reaches only as far as our anthropomorphism. We have tried to ascertain in what sense this might be true. Our conclusions are:

1. There is an anthropomorphism in our clinical psychoanalytic theory, which serves a real function in organizing the introspective and experiential clinical data.

2. Those clinical psychoanalytic propositions which are most immediately related to the experiential data of inner conflict are especially dependent on anthropomorphic language. Certain structural propositions are particularly prominent in this respect. However, to the extent that any proposition is modeled on the experience of inner conflict or an inner division, it will tend to be anthropomorphic.

3. It is not necessary to "purge" the clinical theory of anthropomorphic language. Anthropomorphic language is in no way incompatible with systematic study of individual cases, or of groups of cases, or with any number of ways of grouping and organizing clinical observations. Anthropomorphism per se is not "unscientific." It serves a number of useful purposes, including that of inviting empathic participation by the analyst. Its value lies in providing process terms for explanation according to motives. So long as the only processes of which we speak are wishing, intending, and needing, and their defensive counterparts, there is no other language available.

4. The place of anthropomorphic language in higher-order explanatory propositions constitutes a different problem. We expect of such propositions that they begin to explain and place in a larger framework the clinical findings that are stated in the language of wish, intention, and need. From this viewpoint, attempts to eliminate or minimize the anthropomorphism of metapsychological propositions have not been successful. The various terms intended to replace anthropomorphic terms are deficient in one of several respects, the outstanding ones being:

(a) They represent a model based on physical systems, for instance, which has no other set of referents than the clinical data from which they are derived and which they are intended to explain.

(b) Some suggested terms, such as "tension," are in fact a kind of hybrid. They still bear the essential characteristics of their anthropomorphic lineage.

5. The major route by which the language of metapsychological propositions has been developed is by the use of "bridge concepts." These are terms which by *definition* bridge the gap between experience and theory but do not per se solve problems inherent in using two logically different realms of discourse.

6. A study of the place of anthropomorphism in psychoanalytic propositions, then, is of value both clinically and theoretically because it highlights the need to keep separate issues relating to *meaning* and *motive* from issues relating to *causation*.

7. Our approach to anthropomorphism is of assistance in appreciating certain other facets of Freud's thinking, especially his particular use of the study of history, of biology, and of the nature of society. Using anthropomorphic formulations, he constructs a framework in which theories about the nature of history, biology, and society become "isomorphic." Behind the anthropomorphism and "isomorphism" is Freud's aim of expounding how these realms are represented in the *mental life* of the individual, and particularly how they influence the nexus of meaning and motive, rather than of causality.

8. The distinction between discourse in terms of "meaning and motive" and discourse in terms of "causality" is only partly explained by regarding them as two different languages that describe the same phenomena. Far more important is that each describes fundamentally different sets of data and their related concepts, as exemplified in the distinction between "subjective" and "objective."

9. The contrast between "meaning" and "causality" also points to a major difficulty in developing psychoanalysis as a general psychology. The same problem, however, besets any one psychological approach that attempts to become a general psychology. If psychoanalysis, or any other psychological approach, is to become a comprehensive psychology, there must be some superordinate conception which could encompass both kinds of discourse. Such a schema has yet to be formulated.

BIBLIOGRAPHY

Breuer, J. & Freud, S. (1893-1895), Studies on Hysteria. *Standard Edition,* 2. London: Hogarth Press, 1955.
Brierley, M. (1951), *Trends in Psycho-Analysis.* London: Hogarth Press; see especially Ch. V, Metapsychology and Personology.
Eidelberg, L., ed. (1968), *Encyclopedia of Psychoanalysis.* New York: Free Press.
Eissler, K. R. (1968), The Relation of Explaining and Understanding in Psychoanalysis. *This Annual,* 23:141-177.
Erikson, E. H. (1964), *Insight and Responsibility.* New York: Norton.
Freud, S. (1891), *On Aphasia.* New York: International Universities Press, 1953.

—— (1894), The Neuro-Psychoses of Defence. *Standard Edition*, 3:43-68. London: Hogarth Press, 1962.

—— (1895), Project for a Scientific Psychology. *Standard Edition*, 1:283-397. London: Hogarth Press, 1966.

—— (1900), The Interpretation of Dreams. *Standard Edition*, 4 & 5. London: Hogarth Press, 1953.

—— (1901), The Psychopathology of Everyday Life. *Standard Edition*, 6. London: Hogarth Press, 1960.

—— (1907), Delusions and Dreams in Jensen's *Gradiva*. *Standard Edition*, 9:3-95. London: Hogarth Press, 1959.

—— (1909), Notes upon a Case of Obsessional Neurosis. *Standard Edition*, 10:153-318. London: Hogarth Press, 1955.

—— (1911), Psycho-Analytic Notes on an Autobiographical Account of a Case of Paranoia. *Standard Edition*, 12:3-82. London: Hogarth Press, 1958.

—— (1912), A Note on the Unconscious in Psycho-Analysis. *Standard Edition*, 12:255-266. London: Hogarth Press, 1958.

—— (1913), Totem and Taboo. *Standard Edition*, 13:1-161. London: Hogarth Press, 1955.

—— (1915), The Unconscious. *Standard Edition*, 14:159-215. London: Hogarth Press, 1957.

—— (1916-1917), Introductory Lectures on Psycho-Analysis. *Standard Edition*, 15 & 16. London: Hogarth Press, 1963.

—— (1917), A Metapsychological Supplement to the Theory of Dreams. *Standard Edition*, 14:217-235. London: Hogarth Press, 1957.

—— (1919), The 'Uncanny.' *Standard Edition*, 17:215-256. London: Hogarth Press, 1955.

—— (1920), Beyond the Pleasure Principle. *Standard Edition*, 18:3-64. London: Hogarth Press, 1955.

—— (1921), Group Psychology and the Analysis of the Ego. *Standard Edition*, 18:67-143. London: Hogarth Press, 1955.

—— (1923), The Ego and the Id. *Standard Edition*, 19:3-66. London: Hogarth Press, 1961.

—— (1933), New Introductory Lectures on Psycho-Analysis. *Standard Edition*, 22:3-182. London: Hogarth Press, 1964.

—— (1937), Analysis Terminable and Interminable. *Standard Edition*, 23:209-253. London: Hogarth Press, 1964.

—— (1939), Moses and Monotheism. *Standard Edition*, 23:3-137. London: Hogarth Press, 1964.

—— (1950), *The Origins of Psychoanalysis*. New York: Basic Books, 1954.

Grossman, W. I. (1967), Reflections on the Relationships of Introspection and Psycho-Analysis. *Int. J. Psa.*, 48:16-31.

Hartmann, H. (1927), Understanding and Explanation. *Essays on Ego Psychology*. New York: International Universities Press, 1964, pp. 369-403.

—— (1947), On Rational and Irrational Action. *Essays on Ego Psychology*. New York: International Universities Press, 1964, pp. 37-68.

—— (1959), Psychoanalysis as a Scientific Theory. *Essays on Ego Psychology*. New York: International Universities Press, 1964, pp. 318-350.

—— Kris, E., & Loewenstein, R. M. (1946), Comments on the Formation of Psychic Structure. *This Annual*, 2:11-38. See also *Psychological Issues*, Monogr. 14:56-85. New York: International Universities Press, 1964.

Holt, R. R. (1965), Freud's Cognitive Style. Paper presented to Psychological Colloquium, University of Michigan, February 21, 1964. (Shorter version in *Amer. Imago*, 22:163-179.)

Jones, E. (1955), *The Life and Work of Sigmund Freud*, Vol. 2. New York: Basic Books.

Klein, G. S. (1966), Two Theories or One? Perspectives to Change in Psychoanalytic Theory. Draft, April, 1966, presented at Conference of Psychoanalysts of the Southwest, Galveston, Texas, March, 1966.

—— (1968), Freud's Two Theories of Sexuality. Draft, November 18, 1968, based on a chapter of a book in preparation, *Psychoanalytic Theory: An Exploration of Essentials.*

Kohut, H. (1959), Introspection, Empathy, and Psychoanalysis. *J. Amer. Psa. Assn.,* 7:459-483.

Langer, S. K. (1967), *Mind: An Essay on Human Feeling,* Vol. 1. Baltimore: Johns Hopkins Press.

Laplanche, J. & Pontalis, J. B. (1967), *Vocabulaire de la Psychanalyse.* Paris: Presses Universitaires de France.

Lewis, C. S. (1967), *Studies in Words.* Cambridge: Cambridge University Press.

Masserman, J. H. (1946), *Principles of Dynamic Psychiatry.* Philadelphia: Saunders.

Meissner, W. W. (1966), The Operational Principle and Meaning in Psychoanalysis. *Psa. Quart.,* 35:233-255.

Mischel, T. (1964), Personal Constructs, Rules, and the Logic of Clinical Activity. *Psychol. Rev.,* 71:180-192.

Nash, H. (1962), Freud and Metaphor. *A.M.A. Arch. Gen. Psychiat.,* 7:25-29.

Nunberg, H. & Federn, E., eds. (1962), *Minutes of the Vienna Psychoanalytic Society,* Vol. I, 1906-1908. New York: International Universities Press.

Rubinstein, B. B. (1965), Psychoanalytic Theory and the Mind-Body Problem. In: *Psychoanalysis and Current Biological Thought,* ed. N. S. Greenfield & W. C. Lewis. Madison: University of Wisconsin Press, pp. 35-56.

—— (1967), Explanation and Mere Description: A Metascientific Examination of Certain Aspects of the Psychoanalytic Theory of Motivation. In: *Motives and Thought: Psychoanalytic Essays in Honor of David Rapaport,* ed. R. R. Holt [*Psychological Issues,* Monogr. 18/19]. New York: International Universities Press, pp. 18-79.

Rycroft, C., ed. (1966), Introduction: Causes and Meaning. In: *Psychoanalysis Observed.* New York: Coward-McCann, pp. 7-22.

—— (1968), *A Critical Dictionary of Psycho-Analysis.* London: Thomas Nelson & Sons.

Sarbin, T. R. (1964), Anxiety: The Reification of a Metaphor. *Arch. Gen. Psychiat.,* 10:630-638.

—— (1968), Ontology Recapitulates Philology: The Mythic Nature of Anxiety. *Amer. Psychol.,* 23:411-418.

Schafer, R. (1967), Ideals, the Ego Ideal, and the Ideal Self. In: *Motives and Thought: Psychoanalytic Essays in Honor of David Rapaport,* ed. R. R. Holt [*Psychological Issues,* Monogr. 18/19]. New York: International Universities Press, pp. 131-174.

—— (1968), *Aspects of Internalization.* New York: International Universities Press.

Spiegel, L. A. (1966), Superego and the Function of Anticipation with Comments on "Anticipatory Anxiety." In: *Psychoanalysis—A General Psychology: Essays in Honor of Heinz Hartmann,* ed. R. M. Loewenstein, L. M. Newman, M. Schur, & A. J. Solnit. New York: International Universities Press, pp. 315-337.

Stewart, W. (1967), *Psychoanalysis: The First Ten Years.* New York: Macmillan.

Sutherland, J. D. (1963), Object-Relations Theory and the Conceptual Model of Psycho-Analysis. *Brit. J. Med. Psychol.,* 36:109-124.

ASPECTS OF NORMAL AND
PATHOLOGICAL DEVELOPMENT

LEVELS OF VERBAL COMMUNICATION IN THE SCHIZOPHRENIC CHILD'S STRUGGLE AGAINST, FOR, AND WITH THE WORLD OF OBJECTS

RUDOLF EKSTEIN, Ph.D. and
ELAINE CARUTH, PH.D. (Los Angeles)

> He who has mastered any law in his private thoughts, is master to that extent of all men whose language he speaks, and of all into whose language his own can be translated.
> —RALPH WALDO EMERSON, 1837

As has often been pointed out, although speech is central to the analytic process, few psychoanalytic studies have been devoted to language and its evolvement. What analytic work on language development exists reflects the history of psychoanalytic theory. We can distinguish six phases in the psychoanalytic conceptualizations of language evolvement (Ekstein, 1965). The early Freudian model of 1895, developed in the context of neurophysiological considerations, attributed the emergence of speech—the means of *Verständigung*—to the early helplessness of the infant, and has indeed been a useful first framework, allowing subsequent generations of workers in this field to fill in the details. This initial helplessness—that "primal source of all moral motives"[1] (Freud, 1895)—will again be

---

[1] As Freud described the baby's cry in the face of hunger, thirst or pain, and when outside help is required in order to relieve or satisfy his needs, and thus to restore a state without tension, he stated: "At early stages the human organism is incapable

Director of Project on Childhood Psychosis, Reiss-Davis Child Study Center, Los Angeles, California; Clinical Professor of Medical Psychology, University of California at Los Angeles; Training Analyst, Los Angeles Psychoanalytic Society and Institute.

Senior Clinical Research Psychologist, Project on Childhood Psychosis, Reiss-Davis Child Study Center, Los Angeles, California.

of central concern in our present task of describing a developmental language profile, as it were, for the psychotic child.

In the second phase the conceptualization of language development was strongly influenced by prevailing theories of psychosexual development, and the origin of language was speculatively related to various sexual factors. Work in the third phase, utilizing reconstructions from the analysis of adults and children, stressed the preoedipal mother-child relationship and the importance of the "primitive love talk" (Chadwick, 1928) in terms of needs to be met by the "mother tongue." The fourth phase was under the growing dominance of ego psychology, the adaptive point of view, and notions of differentiation of psychic functions. Molecular considerations of speech mechanics and often too-literal assumptions about the origin of speech elements gave way to more sophisticated models relating the origin of speech to the development of ego functions. The genetic reconstructions of early preverbal experiences were utilized as blueprints for further investigation. The fifth contribution, developing out of the analyst's growing readiness to collaborate with and to learn from other behavioral scientists, came from direct observation of infants under both empirical and experimental conditions. A sixth source has been the study of language in schizophrenia and related disorders, particularly as they occur in childhood; this research has led to improved models of thought and speech development which permit us to see Freud's early and dramatic germinal insight of 1895 as one which has borne rich fruit and which invites new work in the same direction.

The following presentation centers around some new work in that direction. The data derive from the intensive study of long-term psychoanalytic treatment processes with schizophrenic and autistic children. We shall describe our attempts to redefine and delineate the variety and degrees of disturbances in communication that we find in different kinds of schizophrenic and autistic children.

---

of achieving this specific action [the supply of nourishment]. It is brought about by extraneous help, when the attention of an experienced person has been drawn to the child's condition by a discharge taking place along the path of internal change [e.g., by the child's screaming]. This path of discharge thus acquires an extremely important secondary function—viz., of bringing about an understanding with other people; and the original helplessness of human beings is thus the primal source of all moral motives" (p. 379).

This venture into the area of psycholinguistic problems germane to psychotic children requires some ideas of the philosophy of linguistics and science, some concepts of psychoanalytic ego psychology, and some knowledge of the technical interventions one experiments with in trying to bring about a *Verständigung*—a system of communication—between oneself and the schizophrenic child. These notions may help us understand the meaning of the schizophrenic child's language and discover the latent order behind the manifest thought disorder, the communication illness of the patient who struggles with, for, and against language, just as he struggles for and against object and self in the prolonged autism-symbiosis conflict that characterizes the central difficulty of the schizophrenic child—the one which is re-created in and through the transference during the course of analytic treatment.

We are referring to the fact that autism and symbiosis may be understood as normal phases in the development of object relations (Mahler, 1968). If these are successfully mastered, the infant gains the capacity to differentiate self from nonself and eventually to perceive the people around him as separate objects. The relationships he develops with them change in nature as his psychological development proceeds. This progression in object relations optimally moves from the initial objectless autistic state to the early symbiotic position of communion with the maternal figure, and then to one in which the child gradually begins to separate—"to hatch" in Mahler's words—from the object through processes of differentiation and individuation which lead ultimately to the capacity to achieve object and self representation, stable identifications, and to a psychic organization that is capable of functioning on the level of the secondary process and according to the reality principle. In the schizophrenic child, however, we see instead a prolonged and pathological version of the normal symbiotic-individuation struggle of the infant. The pathogenic symbiosis, while maintaining the delusional omnipotence derived from the fusion of mother and self, is also experienced as an engulfment and annihilation of the beginning self representation within the normally protective symbiotic sac.[2] In an earlier publication (Ekstein and Friedman, 1968), we said: "We can

2 Comparable to what Mahler has referred to as the symbiotic membrane.

thus visualize the psychotic state as one in which self and object representations are enclosed within the symbiotic sac, separated by a porous osmotic membrane. It is undergoing, without yet having achieved, separation, nor stable cathexis and differentiation of self and object. In this stage only primitive ego functioning exists. It is dominated by primary process and unstable impulse control, in which the thought disorder is characterized by the equations: thought $=$ action; inner reality $=$ outer reality; self $=$ object" (p. 109).

However, the moves toward separation lead regressively toward the autistic position and thus inevitably to the loss of self in an empty, objectless world which may become seemingly static and immovable or may be a fleeting and fluctuating phase. The schizophrenic adaptation consists of the attempt to restore the symbiosis through fusion experience, as well as the attempt to achieve some kind of separation through an autisticlike avoidance of the object.

CASE ILLUSTRATIONS

The following clinical material will demonstrate the specific ways these core conflicts of the schizophrenic child find different forms of expression at different stages of psychic maturation and development. We might even think in terms of a normal developmental line (A. Freud, 1965) of language from silence and communion to speech and symbolic communication. This would include such stages as babbling, echoing or echolalia, delayed echolalia, self-echoing, expressing, appealing, and finally symbolic communication. Specific developmental disturbances for each stage can be described, several of which are depicted below. The clinical data will also highlight the relationship between the development of early object relations and the beginning development of language.

Case 1

We start with a "classically" autistic, nonspeaking three-year-old, Nanny, the kind of child that Kanner, Bender, Mahler, and others would describe as autistic. Clinically, these children are extremely withdrawn; their relationships have a mechanical quality in that they use the other person like a deanimated tool. Language, when available, is not used in the service of communication but rather in a beginning attempt to contact the external world, still barely perceived as separate from themselves. We refer here to the imitative and mechanical, stereotypic, repetitive speech known as echolalia. These children do not seek symbolic communication through their language, but rather attempt to establish a symbiotic fusion relationship with the maternal figure. The imitative behavior of echolalia and echopraxia can be understood as an attempt to introject the object, but it occurs at such a primitive level of imitation that the child experiences no psychic differentiation from the object; he cannot swallow you because there is no stable, separate "you"; yet he experiences the process as himself becoming "you." Thus the inevitably unsuccessful attempt at incorporation leads instead to fusion or loss of self. Nevertheless it must be understood as the forerunner of identificatory processes in an as yet primitive, undifferentiated psychic structure.

We have previously described the difficulties of treating such children who must constantly destroy the very contact they seek, and whose efforts at establishing this contact lead to this loss of self in the fusion experience (Ekstein, 1966). They seem to have available only the "choice" between becoming the senseless, selfless, albeit delusionally omnipotent echo of the therapist, or else of rejecting the therapist who has become a terrifying engulfing threat. We then see a retreat to the precarious precursor of identity which the autistic position seemingly offers to such a child, whose pathogenic experiences within the maternal symbiosis have not allowed for the development of sufficient ego structure to move toward true separation.

In Nanny's treatment we could observe changes in her symptom of echolalia from an initial form of imitating without understanding to more advanced forms of delayed echoing that became precursors of descriptive language functions in that she would also verbalize her own activities in the third person. Her first echoing was comparable to the imitation games and imitative sounds of very small, preverbal children. At the beginning of treatment, the little girl seemed to be dominated by the peremptoriness and choicelessness of impulse as she wandered everywhere throughout the clinic, guided not by any intention or understandable and meaningful search, but driven by utter chaos, or so it would appear to the casual observer. As she wandered about, the therapist[3] would follow her, observing that chaos and seeking to discern the hidden order or meaning behind it. At the same time the therapist described Nanny's actions in very simple phrases. The therapist's "verbal echopraxia," so to speak, of the child's motor activity—a choiceful regression in therapeutic technique from more advanced technical interventions to a repetitive description of the child's actions—was responded to by the child with echolalia, her beginning way of taking the psychotherapist in, comparable to the peekaboo game between mother and child. The therapist would say, "Here Nanny goes, here Nanny stops." After a while it was observed that Nanny had developed rudiments of speech in the nature of echolalia, a mechanical and repetitive speech which seemed to echo some of the therapist's words.

Nanny, after acquiring echolalic speech, remained for a long time on this imitative level, without truly understanding the meaning of the words. After many months of effort, the child's mother reported that the echolalic speech had developed into *delayed echolalia*. She would comment, for example, "Here Nanny go," which could be understood as the delayed echo of the therapist, who, as we have seen, had chosen to establish contact with the child by describing her actions to her, much as a mother interprets the expressions of the infant in such a way as to echo the inner need they express. The therapist's remarks could also be understood as an immediate echo of the child's own action which was in the nature of a trial thought, albeit a very primitive one, expressing a beginning awareness and recognition of the self experienced through the action.

Shortly thereafter, while the mother was driving with the child, she heard Nanny say: "No, no, you mustn't do it" and "That's the way," imitating the therapist's words. The mother knew that neither she nor anybody else in the family had used these phrases, and that even the intonation was a parrotlike imitation of the therapist. From this report we surmised that the therapist had made contact with the child, who could now maintain an image of her even when the therapist was out of sight. We suggest that the therapist's phrases—

[3] Mrs. Leda Rosow, M.A., has contributed this case illustration.

one phrase of delaying and one phrase of approving—could be considered external organizers by means of which the child had developed a steering device, a kind of primitive red and green signal for restriction and for permission. A germinal delaying apparatus had been created which could serve as a beginning kind of internal control of impulse expression. In some mechanical fashion the therapist had been taken in, even though for a long time this attempt to introject the therapist would continue to deteriorate into a primitive fusing with the therapist's voice and speech instead of leading to more appropriate identificatory processes. We understood this as an attempt to restore the lost introject (in the absence of the object) by means of maintaining it as a quasi-auditory hallucination expressed verbally in the delayed echolalia. The child had turned echolalia into delayed echolalia, which can be understood as the expression of a memory in a mental organization which still lacked the capacity for symbolic and cognitive representation.

Later in the treatment, as the child and therapist were walking out of the building one day, they discovered that it was raining. The therapist said: "Nanny, it is raining." The child's response was, "It is wet." We understood that she had acquired the beginning of symbolic representative speech through a temporary identification with the therapist's symbolic functioning. In this one short sequence she paralleled the development of Helen Keller when at eight years she understood the meaning of the verbal symbol "water" through the persistent efforts of Anne Sullivan Macy and had thus acquired symbolic speech, that "unique hallmark of man" (Kubie, 1953). Both children had thus indicated their capacity to establish the continuity between the concrete experience and the abstract generalization.

In discussing the child's moves during a long span of intensive therapeutic work, we saw the following three steps: echolalia, delayed echolalia, and finally simple descriptive symbolic speech, accompanying her struggle for, against, and with objects, out of which evolved the capacity to master primitive speech functions. Once the therapist had become a sufficiently stable part of the child's inner world, there emerged a beginning "voice of the conscience," and the beginning of higher mental processes which could lead toward identification and superego development. The therapist, by her choice of initially echoing the child in an attempt to empathize with the child's autistic, deanimated world, had gradually gained entrance into that world as a kind of living tape recorder of the child's unspoken, unverbalized, and, as a matter of fact, preverbal needs and experiences. The therapist could then become a creative echo and ultimately translate these needs into a higher form of communication, after she and the child had first restored a communionlike relationship in which the child's need for reunion with the maternal image was restored via the transference.

We would now like to discuss that struggle toward understanding and genuine *Verständigung* against the background of Karl Bühler's (1934) Organon model of language. He distinguishes three functions of language: expression, appeal, and representation. This model is utilized in order to give a graphic illustration of the genesis of speech and learning of language. In the beginning, Nanny's imitation, her echolalic gesture, cannot be understood in terms of object relationship. Nanny does not consider the therapist a person. The child at this point is frozen in an autistic mode. Nanny imitates but cannot animate the therapist and she does not attach meaning to the imitative speech. She talks to herself via the speech element she had received from the nurturing person whom she has now joined within the symbiotic sac. If she could interpret her behavior, she might be saying: "As I become conscious for the first time of the fact that I am walking up and down, I become conscious of it through a kind of auxiliary ego, the eyes of the undifferentiated mother object. I-we have learned to imitate, and I-we start to observe myself. I start to become aware of motor activity as a part of me. I can do no more than echo language without really understanding it, but in doing so I get approval from the person who loves me and therefore I can acquire the beginning of language function."

In the establishment of communion between therapist and child, an attempt to use sound as a bridge between the nurturing person and the child is the first step in bringing about primitive understanding which leads to imitative speech. This kind of *Verständigung* is really reunion, a restoration of that early unity of feelings, and thus has appeal function. One could say that the child's first imitative speech is meant to restore unity with the mother, a unity maintained and limited by and within the symbiotic sac.

When echolalia develops into delayed echolalia, a kind of hallu-

cinatory equivalent expressed in sound, it becomes evident that delayed echolalia serves as a beginning attempt to negotiate between
impulse and delay. Nanny used delayed echolalia as a steering device
to approve and disapprove of impulse expression. To that degree,
she had internalized the therapist and was building up an intro-
jected steering device, a crude ego function to make her independent
of the therapist. Nanny restored the therapist by talking to herself
when the therapist was absent, through describing her own behavior
in similar approving and disapproving terms, but without really
being able to regulate the behavior. Impulse was not yet modified
by this primitive control device of description. Where impulse rules,
there is no need for communication with the object via verbal language. Once she had started to experience the person, primitive
precursors of object relations developed and she could begin to
acquire the first elements of language. But such language was still
only a signal. It was as if Nanny were saying to us: "I notice what
I am doing and I remember whenever you approve or disapprove
of it. It is almost as if you were there. But your disapproval or
approval is as yet an ineffective signal. The language that I use does
not truly guide me. It is a quasi-steering device after rather than
before the fact. I still cannot remember our past experiences together to guide me before the act, but through the act and through
the accompanying delayed echolalia I can restore them and begin to
reconstitute or, more aptly, constitute the beginnings of a separate
psychic organization. For me, language does not serve thought as
trial action but only as *post facto* description."

Case 2

We now turn to an episode from the beginning phase in the
treatment of five-year-old Danny, a somewhat more advanced schizophrenic child with both autistic and symbiotic features. Whereas
Nanny had initially been almost totally withdrawn into an objectless, contactless world so that the therapist had had to spend many
months seeking to find some means by which to intrude herself even
into the child's awareness, Danny demonstrated more responsiveness
to the therapist as an object, albeit primarily as a deanimated thing
that he used as a tool both to satisfy his needs and to serve as a toy
around which to weave his fantasies. Danny had shown signs of deep

disturbance as early as age two, convincing his mother that he was mentally retarded. By the age of three the difficulties in feeding and sleeping and other signs of disturbance such as head banging, rocking, resistance to being held, and slowness in the development of language resulting in an inability to communicate emotionally with others, had led the parents to seek help. Supportive treatment on a weekly basis had led to some improvement in his language development and communication ability, reflecting a growing appreciation of his own identity previously experienced more as a thing than as a human being. Two years later, he appeared to be a seriously disturbed child, who, at the time of evaluation, demonstrated continuous activity of a primarily repetitive and apparently purposeless nature. He gave the impression of having difficulty in differentiating between himself and the external world; he appeared to have shut out most of the human object world, using it primarily as an inanimate tool in relationship to his own needs. His spoken language, usually of an echolalic quality, was scarcely intelligible, but he reacted appropriately to those commands which were satisfying to him. The initial diagnosis was infantile autism, although elements of minimal interhuman relationships were noted; e.g., he could indicate verbally certain basic needs such as "I want candy," his wish to remain in the office, or his desire for his mother to come.

Danny thus was psychologically more advanced than Nanny, who initially had been incapable of symbolic communication of her wishes and concerns. After some months of treatment Danny began to engage the therapist in a kind of continuous mutual echoing, as he indicated clearly his wish for the therapist to echo his "Hello dolly," just as he clearly was himself echoing, like a prerecorded tape of a tape, an earlier experience. When after many weeks he replaced "Hello dolly" with "Hello grandma," it became clear that he was re-creating with the therapist the memory of an earlier experience with a primary figure. He now revived this in the treatment[4] by assigning to the therapist the role of the delayed echo of the earlier object; and just as the earlier experience had not truly been a dialogue between himself and the object but had been experienced in a mechanical, deanimated fashion, so did he mechanically repeat

4 Morton Bramson, M.D., contributed this case illustration.

the memory through the mutual delayed echolalia shared with the therapist. The therapist was allowed to enter into the fantasy not as a separate object but as a re-edition of the earlier maternal figure with whom there apparently had existed only a meaningless, contactless kind of interaction.

Normally, the infant's speech development proceeds via "echoing," that is, imitating the mother, within the context of an emotionally meaningful mother-child relationship in which the child echoes the mother, who in turn, through her loving "baby talk," echoes the baby in the early, satisfying preverbal communion relationship which slowly allows for the development of meaning.

In therapy, Danny was reliving such early experiences, but in his case they lacked the positive affective contact necessary for the development of true communication. He ascribed to the therapist the role of his echo, in the attempt to restore the memory of the earlier experience in which there apparently had begun to evolve some awareness of the object as somewhat differentiated from him although still partially fused within the symbiotic sac, i.e., "separated by a porous osmotic membrane . . . undergoing, without yet having achieved, separation, nor stable cathexis and differentiation of self and object" (Ekstein and Friedman, 1968). In Danny's assigning to the therapist the task of echoing him, as he himself echoed a seemingly meaningless phrase from a record, we see a re-enactment of the past: in response to Danny's delayed echo the therapist must become echolalic, just as originally the child himself echoed a mother who herself could not furnish any spontaneous communication with him but could only repeat—i.e., echo—words to him that did not truly convey any inner emotional meaning. Thus this play was an echo of what should have been a dialogue but which was in fact a monologue that the child had internalized and now was projecting. It was as if there were two introjects, or extrojects, talking together; although to the extent that Danny was not satisfied with the inner monologue and sought the external object around which to weave the fantasy role of one of the introjects, we realize that he was approaching the stage where he might become capable of a true dialogue.

In the nonpathogenic therapeutic relationship, a different resolution becomes possible so that instead of merely going through the motions of a relationship, similar to actions on a stage, there can eventually develop true contact and communication. In the early stages of treatment, however, the child's precarious precursors of ego functioning still needed omnipotently to control and maintain sameness with his surroundings, and the only safe "dialogue" was the prewritten monologue whose story is woven around the therapist, who must act it out with the child as if it were their shared memory.

Danny initially made contact on the level of the desired communion, the preverbal language of the symbiotic phase in which there is still "connection"—to use the language of an eight-year-old borderline schizophrenic child, Johnny—rather than symbolic communication. We might think of the child's development with respect to the capacity for object relations as a process moving from autism to complete fusion, to increasingly greater degrees of differentiation and individuation within the symbiotic sac, until finally, emerging from the symbiosis, there remains only the "connection"—the post-neonatal but still unsevered umbilical cord, so to speak, prior to the final severing and separating. As a consequence we understand that thought and language development proceeds in a parallel fashion.

Case 3

The above-mentioned borderline schizophrenic child, Johnny, had an extremely labile, fluctuating psychic organization. Occasionally he was capable of higher levels of object-related communication. At other times he was dominated by regressive conflicts over differentiation and separation which, in the transference, were reflected in fluctuating fusion experiences and deep regressive shifts to primary process thinking and language. At such moments Johnny ordered the therapist to "copy"—i.e., echo—him. Johnny's more advanced psychic organization enabled him to observe these massive but still partial regressions and to experience the threat of object loss, which he attempted to forestall by "regressing" the therapist with him as she echoed his psychotic thoughts and language. In this way he apparently could experience fusion with her. For example, he would start to bandage his own finger and end by bandaging hers, without concern for or awareness of where he ended and she began (Caruth, 1968). His request that she echo him also reflected an attempt to exert some modicum of ego autonomy over the passively experienced regression "in his private thoughts" and language, a regression which he actively tried to impose upon the therapist (Ekstein and Caruth, 1968). This child was able to communicate his feelings of being "disconnected" as he graphically portrayed on the "connection board" (his word for blackboard) or in his repetitive attempts to connect up various train-track layouts, which he rarely completed in time to run the train, just as it was initially difficult for him to maintain and complete a connected secondary process train of thoughts. On the "connection board" he projected his changing self and object representations or, more aptly, images, as they fluctuated from connected to disconnected, from teeny mouth to devouring monster, from Jonah to the whale. When these archaic fantasies took over, he sought to fuse with the therapist, who, by copying or echoing him, became a projected reverberation—an echo of this threatening inner world into which she had intruded. Moreover, since she now was one with him, she was less likely to fly away and disappear—one of Johnny's prevailing fearful fantasies. However, like any echo, she was at the same time "always so far away," because in becoming an echo she no longer was really there as a separate object. Johnny, however, was able to recognize his desire for the therapist to echo him, and his observing ego—in his words, his rudder world that steered him through life—frequently permitted the therapist to become more than an echoing primitive introject fused with his primary process world. He could gradually let her become an advanced creative echo, an interpreter capable of adding new dimensions to the communication.

Early in the treatment, Johnny brought to the hour his record player—a kind of free-associating machine, as it were, which permitted total fusion between inner fantasy and external reality. The record player represented an extension of the child's delusional omnipotent control over his environment, which he sought to create in his own image, as well as the omniscient and omnipotentially controlling environment, which told him what to think. He also brought the record "Mary Poppins," his choice of an animated but not truly animate extroject onto which he projected his fears that both he and the object might disappear. He presumably brought the record so the therapist could "tell me the words," a request that grew out of a previous session; he had indicated that his singing of a song was an echoing of sounds rather than meaningful words, as indeed was true of the songs themselves, which ranged from the primary process language of "Supercalifragilisticexpialidocious" to the rational secondary process cautionary tale of the "spoonful of sugar that helps the medicine go down," which is to say, helps the demands of external reality become internalized. However, behind his request for the therapist to tell him the words lay, of course, the need to tell her what words to tell him. She was permitted to speak only if she spoke what he had programmed for her; but to the degree that he acknowledged a need to have her explain his language to him, he was opening up the possibility that, as they reconnected, she could begin to disconnect.

Several years later, however, more firmly differentiated and secure in his own identity, he was able to suggest that "we are going to start a new life in outer space, and bring a telescope, camera, and telephone to call Mommy." With this, Johnny diagnosed and prescribed his own conditions of health, which were quite appropriate for a nine-year-old: to be far enough away to create a new life and still close enough to contact Mommy. This may well be the optimal improvement to be expected in the treatment of certain schizophrenic conditions.

Case 4

We now turn to a somewhat different clinical illustration. Don, an eighteen-year-old schizophrenic adolescent, possessed speech and sometimes used a convincing obsessive façade of secondary process thought. During the last few years of treatment he emerged from his former social isolation, in which he had been unable to make use of school or community facilities, and had remained alone in a darkened room communicating with his delusional objects. He improved sufficiently to finish high school and to maintain a number of college courses, drive a car, and attempt social contact with people.[5] The main delusional object of his inner dialogues and "pluralogues" was a Mr. Punishment (Ekstein, 1966), who changed his color like a chameleon as he gravitated back and forth between primary and secondary processes.

[5] This case was treated by one of the authors with the assistance of concomitant casework carried out by Mrs. Beatrice Cooper, M.A., who focused on reality issues.

Don, who is still in treatment, has recently been engaged in building an obsessive-compulsive cognitive structure by means of which he can learn to differentiate between his internal and external world, so that he can begin to bring about a compromise between his impulses and the demands of reality. He tried to build a system to help him cope with his awareness of the need for appropriate delay mechanisms. He literally worked on his treatment day and night, and during a time away from treatment he composed a document entitled *Constitution of the Inner World,* which contains ten amendments as well as a ten-day truce pact. These documents, essentially an intrapsychic Bill of Rights, describe how a schizophrenic deals with his impulses, in this case the seemingly insatiable compulsion to masturbate:

> It has been decided that Don shall stop doing the habit for a period of ten days. This will be an experiment to determine whether or not the habit is the cause of the anxiety and nervousness. I hereby agree to such terms.

This document was signed by Don, later to be witnessed and endorsed by his therapist, to whom he brought this as well as the second document, *The Constitution of the Inner World,* with the subtitle, "Don, President and Ruler—Amendments." We see here this schizophrenic adolescent's philosophy of life: he is the ruler of his own world, who dispenses with the usual power apparatus needed to achieve power leverage in the real world. By emptying it of outside influence, he can maintain the integrity of his megalomanic inner world which is dominated by the pleasure principle. Yet he presented his ideas by using the language of the outer world. One is reminded of Leary's slogan for the hippies: "Tune in, turn on, and drop out." However, to maintain his megalomanic delusional *Weltanschauung,* Don needed to make rules which reflected his way of thinking, delaying, and dealing with conflicting impulses. As we read his rules, we find that they are inner replicas of outside conditions, even though, like dreams, they go beyond what is possible in the waking world; nevertheless the basic material is derived from the real world, from day residuals. Don's inner world was actually a shadowy replica of the outside world, just as Don's *Constitution* represented a distorted version of the conditions of psychotherapy, revealing how he internalized the words of the therapist. While he may say whatever he wants in the therapeutic hour in the "green-light" room, he also knows he must still keep to some limits and cannot act out what he thinks. He thus worded his statement as follows:

1. All private thoughts and actions shall be kept between Dr. E. and members of the inner world only.
2. Each force, punishing or rewarding, is permitted to demonstrate the reason for believing what is best. All forces have equal rights in expression.
3. No severe punishments are permitted at any time. Spanking hard for real is hereby forbidden except in light demonstrations. All actions are for use only in fantasy and private unless they are important in helping a person gain a victory or a rewarding life.
4. All heroes shall be elected by the majority vote of the inner world. No person or reality can be used for any purpose in the inner world except honorary heroes such as the Beatles, or if their names are changed to names used in fiction or television.

We want to call special attention to the "4th amendment," inasmuch as it makes clear the precarious balance of the boy's capacity for object constancy, the nature of his object relations, and the parallel nature of his level of communication in which he still tries to maintain the denial of the existence of the separate object. Don developed this *Constitution of the Inner World* when he was alone at night, working through what had transpired during the treatment process. He reviewed the implicit demands and conditions of treatment and started to "meet" people, but only on condition that they be fantasy people. He developed an inner dialogue with their differing points of view—fantasy figures who played roles he had assigned to them—in a fashion similar to that of the younger child who assigned the singing role to his therapist. He gathered these people around him and "chaired" the meeting. By giving each introject the right of discussion, he hoped to delay the impulse to masturbate, and he did so for several hours. He started his meeting at 9 o'clock in the evening and delayed until midnight, when he succumbed happily and masturbated, having worked out in these meetings of the inner mind an unassailable alibi of a group decision, as it were. The truce was broken, but the discharge of the impulse had been delayed for three hours. One might also say that the masturbatory act had been preceded by the foreplay of the dialogue of the introjects, who "protested too much."

In this essay we are not concerned with the issue of masturbation, the expression of instinctual desires, or Don's use of his penis as a reassuring transitional self-object, but we are concerned with the method Don used to resolve an internal conflict and its relationship to the nature of schizophrenic language and communication. We may ask why the internal conflict during these evening hours was not resolved by permitting Dr. Ekstein, or the parents, or any other "real" people from the outside world to be at the meeting even in fantasy. Why are these figures that Don gathered around not really internalized representations of objects of the external world, but are rather internal representations of earlier unstable introjects, now represented as free-floating, dreamlike personages in his inner fantasy world? We only know that it was easier for Don to reach what appeared to be a compromise with the requirements of the external world. In fact, he circumvented them by creating a "ghost parliament," in which no one from the real world could really communicate by challenging the inevitable breaking of the truce, which was after all but a token identification with the perceived demands of therapy.

We thus see how he dealt with his "pursuit of reality" (Meyer and Ekstein, 1967) and how he stopped short of reaching that very reality, in his inability to let the external object become other than a replica of his internal representations. Reality testing was not yet an inner condition for him, beyond this token gesture, and his system of communication reflected this situation: the use of secondary process language was a token gesture and a token identification—a "ghost language" spoken by a plurality of one. This limited capacity for reality testing merely maintained the precarious balance with the outside world, which was experienced as but a shadowy reality of his inner ideas. Of dreams it is said that the latent dream thought can pass the censorship only if it ventures forth in the disguise of the manifest content. In Don's life the real person can pass by the censorship only if he reappears in the patient's dream world in disguise, in a temporary merger with the delusional object.

Don's future progress depends upon whether he can enter into a true dialogue with the therapist—the real person—and his fantasy characters, which would enable him to acknowledge the existence of a separate person and to accept the conditions for a real exchange with outer reality. We have seen that Don's inner world has to some extent come to resemble the outside world, but it is still only a delayed echo, merely imitative and sterile, and without the spirit of genuine identification. His acceptance of the interpretations is more a caricature of the psychoanalytic process, not too different from the imitating devices that Nanny utilized in internalizing the mother figure whom she then used as an internal steering device.

DISCUSSION

While it is true that these children differ in important respects, we wish to point out certain similarities. Bühler's Organon model can be used as a basic blueprint, except that we have to account for the fact that the language structures of such patients cannot be characterized as stable structures, as was originally maintained during nineteenth-century faculty psychology. Instead of rigid systems, we find that dynamic notions of process give us better insight into the language, communication, and thinking problems of these patients.

Before the acceptance of the object and the emergence of the concept of self, we have an example of the original struggle between impulse and delay carried out on a primitive level. "Here Nanny goes," is in the service of the impulse, while "Here Nanny stays" seems to be characteristic of beginning delay functions. Nanny made these precursors of self-observations away from the therapist and as a delayed echo of the therapist's echoing behavior; hence they represented a somewhat more advanced level of communication than the immediate echolalic repeating of whatever is heard. They reflect the beginning of some experience of self as differentiated from the environment, as if the child had now left the empty, autistic, objectless world through the total fusion with the therapist, which enabled her to begin to discriminate between the animate and the inanimate. At the same time the child not only observed concretely the impulse and the delay—i.e., "Here Nanny goes . . . stops"—but also, via the auxiliary ego of the therapist, began to experiment with the somewhat more abstract notion, "Nanny shouldn't do that," as if in preparation for the future when she would be able to attach that notion which implies some modicum of autonomy and control to her impulsive behavior.

With Danny, the more advanced autistic-symbiotic child, we saw how the more stable symbiotic attachment to the object enabled him to use the therapist as an extension of himself, as an extroject to act out the inner situation, which was but an empty delayed echo of an earlier emotionally meaningless, hence echolalic system of communion with the mother. With Johnny, a borderline schizophrenic child whose fluctuating ego functioning at times led to regression to autistic levels of object relations even though the remaining psychic structures continued to function on a more advanced level, delayed echolalia occurred in the form of self-echoing, as his more critical ego functions observed the intrusion of primary process fantasies over which he exerted some autonomy by "echoing" them, much as the neurotic patient feels his problems are under his control if he labels or names them. In addition, Johnny assigned the role of echo to the therapist as an aid in his struggle against the autistic withdrawal into primary process fantasies away from external reality, and to strengthen his active mastery over the passively experienced regression and eruption of impulses.

We can now see the relationship between echolalia, delayed echolalia, and the "4th amendment" in Don's "ghost parliament." Nanny, for example, observed in sound her impulsive acts and their delay via the echolalic means described above. Don put down in writing the observation, "Here Don goes masturbating" and the delayed pseudoechoing of the outside world's implicit demand for delay. He put down "rules" for his inner world which were a token acknowledgment of the outside world—advanced echoes, so to speak, that fused the impulse with the delay mechanism. Don's essential communication, though seemingly couched in symbolic language, was actually determined by primary process thinking. He excluded reality objects except as an echo of the inner introjects, which had achieved a frozen and immutable psychotic object constancy.

Schizophrenic communications of the more psychologically advanced child contain within them the equivalent motivation of more primitive echolalic speech, expressing both the search for and the autistic defense against the fusion experience. Even though language is acquired for seemingly interpersonal interchange, it fails to become a permanent acquisition brought about by lasting internalizations. The illness makes it impossible to bring about these enduring internalizations which depend on stable object relations. Without these, secondary process language does not develop. Words are then experienced as a kind of "sell-out device," as a fourteen-year-old schizophrenic girl said who complained that the words she used failed to express what she meant on the three different levels of her brain.

The systems of communication which these children use and by which they establish a life line—the "connecting" security line —have ingredients of our thinking, but they are to a large extent attached to the appeal and holding-on aspects of language. Their language is oriented primarily toward conveying an appeal—to join with them in their regression—and not to conveying a thought. It is under the sway of the regressive tendency to restore the early mother-child unity which can dispense with symbolic communication. It is the therapist's ultimate function to translate preverbal experiences into language. Eventually he must interpret, even though the patient initially may want to destroy the representational meaning.

We finally come to what we can do to strengthen that function of language which is task-oriented, solution-oriented, and resolution-oriented; which permits learning and mastery of reality to take place, so that instead of a chasm there will be a viable bridge between self and external reality. That bridge is, of course, the advanced capacity for communication. The language of the schizophrenic is burdened by the primary functions of appeal and of holding on, and is dominated by the need to revert to communion, whereas the acceptance of the need for communication implies the existence of separation between self and object. The schizophrenic struggles with us against the acceptance of our language. Such a child seems to say: "I talk in my language; my language is *the* mother tongue, the child-mother tongue. I have changed the rules of grammar completely and have distorted them in such a way that they restore the early relationship between mother and me, where the object was not an object, where the self was not a self but where self and object are fused in a symbiotic arrangement which is main-

tained in my thought disorder which dispenses with reality testing."
As a matter of fact, words fuse with their referent and become
object-symbols, no longer cathected as object representations (Wexler, 1960).

Thus the schizophrenic, if we may state it in the language of the
philosophy of science, is opposed to the position of radical empiri-
cism, which insists that there is meaning only where there is opportunity for operational verification. We suggest that there are two
extremes of communication: that of the radical empirical, a position
reiterated by Sidney Hook (1959), who insists on operational verification and would force out of language all those aspects that describe
the inner psychological world of people, sick and well; and that
of the schizophrenic child who is in the diametrically opposite position so that in his system of communication there is no place for
reality testing and verification.

The linguistic philosopher, Waismann (1965), speaks about the
chasm which exists between "soul and soul." Could he have meant
the distance between self and object representation? How can this
chasm be bridged without a stable separation, which is the problem
we face in communicating with the schizophrenic child who has not
yet cathected outer reality. We develop a compromise language,
a kind of Esperanto of the mind, which does not quite rule out
reality testing but neither insists on it nor prohibits it. In this
compromise language we do not probe too deeply and we do not
force the patient back to reality testing, because this would prevent
contact. On the other hand, he could not reach us if he were unable
to talk our language just a little bit. But this neutral language—
this Esperanto for the separated minds, this bridge between the two
kinds of language—is made possible through metaphor. Metaphor
becomes a link between the language of inner and outer reality,
and brings about primitive understanding, tolerable contact under
optimum conditions (Ekstein and Wallerstein, 1966; Caruth and
Ekstein, 1966).

At times our patients are people who echo us but who do not
think like we do. They establish their precarious identity not via
cogito ergo sum, but, as Edelheit (1969) phrases it, in terms of
resono ergo sum: I echo, therefore I am; but parenthetically we
might add: "But am I, or am I you, since I echo?" Sometimes the

therapist must play crazy in order to echo the schizophrenic's language, and in the countertransference he, too, may at times ask this question (Caruth and Ekstein, 1964), as in his quest for understanding via the suspension of disbelief he temporarily gives up outer reality testing for inner reality communicating. Despite the fact that the patient's system of thinking follows a different order from ours, we can talk with him because we find certain coincidental points between his way of thinking and our way of thinking which permit a kind of vague and primitive understanding. Carnap (1928) spoke about the possibility of two people understanding each other, in spite of the fact that the inner experiences which are at the basis of their thoughts can never be compared, in terms of the availability of coincidental points. He likened such different inner sensual experiences to one in which two persons, each viewing a different map of the world, would visualize the earth differently. One might see it in the global form pictured on his map, while the other might envision the earth in terms of the flat map he was viewing. Nevertheless, they could understand each other to some extent since they would find certain points of coincidence on each map, and thus could establish relationships of similarity—complementary *Gestalten,* an important aspect of all interpretation (Ekstein, 1966).

We would like to sum up our comments on the psychotic child's struggle with language by citing Waismann (1965), a linguistic philosopher identified with the Vienna Circle, known to us through the names of Carnap, Schlick, Wittgenstein, and others. He says:

What, then, are we to say in reply to the question how far language serves the purposes of communication—as a bridge built by the mind to lead from consciousness to consciousness? Is it really established that every thought which is expressed in this language is intelligible to everyone else who uses it? In the face of the examples just given, such a view can hardly be advocated. Is everyone, then, in possession of a private language comprehensible to him alone? Not that either. It would be truer to say that our language is suited equally to the purposes of communication. On the whole we manage to make ourselves understood passably. But there are cases, for instance, in conveying certain rare moods and states of minds, where it is doubtful how far language really bridges the chasm between soul and soul.

It is perhaps convenient to think of the vast domain of language as a photograph taken with a long-focus lens. A certain area of such a photograph would be sharp, corresponding to the area of language in which words are adequately fitted for purposes of communication. Such is the language of physics. But beyond this as beyond the sharply focused area of the picture, clearness, definiteness gradually decrease, till the edges of the picture, like the uttermost attainments of language, are blurred into indeterminacy [p. 268].

BIBLIOGRAPHY

Bühler, K. (1934), *Sprachtheorie*. Jena: Fischer.
Carnap, R. (1928), *The Logical Structure of the World and Pseudo-Problems in Philosophy*. London: Routledge & Kegan Paul, 1967.
Caruth, E. (1968), The Onion and the Moebius Strip: Rational and Irrational Models for the Secondary and Primary Process. *Psa. Rev.*, 55:415-425.
—— & Ekstein, R. (1964), Certain Phenomenological Aspects of the Countertransference in the Treatment of Schizophrenic Children. *Reiss-Davis Clin. Bull.*, 1:80-88.
—— —— (1966), Interpretation within the Metaphor: Further Considerations. *J. Amer. Acad. Child Psychiat.*, 5:35-45.
Chadwick, M. (1928), Die Unterscheidung zwischen Ton und Sprache in der frühen Kindheit. *Z. psa. Päd.*, 2:369-383.
Edelheit, H. (1969), Speech and Psychic Structure: the Vocal-Auditory Organization of the Ego. *J. Amer. Psa. Assn.*, 17:381-412.
Ekstein, R. (1965), Historical Notes Concerning Psychoanalysis and Early Language Development. *J. Amer. Psa. Assn.*, 13:707-731.
—— (1966), *Children of Time and Space, of Action and Impulse*. New York: Appleton-Century-Crofts.
—— & Caruth, E. (1968), The Relation of Ego Autonomy to Activity and Passivity in the Psychotherapy of Childhood Schizophrenia. *Reiss-Davis Clin. Bull.*, 5:89-95.
—— & Friedman, S. (1968), Prolegomenon to a Psychoanalytic Technique in the Treatment of Childhood Schizophrenia. *Reiss-Davis Clin. Bull.*, 5:107-115.
—— & Wallerstein, J. (1966), Choice of Interpretation in the Treatment of Borderline and Psychotic Children. In: Ekstein (1966), pp. 148-157.
Freud, A. (1965), *Normality and Pathology in Childhood: Assessments of Development*. New York: International Universities Press.
Freud, S. (1895), Project for a Scientific Psychology. In: *The Origins of Psychoanalysis*. New York: Basic Books, 1954, pp. 347-445.
Hook, S., ed. (1959), *Psychoanalysis: Scientific Method and Philosophy*. New York: New York University Press.
Kubie, L. S. (1953), The Distortion of the Symbolic Process in Neurosis and Psychosis. *J. Amer. Psa. Assn.*, 1:59-86.
Mahler, M. S. (1968), *On Human Symbiosis and the Vicissitudes of Individuation*. New York: International Universities Press.
Meyer, M. & Ekstein, R. (1967), The Psychotic Pursuit of Reality. Abstr. in: *Amer. J. Orthopsychiat.*, 37:399-400.
Waismann, F. (1965), *The Principles of Linguistic Philosophy*. London, Melbourne, Toronto: Macmillan. New York: St. Martin's Press.
Wexler, M. (1960), Hypotheses Concerning Ego Deficiency in Schizophrenia. In: *The Outpatient Treatment of Schizophrenia*, ed. S. Scher & H. Davis. New York: Grune & Stratton, pp. 33-43.

FILM REVIEW

John, Seventeen Months: Nine Days in a Residential Nursery by James and Joyce Robertson

ANNA FREUD, LL.D., D.Sc. (London)

We owe James and Joyce Robertson a considerable debt for confronting us with happenings in the lives of young children which otherwise are brought to our notice only once removed through the verbal accounts of adult witnesses, or removed in time through their later revival and reconstruction in analytic therapy. The demonstrations *ad oculos* offered by the Robertsons' films are, to my mind, "direct observation at its best."

These films have gained wide acclaim and have engaged their viewers' interest in a whole range of topics. There was *Laura,* aged two, doing her inadequate best to cope with the double experience of separation and hospitalization; *Sally,* aged twenty-one months, meeting bodily discomfort, medical interventions, and the strangeness of hospital life, supported by her mother's presence; *Tom,* the thalidomide victim, growing up painfully but courageously as the only cripple in the tumultuous world of normal nursery children; there were *Kate,* two years and five months, and *Jane,* seventeen months, in brief separation from their own homes, their distress handled and alleviated by an exceptional type of foster care.

What was brought home to us in each instance was the impact of the external circumstances on the children's inner experience, as evidenced by their facial expressions, their motor responses, their outbursts of emotion, and, quite especially, the relationship between their general behavior and the length of duration of the stressful situation.

However, whatever lessons have been learned from these earlier productions, they have been far surpassed by the latest documentary, devoted to *John,* seventeen months, and his nine days' stay in a residential nursery. The "nine days" are emphasized with justification. We can never be reminded sufficiently that such a period of time, short by adult standards, may be long enough for a child under two to shatter his existing personality, to disrupt the ongoing course of development, and to do long-lasting harm to his normality.

Judged by the prevailing standards of knowledge of a young toddler's needs, no blame attaches to the parents for placing John as they did during the mother's unavoidable absence in the hospital for the confinement with her second child. Whether fathers can stand in for the mother in taking care of a seventeen-months-old for twenty-four hours a day is a question still under exploration. However that may be, John's father was prevented altogether from attempting this due to exacting professional demands. In the absence of supporting relatives, the parents took the family doctor's recommendation to place John in this institution with small groupings, sufficient staff, and an overall efficient, friendly, and nonpunitive atmosphere. They could feel certain that John would receive very adequate body care and that he would be kept safe during the brief interval until his mother could receive him back.

Nevertheless, in the prevailing standards of knowledge it tends to be overlooked that even toddlers, and quite especially toddlers, "do not live by bread alone." Their needs for nourishment, cleanliness, comfort, and security are inextricably bound up with the feelings which tie them to their mothers, who carry out the function of ministering simultaneously to both sides of their natures, the material as well as the libidinal requirements. Only while this happens will the child be sufficiently at peace for internal growth and for increasing interest in and adaptation to the external world.

The film sequences on Kate and Jane left us no doubt that it is difficult for any fostering agency to assume the role of the familiar love object in a child's life. Young children under the impact of emotional loss and deprivation make demands which are excessive by any ordinary standards. We witnessed that it was only by not sparing herself and by being fully available to respond to the mothering needs of her foster children that Joyce Robertson en-

abled them to come through the separations without being overwhelmed and to return unharmed to their mothers. We can feel
convinced that under the conditions of communal life, as in a residential institution, there is not the slightest chance to meet the
separated child's requests in terms of time, effort, patience, and exclusive attention.

Moreover, the change from family life to communal life is never
advantageous at this age. A cherished only child such as John is unprepared for the aggressive atmosphere of an institutional toddler
group. He is not versed in the reigning modes of attack and defense; he has not learned to grab what he wants; nor is he used to
having some precious possession unexpectedly snatched from his
grasp. The concept of sharing, so essential in group life, is still far
removed from his understanding.

Consequently, instead of profiting from the availability of potential playmates, John can only experience the presence of the
other children as a constant threat from which he would like to
withdraw to a protecting adult. While, initially, his retreat and
search is directed toward a "familiar" face, the constant change of
nannies soon makes him more promiscuous, i.e., less discriminating:
any adult will serve the purpose so long as she pays attention (such
as the nanny who bathes him). However, any individual attention
received is either too impersonal in nature or too fleeting in duration to counteract John's growing bewilderment, frustration, and
withdrawal into himself. Nor do the father's visits help much to
improve the situation. His coming and going which is unrelated to
the child's needs and wholly beyond his control seems to aggravate
rather than to decrease tension.

While following the film sequences, we cannot help but think in
terms of two concepts which played an important part in Ernst
Kris's studies of the behavior of young children; in the first instance
their *regression rate* (1950), in the second instance the connection
between *strain and trauma* (1956).

As regards *regression,* I believe that Ernst Kris would have
assessed John's reactions as fairly normal and predictable. Far from
losing his developmental gains indiscriminately, he proceeds on a
retrograde course gradually. From constructive play (according to
description, a child "who amused himself") he returns to cuddly toys,

from there to aimless wandering and manipulating. From babbling words he regresses to toneless whining and whimpering; from interest in his surroundings to thumb sucking. Whether the disruption of bodily functions (vomiting, diarrhea, food refusal) should be classed under the same heading is an open question.

As regards *trauma*, we have to guard here against using the term in the most ordinary sense. What has happened to John is not, according to the common definition of trauma, "a sudden overwhelming experience with an influx of stimuli by which his ego is temporarily (or lastingly) put out of action." Even though the separation from home and his arrival in the new surroundings must have seemed sudden to him, he was by no means overwhelmed by them. This "easy to manage" and "undemanding" child (as he was described) for a considerable time kept to his own manner of reacting, his good ego development permitting him to express puzzlement and distress in a sensible fashion, such as conveying his hope to leave by going to the door, by waving "bye-bye." Similarly, the reported "quiet and harmonious relationship" which existed with his mother had equipped his ego to make appropriate bids for attention and to search for substitutes, both functions remaining quite intact also after the experience of separation. On the other hand, it is the constantly repeated frustration of these ego efforts which puts him under strain, and it is the mounting up of the strain which reaches intolerable proportion and finally disrupts his ego. John suffers from a "strain trauma" as defined by Ernst Kris (1956). By the ninth day, all coordinated ego functioning has disappeared; the returning mother finds him almost totally regressed and, without doubt, severely traumatized.

Fascinating as these glimpses are, to me a particular aspect of John's picture supersedes others in importance. What I have in mind is the following:

At the outset of the film story, in Joyce Robertson's words, John is introduced to us as a "bonny and attractive child." There is no doubt that he is well adjusted for his age, his feelings object-directed, his interest in the external world phase-adequate. At the end of the sequence, we see him withdrawn, uncommunicative, out of reach of parental affection, his behavior fluctuating between apathy and listlessness, on the one hand, and wild, aggressive, animallike screaming and struggling, on the other hand. He shows all the characteristics of behavior which are known to us from our contacts with autistic children, a personality change to which we are first alerted in the film when he turns from his search for human objects who are unavailable to the available inanimate ones. To my mind, the most impressive and disturbing scene in the film is the one where he cuddles up to the oversized teddy bear as if it were the mother, not different from the Harlow monkeys who accommodate themselves to the "wire mother" or "cloth mother" offered to them as a substitute.

Autistic children also take the same turn from the animate to the inanimate (or treat the human object as if it were inanimate). Autism, on the other hand, is a disorder of uncertain origin which many of us are reluctant to ascribe to purely psychological, i.e., emotional, causation. The question arises here whether the personality change undergone by John before our eyes should cause us to revise such previously held opinions. Perhaps all autistic children have been potentially normal once, and have been forced back into this ominous state (or kept back in it) by a similar experience of constantly repeated frustration of legitimate needs and expectations. Experiences which at a later and more settled stage may be no more than unhappy, distressing or depressing may well prove devastating at a time when libidinal and ego functions are on the point of unfolding, i.e., are at their most precarious.

However that may be, we have to feel grateful to the film and the implied urge to keep an open mind, not only on the circumscribed question of autism but on the whole wide problem of environmental harm.

Whether such early damage to development is irreversible or, if reversible, what traces of it are left behind is a question with which John's parents are much concerned. A follow-up on the child's growth would teach us much in this direction.

BIBLIOGRAPHY

Furst, S. S., ed. (1967), *Psychic Trauma*. New York: Basic Books.
Kris, E. (1950), Notes on the Development and on Some Current Problems of Psychoanalytic Child Psychology. *This Annual*, 5:24-46.

—— (1956), The Recovery of Childhood Memories in Psychoanalysis. *This Annual*, 11:54-88.

Robertson, James (1952), Film: *A Two-Year-Old Goes to Hospital;* 16 mm., sound, 45 mins., English and French.*

—— (1958), Film: *Going to Hospital with Mother;* 16 mm., sound, 40 mins.

—— & Robertson, Joyce (1967), Film: *Kate, Two Years Five Months, in Foster Care for Twenty-Seven Days;* 16 mm., sound, 33 mins.

—— —— (1968), Film: *Jane, Seventeen Months, in Foster Care for Ten Days;* 16 mm., sound, 37 mins.

—— —— (1969), Film: *John, Seventeen Months, in Residential Nursery for Nine Days;* 16 mm., sound, 45 mins.

—— —— (not released), Film: *Tom, a Legless Child Reared in a Normal Group.*

* All the Robertson films are distributed (a) in London by the Tavistock Institute of Human Relations; (b) in New York by the New York University Film Library.

THE FETISH AND THE TRANSITIONAL OBJECT

PHYLLIS GREENACRE, M.D. (New York)

The main focus of this paper will be a comparison of the clinical forms and functions of the transitional object and the fetish. The understanding of the differences and similarities may be facilitated by a consideration of the developmental backgrounds.

The transitional object and the fetish resemble each other in certain formal aspects: both are inanimate objects adopted and utilized by the individual to aid in maintaining a psychophysical balance under conditions of more or less strain. But there are rather striking differences in their origins and roles. The transitional object appears in and belongs to infancy, and is generally relinquished when infancy merges into childhood. The fetish, on the other hand, is commonly adopted as a necessary prop or adjunct to insure adequate sexual performance in adult life. The term *fetish* is here used in the limited sense of the perversion of fetishism. While this condition becomes manifest under the demands of adulthood, it has its roots in disturbances in infancy. The transitional object is almost ubiquitous and does not generally forecast an abnormal development.

There are other fetishistic phenomena in which the differences from the transitional object are not so clear-cut. This is especially true in conditions where the fetish is not related specifically to the genital sexual performance. It would be helpful, then, to study the fetish as an amulet or magic object, as a symbolic object in religious rites, as a token in romantic love, and as a special property in children's play. There may be an overlap between the functions of the transitional object and the fetish. The use of the transitional object seems then to be prolonged and ultimately serves a fetishistic need.

144

Such situations and other aspects of the relationship between transitional object and fetish will be dealt with in a second paper.

Winnicott, to whom we are indebted for the conception of the transitional object, first described it in 1953, emphasizing that it is regularly the first not-me possession of the infant and serves as a bridge between that which is comfortably familiar and whatever is disturbingly unfamiliar. It facilitates the acceptance of the latter. It is therefore of help in the beginning of individuation, the separation of the infant from the mother. To fulfill its role, the transitional object itself must have certain qualities. First of all, it must be part of the baby's intimate environment and be readily at hand. This appeal of the familiar depends not only on visibility but even more on texture and odor.

The preferred transitional object is commonly something soft which has been used in the infant's care, e.g., an old blanket, warmly impregnated with body odors, or a bit of wool or fluff, which may be a reduced version of the blanket, or actually a piece of it. Sometimes a smooth and pliable object is chosen, such as a ribbon or the satin binding of a blanket. It is significant, however, that the infant definitely selects the object for himself, in accord with his own needs, and is thereafter intensely loyal to it, refusing substitutes and showing signs of distress if this uniquely desirable object is not at hand. Durability is a built-in requirement commensurate with the degree of familiarity demanded. Individuality of odor (or blend of odors) seems especially important. Many infants will reject a beloved object if it has been washed and only become reconciled when it has again attained its familiar smelliness. Easy movability is also a basic requirement.

The transitional object absorbs neglect and even abuse as well as the most loving closeness; responds sensitively to the impulses and needs of its infant owner; and so in general makes strangeness and solitude more acceptable. While the transitional object takes a great deal of mistreatment, in the sense of being tossed, thrown about, pulled at and fingered, or occasionally sucked or chewed, and so goes to pieces, it is rarely, if ever, destroyed in violence. It may be that the infant who is subject to violence of ragelike proportions, sometimes due to physical distress, cannot use the comforting object, if at all, until he has exhausted himself through movement or attack on his own body. The very sensitive and polymorphous pliability of the transitional object may save it from such violence. For there are times and kinds of infantile distress in which the infant seems to demand something harder to beat against or bite upon, probably with a need to define the body surface rather than to blur it. It is interesting to compare this situation with the fetishist's demand for indestructibility of the fetish. There the distinctiveness and dependability of the form of the fetish give a reassurance as to the reliability of this supplement to fill a sense of lack in the body image.

In this connection, one notes that while the transitional object is the first not-me object, it is never totally not-me. Even its blend of odors seems to be a fusion of me-odors and mother-odors, while its softness is not only from the mother's body and breast but from pillows and blankets which are at hand when the mother is not there. It is likely, too, that the sensations from the mother's breast combine with the fingertip and hand sensations when the infant touches his own cheeks or his own lips, which may not yet be fully appreciated as exclusively part of his own body, but remain with him when he is separated from his mother.

Perhaps the crux of the function of the transitional object lies in its being a tangible object which is neither just infant nor just mother. It may be separated from both but has attributes of both; and through the combination of smell and visibility can convey closeness even when the infant is not in direct contact with it. Thus it is the larval representation of the self, arising from already experienced needs of the infant which have been satisfied by the mother.

If the object disintegrates or is lost, the infant suffers a period of withdrawal, assuaged usually only when he finds a new object closely resembling the first. Even then the acceptance may appear grudging. It is clear from the infant's behavior that this magic appurtenance, although coming from the environment, is absolutely at the disposal of the infant's own inner feelings. Thus, the transitional object may represent the most ideal mother imaginable—one who is constantly on call, is intuitively and almost omnisciently aware of and faithful to the infant's needs. In a sense, no mother can be *that* good. Winnicott indicates that there is a fairly wide range of good-enough mothers, on whose model the transitional object is based. That it should be an improved, magically idealized inner representation of the mother which is materialized is to be understood by the fact that the infant now needs to separate himself from the actual mother. So he creates this extra-good mother representative who will always be on duty whenever the other world becomes too strange.

The selection of the transitional object usually is made in the first year, less frequently later. The timing of its initiation, the way in which it is at first used (close to the mouth and face, sometimes accompanied by a rhythmic tickling of the nose), as well as the nature of its tactile qualities bespeak clearly its role as a bridge between states of body closeness with the mother and separation from her: from the stage of falling asleep at the mother's breast or in the mother's arms to the stage of having to fall asleep away from the mother. Then the transitional object becomes her magic symbolic representative lending assurance for the separation of going to sleep. The importance of the odor depends probably largely on the fact that it adds a potent intangible link between the infant and the breast, in that it is usually compounded of body smells from both sources. But further, it is biologically grounded in the general importance of smell in the first months of life. For until the baby can maintain an upright position in walking, he functions locomotorwise pretty much like a quadruped, with the nose closer to the ground and to his own genitoexcretory area than he will later on. He then seems to accept the body odors as pleasant rather than disturbing. Observations of nurslings indicate that the young baby may find the breast by nosing it out as much or more than from the sense of touch.

This capacity for communion through odors, first aroused in relation to the mother—her breast and general environment—later becomes externalized and extended to the outer world to include emphasis on air-borne sensations. Occurring gradually, it is definite by the fourth year when there is already an extension of the range of vision through increased locomotion. In addition, with the gaining of bowel control, through spontaneous maturational processes, fortified perhaps by the demands of bodily comfort associated with walking, and by the dividends of familial social approval, a more sophisticated awareness of odor develops in connection with air in general. This contributes to the already developing sense of the relation between intangible mental imagery and concrete objects. By then the child is aware of his thoughts, has some idea of time, and of his own memory, and can differentiate dreams from events. This is a period which is significantly vulnerable to disturbance in the early life of the future fetishist.

Winnicott indicates consistently in his writings that while the use of the transitional object is initiated by the infant, it results from an interaction of maturational progress in the infant with the mother's ability to lend herself to the infant's growing independence and to satisfy rather than be alienated by the seeming ambivalence in his behavior while the process of separation is going on. He also mentions other "transitional phenomena" and speaks of the fact that the mother herself may serve as a transitional object if she is available and finely attuned to both sides of the baby's individuation progress. One must assume that when this occurs, the mother is not merely a "good-enough" mother, but that she is also extraordinarily free of other conflicting intrafamily demands, e.g., from the emergent needs of other children.

It can also be seen that the finger sucking accompanied by rhythmic tickling of the nose and lip, which not infrequently precedes the adoption of the transitional object, may be replaced by the use of some other part of the baby's own body. The rhythmical caressing of a lock of hair or of the penis may suggest their use as transitional objects. In such instances the touching, while rhythmical, is gentler and less pressured than when the same body parts are used with a higher autoerotic component in the activity, as may occur in an infantile form of masturbation, most often beginning in response to the stimulation of extreme distress. In any case, whatever serves directly or indirectly as a transitional object, behavior of this gentler nature is to be regarded as healthy insofar as it furthers natural development.

The way in which the use of the transitional object comes to an end is also noteworthy. Usually the need seems just to fade out: it ceases to occupy the child's attention and drops out of sight. Or it may graduate into becoming a favored toy which retains the desirable qualities, is played with for a time, and then is retired to the position of a memento of things past. Winnicott notes that, characteristically, it is not shamefully banished; nor is the memory of it subjected to active repression. I recently had occasion to mention the phenomenon of the transitional object to an eighteen-year-old boy. After a moment's thought, he remarked that he had a faint memory of having had something like that, but it was a smooth strip of plastic almost like a ribbon, perhaps from some early toy. It was not a clear memory and he did not know when he had last thought of it. Yet he knew it was true. He did not think that he had used it over a very long period, and he did not think that his parents had spoken of it to him since, but the mention of the transitional object had brought back a definite feeling memory of it.

The healthy use of the transitional object as a companion with which to meet the unknown was further illustrated by a little boy of two and a half who kept a blue blanket with him, especially when traveling. On a visit to a strange household, he went to get his rubbers from a closet where he had seen them put. On opening the door, he threw the blue blanket in first before venturing in himself. When this same child learned of the birth of a younger sister a year later, he responded, "Get her a blue blanket; she wants it." This suggests a further step in the development of the transitional object. It appears here as more definitely a projection of the self, that version of the self in which the mother's presence still lingers. It would appear as the forerunner of the imaginary companion. Winnicott mentions that while the transitional object is characteristically soft, warm, absorbent, and resilient, there are some instances, especially in boys, in which a hard object is chosen instead. It would be interesting to know whether this occurs in the first year of life or later, and in what setting. It strongly suggests an element arising from early phallic sensations, which may be stronger in the boy than in the girl and more important in that they may be associated with a visible erection.

I turn next to phenomenological considerations concerning the fetish, with special reference to comparison with the transitional object. The fetish is an inanimate object, the presence of which is necessary for certain persons, usually males, in order for them to sustain a sufficient potency to complete intercourse. It too is usually some specific object which is especially preferred and individually chosen, and is commonly but not invariably something associated with the female body. Often female attributes are combined with male ones. Whereas the transitional object is derived from the mother-me association and is somewhat focused on the mouth-nose and breast, the fetishist's mother-me combination is distinctly concerned with the genitals.

Much more variability in the qualities of the fetish is permitted than in the transitional object. In some cases different fetishes may be used alternately. Articles of clothing are most common and include soft silky feminine undergarments. But the commonest fetish of all is the shoe. Some special type of shoe is chosen, sometimes a shoe provided with straps and buckles or often a shoe which combines hardness and softness, e.g., a soft kid slipper with a hard spike heel. The color black may play an important part in the attractiveness of many fetishistic objects: black shoes, black underwear and stockings often being more stimulating than white or pastel shades. The contrast may enhance the visible dependability. The black is associated with pubic hair and with the illusory fecal phallus. It may also add to the definite visible outline of the fetishistic object, causing it to stand out conspicuously against the background of the adjacent skin. Other leather objects—straps, leather jackets, leather hats and helmets—all have their place. While leather itself may have a characteristic pungent odor, it is a usual requirement that the fetishistic leather object should not be new, and should have been worn by some woman even when it has a somewhat masculine form.

Visibility is a more important condition for the use of the fetish than in the case of the transitional object. Further, while the latter is the first *not-me* possession, it must also carry qualities that serve as a link to the *mother-me* state. There is a certain resemblance to this Janus-facedness in the fetish, but in a different setting. The fetish is conspicuously a bisexual symbol and also serves as a bridge which would both deny and affirm the sexual differences. Both fetish and transitional object are security props which serve to bring the current anxiety-provoking situation under the illusory control of the individual infant or man. But the fetishist becomes addicted to the use of his prop, for his dilemma is clearly due to an extraordinarily stubborn fixation and arrest of development with a special infarct in the reality sense. Fetishists habitually treat the vagina as an unknown and dangerous territory. Even years of experiencing intercourse does not teach them that the vagina is a safe, warm, and happy environment for the penis. I have not known of spontaneous recovery from fetishism once it has become established in adult life; and treatment, though sometimes successful, is an arduous undertaking for both analyst and analysand. Without treatment the fetishist does not ordinarily outgrow his need for the fetish as the infant gradually relinquishes the transitional object.

The attitudes toward the transitional object and the fetish by their respective users are conspicuously different. The infant stakes out a claim to his preferred object and openly and doggedly asserts it. Later, as he grows older, when he has reached a stage of finding other friends, first through more complex toys and then through contemporary companions, the transitional object is allowed to fade into the background. If it reappears at all in later forms, it may be regarded with tender amusement. In contrast, the fetishist usually regards the use of the fetish as abnormal, and is somewhat ashamed of it to the extent of hiding it. But since he feels it to be his only way to sexual gratification (and in a less clearly recognized way to the feeling of being a whole man) he accepts it as an abnormality rather than as a symptom. Treatment is sought rather because of secondary anxiety due to secrecy and fear of discovery, together with periods of anxious depression. The underlying feeling of self-distrust and the nagging sense of abnormality may be defended by the development of ruthless competition in the business world through which sadistic drives find a discharge. Narcissistic gratification in "success" and the gaining of possessions may substitute for any developed love relationhip. Even these generally "successful" fetishists may still require the fetish for sexual performance.

Let us turn next to examining the earlier elements of the life situation. It is generally agreed that the human infant requires a longer period of dependence after birth than the lower animals. This is the price that is demanded for the development of his mental functioning with the capacity for memory, speech, reasoning, and imagination. We must rely for our understanding a good deal on what postulations we can make based on observations of the behavior of the young baby in the preverbal era, supplemented by careful scrutiny of the ways in which these early reactions develop, become modified, amplified, and organized in accordance with the progress of maturation and the nature of the environment. Variations in responsiveness even at birth may be due to differences in prenatal life, in the process of birth itself, and in constitutional endowments.

Some of the potential responsiveness which the infant brings into this new world, even though patterned, is not of much use to him. Although seemingly precocious, it is really outdated, belongs to prehistoric eras, and will soon vanish in the strange new environment. But it will be relearned and reassembled to whatever degree it is needed at some later time. I refer here to the grasp reflex and the swimming movements of the newborn. The young infant reacts with seeming comfort to warmth, to gently firm support (as in being held), and to even rhythm. The reaction to rhythm may be to the rhythm of the mother's body as she walks or rocks with the baby in her arms, or to a rhythm granted to the baby separately as when he is rocked in a cradle where he is snugly warm. All of these conditions probably have some relation to experiences in prenatal life as well as to certain constitutionally grounded potentialities.

The reactions to sound, which can also be noted prenatally, vary a good bit between different infants, especially as to the quality of sound which may produce a disturbed reaction. But I am also impressed with the early age at which babies react with ease and seeming relaxation to unsharp sounds such as crooning, or to the rhythm of simple tunes. By six months of age or even earlier the baby may initiate a swaying or rocking motion as he sits on the floor, if a rhythmic tune is played on a victrola. It is common to see a baby jiggling or "dancing in tune" when he has been able to pull himself up into a standing position but cannot yet walk independently. Certainly, the rhythm of walking is ordinarily basically an even one. Winnicott has remarked that sometimes a tune serves as a transitional phenomenon.[1]

Important too is the patterned sucking reaction of the lips and mouth present at birth, followed soon by fumbling hand-to-mouth movements. Here it seems probable that the baby is using his fist or fingers for gratification before the centrally organized representation

---

[1] It is probably the dependability of the rhythm, the familiarity of the sound, and the conditions associated with comfort from the mother which are the basis of selection of such a transitional phenomenon as a tune.

of his own body is well enough assembled and put together for him to distinguish whether they belong to him or are a gift from the outside.

But in general, early stimulations from the environment to which the infant is unaccustomed are met with disparate, not much organized reflex reactions. If the stimuli are multiform and strong, then signs of infantile distress may appear. In the first weeks of life, the infant is simply not sufficiently organized to cope with a very wide range of unfamiliar stimulations. An attentive and intuitive mother at first lends herself very fully to the infant's needs. Through contact with her breast and body, and after a few weeks through the visual contact with her face, these parts of the mother's body become the infant's most intimate environment. Familiarity is a first step to possession. The mother and infant form a dyad, and it may not be quite clear what belongs to mother and what to baby. This is the early part of the introjective-projective period of development for the baby (the symbiotic stage described by Mahler). But the inner pressure of maturation and growth are exerting a continuous and rapid change in this relationship as the infant's increasing abilities bring him spontaneously to new experiences of a widening environment.

By the time of the emergence of walking and talking at the end of the first year and the beginning of the second, the infant is more nearly a going concern on his own: the general introjective-projective stage is giving way to more definite identification by imitation of the mother and those who share the intimate environment. Such imitativeness has its own Janus quality, looking in both directions, concerned with both beginnings and endings. While it furthers the development of channels of communication separate from the mother, it may also contribute to an illusion of her being at hand —an illusion which is fortified by the presence of the transitional object. Especially the spoken words may seem both as coming from the infant himself and experienced from the outside. Athena bursting fully armed from the forehead of Zeus may thus represent the birth of an independent intellectual life rather than the physical birth some months earlier from a less exalted body area.

The importance of speech as a critical point in the development of the species and of the individual is proverbial. There are many quite useful and even complicated communication routes and methods in nonhuman species. But speech allows a more precise, economical, and complex communication probably with more expression of nuances than may be found elsewhere in the animal kingdom. As the infant's communication through speech develops, he spontaneously tends to limit the use of the transitional object to situations when he is out of sight or hearing of the mother. Still, the acquisition of speech does not mean the cessation of need for nonverbal communication, which is achieved in an illusory way through the continued resort to the transitional object.

To digress a bit to consider the relation of speech and nonverbal communication to psychoanalytic therapy. The psychoanalytic situation is built around the emphasis on speech as the cornerstone of therapy. The analysand's position on the couch, by subtle suggestion, limits the extent of active movement. This is further emphasized by the direction to *speak* whatever thoughts or feelings he becomes aware of during the analytic hour. It is thus implicitly assumed that the analysand will be able to describe or at least mention his feelings, involved and painful though they may be. Any experienced analyst realizes, however, that movements on the couch, postures, changes in tone and intensity of voice, flushing, sweating, and special states of body tension are all part of the expression of feeling and may represent explicit communication. As the analyst's experience enlarges, he automatically takes these into consideration in making an interpretation to the analysand. (It is the importance of these elements in the psychoanalytic situation which makes me realize the limitation of teaching through tape recordings of "sessions.") In his awareness of the analysand's nonverbal communications, the analyst is acting—intuitively, as we say—like Winnicott's "good-enough" mother, except for the fact that *his* response is predominantly in words and is rightly so limited.[2] For in this way he is

---

[2] Winnicott (1965) has also mentioned that the fundamental relationship between analysand and analyst partakes of the older relationship between infant and mother, and that the analysand may sometimes use the analyst as a transitional object. There are patients who resist moving from this position. This occurs when there has been severe and persistent disturbance of the early relationship to the mother: she has not been a "good-enough" mother for one set of reasons or another. In dealing with another aspect of the analyst as a transitional object, he says, describing the opening of an analysis, "I do adapt quite a little to individual expectations. Yet I am all the time manoeuvring into the position for standard analysis. . . . For me this means

bringing the content of the behavior and feelings of the analysand into a focus which will utilize the latter's judgment and self-critique. This very process of interpretation inherently tends further to build up and bring into service the underlying therapeutic alliance. When this kind of intercommunication (i.e., nonverbal into verbal form) is lacking, analytic therapy is in danger of becoming a didactic and persuasive affair. It is not only the content of what the analyst says that is significant, but the way in which it is said, and that hard-to-define spirit in which the interpretation is offered. If this kind of rapport is absent or tenuous, the nonverbal needs of the analysand become grounded in too strong an identification with the analyst or too obedient a dependence on him; and the superstructure of the analysis becomes highly intellectualized.

I have thought also that the central position of speech in psycho-analytic therapy has tended to reinforce an attitude of excluding considerations of events from the early verbal or preverbal era of the analysand's life. The implication is that these have taken place before the dawn of clear (mental) memory and that they are there-fore unreachable. Certainly, we deal most often with fantasies or even parts of family myths which are part fact and part rationaliza-tions concerning this period. They may then be derived mostly from what the patient has been told or has overheard or only fantasied about his early infant days. Nonetheless, actual events from so early a time may leave residual patterns of sensory response and reaction. These appear sometimes fused with or incorporated into later memo-ries and fantasies and sometimes as rather stark body reactions, to be re-enacted under the influence of the transference relationship—if one considers this to include the basic rapport between analyst and analysand merging into but not exclusively limited to the trans-ference neurosis which is constellated around the oedipus complex. I would regard these reactions as a special form of body memory which may take on a primitive form of communication.

This leads to further thoughts regarding the early history of the

communicating with the patient from the position in which the transference neurosis (or psychosis) puts me. In this position I have some of the characteristics of a transi-tional phenomenon, since although I represent the early reality principle, and it is I who must keep my eye on the clock, I am nevertheless a subjective object for the patient" (p. 166).

child with a (healthy) transitional object; and presently to a comparison of this with the same periods in relation to events in the child who may be a potential fetishist.

The early incomplete separation of the infant from the outer world has been generally accepted since it was first postulated by Freud. It is conceived of as a period of marked helplessness which lessens rapidly as the infant's growth and strength assert themselves according to biologically preordained patterns of maturation. Certainly, this development is influenced and somewhat reshaped by interaction with the environment, both inanimate and animate. It is clearly the mother on and with whom the most important problems of separation and individuation must be played out. At first the breast is the most important part of her, satisfying not only feeding needs, but offering a soft warm cushion which may blur the sense of separateness; and in offering so comfortable a spot it becomes the germinal center of tender love. This was stated or forecast in Freud's description of the oral phase in the *Three Essays on the Theory of Sexuality* (1905). All this has of course been both documented and amplified during the last two to three decades by the careful observation of infants in longitudinal studies. It is interesting to note that the conception of the origin of the transitional object, expressed in a body memory of the relation of mother and infant, which is carried in the merest but effective illusion, is the very heart of Freud's extraordinary description of the *Mona Lisa* (1910). It is my intention to come back to this in some future paper having to do with the role that the transitional object plays in the creative function in the developing infant.

I want now especially to emphasize two other conditions which influence the need for and the development of the transitional object. The first is concerned with the role of speech in thought and memory; and the second involves a consideration of certain influences on infantile perception. As I have already hinted, I think there may be a fallacy in speaking too definitively of the preverbal and the verbal periods as though there were a line of sharp demarcation between them. I believe that there are many infants in whom speech emerges very gradually and that different ingredients of body reactions become involved or associated with it. Later in life, thinking may correspondingly still contain a variety of sensorimotor components which may tend to give a high capacity for symbolism, even when the final expression in speech is both precise and rich. Individuation too is a gradual and sometimes faltering process, not just clicking into place with the attainment of communicative speech. The development of the latter seems to be promulgated or interfered with by body states as well as by emotional and psychologically expressed ones. But my point now is that the transitional object is most needed during the period when speech is not yet secure. With its protean potentialities, the transitional object can take almost any form and thereby communicate in the me or not-me direction in a way which may or may not involve speech.

Winnicott's work opens the way for further exploration of many questions. André Maurois has remarked in his *Essay on Illusion* (1968) that every perception is in itself an interpretation. It is this capacity for illusion, established through the subjective contribution to observations of the external world, which is of special importance in the forming of both the transitional object and the fetish. After the infant's recovery from the process of birth, he enters a world for which he is not at once prepared. It seems probable that the sensory impacts of his emergence are soon registered in bits and pieces which in the course of time are gradually assembled into some kind of form out of manifold fragmentary and overlapping impressions. It is likely that the rate and degree of completion of the assembled inner representations of the external object depends, not only on the frequency, extent, and intensity of contact with the object, but also on the needs that are directly satisfied by it or are asking for satisfaction.

Further, it may be that we do not adequately take into account that the continually changing actual size of the infant (due to the rapidity of the early growth) is an important factor in the subjective situation, combining as it does with the responses determined by the maturational stage of specific functions. This complicates the central registration of the infant's perception of the outer world. This is a confusing situation which is probably difficult for most adults to appreciate.

While smell, touch, vision, and hearing are the important orienting senses in the early weeks, it appears that visual focusing becomes the most important factor in the process of gathering and unifying the impressions from other sense stimulations. However, the visual focusing acts in combination with increasing strength and coordination of the muscles to produce the inner picture.

Reality testing is a repetitious affair in infancy before the subjective representation is sufficiently *reliable* and yet flexible for the object to be accepted and taken for granted. Reality testing begins when the infant still fluctuates between relative helplessness and the uncertain degree of omnipotence granted him by the environment. Even as he gains control over external objects, these may seem to vary in size and shape as his perception of them changes with his own growth in size and increasing control of his own body movements. It seems to me that the attainment of a fair degree of reality testing is concomitant with the dawn of memory in the sense in which we ordinarily use the term. *I would see the transitional object—pliable, uncomplaining, and rich in its protean possibilities— as promoting a kind of psychophysical homeostasis as individuation progresses.* The need for this must vary greatly in different infants. There seems little doubt that the early object most focused on is the mother, first according to the mouth-breast axis, and later with a face-to-face and even an eye-to-eye communication. It is chiefly the relation to the mother which can be relaxed or tightened up according to the baby's need, by his use of the transitional object, with its enormous illusory value.

Winnicott stresses that the adoption of the transitional object is a normal creative act on the part of the infant; and I believe that his point is well taken. The infant definitely chooses the object from what is at hand and will not accept any other object that is given to him. Neither can he generally be trained to use an object which someone else might consider more appropriate. In some way he seems to endow his chosen object with illusory life. He is tender toward it and acts as though he felt a return tenderness from it. He may wear it out but rarely destroys it otherwise. Preferably it is soft, easily moved, and can take many forms, be molded by chance as it is tossed about or by illusion to meet its young creator's needs. Here we may think of Leonardo and the paper which he crushed and threw to the floor until its wrinkled form seemed to take a shape in his mind's eye that invited him to work again. This takes us into the realm of the creativeness of the specially gifted person, and the role of illusion and ambiguity there. It is too big a subject for my present paper.

To turn next to consider the prehistory of the fetish; I realize here that my knowledge of the fetish has come to me in a quite different way from that having to do with the transitional object. The data regarding the transitional object have come largely from the observations of Winnicott, who as a pediatrician-turned-psycho-analyst has had extraordinarily rich opportunities for clinical obser-vation over a long period of time. My own experience has also been by direct observation, but much more limited in scope. The con-clusions regarding the development of the fetish, on the other hand, have come from the need to understand adult patients and are based on reconstructions arrived at in the course of psychoanalytic treat-ment.

As I have discussed the genetic background of fetishism in a series of papers (1951, 1953, 1955, 1960, 1968), I shall give only a con-densed résumé here.

Fetishism develops against varying backgrounds. Some, but by no means all, such patients have disturbances in the first two years of life. But these are of a more specific type and may stem from a variety of causes: illness in babyhood; illness of one kind or another in the mother which may have made her unreliable or unavailable for consistent mothering; or a deprived or violent family atmosphere which upset things generally. One might say that in a fair proportion of cases the mothering is not good enough or at least not quite good enough. But these conditions form a background for neurotic dis-turbance, not always severe, and cannot be more than contributing etiological factors. They are seen in the transference during analytic treatment in the appearance of an unusual degree of primary iden-tification and a diffuse and rather simple type of envy, jealousy, and projection. There may be some impairment of object relationship and evidence of magic expectations and apprehensions.

The conditions which specifically contribute to the neurotic dis-tortion of development against which the fetish becomes the unique and seemingly obligatory defense are of two types. There are those which may combine to interfere with the adequate awareness of the nature of the own genitals resulting in a focal disturbance in the sexual identity and at least an infarct in the reality sense. *First*, there is the exposure of the infant during the first two or three years, frequently or even consistently, to awareness of the genitals of the opposite sex, whether of the parent or of a sibling.[3] *Second*, there is the acute experience of witnessing an injury (usually bloody) to the self or even more importantly to another, more often the mother, another child, or a pet.

Vision plays a dominant role in both sets of experiences. These attain importance only after visual focusing is well matured. In the first instance, what is seen of the genitals of the other, the *not-me*, is by far clearer than what is seen on the *me*, and supersedes in definiteness and vividness the impression made by the endogenous feelings from within the infant's own body producing thus a confusion about the nature of his own genitals. Similarly the injury to the *not-me* may add to larval fantasies forming a confused impression of the own body and of the existence or danger of injury to it. As vision assumes an increasingly important role in exploring the outer world, it also aids in exploring the outer aspects of the own body, but is least effective in regard to the own face and genitals. At any rate, the continuation of confusion about the nature of the genitals and the witnessing or experiencing of body injury, especially at certain periods of sensual expansion and susceptibility[4] in the infant, cause delay in consolidating the body image and the developing of autonomous drives in the infant, particularly if the maternal environment is also of marginal adequacy. This combination of influences results then in an unusually severe castration fear. It is because this intense fear with its seeming reality reinforced at each attempt at intercourse that the fetish becomes a necessary adjunct to sustain even the semblance of normal sexual life in adulthood.

There is a slight correction to be made here. It is emphasized that the fetish is usually a durable object in which its very hardness

[3] This is discussed in detail in my paper on "Respiratory Incorporation and the Phallic Phase" (1951).

[4] These periods are preponderant in the latter part of the second year and during the fourth year. The first is synchronous with the expansion initiated by walking and talking, and the second with the rising phallic pressure.

and concreteness play a part as though to leave no doubt about its existence. Further, it is desirable for it to be readily at hand or recently seen for it to function properly. Yet there are some cases in which a fetishist has developed the capacity to form a strong visual picture of the fetish, or more frequently a fantasy in which the fetish plays an important part and which must be sustained firmly or in some way acted out in foreplay to serve in place of the concrete fetish. The need for clear awareness of the concrete object is derived from the almost universal assumption that the mother has or has had a penis, with a shock at the hint of this being untrue. The confrontation with the actual female genitals in anticipation of intercourse is counteracted by the presence of the fetish-penis. This can be reincorporated visually and tactilely to strengthen the sense of the own penis in the young male.

Freud (1927) pointed out that the fetish usually consisted of some part of the mother's costume which the boy had seen when in latency or prepuberty he attempted to look under her skirt or that of her substitute. He fixated then on a safe object which warded off the the actual sight of the female genitals much in the fashion that a screen memory utilizes safe or peripheral parts of an experience to repress and conceal the disturbing central parts.

And finally in summing up the utilization of the transitional object in comparison with that of the fetish, I would wish to deal with three additional aspects, viz., the nature of the magic involved; the relation of fetish and transitional object to aggression; and their general relation to the total functioning of the individual, especially the role of illusion.

That symbolic magic is involved in both instances is clear enough. That of the transitional object is extremely primitive. Belonging to the earliest period in life, it offers an illusory bridge— or bridges; it comforts and fortifies the young venturer in taking his first steps into the expanding realities of the outer world. Its effect is as diffuse, multiform, changeable, and evanescent as a fog, but far more reliable. It offers a cushion against distress of frustration before reality testing is at all secure, and provides dosages of omnipotence according to infantile needs. But when infancy is past, the investment in the transitional object generally is gradually dissipated. In contrast to this, the fetish appears and exists in adult life, as a definite, durable, and necessary piece of property, which should leave no doubt as to its actual existence. Its function is a focal one —to represent the female phallus and thereby through visual, tactile, and olfactory incorporation to insure the fetishist of his own possession of it. This is a much more complicated magical procedure, related to fascination and self-hypnosis, than is true in the owner of the transitional object. It combines magical materialization and obliteration, a figurative bringing to life or killing, and it very much influences tumescence and detumescence. Its scope of operation is generally relatively fixed and limited, but the fantasies associated with it are manifold.

The transitional object and the fetish differ also in their relation to aggression. The transitional object arises out of that early period when aggression has not yet become a me-directed hostility, but is an expression rather of the pressure of the expansion of growth. It is both the recipient and the donor of tender feelings, especially in its earliest forms, and is the medium through which feelings aroused in the own body are fused with the touch, smell, and memory of the soft breast; the comfort of being held in the mother's arms; the familiar touch and smell of her clothing; and later perhaps the touch of a helping hand. Such illusory memory feelings then would tend to reassure the child "You are not alone" and would aid him in whatever necessary infantile attack he must make on the outer world. The transitional object itself may suffer from neglect and hard usage, but it is not attacked in anger. Later on it may give way to a favorite toy which represents the child himself or an imaginary companion toward whom he may assume parental moralizing or punitive attitudes. But even this is usually a part of play and self-mastery and not of direct raw anger.

The fetish, on the other hand, contains congealed anger, born of castration panic. While the fetish function is limited to concern about the genitals, it too has a relation to the mother and sometimes there are indications of memories of her breast. But these seem to have been derived mostly from an early period of confusion between breast and penis. While the fetishist needs his fetish to complete the sexual act, it is often the narcissistic need rather than the expression of tender love which is satisfied. Some fetishists seem incapable of tender, object-related love. Those patients of my own who did have genuine tenderness toward the mate expressed it in more peripheral ways than through intercourse. The fullest meaning of the sexual relationship could not be realized because of this narcissistic need to prove adequacy as a man and to get sexual relief.

Sadomasochistic fantasies and practices are quite commonly associated with fetishism. Even where no clear overt sadomasochistic rituals or activities have appeared, such feelings were implicitly and rather slyly expressed in the magic killings, of not looking, silence, and similar attacks by denial or deprivation. It has seemed reasonable, too, that strong sadomasochistic tendencies should exist and in some instances are clearly traceable to derivative repetitions of the original actual traumata which have contributed to the intensification of the castration panic.

In closing I would emphasize that the transitional object is a temporary construction to aid the infant in the early stages of developing a sense of reality and establishing his own individual identity. It is of positive value in monitoring growth and expansion. It is dispensed with when it is no longer needed. In contrast, the fetish serves as a patch for a flaw in the genital area of the body image. While necessary for the approximation of an adequate sexual function, it is not otherwise useful. Like many patches it is circumscribed, aims to be durable, but is not always successful. In that case it must be renewed, sometimes with even larger patches.

BIBLIOGRAPHY

Freud, S. (1905), Three Essays on the Theory of Sexuality. *Standard Edition,* 7:3-122. London: Hogarth Press, 1953.
—— (1910), Leonardo da Vinci and a Memory of His Childhood. *Standard Edition,* 11:59-137. London: Hogarth Press, 1957.
—— (1927), Fetishism. *Standard Edition,* 21:149-157. London: Hogarth Press, 1961.
Greenacre, P. (1951), Respiratory Incorporation and the Phallic Phase. *This Annual,* 6:180-205.
—— (1953), Certain Relationships between Fetishism and the Faulty Development of the Body Image. *This Annual,* 8:79-98.
—— (1955), Further Considerations regarding Fetishism. *This Annual,* 10:187-194.
—— (1957), The Childhood of the Artist. *This Annual,* 12:47-72.
—— (1960), Further Notes on Fetishism. *This Annual,* 15:191-207.
—— (1964), A Study on the Nature of Inspiration. *J. Amer. Psa. Assn.,* 12:6-31.
—— (1968), Perversions: General Considerations Regarding Their Genetic and Dynamic Background. *This Annual,* 23:47-62.

Mahler, M. S. (1963), Thoughts about Development and Individuation. *This Annual*, 18:307-324.
Maurois, A. (1968), *Illusions*. New York & London: Columbia University Press.
Winnicott, D. W. (1953), Transitional Objects and Transitional Phenomena. *Int. J. Psa.*, 34:89-97.
—— (1959), *Collected Papers*. New York: Basic Books.
—— (1965), *The Maturational Processes and the Facilitating Environment*. New York: International Universities Press.

THE IMAGINARY COMPANION

Its Significance for Ego Development and Conflict Solution

HUMBERTO NAGERA, M.D. (Ann Arbor)

During the last few years at the Hampstead Clinic we have studied a small number of children who had at the time of their diagnostic assessment or previously had an imaginary companion. In no case was the imaginary companion the cause for referral. Usually, its existence was elicited more or less accidentally during the course of the diagnostic investigation.

When we explored this fantasy further, we were surprised to learn that only rarely did the imaginary companion play a significant role in the analysis of these children. In fact, we know of only two children who directly and frequently referred to their imaginary companions during the analytic sessions. One such case was described in the literature (O. Sperling, 1954). Since our clinical material is limited, we can only state what our experience was,

In collaboration with Alice Colonna and the Clinical Concept Research Group whose members are: H. Nagera (Chairman), A. Freud (Consultant), S. Baker, A. Colonna, R. Edgcumbe, M. Foote, W. E. Freud, A. Gavshon, A. Hayman, S. Ini, R. Putzel, and I. Rosen. In addition, a number of colleagues helped with the review of the literature and gave permission for the use of their clinical examples. I wish to thank Eva Bry, Lottie Kearney, Elizabeth Model, Dr. Josephine Stross, and T. de Vries.

The paper forms part of a research project entitled "Childhood Pathology: Its Impact on Mental Disorders in Adulthood," which is being conducted at the Hampstead Child-Therapy Clinic, London. The project is financed by the National Institute of Mental Health, Washington, D.C., Grant No. 05683-07.

At present the author is professor of psychiatry at the University of Michigan Medical Center, and Director of the Child Analytic Study Program at Children's Psychiatric Hospital, Ann Arbor, Michigan.

without drawing any inferences or conclusions as to the meaning of this observation or its general validity.[1]

One possible explanation for the absence of references to the imaginary companion, at least in the treatment of the younger child, is that the imaginary companion frequently plays a specific positive role in the development of the child, and once that role is fulfilled, it tends to disappear and is finally covered by the usual infantile amnesia. Although this assumption is probably correct, several puzzling elements remain.

First, in a successful therapeutic analysis of adults, much of the infantile amnesia is lifted. In fact, the success of the analysis usually depends in part on achieving this to a sufficient degree. Nevertheless, in our experience and in that of a considerable number of colleagues whom I have consulted, memories of an imaginary companion are recovered only rarely. Yet we know that the phenomenon of the imaginary companion is not a rare occurrence in children. According to Harriman (1937), for example, one third of the children he studied had an imaginary companion. Why then is it so rarely recovered?[2]

Second, in a large number of individuals the imaginary companion makes its first appearance in later developmental stages, e.g., in latency, a period that usually is not covered by the infantile amnesia. What has become of these imaginary companions?

Third is a point related to the above. We have come to know of a few adults who clearly and consciously recollected having had an imaginary companion in their childhood and who nevertheless managed to go through what they considered a satisfactory analysis

---

[1] Bender and Vogel (1941) have described a large number of children mostly in latency and late latency who talked quite freely of their imaginary companions in a therapeutic situation. But these children were not in analysis (with its special setting and conditions); they were studied in hospitals where they seem to have been very actively questioned.

[2] Perhaps the answer lies (in the case of the very young child) in the fact that what is important is not the content of the fantasy associated with the imaginary companion but the developmental purpose it is designed to fulfill. In this sense it has to be considered part of a developmental process and that is not the type of thing that is recovered by the lifting of the infantile amnesia. Furthermore, what cannot be recovered has to be reconstructed, and there are obvious difficulties in reconstructing the early existence of an imaginary companion. Another possible reason is that in the analyses of adults we do not pay as much attention to this phenomenon as we should.

of several years' duration without ever referring in the analysis to their memories of their imaginary companions.

While we have no definite answers to many of the questions raised, we believe that further inquiry into this phenomenon has long been overdue.

A review of the psychoanalytic literature discloses only one paper devoted entirely to imaginary companions (Sperling, 1954). In addition, several analysts have occasionally referred to this phenomenon (Anna Freud, 1936; Selma Fraiberg, 1959; Murphy et al., 1962; Harrison et al., 1963). The situation is quite different outside the psychoanalytic literature where one finds a variety of publications by sociologists, psychologists, and educators. "A Study of Imaginary Companions" was published by Vostrovsky as early as 1895. Several authors devoted special chapters or even an entire book to this topic (e.g., Harvey, 1918; Hall, 1907; Green, 1922).

In our experience, the phenomenon of the imaginary companion is observed most frequently in children between the ages of two and a half to three years and nine and a half to ten years, the majority being found in the earlier range. Some authors, e.g., Vostrovsky (1895), claim that the first appearance of the imaginary companion varied from the first to the thirteenth year of life, but her conclusions are not based on direct observations of children.

Hurlock and Burstein (1932) placed the first appearance of the imaginary companion much later. They concluded, "Among the girls, the age at which the imaginary companion is most likely to appear is between five and seven years of age. Boys experienced this phenomenon at a considerably later age than did girls. One third of the group of people studied fixed the age of first appearance of the imaginary playmate at the stage between seven and nine years of age" (p. 385). The discrepancy between our findings and those of Hurlock and Burstein is, I believe, a result of the procedure followed by these authors. Their study is based on questionnaires given to 701 high-school and college students whose age varied from fifteen and forty years, with the median being eighteen to nineteen years. Hurlock and Burstein were not aware of the fact that infantile amnesia usually covers the earlier years; if a person nevertheless remembers the imaginary companion (possibly because he was told about it by his parents), he will tend to place it outside the period covered by the infantile amnesia. Our experiences and that of others whose data were obtained through direct observation of children demonstrate that the imaginary companion appears from two and a half years onward.

Bender and Vogel (1941) described fourteen cases of imaginary companions. At the time of admission to the Children's Ward of Bellevue Psychiatric Hospital the children were five to ten years of age, but in some cases the imaginary companions had been active for several years prior to admission. Harvey (1918) thought that the imaginary companions tend to disappear at two points, either at the ages of seven to eight, or between eleven and twelve. Svendsen (1934) stated that "anything approximating accurate information in regard to the time at which imaginary companions disappear is difficult to obtain, owing to the gradual character of the process" (p. 996).

The imaginary companion phenomenon is not restricted to the age groups so far described. Harriman (1937), for example, reported the experiences of a number of college students in psychology who kept their imaginary companions longer than is usually observed. In one case, the imaginary companion made its appearance when the student was twelve to thirteen years of age and remained active for several years thereafter. In another case, the fantasy of an imaginary companion remained active until the student, a male, was eighteen years of age. In some of the cases described by Harriman the fantasy of the imaginary companion was as vivid and clear at this later age as it had been at the beginning; while in others the fantasy, though still present, had lost much of its former distinctness.

We should add that only two analysts among the many we consulted, remembered adult patients who referred to a childhood imaginary companion during their analyses. The special interest of one of these cases is that the patient not only referred to the imaginary companion in his analysis but in fact retained his imaginary companion throughout adulthood. It was the analyst's impression that although this patient's imaginary companion had lost much of its distinctness, it nevertheless continued to play an active role in the patient's psychological life.

Some authors, e.g., Svendsen (1934), believe that the imaginary companion is accompanied by strong visual imagery. Harvey (1918) believes that the imaginary playmate is a visual or auditory idea that becomes as vivid and real as a visual or auditory percept, but that the child nevertheless always recognizes its unreality.

Bender and Vogel (1941) state that they never observed the imaginary companion phenomenon in psychotic children and that they found no instance in which they had any reason to believe that it represented a feature in a prepsychotic state.

Different authors cite different figures with regard to the frequency of the imaginary companion. Svendsen (1934) thinks that about 13 percent of all children show this phenomenon. She arrived at this percentage on the basis of the following definition: "the term imaginary companion, as it is used in this study, implies an invisible character, named and referred to in conversation with other persons or played with directly for a period of time, at least several months, having an air of reality for the child but no apparent objective basis. This excludes that type of imaginative play in which an object is personified, or in which the child himself assumes the role of some person in his environment" (p. 988). Hurlock and Burstein (1932) maintain that as many as 20 percent of all children have imaginary companions, while Harriman (1937) believes that this phenomenon can be observed in about one third of all children between the ages of three and nine. Kirkpatrick (1929) was of the opinion that practically all children have imaginary companions in one form or other.

The discrepancies in these figures, it seems to me, are largely dependent upon the criteria used to define an imaginary companion. A review of the literature makes it clear that there are no uniform criteria and that a variety of fantasy manifestations in children are included by some authors and excluded by others. In what follows I shall use some familiar imaginative activities of children to highlight the difficulties in deciding what constitutes an "imaginary companion."

All child therapists with experience in the treatment of children between the ages of two and seven know how frequently they find an ally among their toys or in a lion, a tiger, a crocodile, Superman, etc. These different animals and persons blindly obey their commands and are ready to attack anyone by whom the child feels threatened. Such dangerous beasts frequently appear at those points in the treatment when the child displaces onto the therapist a fear that belongs in the child's relationship to his father, for example, especially when he has managed to project onto the father and therapist his own hostile and aggressive designs.

One of my patients, a four-year-old boy, used a crocodile and a tiger whenever he felt particularly aggressive toward me. I could observe the following sequence: at first he either verbalized his hostile intentions or tried to attack me physically by kicking or hitting. Shortly afterward he would become frightened by his actions and fearful of retaliation by me. He then looked in his cupboard for his crocodile and tiger, warning me that these two powerful allies were ready to defend him and would destroy me if I meant any harm.

Such behavior is common and frequent enough during therapy; although it seems as if this child had provided himself with an "imaginary companion," it was at first confined to the analytic hour and, within the analytic hours, to those occasions when his aggression was aroused and he feared my retaliation. This type of "imaginary companion" is an ad hoc construction designed to deal with a specific situation such as that described and may not even have arisen were it not for the special conditions of the analytic treatment. It is doubtful whether this type of phenomenon in this limited form really deserves to be considered a true imaginary companion.[3] If one does so consider it, then one must agree with Kirkpatrick (1929) that all children at one age or another have the fantasy of an imaginary companion with greater or lesser intensity.

My little patient's use of the animals, however, did not remain confined to the analytic session. Somewhat later in treatment when his fear of being smacked by the father increased—a fear that had a reality basis—he began to protect himself further by taking the two powerful allies home. If this was not allowed, he took them home in his "imagination" by pretending that he had put them into his pocket. In the following session he would comment spontaneously or in response to my questions how these animals had frightened his father, who then did not dare smack him. With these developments, the defensive ad hoc fantasy had obviously assumed a

---

[3] Furthermore, my patient used concrete objects, a toy tiger and a toy crocodile, while in most cases the real imaginary companion does not require concrete representation.

more integral part of the child's fantasy life; for a while these two animals were his constant and reassuring companions at school, at home, and, when necessary, during the analytic sessions. Even though this type of behavior is closer to the imaginary companion phenomenon than the former, we very much hesitate to consider it a typical example of imaginary companion.

The literature also contained some figures relating to the incidence and nature of the imaginary companion in boys and girls. In Svendsen's (1934) sample of forty cases with clearly defined imaginary companions, the ratio between girls and boys was three to one. In the fourteen cases that Bender and Vogel (1941) described as a heterogenous and unselected group, there were seven girls and seven boys. Bender and Vogel also quote Jersild et al. (1933) who in their study of 143 children with imaginary companions found that girls gave more definite descriptions of their imaginary companions than boys. Further, the imaginary companions of girls were more frequently of the opposite sex than was the case with boys. However, the majority of both boys and girls had companions of the same sex.

Jersild et al. (1933) found that 79 percent of the 143 children had imaginary companions that were human beings, characters from stories, and, in a few cases, elves and fairies.[4] In 21 percent the imaginary companions were anthropomorphized animals, dolls, and other special objects. In a large majority of cases, the imaginary companions went through a variety of metamorphoses and changes in accordance with the child's wishes. Only a few children experienced a strong feeling of a "real presence" in association with the imaginary companion. Burlingham (1945) referred to the fantasy of having a twin, which is occasionally "built up in the latency period as the result of disappointment by the parents in the oedipus situation, in the child's search for a partner who will give him all the attention, love and companionship he desires and who will provide an escape from loneliness and solitude" (p. 205). Although the wish to have a twin usually appears as a conscious daydream (similar to the family romance described by Freud) rather than as an imaginary companion fantasy, we know of a prelatency girl whose imaginary companion was a twin.

[4] The theme of an imaginary companion has frequently been used in literature. For a good survey see, for example, Bender and Vogel (1941).

We also know that some children have only one imaginary companion, while others have a great number of them simultaneously. Harriman (1937) reports the case of a young woman who as a student still had imaginary companions, though they had lost some of their distinctness. At the age of nine she created three imaginary companions, three beautiful girls who in her fantasy lived next door to her own house. These three imaginary girls would visit her in the evening, engage in long conversations, and, among other things, introduce their "friends" to her. According to this student's account, she soon had about twenty-five imaginary companions including a few male ones. She had filled several diaries with a large number of stories about them.

The imaginary companions of some children play a most active role in the household, tending to interfere a great deal with many of the everyday routines. Some children demand a place at the table or in the car for their imaginary companions and make other elaborate preparations in order to satisfy the "needs" of their companions. All this may greatly interfere with such activities as going out, eating, and sleeping—much to the annoyance of the parents—even if we leave to one side those imaginary companions who are all out to be deliberately mischievous and provocative.

One of our cases, Roberta, a girl of two years eleven months, has created her own imaginary family which consisted mostly of TV characters appearing on such programs as *Merlin and Goofy, Donald Duck,* and *Pluto.* They were living in the bathroom cupboard or just under a cot. Once, when the mother had just steered Roberta and the pram across a busy road, Roberta started to howl because "Merlin" had been forgotten on the other side. The mother said that she simply had to go back and get "him."

Katherine, aged three, also had many fantasy animals and people who accompanied her even on the street. The mother described to us how after crossing a street they had to wait until Katherine was satisfied that all her imaginary companions had crossed the street as well.

In other cases, the imaginary companions remain unobstrusive and do not much interfere with the daily routines of mother and child. The clinical manifestations of this phenomenon are enormously rich and varied. Naturally, the experienced clinician finds in all the individual details a useful source of information about the inner difficulties, struggles, developmental stresses, and conflicts of the child.

Several authors agree that there exists a relationship between the level of intelligence and the production of imaginary companions. It is generally assumed that the better endowed children produce the most distinct and vivid imaginary companions as well as the most complex and better elaborated stories around them. Thus, Jersild et al. (1933) found that the children capable of describing well-defined imaginary companions had higher IQs than the others. Svendsen (1934) believes that the phenomenon of the imaginary companion is not limited to highly intelligent children but that it is more prevalent among them. Bender and Vogel's findings on the intelligence level of their group of children would tend to support Svendsen's opinion. Most of the cases we have examined belong in the group of high-average or superior intelligence, but our sample of cases is not a representative cross-section of the population.

Harriman (1937) expressed the opinion that "the phenomenon of imaginary companions may well have a genuine relationship" to creative writing (p. 370). We have already referred to one of his cases, the young woman who developed a series of twenty-five "imaginary companions." She explained that her elaborate fantasy life was in part motivated by her desire to write novels and her hope to utilize this material for plots later on.[5]

The imaginary companion usually is of the same age as the child, or slightly younger. In a few instances, they were somewhat older than the child, but we have not come across a single case in which a child's imaginary companion was an adult. On the other hand, the imaginary companions may possess some adult characteristics (strength, power, knowledge, authority, etc.) or be referred to as growing up fast.

Although the significance of the imaginary companion is usually

---

[5] According to Harriman, she did in fact keep her records up to date as these imaginary friends progressed through college and became established in life. This case illustrates a shift in the use of this phenomenon: at nine years of age it was used to cope with specific personality problems; later it was in the service of more neutralized aims. One also suspects that, in this case, the earlier phenomenon of the imaginary companions was transferred into what is more properly called a continuous daydream.

determined by a variety of factors, it seems to play a special role in the development of the child at the age of two and a half to five years. For this reason we have singled out this group from the latency group in which this phenomenon serves different functions.

Selma Fraiberg (1959) described the imaginary companion called "Laughing Tiger," of Jannie, aged two years eight months. He was the last in a long series of imaginary companions. In tracing his origin Fraiberg correctly states that he was "the direct descendant of the savage and ferocious beasts who disturb the sleep of small children" (p. 17). Laughing Tiger had in fact appeared at a time when Jannie had been very frightened by animals who could bite, including some neighborhood dogs. Confronted with the "ferocious" animals (which embodied the projection of her own hostile and cannibalistic fantasies), the little girl chose an active way of dealing with her fears. Aided by her capacity to use imagination and fantasy, she was finally able to master her conflicts and anxiety—at least, it gave her the necessary respite for a sufficient length of time, until her development in other areas allowed for a better control of the impulses and fears that, to start with, she had been unable to manage in any other way. Fraiberg remarks that Jannie could have used a variety of other mechanisms, as children frequently do, in order to deal with the problem. For example, she could have avoided animals in general, she could have avoided leaving her home and the safety of her parents, or going to sleep (i.e., developed a sleep phobia) in order not to meet the feared animals even in her dreams.

By means of fantasy Jannie transformed the ferocious beast into a friendly animal, who showed his teeth not in anger but in laughing. This laughing tiger was afraid of children and he particularly feared his mistress and obeyed her every command. All this naturally allowed Jannie's ego to operate freely, without having resort to the restrictions imposed by avoidance and phobic symptoms. Fraiberg further states: "Laughing Tiger was a very important factor in the eventual dissolution of Jan's animal fears. When he first made his appearance there was a noticeable improvement in this area. When he finally disappeared (and he was not replaced by any other animal), the fears of animals had largely subsided and it was evident that Jan no longer needed him. If we watch closely, we will see how the imaginary companions and enemies fade away at about the same time that the fear dissolves, which means that the child who has overcome his tigers in his play has learned to master his fear" (p. 19f.).

Anna Freud (1936) described an older child (seven years) who used very similar mechanisms. This boy's imaginary companion, a tame lion, terrified everybody else, but loved and obeyed him. She says:

> From the little boy's analysis it was easy to see that the lion was a substitute for the father, whom he, like Little Hans, hated and feared as a real rival in relation to his mother. In both children aggressiveness was transformed into anxiety and the affect was displaced from the father onto an animal.[6] But their subsequent methods of dealing with their affects differed. Hans used his fears of horses as the basis of his neurosis, i.e., he imposed upon himself the renunciation of his instinctual desires, internalized the whole conflict, and, in accordance with the mechanism of phobia, avoided situations of temptation. My patient managed things more comfortably for himself. Like Hans in the fantasy about the plumber, he simply denied a painful fact and in his lion fantasy turned it into its pleasurable opposite. He called the anxiety animal his friend, and its strength, instead of being a source of terror, was now at his service. The only indication that in the past the lion had been an anxiety object was the anxiety of the other people, as depicted in the imaginary episodes [p. 74f.].

The imaginary companion serves a variety of functions depending upon the special needs of the child who creates it. Not infrequently imaginary companions are used as superego auxiliaries. It is well known that the younger child needs external controls before his superego is fully established; therefore, many young children use the imaginary companion as an intermediate step between the external controls (in the form of the parents) and their own fully developed superego structure. Such children "consult" their imaginary companions, who in turn instruct them to control their behavior in general or certain impulses in particular. Katherine, one of our

---

6 Freud (1909) pointed out that this step has great economic value for the whole personality. Little Hans had to see his father constantly, while by displacing his fears onto horses he felt anxiety only when confronted with them; and even this could be escaped by avoiding to go out, as he in fact did for some time.

patients, consulted Susan (the imaginary companion) about whatever she planned to do.

Hammerman (1965) described this phenomenon clearly in his
paper on "Conceptions of Superego Development":

> Obedience and self-control, however, are not yet the same as self-
> criticism derived from moral judgment, which is the hallmark
> of a discrete intrapsychic structure. It seems reasonable that ini-
> tially the developing superego organization works only under
> the actual supervision of external objects. *In the well-known
> imaginary companions of children, we note the projection of
> prestages of the superego. Even though imaginary, the need for
> an actual external object is still great* [p. 327; my italics].

He also referred to the regressed agoraphobics who frequently need
the companion as an external, actual authority.

The use of the imaginary companion as a superego prop or
auxiliary is by no means limited to the younger child. Many older
children with reasonably well-established superegos use such companions in their attempts to cope with particular impulses that seem
to escape control because of special situations of frustration, stress
or conflicts. Thus Bender and Vogel (1941) describe a ten-and-a-half-
year-old boy who had a history of rejection and neglect by his parents. His imaginary companion would ask him why he had been bad
all the time and simultaneously threaten him by saying that if he
continued to be bad, his parents would never come again.

The differences between the young and the older child's use of
this mechanism deserve attention. In both cases the imaginary companion fulfills the purpose of controlling their behavior, but in the
young child the imaginary companion is at times an integral part of
the developmental steps taken in the direction of internalization and
introjection of external commands, and thus contributes to the
building up the superego structure. In the older child the imaginary
companion acts as a necessary (though temporary) "prop" or "superego auxiliary" to assist an already established superego. In the first
case, the phenomenon of the imaginary companion highlights the
role of *fantasying* as well as that of the resultant fantasies in further-
ing the development of both ego and superego structures. This

particular role of fantasying, to my knowledge, has not yet received sufficient attention.

Some children use the imaginary companion for purposes that can be considered the opposite of those described above. In their case, the imaginary companion is a vehicle for the discharge of impulses that are no longer acceptable to the child either because he has internalized the parental prohibitions or because he fears the parental attitude to such impulses (before internalization has taken place). By this means the child justifies his "naughty" behavior to himself or the parents, or at least tries to do so when he is accused, for example, of his dirty, messy, destructive behavior. He may excuse himself by saying that "Sam" or "Peter" (the imaginary companions) ordered him to do so. It was not his fault, naturally. This type of response is more frequent in the younger child, but even older children will occasionally try to justify some of their actions in this way.

The following case of Maritza is another example illustrating not only the use of the imaginary companion for drive discharge but also its origin and the sequence that led to its establishment.

Maritza was the youngest child in her family. She had two brothers, Paul, six years older, and Peter, eight years older than she. When she was just over two years old, her brothers taught her to say some dirty words, among them "pupu" (feces). At their suggestion she would repeat this word with a great deal of pleasure. Shortly thereafter Maritza began to tell stories about "Pupu," an imaginary boyfriend with whom she enjoyed doing forbidden things and who could do all the naughty things she did not dare do. Pupu frequently made his appearance at moments of frustration in Maritza's life. For example, on one occasion when her brothers were to go away for the weekend while she had to stay home, she said: "I am going with Pupu to a cottage where there is no lawn mower" (on a previous occasion she had stayed with her family in a cottage and had been frightened by the noise of the lawn mower). From the time Maritza was two and a half years old, Pupu was an active member of the family. The mother felt that Pupu was in many ways a personification of Paul with whom Maritza had an ambivalent relationship. They played a great deal together, tending to tease each other. Maritza admired this older brother and was very jealous and envious of him. On one occasion Paul's shoes had been left in the middle of the room and the brother was about to pick them up when Maritza objected: "No, they have to stay there; Pupu wears those shoes."

On another occasion Maritza was building a village with her wooden blocks. Suddenly she turned to her mother, indignant and crying, "Now Pupu destroyed my village" (the structure she had been building had collapsed). The mother answered: "Well, if he disrupts your buildings, he has to go to his own mother so that you can play in peace." Thereupon Maritza opened the door, pretended to pick up Pupu, and threw him outside. That day she did not refer to the imaginary companion again, but on the following day he was back.

During the next few months Pupu's identity began to change. "Pupu has a new suit," she said, just after her father had bought a new suit. Thus, Pupu represented aspects of her father. She now demanded that Pupu sleep by her bedside, and every evening a cupboard had to be moved close to her bed because "That is Pupu's bed."

Some time later her brother Paul had to go to the hospital for treatment—an event that reactivated in Maritza an early hospitalization experience when her mother had not been able to stay with her. The mother sympathized with Maritza's renewed anxiety and explained that Paul would not have to stay in the hospital. It was very unfortunate, the mother added, that Maritza had had to go to the hospital and that she had not been able to accompany her. Maritza answered immediately: "Pupu's mother did stay with him."

More recently Maritza became ill on a day when she expected to visit her grandfather. She asked her mother to let Pupu know that she could not go. The mother promised to do so, but Maritza insisted, "But he is standing outdoors, you have to tell him now, you see he is waiting for me." Maritza was content only when the mother opened the door and delivered Maritza's message to Pupu.

It should be noted that to start with Maritza uttered the anal word with great delight. Shortly afterward, when she was told this was not nice, the word Pupu was used to refer to her newly created companion who could do all the naughty things she did not dare do any longer, thus allowing her some vicarious gratification of forbidden impulses. Still later Pupu acquired additional roles that in part represented wishes she had in relation to her brother and father.

The case of Jimmy is included here by way of contrast. It illustrates how a very gifted child used a different type of fantasy activity to master a variety of situations in which other children might have created an imaginary companion. Jimmy was an extremely gifted four-year-old child. He had great verbal facility: at the age of eighteen months he already was in command of sixty words, and at two years he was quite capable of carrying on a real conversation.

Jimmy had shown no interest in teddy bears or dolls until his second birthday, when his mother was about six months pregnant. When his first baby sister Julia was born, he became very attached to such toys and always wanted one as a companion. He showed no particular preference for anyone of his many gollies, tigers, and teddies. All he wanted was to keep one of them with him for most of the day.

At bedtime Jimmy would say, "Teddy go sleep." He may in fact have placed several gollies and teddies in his cot, but he usually threw all of them out when he wanted to go to sleep. He was intensely jealous of his sister and frequently tried to interfere when his mother was nursing Julia. He had learned from experience that noises made Julia break off feeding and sometimes cry. Armed with this knowledge, he would come bouncing into the room where his mother was trying to feed the baby, shouting, "Let's make a noise, Teddy," while he and teddy proceeded to bounce up and down the bed, pretending to be "lions." It should be noted that he always use one of his real teddies or gollies for this purpose and never resorted to an imaginary companion.

Some time later Jimmy was trying to sort out whom he could marry. He also wondered whether his grandfather (a widower) could marry a student lodger living in their house. He finally produced his two gollies and asked that one be dressed as a boy and the other as a girl. He had them married and demanded that they make some golly babies. When he was three he met Jennie, a three-and-a-half-year-old girl. He saw her altogether on three or four occasions and they got on very well together. At first he asked, for example, where Jennie was when she was not in the block of flats where he lived (she came there only to visit her grandparents). Where did she live? Could he go there? He wanted to see her very badly. Finally, he stated that he was Jennie. This represented an identification with the lost object, a mechanism that he frequently used in dealing with losses.

A similar situation developed with another little girl, Katie, whom he saw only very rarely. For months, two or three times a day he demanded to be told a story that had to include Jennie and Katie. During this period he often said that he and his sister were Jennie and Katie, "two sisters living with their parents."

Still later a cousin, about the same age as Jimmy, visited for a few days. After Alexander's departure Jimmy was for two days several times close to tears. By the third day he brightened up after he told his mother that he now was Alexander and should be called by that name.

Jimmy had always liked books, and at about two and a half began to be interested in the contents of the stories rather than the pictures illustrating them. He enjoyed acting the stories over and over again. He became Tom the Kitten and assigned different roles and names to his mother, father, sister, and various visitors. He became extremely annoyed if he was not always addressed as Tom the Kitten or by the name of the character he was impersonating at the moment. Similarly, the father, mother, sister, etc., had to be addressed by their role names. In turn, he became Percy (the small engine), James (the red engine), and a variety of other characters.

Jimmy's attempt to master through play and fantasy those situations that he found difficult to handle could also be seen in his personification of Pepito. Pepito was "a bad hat" because he did not know how to make friends with girls and went about it in all the wrong ways. At this time Jimmy was most anxious to relate to other children, but found it nearly impossible to do so. Jimmy then asked his mother to invite some girls so that he could learn how to make friends with them. He frequently pretended to have friends around to play. When his mother mentioned in the morning that she had invited two children to come to tea, he would immediately pretend, "The doorbell is ringing! Come and see who it is. Come on in! Mother, we are having a tea party for all our friends." He would then bounce around the room, playing games with these "friends."

Yet, as soon as the real ones came, he began to scream because they touched his toys or even because their mothers started to talk to his mother. Yet, after practicing this fantasy game for some time, he did overcome his difficulties in relating to other children.

Imaginary companions are very frequently used as scapegoats, the recipients of all the badness and negative impulses of the child. This mechanism of externalization is seen more frequently in the young child than in older ones. To externalize, five to six-year-old children generally select a "real" child or an *ad hoc* imaginary one, but usually not an *imaginary companion*. In the young child, the imaginary companion seems to represent a prestage or precursor of externalizing onto a real object. This process is probably favored by the very young child's belief in magic, omnipotence, and his animistic conception of the world.

Selma Fraiberg (1959) described this use of the imaginary companion very vividly. She says, the child "acquires a number of companions, imaginary ones, who personify his Vices like characters in a morality play. (The Virtues he keeps to himself. Charity, Good Works, Truth, Altruism, all dwell in harmony within him.) Hate, Selfishness, Uncleanliness, Envy and a host of other evils are cast out like devils and forced to obtain other hosts. . . . When Daddy's pipes are broken, no one is more indignant than the two-year-old son who is under suspicion. 'Gerald, did you break daddy's pipes?' he demands to know" (p. 141).

As Fraiberg points out, although the child knows that Gerald is an invention of his, he achieves a number of gains in this way. First, he tries to avoid criticism from the parents for his misdeeds and unacceptable impulses. Second, he can maintain his self-love. Third, though he cannot yet control his impulses, he addresses the imaginary companion as a naughty boy is addressed by his parents. He shows in this roundabout way the emergence of a self-critical attitude, which eventually will enable him to control his impulses.

One can hardly avoid the impression that in such cases the imaginary companion acts as a "developmental buffer," that is, as something that mitigates for the child's primitive ego what is at times an impossible situation. The young child acts on impulses whose strength can override his primitive and precariously defended ego at a time when he is already aware of the parental displeasure occasioned by some of his actions. Thus, by means of the imaginary companion, he strikes a compromise that makes the situation more tolerable for his helpless ego and temporarily restores some balance. Perhaps we will be less inclined to underestimate the value of the imaginary companion if we take into account that many of the controls that we demand of the very young child are often beyond his limited capacities. In this respect we can again observe definite similarities with the role played by fantasying and fantasies in later life. Both are used in the attempt to solve conflicts and to restore, at least transitorily, the inner equilibrium before excessive stress forces a path into symptom formation, regression, or other disturbances.

Other examples suggest that a few children use the imaginary companion as part of an attempt to prolong their own feelings of omnipotence and control. For a few, the imaginary companion is a necessary, intermediate step before they can transfer, at least in certain areas, control to their parents while simultaneously accepting limitations to their own previously omnipotent feelings (which now have to be ascribed to the parents). This move from the child's belief in his own omnipotence to a belief in the parent's omnipotence is, as we know, a slow, gradual and difficult process, the intimate nature of which still escapes us. I suspect that in this achievement fantasying and the world of fantasies play a more significant role than is generally ascribed to them.

Not infrequently the imaginary companion is an impersonation of the child's primitive ego ideals, ideals that may be beyond his reach. The companion is good, clever, strong, clean, unaggressive, lovable, etc. This function of the imaginary companion can occasionally be observed in children who for a variety of reasons feel rejected. By endowing the companion with all the attributes the child lacks, he can vicariously participate in the companion's loving relationship with parents. Occasionally too, the imaginary companion is used as a weapon for defiance and provocation, as a vehicle of the negative aspects of the young child's ambivalence, etc.

Feelings of loneliness, neglect, and rejection frequently motivate the child to create imaginary companions. In his sample of forty children, Svendsen (1934) found that 55 percent of the children were "only" children at the time they created the companion. Many of the examples given by Bender and Vogel (1941) show a clear relationship between the imaginary companion and loneliness, neglect or rejection. Thus, Charles, a ten-and-a-half-year-old colored boy, said: "They [the imaginary companions in the form of a brother and sister] come when I am very lonely, not when I am playing with the boys. . . . They are a great comfort to me when I am all alone" (p. 59).

Several of our own examples also illustrate this point. The obvious importance of loneliness for the creation of imaginary companions may have induced several authors to note the frequency with which they disappear when the child finds suitable real companions. Green (1922) found that this fantasy usually vanishes when the child goes to school. He explained the imaginary companion phenomenon as part of an unsatisfied instinct of gregariousness that is fulfilled by the friendships established at school. Nevertheless, as we have seen, the imaginary companion owes its existence to a great variety of factors; therefore, it can be expected to disappear at entry into school only in those cases where it arose as the result of "loneliness" and for no other reason. Furthermore, the imaginary companion can frequently be observed in children who are by no means lonely, as I hope to show below.

In several of our cases the child developed imaginary companions immediately after the birth of a sibling. Tony, ten years old, was refered to the Hampstead Clinic because his teacher complained that he was "terribly dreamy and not with it." As a result his schoolwork was not up to standard. At that time he was suffering from sleep difficulties. The history of Tony's imaginary companion was as follows:

Tony was about three years old when his first sibling, a boy, was born. He was totally unprepared for this event. When Tony saw the baby for the first time, he looked away and from then on continued to ignore the baby. Immediately after the brother's birth Tony pretended to have an imaginary friend by the name of "Dackie," with whom he played and talked for hours at a time. Dackie was around most of the day, getting up in the morning with Tony and going to bed when Tony did. Dackie remained with Tony until he was five years old. Yet, at the age of ten, Tony still remembered Dackie, and when he was reminded of his imaginary companion, he laughed in a shy way.

Caroline was about three years, eight months, when her brother Barry was born. Shortly thereafter Caroline invented an imaginary playmate called "Dooley." At first the mother paid little attention to this, but she became increasingly concerned when this playmate took up more and more of Caroline's time and thought. The mother felt that this preoccupation was "beyond the realm of make-believe." Caroline attributed many of her actions to Dooley's suggestions and during the day would spend hours talking to "her." Dooley also was a girl, a fact in which the mother recognized a compensatory factor, for Caroline had wanted a sister, not a brother.

Dooley would tell Caroline "to eat dinner with a spoon and fork because it is quicker." In the beginning Dooley was a little girl, presumably like Caroline, but later Caroline said that Dooley was growing up "like her mother."

Later on, Caroline had other imaginary companions such as "Feeler," who was a big girl, and "Jane," whose characteristics were not known to us. These three, Dooley, Feeler, and Jane, were permanent members of the household, while several additional characters visited each day.

When Caroline was tested at the Clinic, she told the psychologist that "Dooley does not want to do any more." Furthermore, she asked the psychologist what *her* Dooley's name was, taking it for granted that the psychologist also had an imaginary companion.

Graham was about two years, eleven months when his brother Peter was born. Shortly afterward, within a period of two months, Graham created an imaginary companion who was also called Peter. Graham, who had expected a playmate, was very disappointed by the size of the baby. He had resented his mother's absence during the delivery, and had clearly shown his dislike of the newcomer by telling his mother: "Put it back in your tummy." When Peter was born, Graham was given a doll called Becky. Becky soon was involved in the accounts Graham gave of his doings with his imaginary playmate "Peter." They were shortly joined by another imaginary companion, a "baby Peter," and thereafter Graham spoke of "my two boys" as he had heard his mother do. He included his companions in all preparations that were made for outings and in all plans for spending the day at home. While Graham openly talked about his companions with members of the family, he did not refer to them in the presence of other people.

On the basis of such examples it is tempting to assume that some sensitive children find the mother's limited withdrawal of attention (that follows the birth of another child) more than they can bear and that they react to it by creating a more faithful and reliable figure in the form of the imaginary companion. These children may well feel lonely because after the arrival of the newcomer the previously undivided attention of the mother must be shared.

Where the memory of an imaginary companion is revived in the analysis of an adult patient, it is instructive to see it in all its complexities, fulfilling more than one need experienced by the child. For example, in the following material we can see that it simultaneously serves the purpose of correcting painful reality, denying and relieving loneliness, and assuaging guilt.

The patient, a man in his fifties, was the fifth of seven children. He had one older sister, three older brothers, and two younger ones. In the fourth year of his psychoanalytic treatment he became much concerned with the fact that, whenever he thought he had found a friend, it did not take long for him to experience a deep disappointment, as the friend about whom he had been so happy at first turned against him. The relationship soon deteriorated, he was enraged about being "let down," no longer wanted, and he found himself as friendless as before.

At this point he mentioned that as a child he had had a fantasy brother. He had been smaller and younger than himself, and totally blind. He thought that he had kept this fantasy going for about two years, between the ages of eight and ten. Work on this imaginary brother brought to light the following main aspects. The patient had been severely disturbed about the arrival of a brother when he was eighteen months old. This experience had been revived and more clearly remembered again two years later when another baby brother was born.

The mother had given each of the seven children all her attention and love as long as they were small. She adored babies, would never hand over their care to anyone else, but as soon as the next child came this happy state was suddenly brought to an end and she turned all her interest and care to the newcomer. It seems that by the time the sixth and seventh child arrived she no longer felt able to give the older ones enough interest until much later when she had stopped having babies.

After a phase of great unhappiness and jealousy, in his second to fourth years, the patient developed a reaction formation against his jealousy of the younger brothers: he became a fatherly older brother, trying to make them into his friends, hoping that they would follow him, love him, and be with him constantly. This seems to have been a very successful and happy time at first, when the younger brothers were delighted about his attention and willing to conform to his wishes. However, as they grew up, they refused to be ordered around as before. They freed themselves from their dependence on him and turned against him aggressively. He suffered intensely from "losing" them and tried more and more aggressively to regain control over them.

It is during these years that his "blind rages" occurred. Among his memories there was one in which he violently punched one of his brothers and was accused by the nurse of "nearly blinding him." It appears that the development of the fantasy about having an imaginary blind brother began soon thereafter. Its main features were:

The brother is younger, like his own brothers, but his blindness makes him totally dependent on him; he cannot go anywhere without him and never wants to leave him. Being with his older brother, walking with him, feeling his arm over his shoulders, or sitting close to him, is the happiest experience for the blind brother. There is no one else he wishes to be with, not anyone else who understands him as well. As they walk together they arouse everyone's attention. At first people say, "Look at the blind boy," but immediately afterward they say: "How fortunate he is to have this wonderful big brother, what an unusual child he is to be so good and helpful to his blind brother!" This part of the fantasy gave the patient the greatest satisfaction each time he thought of it, as it contained both the gratification of his exhibitionistic wishes—everyone looked—and the relief about his guilt for his destructive wishes, when he was praised for his kindness toward the younger brother.

A large part was played by the imaginary brother's constant presence, as the patient had felt extremely lonely among the crowd of children in the house. He had felt so hostile against them that he could hardly bear their company at times. To be alone had been especially threatening during and after the phase when he experienced the turning away of the younger brothers.

The "blind brother" also stood for the incapacitated aspect of himself. The defensive function of this fantasy became clear when the patient accepted his own regressive longing for dependence and saw that the wish to be wanted as a "blind child" by his father had been an important factor in retreating from his dangerous hostility against him.

In the role of the blind brother he also felt relief from his guilt about the fantasies of blinding the favorite brother whose "loss" had caused him intense pain.

The next example shows some aspects of the coping mechanisms that a little girl evolved as a reaction to a sudden change in her living conditions that also involved losses. She engaged in a continuous daydream involving the participation of a variety of subjects (animals and people), many of which acquired the status of imaginary companions.

Zeeta was one of the children at the Hampstead War Nurseries,[7] where she had been for eighteen months, from the age of seventeen months to three years. She was a colored baby girl whose cultural background was especially good. Zeeta was described as a delicate and gifted child whose emotional and intellectual development showed some unusually interesting features.

At the end of World War II Zeeta left the Nursery and went to live with her mother and a new father, a man she had met many times before. The first few weeks at home were difficult. Zeeta missed her nurse intensely and found it difficult to make friends with her new daddy. It was then that she began to play elaborate fantasy games. The mother reported that at three years, two months, Zeeta developed a new animal fantasy. "She has a brood of imaginary animals, cats and chickens which live with her and share all her activities. It is quite uncanny the way she looks at them, just as though

---

[7] The account here given of this case is a condensed version of the Fifth Half-Yearly Report (1949) of the Hampstead Nurseries (After Care) written by Dr. I. Hellman.

she could really see them. Often she tells me off for clumsily kicking
one of them or I have to lift them up over the pavement and am told
that 'they are too small, they can't manage.' " In her report Dr. Hellman wondered whether this child had replaced the group life at the
Hampstead Nursery by the imaginary chicks and cats that accompanied her everywhere and, for example, made her walks very similar to those she had taken with the other toddlers whom she had
had to leave at the Nursery.

In the ensuing weeks Zeeta's fantasies developed further, as the
mother reported: "The cats have gradually disappeared, but the
chickens have remained and a husband and father have been added.
The husband's name is Percy and the father's Ninny. They seem to
be very feeble characters; she only allows them to call at the back
door and, when asked about their occupation, she says: 'They do
washing up at the office where my Daddy works.' Sometimes they
bring rings and brooches to her, but they usually take them away
again. On the whole she treats them more like a burden or even a
liability, whereas the birds and cats she liked to care for and was
most loving with."

Until her fourth year Zeeta was surrounded by an ever-changing
population of small animals and tiny babies. They needed a great
deal of care and comfort and accompanied her everywhere. By that
time she had overcome her initial difficulties with her new father
and was on extremely good terms with him. The mother said: "She
absolutely idolizes her Daddy; it amuses me to see how her former
hostility has changed." Zeeta then had a husband, George, who
stayed with her for many months. During the second half of the
fourth year the mother wrote: "You will be interested to hear that
we now have a pony living with us. It has red ears, a red nose, and
red legs, and sleeps in the corner standing on two legs. Of course, he
accompanies us everywhere, buses included, but I can generally persuade him to go into my shopping bag when the bus is too full."

Anna Freud and Dorothy Burlingham concluded the report on
Zeeta by stating: "Life in a community, which to many young infants
is merely a burden, evidently stimulated Zeeta's fantasy life to an
unusual degree. . . . As Dr. Hellman remarked, these daydreams
seemed to reflect her early attitude to her small companions; they
reveal at the same time that this attitude was a motherly one. In

comforting the other infants, in helping them and in looking after their needs, Zeeta seems to have given the others the intimate care and protection which she missed owing to the absence of her own mother."

The following example is particularly instructive in that it shows how a child at a time of serious stress in her life managed to create an imaginary companion who helped her avoid regression and symptom formation. This was in sharp contrast to the reaction of her two older siblings who responded to the same traumatic situation with regression and symptom formation. In this case the imaginary companion fulfilled the same role as that ascribed by Freud (1908) to many daydreams: they are temporary measures compensating for a frustrating or difficult external reality and prevent the development of a full-blown neurosis. That this child's imaginary companion fulfilled the same function is not as surprising as it may seem if we consider that this phenomenon is a special type of fantasy with specific characteristics that distinguish it from other daydreams. In her case, the imaginary companion served a variety of functions such as superego auxiliary, scapegoat, for externalization, etc.

Miriam was the youngest of three children; her sister Laura was eight years old; her brother, nine and a half years old. The parents were a highly intelligent, young, professional couple.

The imaginary companion, Susan, appeared when Miriam was five years old shortly after her parents divorced each other and the mother suffered a mental breakdown that required several months of hospitalization. The children were sent to their grandparents. At first they lived in the grandparents' cottage, but they were soon moved to a caravan (with an au pair) just outside the grandparents' cottage. The situation was further aggravated by the fact that at that time in her life Miriam was extremely attached to her father. The latter left soon afterward for America, where he has since remarried. The two older children reacted to the events described with different overt symptoms such as school difficulties, sleeping disturbances, and regression (bed wetting), while Miriam developed no such symptoms but created Susan, her imaginary companion, who stayed with her for almost nine months.

Miriam had been very close to Laura, but with the advent of Susan she withdrew markedly from her sister, much to the latter's distress. Laura would beg Miriam to play with her. Miriam, engaged in lengthy conversations with Susan, would reply: "Leave us alone." In contrast to Laura, the elder brother took no notice of the imaginary companion.

Miriam was described as a competent, well-organized, active, and friendly child. Nevertheless, during the difficult period at home she had to attend a new school where she was unable to make friends. Further, according to the reports, she was very reality-oriented and had a clear knowledge of what is reality and what is fantasy, but she always tended to deal with difficult experiences by temporary withdrawal into intense play with her dolls. She usually emerged from this preoccupation after some time and re-entered her active life at school. She repeated this behavior after a recent visit with her father in the States, which had been more disturbing to her two older siblings than to her.

Miriam had always been devoted to the maternal grandmother. She used to ask her mother to be allowed to stay "at the hotel with Gran," taking her doll and Susan with her. The grandmother entered into the fantasy of the imaginary playmate and consequently heard a good deal about Susan. For instance, when asked whether she had slept well, Miriam would reply in the affirmative, adding: "Susan slept well too. In the night she was cold and I put an extra blanket on her bed." At meals she might say, "We have to think about Susan [who might be hungry]. . . . Ah, well, never mind. I will make her some dinner later." She and Susan would go off to play together in the woods for the afternoon. At other times she talked for hours with Susan. Miriam made it clear that Susan had no family and belonged exclusively to her.

It was obvious that Miriam mothered Susan, thus restoring in fantasy, at least to some degree, her earlier relationship to her now withdrawn, depressed, and absent mother (who was hospitalized). That Susan was created to cope with the puzzling events and the sudden absence of the mother was further confirmed by the many conversations in which Miriam asked her imaginary playmate what had happened to her mother. She was heard saying, "What happened to Mummy?" and "Mummy wants us to do———." We do not know what factors in Miriam's personality determined her choice of this specific fantasy as a way of coping with the stress situation; nor do we

know why, in her case, this was a sufficient and apparently very successful device.

The imaginary companion also embodied some superego aspects
and in this sense occasionally took the mother's place. Miriam would
frequently say: "I have to consult Susan about doing [whatever it
may have been that was on her mind] or "Susan would like me
to———."

By means of the mechanism of externalization[8] Susan also became an outlet for feelings that Miriam could not have expressed
otherwise. For example, she said: "I think Susan is very unhappy
these days" or "Susan has no family, poor Susan." At other times
Miriam stated: "Susan is terribly angry, she hates her teacher. She
even hates me. Of course, I am angry with her too, but we will make
it up later." I have mentioned earlier that Miriam found the change
of school when her parents separated especially difficult. At that
time she said: "I hear Susan. She doesn't want to go to school," thus
expressing her own difficulties by attributing them to Susan. In
fact, with the exception of this brief period, Miriam enjoyed and
loved school.

Miriam's imaginary companion faded away when she acquired a
very close friend at school. Now, nearly four years later, Miriam says
of her imaginary companion, "I invented her . . . of course, she was
real."

The following example shows clearly the simultaneous presence
of an imaginary companion and a transitional object.

Mary, a young adult, had no conscious recollection of her imaginary companion. Her knowledge of it came from stories her mother
had told her at different times. In contrast, she had clear memories
of a rag doll named Whoopee, her transitional object.

The imaginary companion (whose name was forgotten) appeared
when Mary was two to three years old. At that time the family consisted of the father, the mother, and three children, Mary, Paula
(age ten), and Eva (age eleven). Mary was actually an only child;
the two older girls in the family were close relatives of the parents
who adopted these two children when they became orphans. When

---

[8] Sperling (1954) pointed out that the "child finds it easier to project his own fears
and hopes onto the imaginary companion and to communicate them in this form
instead of confessing that they are his own fears and wishes" (p. 252).

Mary was born, Paula was already a member of the household. Eva joined the family two and a half years later—at about the time when Mary created her imaginary companion. Unfortunately, the exact sequence of events could not be ascertained.

Due to the gap in the ages between Mary and the two older girls, on the one hand, and the closeness in ages of Paula and Eva, on the other, the latter naturally tended to play together and to exclude Mary. As an adult, Mary distinctly remembered playing by herself while Paula and Eva played together.

When the imaginary companion made its appearance Mary's mother was under severe strain and perhaps somewhat depressed following a quick succession of several serious accidents, illnesses, and various deaths in her immediate family. Mary probably felt very lonely at this point because the mother's attention was concentrated on nursing relatives.

The mother remembered that the imaginary companion had been a little girl with whom Mary played in the garden and the house. The imaginary playmate had to have a place at the table and be given meals; however, Mary did not take her along on outings. The mother was not worried about the imaginary playmate and gladly provided food, etc. The imaginary companion began to disappear about a year or so later when Mary acquired two real companions. One was a girl of her own age, and the other a boy about a year older; both lived near her.

What is of special interest in this case is that throughout the period in which the imaginary companion fantasy was active Mary also had a transitional object, the rag doll called "Whoopee" which she had been given when she was a baby and which she remembered very well. Whoopee had acquired her name by virtue of the way in which she had been mistreated. While throwing her up in the air, Mary would yell: "Whoopee." She kept Whoopee until she was six or seven years of age, in contrast to her imaginary companion whom she kept for only one year. It should be noted that the transitional object was important before, during, and after the phase of the imaginary companion.

This example, as others, shows that an imaginary companion appears in situations of special stress or of a traumatic character. Murphy (1962) described the stress situation during which Sam, three

years, three months old, created his imaginary companion "Woody."
Sam had had an unfortunate accident in the bathroom. The tip
of his finger had come off when the door was shut on it. The day
the stitches had to be removed the doctor proceeded forcibly to take
the screaming child away from the mother. Murphy says:

> As an outgrowth of this separation situation a little elf named
> "Woody" appeared in Sam's fantasy. On August 22 Sam told
> me about him—that Woody was with him in the treatment room
> because I couldn't be there. In the next three weeks Woody
> turned up in many different situations and served many different
> purposes—sometimes a companion, sometimes a helper, some-
> times a scapegoat:
>
>> Playing doctor, Sam said to me, "You take your medicine
>> and you won't have to have penicillin." "You'll have to stay
>> in the hospital all day and all night." When I asked him
>> how I could manage to do that he told me there was a little
>> elf, "Woody," who would stay with me, just like it was at Dr.
>> H's office—Woody was there with him because I couldn't be
>> with him.
>>
>> At Dr. H's office he cried hard when leaving me and
>> while soaking his finger—this was one of the times when he
>> had gone to sleep on the bus on the way to the office. Before
>> putting a bandage back on today, Dr. H held up Sam's two
>> little fingers next to each other to compare the length. Later
>> Sam asked about this, "Why did Dr. H *measure* my finger?"
>> "Why is it pink at the tip?"
>>
>> I asked him why he had made a fuss at the doctor's office,
>> and he said "Because Woody wasn't there—he was on va-
>> cation."
>>
>> Later, when we were making brownies he said, "Woody
>> used to make brownies when he was a little boy—he told me
>> that up at Dr. H's office."
>
> The creation of such a satisfying externalized image to stay
> with him at the time his mother was forced to leave suggests
> both the importance of the strong support from mother, and the
> strength in his own struggle to maintain the feeling of support
> during her absence. Later he said to his mother one day, "You
> know Mommy, Woody was really you" [p. 124f.].

Some time later when he was introduced to nursery school,
he showed considerable hesitation and uncertainty and was overwhelmed by the large group of children. Murphy described how

"Once in a while his imaginary elf-friend, 'Woody,' showed up; on October 3, 'Woody was at school today—nurse said he didn't have to open his mouth—he's still a little shy,' but he didn't seem to be needed much of the time" (p. 64). "He used his mother as an anchor to familiarity, for help, as a playmate, and as a love-object during the early period of getting acquainted in the new situation. His imaginary companion 'Woody,' an elf, also helped him" (p. 66).

I have earlier stated that the imaginary companion phenomenon is a special type of fantasy (and fantasying) that has all the characteristics of daydreams. Like ordinary daydreams, the imaginary companion fantasy is an attempt at wish fulfillment of one sort or another, is ruled by the pleasure principle, can ignore the reality principle, and need not be reality adapted, yet the fantasying person remains fully aware of the unreality of the fantasies that are being indulged in. In other words, reality testing remains unimpaired.

Nevertheless, there are a few significant features that are typical of the imaginary companion phenomenon and which are not necessarily characteristic of other forms of fantasy. First, although the imaginary companion is an attempt at wish fulfillment, the type and quality of the wishes involved, especially in the case of the younger child, are different from those that give rise to fantasies in older children. In the latter the wishes are concerned with the gratification of instinctual impulses or specific component instincts that have become conflictful. In many young children, the imaginary companion fills the emptiness, neglect, loneliness, or rejection which the child seems to be experiencing. In this there is nothing conflictful in the neurotic sense. The child is claiming what is after all a genuine right of his—attention, love, and companionship. For this reason he probably can talk quite freely about the imaginary companion, a fact that is in sharp contrast with the reluctance of older children to communicate their fantasies, which are so jealously guarded precisely because they involve impulses that are conflictful (in the neurotic sense) and objectionable. Consequently, they must be kept as secrets. This difference in attitude is one of the most significant differences between the imaginary companion fantasy and other fantasies. While other fantasies can be vivid and intense, that of the imaginary companion has a special quality in this respect. This can perhaps be better understood if we take into account the

younger child's animistic conception of the world and his strong belief in magic and in the omnipotence of thoughts. This does not
imply that even the young child is not aware of the unreality of the
companion; rather I wish to emphasize that in spite of this awareness and coexisting with it, these fantasies have a special quality of
vividness and reality for him.

A related factor is the frequency with which the imaginary companion seems to occupy a physical space in the actual world of the
child, while other fantasies involving objects are better and quite
clearly contained within the realm of imagination and do not require a quasi-physical presence.

We should also note that an intense fantasy life frequently implies a withdrawal from the unpleasant real world into a more satisfactory inner world. This use of fantasying usually also involves a
certain withdrawal from the world of real objects. In the imaginary
companion fantasy, however, the initial withdrawal from the real
world of objects is quickly followed by a return to reality and to
the object world. Having found a new solution, the child brings his
imaginary companion back into his real life and tries to have it
integrated with and accepted by his object world.

I shall end by quoting from Selma Fraiberg (1959):

> There is great misunderstanding today about the place of fan-
> tasy in the small child's life. Imaginary companions have fallen
> into ill repute among many educators and parents. Jan's "Laugh-
> ing Tiger" would be hastily exiled in many households. The
> notion has got around that imaginary companions are evidence
> of "insecurity," "withdrawal" and a latent neurosis. The imagi-
> nary companion is supposed to be a poor substitute for real
> companions and it is felt that the unfortunate child who pos-
> sesses them should be strongly encouraged to abandon them in
> favor of real friends. Now, of course, if a child of any age
> abandons the real world and cannot form human ties, if a child
> is unable to establish meaningful relationships with persons and
> prefers his imaginary people, we have some cause for concern.
> But we must not confuse the neurotic uses of imagination with
> the healthy, and the child who employs his imagination and the
> people of his imagination to solve his problems is a child who is
> working for his own mental health. He can maintain his human
> ties and his good contact with reality while he maintains his
> imaginary world. Moreover, it can be demonstrated that the

child's contact with the real world is *strengthened* by his periodic excursions into fantasy. It becomes easier to tolerate the frustrations of the real world and to accede to the demands of reality if one can restore himself at intervals in a world where the deepest wishes can achieve imaginary gratification [p. 22f.].

BIBLIOGRAPHY

Bender, L. & Vogel, F. (1941), Imaginary Companions of Children. *Amer. J. Orthopsychiat*, 11:56-65.

Burlingham, D. (1945), The Fantasy of Having a Twin. *This Annual*, 1:205-210.

Fraiberg, S. (1959), *The Magic Years*. New York: Scribners.

Freud, A. (1936), *The Ego and the Mechanisms of Defense*. New York: International Universities Press, rev. ed., 1966.

Freud, S. (1908), Creative Writers and Day-Dreaming. *Standard Edition*, 9:141-153. London: Hogarth Press, 1959.

—— (1909), Analysis of a Phobia in a Five-Year-Old Boy. *Standard Edition*, 10:3-149. London: Hogarth Press, 1955.

—— (1910 [1909]), Five Lectures on Psycho-Analysis. *Standard Edition*, 11:3-56. London: Hogarth Press, 1957.

Green, G. H. (1922), *Psychoanalysis in the Classroom*. New York: Putnam's.

Hall, G. S. (1907), *Aspects of Child Life and Education*. Boston: Green.

Hammerman, S. (1965), Conceptions of Superego Development. *J. Amer. Psa. Assn.*, 13:320-355.

Harriman, P. L. (1937), Some Imaginary Companions of Older Subjects. *Amer. J. Orthopsychiat.*, 7:368-370.

Harrison, S. I., Hess, J. H., & Zrull, J. P. (1963), Paranoid Reactions in Children. *J. Amer. Acad. Child Psychiat.*, 2:677-692.

Harvey, N. A. (1918), *Imaginary Playmates and Other Mental Phenomena of Children*. Ypsilanti, Mich.: Michigan State Normal College.

Hurlock, E. B. & Burstein, W. (1932), The Imaginary Playmate. *J. Genet. Psychol.*, 41:380-392.

Jersild, A. T., Markey, F. V., & Jersild, C. L. (1933), Children's Fears, Dreams, Wishes. *Child Developm. Monogr.*, 12. New York: Teachers College, Columbia University.

Kirkpatrick, E. A. (1929), *Fundamentals of Child Study*. New York: Macmillan.

Murphy, L. B., et al. (1962), *The Widening World of Children*. New York: Basic Books.

Nagera, H. (1966), *Early Childhood Disturbances, the Infantile Neurosis, and the Adulthood Disturbances*. New York: International Universities Press.

Sperling, O. E. (1954), An Imaginary Companion Representing a Prestage of the Superego. *This Annual*, 9:252-258.

Svendsen, M. (1934), Children's Imaginary Companions. *Arch. Neurol. Psychiat.*, 2:985-999.

Vostrovsky, C. (1895), A Study of Imaginary Companions. *Education*, 15:383-398.

TERRIFYING EYES

A Visual Superego Forerunner

ANDREW PETO, M.D. (New York)

Many years ago a patient of mine, a man in his late twenties, had the following dream as he approached the end of a rather successful analysis: He was lying on a bed or operating table and looked at his wide-open abdominal cavity which was filled with his bowels and his liver. Somehow, at the same time, he was also another person, surgeon or prosector, who coolly looked at his entrails and pulled them onto the table or bed. His body was not clearly delineated and it was blurred and fused with the other person, who might or might not have been he himself. There was no sign of anxiety in the dream or after awakening.

I bypass here the dream material that served as a useful basis for working through once again several of the patient's essential conflicts. I want to stress only that the analysis of this dream served to clarify important adaptive functions of the ego, contributed to the strengthening of the self, and proved to be useful in gaining territory from threatening archaic superego elements. Thus, this dream indicated an important final step in the integration of those changes that are the inherent mark of successful termination.

Since making this observation, I have repeatedly come upon the same type of dream toward the end of a successful analysis; that is to say, dreams which show in their manifest content a severe disturbance of the dreamer's own body image, like bizarre dismemberment, disembowelling hallucinations or random transpositions of various

Presented at the Fall Meeting of the American Psychoanalytic Association, December, 1968.

Clinical Professor of Psychiatry, Albert Einstein College of Medicine, New York, N.Y.

body parts. In contrast to my first observation, however, there usually is manifest anxiety in the dream. I have the impression that when these dreams occur at the end of an analysis, they always indicate a high degree of trust which the patient has developed in the strength of his ego as well as in the protective role of the analyst. This type of dream invariably signals that a reality-adapted ego and a corresponding self image have firmly established themselves vis-à-vis a hitherto oppressive superego that contained elements of a rather archaic nature.

I must add here that the same type of dream may occur in the early phases of an analysis. At this stage, however, it may have a different meaning, which is not always easy to assess. The experienced clinician will then suspect that the patient is suffering from a psychosis or psychotic character disorder, though he will not be able to establish a firm differential diagnosis unless there are other convincing indicators pointing in the direction of psychosis. Moreover, even patients who suffer only from a neurotic illness may present this type of dream in the early phases of their analyses and may manifest the same anxieties as psychotic patients.

In view of this diagnostic uncertainty I always refrain from going into the analysis of this dream if it appears in the early phases of treatment. However, I consider it propitious if it is dreamed in the terminal phases of a satisfactory treatment.

I

This briefly sketched "struggle" between ego and superego is, of course, an oversimplified presentation of a complicated, stratified process that is an integral part of the transference neurosis. It also represents one aspect of what I have previously described as the ego's fragmentizing function, i.e., a process that aims at the extreme splintering of the dynamic complexes of drives, object representations, and affects permanently or loosely connected with them. This function, presumably, precedes and accompanies all the known defense mechanisms and indeed is, I believe, the necessary precondition which makes them possible.

I have assumed and attempted to demonstrate in the frame of the transference neurosis (1961) and also in the course of a single session

(1963) that the ego persistently aims at fragmenting various facets of the internalized object representations and different layers of the superego, in particular the archaic ones that emerge in the course of the analytic process.

I have shown (1962) that the same fragmentizing ego function operates against emerging archaic superego layers in the course of dreaming as well as in the course of the analysis of a dream. I used the Irma dream as a model for this demonstration of one aspect of the dream work, as it was presented in Freud's analysis of the "specimen dream."

These observations and assumptions enhanced my interest in dismemberment dreams because some of their characteristics could be conceptualized as a fragmentation process which, combined with other defenses of a complicated nature, demonstrated the struggle between ego and superego in the final, critical phase of the analytic process.

II

Two groups of phenomena have features that correspond to these dreams: (1) a variety of altered ego states; and (2) certain manifest dreams.

1. Depersonalization, derealization, and similar ego states as well as hypnopompic and hypnagogic phenomena (the best known being the Isakower phenomenon) are in this category. Moreover, a variety of regressions occurring in and outside of analysis may lead to severe fluctuations of the body image, including its dismemberment and dissolution.

However, the dream research of the last twelve years points to a fact that may prove a significant difference between phenomena of the REM state and those of the waking and awakening-falling asleep states. Although the latter show structural and economic as well as dynamic and adaptive parallels with the dreams under discussion, we have to acknowledge that "dreaming is the subjective concomitant of a pervasive and distinctive physiological state, a third basic biological mode of existence, of the same order yet different from sleep or waking" (Snyder, 1965, p. 377). A recent statement by Ernest Hartmann (1968) is even more sharply formulated: "On the

basis of the ontogenetic and phylogenetic relationships, it appears
that the sleep-dream cycle is one of the basic metabolism-linked
cycles of the mammalian body" (p. 282).

2. I wish to distinguish dreams in which the dismemberment
occurs to the dreamer's body while he is looking on from dreams in
which the dissolution or dismemberment or severe disturbance of
the body image occurs to somebody else while the dreamer looks on.
Freud's *"non vixit"* dream is an example of the latter. It may be of
interest that I found only three publications dealing with this type
of dream (Hitschmann, 1914; Winterstein, 1954; and Pollock and
Muslin [1962], who report dreams under anesthesia, i.e., abnormal
conditions of sleep). To some extent the Irma dream belongs in this
category ("curly structures" in Irma's mouth).

While denial, splitting, and fragmentation are used in both types
of dreams, the style of the dream work distinguishes them. In the
dreams in which the dreamer's own body is dismembered, the dream
work is characterized by the following striking features: (1) the dissolution of the boundaries of the ego and of the self; (2) a fluid and
reversible transposition of parts of the body image; (3) a resulting
general feeling of eeriness, which pervades the whole dream or at
least part of it. These, I believe, should be taken into consideration
and be registered as specific indicators of the ego-superego relationship at the time of dreaming.

III

I have checked rather thoroughly the German and English analytic literature[1] and have found two works with reports of similar
dreams; *The Interpretation of Dreams* (1900), where the dreamer's
own body is subjected to some form of dismemberment while the
dreamer watches what is going on, and a publication by Flournoy
(1920).

In Freud's book, one is his own "strangely enough" dream, the

---

[1] Apart from the well-known and more important books on dreams I consulted
all volumes of the following periodicals: *Zentralblatt für Psychoanalyse, Jahrbuch für
psychoanalytische und psychopathologische Forschung; Imago; Internationale Zeit-
schrift für Psychoanalyse; International Journal of Psycho-Analysis; Psychoanalytic
Quarterly; Journal of the American Psychoanalytic Association; This Annual.*

other is that of a chemist (added in 1909). I shall quote only those parts of Freud's own dream that are relevant to my discussion:

Old Brücke must have set me some task; STRANGELY ENOUGH, it related to a dissection of the lower part of my own body, my pelvis and legs, which I saw before me as though in the dissecting-room, but without noticing their absence in myself and also without a trace of any gruesome feeling. Louise N. was standing beside me and doing the work with me. The pelvis had been eviscerated and was visible now in its superior, now in its inferior, aspect, the two being mixed together. Thick flesh-coloured protuberances (which, in the dream itself, made me think of haemorrhoids) could be seen. Something which lay over it and was like crumpled silver-paper had also to be carefully fished out. I was then once more in possession of my legs and was making my way through the town. [The dream continues to relate several events and finally ends with:] I awoke in a mental fright [p. 452f.; italics omitted].

Freud's dream indicates, according to his own analysis of it, a definite step in overcoming archaic superego prohibitions: "I woke up in a *'mental fright,'* even after the successful emergence of the idea that children may perhaps achieve what their father has failed to—." Afterward Freud was able to follow the principles of a conscious, social superego representation, i.e., those of "old Brücke," and publish *The Interpretation of Dreams.* This dream of Freud's belongs to exactly the same category as those I observed in my patients at the end of a successful analysis and it points to the same ego achievements.

It is of particular significance that Freud dreamed this dream in the final stages of his self-analysis and that the dream dealt with problems the solutions of which provided the final impetus to go ahead with the publication of the dream book and to reveal his self-analysis.

The dissection meant the self-analysis which I was carrying out, as it were, in the publication of this present book about dreams— a process which had been so distressing to me in reality that I had postponed the printing of the finished manuscript for more than a year. A wish then arose that I might get over this feeling of distaste; hence it was that I had no gruesome feeling ['*Grauen*'] in the dream. But I should also have been very glad to miss growing grey—'*Grauen*' in the other sense of the word. I was already growing quite grey, and the grey of my hair was another reminder that I must not delay any longer. And, as we have seen, the thought that I should have to leave it to my children to reach the goal of my difficult journey forced its way through to representation at the end of the dream [p. 477f.].

[Earlier in the analysis of the dream, Freud had said:] I reflected on the amount of self-discipline it was costing me to offer the public even my book upon dreams—I should have to give away so much of my own private character in it [p. 453].

And then Freud referred to Brücke who, in the "*non vixit*" dream, had been characterized by his "terrible blue eyes"—i.e., as the threatening, demanding idealized figure of Freud's younger years when he was admonished and punished by this great man.

Schur, in his paper on the Irma dream (1966), stresses that Freud's liberation from Fliess, who somehow was functioning in the role of the analyst in the transference of Freud's self-analysis, was accomplished at the end of this analysis. The patient of this self-analysis was caught, as all our patients are, in the vise of the demanding *and* forbidding superego.

In some of my patients, this liberation manifested itself in a final adaptation of sexuality and aggressive trends to inner and outer reality; in other cases, it freed energies for better professional adjustments or resulted in a more harmonious balance between desires and capabilities. In still other cases it led to an enhanced sublimatory capacity that had been impeded by archaic superego pressures in the past. In all cases, however, this liberation marked the final integration of those results that were achieved in the course of the treatment.[2]

"A Chemist's Dream" should be mentioned here for the purpose of illustrating a variation of dismemberment:

He was supposed to be making phenyl-magnesium-bromide. He *saw* [my italics] the apparatus with particular distinctness, but had substituted himself for the magnesium. He now found himself in a singularly unstable state. He kept saying to himself: 'This is all right, things are working, my feet are beginning to

[2] Hitschmann (1914) mentions that the analysis of a similar dream had liberated his patient from his father.

dissolve already, my knees are getting soft.' Then he put out his hand and felt his feet [p. 382; italics omitted].

The dream continues and after a state of anxiety-ridden "semi-sleep" is followed by a second dream.

IV

In these dreams, as illustrated by Freud's dream and by my own observations, an ever-present feature of the manifest dream is the prominence of "seeing."

We know very well the role that Brücke's "terrible blue eyes . . . which retained their striking beauty even in his old age" played in the most important formative years of Freud's scientific career. "No one who can remember the great man's *eyes* . . . and who has ever *seen him* in anger, will find it difficult to picture the young sinner's emotions" (1900, p. 422; my italics).

This "watching" or "being watched" represents the functional variation of Silberer's autosymbolic phenomenon (1909). Freud stresses that only the functional symbolism has its special role in dream formation.

I would not describe it as "functional" simply because his [a patient's] dream-thoughts related to his attitude in the treatment. Thoughts of that kind serve as "material" for the construction of dreams as anything else. It is hard to see why the thoughts of a person under analysis should not be concerned with his behaviour during treatment. The distinction between "material" and "functional" phenomena in Silberer's sense is of significance only where—as was the case in Silberer's well-known self-observations as he was falling asleep—there is an *alternative* between the subject's attention being directed *either* to some piece of thought-content present in his mind *or* to his own actual psychical state, and not where that state itself constitutes the content of his thoughts [p. 412f., n.].

A passage in "A Child Is Being Beaten" (1919) does not leave any doubt about the agency that exerts this watchdog function. "According to our present orientation in the structure of the ego, which is as yet uncertain, we should assign it to the agency in the mind which sets itself up as a critical conscience over and against the rest of the ego, which produces Silberer's functional phenomenon in dreams, and which cuts itself loose from the ego in delusions of being watched" (p. 194).

This "seeing" and "being seen" point to the role of the superego, which "watches" the self image and what is going on in other structures and organizations. The dreamer watches in the regressive somatic symbolization his entrails or other organs or limbs that are distortedly represented.

These dismemberment dreams combine both of Freud's criteria concerning the functional symbolism of "being watched" and "watching" on the one hand, and the actual "psychical state" of being critically "torn to pieces" by the observing agency, on the other hand.

V

I believe that this "psychical state" is a new edition of a particular developmental phase of the ego's struggle with an archaic superego forerunner. It may come about as a matter of course in various circumstances at any critical stage of life. It often appears in the final months of a relatively successful analysis when, in the frame of the transference, the working through reaches a stage where certain aspects or functions of the ego are liberated from the archaic shackles of the superego. This is, as it were, a variation of Freud's dictum (1933), "Where id was, there ego shall be"; where the most archaic, instinctually rooted layers of the superego prevailed, a more reality-adapted ego takes over.

As a result of the dreamer's somatic regression, this struggle is represented as a relationship between the body ego and the archaic superego symbolized by the onlooking eyes. The phenomenon functions in the frame of "being looked at" on the part of the regressed ego and "looking at" on the part of the regressed archaic superego representation. On the basis of my analytic material and that of Freud's published dream, it is my hypothesis that the looking, glaring eyes represent the threatening destroying superego in one of its archaic somatic forerunners: the destroying, annihilating eye before which there is no secret and which sees the inside, i.e., what is going on in one's own body.

When we find this representation in the manifest dream, it indicates an operating mode of poorly neutralized aggression that acts through both archaic ego *and* superego. In this instance the functional phenomenon is the combination of "looking at oneself" and of "being dismembered" at the same time. This complex relationship is embedded in the functioning of relatively unneutralized aggression, which is directed against the ego and the self by the superego, on the one hand, and against the superego by the ego, on the other hand.

The dreaming ego's defensive work against this superego action is expressed by the extreme splitting off of the body image from the watching eye that tears it to pieces. This in turn makes possible the denial of the threat of the destructive eye, and this brings about the initial complete lack of anxiety in the dream. Subsequently the strength of the ego determines whether these defenses are able to counteract the destructive action of the archaic, regressively somatized superego.

The threatened ego, in its regression to an archaic body ego, represents the self which functionally is in a state of destruction, dismemberment, evisceration, and exposure in its most concrete form. However, this is only one aspect and one layer of the struggle. The primitive defenses that are mobilized, i.e., splitting and fragmentation, enable the ego to deny any connection between the destructive eye and the dismembered body; therefore anxiety either does not appear or is considerably postponed in the course of dreaming, as, e.g., in Freud's dream.

The precarious balance is then one representation of the ego's struggle for liberation from entrenched archaic superego pressures, which come to the fore in the manifest dream in the form of somatic symbolization. This splitting in conjunction with regression re-creates a state that may be a structuralized new edition of that earlier developmental state in which the infant is not aware of the fact that different parts of his body belong to the same self. It is the mental state of an infant who looks at his hand or foot with interest but does not recognize the connection between the onlooking eye and the observed limb.

The first complex coordinations of motivation, stimulation, intention, and perception that lead to structuralization relate to the visual function. It is mainly through the eye that the infant is capable of registering and recording, activities which lead to the establishment of the initial organizers—i.e., the three-month smile and the stranger anxiety (Spitz, 1959). The visual function is also the main vehicle in establishing the dialogue between mother and child.

A further important factor in this predominant role of the eye and vision is the well-known fact that the infant reacts mainly to the upper part of the human face: the eyes and the forehead. Thus these are the earliest channels of recognition and communication. The most important origins of the nonself are introduced through these visual experiences, as the three-month smile and the stranger anxiety prove. In all these instances it is vision that conveys to the child either the presence of the mother or the anxiety-provoking traumatic experience of the stranger's presence, which is interpreted by the infant as an abandonment by the mother.

VI

In what follows I attempt to prove that this representation of archaic superego elements by the threatening eye is a remnant of an organization whose beginnings go back to the earliest phases of the child's development.

In 1924 Heinz Hartmann hypothesized the existence of "elementary hallucinations." One of his cases was a patient whose hallucinations of red color were, Hartmann assumed, of an elementary visual nature in the strictest sense, since they were only secondarily structuralized and attached to dynamically meaningful objects. These primary visual hallucinations, in particular red ones, were initially perceived by the patient as "free," "like a shine"; "they were experienced not as qualities of objects but as pure sensations." They were linked to an object only secondarily, during the patient's stay at the clinic; she then perceived the red glow in the glare of the eyes of one of the doctors and later as the threatening red-glowing eyes of her angry father, of whom she had always been very much afraid.

Schilder (1942) corroborated Hartmann's hypothesis and agreed with him that it is only "under the influence of experience that the primitive hallucination is bound to a specific object."

In 1934, in a preliminary publication, Hermann discussed what he called archaic primary perceptions *(Urwahrnehmungen)*. These are perceptions to which the very young child is exposed and which later, for external or internal reasons, become repressed. One of these archaic primary perceptions is the red glow that glares up in the pupil of the eyes of a person who is not accommodated to the observing child.[3]

This archaic perception is a subliminal experience and is not registered consciously. Hermann observed its vestiges in screen memories that were structuralizations of parental threats, castration anxiety, and direct retaliatory rage shown by a parental figure. The fact that this phenomenon is found in literature, folklore, and myths accords well with these analytic findings. Hermann assumed that myths about the origin of fire indicate that primitive man was aware of the red glow of the eye. The identification of the sun with the paternal eye gives further weight to the significance of Hermann's assumption.

Hermann found that the analytic reconstruction of this archaic perception in childhood memories made these memories more meaningful. It may add to the significance of this perceptive experience that rage and anxiety dilate the pupils of the adult's eye and therefore enhance the possibility that the child would be exposed to this traumatic experience.

Hermann made the further assumption that the threatening red-glowing eyes of the parental image induce through their fiery effect a corresponding fire of shame in the child, who experiences the warm blushing of the face and of the whole body. In view of the close relationship between shame and guilt, this suggestion is rather convincing and is relevant to my hypothesis concerning the genetic role played by this phenomenon in the development of the superego.

---

[3] I discussed Hermann's statement with a leading opthalmologist and he corroborated its accuracy. In addition, he drew my attention to the fact that Ernst Brücke published two papers on the red glow of the eye in animals and man (1845, 1847). In his youth Brücke carried out trailblazing anatomical and physiological research on the eye. He failed to carry his achievements to their conclusion: the discovery of the opthalmoscope was left to Helmholtz. Brücke, an extremely close-lipped man who was as awe-inspiring to everybody as to Freud, told Exner toward the end of his life: "The most stupid thing of my life was that I did not discover the opthalmoscope" (see E. T. Brücke, 1928).

Twenty years later, unaware of Hermann's paper, Székely (1954) approached the problem of anxiety from the point of view of the phylogenetic and ontogenetic significance of the glowing eye. Taking up the observations of Kaila, Spitz and Wolf, and those of contemporary ethologists, Székely elaborated on the evocation of the three-month smile and the eight-month stranger anxiety by the two-eyes-forehead schema. He proposed that this schema serves as a biological key stimulus for the human being; i.e., it arouses anxiety in a phylogenetically precoded danger situation at three as well as at eight months.

Székely assumed that the three-month smile is actually a phylogenetically developed substitute for the originally imprinted danger signal of anxiety, which became meaningless for the human infant and therefore disappeared in the course of phylogenetic development. In support of his hypothesis he quoted Spitz to the effect that children with a disturbed mother relationship display a "reversal of smiling"; i.e., according to Székely, they show the original anxiety reaction.

Székely believes that stranger anxiety is not provoked by the loss of the object, since it also occurs when the child sits on his mother's lap; rather, it is an anxiety sign provoked by real danger: the partial object of the two-eyes-forehead schema of the unknown person. The key stimulus arouses the proper anxiety in the eight-month-old child, but is lost for the three-month-old.

Thus, as Hermann again pointed out in 1957, Székely corroborated Hermann's views.

Székely's assumptions are important for my thesis because they stress the primary significance of the glaring eye for the subsequent structuralization of anxiety in a biologically determined real danger situation for the human infant. Thus the eyes play a paramount role in the archaic traumatic danger situation and in their internalized organization.

VII

The significance of Hartmann's, Hermann's, and Székely's work lies in the fact that these authors stress the archaic primordial phylogenetic and ontogenetic role that the threatening eyes play in the structuralization of the sense of reality, in coping with danger situations, in adaptation, and—what is most important—in the internal integration of an originally external punitive and dangerous agency that will become part of the system superego. In my experience the repressed archaic thoughts and functions are identical with those that brought about Freud's dream at a particular phase in his self-analysis.

The survival of the partially destroyed body ego and body self in these dreams symbolizes the challenge to the archaic visual superego element and the will to survive. This body self does not succumb to being "stared down" by the terrifying archaic eyes of the internalized parental image. (In Freud's case, this was signaled by his publishing *The Interpretation of Dreams* and by his overcoming his absolute devotion to Fliess.) In one of my patients, it signaled the final tearing away from the loved-hated mother aspects of the inhibiting superego. In another case, it paved the way for the release of sublimated energies for specific professional activities. In a young woman, it indicated the cessation of the unconscious incestuous bondage that was dissolved with the working through of strict archaic inhibitions.

I have attempted to point to *one* of the genetic forerunners of the superego without implying that this forerunner plays a role in the actual functioning of the mature superego system. Hartmann and Loewenstein (1962) emphasize the difference between function and genesis; furthermore, they stress: "Clinically relevant is the question, how much of the antecedents survive and, in connection with this, the problem of regression" (p. 73).

I believe that I have given a satisfactory surmise about the "survival of the antecedents" of the superego. In the combined regression of the transference neurosis and the dream at a particular constellation in the analytic process, there is a stage during which we are able to spot "early identifications and early object relationships taking the place of the contents and the functions of the superego" (Hartmann and Loewenstein, 1962, p. 73).

After these general considerations I want to go further and investigate the specific significance of the eye, of the "terrifying eye," for the mature structure of the superego. And here again I wish to quote Hartmann and Loewenstein:

> Freud himself has sometimes spoken—and we think convincingly —of inner perception as a function of the ego. On the other hand, it is also true that even as late as in the *New Introductory Lectures* (1933) he allocated self-observation to the superego as one of its main functions [p. 57].

My endeavor has been to indicate that self-observation as a superego function can be traced to very early traumatic experiences and to the subsequent defensive identifications. Hartmann and Loewenstein feel that one is justified in calling "archaic" . . . "those pre-oedipal identifications and early drive derivatives and ego activities which, in an unmodified form, survive in the superego system" (p. 73). I hope I have been able to trace the genesis of one of these surviving structures which may appear in a regression if the latter is a combined manifestation of the transference neurosis, the dream process, and a certain critical phase in the termination of the analysis.

Hartmann and Loewenstein point to a further essential consequence of these regressions: "the possibility that there exist variations, partly independent of the contents, in the mode of energy used by the superego—a 'regression,' that is, to a form of energy closer to the pure instinctual mode" (p. 74).

The evisceration dream points to a far-reaching operation of relatively pure aggressive energy through the mediation of the threatening, terrifying eyes. The latter represent the visual, archaic forerunner of the superego, which is in a state of extreme regression in these dreams. In addition to this aspect of the evisceration dream, it also signals a relative breakdown of the ego's capacity to use aggressive energy for the defensive measures of splitting and fragmentation. While the ego uses mainly aggressive energy for its defensive mechanisms (Peto, 1968), as was originally suggested by Hartmann, this mode of channeling, in the case of the dismemberment dream, breaks down to some extent. Therefore, dismemberment and fragmentation operate beyond the usual scope and appear in the manifest dream.

SUMMARY

I have attempted to blend into a meaningful genetic sequence clinical and theoretical material from a variety of observations and speculations. I have shown that a special type of dream, when it appears at a decisive phase of the transference neurosis, represents a crucial re-edition of an earlier ego-superego struggle. This conflict has its roots, I assume, in one particular element of the superego structure, namely, in its visual origins, as represented by the threatening, red-glowing parental eye. According to my hypothesis, this external traumatic agent becomes internalized into the developing superego and is among other factors at the genetic root of the complex critical internal watching agency of the adult.

BIBLIOGRAPHY

Brücke, E. T. (1928), *Ernst Brücke.* Vienna: Springer.
Flournoy, H. (1920), Dreams on the Symbolism of Water and Fire. *Int. J. Psa.,* 1:245-255.
Freud, S. (1900), The Interpretation of Dreams. *Standard Edition,* 4 & 5. London: Hogarth Press, 1953.
—— (1919), 'A Child Is Being Beaten.' *Standard Edition,* 17:175-204. London: Hogarth Press, 1955.
—— (1933), New Introductory Lectures on Psycho-Analysis. *Standard Edition,* 22:3-182. London: Hogarth Press, 1964, p. 80.
Hartmann, E. (1968), The 90-Minute Sleep-Dream Cycle. *Arch. Gen. Psychiat.,* 18:280-286.
Hartmann, H. (1924), Halluzinierte Flächenfarben und Bewegungen. *Mschr. Psychiat. & Neurol.,* 56:1-14.
—— & Loewenstein, R. M. (1962), Notes on the Superego. *This Annual,* 17:42-81.
Hermann, I. (1934), Urwahrnehmungen, insbesondere Augenleuchten und Lautwerden des Inneren. *Int. Z. Psa.,* 20:553-555.
—— (1957), Augenleuchten, Schamgefühl und Exhibitionismus. *Schweiz. Z. Psychol. & ihre Anwend.,* 16:50-53.
Hitschmann, E. (1914), Weitere Mitteilung von Kindheitsträumen mit spezieller Bedeutung. *Int. Z. f. ärztl. Psychoanal.,* 2:31-32.
Peto, A. (1961), The Fragmentizing Function of the Ego in the Transference Neurosis. *Int. J. Psa.,* 42:238-245.
—— (1962), Superego Fragmentations in the Irma Dream. Presented at the American Psychoanalytic Association.
—— (1963), The Fragmentizing Function of the Ego in the Analytic Session. *Int. J. Psa.,* 44:334-338.
—— (1968), Aggression, Defense and Adaptation. Presented at the New York Psychoanalytic Society.
Pollock, G. H. & Muslin, H. L. (1962), Dreams during Surgical Procedures. *Psa. Quart.,* 31:175-202.

Schilder, P. (1942), *Mind: Perception and Thought in Their Constructive Aspects.* New York: Columbia University Press.

Schur, M. (1966), Some Additional "Day Residues" of "The Specimen Dream of Psychoanalysis." In: *Psychoanalysis—A General Psychology: Essays in Honor of Heinz Hartmann,* ed. R. M. Loewenstein, L. M. Newman, M. Schur, & A. J. Solnit. New York: International Universities Press, pp. 45-85.

Silberer, H. (1909), Report on a Method of Eliciting and Observing Certain Symbolic Hallucination-Phenomena. In: *Organization and Pathology of Thought,* ed. D. Rapaport. New York: Columbia University Press, 1959, pp. 195-207.

Snyder, F. (1965), Progress in the New Biology of Dreaming. *Amer. J. Psychiat.,* 122:377-391.

Spitz, R. A. (1959), *A Genetic Field Theory of Ego Formation.* New York: International Universities Press.

Székely, L. (1954), Biological Remarks on Fears Originating in Early Childhood, *Int. J. Psa.,* 35:57-67.

Winterstein, A. (1954), A Typical Dream-Sensation and Its Meaning. *Int. J. Psa.,* 35:229-233.

VICISSITUDES OF INFANTILE OMNIPOTENCE

EUGENE PUMPIAN-MINDLIN, M.D. (Oklahoma City)

The role of fantasies of omnipotence in human psychic life was first delineated by Freud in his discussion of "omnipotence of thought" in relation to the Rat Man (1909). Later he discussed the same topic in relation to the magical power of words and of religion in *Totem and Taboo* (1913) and in *The Future of an Illusion* (1927). About ten years ago my attention was attracted to a phenomenon in youthful patients to which insufficient attention had been paid. This relates to a developmental recrudescence of omnipotent fantasies and feelings (transmuted, to be sure) which occurs in the late adolescent period. I have termed this phenomenon "omnipotentiality" (Pumpian-Mindlin, 1965, 1968).

Until recently there had been no systematic exposition or study of the vicissitudes and fate of infantile omnipotence, in spite of the fact that in psychoanalytic literature frequent reference is made to it as a continuing significant factor in psychic life, principally, however, in a pathological sense. Recently, in a paper on "The Normal Personality in Our Culture and the Nobel Prize Complex" (1966), Helen Tartakoff presented some observations that are similar to mine.

The concept of omnipotence, as it is usually discussed, very quickly becomes fused with the constructs of narcissism and self-esteem, so that it loses its separate identity. If my hypotheses have any validity, omnipotence must be separated out and re-examined, to see if it casts any new light on certain aspects of psychic development.

Based upon a paper presented at the Twentieth Anniversary Program of the New Orleans Psychoanalytic Institute, October 5, 1968.

Vice-Chairman, Department of Psychiatry and Behavioral Sciences, University of Oklahoma Medical Center.

Infantile omnipotence is the primordial state of the psyche as it begins its long maturational and developmental journey through life. It represents the primal state at birth before any recognition of objects. The infant cannot distinguish between self and external world with which he feels merged. There is still no ego and therefore no nonego. In this state he is therefore the whole world and the universe.

This first proto-fantasy and feeling of unlimited omnipotence (often also referred to as the "oceanic feeling") represent the primary narcissistic need. But this initial state of unlimited objectless infantile omnipotence rapidly passes. It exists only as long as there is no concept of external objects. It is belied by the actual realistic helplessness of the infant. Under the stimulus of inner excitations which cannot be ignored or removed, random uncoordinated discharge movements occur. These are perceived by the environment (i.e., the mother) as signals. Her response results in a change, a relief of tension, a diminution of disturbing excitation. Ferenczi (1913) characterized this stage as one of "omnipotence of movements." Tartakoff (1966) states: "the inference has been drawn that the forerunners of fantasies of omnipotence and causality have a common origin in the infant's own activity" (p. 241). She quotes Spitz (1965) in this connection as follows:

In this achievement of enlisting the mother's help . . . through screaming, the human being experiences for the first time the *post hoc ergo propter hoc* in connection with his own action. . . . [This] principle will subsequently branch into two directions. One of them will remain in its crude form as a basic mode of functioning of the primary process. The other will be progressively refined until it becomes one of the most potent ideational tools of man in the form of the principle of determinism [p. 153f.].

Due to unavoidable frustrations, and inevitable delays in tension reduction which the infant experiences, he is forced into a recognition of the existence of the external world. This is the earliest beginning of ego formation. With the awareness of externality the rudiments of ego structure are developed.

Parenthetically, I am, of course, aware of the concept of autonomous ego functions, particularly those connected with the various perceptual modalities. We are dealing here with the development of psychic reality rather than of perceptual or cognitive reality. We are concerned with the earliest phases of the development of psychic processes, which may be called proto-thought (preverbal) processes. Much of the work of recent years in the study of infants and children by psychoanalytically trained observers relates to observations concerning sense organ perceptions and motor responses. Such work must perforce be confined to these areas since the inner (psychic) processes cannot, by their very nature, be observed, but can only be inferred.

Let me briefly present some of the bases upon which these inferences rest. The earliest stage of unlimited objectless omnipotence can be seen reflected in various mystical sensations of being at one with the universe, which have been described through the ages. Although they are extremely difficult to describe and to analyze scientifically in a satisfactory manner, these feelings undoubtedly represent genuine experiences reported by numerous people at various times. They may be dissociative abreactions of the infantile "oceanic feeling." With no apparent cause, one may experience a sense of fabulous joy and well-being, in which all of the emotions that go with delightful discovery, profound insight, and a sense of immortality are rolled into one.

Various drugs, including the hallucinogens or psychedelics, may produce such reactions as illumination, cosmic consciousness, or oneness with all things. Some time ago a graduate student at a large university attempted to depict for me his experience on "trips" under the influence of LSD. Although couched in highly sophisticated and partly scientific language, it was a vivid description of an unlimited objectless omnipotent (and omniscient) sensation. He stated (and I paraphrase, but I believe with fair accuracy) that under the influence of LSD his body lost its limited defined boundaries; it became fused with the molecules and atoms of all the world around him (all people and all things) so that there were no separate and distinct entities, but only the universe, which was himself, and himself, who was the universe and all that was in it. He stated that although he *perceived* all this, he did not use the word "perceive" to mean through his sense organs, but intended rather to imply a fundamentally primitive yet highly sophisticated comprehension, beyond the limits of the ordinary functions of the human mind. He characterized the experience as that of becoming all-powerful, as if one were the "hub of the universe." He ended by bemoaning the inadequacies of words to formulate this remarkable state of being. It is the very primal preverbal nature of the experience of infantile omnipotence which makes it so difficult to express verbally or to formulate clearly and precisely.

While it is true that much of what has been said is speculative and not based upon empirical observation, we have ample data from neurotic and psychotic patients which justify such theoretical assumptions.

The phenomenon of "omnipotence of movements" we see manifested on occasion in the catatonic schizophrenic patient, who later tells us how he felt that any movement he might have made would have affected, even destroyed, the whole world.

Certain aspects of compulsive rituals, in addition to the usual factors of anxiety reduction with which we are familiar in individual patients, contain elements of the "omnipotence of movements" in a primitive magical effort to control and dominate the world and thereby reduce tensions while magically fulfilling inner needs of which that patient is, of course, unaware.

In the manic patient, we see the omnipotence and omniscience of words and movements. The illusion of invulnerability, the enormous pathological self-aggrandizement and self-esteem, the supreme confidence in their ability to do anything and everything, all betray their infantile omnipotent narcissistic origins.

Returning to the infantile developmental aspect of omnipotence, we find that the resultant development of the ego forces the infant to recognize the existence of the seemingly all-powerful adults outside of himself, and his own weakness and helplessness. A "reversal into the opposite" occurs whereby the infant now attributes to the adult the omnipotence he once felt was his. It is in this stage that Freud's concept of the "purified pleasure ego" belongs. The primitive mechanisms of introjection and projection begin to develop, in which that which is pleasant (i.e., reduces tension and unpleasure) is incorporated into the ego, and that which brings unpleasure is attributed to the external world (i.e., nonego). Thus the beginning recognition and cathexis of objects are achieved.

The child now tries to participate in the omnipotence attributed to the adult by partial or total incorporation of the object, or by the reverse fantasy of being incorporated by the omnipotent adult and thereby sharing in his omnipotence. The contrast between the child's growing awareness of his own relative helplessness, and the adult's presumed omnipotence, further enhances the need of the child for objects, through which he seeks to regain his lost omnipotence.

It is during the stage at which the child attributes omnipotence to the adult that language begins to develop. Omnipotent feelings and fantasies become linked with words and verbal concepts. Since the adult exercises his omnipotent power principally through verbal productions, words come to acquire magical powers of their own. The acquisition of language, then, aside from being a powerful tool in dealing with the external world, also at an unconscious level represents an attempt to acquire the power which the child realistically sees his parents possess, as well as an attempt to regain his own earlier omnipotence, with which he has now invested them.

If the child becomes involved in too fierce a struggle for power at this time, the result may be a fixation at this level, in which the omnipotence of thought and the magic of words which we usually associate with the obsessive-compulsive character become dominant. The magical potency that the obsessive-compulsive patient attributes to words is well known and need not be described in detail here. Suffice it to say, on the basis of clinical experience, that the fantasies of omnipotence and the magical power of words are factors that must be dealt with as significant issues in the psychoanalysis of obsessive-compulsive neurotics if therapy is to be successful.

It is interesting to recall that Freud (1939) attributed unusual significance to the magic of words and the omnipotence of thoughts, as evidenced in the following statement from *Moses and Monotheism:*

In our children, in adults who are neurotic, as well as in primitive peoples, we meet with the mental phenomenon which we describe as a belief in the 'omnipotence of thought.' In our judgment this lies in an over-estimation of the influence which our mental (in this case, intellectual) acts can exercise in altering the external world. At bottom, all magic, the precursor of our technology, rests on this premise. All the magic of words, too, has its place here, and the conviction of the power which is bound up with the knowledge and pronouncing of a name. The 'omnipotence of thoughts' was, we suppose, an expression of the pride of mankind in the development of speech, which resulted in such an extraordinary advancement of intellectual activities. The new realm of intellectuality was opened up, in which ideas, memories and inferences became decisive in contrast to the lower psychical activity which had direct perceptions by the sense-organs as its content. This was unquestionably one of the most important stages on the path to hominization [p. 113].

A few parenthetical comments must be made here. Freud limits the omnipotence of thoughts to children, adult neurotics, and primitive people. While it may be true that this phenomenon is of special significance in these groups, it is certainly not limited to them. The fantasy of omnipotence remains a significant factor in all individuals and societies regardless of stage of development, with only its relative dominance varying to some degree. Certainly, we see the fantasy of omnipotence manifested in religion, of whatever faith. All religions, as was long ago pointed out, have in common either a pantheon of omnipotent gods, or one godly figure to whom omnipotence is attributed. The believer presents himself as helpless in order to appeal to the omnipotent figure to use his power in favor of the supplicant. In fantasy, unconsciously, the individual not only regains his omnipotence by identification with his god, but also extends it by having the god act in his favor, thus in a magical way becoming more powerful than the god himself.

This is a maneuver which one often encounters in compulsive and borderline patients who oscillate between fantasies of omnipotence and total helplessness. As a patient once stated, "If I can force you to use your all-powerful magic to help me, by making myself so helpless that you must do something, I will be more powerful than you—superpowerful."

The same fantasy in highly institutionalized form can be found in the most sophisticated religious practices, even in our current society, which, while it may be savage, cannot be considered by other, more usual criteria, primitive. After all, it is not only incantations and spells which depend upon the magic of words;

prayers also attest to the underlying longing for the belief in omnipotence.

In addition, we see similar psychic maneuvers in social systems dominated by powerful political figures to whom followers attribute omnipotent powers in which they share by identification. It would be comforting to feel that this occurs only in societies and social orders which differ from our own, but this element is certainly not absent in our own society, although perhaps it is somewhat more disguised than in an obviously authoritarian social order.

Let me add one further parenthetical remark regarding Freud's statement quoted above. It is an interesting and curious fact that, while language and verbal concepts are among the most significant attributes of human beings, we have very little systematic psychoanalytic knowledge of their origin and development. A most interesting area of study would relate to the question of how the omnipotence of thought and the magic of words become decathected and lose their primitive potency, not only in terms of the further development of the ego, but also in relation to the inner dynamics and outer pressures which change their valences, so to speak. Certainly a systematic psychoanalytic study of the evolution of the shift from predominantly primary process activity and verbalization to predominantly secondary process functioning would represent an enrichment in our knowledge of the human psyche.

From what has been outlined above it appears then that infantile omnipotence is a major component of the most primitive core (or nucleus) of ego structure, around which primal psychic activity evolves. It is the prototype for the primary process which mediates the direct discharge of tension. It is also an analogous force in the development of primary process activity with its modes of condensation, displacement, etc., and in the most primitive mechanisms of defense. It continues throughout life in many different forms as the background for magic, fantasy, dreams, myth, and legend, not to mention multitudinous aspects of our daily lives— now more submerged, now more dominant, but always present. It might even be stated that infantile omnipotence represents the primordial fantasy, the anlage, from which all fantasy formation stems, the deepest underground stream from which our rich and varied fantasy life derives.

As the infant matures and develops, the dominance of the omnipotent fantasy becomes further submerged (repressed) in the
increasing awareness of external reality. With the realization of his
own impotence, and the attribution of omnipotence to the adults
around it, the child comes to depend upon them for his self-esteem,
originally based upon his own narcissistic omnipotence. In transferring omnipotence to the adult, the child then comes to depend
for love upon the all-powerful adult, who becomes thereby the
regulator of his self-esteem. Fenichel (1945) agrees with Rado (1928)
that " 'Self-esteem' is the awareness of how close the individual is
to the original omnipotence" (p. 40).

In the oedipal situation the intense struggle for narcissistic
gratification in relation to the parental figures results finally in the
internalization of the conflict, and in the establishment of the
uniquely human institution which we call the superego and its
supremely sapient concomitants, guilt and shame. The superego
becomes the repository for omnipotent needs, fantasies, and strivings, and also becomes the storehouse for the magical modes of
thought through which it manifests itself. I omit here any discussion of the ego ideal as it is frequently differentiated from the superego. However, *pari passu*, it also shares in absorbing some of the
omnipotent fantasies and feelings. Tartakoff (1966) in her article on
the Nobel Prize complex, discussed significant aspects of the relation of the development of the ego ideal to omnipotent fantasies,
particularly as it relates to the gifted child in whom these fantasies
are reinforced by the environment.

The resolution of the oedipal situation, which uniquely stamps
each individual, institutes the beginning of the struggle for dominance on the part of the secondary process psychic activity over
the primary. With the establishment of the superego-ego ideal as a
separate psychic system to which magical (primary process) psychic
activity is relegated, the child is in a position to begin the systematic acquisition of secondary process thinking—i.e., reality-
oriented thought and action. I do not mean to imply in any sim-
plistic way that secondary process function is not present long before
the oedipal period. What I am discussing here is its relative dominance and significance at different periods.

From this point of view the so-called latency period assumes a

somewhat different significance. It is a period of rapid ego development, primarily related to mastery of the secondary process which is
necessary for the acquisition of the specifically human skills required by the particular social and historical environment in which
the child is growing. But always, in the background, can be
discerned partially submerged omnipotent needs, in the form of fantasy, play activity, the delight in fairy tales (or, in more modern
terms, cartoons), etc. At puberty, this relative dominance of the
cognitive aspects of ego development is disturbed by the emergence
of the powerful sexual drives, together with the characteristic final
growth spurt. The earlier psychosexual stages are recaptitulated at
this new level of development. Under this impetus the ontogeny of
omnipotence is also recapitulated, with much greater resources at
its disposal.

We are all familiar, perhaps too familiar, with the turbulence
of adolescence precipitated by biological maturation. One of the
most striking and disturbing aspects of adolescence is the apparent
fluidity of the psychic apparatus. The boundaries of the psychic
structures which had achieved some relative stability and demarcation now seem to loosen significantly. It is this aspect of youthful
development which creates so much difficulty for us in evaluating
these youngsters. Primary process psychic activity breaks through
unexpectedly. Conflicts from earlier levels of development are suddenly activated in order to be worked through again. It is not surprising, then, that infantile omnipotence with all of its ramifications should reappear in some form at this time. I coined the term
"omnipotentiality" to indicate the relationship of this seemingly
new manifestation to the omnipotence of infancy which, after all,
had never truly disappeared, and (as we have just seen) exercises a
significant and continuous influence beneath the surface.

The fundamental thesis of my previous presentation (1965) was
that there exists a particular facet of development of the ego, or
perhaps more appropriately of the "self" (Hartmann, 1950), during
the period which we now call late adolescence (roughly from sixteen
to twenty-two) which was heretofore largely unnoted, except perhaps
in a negative sense, or at most in passing. This aspect of development is sufficiently characteristic to warrant a separation of adolescence into two relatively distinct periods: (1) adolescence proper,

which dates from the onset of puberty to the age of about sixteen; and (2) youth, from sixteen until approximately twenty-two by which time the transition to young adulthood is usually complete. Naturally the chronological age is only approximate in any specific case. It may be noted that this dividing line is institutionalized in our society by our national "pubertal rite" of the automobile license at sixteen.

During this particular aspect of youthful development emerge many of the phenomena of "omnipotentiality." It appears to be an essential and vital element in the maturation of certain aspects of ego development, particularly as these relate to the concept of the "self." It consists primarily of the feeling and conviction on the part of the youth that he can do anything in the world, solve any problem in the world if given the opportunity. If the opportunity is not given, he will create it. There is no occupation which is inaccessible, no task which is too much for him. As his perspective of the world broadens, as his horizon widens, he begins to question everything which his elders have come to accept. Nothing is impossible, nothing can be taken for granted. He can indulge in wild flights of the imagination, soaring speculations, incredible adventures. He knows no limits in fantasy, and accepts grudgingly any limits in reality. Yet, at the same time, he finds it difficult to do one thing and follow it through to completion, because to do so would mean to commit himself to one thing primarily, and this he is not yet prepared to do because it would mean abandoning all the other possibilities, thus restricting his potentialities.

Limitation, reining in, focusing, remain for the future, for the next stage: the transition to young adulthood. This characteristic coming to grips with one's real potentialities, and the willingness to apply them to a specific line of achievement, may be characterized psychologically as *commitment.* This represents the recognition of limitations (both external and internal), the acceptance of the fact that one must forego one's omnipotentiality for the sake of the acquisition of a particular skill or accomplishment, the realization that one cannot do anything and everything equally well, the understanding that one must establish priorities for oneself in life. The step from omnipotentiality to commitment channelizes the diffuse omnipotential energy into specific directions. If the individual finds the conflict too great to be more or less successfully resolved, he may retreat into fantasy, often regressing to the level of infantile omnipotence and magical thinking.

The resolution of omnipotentiality in the normal healthy youth comes about from the "acting out" of omnipotential fantasies in reality, thereby submitting them to testing. Gradually, as they are tested and retested against reality, the diffuse omnipotential energies are bound to modify the omnipotential fantasies in keeping with the demands of reality. Only then can the youth establish for himself his own priorities and commit himself to some specific task, i.e., assume some specific role and place in society—in short, make the transition to adulthood.

It is exactly this continuous testing against reality which appears so bizarre, and so disquieting to the adult, who has already committed himself. It leads the youth into what the adult calls "excesses." The fantastic confidence of the youth in his ability to do things which the adult has come to accept as impossible is genetically related to the roots of omnipotentiality in infantile omnipotence.

The anxiety of the adult about the omnipotentiality of the youth stems both from its genetic relation with and its basic difference from the omnipotence of the infant. The latter is a wish-fulfilling fantasy belied by and related to the infant's actual physiological and psychological impotence. The youth, however, is both physiologically and psychologically potent—in fact, more potent than most adults. His omnipotentiality is therefore threatening and anxiety-producing to the adult, because it is closer to that of the adult and can therefore be more easily reactivated, and because it is much more real than infantile omnipotence. Infantile omnipotence lies in the realm of unrealizable fantasy; however, the youth, with his omnipotentiality, is much closer to the reality of the adult in time, and thus has the physiological and psychological potential of being a threat. The adult, having struggled to master his own youthful fantasies, is made uncomfortable and anxious in the presence of the fantasies and activities of the youth, particularly if it appears that the youth might be able to realize and fulfill them. In order to control their own anxiety many adults vigorously suppress such tendencies in the youth. The wildness, the exuberance, the excesses, the dedication, the intensity, the devotion, the single-minded pursuit, and, above all, the fantastic confidence which characterize so many youthful activities are exactly those qualities which such adults find secretly fascinating and consciously frightening. Other adults may deal with the threat in other ways, ranging from ignoring—and neglecting—the youth, to an inappropriate clinging to (or attempting to return to) what amounts to the phoney youthfulness of the aging but perennially uncommitted adult.

Another common adult reaction to the expressions of omnipotentiality in the adolescent is that the young person is pursuing will-o'-the-wisps, holy grails, vain illusions. From his own position of commitment he reacts with scorn or alarm to youth's ecstatic involvement, unreserved hero worship, glowing faith, idealistic devotion to the pursuit of "the impossible dream." For the adult who has committed himself to a specific course in life, often irreversible, it all appears to be an illusion. But for the youth, not yet having made his commitment, it is not illusion. It is very real, very meaningful, very important, and at this stage of development very valid.

Adults tend to stress the turbulence, the distress, the helplessness, and the confusion engendered by the maturational psychophysiological surge during this period. At the same time they underestimate the gratifications which arise from the process of growth, maturation, and the eventual attainment of adult status. Youths do not challenge merely out of perversity, defiance, rebellion, and spite, but rather out of a definite inner need to question, to "challenge an axiom," to use Einstein's wonderful phrase, because of their omnipotential strivings. Only by testing his newly acquired strengths, his new mastery, can the youth temper himself to the reality of the adult world, on whose threshold he stands.

The very suddenness with which young people shift their vocational goals, immerse themselves in one field, and work assiduously therein for longer or shorter periods of time, only to discard such involvements just as suddenly and turn to something else, with equal or greater intensity, is related to the feeling of omnipotentiality and to their inability as yet to accept the commitment which is necessary for the passage from youth to adulthood. The feeling of omnipotentiality, while it continues, permits the teen-ager to roam far and wide in many fields before responding to the social and maturational necessity of commitment.

Indeed, the free exercise of this omnipotentiality is a necessary and salutary occurrence in youth. The wider the range of exploration, the more adequately prepared is the youth to relinquish his omnipotential strivings and channelize them into specific priorities, to choose the necessary, appropriate, inevitable commitment. Unfortunately, adults, out of their own anxiety, often make this essential exploration and experimentation as difficult as possible for the youth. The youth resent this and they rebel against it—which leads to further repressive measures, both social and individual.

Herein perhaps lies a major implication of the concept of omnipotentiality: that the omnipotentiality of youth arouses fear and hostility in many adults through reactivation of their own struggles therewith. This unrecognized resentful anxiety in the adult is rationalized both socially and individually. It manifests itself in external complaints against the rashness and folly of the younger generation, and more seriously in repressive measures which take the form of narrowing and restricting the opportunities for expression of these impulses by the young and demanding a commitment from them at an earlier time than they are prepared to make it, or than it is possible for them to accept.

The resultant anger of youth manifests itself in many ways, all of which have as their common denominator the expression of the omnipotential desire to be free and able to do anything—whether in earlier generations as seemingly bizarre as goldfish eating, as risqué as panty-raiding, as dangerous as hot-rodding, or any other activity which expresses the contempt for the limitations and commitments of adulthood. In our current turbulent scene, one can see elements of these feelings of omnipotentiality in the background of many of the social struggles which grip our society. It is very much to the point that these involve predominantly the youth who do not accept the impossibility of change. In the colleges and in the ghettoes alike it is the youth who dare to "challenge the axioms" accepted by their elders.

If the red thread of infantile omnipotence runs through all developmental periods up to the point of young adulthood, one might well ask what its further fate is in the adult life.

We know quite well the varied neurotic and even psychotic forms it may take if it has not been adequately worked through in earlier stages of development. But its persistence universally in some form or other into the years of maturity is an area that has been ignored. Even in the healthiest and best-adjusted people, infantile omnipotence ultimately triumphs in the form of immortality through the propagation of children.

BIBLIOGRAPHY

Fenichel, O. (1945), The Psychoanalytic Theory of Neurosis. New York: Norton.
Ferenczi, S. (1913), Stages in the Development of the Sense of Reality. Sex in Psychoanalysis. New York: Basic Books, 1950, pp. 213-239.
Freud, S. (1909), Notes upon a Case of Obsessional Neurosis. Standard Edition, 10:153-318. London: Hogarth Press, 1955.
—— (1913), Totem and Taboo. Standard Edition, 13:1-161. London: Hogarth Press, 1955.
—— (1927), The Future of an Illusion. Standard Edition, 21:3-56. London: Hogarth Press, 1961.
—— (1939), Moses and Monotheism. Standard Edition, 23:3-137. London: Hogarth Press, 1964.
Hartmann, H. (1950), Comments on the Psychoanalytic Theory of the Ego. This Annual, 5:74-86.
Pumpian-Mindlin, E. (1965), Omnipotentiality, Youth, and Commitment. J. Amer. Acad. Child Psychiat., 4:1-18.
—— (1968), Omnipotence, Omnipotentiality, Conformity and Rebellion. Sandor Rado Lecture, reported in: Bull. Assn. Psa. Med., 8:31-34, 38, 1969.
Rado, S. (1928), The Problem of Melancholia. Int. J. Psa., 9:420-438.
Spitz, R. A. & Cobliner, W. G. (1965), The First Year of Life. New York: International Universities Press.
Tartakoff, H. H. (1966), The Normal Personality in Our Culture and the Nobel Prize Complex. In: Psychoanalysis—A General Psychology: Essays in Honor of Heinz Hartmann, ed. R. M. Loewenstein, L. M. Newman, M. Schur, & A. J. Solnit. New York: International Universities Press, pp. 222-252.

ON THE PSYCHOLOGY OF ARTISTIC CREATIVITY

MICHAEL D. ROBBINS, M.D. (Belmont, Mass.)

This paper is an attempt to formulate the metapsychology of the creative process in a serious adolescent artist. Material from the first two years of his hospital-based intensive psychotherapy is presented and integrated with a review of the literature in an effort to understand the use this young artist has made of his unusual ability.

REVIEW OF THE LITERATURE

The psychoanalytic literature on artistic creativity is immense and will not be comprehensively reviewed here. It is easy to pass over the bulk of the literature which deals with the unique personality structure of various artists and attempts to find some reflection of their particular problems in their work, to which causal significance may or may not be imputed. The literature pertaining to the question of what makes a gifted person create art is more limited, and from it I shall select certain representative approaches: the work of Sigmund Freud, who was responsible for the subsequent interest of psychoanalysis in art; papers by authors whose interest in creativity relates to a more general interest in adolescent psychology; and the more recent contributions of Ernst Kris, based on ego psychology, and Phyllis Greenacre, whose orientation is somewhat at variance with that of Kris.

One of Freud's earliest contributions to the literature on creativity is his 1908 paper entitled "Creative Writers and Day-Dreaming" in which he links the genesis of art to the adult's fantasy, which in turn is derived from infantile wishes. He states that the artist is able to couch his fantasy wishes in socially acceptable forms so that they can be presented to an audience in which they in turn arouse pleasure by stimulating repressed wishes.

In 1910 Freud left his mark on the history of art criticism by inaugurating the psychological biography. In his study of Leonardo da Vinci he utilized primarily the concepts of the oedipus complex and the family romance. He anticipated structural formulations and other contributions of ego psychology while also expressing pessimism about the possibility of understanding the creative process when he said:

> Since artistic talent and capacity are intimately connected with sublimation we must admit that the nature of the artistic function is also inaccessible to us along psycho-analytic lines [p. 136].

In "Formulations on the Two Principles of Mental Functioning" (1911), Freud formulated the artist's achievement in terms of bringing about a reconciliation between the pleasure and reality principles—an achievement that is accomplished by combining the wish-fulfilling and reality-adapted use of fantasy. Freud elaborated these ideas further in his *Introductory Lectures on Psycho-Analysis* (1916-1917):

> I should like to direct your attention a little longer to a side of the life of phantasy which deserves the most general interest. For there is a path that leads back from phantasy to reality—the path, that is, of art. An artist is once more in rudiments an introvert, not far removed from neurosis. He is oppressed by excessively powerful instinctual needs. He desires to win honour, power, wealth, fame and the love of women; but he lacks the means for achieving these satisfactions. Consequently, like any other unsatisfied man, he turns away from reality and transfers all his interest, and his libido too, to the wishful construction of his life of phantasy, whence the path might lead to neurosis. . . . Their constitution probably includes a strong capacity for sublimation and a certain degree of laxity in the repressions which are decisive for a conflict . . . he understands how to work over his day-dreams in such a way as to make them lose what is too personal about them and repels strangers, and to make it possible for others to share in the enjoyment of them. He understands, too, how to tone them down so that they do not easily betray their origin from proscribed sources. Furthermore, he possesses the mysterious power of shaping some particular ma-

terial until it has become a faithful image of his phantasy; and he knows, moreover, how to link so large a yield of pleasure to this representation of his unconscious phantasy that, for the time being at least, repressions are outweighed and lifted by it. If he is able to accomplish all this, he makes it possible for other people once more to derive consolation and alleviation from their own sources of pleasure in their unconscious which have become inaccessible to them; he earns their gratitude and admiration and he has thus achieved *through* his phantasy what originally he had achieved only *in* his phantasy—honour, power and the love of women [p. 375ff.].

In summary, Freud's contribution to the psychology of creativity has two aspects, theoretical and attitudinal. Theoretically, he viewed artistic achievement as a sublimation, an unusual reconciliation of the pleasure and reality principles in which fantasy is not repressed. The artist, he believed, is motivated by unusually powerful instincts and rich associated fantasies, derived especially from the oedipal conflict, which he is unable to gratify. He might become neurotic, claimed Freud, were it not for his artistic sublimation in which fantasy, appropriately disguised and elaborated, is employed as a vehicle with which to win his objects. Equally as important as his theory is Freud's attitude about the value and possibilities of psychoanalytic exploration in creativity, a juxtaposition of curiosity and pessimism which certainly has influenced subsequent investigators.

Siegfried Bernfeld (1924) has made an extensive study of literary creativity in adolescence. Commenting on the preadolescent roots of artistic creativity, Bernfeld asserts that making things first becomes an important activity in the anal-sadistic phase, which is also when words are invested with magical qualities. Fantasy becomes important as a vehicle of wish fulfillment in the oedipal period, during which the fairy tale is presented to the child as a prototype of literature consisting of thinly disguised fantasy. During latency the ego develops those capacities which are later required for carrying out artistic work. With the abandonment of the incestuous object in puberty there is narcissistic recathexis of ego and ego ideal; the ideal of poet-hero may be created by the adolescent at this time to fulfill megalomanic ambitions. The preadolescent anal regression may add further impetus to the urge to make things and to create. If the adolescent's initial object choices are disappointing because his high ego ideals have led to unrealistic expectations, there may be narcissistic withdrawal and the ego ideal may make the ego its object and make demands on the ego to become a poet. The resulting creative efforts bind mood, which itself is a defense, onto words, effecting a stable displacement of libido. As the ego elaborates fantasy in writing, libidinal drives are satisfied. If the wish fulfillment appeared in pure daydream form the adolescent would experience guilt; but when the public accepts the disguised literary elaboration, guilt is relieved. Thus Bernfeld explores the infantile origins of creativity and the specific relationship between adolescent creativity and the recrudescence of infantile wishes in puberty. He also questions why during adolescence so many people engage in artistic activity which they later drop. For the answer to this question he refers to the form of the product, taking for granted that the content is always related to fantasies, moods, and personal experiences.

Anna Freud (1922) utilized Bernfeld's ideas about the adolescent's wish to be a poet in order to have an audience to help explain the progression of a beating fantasy in a latency age patient through daydreams in which the beatings were sublimated into reconciliations, to stories written by the patient in adolescence in which the attainment of pleasure is much further delayed.

Spiegel's work (1958) concentrates on the vicissitudes of the libidinal cathexis in adolescence, in particular the theme of loss and depression and subsequent artistic endeavor. He believes that the adolescent's art product represents a new object cathexis, a pseudopod of libido from the narcissistic cathexis which has resulted from withdrawal of libido from parents; the artwork may also be a love gift to a new personal object.

While these ideas about creativity and adolescent development are interesting, they are of little help in understanding the unique psychology of the creative artist, the reason why one adolescent becomes an artist whereas another does not.

The most provocative contemporary thinking about creativity is to be found in the work of Ernst Kris and Phyllis Greenacre. Spanning a period of about two decades Kris published a series of papers which culminated in his book *Psychoanalytic Explorations in Art.* Kris brought the insights of a developing structural theory to bear on the question of creativity. He coined the term "regression in the service of the ego" or "controlled regression" to distinguish the means whereby the ego gains access to primary process material, which can then be worked over and elaborated, from psychotic regression, in which the ego is overwhelmed by the primary process. He elaborated Freud's ideas about the flexibility of repressions and postulated that the existence of unusual talents fostered by early experiences determines subsequent capacities for sublimation. He concluded that creative inspiration is based on a process of projection and reintrojection which utilizes neutralized energy derived originally from breast hallucinations of the oral period and later homosexual conflicts. As the artist employs this projection-introjection mechanism, activity is converted into passivity, and guilt over the forbidden impulses employed in the creation is thus avoided.

In his 1941 paper "Psychic Trauma and Projective Experience in the Artist," Lowenfeld remarks on the conversion of passivity into activity, the repetition of trauma in the service of mastery. But he also underscores Kris's contention that the distinguishing characteristics of the artist are not so much his conflicts but rather his gifts, his capacity to sublimate. Louis Fraiberg (1956) also emphasizes the strength of the artist's ego and his capacity to synthesize very large quanta of energy. Adapting Hartmann's concepts, Fraiberg believes the artist works with neutralized energy and the artistic activity takes place in the conflict-free sphere.

Some of the most significant contemporary contributions to the theory of creativity have been made by Phyllis Greenacre (1957, 1958, 1963). She questions the view that the creative process employs neutralized energy and represents a conflict-free ego function. Greenacre believes that the psychosexual development of the artist differs from that of other people in that the artist achieves only a partial and incomplete resolution of the various developmental phases, particularly the oral and oedipal. In the adult artist, there is continued conflict, incomplete repression, unusual access to childhood fantasy, and availability of great quantities of unneutralized aggressive and sexual energy. The psychic economics of the artist are uniquely characterized by rapid shifts from the primary process, in which energy is freely mobile in accordance with the pleasure principle, to the secondary process, in which energy is bound to thought and controlled by the ego in accordance with the reality principle.

She believes that the artistic creation is conceived by the primary process, by instinctual energy displaced in aim and object, and is then elaborated by the secondary process. To be more specific, the aim and object of infantile libidinal strivings are displaced from the original personal object to what Greenacre terms the "collective alternates" which the child endowed with unusual sensitivities perceives in the external world—hence "the artist's love affair with the world."

Greenacre elaborates her views through a study of the state of artistic inspiration, the created artwork, and the meaning of the artistic profession. She differentiates two types of inspirational states, the oral and the oedipal. In the former the artist seeks in his work that primitive oceanic fusion feeling characteristic of nursing at the breast. Oedipal inspiration states are divided into two types related to the manner in which the conflict is being resolved. In the passive feminine resolution, the artistic inspiration is experienced as a divine gift from a father-god. The active masculine state of oedipal inspiration is based on the family romance. Either there is a quest for a father figure in the person of an art patron or else there is the myth of special permission or endowment from a powerful god or foster-father figure who approves of the otherwise forbidden wishes and permits the active male penetration by the artist or creator into the mysteries of the cosmic mother. Examples of oedipal inspiration abound in theology and mythology. Greenacre sees the artist's creation as the displacement of his libidinal strivings, and the professional activity of being an artist with a public, the audience, as the provenance of a love gift to the audience, which represents the collective alternates to the original libidinal object.

Greenacre's concept of collective alternates and oedipal inspiration states may account for the well-known observation that women are not so artistically creative as men, since it is more culturally sanctioned for women to continue to have some conscious or preconscious attachment to the original object of libidinal strivings. She comments further on sex differences in creativity in her 1960 paper "Woman as Artist."

Case History

Alan was seventeen years old when he was referred to the hospital, in December, from a local private school he had been attending; he was suffering from an acute psychosis. The history presented below is derived almost exclusively from the first two years of his intensive four-times-a-week psychotherapy, and especially from the analysis of repetitions in the transference and of anniversary phenomena.

I first met Alan two and one half months after his admission to the hospital, at which time I wrote:

> He appears to be an extremely intelligent boy. He reminds me of a youthful anorexic version of Albert Einstein, and he is alternately childishly charming and placating, or else aloof, contemptuous, and sarcastic. He is extremely skeptical of the possibility of any meaningful human interchange occurring through words. He paints a picture of himself as one who is hemmed in, constricted, forced by the environment, and unable to trust people. "You people won't let me by myself. I don't trust people. You're trying to make something out of me I don't want to be. I have more faith in Jungians because they believe in the spirit."

Family History

Mrs. B., Alan's mother, was described by the admitting doctor as domineering, guilty, and very threatened. Alan has alternately viewed her in the course of therapy as a person who dominated and controlled him and did not allow him a separate identity, or else as a person who was depressed, withdrawn from the family, and unable to create a secure, warm, controlled, and disciplined environment. At the time of admission she described having a "special" relationship with the patient, which the stepfather, Mr. O., compared with that of two lovers. Mrs. B. came from a very wealthy family and had a progressive education. She was interested in the arts, and indeed did beautiful drawing and craftwork herself. She met the patient's father, Dr. B., when both were students at the same private school which Alan was attending at the time of his admission. After the death of her first husband, the patient's father, she became an alcoholic and underwent psychotherapy.

Dr. B., Alan's father, died in an auto accident when Alan was seven years old. At the time of his death Dr. B. was a renal surgeon who was just beginning practice in a northern New England college community. He was described as an extremely active, hard-driving, intensely curious, somewhat compulsive individual of sanguine disposition. He must have been remarkably talented. He was an athlete, played the harmonica and the accordion, was a photographer, and a skilled artistic craftsman. When he was a student at the private school which Alan later attended, he composed and illustrated an elaborate paper on insects, and the drawings are of an accuracy and quality which one would expect to find in a first-class biology textbook.

On the paternal side of the family Alan's great-grandmother was a professional artist.

Alan had four younger siblings. He was rather close to and rivalrous with his one-year-younger brother who, he felt, was favored by his father and who excelled him academically and athletically. His relations with the three youngest, a boy four years his junior and sisters six and seven years younger, have been more distant except for some sexual experimentation with the girls in early puberty. Alan's youngest sister was born only about a month before his father's death.

The other important family member is the stepfather, Mr. O., who married Alan's mother when Alan was eleven, about four years after Dr. B.'s death, and was divorced by her about a year following the patient's hospitalization, the definitive separation occurring almost exactly at the anniversay of Dr. B.'s death. Mr. O., a teacher, was never really accepted by either the mother or the children as a member of the family and was perceived by Alan as a harsh, threatening critic. Apparently, Alan's mother and stepfather fought for the allegiance of the children, and Mr. O. was decisively defeated.

Personal History

There is little information about Alan's infancy and early childhood. The family moved frequently while Dr. B., who was away from home much of the time, acquired his medical training. Alan described his mother as an insecure and inconsistent person who precociously attempted to endow him with adult capacities. On the other hand, he had fond memories of his mother reading to him what he referred to as "quest" fairy stories. Mrs. B. has described Alan as a tense, thin infant.

Alan told me that he was able to induce and control what appear to be hallucinatory experiences since early childhood; for example, he described being able to perceive a green, froglike jelly mass under tables. Alan recalled from his early childhood terrifying experiences of gradual, uncontrollable identity loss; a passive sensation of paralysis and merger with a larger cosmic unity. He claimed that this experience came increasingly under his control and, as he grew older, changed affectively from a terrifying one to something he often induced for pleasure. It is of note that he lost control of both the hallucinations and the merger experiences during his acute psychosis.

Alan's significant, continuous memory dated to approximately the year preceding his father's death, his sixth year, an era he tended to look upon as an idyllic one and which he longed to recapture. He was intensely involved with his father, trying to bridge the gap which he felt separated them; in fact, it would not be an exaggeration to say he was living for his father's approval and for closeness with him. As Alan's postweekend and early morning depressions were scrutinized in therapy, it emerged that these were the times he customarily had spent with his very busy father, who had awakened him and cooked breakfast in the morning while simultaneously practicing the tying of surgical knots with one hand. Dr. B. was greatly admired by Alan for his many accomplishments, but was perceived as being distant, either withholding his approval of Alan or else actively criticizing and punishing him and preferring the younger brother; in short, he was a frightening figure. Alan tried desperately to live up to what he perceived to be his father's standards in order to win closeness and approval. As he was awkward and uncoordinated at sports he tried to draw pictures like his father did. He knew his father was a doctor, and remembered one occasion when he had drawn an elaborate skeleton for father, only to have father burn it.

As Alan recalled the summer before his father's death, during which his mother was pregnant with his youngest sister, it was apparent that he wanted to be like father in other ways as well. At that time the family lived in the Midwest where Dr. B. was just completing his surgical residency. Alan recalled sleeping next to his parents' bedroom and wondering what went on there. He remembered his own sexual curiosity and his perception of the female genital as a wound, a castration. He wanted to do what father did to mother, but felt incapable and wanted to talk to his father about it and get help. At this time in Alan's life Dr. B. moved to New England to get established, leaving his wife and the children behind for the summer. Alan and his mother achieved a special closeness during that summer of his father's absence. He recalled staying up late at night with her in her bedroom eating ice cream and talking. She told him stories of German concentration camps and Nazi atrocities, and she also told him much about sex and that it felt good.

Dr. B. returned to the family in the fall, about a month prior to his death, around the birth of his youngest daughter, to help move the family to New England. Alan resented that his father was away so much and did not spend more time with him, felt guilty about his closeness with and sexual wishes for mother, and was angry that his father had returned and spoiled the fairy-tale world of expectation mother had created. He blamed his father for the unwanted move to New England. Alan recalled a long, silent motor trip across Canada alone with his father, probably at the time of the move, during which he felt quite estranged; there was no verbal communication except for occasional remarks by father about the beauty of the landscape, and little interaction except for occasional stops for father to photograph trees.

Shortly after the move to New England Alan, then seven years of age, sustained a painful injury to a finger when he put his hand through a pane of glass, and his finger had to be splinted and bandaged in a curved position. He recollected fear that the finger might never straighten out again, and anger at his father who had seemed unsympathetic to his pain.

One evening, several weeks after the family had established itself in the new home, Dr. B. yelled at the children because they did not go to bed on time. On the following morning Alan remained angry at his father. As Dr. B. prepared to leave for work, Alan deliberately busied himself with his toys and ignored his father. Dr. B. said good-bye, but Alan ignored him. Dr. B. was killed when his

Volkswagen collided head on with another car crossing a bridge. Ironically, Dr. B.'s final medical certificate arrived in the mail that very morning.

Alan learned of his father's death when his mother collapsed on his lap and cried. She told him he would have to be a man and take over for his father, and he recalled looking around him fully expecting to find that the world had disappeared, and reacting to his mother's announcement with a trapped, paralyzed feeling. Indeed, his father had meant the world to Alan; and when he learned that his father had died he became confused about what was going on inside of him and what was happening outside, a confusion that was interwoven with ideas about life and death and with his own guilty need for punishment. In short, he was not sure what had happened to whom, but something central to his being was dead. He also felt betrayed that he had made such an enormous investment in someone and had been left. At the same time he did not really accept that his father was dead; even after his therapy was far advanced he still harbored the fantasy that his father had gone on a trip and would return.

Alan was extremely guilty about what had happened. He felt that his father had died because he had been a bad boy whose feet were too big, who was not good enough in school, who fought with other children, and who harbored forbidden wishes about his mother. The death was interpreted as caused by his badness and as a punishment for it. He recalled the family gathering and eating food, and being kept from school for several days, events that he viewed as a celebration and which therefore enhanced his guilt. After Dr. B.'s death the family obtained a Catholic housekeeper whose literal morality fit in with Alan's fantasies about crime and punishment. He felt that he was destined to go to hell, and indeed experienced his life after his father's death as a hell. In treatment he realized that his "flip-outs" were a hell of alienation, meaninglessness, and dreariness, peopled by monsters, a hell like that which he had experienced and interpreted as condign punishment after his father's death.

In another sense his father's death was a wish fulfillment, the sexual implications of which overwhelmed him. As previously mentioned, during the preceding summer he had been striving to have intercourse with his mother the way father did, and the events of that summer had inflamed his wishes. They were intensified by mother's comments that he would have to take father's place, and by the actions of his paternal grandmother who would steal into his bedroom at night inebriated and whisper to him that he should grow up to be like his father. During therapy, around the anniversary of his father's death, he had a dream in which he was growing a second penis; this dream revealed that with father gone he had felt he had to do the job of two men, that he also had to be his father's penis to mother. But he felt "dead, nothing, drooping, dangling. I couldn't handle my mother, I was only seven; even with the two phalluses in that dream I couldn't do it." He gave up and sat, passive and depressed, watching television and the barren winter landscape, which he recalled in vivid detail. For a whole year after Dr. B.'s death Alan could not do his schoolwork; he had a specific reading difficulty and was not promoted from second grade. His relationship with father had been based on activities; watching father, doing things with father and for father, not on verbal communication, in which he had no faith. With the loss of his father, Alan lost the wish to do things; and when this wish returned he felt empty inside, the things he would make had no meaning because father was not around to give them to, so that when he started serious artwork, in the year following his father's death, he gave whatever he made to anyone who wanted it.

Nor did Alan receive much support from his mother. Following Dr. B.'s death, she seems to have been severely depressed, having to cope with a newborn and the care of four other children. She cried frequently and was withdrawn. She was emotionally unavailable to Alan so that he had no one with whom he could share what sounded like psychotic grief of his own. Furthermore, Alan remembered how his mother would knot his father's tie, and how after his death she wore father's clothes, did his chores around the house, and adopted some of his mannerisms. These memories interwove with Alan's fantasies and led him to wonder whether his mother was a monster, witch, vampire or spider who had devoured father in order to have Alan to herself. This frightened him. He was also angry when his wishes to have mother to himself were not fulfilled. He was further confused when after what he experienced as preparation for his new role, the following summer mother sent him off to camp, where he felt rejected, homesick, and frightened, and was enuretic. Life with mother not only was filled with these contradictions, but it was insecure. Alan recalled with fright how his mother had burned the Christmas tree in the fireplace of a house with wooden shingles. She did not discipline the children but believed in letting them fight things out until she got so angry that she would explode. And open nudity was sanctioned in the family, so that the siblings regularly saw one another undressed.

At that time Alan also felt alienated from his peers. He had no father, and they did. He wore glasses. He had pinworms and was called dumb by his schoolmates because he learned to read and tell time much later than they did. His brothers would taunt him because of a supposed curvature of his penis. He had some breast development at puberty and his genital development was delayed; he felt further alienated by his intense, guilt-ridden incestuous concerns.

When Alan was eleven years old his mother remarried. In one sense, because he considered his mother so undependable, Alan welcomed Mr. O., his stepfather, but for the most part he resented him as an intruder. It is of interest that although Alan's schoolwork had improved by the time of the remarriage, he subsequently lost all interest in both personal and world history. He began an incestuous relationship with his sisters which included ejaculation but not penetration and lasted for three years. He felt that the impetus for this relationship came in part from a demotion from a more challenging to a less challenging group in school.

The parents' marriage was not happy. They had explosive and frightening arguments, each vying for power and trying to get the children on his or her side. The children, if punished by one parent, would turn to the other for support. At this time Alan engaged in a considerable amount of denial and projection, using the landscape as his screen, and this will be elaborated in the section on his artistic activities. He became a behavior problem at home, was insolent to his parents, sneaky and untruthful, and often ran away without permission. The parents, in turn, would interrogate Alan in the room formerly used by Dr. B. as a study, and there Alan recalled his stepfather threatening him with the police.

When Alan was thirteen, his parents sent him away to a private school, which he interpreted as a rejection. Although he made several friends there, he was disliked by most of his teachers, who considered him lazy and undisciplined. He felt increasingly isolated and different from other people, and turned to his artwork with renewed vigor.

At the age of fifteen Alan returned to a public school in his home town, where he remained until the fall preceding his hospitalization. There he felt depressed and estranged from family and peers alike. He made some attempts to be accepted by the group by drinking, playing football, and even an episode of car-stealing, but he experienced these activities as superficial and unsuccessful. His grades were very poor, but he did a great deal of painting and drawing. He began to drink and to experiment with drugs, though not on a regular basis.

During the winter of his sixteenth year, about one year prior to hospitalization, Alan experienced mood swings of increasing frequency and amplitude, with vivid pleasant and unpleasant hallucinations accompanied by elation and artistic productivity, at one extreme, and an episode of depression and suicidal ideation during which he slashed his left wrist, at the other. He hallucinated skulls and frogs under the tables. He did not tell anyone about this, but did ask to see a psychiatrist. His parents, who were very upset with almost everything about him at this point, did not permit him to do so. Alan became increasingly attracted to the drug cult and to mystical philosophy. Periods of activity and painting continued to alternate with periods of depression and immobility, and his life pattern became increasingly disorganized with inversion of the sleep pattern and habit deterioration.

Just prior to his seventeenth birthday, he was sent away to the private school where his parents had met. He felt lonely, alienated, depressed, and incapable of doing as well as his parents had done. As the anniversary of the move to New England and the death of his father, always a most difficult time, approached, things worsened. After Thanksgiving he began medicating himself regularly and heavily with a variety of drugs including amphetamines, which he took first to combat his depression, marijuana, and LSD. He had almost continuous hallucinations involving all his senses as well as other disturbing distortions of his sensory experience. The hallucinations became increasingly alien, frightening, and attacking, often in the form of animals and monsters. One hallucination of being buried represented his sense of vulnerability in relation to his stepparent. He also experienced sensory distortions in which walls would bulge, floors undulate, and rugs sparkle, which were a projection of his own feeling of weakness. Finally, the school consulted a psychoanalyst who referred Alan to the hospital.

On admission Alan was oriented but confused and frightened, guilty and ashamed. His associations were loose and his often contradictory thoughts indicated primary process functioning. He believed that he had lived other lives in the past and that his flesh was being torn apart and eaten. He had visual hallucinations of little men and rabbits. He strongly cathected his pleasant hallucinations and related them to art and to his identity. He was reluctant to remain in the hospital, and wanted to undergo a Jungian analysis. Psychological tests performed two weeks after admission hinted at an organic problem, probably drug residual, and an electroencephalogram was mildly and diffusely abnormal. The psychologist commented on the patient's disorganized appearance and speech, his poor reality testing, his hallucinations, his ideas of influence which were at times overtly paranoid, his withdrawal from object relations and loss of sense of self, and his tendency to live amidst the events his mind would create.

MATERIAL RELATED TO THE PATIENT AS AN ARTIST

Of particular interest are those aspects of Alan's endowment which might help us to understand what made him an artist. The most obvious and basic of these is his heredity. Both parents were extremely talented artistically, and there is a striking similarity among some of the pen-and-ink drawings done by mother, father, and Alan.

One of the most important characteristics of the patient as an artist is his hypercathexis of the visual apparatus and experience, whether it be current perception, memory, dream, or psychotic hallucination, as opposed to verbal thought and communication, about which Alan was very skeptical until he was well advanced in therapy. At the very start of therapy he stated that there were two worlds: the superficial social and verbal world; and the world of vivid Jungian, artistic fantasy deep inside, which was not susceptible of verbal translation and description. He also said that the outer perceptual world was all important, and the inner world of thoughts and feelings unimportant or perhaps even nonexistent. Even his memories were pictorializations. Indeed, he showed an extraordinary capacity for vivid visual recall of early childhood experience; it was' as though he had somehow taken and stored away pictures which might later be reviewed in all their original freshness. It is also impressive how many dreams of unusual richness and complexity Alan regularly remembered and could reproduce in detail, often six or seven in one night. Two other aspects of Alan's visual hypercathexis, his apparent continuing capacity for hallucinatory experiences from childhood on, and his artistic interest itself, have already been mentioned.

It is possible to identify three determinants of Alan's perceptual hypercathexis that derived from the period of infantile self-object differentiation: fusion experiences, projection, and manic denial. The experience of self-object merger or fusion was described by Alan during the first month of therapy when he told of a pleasant hypnagogic hallucination reminiscent of the blank dreams described by Lewin (1950), or the Isakower phenomenon:

> I saw a blue ocean with a multitude gathering on the shore. The multitude forked in two and a huge black chest was revealed. I opened it and saw an immense sparkling endless round sleep-inducing diamond.

Around the same period of therapy he described his repetitive childhood terror involving a gradual diffusion of his identity and boundaries and a sense of being overcome by or merging with a cosmic unity, so that he felt paralyzed and carried inexorably along by a slow movement, a pervasive silence, with which he would unite. In his psychotic experiences he reported loss of the sense of self and merger with the world, or loss of the world and feeling that everything was a movie in his head. At times he associated this with loss of the self here and now, and return to something in the past; at other times this sense of identity loss and merger with or capture by a larger entity was graphically associated to his relationship with his mother. Finally, sixteen months after the start of therapy, following a period of artistic unproductivity, he returned to the studio only to make the frightening discovery that he must lose himself in the experience just described in order to create, and that he would actually remain disoriented for a few minutes after he stopped working.

The mechanism of splitting off parts of the self, or projection, also seems to be an important determinant of the richness of Alan's visual experience. The outer world and the dream world became a screen onto which he could project unpleasant affect. After three months of therapy he realized that he dealt with anger by making it an object, taking distance from it and alienating himself, so that it would then reappear in the form of nightmares about monsters and war. He could recall the exact external situation at the time of his father's death, and he remarked, "My feelings were a cinema-scope in my mind, they were out there." While others grieved for his father, he was not aware of feelings, but was acutely sensitive to changes in the bleak winter landscape, which he found sad and hated. Subsequently he characteristically perceived fall landscapes as dead and empty. After about a year of therapy he was more aware of his projective tendencies, so that he could sometimes infer his inner feelings from the way the outer world looked to him. He also concluded that his hallucinations were the product of concentrating on the outside when he was upset and projecting things out there.

Finally, the third determinant of Alan's intense perceptual cathexis of the external world was a maniclike denial of inner feelings. Early in therapy Alan's tendency to cope with painful subjects by talking about the beauty of the landscape became evident. During the first month he described how he was able to make things into great aesthetic wholes, cosmic canvases, of which he was a detached observer, in order to avoid feelings. In this context he described a dream he had had one year before hospitalization. In his dream Alan was lying on the floor of a large cave staring at the ceiling, where a panorama of hundreds of years was passing by, and feeling a sensation of cosmic beauty and peace. After his father had died, he survived his terrible depression by looking "out of my eyes at the world. It's like everything is a hallucination. I looked at the December day and occupied myself with thoughts of out there. I guess I became unreal, in my feelings, that is." A similar mechanism was employed after his mother remarried. The parents were arguing, and Mr. O. accused Alan's mother of drinking and spoiling the children. The children cried and ran out of the house. Alan hid in the bushes, petrified with fear and a feeling of impending catastrophe. He protected himself by looking off toward a distant mountain and focusing his attention on its scenic beauty. This became a characteristic way of dealing with their arguments. That this determinant of Alan's perceptual hypercathexis, namely, denial of affect, relates to manic denial is supported by his use of flight into activity as a way to negate his inner life in treatment. Once he told me that when he was restricted to the ward, his inner self became much more important; but when he was outside and active, "I lost myself externally."

Up to this point the discussion has centered on Alan's perceptual hypercathexis and his predilection for the creative sensory experience, viewed as derivatives of the mechanisms of fusion with the object, projection of emotion, and manic denial common to the period of infantile self-object differentiatior. The determinants of his creative activities derive from a different level of development; namely. Alan's fixation at the point of incomplete identification with his father in resolution of the oedipus complex at the time of his father's death. A photographic technique used skillfully in such recent movies as *The Pawnbroker, Blowup,* and *Elvira Madigan* may help us to visualize Alan's taste. In these movies the filmstrip is stopped at a critical point, indelibly capturing the subject immobilized in the midst of an important action. In this manner Alan may have been arrested in the act of identifying with his father. He said on many occasions that "things don't exist in words" and that he had no faith in verbal communication. As he remembered it, he and father did not communicate in words. Instead there was an intense visual-motor cathexis of father and his interests. He watched father intently and tried to emulate him and gain his approval by playing sports, which he was not good at, and by drawing pictures as gifts for father. When he and father were together they would do things, or father would comment on the beauty of the landscape and Alan would pay close attention. Thus looking for father, looking at father, looking at beautiful things with father, doing things with and for father, and giving to father were important unfinished issues at the time of father's death. During his treatment Alan brought in a cut-out-and-paste collage picture of his father which he had made when he was five years of age. It was reminiscent of the experience of standing at the base of a huge skyscraper and looking upward. The legs and penis were immense. Father was obviously a giant to the boy.

After the bitter disappointment of losing his father, Alan did not transfer his affection to another person. Apparently he remained depressed and immobile for some time, although he had intense experiences of the beauty of the visual world. He did continue to hope that his father would return, and he retained the idea of a golden era in the past associated with vivid memories of his parents and perceptual recollections of beautiful landscapes in places where the family had lived. His hitherto casual drawing blossomed into a serious interest in art when his paternal grandmother came into his room one night not long after the tragedy, drunk, and exhorted him to be like father, not to waste his life and his artistic talent. The subsequent resemblance between his artwork, his dreams, and his hallucinations is noteworthy. He made elaborate pen-and-ink drawings of crickets which resembled very much Dr. B.'s drawings of grasshoppers in his biology paper. It is striking that Alan placed no value on his art productions and invariably gave them away without thought of payment to anyone who showed interest. When the anniversary of his father's death approached one year prior to his hospitalization, Alan began to experience dramatic mood swings from periods of depression and suicidal ideation to periods of elation marked by vivid hallucinations and increased artistic productivity. When the anniversary recurred the following year, just prior to admission, Alan began to take mood-elevating and hallucinogenic drugs in order to combat the depression and foster elation, and to produce vivid sensory experiences which he associated with the wish to reinstate the world as it was prior to the death of his father.

After about ten months of psychotherapy, the first portion of which was devoted to the establishment of a trusting relationship and the latter portion to the work of grief over his father's death, Alan began to complete via the transference the process of identification with his father which had been arrested when Dr. B. died. Alan began to ask me how he could please me. After eleven months of therapy he said that for the first time in his life words had become important. He was now able to think in therapy because he felt that he was doing it for me, though between sessions he remained unable to think verbally. But at the same time he lost his artistic inspiration and creativity. This he attributed to therapy, the goal of which he believed to be to have him *think* things through. He added that the only reason he had created was for his father, and he felt he was in an intermediate period between doing it for his father and doing it for himself.

About a year later Alan did resume his artwork which then had acquired new meaning. After twenty-two months of therapy he said that he was not completing anything he started because finished works of art had a life of their own like children, and he was afraid of the responsibility which producing them might entail. He added that artistic creation was like sexual procreation: that artists are insecure people who fear for their potency and express it through their hands, the finished work being like an ejaculation or a child. After two years of therapy there ensued another period of artistic unproductivity, although Alan was then actively learning and doing many new things. At that time he said jokingly that he identified with his therapist. He copied my mannerisms, and thought as he believed I did. He borrowed particular phrases and words I had used when he dealt with people important in his life, presenting this language as his own. He said, "Words have a zing, they're sexual, electric. Words are *mine* now." He felt as though he had been on a kind of Pilgrim's Progress since his father's death, looking for a magic diamond; a roundtrip which would eventually lead back to the family as it had been before his father died. In the process he would learn that although he wanted mother for himself, he could not have her because she belonged to father, so "I will have to find my own thing to do."

After two years of therapy, he was happier, and felt he no longer was a child. But he was depressed and longed for close human relations. About art he said, "There's nothing I want to make. Art seems silly, futile, an imitation like a portrait. You know, I want the real thing." During the interview in which he related this he described a series of dreams of the previous night, the content of which he could not recall, but from which he awakened laughing. He associated the mood to that which he might feel were he with his current girlfriend, who lived in another city.

DISCUSSION

What follows is an attempt to describe Alan's creativity in theoretical terms which may be applicable to other artists as well.

The artist may be a person who has particular problems involving the resolution of those phases of development that involve the self-object separation, first the differentiation from mother in infancy, and later the selective identifications in the oedipal phase. The self-object differentiation phase remains the fixation point for his regression under stress, and such adaptive mechanisms as the inclination to fusion, the projective mode, and manic denial, which are employed at that time to forestall the painful affect associated with individuation and thereby to retain the security of primal unity, later also serve the perceptual apparatus of the artist. The usual mode of resolution by identification of the ensuing oedipal conflict is rendered more difficult by primitive tendencies to fuse with, on the one hand, and to project onto and repel, on the other, both the mother who must again be relinquished and the afther who is to be the object of identification. If conflict resolution is then arrested by the trauma of real or imagined loss of the object of identification, adaptive, depressive, and regressive mechanisms determine the crystallization of artistic endeavor. In other words, the oedipal trauma sets the stage for doing art. There may be a partial identification with aspects of the lost object of identification that relate specifically to art. As the identification process is incomplete, however, there is a characterological arrest in the posture of questing, taking in, or inspiration, in an attempt to restitute the lost object and complete the task of identification. It will not escape notice that there is a peculiar resonance or reverberation between this characterological questing after the oedipal object of identification and the more primitive mechanisms invoked to prevent separateness, loss, and depression, and to maintain the primitive unity of the preobject period of development. In other words, the artist has a primitive perceptual orientation, an inspirational or questing character derived from trauma incurred during both periods of self-object separation, and a creative attitude involving partial oedipal identifications.

Furthermore, the trauma of renunciation of the oedipal love object plus the loss of the object of potential identification institute a regression to a more primitive mode of ego and instinctual organization involving the use of projection, fusion, manic denial, and primary process thinking. In this attempt to re-establish a state of unity there occur more or less controlled rapid ego regressions to this more primitive mode of functioning analogous to the perceptual regression which occurs during dreaming. These ego regressions can continue to occur in a controlled manner during the creative process and, if the trauma is sufficiently severe, in psychotic periods as well. The creative process is set in motion when painful affects related to object loss and object hunger threaten to become conscious. The ego's defenses set in motion by the internal signal as well as the unavailability of the real objects striven for block the path to consciousness and motor discharge much as in the dream state. Regression according to the laws of primary process to the perceptual-visual apparatus then occurs, as in the dream. Whether this hallucinatory-like wish fulfillment is not sufficient, as in severe anxiety dreams which lead to waking, or whether this whole process remains under some ego control, or both, there ensues an attempt on the part of the ego using secondary process mechanisms to reproduce the perceptual experience as art, analogous to the attempt of the dreamer on awakening to recall his dream. In this way the artist creates his own world of objects which he may then possess and maintain, thus avoiding for the time the pain of loss.

The adolescent whose history was presented did not resolve the problems of self-object differentiation completely, and during periods of regression initiated by the threat of experiencing painful affects consequent to object loss, his ego would function in ways appropriate to this level, with fusion experiences, projection, affect denial, and primary process thinking. These mechanisms were partially responsible for his remarkable capacity for visual imagery and symbol formation, although they also contributed to his skepticism and indifference regarding the possibility of communication in words.

During the oedipal conflict Alan's unusual openness to fusion experiences must have heightened his cathexis of his father, whereas his reliance on projection must have sharpened the negative aspect of the ambivalence and made the identification with father more difficult. Dr. B.'s emphasis on art must have been especially meaningful for Alan because of his constitutional endowment and his predilection for perceptual experience derived from his own early history and utilized in his real relationship with his father. Thus, before Dr. B.'s death Alan's artistic endeavor served as a partial identification with him and a love gift to him. When Dr. B. died suddenly, in mid-identification, so to speak, the quest for father via art and the proneness to inspiration became parts of Alan's character structure; a kind of set oriented toward solving the uncompleted problem and reinforced by a similar, but more primitive set derived from the earlier self-object differentiation period. At the same time there was a regression to a more primitive organization which facilitated his artistic perceptiveness and his capacity to form visual images. The result was a precarious balance in which the regressions to the more primitive modes at one time served the creative process and at other times led to an overt psychotic state, depending on the degree to which the ego controlled them. In both instances, however, they helped deny and prevent the pain of loss and maintain the object relationship as well as the preobject state of unity.

Conclusion

The hypothesis presented here is not inconsistent with the theoretical formulations found in the literature. There are similarities between the patient presented and artists studied by other authors. A comparison of material suggests that common psychological factors are involved rather than unique and fortuitous relationships. Of course, one may speculate that the traumatic events in Alan's life interfered with his development as an artist rather than contributed to it, or that his pathology and his artistic endeavors just happened to coexist without being related. It is equally possible that the severity of his pathology has thrown into bold relief some of the creative mechanisms, much as a partial paralysis may offer the physiologist unexpected opportunities to study muscle function. In the course of psychotherapy the grief-work related to his father's death was completed, and the arrested oedipal conflict was resolved through the transference completing identifications and superego formation. At the same time some doubt arose whether Alan would continue with his artistic pursuits. If he should not become an artist it might be not because he lacked the talents and psychological makeup of an artist, but rather because the oedipal trauma he sustained was so severe that the defensive and restitutive value of art alone was not sufficient to allow him to form a stable identity as an artist. His tendency to psychotic regression characterized by loss of the capacity to make self-object differentiation and restitutive attempts involving vivid dreams, fantasies, and hallucinations led him into treatment. This treatment, insofar as it resolved the problems which tended toward artistic endeavor, may have proved to be his downfall as an artist, though certainly not as an active, productive, and hopefully nonpsychotic individual.

BIBLIOGRAPHY

Bernfeld, S. (1924), *Vom Dichterischen Schaffen der Jugend: Neue Beiträge zur Jugendforschung. Vienna:* Internationaler Psychoanalytischer Verlag. Unpublished English summary by Peter H. Wolff.

Fraiberg, L. (1956), Freud's Writings on Art. *Int. J. Psa.,* 37:82-96.

Freud, A. (1922), The Relation of Beating-Phantasies to a Day-Dream. *Int. J. Psa.,* 4:89-102, 1923.

Freud, S. (1900), The Interpretation of Dreams. *Standard Edition,* 4 & 5. London: Hogarth Press, 1953.

—— (1908), Creative Writers and Day-Dreaming. *Standard Edition,* 9:141-153. London: Hogarth Press, 1959.

—— (1910), Leonardo da Vinci and a Memory of His Childhood. *Standard Edition,* 11:63-137. London: Hogarth Press, 1957.

—— (1911), Formulations on the Two Principles of Mental Functioning. *Standard Edition,* 12:213-226. London: Hogarth Press, 1958.

—— (1916-1917), Introductory Lectures on Psycho-Analysis. *Standard Edition,* 15 & 16. London: Hogarth Press, 1963.

—— (1928), Dostoevsky and Parricide. *Standard Edition,* 21:175-196. London: Hogarth Press, 1961.

Greenacre, P. (1957), The Childhood of the Artist. *This Annual,* 12:47-72.

—— (1958), The Family Romance of the Artist. *This Annual,* 13:9-43.

—— (1960), Woman as Artist. *Psa. Quart.,* 29:208-227.

—— (1963), *The Quest for the Father*. New York: International Universities Press.

Jones, E. (1953-1957), *The Life and Work of Sigmund Freud*, 3 Vols. New York: Basic Books.

Kris, E. (1950), On Preconscious Mental Processes. *Psychoanalytic Explorations in Art.* New York: International Universities Press, 1952, pp. 303-318.

—— (1952), *Psychoanalytic Explorations in Art.* New York: International Universities Press.

—— (1953), Psychoanalysis and the Study of Creative Imagination. *Bull. N.Y. Acad. Med.*, 2nd series, 29:334-351.

—— (1955), Neutralization and Sublimation. *This Annual*, 10:30-46.

Lewin, B. D. (1950), *The Psychoanalysis of Elation*. New York: Norton.

Lowenfeld, H. (1941), Psychic Trauma and Productive Experience in the Artist. *Psa. Quart.*, 10:116-130.

Mooney, W. E. (1968), Gustav Mahler: A Note on Life and Death in Music. *Psa. Quart.*, 37:80-102.

Spiegel, L. A. (1958), Comments on the Psychoanalytic Psychology of Adolescence. *This Annual*, 13:296-308.

URINE or YOU'RE IN

An Ambiguous Word and Its Relation to a Toilet Phobia in a Two-Year-Old

MILTON SIROTA, M.D. (New York)

This paper will present the pertinent clinical history which led to a toilet inhibition in a twenty-seven-month-old boy after the word "urine" was introduced for the first time. Such manifestations as a precocious heightening of phallic drive derivatives, oedipal interests, castration anxiety, and phobias at so early an age raise questions regarding their genetic determinants. I shall present some theoretical considerations which may explain the phenomenology.

In his book on wit, Freud (1905) wrote, "children, who as we know, are in the habit of still treating words as things, tend to expect words that are the same or similar to have the same meaning behind them—which is a source of many mistakes that are laughed at by grown-up people" (p. 120).

In a footnote to the case of Little Hans, Freud (1909) wrote, "It must never be forgotten how much more concretely children treat words than grown-up people do, and consequently how much more significant for them are similarities of sound in words" (p. 59).

During the course of development in an environment where distortions in interpretation are corrected the child learns to appreciate the abstract and figurative use of language and comprehend ambiguity and innuendo. Prior to that time the toddler gropes in a mysterious maze of sight and sound, trying to make some sense out of the confusion of the adult world of communication. When a child seems to misinterpret a concept, a corrective remark will

Department of Psychiatry, State University of New York, Downstate Medical Center.

often lead to a clearer understanding. For example, twenty-month-old Samuel, while walking along with his father on a sunny afternoon, looked up at the sky and asked, "What is that?" "That's the sun," his father replied. Samuel, who had heard his father call him son then asked, "Me up in the sky, Daddy?" His father recognized the confusion and made the necessary clarification so that Samuel could appreciate that there were two meanings to the word. He learned that the meaning could be inferred only from the context in which the term was used.

Such misinterpretations are ubiquitous and can be ascribed to a stage of language formation. One need merely talk to a two- or three-year-old child to realize the extent of such distortions. However, a stage in language development is not the only determinant for such distortions. Why particular concepts are chosen for distortion and why the distortion takes a particular form cannot be fully explained in developmental terms. These distortions are overdetermined and should be understood within a genetic-dynamic frame of reference. Ferenczi's remarks (1913) are pertinent: "one was formerly inclined to believe that things are confounded because they are similar; nowadays we know that a thing is confounded with another only because certain motives for this are present; similarity merely provides the opportunity for these motives to function" (p. 281).

This work was originally undertaken to study features of childhood ego and drive development through direct observation by a parent. The parent in this case was a psychiatric resident supervised by the author. His wife had just delivered their first son when he began his observations in his home and recorded them in a diary. The following history was obtained largely from the diary but was also supplemented by several discussions with the parents.

CASE HISTORY

History of Lion Phobia and Toilet Inhibition

Samuel began to use the toilet to urinate when he was eighteen months old. Following a visit to the zoo when he was twenty months old, he developed a transient reluctance to use the toilet. After he described his fear that a lion would come out of the toilet and bite his penis, he was reassured by his parents that this would not happen to him. Samuel persisted in reiterating more vigorously that a lion was indeed in the toilet. His father told him that this was not so and that he could not understand why Samuel felt that way. During the next several days Samuel persisted in his belief. Having observed Samuel attempt to bite his mother and being scolded for it, his father decided to interpret the fear. He told Samuel, "Just because Mommy is angry at you for biting her it doesn't mean that the lion in the zoo was angry at you too. I think you feel that the lion will bite you because you so much want to bite Mommy." Samuel seemed relieved and smiled. His father added that his mother would not permit him to injure her by biting and that he, Samuel, was not going to be injured for wanting to bite. Samuel immediately began to urinate into the toilet and no longer showed apprehension. Occasionally, he would jokingly say, "There is the lion, me lion," and then he would laugh.

At the age of twenty-three months, Samuel used the toilet to urinate fairly regularly. By the time he was twenty-seven months old he had achieved full daytime bladder control. He would either go directly to the bathroom and say, "Me make wee wee," or, upon clutching his groin while at play, he would be asked if he had to "make wee wee," and he would respond according to his needs. Then suddenly a dramatic change took place, in that Samuel began to wet his training pants. He would obstinately refuse to use the toilet when it was suggested to him. Occasionally, he would acquiesce and stand before the toilet for a minute or two, only to demand to leave the bathroom and urinate in his diapers, which had to be once more introduced.

After about a week of this regressive return to enuresis, or more accurately, a refusal to use the toilet, a curious thing took place. His father, who was a loving and ordinarily a perspicacious man, was encouraging Samuel to use the toilet after Samuel had indicated his desire to make "a wee wee." While standing before the toilet his father noticed a definite apprehension on the young boy's face, and remarked in a kindly and interested fashion, "Are you scared of something?" Samuel gave the unusual reply, "What it called?" "What, what called?" the confused father asked. Samuel obligingly responded with, "What wee wee called." Still bewildered, the unknowing father replied, "Wee wee is called wee wee." Samuel persisted by asking, "What else wee wee called?" At this point Samuel's father suddenly realized what had taken place. He remembered that on the day when the symptom started he had introduced the term "urine" to refer to wee wee. He recalled having asked Samuel, "Do you want to make urine?" He also recalled that he attempted to explain that urine was another word for wee wee.

Realizing the probable source of the symptom, his father then asked Samuel whether he meant the word urine, to which Samuel replied, "Yes." Having sensed the ambiguous meaning of the term, his father asked Samuel whether he was scared because of the word urine. Another affirmative reply indicated that he was on the right track and he asked, "Samuel, were you scared that when you make a wee wee you will fall into the potty?" "Yes," was the reply. His father then said, "Urine does not mean that you will fall in. It is another word for wee wee. When you make urine or a wee wee it does not mean that you will fall into the potty. The wee wee or urine goes into the potty. Samuel with his penis and his bladder stay here. Let's just call it wee wee from now on, O.K.?" Samuel, whose precocity in other areas was quite prominent, did what was characteristic for him when he discovered a bit of foolish reasoning in himself. He laughingly exclaimed, "That silly. Me no go in potty. Wee wee go in potty." Samuel urinated, began to use the toilet regularly, and proceeded to achieve nighttime bladder control during the next six months.

Pertinent Clinical Material

Samuel was the first child born to a psychiatric resident and his wife, a college graduate who majored in biology. Pregnancy was normal but delivery was prolonged to ten hours and required a mid-forceps extraction. Breast feeding was continued until ten months. At the age of four and one half months Samuel began to teethe, and shortly thereafter he would vigorously bite his mother's breast. This was handled by a gentle admonishment consisting of pressing on his lower jaw to unclench his teeth, shaking of the mother's head in a negative way with the word "no" clearly but not loudly uttered. The breast was then removed for a few seconds and then returned to his mouth. A sly grin appeared on Samuel's face just prior to each episode of vigorous biting. These biting episodes persisted for several months with one minor complication, which consisted of a mild transient unilateral mastitis.

Further inquiries about his biting behavior revealed an event that occurred while Samuel was still in the hospital nursery. The nurse there, who was a warm, interested, and patient woman, noticed that Samuel chewed vigorously during breast feeding, and the breast had to be repositioned in order to get him to suck properly.

When Samuel was about five months old he began to cry at night. He received only partial comfort from his mother, who would go into his room, pick him up for a short time, and return him to his crib only to see him cry once again. This procedure usually occurred several times in succession. Samuel cried during the next few nights and his father noted that the cry began with an intense high-pitched sound quite different from the usual gradual awakening, which consisted of progressively louder moans and groans. Furthermore, the crying did not seem to be related to painful teething inasmuch as aspirins, which ordinarily relieved such pain, were of no help. His father assumed that Samuel had a frightening dream. He conjectured that Samuel's anxiety about being separated from his parents contributed to this dream and he rushed into the room, saw Samuel lifting himself to stand and said, "Samuel! Mommy and daddy are here. There is nothing to be afraid of." Samuel looked at his father with some amazement, relaxed completely almost immediately, and soon fell asleep again. The night awakenings ceased abruptly.

When Samuel was six months old he began to stand with some support and made walking motions. A significant internal torsion of his left tibia was treated with a series of three Plaster of Paris casts applied at two-week intervals. The casts, extending from toes to mid-thighs, were removed with a high-pitched drill, which Samuel was permitted to manipulate prior to its use. He was not permitted to stand while he was wearing the casts, although he made several attempts to do so. He crawled about vigorously and suffered some discomfort while being bathed. Shortly after the casts were removed when he was eight months old he began to stand and then soon started to walk with support.

Language development began before his first birthday, at which time he was regarded as precocious in handling and manipulating various objects. He could speak full sentences at about eighteen months. At twenty months he spoke of an event which had taken place six months earlier when he still could not talk. He said, "Me play with Lois around flagpole with gun." Samuel was referring to his having run around a flagpole saying "bang-bang" when he was fourteen months old.

Although he could not speak full sentences until he was eighteen months old, he seemed to comprehend a great deal and often listened to his parents read to him. Once again he developed night awakenings at sixteen months after he was read a story about a young boy who had to prepare for the arrival of a new brother or sister. Samuel awakened at night with the cry, "Baby, baby!" These awakenings persisted for several days until Samuel's parents informed him that he, too, would get a baby brother or sister when he was two years old.

At the age of eighteen months a small flat nevus on Samuel's scrotum was excised under local anesthesia in a doctor's office with both parents present. Samuel played with some toys and was told that he would feel a slight stick on the skin of his scrotum. The procedure was tolerated without noticeable discomfort or anxiety.

Shortly after the nevus operation he was started on the potty in an attempt at bowel training. He developed a moderate constipation and blood-tinged stool and the use of the potty was discontinued.

A few days later, he expressed his awareness of his mother's growing abdomen. At twenty months he developed another series of nightmares. When awakened he would exclaim "Baby!" as he pointed to his mother's abdomen. He was told in some detail that the baby was in his mother's womb and the nightmares soon disappeared. During that month, bowel training was resumed. He listened to stories read to him as he sat on the potty and soon he began to defecate.

During his twentieth month he became increasingly aggressive, cried more readily, and tried to bite his mother, particularly on her buttocks. He used the toilet to urinate until the phobia of the lion biting his penis developed and remitted as was previously described. Although he continued to urinate into the toilet, he began to withhold his stool but defecated into the diaper after he left the potty. His parents felt that the bowel training and the forthcoming new baby were too much for him to tolerate at the same time and once again, they decided to postpone the bowel training. However, Samuel very much wanted to wear shorts instead of diapers and this required that he keep dry. As a result, he insisted upon achieving bowel control when he was twenty-three months old. By the time his mother entered the hospital when he was twenty-four months old, Samuel was almost completely toilet-trained.

During the months preceding delivery he was very curious about the expected sibling. He asked numerous questions; most of them were answered in a manner which could be fairly well understood by a child with his language development. How the baby would eat, where he would sleep, and what toys he would play with were easy to answer. Where the baby would come from was less easily answered. He was told that his mother had a special place in her "belly" called a womb in which the baby would grow for nine months, and would then come out through the vagina. She would have to go to the hospital where her doctor would help to deliver the baby. Samuel speculated that he too could have a baby in his abdomen and that it would come out of his umbilicus. He was then told that men do not have babies and that they do not come out of the mother's belly button, but through her vagina. No elaborate description of the vagina was made at that time.

During the course of the pregnancy, Samuel would often tap and lightly punch his mother's growing abdomen. Shortly before he was told about the new sibling he was very patient, attentive, and interested in listening to a storybook read to him by his parents. The story was about a boy who was awaiting the birth of a new baby sister and ended with the boy playfully holding his baby sister on his lap. When Samuel's mother was in her last trimester, Samuel was as interested as ever in hearing the beginning of the story about this little boy getting a new bed and chair for his bedroom, but Samuel insisted that the story end when the page was turned to show the little baby sister being brought home.

His negative feelings were demonstrated in a more painful way when at the age of twenty months he started to sneak up behind his mother and attempted to bite her buttocks. On two occasions he succeeded, and his mother vociferously reprimanded him. However, his feelings toward his mother were ambivalent. He was annoyed with his mother's pregnancy, but his positive feelings toward her intensi-fied. He would often say to his father, "Daddy you stay at work all night and I'll take care of Mommy." He enjoyed climbing upon his mother's lap, straddling her legs while facing her, and tried to push her down onto the couch. He would also lean on her from the side in order to use better leverage to push her onto the couch. When such behavior was curtailed he would turn to some dolls, particu-larly a teddy bear, upon which he would climb, rock up and down, and say how much he loved it. Periodic masturbatory activity with his hands increased at that time. It should be noted that Samuel was never exposed to parental intercourse and from birth slept in a separate bedroom.

During the week that Samuel's mother was away in the hospital delivering his younger brother, his father handled many of the household chores. Samuel liked pretzels, particularly long ones. While sitting at the table one day, he asked for a pretzel. He in-sisted on taking it out of the wrapper by himself, and inadvertently he broke it in half while trying to remove it. He burst into tears, and insisted that he be given another whole pretzel. This time his father insisted on removing the wrapper in order to guarantee his son his desired "whole pretzel." To his chagrin, Samuel's father dis-covered that the pretzel had a small, darkened, indented mark near its center. Knowing how much Samuel disliked blemishes on pret-zels, his father stealthily presented Samuel with the pretzel so posi-tioned as to obscure the blemish. Samuel began to gaze at his pretzel and slowly turned it in order to inspect the entire surface. When he discovered the site of damage, he again burst into tears, put the pretzel to the side and insisted on being given a whole un-blemished one. His father ordinarily would call a limit to this non-sense, but with his wife in the hospital, and directed by strong urgings from catering grandparents, he made his way to the local candy store to replenish the pretzel supply. He then presented Sam-uel with the carefully selected, unblemished pretzel. Hoping to get some note of appreciation and thanks from his son, Samuel's father noted the still apparent scowl on Samuel's face, while he munched on his "whole pretzel."

Father: What's the matter, Samuel? Don't you like the pretzel?
Samuel: No.
Father: Why not?
Samuel: Me want bigger pretzel.
Father: How much bigger can a pretzel be?
Samuel (with his arms outstretched): Me want pretzel up to
    ceiling.

While his mother was in the hospital, Samuel showed an unusually aloof and rejecting attitude toward his grandparents, who
spent a great deal of time taking care of him while his mother was
away. This attitude was in marked contrast to his previous close
attachment to them. It appeared that Samuel was angry at them
because he blamed them for his mother's absence and they were
regarded by him as unwanted replacements. This seemed to be demonstrated by his affectionate response when he was told by his grandmother that his mother was coming home, following which he offered his grandmother an apple in a most generous fashion.

Samuel's negative feelings toward his mother persisted during
her stay in the hospital. He manifested a reserved, cold attitude toward her when he spoke to her on the telephone. His major concern
was with a gift she had promised to give to him upon her return
home.

Following his mother's return home with baby Richard, Samuel
ignored his younger brother and mother for the first day or two and
instead played with his gifts. Finally, during a luncheon meal, he
asked his mother, "Where is your penis?" After a short silence Samuel reiterated, "I want to see your penis. Show me your penis." His
mother replied, "Samuel, I don't have a penis. I'm a lady and I have
a vagina. Men have penises and boys have penises, but ladies and
girls have vaginas." Samuel then demanded, "Then show me your
vagina, I want to see it!" His mother replied, "The vagina and penis
are private parts, and we don't go around showing them to each
other. We can talk about it, but we don't show our private parts."
To this Samuel retorted, "I'll show you a vagina; pick me up!"
Samuel's mother picked him up and in response to his direction she
opened the closet, whereupon he reached into the top shelf to obtain a ten inch by four inch cylindrical attachment to the vacuum

cleaner. Samuel pulled out a plug, pointed into the cylindrical opening, and said, "Mommy! That your vagina!"

During the three months following his brother's birth, Samuel was curious about how his younger brother was handled. He was very disturbed when Richard cried and urged that he be fed. He was somewhat shy but curious about watching Richard being breast-fed, but soon overcame his reserve, largely because his mother was relatively nonchalant about the procedure. On several occasions he asked to suck on the breast. Then Samuel developed more negative and aggressive behavior. In addition to pushing Richard's nose and kissing him on the cheek, Samuel would tightly squeeze Richard's head, and vigorously and annoyingly rattle the various objects over the baby's crib, even when told to stop.

One day, when Richard was about one month old, Samuel accompanied Richard and their mother to a local park for the first time. Upon returning home, Samuel noticed a group of children on a swinging amusement ride attached to a truck with loud music blasting from a speaker. On the side of the truck there were pictures of clowns. Samuel became frightened and wanted to get home quickly. One aspect of this fear was clarified several days later, when he saw a horse merry-go-round and wanted to run from the sight. He was encouraged to remain until the children got off. Although he was relieved when the children were safe, he continued to show an unusual fear of vehicles that played music or gave rides, and his fear of clown faces persisted for more than a year. He also developed a fear of barking dogs, which started when his grandmother, while walking with him, suddenly startled when a dog began to bark.

At twenty-six months Samuel insisted upon doing many things by himself. He was more negativistic at mealtimes. He was particularly annoyed about eating meats and was reluctant to chew his food.

During the following month Samuel developed the toilet inhibition when the word urine was first used.

Discussion

Although Samuel's various fears and inhibitions were relatively transient in nature, his two toilet fears and his fear of the swing ride share certain phenomenological similarities with adult phobias.

The idiosyncratic nature of Samuel's fears separates them from the ubiquitous anxieties of childhood which are believed to be due to a traumatic flooding of the immature ego. Anna Freud (1965) described these anxieties as archaic; they occur before the increasing structuralization of the personality and cannot be traced to any previous frightening experience.

> Descriptively, they are fears of darkness, of loneliness, of strangers, of new and unaccustomed sights and situations, of thunder, sometimes of the wind, etc. Metapsychologically, they are not phobias since, unlike the phobias of the phallic phase, they are not based on regression or conflict or displacement. Instead, they seem to express the immature ego's weakness and paniclike disorientation when faced with unknown impressions which cannot be mastered and assimilated.
>
> The archaic fears disappear in proportion to the developmental increase in the various ego functions such as memory, reality testing, secondary process functioning, intelligence, logic, etc., and especially with the decrease of projection and magical thinking [p. 161].

The archaic fears described by Anna Freud differ both descriptively and dynamically from some of Samuel's specific fears. For example, Samuel's lion fear did not clear up with clarification or reassurance but remitted only in response to an interpretation of the dynamic mechanisms involved. Initially, Samuel's father had assumed that the phobia was simply an externalization of fantasy upon reality. When his reality-testing maneuver failed to dispel the phobia, he assumed that a reality-testing deficiency appropriate for that age was not the only cause for the difficulty. When the father interpreted the projection of oral-sadistic impulses, therapeutic results did occur. The impulse to bite was projected onto the lion and the object of the impulse was displaced, indicating some internalization of external controls and prohibitions. Therefore, Samuel's distortion could not be due to the immaturity of several ego functions exclusively. Rather, the involvement of dynamic and genetic factors is suggested. In the presence of conflict and defensive operations of the ego, some psychic structuralization must be postulated. Furthermore, the conflict between id derivatives and partially internalized superego nuclei suggests that the symptom had many of the attributes, dynamically, genetically, structurally, and descriptively, of an adult phobia.

The importance of the immature ego state as a contributing factor to these phobias must not be minimized. This ego state provides a fertile ground upon which the specific behavioral, cognitive, and emotional characteristics of the child develop. The following discussion, however, will focus on the motive forces for some of the specific phobias described.

Three events should be recalled. At twenty months there was a fear that a lion would come out of the toilet and bite off Samuel's penis. At twenty-six months he was afraid of a swinging ride and clown faces. At twenty-seven months he was afraid that he would fall into the toilet soon after the word "urine" had been introduced.

There are some striking similarities between the first and third phobia, but an interesting difference is present. In both phobias the toilet was the engulfing object, and the aim of the projected impulse orally to destroy the self or part of the self was the same. However, the object to be engulfed shifted from the penis to the body. In general, children develop fears of danger to the whole self much earlier than fears of castration. Later in life fears of body injury are often displacements of castration anxiety. What in Samuel's case requires explanation are: the rather early origin of the fear that the penis would be bitten; the meaning of the fear of the body falling into the potty at the age of twenty-seven months; and the nature of the intense oral-sadistic impulse as it developed in Samuel.

The first of the three fears, the fear of the lion, will be considered in greater detail. As mentioned earlier, the interpretation given by Samuel's father reflected his concept that Samuel used the mechanisms of displacement and projection. Angry and threatened by his mother for bearing a new sibling, Samuel developed heightened oral-sadistic impulses directed against her. Prohibited from discharging these impulses directly and fearing retaliation for his wish, he projected the source of the impulse to bite from himself onto the lion. The initial anxiety in the zoo was also an archaic fear in that there was a sudden noise which was not comprehended by little Samuel. Another genetic factor that may have accentuated this anxiety was the noise of the drill which was used to remove his cast during his first year.

Samuel's increasing interest in his penis, the object to be bitten, was demonstrated in several ways. Before the lion phobia developed Samuel began phallic masturbation, was interested in the differences between the sexes and the origin of babies, jumped upon his mother and the substitute doll, and remembered holding a gun and chasing a girl.[1] After the lion phobia he showed continued phallic preoccupations, which included a concern about a big pretzel and its blemishes, a belief that his mother possessed a penis, a wish to replace his father, and a very strong desire to master bladder control at twenty-three months. These manifestations suggest phallic and oedipal interests, which occurred at an unusually early age. The premature heightening of phallic interests may be related to the rather frank and open discussion about the forthcoming sibling carried on with a precociously verbal child. The parents actively attempted to encourage and perhaps stimulate curiosity. The penis as a unique possession of the male which differentiated him from the female was described to Samuel at the rather early age of two years. Mention of the female's uniqueness in having babies was made even earlier at a time before the ego had the ability effectively to assimilate such information.

Another factor implicated in producing a hypercathexis of instinctual impulses is the effect of trauma. The operation on the scrotal nevus might have intensified Samuel's concern with blemishes such as the one on the pretzel. His anxiety centering around the scrotal surgery seems to have been displaced "anteriorly" to the penis.

Loewenstein (1950) focused on the forces which produce early manifestations of castration anxiety. He reported an illuminating observation of a patient of his, the mother of a ten-month-old boy. He summarized the event as illustrating two stages in the formation of the body image:

> one is the discovery of the penis, contact with which produces a pleasurable sensation; the second step consists in finding, experimentally, that this object, the penis, is not being left behind, lost, when crawling away, but stays with the body, belongs to it.

---

[1] It is of interest that Samuel showed clear evidence of having recalled an event from his preverbal days. It may be assumed that visual memory traces can be structuralized prior to language development and are available for later communication.

[Loewenstein theorized that] During the formation of the body image, the infant goes through moments of uncertainty, which are resolved by the confirmation that the penis is an indissoluble part of his own body. We suppose that under the impact of castration anxiety this uncertainty might be reactivated in the form of doubts and fears that the penis could fall off or be lost. [However, he added that prototypical elements may come from other sources:] It has been stressed that castration is preformed earlier, at the oral and anal stages. The loss of feces was considered as an anal castration, and the repeated loss of the breast or the bottle at the end of feeding has been called oral castration. . . . Such instances of incomplete or interrupted gratification during feeding must constitute experiences in which the infant learns that the gratifying object can be lost, does not belong to its own body. Thus, in contrast to the reported observation of finding that the penis belongs to one's own body, the oral frustration might indeed be the earliest prototype from which the process just described as well as the content of the later castration borrows certain of its elements [p. 48f.].

These observations concerning ego processes of cognition that take place during the course of the changing mental representations of body image may help to explain Samuel's castration anxiety at so early an age. In addition to the usual loss of breast and gratifying objects, other prototypical elements may be genetically related to Samuel's premature, fairly intense castration anxiety. Noted earlier was the heightening of a narcissistic cathexis of Samuel's penis, the consequence of which was the fear that the precious part could be lost. This fear was further accentuated when Samuel projected oral-sadistic impulses. However, upon a foundation containing such instinctual and developmental traces, Samuel experienced another trauma that further fixed for him the concept of loss of the hyper-cathected object. He watched the removal of Plaster of Paris casts from his leg at the time when he was deriving pleasure from locomotion. It may be conjectured that when Samuel moved about with these casts for several weeks, he incorporated them into the mental representation of his own body image. When he witnessed their removal he experienced a multiple castration of what was for him part of his own body. A narcissistically valued body part and a pleasurable activity were traumatized, and the fear of losing narcissistically valued objects in the future was accentuated.

Two events which antedated the lion phobia may have stimulated the fear of loss of a specific part of the body rather than the whole body. The scrotal operation and the casts applied to his leg could have prematurely and too intensely entrenched in Samuel's mind the concept of loss of a body part.

Some possible genetic determinants of the lion as the castrating object and the penis as the object for the assault have been described. The dynamics of the projection and displacement with the antecedent event in the zoo was also discussed. What can be said about the toilet as the general setting for conflict and the displaced source of Samuel's oral impulses? The sound of the toilet was similar to that of the lion's roar and both were perceived as engulfing. Samuel used the toilet which engulfed his other prized possessions, his feces and urine. Initially, he was reluctant to part with these objects, which he considered parts of his body, and he viewed the toilet as the place where he was made to give up parts of himself.

The genetic determinants of Samuel's oral impulses may be traced to events which preceded his biting behavior at the time of his sibling's birth. A constitutional predisposition to bite was apparent soon after his birth when he chewed rather than sucked the breast. Samuel showed signs of a heightened oral biting impetus from earliest infancy, and it may be postulated that his propensity for an oral biting discharge when frustrated was due to an inherent accentuated strength of this drive. Shengold (1964) suggested a factor which may contribute to the strength of the oral biting drive. He compared teething to the birth process as a traumatic situation. The absence of an ego at birth precludes the use of characteristic defensive operations in this traumatic situation; instead, the infant uses reflexlike automatic adaptations. In contrast to birth, at the time of teething, rudimentary ego functions do operate, which may result in characteristic ego defensive maneuvers such as a heightening of aggressive cathexes which, when turned against the self, produces heightened masochistic fixations.

Thus, the teething situation may be viewed as a kind of generator that stimulates the heightening of oral biting impulses (Kucera, 1959). This is seen clearly in adults who, when in pain, clench their teeth or wish to bite on something. Also, during the teething stage, the infant appears to be relieved after he bites upon a hard object.

How can this possible linkage between the teething situation and the oral biting stage be applied to the strength of Samuel's oral biting impulses? In addition to such anatomical-physiological factors as gum structures and pain-threshold barriers, can the age of the infant at the time of teething be related to the ability to cope with the pain and partially determine the strength of the reactive oral biting stage? It cannot be oversimplified to comparing age of teething onset as an independent variable to subsequent signs of heightened oral-sadistic traits or defenses against these traits as a dependent variable. A complex set of factors including relative maturation of many ego functions would determine the quality of the reaction. Nevertheless, it is noteworthy that Samuel's teeth first erupted at the age of four and one half months, which is on the very early side of normal. A harbinger of the early teething may have been the kind of sucking that was initially noticed in the nursery. It is suggested that as a result of the early teething, Samuel could have developed an abnormally heightened oral biting impulse and subsequently was more prone to a reactivation of these impulses during times of stress or pain. Thus, a biological matrix, the inherently varying traumatic situation of teething, may be viewed as an anlage upon which developmental processes can be traced to the onset of symptoms.

Should the terms castration anxiety and phobia be used in this case? These terms generally refer to the effects of the phallic-oedipal conflict, and imply the presence of some structuralization, internalization of external controls, and elements of superego nuclei. Samuel's attachment to his mother was mainly oral rather than phallic, but following the scrotal operation, phallic impulses and oedipal strivings emerged. Samuel's symptoms were both phenomenologically and dynamically similar to phobias which occur during and after the resolution of the more fully developed oedipal phase. He apparently believed there would be punishment to a pleasure-giving organ if his aggressive behavior persisted. It was only upon interpreting the talion principle that the phobia dissipated. Inasmuch as the talion principle is the unconscious mechanism by which the superego operates, and postdates the pleasure principle, its presence indicates some structuralization. In the presence of both an id-superego conflict and ego defensive maneuvers, the ensuing symptom may be regarded as a phobia derived from castration anxiety.

In summary, Samuel's castration anxiety at so early an age may be examined with the use of the structural model. From the side of the instincts, it represents a manifestation of the projected oral-sadistic impulses in which the aggressive drive plays the dominant role. From the side of the rudimentary superego, it represents the prohibition of the direct aggressive discharge. From the side of the ego, it is a result of a previously learned experience of loss and is the manifestation of a defensive operation aimed at protecting both self and the ambivalently loved mother.

Samuel's fear of falling into the toilet at the age of twenty-seven months may now be considered. Here the toilet was the engulfing object, no lion intermediary was present, and the object to be engulfed was the entire body. The person who suggested this possibility of engulfment by introducing the word urine was the father.

Laying the foundation for this transient phobia and concomitant inhibition was the birth of Richard followed by the noisy swing-ride and the fear that something would happen to the children. Recall now Samuel's question concerning the "son-sun" ambiguity six months earlier. At that time, before Richard was born, Samuel quite laughingly joked about the possibility of being far away, "up in the sky." After the birth of his brother he saw children swinging quite high in the air while he was walking beside his unwanted rival. Samuel's fantasy is not available, nor is there any evidence from interpretive work. However, it may be speculated that he wished to see his father's other son up in the sky and via displacement and reaction formation developed a fear that this would happen to other children. The strangeness of the situation was the fertile ground upon which two concerns were manifested: the fear for the children's safety and the subsequent fear of the strange clown face. The fears of noise, swing, and clown face may be regarded as archaic fears, but they may also reflect a heightened concern about body change. Antedating this event by two months Samuel witnessed two other changes. His mother changed shape remarkably and a new face appeared on the scene. It was out of the former that the latter occurred and Samuel knew this quite well. In fact, he did ask questions about the sleeping state of his unborn sibling and what it was like inside "Mommy's belly." The impact of this knowledge about changes in location of the fetus and appearance of the mother's abdomen may have accentuated his fear of the swing-ride.

During the month following the swing-ride the word "urine" was introduced and the toilet inhibition developed. The toilet still represented the projection of his oral sadism. The talion principle was still operative, but now it was in retaliation for wishing all of Richard gone. In addition, the toilet became the place for parting with his urine. At this stage in Samuel's life he did not yet have a fully internalized concept of a self representation that clearly demarcated it from the mental representations of body wastes and body parts. He still equated urine, penis, body, and self. It was in this fluid state of incomplete ego differentiation and self-object discrimination that the fantasy of being in a hole or womb emerged into the fear of engulfment. It may be assumed that Samuel had a fantasy about being in or coming through the vagina. Certainly, he had been curious about the birth process, was aware of the vagina as a cylindrical opening, fantasied an umbilical birth, and later felt capable of producing children through his own umbilicus. The body going through a cylindricallike tube was understood by him. The introduction of the word urine may have been interpreted phonetically because of his fantasied wish to be inside his mother.

Summary

1. Upon hearing the word "urine" a two-year-old boy developed a toilet phobia, believing he would fall into the toilet when he urinated.

2. Careful observations of this child's development revealed experiential factors which may have contributed to this toilet phobia as well as to earlier phobias.

3. Heightening of phallic impulses and the development of castration anxiety before the age of two years are related to antecedent factors which include body traumas and the birth of a sibling.

4. Intense oral-sadistic impulses are related to the effects of early teething.

BIBLIOGRAPHY

Ferenczi, S. (1913), The Ontogenesis of Symbols. *Sex in Psychoanalysis.* New York: Basic Books, 1950, pp. 276-281.

Freud, A. (1965), *Normality and Pathology in Childhood.* New York: International Universities Press.

Freud, S. (1905), Jokes and Their Relation to the Unconscious. *Standard Edition,* 8. London: Hogarth Press, 1957.

—— (1909), Analysis of a Phobia in a Five-Year-Old Boy. *Standard Edition,* 10:3-149. London: Hogarth Press, 1955.

Kucera, O. (1959), On Teething. *J. Amer. Psa. Assn.,* 7:284-291.

Loewenstein, R. M. (1950), Conflict and Autonomous Ego Development During the Phallic Phase. *This Annual,* 5:47-52.

Shengold, L. (1964), The Rat and the Tooth: A Study of the Central Clinical Significance of Overstimulation. Presented at the American Psychoanalytic Association.

ON SELF, CHARACTER, AND THE DEVELOPMENT OF A PSYCHIC APPARATUS

IRVING STEINGART, Ph.D. (New York)

I

The basic purpose of this paper is to define, psychoanalytically, the concepts of "character" and "self" (or, as I prefer to say, sense-of-self), and to define the interrelationship between these two concepts. My aim is to formulate these concepts so as to make them congruent with—but theoretically and clinically distinct from—the psychic system concepts id, ego, and superego. I understand these concepts to be classificatory terms. For example, Hartmann (1950) states about the term ego: "It is a substructure of personality and is defined by its functions" (p. 75). In employing these terms I also shall be guided by and use a further important distinction introduced into the literature by Hartmann (1950; see also Hartmann and Loewenstein, 1962): We use the same concepts to classify different types of identifications which produce important differences in psychic content (experience).

I believe this, in turn, leads to a more useful, general framework for a thoroughly objective study of behavior and experience—and in particular for the ideals and standards possessed by an individual. For a good number of years now, the literature has contained many

Submitted to the faculty of the Postdoctoral Training Program at New York University. I want to thank Drs. Ruth-Jean Eisenbud and Bernard N. Kalinowitz who served as readers and commented upon an earlier draft of the paper. I want to thank the following individuals who also read and commented upon an earlier version of the paper: Drs. Philip Bromberg, Norbert Freedman, Stanley Grand, Stanley Hoffman, and Lillian Gordon. Finally, I want to thank my wife, Dr. Joyce Steingart, for her numerous helpful suggestions and comments which improved the presentation of these ideas.

theoretical discussions of the relationships between the concepts of ego, ego ideal, and superego. These particular concepts have been in the foreground of discussion; in the background, I believe, are the more basic questions concerning objective psychoanalytic concepts of self and character—their formation, function, and development. A final solution to these more basic questions will, of course, require a complete metapsychological approach. Here, however, I plan to bring forward a psychic-apparatus-development aspect of this problem. I believe that this aspect has been neglected and that its investigation should help clarify other aspects of the problem. My attention to this factor will of necessity lead to the question of self-representation. I shall use the awkward term *self-representation-learning* to designate only a *process,* one about which we know unfortunately little. In varying contexts, I shall use the terms (sense-of-) self, identification, introject, self concept, self image, and self ideation to describe the structured conceptual product of such a complex learning process. Adapting terms introduced by Hartmann (1950) and Jacobson (1964), I shall use the more general term *representation* to designate such *concept formation* as it may pertain both to the self and object world.

It is hardly surprising that ideas in any way relevant to the psychoanalytic concepts of character and self reflect the historical development of the theory itself. In particular, changes in the conceptualization of the process by which character is formed, and what it is that is so formed, reflect a change in the always basic concept of conflict (see especially Rapaport, 1959). For the purposes of this paper it will suffice to indicate only the contours of the literature on this subject.

Freud first thought of conflict as engendered by an environment which was in some way unhospitable to an act of the ego. Thus Freud (1896) could describe how a sexual act committed in childhood could turn into shame through the anticipation that "some one else should find out about it" (p. 171).

As is well known, clinical findings forced Freud to revise the concept of intrapsychic conflict. First, he attributed to the ego a self-preservative instinct which supplied energy for a censorship force to oppose infantile drives (1900). This, so to speak, instinctual interpretation of drive opposition gradually was replaced by one of structure. These structures were seen, on the one hand, to be the result of a process which in some way produced an internalization of environmental delay and/or prohibitions over infantile drives; and, on the other hand, these structures were thought to obtain their energy to do such work from the drives themselves. The development of this structural theme proceeded in several phases. First, the importance of structures was recognized via the concept of defense mechanisms (e.g., 1915). Later Freud elaborated this structural concept of defense into a more comprehensive theory which described the much more complex classification of psychic functions and identifications which he termed the ego. Ego formation, function, and development were seen as related to a genetic series of infantile anxiety (danger) situations (1926). Interpolated between these two phases of the development of a structural theme, Freud (1923) introduced the significant concept of superego-ego ideal.

This momentous development in theory had the following consequences for a psychoanalytic theory of character: (1) Freud coordinated the formation of character with the formation of the superego-ego ideal.[1] (2) The structural constituents of the superego-ego ideal were formulated by Freud as special kinds of identifications made by the child with rewarding, aim-setting, and prohibiting aspects of parental behavior as well as with gratifying aspects of himself. Once formed, the special property of these identifications expresses itself in terms of their general psychic function to influence experiences of self-esteem independent of any external, actual reward and punishment. (3) Freud established the beginning of a genetic timetable for such character formation, in that he considered the formation of superego-ego ideal identifications and functions to arise within the resolution of the oedipus complex (1924). (4) Both guilt and shame experiences are formulated as forms of anxiety referred to the superego-ego ideal (Fenichel, 1945). (5) In 1923 Freud specifically defined an experience of guilt as registering the occurrence of a conflict between ego and superego-ego ideal identifications.

Subsequent disagreement in the literature has to do with differences in the attributes ascribed to the different types of identifica-

---

[1] "We have already made out a little of what it is that creates character . . . the incorporation of the former parental agency as a super-ego . . . is no doubt its most important and decisive portion" (Freud, 1933, p. 91).

tion which are classified according to ego, ego ideal, and superego: the functional relationships considered to exist between these identifications as they affect different types of conflict experience; differences in their general and particular functional relationships to instinctual drives; and their origins.

Piers and Singer (1953) are led from considerations about shame and guilt experiences to argue that ego ideal and (remaining) superego identifications must be classified as separate psychic systems. In the view of these authors, the experience of shame registers a state of conflict between identifications in the ego and ego ideal, whereas the experience of guilt is taken to register a conflict between the ego and the "remaining" superego identifications. Lampl-de Groot (1962), Annie Reich (1954), and others also argue for the preservation of such a distinction. Bing et al. (1959) postulate a distinction between ego ideal and superego identifications on an economic basis. They suggest that only the superego identifications ought to be viewed as possessing psychic energy to initiate cathexis or withhold it, and that ego ideal structures are to be taken only as capable of receiving cathexis from other psychic energy sources. Such a description of ego ideal identifications as only capable of being cathected provides the economic basis for a general dynamic distinction between ego ideal and superego identifications suggested by Lampl-de Groot (1962) and Annie Reich (1953). These authors maintain that ego ideal identifications in their infantile origins and thereafter operate as structures established by and serving drive gratification, whereas superego identifications function only to prohibit instinctual drive expression. Nunberg (1955) too has supported such a general dynamic distinction between ego ideal identifications and those classified as superego. Jacobson (1964) argues that shame, indicative of ego ideal structures, make its appearance genetically earlier than behavior and experience indicative of superego identifications. Novey (1955), in contrast, classifies the superego as possessing earlier, more primitive psychic structures, and the ego ideal as more advanced structures involved with adaptation to reality. Piers and Singer (1953) believe that shame is connected to an earlier anxiety, fear of abandonment, whereas guilt is produced by the later appearing castration anxiety. Correlated with this last idea is a concept of shame as tied to a fear of outer sanctions, whereas guilt involves the development of an inner system of sanctions. That shame and guilt are subjectively different experiences is, of course, obvious. The question is whether such a difference in subjective experience ought to be used—and in what way—to support theoretical distinctions between the concepts ego ideal and superego. Hartmann and Loewenstein (1962) state that this should not be done. They argue that any dynamic, genetic, energic, etc., distinctions which have been drawn between the ego ideal and superego involve a misapplication of the genetic point of view to the issue of structural development. The characteristics of early (preoedipal) infantile structures are being confused with those structures of the superego-ego ideal which normally come to be implicated in conflict experience with the advent of (postoedipal) character formation. Both shame and guilt experiences, these authors point out, can clinically be observed as "reactions to the danger of loss of love, to ridicule, or to anger." Therefore, any differentiation between "shame and guilt in terms of outer and inner sanctions . . . seems to us to represent primarily a distinction in terms of developmental level" (p. 66). Beres (1958) has described cases of extremely immature or ego-deviant children who appear to experience guilt exclusively in terms of outer sanctions and fears of loss of love. Freud (1930) described "a sense of guilt . . . in existence before the super-ego, and . . . conscience" (p. 136). Sandler (1960) states that in early childhood there exists a "warning signal . . . [that] does not yet deserve the name of guilt, though the affective state it produces in the ego may be identical with that which we refer to as guilt, later in the child's development" (p. 152f.).

With respect to the question of the ego ideal, Hartmann and Loewenstein (1962) grant that early infantile (preoedipal) ideals stress drive-gratifying themes of power and strength, but at the end of the phallic phase idealization concerns moral behavior. "We do not want to imply that all contents of the ego ideal are of this kind, . . . these contents may well go beyond the realm of moral demands. Ideals of perfection are not necessarily of a moral nature" (p. 63). However, with the advent of postoedipal development, ideal aims and directions undergo significant change since they become integrated with restrictions upon behavior. "Once this integration has taken place, to act according to a given set of standards comes to mean not only a reduction of guilt feelings but also a narcissistic gratification" (p. 62). "While no doubt there is a genetic continuity between the precursors . . . and the developed ego ideal, . . . what is added is that the 'striving after perfection' of the ego ideal becomes dynamically a partly independent direction-giving function. . . . The aims of the ego ideal are then to a considerable extent no longer identical with the primitive wishes which played a role in its formation" (p. 64).

Sandler (1963) believes that Freud's use of the term ego ideal was too varied, with respect to both the identifications and the psychic functions to which it referred, to permit the assignment of all such phenomena to a single, unitary concept. In terms of psychic function, Sandler points out that when Freud introduced the ego ideal concept in 1914, it was the "conscience" which was described as being involved in maintaining ideal content. In a later paper (1921), Freud indeed used the term ego ideal broadly, to include not only certain psychic content but also the necessity to maintain behavior in accordance with such ideal content. The earlier "conscience" idea became, with the structural point of view, elaborated into the psychic system concept, superego, which included a classification of psychic functions related to maintaining ideal content. At the same time (1923), Freud did indeed use the ego ideal concept to refer both to ideal content and to those psychic functions related to the maintenance of such ideals. In his final formulation (1933), Freud returned to the original, narrower reference for the concept ego ideal. He described the superego as the "vehicle of the ego ideal," i.e., psychic functioning relevant to the maintenance of ideals was referred to the superego concept. This type of formulation, which attributes an "ego ideal aspect" to the superego, is emphasized by Hartmann and Loewenstein (1962). Sandler (1963) contends that these varying connotations of the ego ideal concept obscure "aspects which should also be *functionally* differentiated at all ages" (p. 144), but whatever these supposed, important differences in psychic function actually are is not described. What is clear is Sandler's other contention that Freud used the ego ideal concept to refer at different times to significantly different kinds of identifications. Sandler cites passages from the "Narcissism" paper (1914), in which

Freud described as psychic content elements having to do with the child's own past, gratifying images of himself. Sandler contrasts this kind of psychic content with other ideal content which in later writings Freud derived from the parents as model figures. Sandler proposes that the term *ideal self* be used to refer to the child's own gratifying images of himself, and the term *ego ideal* to refer only to ideal content constructed from parental figures as models; according to Sandler, only ego ideal formations should be classified as belonging to the superego.

Schafer (1967) argues for the need to formulate a distinction, in terms of identification and functions, between "the psychology of ideals and the psychology of morality" (p. 132). This position also leads Schafer to separate the concepts of ideal self and ego ideal (the latter being taken to represent only ideal content of morality). Schafer further states that ideals must be studied from the standpoint of all psychic systems; thus, an ideal of the ego would be, e.g., competence; one example of an "ideal of the id" is "good orgasm." However, the maintenance of these sorts of ideals Schafer considers to be an ego function.

II

Clearly, the literature reflects important and basic differences of opinion about what could be called the conceptual building blocks of character. An outline of the steps by which I shall proceed follows.

I shall examine what I consider to be Freud's view of the super-ego-ego ideal issue, by comparing Freud's use of the term ego ideal in 1914 and in his subsequent writings (1933). It is at this later point that Freud once again narrowed his concept of the ego ideal, distinguished it from the superego, and reformulated their interrelationship. A real difficulty is that Freud did not write about the concepts ego ideal and superego in such a way as to make their development central and explicit, as was true, for example, about his treatment of psychosexual concepts.

I shall define the psychoanalytic concepts of character and (sense-of-) self and describe the process by which self and character are formed as some complex self-representation-learning. One determinant of self-representation-learning will be emphasized: the age-expectable stage characteristics of a psychic apparatus as it unfolds in an average expectable environment (Hartmann, 1939).

I shall then examine whether variations in identifications are related to shame or guilt conflicts.

Finally, I shall examine the identification content of the ego ideal, and present a broader formulation, but one which I believe still follows Freud's basic intention.

With respect to Freud's use of the concept ego ideal, I believe the following passages from his paper "On Narcissism" (1914), in which he introduced this concept, are critical:

> We can say that . . . man . . . has set up an *ideal* in himself by which he measures his actual ego. . . . For the ego the formation of an ideal would be the conditioning factor of repression.
>
> This ideal ego is now the target of the self-love which was enjoyed in childhood by the actual ego. The subject's narcissism makes its appearance displaced on to this new ideal ego, which, like the infantile ego, finds itself possessed of every perfection. . . .
>
> It would not surprise us if we were to find a special psychical agency which performs the task of seeing that narcissistic satisfaction from the ego ideal is ensured . . . ; we may reflect that what we call our 'conscience' has the required characteristics [p. 93ff.].
>
> In addition to its individual side, this ideal has a social side; it is the common ideal of a family, a class or a nation. . . . The want of satisfaction which arises from the non-fulfillment of this ideal liberates homosexual libido, and this is transformed into a sense of guilt (social anxiety). Originally this sense of guilt was a fear of punishment by the parents, or, more correctly, the fear of losing their love; later the parents are replaced by an indefinite number of fellow-men [p. 101f.].

The following should be emphasized in the passages just cited. First, Freud maintained, even in this introduction of the concept of the ego ideal, that its identifications are constructed from both internal and external sources ("In addition to its individual side, this ideal has a social side"). Therefore, any suggested theoretical contrast between ideals which derive from within and those which derive from without is not based upon Freud's conceptualization. Second, ego ideal content is viewed as the repository of all types of aspirations for oneself which are narcissistically gratifying. (Freud describes the ego ideal as "possessed of every perfection.") Therefore, any suggested contrast between moral and nonmoral ideal content as being classified according to separate psychic systems also is not in accord with Freud's formulation. Third, the ego ideal is described by Freud as being associated with a definite psychic advance, with significantly changed pleasure capabilities and possibilities. (Freud distinguishes between the "new ideal ego" and "self-love which was enjoyed in childhood by the actual ego," and he describes the formation of the ideal as the "conditioning factor of repression.") Finally, we see that the concept of the ego ideal was deliberately and specifically linked with a formulation of what became later the superego function of maintaining ideals. Freud (1914) specifically speaks of "the conscience" and states that it "performs the task" of maintaining ideals (p. 95). Thus, I believe, any suggestion that the ego ideal and superego are genetically to be distinguished is not in accord with Freud's thought, nor is a belief that the ego ideal and superego can be functionally distinguished with respect to opportunities offered for instinctual drive gratification.

In contrast, in the *New Introductory Lectures* (1933), Freud stated:

> With his abandonment of the Oedipus complex a child must . . . renounce the intense object-cathexes . . . it is as a compensation for this loss of objects that there is such a strong intensification of the identifications with his parents [p. 64]. There is no doubt that this ego ideal is the precipitation of the old picture of the parents [p. 65].
>   . . . it is entirely in accordance with the emotional importance of . . . such a transformation [of object cathexes to identifications] that a special place in the ego should be found for its outcome [p. 64].
>   We have allocated to it [the superego] the functions of self-observation, of conscience, and of [maintaining] the ideal [p. 66]. It is also the vehicle of the ego ideal by which the ego measures itself [p. 64f.].
>   The super-ego is the representative for us of every moral restriction, the advocate of a striving towards perfection—it is, in short, as much as we have been able to grasp psychologically of what is described as the higher side of human life [p. 66f.].

In these passages Freud indeed emphasizes ideal content which derives from parental figures. But it is quite clear from the entire context that Freud did not believe he was giving a complete description of the sources of ideal content: "We do not suppose, of course, that with the separation off of the super-ego we have said the last word on the psychology of the ego" (p. 68). In any case, this external source of ego ideal content was already anticipated in 1914. Again we note Freud's description of the ego ideal content as being more than moral ("the higher side of human life"). Also, again in terms of psychic function, Freud explicitly linked the superego with such ego ideal content as being "the vehicle of the ego ideal." And, finally, there is a clear indication that superego and ego ideal formation brings about something distinctly new in pleasure capabilities and opportunities ("a special place in the ego"). This kind of comparison reveals, I believe, that throughout his writings Freud remained essentially consistent in his use of the ego ideal and superego (initially conscience) concepts whenever he explicitly employed both concepts and described their relationships to each other.

III

The formation of character can be defined theoretically as the emergence of behavior and experience which we take to reflect the simultaneous influence of id, ego, and superego functions. More specifically, it is coordinated with the formation of superego functions which are "something 'within us,' yet it is not so from the first" (Freud, 1933, p. 61). But how are we to understand the process by which character is so formed? Freud admitted uncertainty about this and indicated only that "The basis of the process is what is called an 'identification' " (p. 63). Sandler (1960), in an ingenious way, has attempted to use this basic idea of Freud's to explain character formation. He suggests we use the term introjects to designate certain very important identifications formed during the oedipal period, particularly those involving the psychic content of parental authority. He further indicates that a child's "ego can use its capacity for identification to obtain a libidinal gain through . . . *identification with the introject*. It changes and modifies the *content* of the self, but does not result in the formation of psychic structure. Where ego and superego work together harmoniously, the harmony may be achieved by such an identification on the part of the ego" (p. 155). Sandler is clear that he is using the term "identification" to refer both to the process of self representation and to the content produced by it.[2] On developmental grounds, Sandler recognizes the need to distinguish between a process of primary identification in which identification attributes can fuse readily with each other, and identifications which derive from a secondary, more advanced self representation. An identification which is acquired through this more advanced self representation, while it can become modified to be like that of an introject, involves no fusion between the introject and itself. This more advanced identification with an introject is likened by Sandler to a kind of internal imitation process. Recently, Beres (1966) also expressed dissatisfaction with our ideas concerning the process by which authentic superego functions emerge. He suggests that the term "internalization" be used to refer to that psychologically more advanced self representation which involves the production of authentic superego functions; and that the term identification as a process be used to describe only that immature process which may be "of a transient nature, such as is characteristic in the young child or the 'as if' character in adult life, without internalization" (p. 488).

Obviously, it is necessary to attribute something distinctive to a process that produces something so unusual as the acquisition of authentic superego functions. However, I do not believe that any process formulation will be adequate to the task of explaining such acquisition, and character formation, unless it emphasizes exactly what is so striking about the actual phenomenon of character—and this is that it is a phenomenon of organization. What exactly do we have in mind about an individual's use of psychic functions when we think of a person's character? Introspection always reveals we are talking about a distinctive way in which an individual *organizes* his

2 Sandler also suggests that self representation (and representation in general) be viewed as an ego function, an allocation that raises questions. To take just one example, self-criticism is commonly regarded as a superego function, yet self-representational processes are implicit in this kind of psychic function. For the present, I shall continue to use the more noncommittal, unclassified term self-representation-learning. Also, to speak about an "ego" which identifies with an introject is to court reification of this psychic system.

psychic functions. For example, if we say that a child demonstrates in latency an "obsessive" character formation, we would expect to be able to forecast something about, say, his impulse control (an ego function) and his self-criticism (a superego function) whether we observe him at school, at a birthday party, or at a place of worship. Very importantly, if this child's character is evaluated as being responsive to reality conditions, we would expect these psychic functions of impulse control and self-observation to vary considerably in these three situations. Hartmann and Loewenstein (1962) have pointed out that superego as well as ego functions can possess relative degrees of autonomy. But if we compared this child's level of impulse control and self-observation to that of his peers, separately in each situation, we would expect this child's *relative position* on these psychic functions to remain about the same (relatively high). We would expect to be able to make similar forecasts for all other psychic functions. Character, then, is defined as the presence of a kind of *strategy* for the use of psychic functions. Character is the presence of an *organizational principle* applied to psychic functions.[3]

Clinically, the formation of character is coordinate with the formation of superego functions, but the functioning and development of character require further consideration. We can employ the terms *automatized character* and *autonomous character* as polar concepts to define a continuum of integration with respect to character functioning.[4] The more character demonstrates automatization, the more will behavior and experience show an organizational sameness not only in the patterning of psychic functions but in the actual level of psychic functions as well (so-called rigidity in character). A highly automatized character can be defined as possessing only that minimal degree of integration which is required for character formation to take place at all. The more a character demonstrates autonomy, the more will psychic functions show a varied responsiveness, i.e., be adapted to the conditions of each reality situation; nevertheless, this diversity will always express a consistent organiza-

---

3 This, of course, is a familiar Gestalt idea, first established in the area of perception and then carried over to learning, and I now apply it to psychoanalytically formulated psychic functions.

4 I am adapting these terms, introduced by Hartmann (1939), to describe attributes of character.

tional strategy in the use of psychic functions. Character which demonstrates a good deal of autonomy can be defined as possessing a high degree of integration.

One thinks of a concept such as the synthetic function (Nunberg, 1930), which is commonly inventoried as an ego function, in order to explain the organizational phenomenon which is character, but such an idea reveals nothing about the actual nature of such an organization-making process,[5] and leaves unclarified an important question. How are we to explain the timing of actual character formation? Appeals to some inferred special characteristics of oedipal or other development phases really cannot explain this question. Anal problems are certainly just as intense, the anxieties of this period are just as severe, identifications with parents obviously are made which involve efforts at prohibitions of drives, and yet character is not formed with the resolution of this psychosexual stage. One can argue that the oedipal stage is unique and different from earlier stages, but the oedipal crisis is at its height at ages three to five and character formation is not evident at this time in childhood. Bornstein (1951), for example, observes that it is not until what she terms the "second stage" (middle years) of latency that character appears really to be established. Anna Freud (1936) holds a similar view with regard to the emergence of authentic superego functions.

We can begin again with Freud's observation (1933) that the process which produces the constant influence of superego functions in behavior and experience "is what is called an 'identification' " (p. 63). It is, then, to a renewed study of self-representation-learning to which we should turn. But self-representation-learning must after all be considered to be a special aspect of a more general symbolizing or concept-forming capability. Of course, the complex learning

---

[5] Waelder (1930) has already made this point: "What impresses one as its characteristic synthetic function is that each act in the ego has a multiple function" (p. 54). This "principle of multiple function" unquestionably is a well-proven guide for clinical investigation. My understanding of this is that the self-representation-learning process (which may eventually produce character) is extremely complex and involves manifold drive, reality, etc., determinants, so that *whatever* character is formed will express such diversity in every experience and act. As I have already indicated, I shall single out for consideration only one such influence, the characteristics of a psychic apparatus.

which produces an identification is never only an intellectual process, but the general development of symbolism surely must be one necessary determinant involved in such a process. Psychoanalytically, the capacity to form and use symbols is attributed to a psychic apparatus which unfolds in an average expectable environment according to definite stages (Hartmann, 1939). However, it will be noticed that I use the term psychic apparatus (rather than describe an ego apparatus, as does Hartmann). I do this to indicate the relevance of this specific capability for other than just ego-classified psychic functions.

Piaget, in a lifetime of work (e.g., 1923, 1937, 1945, 1960) devoted to an examination of intellectual growth, has made a profound contribution to our understanding of the development of this symbol-making apparatus. Piaget has demonstrated that a child reared in contemporary Western society, and exposed to the appropriate learning experiences, acquires at some time in the middle years of latency a significantly new ability to form concepts. Concepts then possess what Piaget terms "conservation" and "reversibility." Piaget does not intend to use these terms "conservation" and "reversibility" to define rules for reasoning with a concept such as inheres in some logical system. It is Piaget's contribution to insist and demonstrate that these are *psychological attributes* which serve to produce powerfully different psychic realities for a child.

A classic (and somewhat oversimplified) demonstration by Piaget concerns the concept of quantity.[6] Each of two beakers, A and B, of identical physical shape, is filled with the same amount of orange juice, producing therefore an identical visible level of juice in each beaker. All of this is done in the child's presence and the child is then asked whether one beaker has more juice than the other, more juice to drink from than the other, or whether both have the same amount of juice to drink. Both the four- to five-year-old and a child in middle latency will answer that both beakers have the same amount of liquid. Now, before the child's eyes the orange juice from beaker B is poured into a third beaker C, much thinner in physical shape than the first two vessels, as a result of which the juice level in beaker C is now considerably higher than in beaker A.

6 Adapted from Hunt (1961, p. 203f.).

Again a child is asked about the relative quantities of liquid, which has more to drink, vessel A or C. The younger, four- to five-year-old child now answers that beaker C has more orange juice than beaker A because the juice level is visibly higher in beaker C compared to A. The middle latency child answers that the quantity of juice has not changed, even though he readily can acknowledge that he sees that this same quantity is very different in terms of juice level for beaker A than beaker C. Finally, the orange juice in beaker C is poured back into vessel B in the child's presence. Again the same question about relative quantity is put to the child, and again both the four- to five-year-old and the middle latency child will answer that the amount to drink is the same. Piaget emphasizes that the four- to five-year-old child *does* have a concept of quantity. What is very different is the way in which his quantity concept gives meaning to his experience. A *perceptually* impelling change in an object's appearance will produce a very different quantity connotation in the young child. Piaget terms this kind of concept "preoperational." The middle latency child comprehends this fluctuation only as a change in perception, and thus the concept of quantity for the older child possesses a conceptual "sameness" whatever variation may occur on a perceptual level. The acquisition of this essential conceptual sameness Piaget terms "conservation." The manner in which such a concept can be "thought back" from any particular thing perception Piaget terms its "reversibility."

I believe it reasonable to conclude that an advance in self-representation-learning also takes place, and that the result for identification formation is akin to this more general advance of symbolism. This means that, typically, a child at some point in middle latency forms a basic sense-of-self which possesses both self-conversation and self-reversibility. All particular identifications are now integrated and therefore experienced as reversible *aspects* of this basic sense-of-self. Such a sense-of-self must be seen to extend as well to the various introjects. Prior to a sense-of-self we can conceive of these introjects as a highly differentiated set of functionally equivalent identifications, which exist among a series of such differentiated identification-sets during the oedipal period and early latency. The introject-set becomes differentiated as an identification-set by virtue of its peculiar ability to release a vivid and impelling pleasure experience of "self-love" (Freud's term). *Each identification-set imputes meaning to self experience in the manner of a preoperational concept (Pi-*

aget's term)[7] *and the same situation obtains for object representation:* a change in the gratification experience, or some other impelling feature associated with what is objectively the *same* self or object, will produce reference to a *different* representation-set for meaning. Whenever a child is representing himself through a member of this introject-set, he vividly experiences, presumably, a special type of narcissistic gratification not available through any other kind of identification-set during the oedipal period and early latency. While all identifications which belong to the introject-set can supply such narcissistic gratification ("self-love"), they have such an equivalent functional relationship only to each other; there is no functional relationship to any other identification-set because no structural arrangement as yet exists for all identification. With the formation of sense-of-self, this special differentiated set of introjects is integrated into an embracing identification structure possessing self-conservation and self-reversibility. Speaking in terms of identification, the possession of these introjects now produces a constant evaluative frame of reference for all other identifications.[8] The operation of this same integrative structure, looked at from the viewpoint of psychic functioning, *is* the internalization of those psychic

---

[7] While the introject-set is critical for future character formation, we must envision other sorts of identification-sets as present during the oedipal and early latency period. For example, "male " versus "female" identification-sets are present, and these probably become differentiated from each other because of vividly different pleasure modalities experienced by the child. Prior to such a stage of differentiated identification-sets, numerous authors assume a stage of fluid percept "identifications" (see, e.g., Jacobson, 1964; Mahler, 1952). At this stage there is really no *conceptual* representation, and this includes the absence of what is a basic and probably initial representation-set which differentiates between the self and object world. Piaget has been criticized for his reliance upon verbal interviewing to demonstrate conservation in concept formation, and such criticism itself has been criticized (Kessen and Kuhlman, 1962). I do not believe such questions of method affect these substantive issues.

[8] I use the term *sense*-of-self to suggest the emotional elements which also enter into the learning process. The application of the conservation concept to personality is not new. R. Brown, for example, has suggested its relevance to the phenomenon of mood, although Inhelder rejects this idea (see Kessen and Kuhlman, 1962). However, Piaget (1967) himself describes how conservation and related concepts are relevant to personality, although his point of view is of course not psychoanalytic. Hartmann and Loewenstein (1962) do not propose any such psychic formation, but I believe their comments about the distribution of narcissism among the psychic systems are highly relevant and raise questions about the necessity for such a formulation: "In this context, another point might become relevant, though little is known about it so far, namely, the habitual or situational representation of the various localizations of narcissism in *the self-image*" (p. 61; my italics).

functions we inventory as superego. Whatever organizational principle for psychic functioning is evident in such an integrative structure *is* a person's character.[9] Henceforth, I shall use the term
"personality" as a more general concept to designate both the
identificatory and functional aspects of this integrative structure
which results from such an advance in self-representation-learning.

Of course, conflict recenters our clinical attention upon the
separate psychic systems. However, these constructs of sense-of-self
and character apply *both* to the presence and absence of conflictual
experience. It is usual to describe conflict as changing from interpersonal to intrapsychic with the advent of personality formation,
and this of course is true. But to this can be added the idea that
conflict becomes intraself as well: one can feel oneself to be *like* or
unlike what one ought or aspires to be, and both kinds of psychic
content can be seen to take place within a (conserved) sense-of-self
experience.[10] That this is so has important consequence for psycho-

[9] It is true that Freud (1933) once defined character differently: "You yourselves
have no doubt assumed that what is known as 'character', a thing so hard to define,
is to be ascribed entirely to the ego" (p. 91). This definition appears quite similar to
Erikson's concept of ego identity (1956), and Hartmann's notion of a "central regulation" (1939), which also is referred to as an ego function. Waelder (1930) defines
character as "specific solution methods which are peculiar to each individual" (p. 53),
and also classifies such activities as belonging to the psychic system ego. See also Glover
(1925) for a similar definition.

But to define character in these ways, I believe, causes clinical and theoretical
confusion between terms signifying subdivisions of the psychic system and what must
be an organizational concept of character as a whole. Such a definition does not do justice to the fact that superego functions also can demonstrate autonomy, or that it is
actually an organizational sameness in the use of *all* psychic functions by which we
can characterize a person over time and place. It is not really difficult to marshall an
argument from Freud himself that character must be recognized as a mechanism inte-
grating all psychic functions. For example: "On the other hand the ego is identical
with the id, and is merely a specially *differentiated* portion of it. If we think of this
part by itself in contradistinction to the *whole*, or if a real split has occurred between
the two, the weakness of the ego becomes apparent. . . . The same is true of the
relations between the ego and the super-ego. In many situations the two are merged;
and as a rule we can only distinguish one from the other when there is a tension
or conflict between them" (1926, p. 97; my italics).

The entire issue of a psychoanalytic conceptualization of psychic functions, their
classification according to our psychic system "ordering abstractions" (Schafer, 1967),
and how to formulate a relationship between the idea of a psychic function and the
concept of a psychic apparatus, is in need of rigorous attention.

[10] Not only can conflict occur within an integrated context, but a lack of such
integration cannot always and completely be explained as being due to psychopathology. The following comments by Freud (1923) are pertinent: "Although it is a
digression from our aim, we cannot avoid giving our attention for a moment longer

pathology in general, and self-esteem regulation in particular (see, e.g., Kernberg, 1966). Normal and neurotic experience of conflict may be regarded as taking place intraself, and since it does so, the existence of the structure which mediates such conservation must exercise a moderating influence upon fluctuations in self-esteem. What, for example, in a normal and neurotic individual remains only an experience of pride can become in a borderline or psychotic person a state of elation over a "new" identity.

Speaking now in terms of the integration of psychic functions, i.e., character, conflict can have various consequences. First, due to conflict, self and object "meaning" remains only perceptual and produces no differentiation of conceptual representation-sets. Consequently, psychic functioning is highly limited or disturbed; in either case the use of psychic functions is highly erratic, dependent upon whatever inner and outer forces prevail in any given situation. Second, a genuine advance in self-representation-learning takes place so that character is formed, but it is minimal, with the result that psychic functioning is highly automatized (character is rigid).[11]

Another interesting consequence is illuminated by the example of behavior which is termed schizoid. Because of conflict, self-representation-learning continues to differentiate representation-sets only

---

to the ego's object-identifications. If they obtain the upper hand and become too numerous, unduly powerful and incompatible with one another, a pathological outcome will not be far off. It may come to a disruption of the ego in consequence of the different identifications becoming cut off from one another by resistances; perhaps the secret óf the cases of what is described as 'multiple personality' is that the different identifications seize hold of consciousness in turn. Even when things do not go so far as this, there remains the important question of conflicts between the various identifications into which the ego comes apart, *conflicts which cannot after all be described as entirely pathological*" (p. 30f.; my italics).

I owe to Dr. Stanley Grand the interesting idea that it is only a regressive *de-differentiation within the introject-set* of identifications which produces (so-called) multiple personality; and that this occurs just at the point when this same introject-set normally undergoes an integration that produces authentic personality formation. The idea, then, would be that a split-off portion of this introject-set is subjected to repression but remains active in the unconscious as a source of primitive, narcissistic gratification (self-love). Periodically, these unconscious introjects assume control of consciousness (and motility).

A related, contemporary question is the extent to which intellectual retardation and/or educational handicap can in itself so limit self-representation-learning that a sense-of-self cannot form.

[11] Some clinical observations suggest that character initially always functions in a somewhat rigid manner (Bornstein, 1951). I am not sure that this must always be the case.

on the basis of impelling surface features of experience. This does include a basic differentiation between self and object representation; however, the psychic content of identifications formed by such a learning process must remain *imitative*. An object is, so to speak, how it *looks* (impressively acts, vividly performs); representation meaning is therefore carried by the *image*. The young child need only imitate the manifest appearance(s) of the object which is so impressive (even if only playfully) in order to promote an identification-set the meaning of which will be *similar* to that of the object. Whether the child so imitates, and with what aspects of which object similarity is sought and experienced, and with what effect—all of these depend of course upon the prevailing dynamic and other conditions.[12]

Anna Freud (1936) indicates that a child in early latency can be expected to form ego ideal and superego introjects which are imagistic-imitative. She terms this result "identification with the aggressor" and considers it to be an age-expectable, necessary prelude to later, authentic superego formation. Schizoid individuals evidently remain on such an imagistic-imitative level of identification formation (H. Deutsch, 1942). Such formation, however, may stabilize an individual's psychic functioning to such a degree that character appears to be present. Nevertheless, the essentially unconserved nature of such an identification structure can be revealed by a sudden change in psychic functioning due to the imitation of a new (love) object.

Individual differences in the formation of a sense-of-self have to

---

[12] Schafer (1968) recently described the complexities which enter into the formation of identification; however, the manner in which he defines and uses imitation as a type of identification is different from that described here.

Piaget (1945) also recognizes such complexity. At the risk of simplification, I will state that he tries to deal with it by contrasting the young child's "symbolic play" with childhood behavior that is expressive of an "adaptive image." The latter would involve an effort continuously to redefine an imagistic-imitative identification to fit ("accommodate") newly encountered features of reality. The former involves an effort to fit ("assimilate") such newly encountered, so to speak, retractable features of reality to an already solidly established imagistic-imitative identification. Various kinds of individual differences in adapted behavior, symbolic play, and the balance between the two, remain to be explained, an explanation that requires a complete psychoanalytic viewpoint. My purpose is to emphasize an imagistic-imitative stage of identification formation which is common to all such activities. Imitative behavior organized by imagistic *concepts* no longer requires (is triggered by) some presented stimulating condition, as is true of the *perceptually* mediated mimicry of the infant. This important distinction requires separate study.

do not only with identification content but also with what one can describe as *identification form*. What already has been described is a general advance in symbolic processes, from concept formation based upon perceptually impelling features of experience to concepts which are formed on the basis of criteria that are more inferential and abstract. Self-representation-learning participates in this general advance in concept formation. We can describe a difference in the structured result of this process as a change in identification form. Earlier childhood identifications (including the introjects) derive from representation based upon visually impelling features of experience. Therefore, what is constructed are perceptually dominated images of oneself (essentially, perception-derived body images, although, perhaps, sensations of taste, smell, etc., also may become implicated in such childhood self concepts). What results from the advance in the self-representation-learning can be described as a change from self image to more abstract *self ideation;* with this occurs a special new kind of emphasis upon the spoken word, which becomes the "carrier" of some such abstract (not visible) connotation. However, it is clear that this more abstract self ideation still can retain and utilize developmentally earlier elements of imagery (and perhaps sensation). The adult use of simile and metaphor to describe oneself is, precisely, a deliberate reference to such imagery and sensation. There is evidence at hand that the ability to comprehend the use of such "double terms" as "sweet," "hard," "warm," etc., as self concepts becomes really evident during the middle years of latency, that is, at the time at which a sense-of-self is formed (Asch and Nerlove, 1960). There is other evidence which indicates preferred "memory modalities" in adults (Wallach and Auerbach, 1955)—for example, visual versus ideational—and this also suggests the further idea that self concepts may in the same manner be typed according to whether they are predominantly visual (sensation) or ideational (and verbal) in form.

This difference in identification form is relevant to whether intrapsychic conflict is experienced as shame or guilt. Various sorts of psychodynamic explanations have been put forth in an effort to comprehend the arousal of shame versus the instigation of guilt experience. For example, Weiss (1933) has emphasized phallic drives in the arousal of shame; but others (Freud, 1931b) emphasize that phallic drives can be observed in connection with guilt experience. Oral drives and conflicts have been observed in both shame (Wallace, 1963) and guilt experiences (Fenichel, 1945). What can be concluded from such disparate reports is not that clinical observation of these psychodynamics is inaccurate, but that it is insufficient. Attention must be paid to a difference in identification form which mediates either a guilt or a shame experience. Whatever psychodynamics clinically are reported in connection with intrapsychic shame or guilt experience, all observers are in agreement as to the phenomenological difference between these two experiences. Shame is described as an impelling visual experience (Erikson, 1950; Feldman, 1962; Wallace, 1963); guilt is described as an experience in which more purely ideational (and verbal) qualities predominate (Erikson, 1950; Freud, 1923; Isakower, 1939). I suggest that identification forms which retain large elements of imagery (and perhaps sensation) mediate shame experience; whereas identification forms which are of a more purely ideational (and verbal) nature bring about guilt experience.[13] There is an obvious developmental implication that has been recognized, e.g., by Erikson (1950). Whatever it is that is being described as a guilt experience in the young child (before the advent of personality formation in middle latency) cannot be based upon the differences in the mediating form of self concept which have just been described.

IV

I shall now comment about a recurring question in the literature: What is it that is to be considered the psychic content of the ego ideal? While Freud did emphasize that various kinds of identificatory psychic content can become idealized and belong to the ego ideal, he contributed to this controversy by his frequently stated conviction (1924, 1925, 1931b) that superego functioning is less pronounced in women (and consequently character is less formed). Freud came to this conclusion logically enough, from a premise that castration anxiety is the critical determinant in character formation.

---

[13] There are other implications to be derived from such variations in identification form: types of interests and defenses are pertinent here, as are issues of clinical technique, but I shall not pursue this further.

He reasoned that castration anxiety could not be as extreme in little girls as it was in boys since girls could not anticipate this fear to the extent that boys could. But the actual evidence that Freud cited for such a conviction emphasized certain psychic content rather than any observation that would suggest a limited presence of those psychic functions which we inventory as superego. For example, in one paper (1925), Freud specifically cited such a typically feminine trait as emotionality as constituting evidence for more limited superego functioning in females. I have already suggested that character formation is not simply due to the resolution of the oedipus complex or any other psychodynamic factors; rather, it is a consequence of significantly new symbolic capabilities which become available for self-representation-learning in the middle years of latency. This, of course, is not to say that oedipal and earlier infantile conflicts have no influence on self-representation-learning and on what becomes the content of the ego ideal. But it seems more reasonable to assume that any and all infantile psychosexual stages have significance for and influence on what ultimately becomes the content of the ego ideal.

Speaking generally, the psychic content of ego ideals can be placed into three broad, probably overlapping, categories. (1) Self and object idealization can take place with respect to representation-learning made in situations in which the renunciation of instinctual drives leads to such values as cleanliness, compliance, etc.; these values can be generalized into a widespread pursuit of asceticism. (2) Idealization of self and objects can occur with respect to representation-learning made in situations in which the management and regulation of instinctual drives result in ideals of control, competence, etc.; these can be generalized into a widespread pursuit of excellence. (3) Self and object idealization can take place with respect to representation-learning made in situations in which *standards of drive gratification* produce ideals of love, bravery, etc.; these can be generalized into a widespread pursuit of taste and sensibility.[14]

14 From the viewpoint of the instinctual drives, the psychology of instinctual frustration is not the same as that of instinctual renunciation. Nor is the psychology of instinctual wish fulfillment simply the same as ideals which involve standards of drive gratification. With respect to the latter, Freud's comments about the "aim-inhibition"

All such ideal content—following Freud, all the "higher side of human life"—is to be referred to the ego ideal. Further, to refer the maintenance of such differences in ideal content to the different psychic systems invites reification of these classificatory terms, obscures further what must be an organizational concept of personality as a (single) whole, and makes more likely a subjective evaluation of behavior. And this includes what has been described here as ideals of drive gratification. For example, the love of food of a gourmet—someone who genuinely idealizes the conditions of (oral) eating pleasure—is significantly different from that of an individual who eats to rid himself of tension, or simply because it is necessary to live. Under certain circumstances a gourmet will refuse to eat, even though he may be considerably hungry or quite tense. Speaking now in terms of psychic function, the superego maintenance of any of these ideals can demonstrate either a measure of autonomy or become subject to extreme automatization. An experienced inability to live up to any such ideals can produce shame and guilt. Very interestingly, *the maintenance of ideal objects* (Schafer, 1967) *would appear to have different degrees of relevance for the various kinds of ideal identifications.* In particular, ideal identifications pertaining

---

of an instinctual drive are pertinent: "we have grounds for distinguishing instincts which are 'inhibited in their aim'—instinctual impulses from sources well known to us with an unambiguous aim, but which come to a stop on their way to satisfaction, so that a lasting object-cathexis comes about and *a permanent trend* [of feeling]. Such, for instance, is the relation of tenderness, which undoubtedly originates from the sources of sexual need and invariably renounces its satisfaction" (1933, p. 97; my italics). One may add that Freud carefully distinguished such "aim-inhibited" instincts from instinctual drives which are subject to sublimation; with sublimation, presumably, no such element of inhibition is present, but instead there is a process of continuous instinctual discharge, although of course with a modified drive aim.

Freud, in a brief but extremely provocative paper (1931a), once suggested a character nosology based upon "libidinal types." He described three basic types of character: "according, then, as the libido is predominantly allocated to the provinces of the mental apparatus" (p. 217). First, an "erotic type," a person "whose main interest . . . is turned towards love . . . this type represents the elementary instinctual demands of the id." The second type is termed the "obsessional type" which "is distinguished by the predominance of the super-ego." The third type is called the "narcissistic type," whose "main interest is directed to self-preservation. . . . His ego has a large amount of aggressiveness" (p. 218). It is interesting that Freud called the superego-dominated type "obsessional." I believe this indicates an insufficient focus upon one kind of psychic content and also an inadequate reference to the superego functions involved in maintaining ideal content. Actually, the ego ideal content typology I have described represents a superego framework for each of Freud's three "libidinal types."

to standards of drive gratification would appear by their very nature
to predispose one much more to maintaining the actual presence of
complementary ideal objects, compared to ideals of instinctual regulation and renunciation. Idealization of one's capabilities to regulate
and manage instinctual drive makes, perhaps, idealization of objects
less necessary, or even less possible. Freud (1912) once seemed to
suggest that ego ideals of renunciation facilitate the development of
"absent" ideal objects (i.e., religious figures).[15] A thoroughly objective theory of personality would exclude any absolute, comparative
judgment of different ego ideal content. However, an examination
of the kind of ego ideal content emphasized in different societies at
particular points in history is of course of great interest. For example, the medieval ideals of courtliness, taken as a whole, may be
considered to represent an institutionalization of ideals of drive
gratification. It is difficult to see how the industrial revolution, and
all that went with it, could have taken place without an emphasis
upon ideals of drive management and regulation, and perhaps even
ideals of renunciation. Now, in an "affluent" society, ideals of drive
gratification would seem once again to become emphasized. What we
consider to be typical of feminine personality undoubtedly emphasizes ideals of drive gratification, especially standards for various
libidinal pleasures.

V

Psychoanalytically, we maintain that personality once established
is not subject to basic change during the latency period. Once superego (and ego ideal) introjects become integrated into a sense-of-self,
the latency child possesses standards and values which produce an
unchanging orientation for both his love and work life. This is so
because, speaking now in terms of psychic function, it is only one

---

15 It is perhaps apparent that a self-ideal of being loving and lovable predisposes
one toward maintaining a complementary ideal object, but the same is true for ideals
which include standards for aggressive discharge, for example, that of bravery. From
the viewpoint of instinctual drives, the psychology of bravery is not simply the same
as that of aggressive release. True bravery involves self-idealization and requires some
idealization of an adversary object (or adverse circumstance). A vivid, institutionalized example of this is the bravery of the Spanish matador—which is impossible
without the adversary presence of the "brave bull."

such orientation which can provide narcissistic gratification.[16] The following comments by Freud (1933) are pertinent in this regard:

> In the course of development the super-ego also takes on the in-influences of those who have stepped into the place of the parents. . . . Normally it departs more and more from the original parental figures; it becomes, so to say, more impersonal. . . . Identifications with these later parents as well . . . regularly make important contributions to the formation of character; but in that case they only affect the ego [p. 64].

I believe that these comments by Freud—that the superego "takes on" (it is not taken on) and that later influences on character only "affect the ego"—ought to be taken to mean that the obvious intellectual and social role development which occurs in latency should sharply be distinguished from a change in the basic sense-of-self. Clinical observation would indicate the correctness of this position. However, in terms of psychic function, changes in the degree of character autonomy are perhaps possible due to latency influences upon the child.

While we do not ordinarily expect personality during latency to change basically, except under unusual, traumatic circumstances, we do expect adolescence to bring with it phase-specific influences which move the child toward personality change. Of course, one such influence is the adolescent's need to reorganize his libidinal and aggressive life, to withdraw attachments from the early introjects. But another source for such personality reformation derives from a startling new stage in the development of that psychic apparatus which enables a person to perform symbolic operations.

Piaget describes this as a change from abstract concepts, which are "concrete," to abstract concepts, which are "formal."

This significant change in conceptualization can be described as follows.[17] Suppose a latency age child is shown a collection of sticks

[16] In terms of learning, the acquisition of a sense-of-self may be regarded as a complex example of Harlow's concept of "learning how to learn" (1949). The latency child now has "learned how to learn" with respect to imputing value-meaning to his interpersonal experience. Looked at from the viewpoint of the integration of psychic functions, i.e., character, this formation may be related to the emergence of cognitive style and type (Gardner et al., 1959). Developmental research ought to be able to answer such questions.

[17] Adapted from Hunt (1961, p. 226).

on a table before him, and asked to arrange the sticks along a continuum expressing the concept of size. This the child is able to do
easily. The child is then told to imagine that each stick is a flagpole.
Suppose then that, in addition, the child is shown a series of card-
board houses of different sizes, and told to align each house with the
proper-sized stick. This the child can also do easily, even if the house
series is presented in an order which is the reverse of the stick series.
But now suppose that the same latency age child is asked to read
and solve a problem such as this: "Edith is fairer than Susan; Edith
is darker than Lilly; who is the darkest of the three?" This problem
a latency age child cannot solve and will not be able to solve until
the approach of adolescence. It is only when children reach eleven to
twelve years, according to Piaget, that they begin to acquire a capacity to use such *purely* verbal (or formal) concepts as a medium
for the expression of abstract thought. Prior to this, a child must
have concrete objects to manipulate, to possess, as a medium for
the expression of his abstract concepts. Piaget (1967) aptly terms the
emergence of such formal abstract concepts as "thought raised to the
second power. Concrete thinking is the representation of a possible
action, and formal thinking is the representation of a representation
of a possible action" (p. 63). Purely hypothetical-deductive propositions are now possible (such as constructing a set of mathematical
axioms and generating their derivatives). Werner and Kaplan's
"lexical concept" (1967) is related to the emergence of such a stage
in conceptualization.

Again, self-representation-learning can be seen to participate in
this more general advance in symbolic capability, and this has important consequences. A self concept now exists formally for an
adolescent as something that is an entity unto itself—*and hence is
man made*—not as something somehow embedded and given in the
very concrete flux of his experience. The sense-of-self, its conservation and range of reversible identification, is now for the adolescent,
in principle, limitless. This significant new kind of identification
for the adolescent—that any and all identification constitutes only a
personal decision and creative tool about meaning—ought not to be
mistaken for the familiar comparison between fantasy and reality. A
latency-age child does of course possess a private fantasy life and
discriminates between it and reality. But for a latency-age child,
reality is defined by interpersonal activities with significant others;
therefore, in complementary fashion, fantasy is actually defined by

such concrete experiences with others. The new capacity of the adolescent is dramatically different. He can define *what* it is that is to be considered real self and *what* it is that is to be considered unreal. I believe that a concept of existential anxiety does have relevance to such a state of affairs, as a phase-specific type of anxiety for the adolescent. (However, it is difficult to see how such an idea of existential anxiety can be relevant for any earlier stage of personality.) The metapsychology of this kind of adolescent experience obviously is not at all the same as that of psychotic disorganization which can emerge in adolescence. The latter is primarily a consequence of withdrawal from the object world and regression in psychic functioning. The former is due to an advance in the form of self-representation-learning, which occurs in part because of a significant new stage in the development of the psychic apparatus that performs symbolic processes.[18]

Several important consequences can result for ego ideal content. First, and probably most frequent, the resolution of adolescence produces a sense-of-self basically in agreement with that of childhood. Second, the psychic content of ideals may change basically, as a consequence of which a person's basic sense-of-self will undergo significant content modification. Third, a broadly based cynicism, nihilism, etc., may emerge; this then involves the paradoxical maintenance

[18] Diagnostically, subtle syncretistic concepts must be distinguished from this new plane of representation about self (and objects) which makes the adolescent both glorious and notorious; this discrimination is not always easy to make.

On the other hand, consider the situation of an adolescent who does not acquire this formal plane of conceptualization because of inadequate intelligence or education. This means that an "existential" plane of identification cannot be experienced. Because such "existential issues" are not available, such an adolescent only has physically direct means of expressing his inevitable adolescent independence.

The stages of self which I have described clearly touch some part of the complex identity growth phenomenon described so beautifully by Erikson (1950). However, I believe it is also clear that I describe stages in the structural development of self and emphasize as contributing to this the growth of symbolic processes, while Erikson emphasizes identity acquisitions that are related to psychosexual stages. It should also be clear that the self constructs described here cannot be considered the same as a perceptual process definition of sense-of-self as suggested by Spiegel (1959). Other psychoanalytic writers who emphasize the importance of cognitive self constructs, although not in the structural developmental terms used here, include Jacobson (1964), Monroe (1955), and Grinker (1957). See especially G. Murphy (1947) for a more general discussion of the ideas of differentiation and integration applied to personality. Lampl-de Groot (1963) includes the idea of integration as essential in the definition of character, but does not describe a framework such as is used here.

of narcissistically gratifying, but culturally contradictory, "negative" values. Looked at from the point of view of psychic functions, the resolution of adolescence can produce change in the degree of character autonomy. We may conceive of still other possibilities. Freud (1933), after describing how anxiety develops from what is originally the objective fear of parental punishment and loss of love to superego anxiety, went on to characterize superego anxiety as a secondary situation that "we are all too ready to regard as the normal one" (p. 62). Even more interestingly, Freud also stated: "Fear of the super-ego should normally never cease, since, in the form of moral anxiety, it is indispensable in social relations, and only in the rarest cases can an individual *become* independent of human society" (p. 88; my italics).

What sort of personality development can we extrapolate from this provocative statement by Freud, keeping in mind an individual's final advance to formally abstract self-representation-learning? First, the essentially *inventive* aspect of this new plane of self-representation-learning of which the adolescent becomes capable can form the basis for a new sense-of-self—that of a *maker of meanings*— and does so in a personality type we can designate as creative. Second, the essentially *instrumental* aspect of this new plane of self-representation-learning also can form the basis for a new sense-of-self—that of a *user of meanings*—and does so in a personality type we may designate as pragmatic. It is not that superego functions and ideals are absent in creative and pragmatic personality types. These are present. But in a creative personality these superego functions and ideals are subordinate and subjected to an integrative principle of psychic organization which expresses a constant question and answer dialectic about life's meaning. In a pragmatic personality, superego functions and ideals are integrated into a psychic organization which expresses them as always provisional tools for the mastery of particular reality situations.[19] Creative and pragmatic per-

---

[19] Pragmatism can be regarded as a philosophical expression of such a personality. Consider, for example, the following by Dewey (1920): "Health, wealth, industry, temperance, amiability, courtesy, learning, aesthetic capacity, initiative, courage, patience, enterprise, thoroughness and a multitude of other generalized ends are acknowledged as goods. But the *value* of this systematization is intellectual or analytic. Classifications *suggest* possible traits to be on the lookout for in studying a particular case; they suggest methods of action to be tried in removing the inferred causes of ill. They are

sonality types should be distinguished from any other kind of personality organization which expresses a basically constant framework for the content and form of ideals and standards, even if such a framework functions with a great deal of character autonomy. A creative personality may be quite conflicted.[20]

The psychic apparatus approach emphasized in this paper leads to a series of further questions not only about personality itself but also about the way in which we conceptualize the treatment process. Some of these are: What is the metapsychology of the self-representation-learning which, in terms of identifications, produces a sense-of-self, and, looked at from the viewpoint of psychic function, produces character? What is the metapsychology of different ego ideal content? What is the metapsychology of that kind of disturbance we find in certain ego deviant children, where no sense-of-self is present, and yet where conceptualization outside this area seems to show conservation and reversibility? What are the different relationships which can exist between the state of consciousness and the sense-of-self? Is self-conservation and reversibility achieved prior to, after, or coincident with, the more general acquisition of such concept formation?

Does psychoanalytic treatment require, if only for the working through part of the treatment, a maker-of-meaning self? Is this not the case in psychotherapy? If so, and since such a maker-of-meaning self cannot be possessed by latency children, how does this affect the concept of child analysis compared to adult analysis? What implication does the maker-of-meaning self have for treatment techniques with the adolescent?

---

tools of insight; their value is in promoting an individualized response in the individual situation" (p. 338).

Spranger (1928) would consider the creative and pragmatic types described here as the religious and the economic types. There is, incidentally, no simple manifest connection between these types of personality and interests or vocation. I believe, for example, that both creative and pragmatic personalities may express scientific interest and have a scientific vocation.

20 Nevertheless, creative torment about the content and form of meaning should not be confused with obsessive doubting; the latter presupposes a fixed framework of ideals and standards, while the former does not.

Conclusion

I have emphasized that personality (self, character) *is* the formation of an integrative structure. An emphasis upon the development and operation of such an integrative structure avoids a reification of the psychic system terms; and this occurs when such classificatory terms are pressed into service to describe the (dis)organizational properties of a total personality. A necessary but insufficient cause of this structure is a symbolic tool which becomes available for self-representation-learning in the middle years of latency. This integration follows the differentiation of various imagistic-imitative identification-sets, a period which is at its height during the oedipal phase but also appears to extend into the early years of latency. I have sought to separate carefully the idea of such integration from the idea of psychic conflict. Psychic conflict may or may not occur within a context of integration. I have suggested a variety of ego ideal content which may become integrated into a personality organization, and this variety is related to varying fates and aspects of an instinctual drive: its renunciation, regulation, and management, or its standards for gratification. Furthermore, I have suggested that a person's sense-of-self can vary in form, and that such variation is related to a disposition to experience shame versus guilt intrapsychic conflict.

I have formulated a concept of character in terms of a dimension of integration, so that increasing integration is indicated by increased character autonomy. The concept of character autonomy is not just a reasonable extension of the theory of autonomy of psychic functions, but I believe a necessary one. When we say that a psychic function operates with some degree of autonomy, we mean that it is available for adaptation, that it is responsive to prevailing reality conditions. But when reality changes the opportunities and requirements for drive gratification, regulation, and prohibition, we observe a response that nevertheless retains an organizational sameness in the patterned use of all psychic functions. Therefore, a "superordinate ego function" of "central regulation" (Hartmann, 1939, p. 95) can be formulated. But such "central regulation" affects superego and all other types of psychic functions. Therefore, I believe, it must be thought of as the operation of an organization which is distinct from classificatory psychic system terms. It is the organizing principle inherent in this structure, viewed in terms of psychic function, which I have defined as character; it is this which can be subject to some degree of autonomy. This concept of character can do "double duty": it can be conceptualized both as a mechanism which integrates psychic functions and as a structural integration of identifications. However, a separate term, sense-of-self, has been formulated to describe the integration of all identifications. First, I believe such a term alludes to Freud's emphasis upon self-representation-learning (identification) as the key process for personality formation, function, and development. Second, varying attributes of such a sense-of-self (for example, its form) appear to have important consequences for psychic content.

Finally, I have raised, but not answered, a series of further questions about personality and its treatment, questions which derive from the psychic apparatus emphasis of this paper.

BIBLIOGRAPHY

Asch, S. E. & Nerlove, H. (1960), The Development of Double Function Terms in Children: An Exploratory Study. In: *Perspectives in Psychological Theory,* ed. S. Wapner & B. Kaplan. New York: International Universities Press, pp. 47-60.
Beres, D. (1958), Vicissitudes of Superego Functions and Superego Precursors in Childhood. *This Annual,* 13:324-351.
—— (1966), Superego and Depression. In: *Psychoanalysis—A General Psychology,* ed. R. M. Loewenstein, L. M. Newman, M. Schur, & A. J. Solnit. New York: International Universities Press, pp. 479-498.
Bing, J. F., McLaughlin, F., & Marburg, R. (1959), The Metapsychology of Narcissism. *This Annual,* 14:9-28.
Bornstein, B. (1951), On Latency. *This Annual,* 6:279-285.
Deutsch, H. (1942), Some Forms of Emotional Disturbance and Their Relationship to Schizophrenia. *Psa. Quart.,* 11:301-321.
Dewey, J. (1920), Reconstruction in Moral Conceptions. In: *Philosophy in the Twentieth Century,* Vol. 1, ed. W. Barrett & H. Aiken. New York: Random House.
Erikson, E. H. (1950), *Childhood and Society.* New York: Norton.
—— (1956), The Problem of Ego Identity. *J. Amer. Psa. Assn.,* 4:56-121.
Feldman, S. S. (1962), Blushing, Fear of Blushing and Shame. *J. Amer. Psa. Assn.,* 10:369-385.
Fenichel, O. (1945), *The Psychoanalytic Theory of Neurosis.* New York: Norton.
Freud, A. (1936), *The Ego and the Mechanisms of Defense.* New York: International Universities Press, rev. ed., 1966.
Freud, S. (1896), Further Remarks on the Neuro-psychoses of Defence. *Standard Edition,* 3:159-185. London: Hogarth Press, 1962.
—— (1900), The Interpretation of Dreams. *Standard Edition,* 4 & 5. London: Hogarth Press, 1953.

—— (1912), On the Universal Tendency to Debasement in the Sphere of Love. *Standard Edition*, 11:177-190. London: Hogarth Press, 1957.

—— (1914), On Narcissism. *Standard Edition*, 14:67-102. London: Hogarth Press, 1957.

—— (1915), Repression. *Standard Edition*, 14:141-158. London: Hogarth Press, 1957.

—— (1921), Group Psychology and the Analysis of the Ego. *Standard Edition*, 18:67-143. London: Hogarth Press, 1955.

—— (1923), The Ego and the Id. *Standard Edition*, 19:3-66. London: Hogarth Press, 1961.

—— (1924), The Dissolution of the Oedipus Complex. *Standard Edition:* 19:173-179. London: Hogarth Press, 1961.

—— (1925), Some Psychical Consequences of the Anatomical Distinction between the Sexes. *Standard Edition*, 19:243-258. London: Hogarth Press, 1961.

—— (1926), Inhibitions, Symptoms and Anxiety. *Standard Edition*, 20:77-175. London: Hogarth Press, 1959.

—— (1930), Civilization and Its Discontents. *Standard Edition*, 21:59-145. London: Hogarth Press, 1961.

—— (1931a), Libidinal Types. *Standard Edition*, 21:215-220. London: Hogarth Press, 1961.

—— (1931b), Female Sexuality. *Standard Edition*, 21:225-243. London: Hogarth Press, 1961.

—— (1933), New Introductory Lectures on Psycho-Analysis. *Standard Edition*, 22:3-182. London: Hogarth Press, 1964.

Gardner, R., Holzman, P. S., Klein, G. S., Linton, H., & Spence, D. P. (1959), *Cognitive Control* [*Psychological Issues, Monogr.* 4]. New York: International Universities Press.

Glover, E. (1925), The Neurotic Character. *Brit. J. Med. Psychol.*, 5:279-297.

Grinker, R. R. (1957), On Identification, *Int. J. Psa.*, 38:379-390.

Harlow, H. F. (1949), The Formation of Learning Sets. *Psychol. Rev.* 56:51-65.

Hartmann, H. (1939), *Ego Psychology and the Problem of Adaptation.* New York: International Universities Press, 1958.

—— (1950), Comments on the Psychoanalytic Theory of the Ego. *This Annual,* 5:74-96.

—— & Loewenstein, R. M. (1962), Notes on the Superego. *This Annual,* 17:42-81.

Hunt, J. McV. (1961), *Intelligence and Experience.* New York: Ronald Press.

Isakower, O. (1939), On the Exceptional Position of the Auditory Sphere. *Int. J. Psa.*, 20:340-348.

Jacobson, E. (1964), *The Self and the Object World.* New York: International Universities Press.

Kernberg, O. (1966), Structural Derivatives of Object Relationships. *Int. J. Psa.*, 47:236-253.

Kessen, W. & Kuhlman, C., eds. (1962), *Thought in the Young Child.* Monogr. Soc. Res. Child Develpm., No. 27.

Lampl-de Groot, J. (1962), Ego Ideal and Superego. *This Annual,* 17:94-106.

—— (1963), Symptom Formation and Character Formation. *Int. J. Psa.*, 44:1-11.

Mahler, M. S. (1952), On Child Psychosis and Schizophrenia: Autistic and Symbiotic Infantile Psychoses. *This Annual,* 7:286-305.

Monroe, R. (1955), *Schools of Psychoanalytic Thought.* New York: Holt, Rinehart, & Winston.

Murphy, G. (1947), *Personality.* New York: Harper.

Novey, S. (1955), The Rôle of the Superego and Ego-Ideal in Character Formation. *Int. J. Psa.*, 36:254-259.

Nunberg, H. (1930), The Synthetic Function of the Ego. *Practice and Theory of Psychoanalysis.* New York: International Universities Press, 1955, pp. 120-136.

—— (1955), *Principles of Psychoanalysis.* New York: International Universities Press.

Piaget, J. (1923), *The Language and Thought of the Child*. London: Routledge & Kegan Paul, 1948.

—— (1937), *The Construction of Reality in the Child*. New York: Basic Books, 1954.

—— (1945), *Play, Dreams, and Imitation in Childhood*. New York: Norton, 1951.

—— (1960), *The Psychology of Intelligence*. Paterson, N.J.: Littlefield, Adams.

—— (1967), *Six Psychological Studies*. New York: Random House.

Piers, G. & Singer, M. D. (1953), *Shame and Guilt*. Springfield, Ill.: Thomas.

Rapaport, D. (1959), *The Structure of Psychoanalytic Theory* [*Psychological Issues*, Monogr. 6]. New York: International Universities Press, 1960.

Reich, A. (1953), Narcissistic Object Choice in Women. *J. Amer. Psa. Assn.*, 1:22-44.

—— (1954), Early Identifications as Archaic Elements in the Superego. *J. Amer. Psa. Assn.*, 2:218-238.

Sandler, J. (1960), On the Concept Superego. *This Annual*, 15:128-162.

—— (1963), The Ego Ideal and the Ideal Self. *This Annual*, 18:139-158.

Schafer, R. (1967), Ideals, the Ego Ideal, and the Ideal Self. In: *Motives and Thought*, ed. R. R. Holt [*Psychological Issues*, Monogr. 18/19]. New York: International Universities Press, pp. 131-174.

—— (1968), *Aspects of Internalization*. New York: International Universities Press.

Spiegel, L. A. (1959), The Self, the Sense of Self, and Perception. *This Annual*, 14:81-109.

Spranger, E. (1928), *Types of Men*. Holle (Saale): Max Niemeyer Verlag.

Waelder, R. (1930), The Principle of Multiple Function. *Psa. Quart.*, 5:45-62, 1936.

Wallace, L. (1963), The Mechanism of Shame. *Arch. Gen. Psychiat.*, 8:80-85.

Wallach, H. & Auerbach, E. (1955), On Memory Modalities. *Amer. J. Psychol.*, 68:249-257.

Weiss, E. (1933), A Recovery from the Fear of Blushing. *Psa. Quart.*, 2:309-314.

Werner, H. & Kaplan, B. (1967), *Symbol Formation*. New York: Wiley.

CLINICAL CONTRIBUTIONS

BORDERLINE STATES IN CHILDREN

E. C. M. FRIJLING-SCHREUDER, M.D. (Amsterdam)

The diagnosis borderline case is frequently used loosely and may point to a confused doctor rather than to a confused patient. It may mean: "I do not know what is the matter with this patient," or: "I was not able to help him; so he must have a more severe illness than I originally thought"; it may be a kind of excuse for the failure of treatment.

Parents of mentally retarded children may cling to the diagnosis autistic syndrome as if that would make for a better prognosis. Institutionalized children showing severe aggressive behavior are sometimes sent to child psychiatric hospitals with the diagnosis psychosis in the hope that they will get more care than the average institution is able to offer. However, I am not concerned with this kind of diagnostics.

In this paper I shall attempt to develop criteria which will help us define the diagnosis borderline state and distinguish it from both neurosis and psychosis. It should be borne in mind, however, that these criteria are not absolute. Individual cases are diverse, and it may be extremely difficult to differentiate between neurosis and borderline state, and even more so between borderline state and psychosis. The differential diagnosis is further hampered by the fact that many psychotic children do not speak, or do not use speech as a means of contact or communication. The absence of speech necessitates very careful evaluation of behavior.

Nonverbal psychological tests and behavioral data may also help us in distinguishing between various psychotic and psychoticlike conditions and organically based disorders such as congenital deaf-

Read at the Symposium on Borderline States, held by the San Francisco Psychoanalytic Institute, Extension Division, on October 13, 1968.

ness or mental retardation. But even in these instances we may be confronted with great problems. Congenital deafness, for example, frequently occurs in conjunction with other congenital abnormalities. I have seen a deaf boy with panhypopituitary disease who was so understimulated that it took a year of residential treatment in the child psychiatric hospital before the diagnosis deafness could be made with sufficient certainty.

Returning to the childhood psychoses, I shall start my discussion with the autistic syndrome. Early infantile autism is the earliest childhood psychosis. In clear-cut cases the children never make any contact from the beginning of life; for example, they never show a smiling response. It is impossible to develop a normal "dialogue" or an object relationship, however primitive, with an autistic child.

The autistic syndrome occurs as a complication of many early abnormalities. We may see it in combination with retardation, as the outcome of early severe neglect or of early and long hospitalization. There is always a strong constitutional factor, although in a family with one autistic child the other children may be normal. Often there are other forms of schizophrenia in the ascendency. The children are completely lacking in human contact; they do not talk; they show stereotyped behavior and much autoerotism. Contact with lifeless objects is made with the mouth, or the fingers may explore the borders of an object without definitely handling it. The stereotyped movements indicate very well developed motility, and in general motor development is normal. Musical stimulation may, in some cases, overwhelm the autistic child and give rise to stereotyped autoerotic movement, i.e., rocking. These autistic children may get addicted to music or develop highly personal choices. One of my autistic patients always chose Bach's music from her parents' records.

Such special interests, the absence of any visible disturbance, and the high motoric skills give rise to the hope that the condition is less incapacitating than mental retardation, whereas in reality autism is far more disabling. The prognosis is related to the underlying illness: I have seen autistic reactions in battered or otherwise neglected children which cleared up with adequate care and mothering. As soon as these children make contact they show intense negative feelings—and these should be respected as a sign of better functioning. I cite as an example the first sentences an autistic hospitalized boy spoke to me with a kind and friendly smile: "Shall I pick your eyes out? Would that hurt you?" This was the first sign of contact given by a boy who until then had been mute.

More important for the understanding of the borderline states are the childhood psychoses rooted in disturbances of the separation-individuation phase. Mahler emphasizes the importance of that phase in which the child grows into a separate being apart from the mother, the period from about four to thirty months. The following case illustrates a symbiotic psychosis.

CASE 1

Developmental History

We saw Alfie for the first time for a short examination at my clinic when he was six years old. He already had a long history of suffering. Until the age of eighteen months his development had been normal. At eighteen months he had convulsions in connection with a febrile illness. He was hospitalized for six weeks, but no signs of encephalitis or meningitis were found. He returned home completely changed. Such a sudden twist in development is typical of the symbiotic psychotic illness in childhood. The mother said he had changed into a wild animal; he had become malicious. However, we have to keep in mind that, apart from the convulsions, there was never any sign of brain damage. The family was extremely disharmonious and during this period the parents' quarrels often were so vehement that the police had to intervene. The father, a Chinese cook who spoke very little Dutch, left the family shortly after Alfie returned home from the hospital. The mother was a chaotic, primitive, confused hysterical woman. She had two children; the elder son was neurotic, but well adapted socially and at school. She felt completely tyrannized by Alfie.

Alfie's history followed a typical course. When he was four years old, the child psychiatric department of the town was unable to place him because he was too difficult for a special school or an institution for neglected children. His aggressive outbursts and unpredictable impulsive behavior were a danger to himself and to his environment. At the age of seven years he underwent a most extensive examination on the children's neurological ward, where he was disoriented, contactless, and catatonic. The neurological examination neither showed nor excluded organic causes of his disturbances, and he was then admitted to the child psychiatric hospital. Initially he could come only for a few hours a day, later on he stayed for the whole day, and after a year he received full residential treatment. I have seen him regularly five times a week since he was eight years old.

In the first months Alfie spoke only a few stereotyped words: "Little ear, little nose," sniffing at the ears of his nurse or feeling her nose. When speech gradually emerged, there were many concretisms and neologisms. However, it became increasingly clear that Alfie's lack of speech was determined by his continuously being flooded with aggresisve fantasies. His concretisms, too, as far as they could be understood, were caused by the fact that every word had aggressive overtones. In the first period his "treatment" consisted of his coming to my room with his nurse, always fingering the same toy car, then somehow feeling attacked, and attacking me or running away. As there was no speech the interpretation of this behavior was very difficult. Sometimes the aggressive outbursts were linked to some event in his life.

Alfie's mother told me that every visit to the barber gave rise to enormous outbursts. Her management of this situation illustrates the type of mishandling which constantly interfered with the child's reality testing. A boy in the neighborhood had been brought to a hospital in an ambulance. Alfie had seen the ambulance and the sick child. His mother told him that the child had become cross-eyed because of his unwillingness to have his hair cut and that now his eyes must be operated upon. Alfie also refused to have his nails cut. The mother managed to do this while he was asleep and then told him that part of the nails had fallen off during the night. This continual interplay between mother and son, each arousing the other's anxiety, led to perpetual overexcitement and always tended toward annihilating the child's reality testing. The mother's anxiety over his temper tantrums was so great that she sought all kinds of quaint solutions to prevent them.

One of Alfie's most intense wishes was to be completely Dutch. This wish meant that everything unpleasant, especially his anxiety about his own aggressivity, was projected onto his Chinese half. The image of the Chinese father had been changed into that of an inhuman monster. Alfie expressed the wish to become Dutch by crying: "I want fair hair, I must have fair hair." His mother told him that his seafaring uncle would bring him fair hair, but that there was no fair hair to be had in the country he just came from. At other times she would urge him to eat his porridge to get fair hair.

In addition to this persistent undermining of his reality testing, he was continuously being overstimulated. This had started in his second year with the ceaseless scuffles between Alfie's father and mother and later continued in the permanent quarrels between his mother and her successive lovers. He slept in his mother's bed when she was alone and was sent to his own room when her friend came. While the mother undoubtedly overstimulated him, Alfie himself constantly provoked abnormal stimulation. He followed his mother to the toilet and was furious when she tried to shut him out. When he used the toilet, she had to go with him and hold his buttocks while he defecated. The mother was convinced that it would be impossible for Alfie to have a bowel movement at the hospital if this ritual were not followed. To the astonishment of everyone he was able to defecate after two days, although he never had a bowel movement at the clinic throughout the time he came only for the day.

This kind of overstimulation is regularly found in the anamnesis of psychotic children. It is of course true that we find abnormal kinds of stimulation in neurotic cases as well; however, in the psychotic patients, both children and adults, the stimulation usually is much more intense and disorganizing.

Alfie did not make contact via speech. His stereotyped sayings, "little ear, little nose," and his sniffing at the people did not give one the impression of his seeking contact with a human object; rather, it was as though he used human beings as extensions of his own body.

After a few months of treatment he began to tell me about his fear of being killed, cooked, and eaten. It is not as strange as it seems that this is so often the main anxiety in childhood psychosis. The psychosis of the separation-individuation phase rests on the faulty distinction between self and object, and the enormous anxiety over losing this distinction expresses itself in the fear of being eaten by the object. The more Alfie could tell me about himself, the clearer became the confusion between self and object. His main mechanism of defense was projection, and this too led to continuous confusion. He spent much of the time with me calling me names; however, just as often he would say, "You are an ape," and then run away to his nurse, crying, "Professor says I am an ape." In the hospital this did not lead to difficulties, but at home his poor mother was the recipient of all his criticism of her or of his projected self-criticism, which he asserted was coming from me: "Professor says you are mad," etc. The social worker had a very difficult time helping the mother maintain some semblance of a positive attitude.

Alfie had no contact whatever with the other children until one day he said to his nurse: "There is a quaint idea in my head that Richie and I could be friends." After another year of treatment he said: "Peter is my friend and I imitate him in everything." I believe this illustrates his growing sense of identity. At the height of an aggressive outburst, however, he could completely lose his sense of identity again. When I once asked him, "Why are you so angry, Alfie?" he answered, "I am not Alfie, I am just anything."

The continuous state of excitation in these children is caused partly by their insufficient capacity for object cathexis. Neither libido nor aggression can be turned away from the self. They are permanently flooded by outer and inner stimuli with which they cannot cope and which thus hamper their ego development. Yet, it is difficult to say what is the cause and what the effect: whether the continuous overstimulation is too great for the ego, or whether the ego's incapacity to bind stimuli leads to overstimulation. Mahler points to the discrepancies in ego development as one of the preconditions of childhood schizophrenia. Psychotic children generally have areas of very defective ego functioning and other areas of highly developed capacities.

Alfie, for example, drew and modeled wonderfully. In the first period the drawing and modeling were completely under the influence of his stereotyped attempts to ward off his anxious fantasies. In the end we had cupboards full of crocodiles, which would give him the magic power to devour instead of being devoured.

In what I have described so far Alfie's oral and anal fixations are clear. In addition, he showed very intense rivalry with his mother's friends. When his mother took a new lover—the third in a period of a few years—Alfie regressed completely, losing bladder and bowel control. He fought very openly over his place with the mother and tried to obstruct this new relationship. The overlapping of early developmental phases is typical of childhood psychosis. There is no clear dominance of any phase; instead, we see side by side unintegrated fragments of oral, anal, and oedipal traits.

In addition to the symptoms described, Alfie had delusional feelings of grandeur, which were not corrected by reality testing. He cried, "I will, I will," and believed that in this way he could really change himself into a completely Dutch boy. He tried to jump out of the window, convinced that he could not possibly be hurt. At the same time, however, he was swamped by hypochondriacal fears. Both attitudes can be viewed as resulting from the hypercathexis of different aspects of the self.

Discussion

The separation-individuation phase is a relatively long period, lasting from the age of a few months to three years. During it the child learns to distinguish increasingly between his self and the environment and develops more and more individuality. Among the first signs of the awareness of the beginning separation is the first smile and later the eight-months anxiety. Soon thereafter follows the first "no," in gesture or speech, signifying the nucleus of the inner differentiation between child and mother, which is more clearly marked with the first use of the word "I." The motor development makes it possible for the child to draw physically away from the mother and to return to her for emotional "refueling," as Furer calls it. In normal development the child of three years is able to continue playing with pleasure if the mother leaves the room. He feels sure that he can find her when he wants her; her object representation is cathected with sufficient object libido to remain stable even in her absence.

In cases of early childhood psychosis these steps in development do not take place, or there is regression to a very primitive level. The differentiation between self and object remains insufficient. The primary defenses used are projection and introjection. Anxiety is warded off by delusions of persecution and grandeur. In outbursts of panic the fear of annihilation breaks through and is defended against by aggressive and impulsive behavior.

I believe that in the literature on childhood psychosis, the enormous importance of speech for the development of the secondary process has not always received sufficient attention. We know that in the beginning speech consists of need-words and of magical use of words. "Mamma" may mean: "I love you" or "I am hungry" or "My tummy aches." This is what we often observe in childhood psychosis if the child is able to speak and is not autistic. During the second half of the second year and during the third year of life speech is normally used as a means of real communication of secondary process thinking, although some magical use of speech may persist. We all know from our daily work how much magical thinking and magical use of words persists unconsciously into adulthood and how vulnerable the reign of reality testing is under the sway of intense affects. In my opinion, the use of speech to convey secondary process functioning and the capacity to tolerate feelings of anxiety constitute the main difference between psychosis and borderline states.

The psychotic child is constantly flooded with stimuli and this overstimulation leads to continuous traumatic anxiety. Panic follows panic; since the child lacks the ability to verbalize his feelings, he does not succeed in binding them in a secondary process mode. His main attempts at regulation, proceeding via projection and introjection, lead to delusions. In this remodeled reality, verbalization becomes possible along the lines of the primary process. In this way the feeling of anxiety may no longer be experienced consciously, even though the child suffers from a fully developed psychosis.

In summary, I shall list the characteristics typically found in childhood psychosis. There is extreme overstimulation, absence of social adaptation, and lack of contact. What contact there is, has a very abnormal form. There is no real phase dominance of any developmental phase, but we see remnants of all the phases. Either objects are cathected with narcissistic libido, or they turn into persecutors; in the symbiotic psychosis, we regularly find signs of persecutory delusion. There is overcathexis of the self and chronic excitation. The great unchecked impulsivity makes the little patient dangerous to himself and to his environment. In the area of the ego important

features are the unevenness of development and the specific disturbance in integration and reality testing. The excessive reliance on in-
trojective projection is one of the causes of the lacking distinction
between self and object representations. The attempts to deal with
the resulting fusion and confusion are hampered by the minimal
capacity for thinking in words. Speech is characterized by concretisms and neologisms. There is a great lack of secondary process
thinking.

In the symbiotic psychosis the need for human contact may persist and we see many restitutive processes. Some of these lead to the
high development of certain skills, e.g., in the case of Alfie, to sculp-
turing and painting. Rituals and stereotyped behavior are used as a
defense against disintegration but also to oppose change of any kind.
Every developmental step leads to regression, so that progress is very
slow indeed even if the child is in treatment. There is no structured
superego, but archaic anxiety is projected onto the outer world. The
frustration tolerance is very low. The loss of reality testing together
with the tendency to restitution makes for a remodeling of reality.

In borderline states the flight from reality may be extreme, but
reality testing is not lost as completely as in psychosis. The use of
the secondary process leads to conscious feeling of anxiety, to the
possibility of the ego's experiencing signal anxiety. The threat of
being overwhelmed and engulfed by the object remains, but thinking in words is used as an attempt at mastery. Persistent but conscious anxiety is very much in the center of the clinical picture, as
the following case report illustrates.

CASE 2

Developmental History

Ben seemed to have had a transitory autistic-symbiotic syndrome
after a very long period of hospitalization in his first year of life.
From the age of six weeks to six months, he was in a hospital with
an incarcerated hernia and peritonitis. After his return home, he
made good progress in his motor development; however, he made
little or no contact, showed much stereotyped behavior, and had
screaming fits during the night. When he was two and a half years
old, the mother saw him smile for the first time. As he did not speak,

a psychiatrist advised speech lessons. He learned to speak and to use speech actively, but not as a means of establishing contact with others. His speech consisted primarily of stereotyped questioning.

When Ben was six years old his parents came to me in despair. He ate only Yogurt. Throughout the day he talked obsessively. He had to have a woolen fluff in his hand with which he caressed his face. He could sit endlessly sorting nails without ever doing anything constructive with them. He showed much autoerotism and no signs of object relations. His parents were very concerned and tried very hard to help him.

The mother was ridden by guilt feelings and very anxious about her handling of the child. With my support and encouragement she began to treat Ben as a much younger child and thus succeeded in regaining contact with him. His quaint food fads faded out and he showed less stereotyped behavior.

It is difficult to describe the difference between early infantile autism and Ben's illness at this stage. However, the rapid reintegration and his enjoyment of the contact he was able to make, differ from the pyschotic resistance to change and from the strong negative feelings children show when they begin to conquer an autistic psychosis. This rapid response to better handling is typical of the borderline case, in contrast to the psychotic and autistic child. I shall come back to this difference.

As soon as Ben was able to express himself it became clear that he was afraid of everything. He was afraid to go out, afraid of dogs, afraid of too much light, afraid of the dark, afraid of other children. The whole day he clung to his parents, with both of whom he had a helpless, dependent, but positive relationship. The regained contact itself represented an enormous achievement for the parents. For the first time after the catastrophe of his early illness they felt that he was again their son and that there was real feeling communication.

The quality of parental caretaking is even more decisive for the functioning of a borderline case than it is for normal children. In his terrified state Ben could always turn to both parents and their availability made it possible for him to achieve some feeling of individuation. Moreover, Ben had a good intellect. Was he able to proceed further on the line toward separation-individuation as a result of his good intellectual endowment, or was the development of object relations the precondition for his intellectual functioning? It is difficult to distinguish between cause and effect. That both factors influenced each other is of course true. The interaction between ego and drive development is so intensive and continuous that it is impossible to know what comes first in the chain of cause and effect.

There is another difference between borderline states and neurotic and psychotic disturbances in childhood. While the borderline patient is constantly tortured by anxiety, it is not castration anxiety (as in the neuroses) but disintegration and separation anxiety. In psychotic states, it is the same type of anxiety, but it is so overwhelming that it completely interferes with reality testing and often even dissolves structure. This means that in psychosis anxiety is no longer a function of the ego; it is not signal anxiety but a traumatic anxiety that can be handled only by the most primitive defense mechanisms of projection and incorporation. In the borderline case, in contrast, the disintegration anxiety remains a function of the ego. This means that the borderline patient is more aware of his anxiety, but also that in coping with the anxiety his ego can resort to the whole scale of defense mechanisms. Ben used displacement, denial, and repression, as was shown in a host of phobic and obsessive symptoms. In borderline cases, the defense organization is not as well structured as in neurosis, but it is not as completely lost as in psychosis. Affective attitudes may serve to ward off other affects, etc. Verbal thinking and inner speech may be used in attempts at mastery.

I do not know whether it is correct to speak of obsessive symptoms in a borderline case. Perhaps stereotyped behavior is a better expression. Yet, from what follows it will be clear that at least some of Ben's symptoms were structured as obsessive symptoms are in neurosis.

When the parental climate had become stable and Ben had developed real contact with his parents and with his two sisters, I continued to treat him for some years. His obsessive symptoms—e.g., the sorting of the nails and his stereotyped questioning—diminished as we worked on them as a defense against feelings of grandeur and a variety of anal impulses. However, although we could analyze the unconscious content in this way and so identify them as obsessive symptoms, it is quite clear that they also had another function and therefore are better described as stereotyped behavior. As in the childhood psychosis, they serve as an inner structure where no normal structuring of the personality has developed. In psychosis, too, stereotyped behavior may function like an inner structure in the attempt to ward off disintegration anxiety or, in a state of disintegration, it may be a restitutive reaction.

On the other hand, in my clinic there is a psychotic boy who sometimes shows stereotyped behavior but who wards off anal-sadistic impulses by obsessive thinking. To my mind, the difference lies in the fact that the warding off of anal-sadistic impulses by obsessive symptoms is an expression of a specific inner conflict, whereas disintegration anxiety concerns the whole personality. It is not a conflict within the structure; rather, anxiety is raised by virtue of the fact that the structure is dissolving. Only psychoanalysis can make clear in a given case whether a certain behavior is stereotyped or obsessive. As a rule there is more stereotyped behavior in psychosis than in a borderline case, but one cannot take this as pathognomonic because both phenomena are seen in psychosis as well as in borderline states. The real difference lies in the fact that the borderline case has the inner awareness of the disintegration threat, whereas the psychotic patient wards this off with delusions.

When we succeeded in bringing Ben to school, which was quite an achievement in view of his enormous anxieties, he developed an obsessive preoccupation with school that took the place of his earlier obsessive questioning. During the whole twelve-year school period his preoccupation with marks helped to fill the inner void and give him a frame to stick to. On the other hand, his anxiety secondarily interfered with motor development. He was afraid to leave the house, to ride a bicycle, to do gymnastics. With enormous patience the parents taught him the usual motor skills: for many months his father went bicycle riding with him every day; his mother devoted endless time and energy to teaching him how to swim. In all this, Ben's wish to be accepted by the other children was the essential force motivating him to acquire a skill which itself had never been a goal; mastery of a skill always was in the service of conformity. In many borderline patients we see a strong wish to be like others in combination with an equally strong feeling of being unable to reach out to another person.

In his struggle for object relationships, the psychotic can only reach the stage of the need-satisfying object. The borderline patient may develop some object constancy, although his relationship to the object remains a very dependent one. I have not seen real dominance of the oedipal phase in a borderline case. The object constancy, insofar as it is reached, is very vulnerable. The inner experience of a tenuousness in the object relationship contributes to the basic anxiety. Here again it is the inner awareness made possible by the development of inner speech and by some development of the secondary process that differentiates borderline states from psychosis. The psychotic child loses his inner objects and sees them as persecutors in the outside world. I do not think we can maintain that a child who develops inner speech is not psychotic; but if a child is able to use thoughts not only in a magical way but for self-awareness, I believe we know that he is coming out of his psychosis.

As a rule, borderline cases have occasional aggressive outbursts. Perhaps on account of the very skillful parental help Ben never had any. What he did show, however, was the constant fluctuation of the level of functioning that is described by Ekstein and Wallerstein (1954). This fluctuation between functioning on an autistic or on a symbiotic level and a much higher level of development gives rise to much diagnostic confusion. Case conferences about borderline cases always tend to degenerate into discussions about such questions as: are we not dealing with a hysterical character deformation, or is it not a severe obsessional case; or is this patient a full-blown psychotic? More important than the psychiatric confusion is the inner confusion of the patient, who experiences this abnormal tendency toward sudden and severe regression as a basic insecurity.

Like most borderline cases, Ben developed micropsychotic states. During his more regular treatment phase he avoided shaking hands with me for months. This is very unusual in Holland where handshaking on coming and leaving is the usual form of greeting. However, Ben's greeting was done so charmingly, with waving and smiling, that I was very slow to see it as an abnormality. At a time when we were discussing his obsessional anxieties about infectious diseases,

I eventually asked him why he avoided touching my hand. He answered, "But you have large poison glands on it." This delusional idea dissolved after a few weeks, but we do not always have the opportunity to understand the background of such ideas. I never learned what occasioned the idea of the poison glands.

In adolescence Ben's anxiety about the pubertal changes gave rise to feelings of grandeur which he experienced as very threatening. With great difficulty he confessed that he sometimes was Napoleon or Hitler for a few days. He could not quite maintain his sense of reality in the face of these intense fantasies. Although these fantasy formations had more reality than an ordinary fantasy, they never changed completely into delusions. But they made Ben aware of the degree to which his sense of reality was vulnerable and how close to delusion he was—factors which could only increase his anxiousness.

Discussion

The micropsychosis of the borderline cases clears up. Speaking metapsychologically, we can say that there is a fluctuation in the severity of regression and that a core of ego functions remains intact, whereas in psychosis the ego, especially its reality testing function, is completely overwhelmed.

If a psychotic child progresses, it is very gradually and with an enormous resistance to change. Every effort at functioning on a higher level leads to new psychotic defenses. In the borderline case the threat of deep regression is present, but progression may be swift and instantaneous if the child feels understood. We may even see him reintegrate within the compass of one hour. Ben often used school as a help in reintegration. Although Ben's schoolwork helped him greatly to maintain continuity, he never became capable of independent thinking.

Borderline cases often develop special interests in one area: e.g., they know everything about paleontological zoology, but nothing about the world they live in. In my clinic Dr. de Levita calls them "moon and star boys." They may know everything about spaceships, but do not know how to get from their homes to the hospital.

In childhood psychosis frustration tolerance is low and impulses are acted out immediately. In contrast, I observed several borderline patients who, living in a good environment, had a very high frustration tolerance and slowly developed rather mature ways of coping with their very severe handicap. Although they are swamped by pervasive anxieties, they sometimes manage to maintain a level of functioning that permits them to adapt socially on a very restricted level.

A survey of the child psychiatric literature shows that there are borderline children who develop into normal adults (Tilton et al., 1966; Brown, 1969). I have seen only one such case where the borderline state came to the fore during puberty, but I have never seen complete restitution in cases of childhood borderline states. My experience is of course limited. Most of the borderline states I have seen remained borderline states forever. When subjected to stress, they may easily become psychotic. Some borderline patients manage in adulthood to find a partner on the basis of mutual dependency if the partner is willing, at least for some time, to play the role of the ever available parent. Very often, however, psychotic periods are provoked by trials to make sexual contact. It is one of the tasks of the psychiatrist to help the parent of the borderline patient not to push the youngster into dating, which is a real and severe danger to his vulnerable organization. The patients themselves should be strongly supported in forgoing the attempt to choose a partner merely out of conformity as long as they otherwise feel no need to do so.

Every borderline case and every psychotic has strong conflicts about bisexuality. However, attempts to deal with these conflicts in psychotherapy may give rise to psychotic outbursts. The therapist should be exceedingly careful in his handling of the transference. In both psychosis and borderline states the extreme anxiety about bisexuality represents at the same time the threat of losing identity.

The neurotic who wards off the castration anxiety engendered by his negative oedipal wishes does not lose his sense of identity. In both psychosis and borderline states, there is intense anxiety about really becoming another, for the boy to become a woman. The psychotic tries to ward off this anxiety by aggressive outbursts and delusions of grandeur. In the borderline case the anxiety is conscious, but the content of the anxiety is warded off. Or, to express this in other terms: in psychosis the masculinity-femininity conflict remains intrasystemic. In the borderline states, the ego tries to handle the conflict, however feebly it is structured, and the conflict is an intersystemic one.

In the borderline cases, it is the arrest in the development of the total personality that hampers the normal maturation of drive development. As long as the object relations remain on the level of the separation-individuation phase it is impossible to achieve mature drive development. For this reason the sexuality of borderline cases shows a variety of perverse traits. For example, when Ben masturbated he had to push small pieces of paper into a purse, an activity that was linked to a primitive identification with his far more successful sister. He had to steal the pieces of paper from her. These fetishes often represent in some way a transitional object.

The feelings of loneliness of borderline patients often are very intense. They feel like toddlers whose mothers are permanently out of the room. They are always reaching out for contact without achieving it. This may give rise to the extreme wish for conformity. Ben filled hours and hours reassuring me how much better accepted he felt by his schoolmates, by his church group, and the like. The intense feelings of grandeur which I have already described may ward off these feelings of loneliness and powerlessness.

Typical of the borderline case is a pananxiety with a continuously changing picture in which panneurotic and psychotic traits alternate. There is more secondary process functioning than in psychotic children, but the primary process easily breaks through. Thinking in words is used as a defense. I believe that this is very important in the inhibition of primitive aggressive outbursts. Object relations remain on a symbiotic level. This means that the patients are in perpetual danger of inner object loss and of disintegration.

In their anxious conformity they may remain undiagnosed and untreated until the onset of puberty. Some of the borderline cases we see in puberty were in fact borderline children whose pathological development remained unnoticed. On the other hand, adolescents may regress to borderline states during the disintegration phase of adolescence. This may indicate a fixation in the symbiotic stage, which remains a weak core in their personality. The borderline state may be passing and ephemeral, as are other things in adolescence, but it may also signify the onset of schizophrenic illness.

SUMMARY AND CONCLUSIONS

I would like to end with the proposal that we try to limit the diagnosis borderline state to the kind of case I have described. Freud's statement that the oedipus complex is the kernel of neurosis can also be used in differentiating between neurosis and borderline state. Hysterical acting-out personalities or disabling obsessive character formations, regardless of how severe, should be grouped under hysteria or the obsessional neurosis.

Both psychosis and borderline states can be seen as arrests of development in the symbiotic phase. However, this statement is misleading unless it takes the great complexity of mental development into account and unless the diagnosis is based on an assessment of the total personality development. We should be very careful to avoid oversimplifications, and I would like to stress again that especially the differentiation between borderline states and psychosis may be extremely difficult. I have tried to plead for basing the differential diagnosis on data from all levels of the personality.

As I see it, both childhood psychosis and childhood borderline states are arrests in the symbiotic stage of development. However, within this stage there are very great differences of development, and these differences may be responsible for the fact that the outcome in one case will be an autistic psychosis; in another, a symbiotic psychosis with more or less autistic traits; and in the third case, a borderline state showing some secondary process thinking and some mastery of impulses by means of inner speech. If we compare the reality testing of a four-month-old, a one-year-old, and a two-and-a-half-year-old normal child, who all may be in the separation-individuation phase, it is clear that the age at which the arrest occurs will determine the differences in the subsequent pathological picture. This factor is also responsible for another difference in the clinical picture; namely, the borderline case has recourse to the whole scale of defense mechanisms. He may use them in a chaotic, disorderly way, but he is not confined, as the psychotic is, to exclusive reliance on projection and primitive forms of identification.

SOME PROVISIONAL DIFFERENTIAL DIAGNOSTIC CRITERIA

	CHILDHOOD PSYCHOSIS	CHILDHOOD BORDERLINE STATES	NEUROSIS
Reason of Referral	Unmanageable at home.	Behavior ununderstandable.	All kinds of difficulties.
Description of Child	Strange.	Strange.	All kinds of descriptions.
Environmental Influences	Overstimulation. Lack of contact or abnormal contact.	Overstimulation. Lack of contact or abnormal contact.	Neurotic family relationship (less intense than in psychosis or borderline cases).
Drive development of the Child	No real phase dominance of any developmental phase Many traits of early phases, all phases overlap and merge. Great difficulties at the transition from one phase to the next. Abnormal libido distribution, with lack of object cathexis or objects cathected with narcissistic libido. Preference for lifeless objects. Too intense cathexis of the self. Chronic excitation.	No real phase dominance. Developmental phases overlap and merge. Difficult transition from one phase to the next. Less disturbance of libido distribution than in psychosis. Great dependency on a few objects. Symbiotic relationships. Too much cathexis of the self, but less chronic excitation. Less vitality. Often fetishistic traits. The fetish may represent a transitional object or a primitive identification with a person by means of something associated to that person.	No real phase dominance. Conflicts stemming from the oedipal phase, with regression. Object cathexis. Self-esteem may be disturbed by neurotic conflicts.
Aggression	High impulsivity. Dangerous to themselves and to the environment.	Open aggression lacking, with impulsive outbursts.	Difficulties in aggression regulation, but as a rule not dangerous to others. Only dangerous to themselves in suicidal impulses or accident proneness.
Conflicts	Severe intrasystemic conflicts. Masculinity-femininity active-passive libidinal-aggressive.	Intersystemic and intrasystemic conflicts.	Intersystemic and intrasystemic conflicts.

	CHILDHOOD PSYCHOSIS	CHILDHOOD BORDERLINE STATES	NEUROSIS
Ego development	Specific disturbances of integration and of reality testing. No distinction between self and object representation. Active warding off of this distinction and of the perception of the object. Speech is not used as a means of contact with the object. Concretisms and neologisms. The need for human contact may persist and this may lead to restitutive processes. Secondary process mainly lacking.	Specific disturbances of integration. Less disturbance of reality testing than in psychosis. Differentiation between self and object representation, but with tendency to regression to nondifferentiation. Disturbance of the use of speech as a means of contact, often with a strong need for contact. Unrealistic ideas of grandeur, but no constant delusions. Secondary process thinking is used defensively. "Star and moon boys."	Disturbance of integration and reality testing only in symptom formation. Speech is used as a means of contact. Secondary process is used extensively.
Defense	Mainly by primitive projection and introjection. In addition, ritualized and stereotyped behavior is used as a defense against disintegration. Open anxiety may be lacking, but there are outbursts of panic and impulsive behavior.	All kinds of defense mechanisms are used. More primitive projection and identification than in neurosis. Phobic displacement and obsessional symptoms. Defense is very ineffective. Pananxiety.	All kinds of defense mechanisms are combined in the defense organization. This may lead to deadlock within the structure.
Superego	No structured superego, but archaic anxiety projected into the outer world.	Primitive superego structure very dependent on outer objects. Some internalization with a tendency to regression and to re-externalization.	More internalization of conflicts with structured superego.
Frustration tolerance	Very low.	May be high apart from specific traumatic situations.	May be high or low.
Progressive tendencies	Great opposition to change. Every developmental step may lead to severe regression.	Much anxiety at every step in development. Danger of psychosis if pushed to take such a step. Especially attempts at adult object relations and at sexual contact may lead to psychotic decompensation.	If adult object relationship and sexual contact are reached, this may be of help in recovery.

In the borderline state there is some differentiation between ego and id. For this reason we find intersystemic conflicts. Conflicts between masculinity-femininity, active-passive, libidinal-aggressive tendencies lead, in the psychotic child, either to delusions or to complete confusion. In the borderline case, however, they may be perceived as intersystemic conflicts and give rise to a confusing mixture of phobic and obsessive and conversion symptoms. The more structured ego is more aware of the threat to its integrity, and this gives rise to the pananxiety of the borderline states. The primitive superego structure is very dependent on outer objects. The object relationships are colored by strong dependency needs which themselves hamper the establishment of genuine contact. The disturbed contact, together with the strong dependency needs, leads to rigid conformity. In a good environment this conformity may help in developing ego skills. Integration is very unstable and there are sudden and severe regressions, but there is also a tendency to reintegration. Every step in development leads to anxiety and may initiate regression, but after such a regression the reintegration may really occur at a higher level.

As a last point I would like to stress that this description is an oversimplification of the real picture. I could have stressed the pre-oedipal traits in neurosis, the onset of oedipal development in a borderline case. I could even have stressed the mature character traits that we find in adult borderline patients whom we have known from childhood. Ultimately, all psychiatric classification may well differ from one country to another, from one clinic to another. I hope that I have illustrated how important it is to use all our analytic knowledge even in the diagnosis of very disturbed children. Only by assessing the total personality and the deviations of development in every area of the personality can we formulate rational treatment programs.

BIBLIOGRAPHY

Benda, C. E. (1968), A Distinctive Metabolic Disorder. *Int. J. Psychiat.*, 5:220-221.
Bender, L. (1968a), Childhood Schizophrenia: A Review. *Int. J. Psychiat.*, 5:211-219.
—— (1968b), A Reply to the Critics. *Int. J. Psychiat.*, 5:234-236.
Blécourt, A. de (1967) Borderline States (unpublished paper).
Brown, J. L. (1969), Adolescent Development of Children with Infantile Psychosis. *Seminars in Psychiatry*, 1:79-89.

Chess, S. (1968), An Interactive Concept of Childhood Schizophrenia. *Int. J. Psychiat.*, 5:222-223.

Ekstein, R. & Friedman, S. (1968), Cause of the Illness or Cause of the Cure? *Int. J. Psychiat.*, 5:224-229.

—— & Wallerstein, J. (1954), Observations on the Psychology of Borderline and Psychotic Children. *This Annual*, 9:344-369.

—— —— (1956), Observations on the Psychotherapy of Borderline and Psychotic Children. *This Annual*, 11:303-312.

Freud, A. (1958), Adolescence. *This Annual*, 13:255-278.

Geleerd, E. R. (1947), A Contribution to the Problem of Psychoses in Childhood. *This Annual*, 2:271-293.

—— (1958), Borderline States in Childhood and Adolescence. *This Annual*, 13:279-295.

Goldfarb, W. (1961), *Childhood Schizophrenia*. Cambridge: Harvard University Press.

Greenacre, P. (1941), The Predisposition to Anxiety: Parts I and II. *Psa. Quart.*, 10:66-94, 610-638.

—— (1954), In: Problems of Infantile Neurosis. *This Annual*, 9:18-24.

Kut Rosenfeld, S. & Sprince, M. P. (1963), An Attempt to Formulate the Meaning of the Concept "Borderline." *This Annual*, 18:603-635.

—— —— (1965), Some Thoughts on the Technical Handling of Borderline Children. *This Annual*, 20:495-517.

Lampl-de Groot, J. (1962), Ego Ideal and Superego. *This Annual*, 17:94-106.

McDermott, J. F., Jr., Fraiberg, S., & Harrison, S. I. (1968), Residential Treatment of Children: The Utilization of Transference Behavior. *J. Amer. Acad. Child Psychiat.*, 7:169-192.

Mahler, M. S. (1952), On Child Psychosis and Schizophrenia: Autistic and Symbiotic Infantile Psychoses. *This Annual*, 7:286-305.

—— (1961), On Sadness and Grief in Infancy and Childhood: Loss and Restoration of the Symbiotic Love Object. *This Annual*, 16:332-351.

—— (1963), Thoughts about Development and Individuation. *This Annual*, 18:307-324.

—— (1968a), The Self-Limitations of Lauretta Bender's Biological Theory. *Int. J. Psychiat.*, 5:230-233.

—— (1968b), *On Human Symbiosis and the Vicissitudes of Individuation*. New York: International Universities Press.

—— & Furer, M. (1963), Certain Aspects of the Separation-Individuation Phase. *Psa. Quart.*, 32:1-14.

Rose, K. E. & Shriver, M. (1954), The Dynamic Significance of the Mother-Child Relationship in the Case of a Young Delinquent with Psychotic Mechanisms. *Amer. J. Orthopsychiat.*, 24:797-828.

Rubinfine, D. L. (1958), Panel Report: Problems of Identity. *J. Amer. Psa. Assn.*, 6:131-142.

Singer, M. B. (1960), Fantasies of a Borderline Patient. *This Annual*, 15:310-356.

Smolen, E. M. (1965), Some Thoughts on Schizophrenia in Childhood. *J. Amer. Acad. Child Psychiat.*, 4:443-472.

Thomas, R., et al. (1966), Comments on Some Aspects of Self and Object Representation in a Group of Psychotic Children. *This Annual*, 21:527-580.

Tilton, J. R., et al. (1966), *Annotated Bibliography on Childhood Schizophrenia, 1955-1964*. New York: Grune & Stratton.

Weiland, I. H. & Rudnik, R. (1961), Considerations of the Development and Treatment of Autistic Childhood Psychosis. *This Annual*, 16:549-563.

A PSYCHOANALYTIC APPROACH TO THE DIAGNOSIS OF PARANOIA

MAURITS KATAN, M.D. (Cleveland)

I

In 1917 Freud wrote: "The form of disease known as paranoia, chronic systematic insanity, occupies an unsettled position in the attempts at classification made by present-day psychiatry. There is, however, no doubt of its close affinity to dementia praecox. I once ventured to suggest that paranoia and dementia praecox should be brought together under the common designation of 'paraphrenia' " (1916-1917, p. 423f.).

Indeed, paraphrenia would have been a much more fitting name than Bleuler's term of schizophrenia, which is now the commonly accepted designation. This term suggests that a splitting of the personality is the most characteristic symptom of the illness, which is certainly not true (Freud, 1911, p. 76). It is a pity that, to my knowledge, no deep analytic evaluation has been made of those symptoms which clinically seem to demonstrate the phenomenon of splitting in the psychotic personality.

In the United States not much attention has been paid to attempts at differentiating between paranoia and schizophrenia, nor does this problem seem to have been settled among German psychiatrists. In this respect, I want only to comment that the prominent psychiatrist Kretschmer developed a picture of paranoia which deviates considerably from the picture as it is usually understood. Strictly speaking, Kretschmer (1950) does not think that paranoia exists; however, there are paranoiacs. He sees the personality of the paranoiac as resulting from a process of long standing. The endogenous factors are influenced by exogenous ones. Kretschmer paints a picture of the paranoiac as coming to full bloom when he has gathered around him a sect or a party of followers. Under such circumstances both the central figure and the others in the group influence one another, and the ideas expressed by the paranoiac are bounced back to him by the group in increased strength. In this situation the paranoiac is intoxicated by the resonance, his value in his own eyes mounts tremendously, etc.

It occurs to me that Kretschmer, in formulating this opinion, had in mind the person of Hitler. By pointing to the mutual excitement between Hitler and his followers, Kretschmer puts his finger on the right spot to start an analytic investigation of Hitler's personality. I would diagnose Hitler as having a narcissistic character disorder. His glaring moral defects show that there is no superego present to keep his narcissism within check. This overwhelming narcissism might lead the observer to consider Hitler psychotic. However, in order to satisfy his narcissistic demands, Hitler needed the approving excitement of the crowd. This feature is lacking in cases of paranoia; on the contrary, these individuals complain bitterly that their rights are continually infringed upon by others. Whereas the narcissistic psychopath craves approval in reality, this kind of approval would not influence at all the delusion of the paranoiac, a point to which I shall return.

The occurrence of a pure case of paranoia is extremely rare, but rarity does not nullify its scientific value. However, we may also emphasize the great number of gradations that exist between this extremely rare picture of paranoia and the more common one of schizophrenia. Moreover, a mental illness may start as a true paranoia and then gradually develop in the direction of schizophrenia. Occasionally one might even observe a development in the opposite direction. Schreber's psychosis will serve as such an example. In the beginning, Prof. Flechsig was Schreber's main persecutor; the men around Schreber were dead and were only fleetingly present as long as they were within the range of his observation. After a number of years his illness took a more favorable turn; he acknowledged that the people in his environment existed in reality, whereupon he developed traits of a paranoiac nature. The mantle of a prophet had fallen upon Schreber; he would make known his new religious insight to the public through his autobiographical account of his illness. Shortly before the publication of his autobiography, Schreber added an Open Letter to Flechsig, in which he took back practically all his previous accusations of Flechsig. Now he was convinced that from the very beginning, God, and not Flechsig, had been the perpetrator of all his miseries. In the interests of mankind, he begged Flechsig to confirm his conviction that Flechsig had had the same visions as Schreber himself. Of course, I do not mean that Schreber's illness had lost its schizophrenic character, but it is as if at that time he took a step in the direction of paranoia.

If paranoia and schizophrenia were basically different illnesses, one might perhaps ask whether paranoiac delusions are different from schizophrenic ones. The fact is that we find no evidence for any difference between them. The many transitions between paranoia and schizophrenia, as I have just pointed out, lead me to the conclusion that there is not a single delusion occurring in paranoia which we cannot also find in schizophrenia. So let us join Freud in calling paranoia a form of schizophrenia. To put things straight, I want to say immediately that Freud never made such a statement. But he did consider paranoia as belonging to the group of paraphrenias, a name which, as we have seen, was never accepted.[1] Let me also stress that I consider paranoia a very special form of schizophrenia. By wording my conclusion in this way, I hope to have gained an advantageous setting which will enable me to examine the similarities as well as the differences between paranoia and the more usual forms of schizophrenia.

The similarity between paranoia and schizophrenia is easy to detect. The delusion development must follow the same course for both.

It will be more difficult to find out in what ways paranoia differs from the usual forms of schizophrenia. Regarding this problem, it is very instructive to become acquainted with Freud's earliest ideas about paranoia. In January of 1895 Freud sent a treatise on this subject to his friend Fliess. In this treatise Freud stated that "chronic paranoia in its classical form is *a pathological mode of defence,* like hysteria, obsessional neurosis and states of hallucinatory confusion"

---

[1] A psychiatric diagnosis of paraphrenia still exists, but this diagnosis covers only a limited number of cases and therefore has nothing in common with Freud's concept.

(1950, p. 109). A woman had been surprised by having a man put his penis into her hand. There had been no sequel to this scene, and the man had left forever. The woman next thought that the neighbors were pitying her because she had been jilted and was still waiting for this man. They were always making hints of this kind to her and kept on saying all kinds of things to her about the man. All this, she said, was of course untrue. Freud guessed that what this woman was repressing was probably the fact of having been excited by what she had seen and by recollecting it afterward. "So what she was sparing herself was the self-reproach of being a 'bad woman.'" Freud concluded: "The purpose of the paranoia, therefore, was to fend off an idea that was intolerable to her ego by projecting its subject-matter into the external world" (p. 111).

It does not matter that today we cannot accept Freud's explanation as being valid for delusion formation. The importance of Freud's early explanation lies in the fact that the content of a paranoiac delusion is the same as the content of a neurotic ego defense. Accordingly, a paranoiac delusion appears as if a feeling of guilt is warded off through projection; instead of the superego expressing its complaint, a person in the environment now accuses the patient of having committed a wrong act. Far more frequently these accusations may appear, *not* as delusions, but as suspicions to which no or little reality value is attached.

We may use this simple fact to draw some conclusions. In paranoia, a common ego defense is used as the matrix for a delusional idea. Let us now consider the symptoms of the more usual forms of schizophrenia. It is often said that in schizophrenia id material penetrates freely into consciousness. A long digressive explanation would be required to show that this observation, which is very easy to make, should not be taken at its face value. Metapsychological reasoning would show that we are not dealing here with a return of the repressed. However, to generalize, we may say that in paranoia the delusion makes use of an ego defense, whereas in the more common forms of schizophrenia the delusion crystallizes around material coming from the id.

This distinction is, of course, a very general one, and we are looking for an opportunity to refine it. The opportunity is offered us in Freud's article on paranoia, jealousy and homosexuality (1922).

In paranoia, Freud distinguishes among three different layers—a normal, a neurotic, and a psychotic form of jealousy—which are all present at the same time.

Obviously, Freud called the first layer normal because a cherished love object is lost to a rival. The patient reacts to this loss with a feeling of jealousy, which feeling is a composite one. The patient might accuse himself of having caused the loss; depression, pain, narcissistic trauma, feelings of hostility and guilt, all figure in this affect of jealousy. What is more important, these feelings are derived from the infantile oedipal situation, and, in addition, normal jealousy may even contain bisexual tendencies. This means not only that jealousy may occur at the thought that the loved woman is lost to a male rival, but that the opposite may also be true; namely, jealousy is felt over the loss of the unconsciously loved male, and here the woman appears as the competitor. We see that what Freud has called the normal form of jealousy already offers, through its infantile origin and its bisexual character, sufficient opportunity for the development of all possible neurotic reactions.

In the first layer of jealousy, a certain amount of guilt can be detected. Therefore, the superego plays a role in the origin of "normal" jealousy.

In the second layer, guilt has an incomparably stronger influence upon the development of jealousy. Here, in contradistinction to the first layer, the jealousy is not centered around the lost object. The patient, in order to discharge his feelings of guilt, accuses his partner of being unfaithful and as a result feels jealous. Here the guilt is formed around committed acts or otherwise conscious fantasies of unfaithfulness, but it may also be present when such fantasies remain unconscious. In the latter case, the ego, through its accusations, tries to keep its own urges toward unfaithfulness unconscious.

At the time Freud wrote his article, attention had not yet switched to the ego defense mechanisms, but we see clearly that this form of jealousy is a defense mechanism of the first order. It makes use of projection. We notice how similar this neurotic ego defense is to the one which Freud formulated as being valid for the mechanism of paranoia in his January, 1895 letter to Fliess.

Freud has drawn attention to the fact that the paranoiac tends to prove the correctness of his accusations in a very special way. The paranoiac interprets unconscious expressions of unfaithfulness quite correctly in his love object, and the only abnormality of his interpretations is that he attaches too much value to them. According to my experience, this type of interpretation is especially to be found within the framework of a neurosis and *refers to heterosexual as well as to homosexual unfaithfulness.*

The third layer constitutes the psychotic form of jealousy. Freud uses the same explanation for the delusional jealousy as he had already given in his article on Schreber, namely, "I do not love him, *she* loves him!"

In my discussion of Freud's views on jealousy and paranoia, I have stressed those points which I think are important for a further investigation of the delusions in that illness. Based on my conclusion that paranoia is a form of schizophrenia, the development of the paranoia delusion must follow the same course as the other schizophrenic delusions. I have tried to describe this development in my article on "The Importance of the Non-Psychotic Part of the Personality in Schizophrenia" (1954).[2] Therefore I shall give only a brief résumé here.

In the development of a psychosis, not the whole, but an important segment of the personality is submitted to a process of total regression, i.e., a regression that leads to a return to the undifferentiated state. What I have tried to describe is the desperate struggle of the ego to ward off this regressive process that leads to a loss of contact with reality. During this struggle the ego is forced to make use of strivings which were previously warded off. Increasingly the ego has to surrender its ties with reality. Thus, focusing upon the libido, we conclude that the ego is forced to regress more and more to infantile narcissistic positions. This regression goes so far that even this part of the ego loses its cathexis, and a return takes place to the undifferentiated state, i.e., the state of absolute narcissism which exists at the beginning of life. The aggressive drive has to follow the same regressive movement as the libido. We may apply Hartmann's viewpoint (1953) that in the prepsychotic development

---

2 At the present time I would change a number of details of this article. For instance, I would no longer say that the male patient's desire to be a woman has its origin in the patient's constitution. Neither would I distinguish any more between a castration danger and an emasculation danger.

the neutralization of instinctual energy is lost; the functions of de-libidinization and deaggressivization are surrendered.

In this process of total regression, a few conspicuous phases are distinguishable. In a neurosis, the ego wards off the danger arising from the oedipal relationships. However, in the first stages of the prepsychotic development, other types of dangers already begin to threaten the ego's ties with reality. The ego is now forced to rely upon the oedipal ties in order to protect its relation with reality, for the oedipus complex represents a solid foundation for this re-lation.

When the regressive process advances further, the oedipal com-plex loses its cathexis, and homosexual urges toward femininity be-come prominent. These urges are of a preoedipal nature and there-fore are different from the instinctual drives of the homosexual perversion. In the origin of the perversion, the oedipus complex always plays an important role.

As long as the oedipus complex is cathected, the ego can strive for genital satisfaction in an attempt to ward off the urge toward femininity. As soon as the oedipal relationships are no longer suffi-ciently cathected, genital orgasm would mean that the feminine urge was satisfied; at this point the ego would be unable to maintain contact with reality, for this would imply transformation into a woman.

Thus, in this stage of the regressive process, the ego is in a peril-ous position. The ego has to ward off the threatening urge toward femininity. However, this urge is directed toward another male object and for this reason could be an ally of the ego in its struggle to maintain contact with reality.

The ego tries to solve the situation by externalizing its male qual-ities and ascribing them to the other man, who now increasingly represents the ego's narcissistic ideal. This feature excites the pa-tient's femininity even more, enormous anxiety breaks out, and contact with reality has to be relinquished.

A sign of further weakening of the ego is the fact that the re-gressive process also affects the patient's object constancy. The ego is unable to maintain secondary process thinking and falls back upon primary identifications and primary projections. These reactions change the relationship to the object. Instead of the representation of the object being a stable one, this representation has now become subject to the influence of primary projections. In this way the representation of the male object may acquire its too stimulating quality.

After contact with reality is surrendered, the psychotic attempt at restitution leads to delusion formation. The energies involved in the conflict which could not be mastered by the ego with reality means are now used in the formation of the psychotic symptoms. Therefore, as far as the range of the attempt at restitution extends, the prepsychotic conflict is decathected, or, in other words, is eradicated. Whereas prepsychotic symptoms are a result of the ego defending itself against urges, etc. from the id, in the domain of the psychosis proper the unconscious strivings, etc. have lost their cathexis. I shall try to demonstrate this point later by describing the formation of delusional jealousy.

Once the psychosis proper has started, the ego attempts to maintain its ties with reality as much as possible. Only in those situations where the ego is unable to do so, will psychotic symptoms be developed. Thus the psychotic patient offers an ever-changing picture, in which almost simultaneously normal, neurotic, oedipal attitudes, preoedipal strivings, and psychotic symptoms may clearly be detected.

These many reactions represent fixations on various levels of the regressive process, which process in the psychotic development comes to a stop when the undifferentiated state is reached. In order to prevent misunderstanding, I repeat that only that part of the personality regresses which is involved in the specific conflict. The differentiation among these many reactions is based upon metapsychological considerations. Descriptive psychiatric concepts are of no value in judging these reactions. Therefore diagnosis no longer should be based upon traditional psychiatric concepts, but upon metapsychological evaluation. Metapsychology has become the core of diagnosing illnesses of the mind.[3]

---

[3] In my contribution to the 1951 panel on Childhood Schizophrenia I defended my conviction that diagnosis should be based upon structural insight and not upon the usual psychiatric concepts. My contribution evoked a lot of resistance. In 1960 Anna Freud concluded that diagnosis should be based upon metapsychological insight. At the

My 1954 article on the development of the psychosis might perhaps today be called a *profile of a psychosis*. I want to use this *profile*
to assess Freud's description of jealousy paranoia in order to deepen
our insight into the structure of this intriguing illness.

1. According to the picture I have just painted, in a psychosis
a mixture of material from all levels of development may be found.
Freud's statement that in jealousy paranoia the three layers of normal, neurotic, and psychotic jealousy are simultaneously present corresponds very well with my description. However, there is an important difference. In Freud's article, these various forms of jealousy
are not described as having anything to do with the regressive process. According to me, in this article Freud stresses the overdetermination of the symptom of jealousy in paranoia.

2. Freud's brilliant new insight, namely, that three different layers of jealousy are overlapping in paranoia, paves the way for further
exploration. Through the comparison with my "profile" of the development of a psychosis, we discover that in Freud's description
the layer which in all likelihood is the most important one is missing. Although Freud explicitly points to the fact that in normal
jealousy the oedipus complex is at the center, and that in the second
form of jealousy the oedipus complex also plays a prominent role,
he does not consider the situation in which the oedipus complex has
lost its cathexis. Thus that part of the personality in which the impoverished ego has to cope with the preoedipal urge of being a
woman in love with a man is not considered by Freud.[4]

We have to fill out that part of the prepsychotic development of
paranoia which Freud does not speak of. It is clear that this preoedipal urge is warded off by the patient's accusation, which has the
same content as the other forms of jealousy, namely, that his wife is
unfaithful: she loves the man with whom unconsciously he is in love
himself. We are now confronted with a confusing picture. How can

December, 1965 panel on Clinical and Theoretical Aspects of "As If" Characters, I
expressed the idea that Helene Deutsch made the first truly metapsychological diagnosis in her description of the "as if" patient.

[4] It is completely understandable that Freud should overlook the presence of
another layer of jealousy. Not having had contact with a large number of schizophrenics, Freud did not have a basis for comparing schizophrenic development with
the development of paranoia. The chief value of Freud's article on paranoia lies in
his discovery of the overlapping layers of jealousy.

we determine whether the ego, through its jealous accusation, is warding off a homosexual urge in the nature of a perversion, or whether the accusation of unfaithfulness is warding off the preoedipal variety of an urge toward femininity? Although the contents of the two accusations are the same, the underlying conflicts are different. The one problem refers to a neurotic, the other to a prepsychotic, situation. Let us try to unravel the metapsychological difference between the two.

In the case of a neurosis, the warded-off homosexuality is of a perverted nature; i.e., the homosexuality in its final development is centered around the oedipus complex. The patient would like to be a woman himself and is jealous of the woman's ability to attract the sexual attention of the man. Accordingly, he accuses her of being unfaithful and, in doing so, wards off his own feminine urge.

The prepsychotic condition is completely different. The oedipal relationships no longer play a role. Especially when object constancy is lost and primary processes start to prevail, the ego tries, through primary projection, to get rid of its instinctual wish to be a woman. In early infantile development, the baby regards everything that is disagreeable as belonging to the outside world. The prepsychotic patient acts similarly. His wife's assumed unfaithfulness represents his own feminine urge; *instead of combatting this urge within himself, he combats it after its externalization in his wife.*

To repeat: in neurotic jealousy, the patient tries to keep his feminine urge unconscious; in contradistinction, the prepsychotic patient behaves as if he were warding off his own unconscious in the outside world instead of in his inner world.

This distinction also illustrates why the ego during the final stages of the prepsychotic phase may so easily lose its contact with reality. If the female partner becomes too excited sexually, the patient will feel that he has lost the struggle against his externalized femininity. The woman's excitement will exert too strong an influence upon the patient, and the ego, through a primary identification with the female partner, will accept femininity. The feminine urge goes through a very interesting circular process. First, this urge is externalized; next, the ego finds itself unable to prevent the woman's real or fancied sexual excitement and, through primary identification with the woman, gives up warding off this urge.

The result of all this is that the ego is forced to relinquish its contact with reality. However, both the ego and the unconscious are also part of reality; therefore the process of total regression will reach its deepest possible level, namely, the undifferentiated state.

3. One can also raise a question about the differences between jealousy in the prepsychotic phase and in the psychosis proper. Freud thought that the *delusional* "She loves him" warded off "I love him"; this formulation, however, can be used as well to explain the formation of *neurotic* or *prepsychotic* jealousy. Therefore I cannot accept this formulation as being valid for the development of a jealousy delusion.

The withdrawal through a regressive process to the undifferentiated state is a flight; the overwhelmingly strong castration danger has forced the ego to disappear. Once the undifferentiated state is reached, the energy is suspended in that part of the personality which is involved in this regressive process. Superego, ego, and id are no longer cathected and no longer differentiated from one another. Thus, a conflict between ego and id no longer exists, and neither does there exist a cathexis of an object. The dangerous conflict has disappeared. When the attempt at restitution sets in, the main task of this attempt is to maintain a state in which this dangerous conflict will not reappear. Therefore no return of a division between ego and id can occur, for this would be synonymous with recathecting this conflict. Accordingly, the delusional formation of a new ego and a new outside world must take shape, one in which any differentiation between ego and id is completely excluded. The newly formed delusional relationship between ego and outside world is patterned after the example of prepsychotic relationships. Thus we see, applying Freud's viewpoint also in this context, that the delusional relation leans upon the still existing prepsychotic relation, both relations, the psychotic and the prepsychotic, having the same content. But whereas in the prepsychotic relation an unconscious cathexis is still present, in the psychotic relation, because of the absence of any differentiation between ego and id, the unconscious is no longer cathected. The delusion is an end product, a product which is removed from the preceding processes by the dropping out of the unconscious cathexis. In this way large amounts of energy which previously were used for the unconscious cathexis are now used for the delusion formation; i.e., they have moved from a cathexis of unconscious representations to a cathexis of conscious ones.

We are now ready to formulate the difference between jealousy in the final stages of the prepsychotic phase and jealousy in its delusional form. In the prepsychotic phase there is still a cathected unconscious homosexual wish to be an unfaithful woman. The ego, through the process of externalization, tries to combat this wish in the outside world. As we have seen, however, this process of externalization does not do away with the conflict caused by the unconscious preoedipal wish. In contradistinction to the prepsychotic situation, in the psychosis the ego, after getting rid of this preoedipal urge, is able through delusion formation to master this conflict.

4. Freud's first contribution to the subject of paranoia, in 1895, emphasized that the ego, through projection, defended itself against feelings of guilt. This statement leads us to examine the role of the superego in the development of paranoia. In connection with this question another one arises. We may ask whether the role of the superego can be this important, for the regressive process very soon reaches levels of development where there is no superego formation. At the utmost, it can be said that at these levels some division between ego and early ego ideal is discernible. Therefore, during the final stages of the prepsychotic development it is impossible to detect anything in the nature of a guilt feeling that causes the patient's ego to react with the projective accusation of the wife's unfaithfulness.

After pondering for a while over this problem, we find ourselves inevitably steered in the direction of the depressive psychosis. To avoid misunderstanding, I want to make a distinction between depression and melancholia. As long as reality thinking is maintained, I prefer to speak of the various depressive states as depressions. When delusions of self-guilt enter the picture, I speak of melancholia. In cases of melancholia, only a part of the personality is psychotic; all other possible phases of depression are simultaneously present.

We observe that the pictures of paranoia and melancholia correspond with each other in many respects. In both, the ego is the

scene of action. In both, various layers of the same content are overlapping; namely, in melancholia the content "I am guilty" is present
in all the depressive manifestations in the same way as jealousy is
present in jealousy paranoia. I want to remark, in passing, that in
1936 I read a paper on the development of melancholia, in which
I pointed to the overlapping of the various layers and the ways in
which these layers were related to one another.

In "Mourning and Melancholia" (1917) Freud revealed the
process of introjection. Through this mechanism it becomes possible
for a conflict with an outside object to be internalized and then to
appear as a conflict between superego and ego. It would lead me
too far astray to point out that in Freud's article the theme of the
overlapping of the various layers of depression is already detectable;
in this regard we may consider "Mourning and Melancholia" a forerunner of Freud's article "Some Neurotic Mechanisms in Jealousy,
Paranoia and Homosexuality."

Next, we may conclude that in melancholia, too, a total regression of a part of the personality takes place to the undifferentiated
state. The ego wards off the aggression toward the object, whereupon
the aggression appears in the tension between superego and ego.
The aggression is aroused because the ego feels narcissistically
wounded. I want to stress that in melancholia, on a higher level of
development, the self-accusations are unable to cope with the conflict. As a result, deeper levels of development are affected. Furthermore, in the *final* stages of the regressive process, the ego is *not* successful in mastering the internalized conflict. This means that the
ego is unable to prevent the hostility, which is turned inward, from
finally leading to self-destruction. At this point, the ego can no
longer prevent the regressive process from taking the final step
toward the undifferentiated state. The conflict caused by the aggression is now decathected. The attempt at restitution recathects the
conflict between superego and ego, with resulting delusional self-
accusations. Thus, in my opinion, a strong similarity exists between
the development of melancholia and that of jealousy paranoia.

I am aware that my account of the development of melancholia
is superficial and in many ways inaccurate. I have given it only to
make possible the understanding of a certain aspect of paranoia,
which I shall now present.

In the early stages of the paranoiac development, when the oedipal relationships are still cathected, we observe, in accordance with Freud's suggestion, that the ego defends itself against feelings of guilt. The externalization of an inner conflict takes place. In the later stages of the prepsychotic development, after the influence of the guilt feelings has increasingly diminished, the ego's defense still follows the example set by the earlier mechanisms of a "higher level."

Melancholia follows exactly the opposite course. An external conflict is internalized. German psychiatrists have regarded paranoia as a buffer between schizophrenia and manic-depressive disorders. We must admit that these German psychiatrists have a point!

It is time to make use of these various deductions in order to determine in what respects paranoia differs from schizophrenia. Let us test these findings by correlating them with a résumé of paranoia, a résumé which I found among my notes written during the last war winter of 1944-1945: "In summing up the characteristics of paranoia, one should stress especially the fact that the delusion is concentrated around the ego. The patient tends to experience his delusion *not* autistically, but in contact with the outside world, during the course of which contact he frequently forms many ideas of reference. A large part of his personality remains intact, a state of mind from which one may assume also arises the tendency to furnish intellectual proofs for the correctness of his ideas. As a rule, the delusion has the same content as the already existing character anomaly, and thus it may appear to the observer as if the delusion develops as a mere intensification of such an anomaly. As a result of this relation, the course of the illness changes frequently and seems to oscillate between the extremes of the character anomaly, on the one hand, and the pronounced delusion, on the other."

I concluded that the ego strives insofar as possible to maintain its ties with reality in order not to be drawn further into the psychosis. It is true that the ego is powerless to prevent the development of a delusion, but at least in this way the ego succeeds in shaping the delusion according to the pattern of a defense mechanism. This last feature is probably responsible for the fact that paranoia seems to a certain degree receptive to psychotherapy, in which respect paranoia distinguishes itself favorably from schizophrenia.

However, at other times the oscillation between the two extremes appears to be absent and the ego gradually loses its unity, the thought processes become increasingly confused, and at the end the illness no longer differs from schizophrenia.

Our metapsychological examination seems to corroborate fully the features mentioned in this résumé of paranoia. The tenacity to cling as much as possible to reality, and as a result not to sink deeper into a psychotic state, we may ascribe especially to the role played by the superego. Under the accusation of the superego, the ego feels forced to defend itself through projection, which leads to a discharge of feelings of guilt. This defense sets the example for the more primitive mechanisms which the ego applies when the personality regresses to deeper levels.

The paranoiac tendency to form delusional constructions seems to follow the example of the more normal part of the ego. This more normal part feels guilty and very soon discovers, by interpreting the partner's unconscious, that the latter is at fault. This discovery forms the basis for the accusations. The psychotic attempt at restitution recathects the ego defense of blaming somebody else. The delusional proofs that the other person is guilty are practically always irrational. For instance, I knew a jealousy paranoiac who accused his wife of giving signals to her lover, a neighbor, by flushing the toilet, arranging the curtains in a certain way, etc.

In this connection a statement by Freud (1926) is relevant: "The delusional constructions of the paranoic offer to his acute perceptive and imaginative powers a field of activity which he could not easily find elsewhere" (p. 99). This statement, however, refers to the narcissistic satisfaction of the function, and not to our goal of finding out why the patient creates these constructions. Thus we have still with us the problem of what constitutes the source of the paranoiac tendency toward these constructions.

5. After comparing the development of paranoia with the separate developments of schizophrenia and melancholia, we might gain a better understanding of paranoia by also comparing it with certain types of neurosis, because the psychotic symptoms of jealousy

paranoia are usually strongly interwoven with the symptoms of various forms of neurotic jealousy.

Whenever, in analyses, I meet the symptom of jealousy, I am always struck by its complicated structure and tenacity as well as by the strength of the warded-off unconscious homosexual urges. The patient's difficulties seem especially to culminate in the act of intercourse. One patient may perform this act only sporadically or seek an outlet in fleeting relations with other women, whereas another patient may attempt to satisfy his partner to such a degree that in his fantasy she will have no incentive to think how much better another man might be able to fulfill her sexual needs. Regularly the other man is a person who only shortly before has impressed the patient as being sexually attractive to women.

It has been my experience that every one of these patients is involved in a strong masturbatory activity. Not that these patients do not try to curtail this activity. They do, but various derivatives of masturbation result from the struggle against it; for instance, the patient may find himself unable to limit his predinner cocktail to a modest intake of alcohol, or, if he is a dilettante at the piano, he may play endless finger exercises. During the analysis, such patients frequently try to refrain from masturbation because they consciously feel ashamed. One gets the impression that, in general, they are warding off the danger that they might reveal their homosexual desires. Even if they are unsuccessful in warding off this danger, they at least try to exclude their homosexual transference fantasies from their acts.

Another phenomenon deserves to be mentioned. While trying to recall some outstanding examples of jealousy, I arrived at the conclusion that these patients betray unmistakable obsessional neurotic traits. For instance, they show a strong need to observe obsessional schedules, or the processes of doing and undoing are clearly present. One patient may be a strict adherent of Jewish dietary laws without believing in God, and another may follow a strict schedule with regard to his use of money and time, more particularly safeguarding the necessary amount of sleep in an obsessional way. Of course, one immediately thinks of these obsessional habits as a continuation of the struggle against certain types of masturbatory fantasies. If all other mechanisms fail to ward off the masturbatory tendencies, the ego forces the genital urge to regress to the anal level. The obsessional symptoms result from the ego's combat with the anal urge.

I would thus conclude that *guilt about unconscious unfaithful tendencies is intimately connected with guilt about infantile masturbation.* Applying these various observations and provisional conclusions to the symptomatology of paranoia, I would suggest that the paranoiac delusional constructions follow the pattern of the obsessional schedules adhered to by the jealous neurotic.

II

In the second part of my paper I shall give some examples to illustrate certain points of my theoretical discussion. I shall first discuss a few examples of psychotic development and conclude with analytic material from a case of jealousy that borders on the abnormal.

I have already stressed that under certain circumstances a sexual orgasm of the female partner can have a disastrous effect upon the patient's relationship with reality. Although the following case from the *Introductory Lectures* (1916-1917) is clearly schizophrenic and not paranoiac, it serves as an instructive example. Freud used this case to demonstrate that the man who became the persecutor had once been the patient's best friend. Presently I think the other aspect of the case is even more interesting.

A young doctor had to be expelled from the town in which he lived because he had threatened the life of the son of a university professor residing there, who had up till then been his greatest friend. He attributed really fiendish intentions and demonic power to this former friend, whom he regarded as responsible for all the misfortunes that had befallen his family in recent years, for every piece of ill-luck whether in his home or in his social life. But that was not all. He believed that this bad friend and the friend's father, the Professor, had caused the war, too, and brought the Russians into the country. His friend had forfeited his life a thousand times, and our patient was convinced that the criminal's death would put an end to every evil. Yet his affection for him was still so strong that it had paralysed his hand when, on one occasion, he had an opportunity of shooting down his enemy at close range. In the course of the short conversations I had with the patient, it came to light that their friendship went back far into their schooldays. Once at least it had overstepped the bounds of friendship: a night which they had spent together had been an occasion for complete sexual intercourse. Our patient had never acquired the emotional relation to women which would have corresponded to his age and his attractive personality. He had once been engaged to a beautiful young girl of good social position; but she had broken off the engagement because she found that her *fiancé* was without any affection. Years later, his illness broke out just at the moment when he had succeeded for the first time in satisfying a woman completely. When this woman embraced him in gratitude and devotion, he suddenly had a mysterious pain that went round the top of his head like a sharp cut. Later on he interpreted this sensation as though an incision were being made at an autopsy for exposing the brain. And as his friend had become a pathological anatomist, it slowly dawned on him that he alone could have sent this last woman to him to seduce him. From that point onwards his eyes were opened to the other persecutions to which he believed he had been made a victim by the machinations of his one-time friend [p. 425f.].

This description, although brief, is outstanding for its vividness, dealing as it does with facts that challenge us to understand this exceptional course of events. First, let us try to make up our minds about the personality of the young doctor before his life took a turn for the worse. Certainly this kind of turn would not have been predicted from the homosexual relationship which had occurred years back when the two friends spent a night together. The doctor's inability to form an emotional relationship with women, and the unfortunate ending of his engagement to a beautiful girl because she found him too cold, might perhaps have served as a warning. On the other hand, however, we are told that he had an attractive personality and that whatever abnormality he had, if any, did not prevent him from becoming a physician. One might have guessed that his strong inhibitions were the result of his warding off perverted homosexual desires, but such a guess would have given no hint at all of a possible development in the direction of a psychosis.

We should not forget that these various facts refer to a period which was separated by "years" from the moment when the patient's illness broke out. First, we are justified in assuming that he had become *definitely* abnormal even before his sexual contact with the woman took place, because one would never expect intercourse to have such a devastating effect upon a personality well anchored in reality. Next, we are confronted with the problem of determining in what way he was abnormal. The act of intercourse, in which for the first time in his life he was able to satisfy a woman, was immediately followed by a precipitous psychotic development. The entire process took place in such a short time that we are unable to differentiate between the various phases of the prepsychotic development. Axiomatically, however, we must assume that these various phases were still present. The abrupt course of the regressive process caused what otherwise would be distinguishable during a slower development to be withdrawn from observation. I shall try to unravel this condensed regressive process by means of reconstructions.

First of all, we may conclude from the sequence of events that the act of intercourse did not prevent the breakdown of the personality. We are so accustomed to seeing a completely or partially successful intercourse as having a beneficial effect that we cannot wonder enough about the totally different outcome in the case of Freud's patient. Using the scheme of the prepsychotic development as background, we may conclude that the patient was relying upon his oedipal relationships to ward off the upsurge of the preoedipal urge toward feminine homosexuality. Thus a shift of cathexis must have taken place: the ego was already considerably weakened and forced to rely upon oedipal relationships in order to defend its hold on reality. Freud's description makes it perfectly clear that the woman's orgasm triggered the subsequent process of deterioration. When she embraced him with gratitude and devotion, he did not react with an orgasm of his own but instead suddenly felt a mysterious pain that went around the top of his head like a cut. Never before had he experienced a woman's full orgastic reaction. In all likelihood, therefore, he must have been unprepared for this phenomenon, and the element of being taken by surprise must have furthered the powerful impact which the orgastic reaction had upon him. After a short *période de méditation*, delusions entered the picture.

At this point I want to remind you that the delusion frequently contains information that throws light upon the prepsychotic conflict which the ego has been unable to master by reality means. Accordingly, from the delusion, we are able to reconstruct what happened during the preceding period. The patient made two successive interpretations. First, the sensation in his head made him feel as though an incision had been made, in an autopsy, to expose the brain. Second, because his friend had become a pathological anatomist, it slowly dawned upon him that this friend had sent this woman to seduce him. It occurs to us who are observers that this last delusion reveals the core of what threw the patient off balance. Thus, only in successive delusions could the patient finally become aware that his friend had sent the woman. This delusional end result proves to me that during his sexual contact with this woman a concomitant process was going on in his mind, in which his experience with the woman was connected with his unconscious homosexual desire for his male friend. *The sequence of his warded-off ideas during the prepsychotic period, which was the period of his intercourse, should be read in the reverse order of the occurrence of these various delusions.*

In an attempt to throw full light on this reversed order, let me repeat the sequence of the occurrence of these various delusions. (1) The patient felt a mysterious pain around the top of his head, like a sharp cut. (2) He made the interpretation, as though at an autopsy, that an incision to expose the brain had caused this sensation. (3) He concluded that this incision had been made by his friend, who had become a pathological anatomist. (4) He concluded that his friend had sent the girl to seduce him for this purpose.

The content of this last delusion reveals that the origin of his difficulties revolved around his friend through the connection between his friend and the girl. When the patient established contact with the woman, he did so in order to ward off his desires for his friend. The orgasm experienced by the woman during intercourse with the patient represented the emotion which the patient wanted to experience in a sexual relationship with his friend. In this way he would become a woman. Instead of forming a delusion in which he would accept transformation into a woman, he accused his friend of wanting to make this fact known publicly. That is to say, by applying his knowledge that his friend had become a pathologist, the patient ascribed to his friend the intention of exposing his brain, which action would be identical with laying bare his thoughts. In order to bring about this result, the friend had to cut his skull, a procedure which caused great pain. The patient felt this pain first, but the processes preceding it remained unconscious. From then on, through a series of free associations which were expressed in the form of delusions, he uncovered these unconscious motives which constituted the basis of his difficulties. His associations about the exposure of his brain by his friend also explain why a displacement occurred from his genitals to his head: instead of feeling the cut in his genitals, he felt it in his skull.

My reasoning will have made it clear that the patient's defense of seeking contact with a woman was undermined from the start, for this defense was undertaken with the feeling that in this relationship it was more attractive to be the woman than to be the man.

Another line of interpretation shows that the woman's orgasm had still another meaning for the patient. We now see that this phenomenon was experienced by the patient in an overdetermined way. Usually, during the final stage of the prepsychotic phase, the patient's orgasm is a sign that the ego is no longer able to maintain its ties with reality. In the case now under consideration, we discover that the psychological damage has been caused by the partner's orgasm, not by the patient's. Accordingly, it is my impression that the woman represents the patient's penis. (That this interpretation does not result from what I like to call a "desk-fantasy" I hope to demonstrate later through the analysis of one of my cases.)

I have already mentioned that during the final prepsychotic stage, the condensation into a period of very brief duration makes it impossible for us to distinguish among the various phases of the regressive process. The results, however, speak clearly. What other conclusion can we draw than that the woman's orgasm made such a strong impact upon the patient that the regressive process took over completely? The identification with the woman's femininity, expressed through the patient's sensation that a cut had been made in his head, led to the severing of contact with reality. Thus this identification must be a primary one; in a split second, the secondary processes were surrendered and the primary processes took over. The regressive process, however, could no longer be stopped and reached the undifferentiated state. Although, for our insight into the paranoiac development, the following will have no meaning, we still want to point to the delusion that the patient's friend and his father had caused the war. This delusion shows that in the persecution a father figure was in the background.

This demonstration of the influence of intercourse upon the development of a psychosis forms the link with another of Freud's cases (1922):

> *Paranoia.*—Cases of paranoia are for well-known reasons not usually amenable to analytic investigation. I have recently been able, nevertheless, by an intensive study of two paranoics, to discover something new to me.
>
> The first case was that of a youngish man with a fully developed paranoia of jealousy, the object of which was his impeccably faithful wife. A stormy period in which the delusion had possessed him uninterruptedly already lay behind him. When I saw him he was only subject to clearly separated attacks, which lasted for several days and which, curiously enough, regularly appeared on the day after he had sexual intercourse with his wife, which was, incidentally, satisfying to both of them. The inference is justified that after every satiation of the heterosexual libido the homosexual component, likewise stimulated by the act, forced an outlet for itself in the attack of jealousy [p. 225].

Again the act of intercourse is responsible for the outbreak of a psychosis. This time, acts of intercourse lead to paranoiac episodes of short duration. In comparison with the preceding case, it strikes us that in the present case the act is satisfactory to both partners.

It seems advantageous to me to deal first with Freud's inference that the homosexual component was likewise stimulated by the sexual act and caused the attack of paranoia.

In the analysis of neurotics, one sometimes meets the phenomenon that the man, after having performed intercourse, longs for a homosexual relationship. This longing is frequently revealed through the analysis of dreams occurring the same night, after the intercourse. Some patients, to their amazement, have a nocturnal emission during the sleep that follows intercourse. Although they consciously defend the point of view that obviously they wanted to repeat the act of intercourse, the analysis of their dreams often tells quite a different story. After the heterosexual desires have been satisfied, the homosexual desires seek satisfaction.

I have found that the longing for homosexual satisfaction may have a surprising origin. Through the homosexual act, the patient tries to restore the damage inflicted by intercourse with a woman. By becoming the anal recipient of the other man's ejaculation, the man makes up for the loss he has suffered in his sexual relationship with a woman.

My analytic experience with these kinds of phenomena has been confined to neurotics. After my long discussion of the preceding case, I feel justified in differing with the opinion Freud expressed in his inference. In the case of the paranoiac who had previously suffered an uninterrupted psychotic attack, we also may assume that this patient had not made a sufficient recovery. His mind was still in a labile state, and intercourse threw him off balance.

In contradistinction to the young doctor who reacted to the woman's orgasm with a displaced castration pain, the paranoiac patient experienced an orgasm in connection with his wife's sexual satisfaction. Applying the same reasoning as before, we may say that the paranoiac identified with his wife by also experiencing an orgasm. Accordingly, at that moment he accepted femininity. We know that this acceptance triggers the regression to the undifferentiated state. Then the delusion takes over.

Thus, in my opinion, in contrast to Freud's, it is precisely because the patient's homosexual desires in intercourse were satisfied that his psychosis broke out. In addition, Freud did not differentiate between the two forms of homosexuality.

This clinical discussion offers an opportunity to tackle the following problem. German psychiatrists still distinguish between primary and secondary delusions. According to these psychiatrists, delusions which are not preceded by any corresponding mental phenomenon result directly from organic factors and are therefore of a primary nature. It is clear that the distinction between primary and secondary delusions fails to take unconscious processes into account. In *An Outline of Psycho-Analysis* (1940) Freud attacked the organic point of view in his discussion of what should be called mental.

It is possible that some psychiatrists might be found who would classify the sudden formation of delusions in the case cited by Freud, which started with the hypochondriacal sensation in the patient's head while he was still engaged in the act of intercourse, as primary delusion formation. However, this assumption of mine may be incorrect, for even these psychiatrists might have the impression that the act of intercourse had something to do with the outbreak of the psychosis.

Let us see whether we can find a better example. A young journalist was standing in a crowd watching a float in a flower parade. A girl from a prominent Amsterdam family was throwing flowers from the float into the crowd. The young man had brought a flower with him and threw it at her, and his flower and one of hers crossed each other. For him, this was a sign that she was in love with him. He started to bother her and her family, and within a very short time he was institutionalized.

At least in this case, intercourse did not trigger the development of the patient's erotomania. Neither can the crossing of the two flowers be held responsible. Rather, the first sign of the patient's erotomania was his delusional interpretation of this incident. The patient regarded this accidental crossing of flowers as a proof that he and the girl were in love with each other. It strikes me that the crossing of the flowers represents symbolically the love act between himself and the girl. I assume the patient became aware of sensations which contained a threat; namely, as a result of his unconscious fantasy of being united with the girl, he was afraid he would have an orgasm. Obviously the picture of the girl attracting the attention of the men in the crowd must have been very exciting to him. The identification with this aspect of the girl would have led to a genital orgasm, and this orgasm would have caused a break with reality. Therefore, in anticipation of this danger, he severed his ties with reality. He then immediately formed a delusion around the observation of the crossing flowers. In his delusional observation he externalized the inner process which had caused the loss of contact with reality. The two flowers represented himself and the girl; he could then feel that they were in love with each other.

In order not to limit my examples to men only, I shall mention the case of a woman who, while passing in front of the city hall in Utrecht, looked through the window of the mayor's room. The mayor was sitting at a table in such a way that his cuff links reflected the sunlight straight in her eyes. This connection through the sunlight between the woman and the mayor would have developed further in an "orgastic" identification with this father figure. At this deep regressive level, reality thinking would have clashed with her idea of being transformed into a man. She, too, severed her ties with reality before the orgasm could develop. At this moment her eroto-mania broke out.

From these various examples we may conclude that sometimes the illness of paranoia appears to develop suddenly without any preceding warning, and at other times the delusions impress the observer as being an outgrowth of already existing character traits.

I have defended my opinion that paranoia should be compared not only with schizophrenia and melancholic depressions but also with neurotic conditions. Therefore I am including an excerpt from the paper I read at the Congress in Paris in 1938. I have not changed the original text, although at the end I have added a description of a few of the patient's other symptoms.

The patient was a man suffering from jealousy of abnormal intensity. He thought that the experiencing of a simultaneous orgasm with his wife would spell for him the greatest danger possible. His first remark during the initial consultation was, "I don't have intercourse with my wife; I only masturbate myself." My patient, as he himself already hinted in his first complaint, anticipated this danger.

The mother of my patient came from a very disturbed family. She and her five sisters were all extremely jealous women. A number of them had been diagnosed by various psychiatrists as having paranoia. The mother's only brother was an alcoholic bum, who had squandered his inheritance and afterward tried to make some sort of living in Paris as a tourist guide.

Practically from birth on, the patient had witnessed how his mother persecuted his father with her accusations. She, and also his aunts, took the greatest pleasure in seducing the little boy into making mistakes, in this way undermining his masculine feelings.

His father was not much better. Once, when my patient was six years old, his father punished him by behaving as if he were mourning his little son's death.

A severely disturbed sister, who was a few years older, completed the family picture.

The patient developed an extreme jealousy of his wife. But he was also aware that if his wife did not continue to attract the attention of other men, she would lose all attraction for him. When, for instance, she left town, he would stand in the railway station waiting for her, the victim of unbearable fantasies that she might have intercourse with a stranger on the train! He quarreled with his wife, repeating what he had witnessed in infancy. When sporadically he did have intercourse, he could perform the act only if he had constant fantasies about other women. This symptom was overdetermined. His wife had too much the meaning of his mother to him! Another meaning will be discussed further on.

Primal scene material was conscious, but in a very peculiar form. Although he knew it was nonsensical, he nevertheless could not free himself from the idea that he had been present at his own conception. It turned out that this conviction served a strong denial. "If I can be convinced that what is obviously nonsense still may have occurred in reality, then what I have actually observed does not have to be true." In this way he denied that he had observed the primal scene. By not having intercourse himself, he could keep up this denial. If he did not commit the sexual act, then his parents might not have done so, either!

By rejecting his wife, he thought he could drive her to another man. But at the point at which he thought he was about to lose her, he could perform the sexual act again in order to win her back. Thus he could have intercourse with her only if he could think of her as a woman belonging to another man. His intercourse therefore represented an act of competition with another man.

According to the deeper meanings of the primal scene, his mother became a preoedipal figure who robbed the patient's father of his penis. This picture the patient extended to himself: the mother took his penis away from him just as she had taken his stools away from him.

In intercourse he had to prevent his wife, in her orgasm, from becoming like his mother. If, notwithstanding his precautions, he perceived that his wife was receiving satisfaction, he lost his erection at that precise moment.

His wife's orgasm would lead not only to his castration but to many other dangers. If she could have an orgasm with him, she might also experience it with another man. This thought produced unbearable jealousy in the patient.

If both the patient and his wife lost themselves in sexual emotions, then neither of them would be able to ward off intruding elements. This anxiety was related to the patient's own spying on his parents. His fear of intrusion could finally be brought back to the idea that he would not be able at that moment to pay attention to the possibility that a man might penetrate his anus! The main significance of the sexual act lay in this connection which was formed between his wife's orgasm and his own passive wishes. The same connection turned up in many other ways.

In infancy the mother's accusations of the father's unfaithfulness convinced the patient that his mother preferred him to his father. Yet this same fact made him feel guilty of having been unfaithful to his father. I have already indicated how his wife's orgasm, which meant the satisfaction of his incestuous aims, led to painful ideas about her unfaithfulness with other men and simultaneously brought his passive feminine wishes to the surface.

What did this patient's masturbation have to do with these ideas, which had in fact much more complicated ramifications than I have pictured here? The main outlet for his sexuality was his frequent masturbation.

One should not think that he had not formed strong defenses against masturbation because he had given in to it from childhood on. I have the impression, however, that the defenses were to a certain degree directed no longer against the masturbation but against the derivatives of it.

This process was especially clear in his relations with his wife. During the course of treatment, there was increasing evidence that in trying to suppress any sexual emotion which his wife might feel, he was in fact fighting certain sexual drives within himself. Suppressing the possibility of getting an erection and warding off the possibility that his wife would have an orgasm seemed to go hand in hand. His wife had acquired the meaning of his penis. The defense against masturbation found its application in warding off her sexuality. Having intercourse with her became synonymous with submitting to a dangerous form of masturbation. I have already mentioned how her orgasm uncovered his passive feminine wishes.

Her orgasm was then the sign that he had surrendered to his femininity; i.e., *her orgasm was the sign of his castration!* Thus we may conclude that, through a projective displacement, his wife became for him the condensation of the representative of his femininity, on the one hand, and the representative of his penis, on the other. Yet the latter was a very special kind of representation; namely, his wife represented his penis as the executive organ of his drive toward femininity.

To demonstrate how complicated the picture of his symptoms had become since intercourse had acquired this masturbatory meaning, the following needs to be pointed out. His masturbation, frequently performed in actuality, much more represented the satisfaction of his heterosexual drive. In intercourse, he had to prevent his femininity from taking over. *Thus, paradoxically, masturbation symbolically represented intercourse, and the act of intercourse acquired the meaning of masturbation.*

During his analysis the patient confessed that he frequently had relations with married women whom he had met through his profession. After the sexual act, he always ran away immediately and did not continue the relationship. Basically the same pattern was present in his behavior toward his wife. A few years before the patient began his analysis, he and his wife consulted an orthodox rabbi. From that time until the beginning of his analysis, the patient adhered to extremely strict dietary laws. When he mentioned this dietary adherence in his analysis, I was surprised because he had told me that he was an atheist. He observed these dietary laws only because they regulated every single moment of his life. Indeed, he had the advantage of taking over a ready-made obsessional system, falling in line with the already existing obsessional traits.

The patient had a strong craving for sweets. He would suddenly yield to this craving and buy quantities of candy, which he would eat in his car until he became nauseated; any candy that remained uneaten he would then throw out of the car window. Upon returning home, he would immediately give himself an enema to expel what he had just taken in, although intellectually, of course, he knew much better. Clearly, this was an example of doing and undoing on oral and anal levels.

The patient was very much overweight. When he finally went

on a diet, his dieting took an obsessional form. His being overweight could easily be interpreted as resulting from masturbation. He would stand on the scales many times a day. It was as if he looked at the scales to see them reflect the doing and undoing of his masturbatory sins in the same compulsive way as Dorian Gray kept looking in secret at the ever-worsening picture of himself.

Although this patient was severely disturbed and expressed the fear that I would institutionalize him,[5] he was still to a great extent responsive to analysis. His jealousy diminished considerably. Yet I would not have been surprised if the result had been different and he had regressed further and become a paranoiac.

I do not want to stress anything else except the one symptom in which his wife became his externalized penis. Keeping previous examples of the psychotic development in mind, we see how easily, if the ego had not been able to maintain secondary process thinking, his wife's orgasm could have marked the beginning of a delusional development.

Let me state some final conclusions. Paranoia can make the impression that a delusion occurs in a personality which otherwise appears to be quite normal. This impression is very deceptive, for those parts of the personality which, to the observer, represent the more normal aspects, form the cover that hides the abnormal core of deeply regressive processes. Insight into these complicated relations has to result from metapsychological thinking. Therefore the diagnosis of paranoia should be based upon metapsychological reasoning and not upon descriptive psychiatric concepts.

The study of the spectacular role which intercourse played in the precipitous development of a case of paranoia brings valuable new insight. The ego used intercourse as a defense against a preoedipal feminine urge. Surprisingly, in intercourse the warded-off urge toward femininity was satisfied. In order to cope with the resulting castration danger, the personality regressed further, whereupon a delusion developed.

This newly gained insight casts light also on those cases where not intercourse, but seemingly inconsequential events, triggered a

---

[5] This fear was especially aroused after he heard I had advised institutionalization for a woman whom he knew. Namely, he could not see anything grossly abnormal in her, so he feared that what I had done to her I would do as well to him.

psychotic development. The case of the crossing flowers, for instance, resulted in the acute development of an erotomania. The crossing flowers symbolized intercourse between the patient and the girl and therefore led to the similar result of instant psychotic development. Finally, through the application of metapsychological thinking, it has become possible to explain cases of paranoia which develop acutely as well as those cases which erroneously appear to be the outgrowth of an already existing character anomaly. When we contemplate the various processes which have to fit together before a pure case of paranoia can develop, we do not wonder that these cases are extremely rare.

BIBLIOGRAPHY

Deutsch, H. (1934), Über einen Typus der Pseudoaffektivität ("Als ob"). *Int. Z. Psa.,* 20:323-335.
Freud, A. (1960), Four lectures presented in New York.
—— (1965), *Normality and Pathology in Childhood.* New York: International Universities Press.
Freud, S. (1911), Psycho-analytic Notes on an Autobiographical Account of a Case of Paranoia. *Standard Edition,* 12:3-82. London: Hogarth Press, 1958.
—— (1916-1917), Introductory Lectures on Psycho-Analysis. *Standard Edition,* 15 & 16. London: Hogarth Press, 1963.
—— (1917), Mourning and Melancholia. *Standard Edition,* 14:237-260. London: Hogarth Press, 1957.
—— (1922), Some Neurotic Mechanisms in Jealousy, Paranoia, and Homosexuality. *Standard Edition,* 18:221-232. London: Hogarth Press, 1955.
—— (1926), Inhibitions, Symptoms and Anxiety. *Standard Edition,* 20:77-175. London: Hogarth Press, 1959.
—— (1940), An Outline of Psycho-Analysis. *Standard Edition,* 23:141-207. London: Hogarth Press, 1964.
—— (1950), *The Origins of Psycho-Analysis.* New York: Basic Books, 1954.
Hartmann, H. (1953), Contribution to the Metapsychology of Schizophrenia. *Essays on Ego Psychology.* New York: International Universities Press, 1964, pp. 182-206.
Katan, M. (1936), Die Übereinstimmungen zwischen den Schizophrenen und den melancholischen Wahnmechanismen. Presented at the Congress of the International Psycho-Analytical Association at Marienbad.
—— (1938), Einige Mechanismen der Eifersucht. Presented at the II Congress of the International Psycho-Analytical Association at Paris.
—— (1951), Discussion in Round Table B: Schizophrenia in Childhood. *Bull. Amer. Psa. Assn.,* 8:149-170.
—— (1954), The Importance of the Non-Psychotic Part of the Personality in Schizophrenia. *Int. J. Psa.,* 35:119-128.
—— (1965), Discussion in Panel: Clinical and Theoretical Aspects of "As If" Characters, rep. J. Weiss. *J. Amer. Psa. Assn.,* 14:569-590, 1966.
Kretschmer, E. (1950), Grundsätzliches zur modernen Entwicklung der Paranoialehre. *Der Nervenarzt,* 21:1-2.

PROBLEMS OF TECHNIQUE OF CHILD ANALYSIS IN RELATION TO THE VARIOUS DEVELOPMENTAL STAGES: PRELATENCY

JUDITH S. KESTENBERG, M.D. (Sands Point, N.Y.)

Analysis offers each patient a second chance to resolve problems that originated in the past. In the analysis of young children, parents have a unique opportunity to undo the developmental distortions they themselves helped create (Balint, 1968; Anna Freud, 1968). If they are able to tolerate living through the past as it unfolds in the young child's analysis and are ready to accept new solutions for old problems, we have a better chance for therapeutic success.

The younger the child we analyze, the more we avail ourselves of the usual adjustments in technique that are dictated by our appraisal of the patient's ego attitudes, his frustration tolerance, state of needs and drives, sense of reality, nature of object relationships, and mode of family life (Anna Freud, 1946, 1965, 1968; Pearson et al., 1968). Once we decide to analyze a young child rather than guide his parents, we uphold psychoanalytic aims and principles of psychoanalytic treatment, as we do with older patients (Bolland and Sandler, 1965; B. Bornstein, 1931; S. Bornstein, 1933; E. Furman, 1956, 1957; R. A. Furman, 1968; Jacobs, 1949; Harely, 1951; A. Katan, 1959; Kolansky, 1960; E. Sterba, 1949; and others). By altering technical devices rather than psychoanalytic methods, we adjust our interventions to individual differences (Ritvo et al., 1963)

Presented at the Meeting of the American Association for Child Analysis, New Haven, Conn., 1969.

and structure interpretations in accordance with the predominant organization of the patient's developmental level.[1] We try not only to remove obstacles to orderly development but to ally ourselves with the progressive developmental forces of a given phase (Anna Freud, 1965). We make use of the organizational principle which the preoedipal child employs in building an independent ego, or which the oedipal child pursues in the formation of an independent superego.

We assist the two- to four-year-old to achieve a meaningful *integration* of units of achievements, memory fragments, body feelings, words, and concepts. We respect the *global growth* of the four-year-old and help him cope with the suddenness and the intensity of his new excitement. We help the five-year-old in his attempts to *differentiate* between children and adults, fantasies and actions, the good and the bad, the socially desirable and the condemned.

By allying ourselves with the child in this manner, we can establish a therapeutic relationship with the very young and can be accepted as removers of obstacles and helpers despite the frustrations we impose during the psychoanalytic process. Excerpts from the analyses of children in the preoedipal and oedipal phases of development will illustrate and amplify these points.

CASE ILLUSTRATIONS

Case 1

Mortimer was two years and ten months old when his mother brought him for treatment with the following complaint: "Either he is impossible to raise or I am not a good mother. My feelings are that he is taking my time away and my life." She had been quite ill during her pregnancy and was not allowed to have any more children. Even though she was depressed and disappointed that she

---

[1] Analyses of young children and a specialized study of the development of movement patterns suggested to me the following subdivision of phases, which follow pregenitality and precede latency: (1) preoedipal-inner-genital phase, in which the influx of genital sensations from the inside of the body promotes integration of functions into a cohesive ego structure; (2) oedipal-phallic phase, in which phallic growth is succeeded by a developmental need to differentiate, a process leading to internalization and to delineation of the superego. For a more comprehensive description and classification of prelatency see Kestenberg (1967, 1968b, 1969).

could never have a daughter, she took good care of baby Mortimer. Since his earliest infancy, she had had to contain him. He was always on the go, touching everything, pushing, rattling, babbling or saying things clearly but endlessly repeating them. He annoyed people by hitting babies, was greedy and selfish.

Mortimer, indeed, had every trait usually associated with pre-genitality. He grabbed and demanded without taking "no" for an answer. He threw temper tantrums, broke or scattered things, pitting his will against the adult's. He ran off flitting to and fro, invading space with a flood of words and "flying limbs," advancing, retreating, and ambitiously reaching for everything. These traits were embedded in a nagging quality, which is characteristic of women (Kestenberg, 1956; Mead, 1956) and generates excitement by contagion.

Mortimer made people very anxious because of his illusory accident-proneness. He seemed in constant danger of "falling apart," losing a limb or dropping to the floor. Nevertheless, he rarely fell or hurt himself, and broke objects only when thwarted. When I annoyed him, he announced pleasantly that he would break me.

In tracking a preoedipal child through the land of his illusions, one feels like an explorer encountering a jungle tribe whose means of communication are different and strange (Balint, 1968). In order to understand the child we have to devise means to reach the inhabitant and creator of the illusory land (Winnicott, 1965) and help him grasp the intent of the outsiders who invaded it. These procedures are designed to give insight and as such may be considered educational. They are analytic when they help to form an alliance between analyst and child in the common task of removing obstacles to ego-building.

From the beginning of his treatment Mortimer willingly left his mother in the waiting room. Sometimes, while he was running through my house, he would say: "Where is mommy?" just as he might say: "Where is the light?" or: "I put it on. You do. I can open it. Fix it. I can fix it." It seemed that each such phrase was sufficient unto itself and equivalent to an action. Through dropping words and things, moving about and creating confusion, Mortimer excited his mother. He controlled her by means of the excitement, the remote control of his thoughts, and a mechanism of fusion which he called *attaching*. Whenever I attempted to draw a figure, Mortimer would scribble over it before it could be completed. When I started another drawing next to the first, he stopped me again. Then he drew a horizontal connecting line between the two incomplete bodies, saying: "I'll attach them."

Throughout his actions and words, Mortimer expressed in rapid succession the desire to disarrange things and to fix them. It was up to me to find a medium suitable for the investigation of this problem. A large flashlight proved to be "just right" to hold his attention and focus it on his concern with the inner mechanics of his body. Mortimer unscrewed the flashlight, opened the top, examined the light bulb, and discovered how the switch operated to make connections inside the flashlight. All through this "work" he chattered incessantly: "I can do it. It's too hard. I can't. You do it. I can, I will. You do." No sooner had he handed a part to me than he took it away again. Under the circumstances it seemed incredible that he disassembled and reassembled the flashlight as well as he did. Still, some of the mechanisms were not clear to him and he needed real assistance. He could not proceed with his explorations without me. This made it possible for me to explain that I could not help him if he could not sit still and watch what I was doing. If I had to look after him, find his fingers between mine, and suddenly see his legs dangling from his chair, I could not work in peace. Not only did this behavior make me anxious, but it confused me when he simultaneously asked me to fix something and then interfered with my attempt to do so. It took of course more than one sitting to convey all this to him.

Gradually I did succeed in proving to him that I could assist him in taking the flashlight apart, putting it together again, and keeping it in good order. At the same time, I confronted Mortimer with the confusion he created and its effect on his environment. He realized and accepted that I could teach him to take the flashlight apart and put it together again only under certain conditions. He understood clearly that I intended to help him in his endeavor to understand the things which seemed scattered, broken, and unrelated. He also knew that I would not engage in excited games of doing and undoing because I neither enjoyed them nor found them useful in my role as helper in putting things together the right way, understanding their inside mechanism, and preserving their function and integrity.

A working alliance (Greenson, 1965; Dickes, 1967) was established between us, an alliance sanctioned by the child's parents who now began to believe that I could get the incorrigible Mortimer to become a useful citizen. At that point the child was able to express a coherent, well-organized fear which interfered with his wish to explore the insides of things. When I tried to take the battery out of the flashlight, Mortimer exclaimed anxiously: *"Don't, don't, the hole will run out."*

Mortimer was now ready for the beginning of analysis proper. His analysis began three months later when he was three years and three months old. During the intervening vacation period he had been weaned and trained and had begun to attend nursery school. These new experiences reinforced Mortimer's new desire to be a big boy like his brothers, whom he admired. To avoid the danger of becoming a baby instead of the big boy he now was, Mortimer assured me emphatically that he never was a baby. He refused to accept as his own the photographs of himself as an infant and younger toddler. He wanted to draw letters, squares and circles, and be a real schoolchild. However, his preoccupation with things falling apart, disintegrating, and breaking interfered with "big boy" ambitions. He scribbled over shapes in great excitement and ruined what he created. He leaned on the typewriter so that the keys became entangled or the chair would fly out from under him. Somehow papers dropped, and erasers, pencils, and scissors disappeared. He refused to pick things up and demanded that mother or I do it for him. When I tried to speak to him, he would interrupt me, mix things up, change the subject and walk away to get something new from the toy shelf. To contain him, I called his mother and asked her to take him on her lap while I talked to him. Looking at his tense, uneasy face and adjusting my tone of voice to be attuned to, yet minimize, his pattern of tension, I said: "Things fall out of your hands and your fingers, your arms fly and don't stop. You need your mommy to pick up all the pieces for you. They are yours. They must stay with you all the time." His mother said with sudden insight: "I used to tell him all the time that either he will break me or I will break him" (Kestenberg, 1969).

After this interpretation Mortimer calmed down considerably and stopped demanding that I pick up the things he dropped. It became apparent that he liked to tease by threatening to break things and people and that he enjoyed the game of breaking and fixing in a sort of "togetherness." Whenever I drew something he was interested in, such as a train, a turtle, a horse or a boy, he invariably scribbled over it, rumpled it or cut parts off. He frequently cut off the right hand of a figure, and did not allow me to complete its outlines. When I drew another figure next to the first one, he quickly "attached" its left arm to the amputated right side of the first figure. No doubt the cutting off was equated with getting away from his mother's holding hand and restoration was accomplished through reattachment of his body to that of his mother.

All drawings were taken as evidence of concrete transformation of bodies into paper images. He did not permit me to complete the outlines of a body until I understood this and could explain to him that he would not become the image I was drawing on paper. Now he was very pleased when I made a cut-out figure of "Mortimer," but soon crumpled it, looking at me mischievously, expecting that I would be upset or injured. It took him some time to convince himself that throughout all this no one was broken. Still, he was happy when I made a new paper-Mortimer and he relied on me to put it away safely to protect it. At this time he was greatly improved at home, acquired a friend, and functioned much better in school.

The next phase of Mortimer's analysis was dominated by his urgent need to play with "mail." He stuffed wads of paper into envelopes and one large envelope into another (preferably smaller than the first), using long strips of Scotch tape to seal the stuffed envelopes. These would become entangled, did not serve the purpose of closing the opening of the envelopes, and had to be discarded. He needed my help to get a piece that was short and straight enough to seal an envelope. On its outside he attached a clean, intact piece of white paper which he Scotch-taped with great care.

Mortimer used to ignore my question whether he wanted to stuff his own body until one day he told me teasingly that his friend had stuffed his belly with "poo-poos." I wondered whether these were the things he did on the toilet and he corrected me soberly: "No, that's duty." Subsequently he had to go to the bathroom in my office. He was somewhat worried about the drain in the sink and the pipes, but there was no evidence of worries about loss of feces. Eventually, the "poo-poos" could be traced to the way the father addressed his boys in moments of affection. No doubt, Mortimer wished to be stuffed with little boys. However, the wish to have a baby was not integrated with Mortimer's representation of his genitals.

One day I discovered that the entangled Scotch tape felt stringy. When I asked whether Mortimer had something stringy in his bal-lies (Bell, 1968), his sac or penis, he offered to take off his pants to show me. When I suggested that he tell me instead, he went straight for a spool of string. He unraveled a large quantity of string, en-tangled, folded, and cut it. He asked me to put it on the table and proceeded to make a replica of it. Then he ordered me to put the twin sections into a plastic bag, and carefully showed me how to close the bag by bunching and rolling it like a fist and putting Scotch tape around it. His construction finished, he began to attach a white piece of paper on the outside of his envelope and instructed me to put a white paper on the outside of the plastic bag as well. Now the plastic bag contained two tangled, stringy balls and was securely closed like a Scotch-taped fist. On the outside, attached with a long piece of tape, protruded a piece of white paper. Even though Mortimer had erected a model of his maleness, he continued to stuff and seal large envelopes, which I took to be an indication of fantasies of having children inside of him.

Although he was intent on separating himself from his mother, he was not yet able to disentangle his own body image from that of his mother. Once he consented to draw a picture of a baby, it became clear from his own words that the entangled scribbles of crisscrossing lines he had produced represented both the baby inside the mother and his mother inside the baby. The scribbling expressed the manner in which he perceived sensations from the inside of his body, sensations that defied verbal description. Because of the in-tensity of his feelings, the uncontrolled scribbling ruined every shape he was trying to create. Unable to contain objects within their boundaries, Mortimer refused to draw or to look at my drawings.

The observation of his brothers' interest in completed figure drawings reinforced Mortimer's hidden wish to create shapes instead of entangling lines. Although some of these lines functioned as "attaching bridges" (Kestenberg, 1969), they destroyed rather than created distinct shapes. Before Mortimer could draw figures with clear outlines, he erected in his mind three distinct sex entities: boys-daddies, girls-ladies, and mommies. In contrast to girls-ladies, boys-daddies and mommies had "penies," a fascinating idea which prompted Mortimer to jump on the couch, manifesting phallic behavior for the first time in his analysis.

In the meantime Mortimer's father became disquietened by what seemed to him a need on the part of his youngest son to create a feminine identity for himself (Lampl-de Groot, 1946). He reported the following dialogue between himself and Mortimer.

Father: What will you be when you grow up?
Mortimer: A mommy.
Father: A mommy? You can't be a mommy, you are a boy. What do you want to be:
Mortimer: A mommy.
Father (amused and irked, decided to reason with him): Are you a boy or a girl?
Mortimer: A boy.
Father: When I was little I was a boy. When mommy was little she was a girl. What will you be when you grow up?
Mortimer: A mommy.

Mortimer did not want to give up his identity as a boy and wanted to be a mommy just the same. He touched his mother's breasts and told her that father had his breasts down below. As long as he could look upon himself as someone attached to his mother, Mortimer did not experience separation anxiety. Once he had made considerable progress in the formation of his body image, his feelings about "his mommy" as a separate entity could crystallize (Mahler, 1968). This became apparent in a series of sessions, beginning with one to which he came with his father instead of his mother.

In contrast to previous sessions, Mortimer was tense and uneasy. Several times he got up from the table to look for new material and two or three times he announced that his work was finished and he wanted to go home. He found clay on the table and told me that he would not play with it. He agreed that I could and instructed me to take a mommy out of clay. When the figure was almost completed, he interrupted his play with envelopes and seized "mommy." When he pulled off the right hand of the figure, I said: "Poor mommy has no hand." He said: "Give me Scotch tape; I will give her another one." I pointed out that he did not need tape to attach clay. When he put the new clay hand on, it had a new shape and the whole arm was foreshortened as a result. I wondered whether Mortimer wanted to change his mommy. He agreed and I suggested that he might want one like grandmother or Georgie's mother. He shook his head. I asked whether he wanted me for a mommy. He looked up as if startled and parried: "Are you a mommy?"

It was most unusual for Mortimer to ask direct questions rather than elicit information indirectly. When I nodded that I was a mommy, Mortimer proceeded to stuff his envelope, but soon he tore the clay-mommy to pieces. I said solicitously: "Poor mommy." Mortimer answered in a matter-of-fact tone of voice: "Mommy is at home." I asked whether she stayed home to take care of Bobby, who was sick. Mortimer mumbled forlornly: "He is very sick and I bring him water but I eat alone. . . ." "You don't like it because mommy takes care of Bobby instead of you?" I asked. He mumbled that he too was coughing. Asked whether mommy liked Bobby better than him he ignored the question, but became more and more anxious to go home.

In this session Mortimer tried very hard to draw a baby. He made a "V" shape that seemed to represent legs, but he crossed it out saying that it was a letter. Then, starting anew, he made horizontal strokes over a vertical line. The horizontal "hair" increased, but there were no facial features. When I asked where they were, Mortimer made a few circles outside of the vertical line. I wondered why they should be outside of the body and he answered a bit sadly: "*I don't know how to attach them.*" The following morning he asked his mother: "*Where do mommies come from?*" Startled, she told him that mommies and daddies made babies when they loved each other. They brought them home from the hospital. The child was interested, but what he really wanted to know was: "How come there was only one mommy for so many children?" implying that each child should have a mommy of his own. Mother told him that parents could make many children.[2]

At the next session Mortimer arrived happily with his mommy. Showing me a new way to open a sealed envelope without damaging it, he said: "*My* mommy showed me how to do it." Still busy stuffing paper into little envelopes and little envelopes into a big one, he used hardly any Scotch tape on that day. He wanted his mommy but instead of getting her, he went to the kitchen, where he opened many drawers and asked innumerable questions about the toaster and the broiler. On the way back to the office, he again neglected to call his mother and yelled for her only when reminded of his original intent. He was pleased that she had brought three pictures he had given her. He explained what he had painted on each side. His mother beamed: not only was her child generous now, but he was also very patient. I remarked that he had many questions on his mind. Mortimer's mother asked him whether she could tell me about the questions he had had about mommies. He consented but was a bit bewildered as if he had forgotten.[3] When she repeated his question, Mortimer's face lit up in recognition and he said quickly: "Where babies come from. From the hospital." In this manner he camouflaged the meaning of his original question which betrayed his search for a mother. Mother continued: "Who makes babies? Daddy and mommy . . ." Mortimer chimed in: "And Mortimer." Mother shook her head in the negative, and I intervened by asking whether Mortimer indeed could make a baby. He became very eager, then a bit confused. He looked at his hands and at the table and muttered: "I don't have. . . ." Then, quickly regaining his customary self-composure, he ordered his mother to take out the crayons she had bought for him. While chosing the right colors, he ordered me excitedly to bring him paper. He systematically cut

2 Regina, two and a half years old, and already a sister of two baby girls, kept talking about "My mommy." She explained that her mommy was just hers and was most eager to provide her siblings with mommies of their own. She too asked her mother where mommies came from and was told that ladies who had babies became mommies.

3 It is interesting to note how often repression is initiated by the child's feeling that his mother does not want to answer a question. Mortimer's mother had not really responded to his question where mommies came from.

off the "holes" at the edge of the pad, carefully dropping them on the floor. He finished the job without a mishap and announced that he would make a baby. Asked whether it would be a boy or a girl, he started saying: "B . . . ," looked at his mother and said: "A girl." He drew a "V," which this time he accepted as legs, and crossed the figure horizontally. For the head he made a very small circle on top and put in still smaller circles for eyes and mouth. He put the nose inside the chest and ended by adding more horizontal lines and scribbles. When he finished he began to play with the flashlight without worry that "the hole would run out."

During the following session Mortimer again wanted to investigate my kitchen. I suggested that he wanted to see whether I had babies there. I took out dolls to represent my babies, but Mortimer ordered me to put them back in the hospital. He wanted to play with the doctor bag, but his wish to explore the kitchen was stronger. Impatiently he punched me, with a maturity of aim and a strength that made his action appear phallic in nature.

At this point of his analysis the quality of Mortimer's transference reactions changed. This conspicuous change coincided with the appearance of phallic-oedipal traits. Whereas previously his mother had been the recipient of his feelings revived from infancy, now he experienced feelings toward the analyst which manifested themselves in the sessions and were absent at home with mother.

During a vacation Mortimer did not seem to miss me. He behaved very well at home. Yet, upon his return to my office, Mortimer disrupted the sessions, regressing to behavior long outgrown. He knew that everything seemed to fall apart again. He agreed that he was afraid that his penis and ballies would fall out because he wanted to open his body to look inside. However, his behavior did not change very much. When I asked him directly why he was so upset, he mumbled: "We are moving." I could then discuss with him how unhappy he had been during my absence and how he feared he would never see me again once they had moved to the new house his parents were leasing. We invited his mother to discuss the new house and help us remember or reconstruct earlier separations. Shortly before he was two, Mortimer was left in the care of a housekeeper while his parents had gone to California. We began to play that he was getting mail from mother; we constructed postcards and drew pictures on them. I could guess from his choice of a colorful horse that he was thinking of a rocking horse. His mother remembered that they used to have one before Mortimer was six months old. At that time they moved and left the rocking horse with a neighbor, where it remained another year before it was finally discarded. Mortimer had condensed the loss of his mother with the loss of the rocking horse. In the transference, he anticipated that he would lose me with the impending move.

As soon as Mortimer began to show increasing evidence of phallic-oedipal trends, his transference reactions toward me became more frequent. In the preoedipal phase, his intense infantile feelings, which were revived during treatment, were primarily discharged at home rather than in the analysis. All events of the past were interpreted as transactions between mother and child and treated as if they were current. In contrast to the usual analytic transference, this type of transfer of feelings during an analysis can aptly be called "transference to the mother."[4]

In the process of separating the representations of self and mother, Mortimer had begun to identify with her instead of fusing with her. Simultaneously with the arousal of his interest in me as a nurturing mother figure, Mortimer became chivalrous and solicitous of his oedipal mother. He began to masturbate and he shared with his mother the joyous discovery that his penis felt "good." He asked to get on top of her and hug her.

As is typical for the end of the "inner-genital" phase and the beginning of the phallic, Mortimer began to deny the existence of "ballies" (Kestenberg, 1967). He omitted them from drawings of male figures and, when asked where they were, he said soberly: "There aren't any." He did draw a long tie on the mother figure, but corrected himself spontaneously and drew another mommy without a tie. He denied that he had a scrotum, discarding it as a

[4] During the discussion of this paper, Drs. Anny Katan, Marianne Kris, and Samuel Ritvo raised questions about this term. Dr. Katan suggested that it would be better to speak of a displacement of feelings (revived in analysis) to the mother. Dr. Kris thought that we might be dealing here with a continuity of behavior rather than a revival of old patterns.

I am grateful to Dr. Annemarie Weil for drawing my attention to a paper by Selma Fraiberg (1966) in which she distinguishes between repetition in the transference and repetition with the original object.

feminine attribute. At the same time he stopped endowing his mother with a phallus. Now, when he regressed to former behavior, he would explain it from a masculine point of view—in identification with his father. For instance, one day he could not pick up things from the floor by himself because he had a backache like his father. Since the latter explained his injury as due to a "torn muscle," Mortimer announced that he was born a girl and was torn. When his father recovered, Mortimer assured him that all the boys in the family would grow up to be daddies. Hesitatingly he added that even mother might become one. He looked upon his babyhood as an era of femininity and feared castration for father and himself. Being big and identified with his father had its perils, but these were relegated to the past, while the future was clearly one of pleasurable masculinity.

I have traced the successive steps in ego-building which were accomplished in Mortimer's analysis by the removal of obstacles to his own integrative efforts. In the analysis of preoedipal children we invent technical devices to help integrate into meaningful units past and present feelings and memory fragments. This allows them to reach the phallic phase without ego deficiencies. New technical devices must be employed to assist phallic children in their next developmental task which calls for the correlation of growing genital excitement with oedipal fantasies.

Case 2

Selected data from the analysis of two phases of Dorie's analysis illustrate the change in technique at the time she entered the phallic phase and a decision to terminate treatment based in large part on the child's need for privacy during oedipal involvement.

In contrast to Mortimer, three-year-old Dorie clung to her mother, and her treatment had to begin with both of them present in the analytic sessions. Dorie understood very quickly that I would help her to resolve problems that prevented her from becoming a big girl, a nursery school child. Her physical separation from her mother could not be accomplished until she remembered and understood past separations and past losses of familiar objects.

For months Dorie drew small circles which she filled with various colors. She asked me to help her with the naming and mixing of colors until she arrived at the desired "reddish-purplish" hue of an object or body part she tried to recover. She was responsive to my drawings of parts of the body, of the whole body, of its outside and its inside. She acknowledged her interest in the phallus but indicated that she was looking for something else. When she was sure that I knew how to help her to re-create the shape that belonged to the "reddish-purplish" color, she gained confidence in me and began to work with me alone. She reconstructed various events from her infancy, paying special attention to objects she had lost and hoped to recover.

When Dorie was twenty months old, the family had moved from one apartment to another. Many of Dorie's possessions had disappeared; her mother had become preoccupied with movers and decorators and, to top it all, a few months later little Nick was born. One day Dorie painted a large red chair. She remembered the place in her parents' bedroom where the chair used to be and recalled that both parents sat on it and held her, when she was a baby. She could not find the red chair in the new apartment. We invited her parents to help us solve the riddle of the missing chair. We discussed at length what had become of Dorie's crib, her bath toys, and her carriage. Dorie supplied bits of information which we used to help her parents remember the red chair. As soon as they did remember it, they explained that it had been reupholstered and placed in the living room of the new apartment.

Dorie enacted without words how the movers had taken things out of the drawers. She did not know what happened afterward because she had been taken to a neighbor's house to keep her away from the turmoil of moving (Kestenberg, 1969). When her parents picked her up, a car took the family to a new place where everything was different. Going places in a car, Dorie was always upset and disgruntled. She associated such trips with losing things she liked and becoming separated from her mother. These losses were connected with her search for a body part which she wanted to identify.

One day Dorie asked me to draw her father in a miniskirt. There was something "reddish-purplish" hanging from his "tushy," something which Dorie had seen and wanted to see again. It seemed that Dorie thought she had a thing like that herself, but it was inside of her and could not be seen. When spring came and tulips began to bloom, Dorie remembered that she had been some place before where there were flowers and dogs, a place where there was no carriage for Nick. It was not the old apartment with the red chair, it was not the new place. Trying to explain, Dorie left the table and came to the couch to draw. With this action she indicated that she had seen something on a bed. She asked me to draw a flower for her. When I drew a tulip, she turned it upside down and beamed. We had found the right shape for the scrotum that seemed to hang from her father's "tushy" (Kestenberg, 1968a). When Dorie understood that she did not have a body part like her father's tulip-shaped scrotum, she began to question her parents about her baby-hood. She scrutinized pictures and helped reconstruct her experiences with an unpleasant baby sitter. She wanted to re-create herself as she had been when she was her mother's baby. Becoming a baby herself became a method of creating one.

As soon as Dorie regressed, she revived early infantile feelings, which she experienced primarily in relation to her mother rather than the analyst. She tried to transform her current mother into "Baby-Dorie's" nursing and diapering mother. When she craved to regain her "oral" mother, she demanded the return of her nursing bottle at home; in the office she played with a doll bottle. When she revived her ambivalent "wooing" of her "anal mother," Dorie resumed soiling at home; in treatment she threw toys around provocatively. When she squirted water on the bathroom floor in the office, Dorie promptly called her mother to admire the beautiful designs (babies) she created.

In the analysis we could see that Dorie reverted to old methods whenever her current needs were frustrated. It was painful to accept that neither the bottle nor the feces brought her closer to her mother. Neither excessive intake of fluids nor withholding of feces could be used to make a baby and reduce the nagging, inner-genital tensions inside her body.

The method of assisting Dorie to remember and think things through had to undergo considerable change when she reached the age of four. Just as Mortimer initiated his move into the phallic phase by denying the existence of his ballies, so did Dorie deny the existence of her introitus when she reached the phallic phase. When

I spoke about the opening for the delivery of babies, which we had discussed many times during the previous year, Dorie indicated that I was nagging her. She called me stupid, put her fingers in her ears or said: "Nothing. Don't talk about it." She ceased to be an investigator. Her need to reconstruct, remember, and re-enact was replaced by a need to project, deny, and repress. She used these defense mechanisms to ward off the nagging excitement that came from her inside. She tried to drown it by surrendering to an all-encompassing, sweeping phallic form of excitement. From a shy, thoughtful little thinker a new Dorie began to emerge: an exuberant, exhibitionistic, outspoken, even bold child.

In many sessions, old and new behavior would alternate. Dorie would draw and write, then play an imaginary game, interrupt it to jump on the couch and ask me to admire her or explain her excitement. She used drawings and phallic stunts to get her mother's admiration, but her excited demands and her angry disappointments became more and more centered upon me as a transference object.

When her interest in how babies were produced flared up again, she reverted to the old method of drawing to explain and reconstruct. She wanted to know why her father had to take mother to the hospital to deliver Nick. She was sure that he played a role in the delivery. We drew the car in which her parents had gone to the hospital, we drew the hospital and the delivery table, and we invited father into the office to help remember the night of Nick's delivery. Dorie was dissatisfied. She complained about a "boo-boo." She politely shrugged off my correct but irrelevant interpretation that she thought deliveries hurt. She walked away from the table which always indicated that a new way must be found to resolve the problem. She stood in the middle of the room, all alone, inspecting her arm and complained again of pain. When I offered her a box of Band Aids, I could see on her face that this was just as right as the flashlight had been for Mortimer.

Dorie proceeded to cover herself with Band Aids until her father exclaimed in amazement: "Oh, she had blotches of poison ivy. I took her to the doctor after I came back from taking my wife to the hospital; as a matter of fact, we both had poison ivy." This was the information Dorie had been waiting for. She beamed; at last we could understand her reasoning: both she and her father had gone to the doctor for the same thing. What had gone wrong? Why had no baby materialized as it did for mother? Dorie left the session still covered with Band Aids. At the door I asked her whether she was going to the doctor with daddy. She looked at me very thoughtfully. It must have struck her with great clarity that it was not true, that she was not going to the doctor, and was not going to get a baby. Then she smiled in recognition of the joke and of the "make-believe" way of delivering a baby.

When Dorie realized that her father gave the seed to create a baby but did nothing to deliver it, she began to see him in a new light. In the transference, she competed with him to gain my admiration. She climbed on tables to be as tall as her father and carried heavy things to be as strong as he was. She was pleased when I addressed her as "daddy." Her new excitement called for an immediate and brief response from me. She could not tolerate longer interventions which she took as rejections. This was also apparent in the way she tried to involve me in imaginary games, in which she linked past and present fears and demonstrated how her excitement evoked new fears of losses.

In a series of sessions, Dorie played with cards which, in her mind, belonged to a big boy she had seen in my waiting room. Each time she spotted a black card, it triggered off her anxiety. She instructed me that we were to be babies and had to go to sleep. We had to put the black cards under our heads the same way Dorie used to arrange her transitional objects when she was younger. Through the night we held the dangerous black cards in check. Still, upon awakening, Dorie would reach for her pony tail to make sure it had not disappeared at night. Upon finding her pony tail, she informed me that our mother went shopping. When I cried too much and would not accept daddy as a substitute, Dorie first reassured me, then scolded me. She herself was not quite ready to turn to her daddy as a love object. She abruptly turned to jumping on the couch. I had to admire the two forms of jumping: high jumps, repeated frequently, and jumps which ended with falling on a pillow.

It seemed that Dorie, despite her exhibitionism, needed privacy to develop feelings for her father which would blend with her genital excitement. She had become secretive. She did not want her parents to participate in her analysis any longer. Neither did she want me to help her understand. She wanted me to be part of her excitement. When I failed to respond properly to her jumping stunts, she experimented with other means to express what she felt inside her body. She drew mysterious designs which she refused to explain.

Eventually I could help Dorie to come to grips with her excitement by suggesting that her two forms of jumping were associated with feelings in two different parts of her body. Dorie showed me the button on the couch to indicate that the high jumps were responses to clitoral sensations. She tried to explain the other form of jumping but could not. I drew several rhythmic designs and encouraged her to choose those that best represented her feelings. Dorie watched me carefully until she spotted the "right" rhythm. She yanked the pencil out of my hand and continued drawing in her own way. She produced two pictures which represented the two sources of her genital excitement. One was a house in which a mother and a baby resided. It was surrounded by wavy scribbles which resembled the "right" rhythm, and was associated with jumping and falling on the pillow. The second picture consisted of concentric circles from which rays emanated, and was associated with repeated high jumps (Kestenberg, 1969).

As soon as Dorie grasped the nature and the sources of her genital excitement, she began to concentrate her efforts on finding a suitable love object. When her mother rejected her daring phallic overtures, Dorie became angry and depressed. Regressive behavior which she had been ready to give up was again intensified. She conveyed to me that I had disappointed her greatly and only her father gave her a new hope.

I agreed that I could not help her to get a baby. She had to wait until she was a big lady to become a mommy. Dorie said: "I hate you and I never want to see you again." She drew for a while in silence as if she needed privacy to formulate her thoughts. Then she said: "Daddy and I are going to plant seeds today." At last Dorie began to concentrate her wishes on her father.

A combination of factors suggested termination of Dorie's treatment at this point. The most important of these was the consideration that an intense transference relationship might interfere with the unfolding of her positive oedipus complex. I expected that Dorie's devoted father would ally himself with the child's progressive developmental forces in order to counteract the remaining pull of regressive, pregenital forms of gratification. After treatment ended, Dorie developed an intense relationship with her father. Eventually she asked him to give her a live baby and was able to accept the fact that her wish could not be fulfilled.

Analysis helps children who reached the phallic phase to cope with their genital excitement. In so doing it liberates fantasies which link phase-specific wishes with phase-specific oedipal objects. A strong relationship with the opposite-sex parent can now become the basis for the differentiation of the superego as a structure.

Case 3

Excerpts from the analysis of four-and-a-half-year-old Charlie illustrate the technique that was used to help a child, well advanced in the phallic-oedipal phase, differentiate sex from aggression and fantasy from reality, which freed him to pursue the formation of an independent superego.

Charlie was a dependent, phobic, and infantile boy. His movements were inhibited and his affect restricted. He was never sad and never cried with tears. When he became excited, he would lose control over his movements and hit out in an indiscriminate way. He did not seem to know the difference between a loving and hostile approach. To approach his mother sexually, he punched her "busom-buppers" in the same way as he hit his brothers when they refused to let him play with their electric train.

I had to show Charlie that for him every excitement was so dangerous and overwhelming that he could only express it by hiding under the façade of a sheltered or sick baby. Once he could tolerate expression of feelings without ego regression, we could focus on the mechanisms of displacement, denial, phobic avoidance, and ego restriction which hampered his judgment and reduced his ability to resolve conflicts. When Charlie's defenses weakened, he regressed to drinking from a bottle, to duty talk, and excessive water play. The bulk of these activities was confined to the analytic sessions.

Charlie used his mother as an anchor point. He had to know where she was at all times. He asked her to function for him when his play became disorganized and he attacked her whenever he failed in something he wanted to do. All analytic interventions were confined to showing Charlie why he failed in his endeavors. He hammered without strength and sawed without direction. Instead he threw the wood away with great force and went directly to his mother to punch her. He breathed heavily or laughed in an embarrassed way while carving clay. When he was sad, he sneezed or had a runny nose. When he was excited or fearful, he invariably vomited and got a cold. When he wanted help, he attacked people and made them angry.

When Charlie accepted me as an ally in his numerous attempts to test and chose what was appropriate and effective or undesirable and ineffective, he settled down to wood carving. He was working quite well, but he still could not live up to his aspirations. I commented: "Your daddy's daddy had a wood-carving shop." When Charlie denied this, I asked him whether he knew his grandfather. He answered: "Yes, I know him. He plays with me." It took some time before he could admit that "gramps died last year." I asked him: "Were you sorry that he died?" and he replied curtly: "Not a bit. He did not even play with me." When I reminded him that he had just told me that he knew his grandfather and had played with him, Charlie avoided the whole issue by saying: "I thought you were talking about my father." Even though Charlie could not talk about this subject any longer, he did show me by his choice of play how much he needed to sort out and unwind things which had been mixed up and entangled. He took a piece of string and began to separate the strands which composed it. When he entangled and knotted the strands, he asked me to help him and was surprised how easy it was to unwind them. However, it took a lot more unwinding before Charlie could face the implications of his grandfather's death.

Charlie then became preoccupied with the killing of animals and being injured himself. He played that he was a hunter or a butcher. He brought books from home to show me how afraid he was of pictures of whales, boats, and fish. When his fish died and were thrown away, Charlie associated this event with the loss of his dog and the loss of his parents when they had gone away on a boat trip. At the same time we discovered that the whale in Charlie's version of *Pinocchio* was referred to as a "dog-fish."

When Charlie was about to enroll in kindergarten, his fears intensified and he had a series of nightmares about whales, fish, and water. When he awoke in fear, he would dream a good dream in which he was Captain Marvel. He now dared to look at the picture which showed how an old man had created Pinocchio out of wood. I asked him whether he knew the name of the old man. Charlie began to stutter: "I . . . I . . . don't remember, but I . . . I . . . think . . . so . . . sometimes he called him father."

Charlie's conflict between his wish to stay with his mother alone and his desire to become a schoolboy evoked a great many fantasies in which he tried to eliminate his father without killing him. He allied himself with his brothers against his father. In the transference I became his fairy mother who flew up to heaven to join the dead grandfather with whom Charlie identified. By helping Charlie differentiate between fantasy and reality I gradually led him to the recognition that he wanted to be his father's father instead of his father's child.

Charlie wanted to eat at home with mother or bring his own lunches to school. When I asked whether this was allowed, he said: "I will take a lot of bricks and build the school, then I will be the director and the children will bring their lunches from home." I sympathized with the little children who were lonesome for their mothers while in school. Charlie consoled me: "I will have a big school. Only fifth and sixth graders" (like his brothers). I said: "The little children will cry, they want to be in school too." Charlie replied quickly: "I will build another school for them. I will be my brothers' helper. We will not work for daddy. . . . John will be the boss and I will do what he says. We will be on the train, engineers. We will have a school on the train." "Who will be the director?" I asked, and Charlie replied: "We will all three run it. I will put John and Philip in the Caboose." I told him that it would not matter so much who was older when they all grew up to be men. He added: "Daddy will teach them what he knows and they will go to college and daddy will teach me and I will work with them." Bearing in mind that his grandfather was a workman and never went to college, I asked: "Will you go to college like your brothers?" Charlie got carried away again: "No, I will be the boss, and we will roll the earth and we will look at Europe. . . . I will be Captain Marvel. He can fly." He stretched out his arms to show me how he and I would fly. "Will we fly to see the world?" I asked. Charlie answered: "No, we can't fly. You could be an angel and go to God to see gramps." Charlie told me about the bad people in hell and the good people who were with God. Then he returned to the practical question how to make wings and how to pin them on me. When I remarked that the fairy in *Pinocchio* had wings, Charlie acted as if I had helped him make an important discovery. He became exhilarated and almost immediately transformed himself into a good and generous boy. He assured me that he would share his new dog with daddy and his brothers, and that mommy would not have to be the dog's nursemaid.

Subsequent sessions revealed that Charlie was not yet content to be just a schoolchild. In a game in which he was a storekeeper, he betrayed his wish to become a father by creating a baby. He sorted out merchandise and money. He cheated me (his customer), gave me the wrong merchandise, and misinformed me. We talked at length about the relative merits of cheating and playing fair, lying and telling the truth, making fools out of people and helping them find out things. At last Charlie told me that babies came from Macy's, that the stork flew them down, but God created them and sent them to the store. Now we could trace the God image to his grandfather and confront Charlie with the fact that he had seen his father cry in helpless grief at the time his grandfather presumably went to God. Charlie had avoided all displays of grief and resorted to sneezing instead. His model might have been the giant puppet master in *Pinocchio* who sneezed instead of crying, or the whale who was forced to sneeze out the wooden Pinocchio and his father. We talked about the relative merits of runny noses and sneezing versus crying and becoming sad and helpless. The latter meant, of course, that one had to give up the unattainable. Charlie now began to use the reformed Pinocchio as a model in his task of building an ideal "real boy" image of himself as a schoolchild.

If we characterize Mortimer as a "touch and go" boy and Dorie as a "sit, see, and think" girl, Charlie can be best described as a "secret power station." These traits were accentuated in certain developmental phases and diminished in others. Some of these traits were welcomed and fostered by a mother or father, others were discouraged. Each of these children had to be treated differently, not only because their treatment covered different stages in their development, but also because they were different people, living under different circumstances. In the analysis of prelatency children, psychoanalytic technique must be geared not only to enhance the child's development, not only to adjust to his individual temperament, but also to the limitations imposed by the environment.

Space does not permit discussion of the influence of teachers, physicians, friends, and relatives upon the parents' and the children's reactions to the analytic process. Nor is it possible to present material to show how parental reactions to the young child's behavior, in analysis and at home, promote or restrict the scope of the child's treatment.

A mother of a preoedipal child may be pleased when she becomes the target of her child's transference because it affords her the opportunity to undo her past mistakes. By participating in the child's sessions she may identify with the analyst and learn new ways of coping with the child's regressions. A mother of several young children may be afraid of her older toddler's regression. Rather than help reveal or remedy her past seductive or aggressive behavior toward her firstborn, she may prefer to undo her "sins" by bringing up her new infants in a new and better way.

Parents who have been successful in helping to minimize the effect of early traumatization are proud of the child's progress and accept as part of this progress their exclusion from the analytic treatment of the phallic-oedipal child. Other parents may become competitive with the analyst just as soon as he becomes the transference object of their child. They may disrupt the therapeutic alliance by their opposition to the child's progress. They may obstruct the unfolding of genitality by open rejection of masturbation and courtship behavior and by hidden invitation to regression.

Premature termination of treatment in prelatency may occur when a parent, usually of the same sex as the child, is unwilling to relinquish his claim on a certain aspect of the child's life which, he justly fears, analysis will remove. The analyst himself may decide to terminate treatment when regression or deflection of wishes from parents to the analyst comes into conflict with the child's progression from one developmental phase to the next. In other cases, treatment may have to be terminated because a parent cannot tolerate regression or withstand the onslaught of intense infantile feelings, which have here been called "transference to the mother."

CONCLUSIONS

Psychoanalytic technique varies in accordance with the predominant organization of a patient's developmental level.

In analysis the preoedipal child needs assistance in the integrative work involved in ego-building, which is his current developmental task.

The young phallic child needs the analyst's help in coping with his global excitement and in correlating it with the fantasies and wishes that are directed to the opposite-sex parent.

The older phallic-oedipal child uses analysis to help him maintain or recoup his ability to differentiate, which leads him away from global excitement to internalization and to delineation of the superego.

For the preoedipal child his mother can easily become a "transference object" on whom he projects his early infantile wishes that are revived in analysis. For that reason, the mother frequently has a second chance to wean or train her child. She may be able to undo the "basic fault" (Balint, 1968), from which her child suffers by helping reinstitute harmony to the ego.

When a child reaches the phallic-oedipal phase, he is less likely to transfer feelings aroused in analysis to his mother. Transference reactions to the analyst become increasingly similar to those of older children. Parents of a child in the phallic-oedipal phase must tolerate their exclusion from his treatment and accept the analyst as a transference object of their child.

In the analysis of prelatency children, more so than in the analysis of older patients, we adjust our technique to the individuality of the child and his family. Our decisions to begin an analysis of a prelatency child or to terminate it are guided by the potentialities and limitations which the parents' personalities impose on the treatment of the child. It may be necessary to terminate a young child's treatment in order not to interfere with his developmental needs or the needs of his family. One may choose not to apply analysis in certain prelatency problems. Once analysis is decided upon the treatment is adjusted to the child's developmental level without giving up the goals and principles of psychoanalysis.

BIBLIOGRAPHY

Balint, M. (1968), *The Basic Fault*. London: Tavistock.
Bell, A. (1968), Additional Aspects of Passivity and Feminine Identification in the Male. *Int. J. Psa.*, 49:640-647.
Bolland, J. & Sandler, J. et al. (1965), *The Hampstead Psychoanalytic Index*. New York: International Universities Press.
Bornstein, B. (1931), Phobia in a Two-and-a-Half-Year-Old Child. *Psa. Quart.*, 4:93-119, 1935.
Bornstein, S. (1933), A Child Analysis. *Psa. Quart.*, 4:190-225, 1935.
Dickes, R. (1967), Severe Regressive Disruptions of the Therapeutic Alliance. *J. Amer. Psa. Assn.*, 15:508-533.
Fraiberg, S. (1966), Repression and Repetition in Child Analysis. *Bull. Phila. Assn. Psa.*, 17:99-106, 1967.
Freud, A. (1946), *The Psycho-Analytical Treatment of Children*. New York: International Universities Press, 1959.
—— (1965), *Normality and Pathology in Childhood: Assessments of Development*. New York: International Universities Press.
—— (1968), Indications and Contraindications for Child Analysis. *This Annual*, 23:37-46.
Furman, E. (1956), An Ego Disturbance in a Young Child. *This Annual*, 11:312-335.
—— (1957), Treatment of Under-Fives by Way of Parents. *This Annual*, 12:250-262.
Furman, R. A. (1968), Excerpts from the Analysis of a Child with a Congenital Defect. *Int. J. Psa.*, 49:276-279.
Greenson, R. R. (1965), The Working Alliance and the Transference Neurosis. *Psa. Quart.*, 34:155-181.
Harley, M. (1951), Analysis of a Severely Disturbed Three-and-a-Half-Year-Old Boy. *This Annual*, 6:206-234.
Jacobs, L. (1949), Methods Used in the Education of Mothers. *This Annual*, 3/4:409-422.
Katan, A. (1959), The Nursery School as a Diagnostic Help to the Child Guidance Clinic. *This Annual*, 14:250-264.
Kestenberg, J. S. (1956), On the Development of Maternal Feelings in Early Childhood. *This Annual*, 11:257-291.
—— (1967), Phases of Adolescence: Part I. *J. Amer. Acad. Child Psychiat.*, 6:426-463.
—— (1968a), How Children Remember and Parents Forget. Read at the Division of Child Psychiatry, University of Colorado, Denver.
—— (1968b), Outside and Inside, Male and Female. *J. Amer. Psa. Assn.*, 16:457-520.
—— (1969), From Organ-Object Imagery to Self and Object Representations. In: *Separation-Individuation: Essays in Honor of Margaret S. Mahler*, ed. J. B. McDevitt & C. F. Settlage. New York: International Universities Press (in press).

Kolansky, H. (1960), Treatment of a Three-Year-Old Girl's Severe Infantile Neurosis. *This Annual,* 15:261-285.

Lampl-de Groot, J. (1946), The Preoedipal Phase in the Development of the Male Child. *This Annual,* 2:75-83.

Mahler, M. S. (1968), *On Human Symbiosis and the Vicissitudes of Individuation,* Vol. I. New York: International Universities Press.

Mead, M. (1956), Personal communication quoted in Kestenberg's (1956).

Pearson, G. H. J., ed. (1968), *A Handbook of Child Analysis.* New York & London: Basic Books.

Ritvo, S. et al. (1963), Some Relations of Constitution, Environment, and Personality, as Observed in a Longitudinal Study of Child Development. In: *Modern Perspectives in Child Development,* ed. S. A. Provence & A. J. Solnit. New York: International Universities Press, pp. 107-143.

Sterba, E. (1949), Analysis of a Psychogenic Constipation in a Two-Year-Old Child. *This Annual,* 3/4:227-252.

Winnicott, D. W., (1965), *The Maturational Processes and the Facilitating Environment.* New York: International Universities Press.

A STUDY OF DRUG-TAKING ADOLESCENTS

DORA HARTMANN, M.D. (New York)

The drug problem is currently approached from many different angles. Not one month goes by without new publications dealing with the increased use of drugs, especially among young people, appearing in the psychiatric journals. The authors of these recent papers look at various aspects of the drug problem, such as: general characteristics of drug users, motivation, self-image, mood, object relations, reality testing, academic performance, social responsibility, psychological dependency; psychotic reactions; relation to homosexuality and crime; relation of LSD and marihuana to heroin addiction (Hekimian and Gershon, 1968; Blacker et al., 1968; Keeler, 1968; McGlothlin and West, 1965; Konner, 1968; Weil, Zinberg, and Nelson, 1968; W. A. Frosch, 1968; Munter, 1968).

Undoubtedly there is a cultural-sociological aspect to the fact that today so many young people, mainly between the ages of sixteen and twenty-five, experiment with various drugs. Less rigidity or even a lack of restrictions and setting of standards on the part of the parents, the greater importance of group formation among the young ones (H. Deutsch, 1967), more freedom in expressing, in publicizing and advertising the satisfaction of impulses which were not even to be mentioned openly thirty years ago—all of these factors are thought to be, in part at least, responsible for drug-taking as a kind of "fashion." The general increase in acting out among adolescents might be attributed to the same reasons. I want to mention here, for example, the greatly increased number of pregnancies and abortions among very young girls which we have seen during the last ten years.

Presented at the Annual Meeting of the American Psychoanalytic Association, Miami Beach, 1969.

While we are quite aware of some of these sociological aspects—the "fashion" of acting out in groups; the pressure of these groups, with their jargon and ritual, on those who are afraid of joining them; the ridicule which the "squares" face—there still remain many questions unanswered for us as psychologists and psychoanalysts; e.g., what reasons can we find for the fact that with all of this group pressure and advertisement, a great number of young people resist the temptation to join the "acidheads" or "potsmokers"; and what psychological factors make an individual either decline taking any drug, or take it once and never again, or experiment a few times with it, or become really sold on it and more and more involved with it.

Have these differences in response of the adolescents anything to do with: (1) the constellation in the family; (2) the attitude of the parents toward their children; (3) early childhood experiences; (4) developmental difficulties; (5) a combination of various factors?

I believe all these are questions which a psychoanalyst can and should ask himself, and which he should try to clarify by comparing detailed psychotherapeutic and psychoanalytic studies of adolescents who are involved in taking various drugs.

Two years ago some members of The American Association for Child Psychoanalysis formed a Study Group to try to find some answers to these questions. We felt that our contributions as psychoanalysts to the subject of drug-taking in adolescence could come mainly from microscopic studies of individual cases. A great variety of cases was reported to our group:

1. Some used drugs only for a short time as a rebellious acting out against a parent or against their analysts.

2. Some were neurotic or depressed before taking drugs, then were involved in and felt compelled to take drugs for a long time, but were able to sustain treatment.

3. In some patients their capacity to function in life was very much restricted and aggravated through their involvement with drugs, and for them drugs became imperative and treatment ineffective.

4. In our group of patients there was one adolescent boy whose main problem was alcoholism. He could not be "seduced" to enjoy the use of other drugs.

Classical psychoanalysis could not always be used or maintained with these youngsters. The therapists had to use various parameters adequate to the conditions of their patients. It also became quite clear to the therapists that prohibition of drug-taking was neither advisable nor possible and would lead only to an immediate interruption of the treatment.

Our interest was focused primarily on the following questions:

1. Can we understand the underlying psychological development and dynamic reasons for the strong impulses of these adolescents to become more or less intensely involved with the taking of drugs?

2. Can we understand the unconscious meaning and the different effects various drugs have on gratifying or inhibiting impulses, in strengthening or in weakening defenses?

3. What is the ego structure of these youngsters who need a constant supply of drugs, and what are the changes in the ego of those who depend completely on drugs?

4. Can we interpret the meaning of the drugs to these youngsters and will our interpretations, aimed at giving them understanding, diminish the need for drugs?

To bring some order into the many data we collected and to concentrate our study on the specific problems outlined above, we worked out a questionnaire. This questionnaire was based in part on some of the headings in Anna Freud's Developmental Profile (1962) as modified by Laufer (1965) for adolescents.[1] We also added questions which we hoped would throw some light on the drug experience itself. In this way we thought we might be able to compare: (1) similarities and differences in the parents' background—especially in its relationship to the development of their children; (2) similarities and differences in the adolescents—their own libido, aggression, and superego development, their ego functioning, affect and object relationships before and after their experiences with drugs; (3) similarities and differences in their drug experiences—onset, conscious and unconscious motivations, genetic determinants, the course of drug-taking, its relationship to other symptoms and to the treatment.

[1] The Profile as envisaged by Anna Freud could not be used in its entirety because our case material did not lend itself to this type of comprehensive metapsychological assessment.

We have so far compared and studied in detail the answers thus obtained in twelve cases.[2] This group included ten boys and two girls ranging in age from fifteen to twenty-five, the majority being about nineteen years. They all belonged to the middle or upper-middle class. Either they themselves or their parents could afford private treatment.

Results of Questionnaire

I shall now summarize the most important aspects of the data collected.

Referral of the Adolescents

Nine of the adolescents were referred by their parents (three of them at the demand of their schools), one by the court, two came at their own request. Of our group of twelve, only seven were referred because of drug abuse, the others because of school difficulties or neurotic symptoms or both, one because of psychotic behavior.

Background Information

In trying to point to the *most conspicuous facts of the background information,* there seems to be more pathology among the mothers than the fathers. Infantile libido and superego development prevailed among the mothers; with regard to aggression, the fathers seemed to show more controlled, the mothers more uncontrolled aggression. With regard to the parents' relationship to their children, only one mother and two fathers were considered adequate. Seductive behavior was more prevalent among the mothers; inconsistency and distance, more among the fathers.

Siblings. As we would expect, drug-taking was found very frequently among the siblings in our group. Drug-takers have a great need to seduce others to join them, and they very often succeed.

[2] The twelve cases discussed in the following pages were treated by: Dr. T. Becker, Dr. P. Blos, Dr. A. H. Esman (two), Dr. E. Kaplan (three), Dr. W. Kelly, Miss E. Landauer, Dr. F. Parcells, Miss K. Rees, and Dr. H. Rosner.

I want to thank them as well as all the members of the Study Group who contributed to our work through their suggestions and discussions. I want to single out only Dr. H. Wieder who was one of the most active contributors to our group and whose paper (with Dr. E. Kaplan) is also published in this volume.

Description of the Adolescents

A high number of these youngsters (ten) were characterized as *orally fixated* (or regressed) in their libido development. The other two, not so described, took drugs only occasionally or transiently as a rebellious acting out against the parents or analyst. I shall first describe these two youngsters.

They did not show much change in their aggressive behavior after they had started to take drugs, although one became somewhat more daring. There was no gross superego pathology, and their superego functioning did not change after they started to take drugs regularly. Their ego functioning seemed age adequate. (We speak here mainly of reality testing, of functioning in school, and ability to work efficiently.) Once they were on the drug, one patient continued to function well, while the other showed some deterioration with drugs. Their affect seemed normal both before and after they took drugs. Their object relations were normal prior to regular drug-taking, and in one case remained so even while he was on the drug; the other patient had superficial relations to friends and associated more with other drug-takers.

If we now look at the ten patients who were classified as orally regressed or fixated, the picture appears much more pathologic.

With regard to their *aggressive* development, six were considered to be very passive, their aggression being inhibited (two of them could express aggression more easily with drugs); four had at times uncontrolled outbursts of aggression, and these four felt that their aggression was dissolved or decreased or under better control while they were on drugs.

Their *superegos* became generally less adequate under the influence of drugs—in some instances, it deteriorated to a marked degree; this was also the case in three youngsters whose superegos seemed to function quite adequately in periods when they were not on drugs.

Their *ego functioning* became less adequate and deteriorated under drugs in nearly all of these cases. Only two youngsters whose ego functioning was impaired to begin with continued to function, when taking drugs, on about the same low level as before.

As to their *affect,* eight of the ten were *depressed* before taking drugs and most of them felt less depressed when on drugs.

The *object relations* of these ten adolescents, with one exception, became much more superficial under drugs, even when they had appeared to be normal before the drug-taking; their social contacts were confined mainly to other drug-takers; in some cases object relations became very infantile under the influence of the drug; fusion fantasies were prevalent. Sex relations were on an infantile level; whether homosexual or heterosexual, they resembled autoerotic, narcissistic, and mastubatory activities rather than a meaningful emotional relation to a specific partner.

The Drug Experience

If I try to pick out those factors of the drug experience of this group which seem remarkable to me, I would mention the following:

Nearly half of our twelve cases (five) *started on drugs during their treatment,* which can only mean that today drugs are very easily available as a means of acting out in the transference and alleviating conflicts or symptoms brought out in treatment through the revival of early memories and traumatic childhood situations and through the re-experiencing of early object relationships in the transference.

The *conscious motivation* for the use of drugs was, in a few cases, the desire to experiment; in most others, it was the wish to avoid painful affects (depression), alleviate symptoms, or a combination of these factors.

Among *the unconscious motivations* (in addition to oral gratification and passive identification with a parent), the need to replace a lost object seemed to play a very important role. Three of our patients had lost one of their parents in childhood; another one had lost his mother due to divorce; and a fifth one lived alone with his mother until he was two years old. Two of these patients began to take drugs during the first vacation of their analysts. In two other cases, the drug-taking stopped during the analysis after early traumata and passive identifications had been worked through; but they started drugs again when their analysts' long summer vacation approached or had started.

Among *the genetic determinants,* it is remarkable how many of these youngsters had to face death, a severe illness, an operation on one of their parents, or themselves had had a severe illness or operation as children. With these traumatic histories we could expect disturbances in the early object relationships and in the early ego development of these patients.

Type of drug. Nearly all of our patients started with marihuana or LSD, but only two remained on these drugs alone. The others also experimented with amphetamine, methadrine, hashish, and some also with barbiturates and heroin. The need for or effect of specific drugs in relation to the psychopathology of some of these adolescents is discussed in another paper by two members of our Study Group (see Wieder and Kaplan, 1969).

Drug-taking in Correlation to Treatment

There were only three youngsters who showed no change in their drug-taking pattern during their treatment. All the other patients either stopped taking drugs when their early object relations were understood and worked through, or started taking drugs when an early traumatic situation was remembered or repeated in the transference; or they stopped at a certain point and started again when frustrations could not be tolerated. Usually, these changes could be understood and analyzed.

Drugs at the End of Treatment

The method of treatment employed in our series of twelve cases was either psychoanalysis (in seven cases) or psychoanalytic psychotherapy (in five cases). The duration of the treatment was from nine months to five years.

Eight patients have finished treatment to date. Of these three were successfully analyzed; two of them worked through the neurotic aspects of their drug-taking and stopped using drugs altogether; one experimented with drugs during his analysis and occasionally still does, but this has never become a real problem to him. Five dropped out or were dropped from treatment, because drugs were much more important to them than gaining insight into and understanding of their conflicts, or because they could not tolerate the frustrations of treatment and of their lives without alleviating their symptoms in an artificial way.

Four cases are still in treatment, three of them in classic analysis; two have stopped taking drugs at the present time.

Summary

If we look at these findings one by one, we must conclude that none of them could be called pathognomonic for drug users or drug addicts.

Neurotic patients, whether or not they take drugs, certainly also have infantile mothers. A mother's seductive behavior may lead to a boy's passivity, sexual disturbances, learning difficulties, and neurotic symptoms either in combination with or without drug-taking. The same can be said about adolescents who show oral fixations and regressions. These factors are not specific to drug-taking but are also found in neuroses, depressions, delinquencies, and even psychoses.

Early traumata such as severe illness and operations, or the loss of a parent during childhood, can be found as causative factors in disturbed adolescents—drugs or no drugs. Low frustration tolerance, depression, and difficulties in establishing mature object relationships are characteristics and symptoms we see frequently during this period of life—drugs or no drugs.

Even though these considerations make it clear that none of the aforementioned data on symptoms, character structures, childhood experiences, background, etc., can by themselves explain the wish or the imperative need for drugs, we felt that it might be of interest to see what significant factors our case material would disclose. This would make it possible for other psychoanalysts treating drug-taking adolescents to compare their findings with ours.

Clinical Illustrations

I shall present two short vignettes, taken from the case histories of two patients who were included in our study, to illustrate some of the points previously made:

Case 1[3]

A nineteen-year-old girl, A., was referred for psychoanalysis by her parents. She withdrew from an out-of-town college, where she had become depressed and, while drunk, had made a suicidal gesture following a disappointment in her boyfriend.

A.'s father was a rather narcissistic, infantile person who had uncontrolled outbursts of aggression. He showed evidence of a fragmented superego in his behavior toward his daughter: he was inconsistent, domineering, and very seductive.

The patient's mother, an alcoholic, was infantile, withdrawn, and concerned only with her own pleasures. She was emotionally unavailable to her daughter, who could reach the mother only through illness or acting out. The patient had a severely disturbed sister who committed suicide while A. was in treatment.

After her return from college the patient stayed at home for a short time, then moved into her own apartment and enrolled in a local college. While A. had taken drinks on social occasions since she was sixteen, neither alcohol nor drugs had been a problem.

She described her early childhood as lonely and terrifying. Nocturnal asthmatic attacks, enuresis, and nightmares were constant symptoms until she was eleven years old. She remembered a series of nurses who responded to her screaming by turning off the lights and closing all the doors. Her parents were absent much of the time. When they came home from a party late at night, it was always her father who would change her wet sheets, or give her medicine for her asthma, or comfort her in her night terrors. He also played very seductive games with her during the day. Later on, A. engaged in a variety of activities to please him and to gain his approval. For him, she worked well in school, and for him she learned to play tennis, to ice skate, to swim, and to dive with almost professional proficiency. But he lacked awareness of her emotional needs to a shocking degree. Both parents saw A.'s childhood as idyllic, every need having immediately been satisfied by gifts. For many years A.'s depression was masked by a fantasy world and her ability to win

---

[3] This case was reported extensively to our Study Group by Dr. Ted E. Becker, who also summarized it at the meeting of the New York Psychoanalytic Society, March 25, 1968.

father's interest through exhibitionism. She wanted never to grow up, but to remain a little girl, protected and cared for by her father. These longings also became quite clear in the transference.

During the first few months of her treatment she used alcohol to combat her loneliness and her nightmares and her sense of being completely abandoned. While alcohol lessened her depression, it also led to loss of control and severe guilt feelings, as a consequence of which she tried to turn away from alcohol. During the first long vacation of her analyst she began to take drugs and thereafter tried out every available drug in the attempt to combat her loneliness and depression, especially at night.

At certain times she was able to work quite well in school, at other times she could not tolerate her depression even during the daytime without turning to amphetamines and to marihuana. She frequently took large overdoses of drugs and had to be hospitalized six times during the following three years. The drug replaced the absent object, the mothering father, the analyst; it helped her forget and lifted her depression and anxiety. As a secondary gain, it also drew the need-satisfying objects to her. Her frustration tolerance was so low that she sometimes took drugs a few minutes before her appointment with her analyst because she could not tolerate waiting that long to relieve her tension. Her goal became instant "highs," instant forgetfulness, making insightful psychotherapy futile.

Case 2[4]

D., a boy aged fifteen, was referred by his parents because of depression, school difficulties, and drinking. His father was a very constricted, tightly controlled person, emotionally very distant from his family. His mother was very immature, drank a great deal while he was a child, and was then emotionally unavailable. After the parents' divorce, D. chose to live with his father.

D. was a very passive, orally fixated boy who because of his severe depression started to drink. While he was not blocked in learning, he was completely indifferent to his schoolwork. He was eager to start treatment, wanted to use the couch, and worked quite

---

[4] This case was presented extensively by Dr. Aaron H. Esman at the meeting of the New York Psychoanalytic Society, March 25, 1968, and was published in the *Psychoanalytic Forum*, Vol. 2, No. 4, 1967.

well in his analysis. He understood his identification with his mother and his fight against it. He stopped drinking, did better in school, and was less depressed.

In the second summer of his analysis, during the vacation of his analyst, he was introduced to marihuana—an event that changed his life. His drug-taking could not be analyzed; it became the central issue of his life. He spent most of his waking hours high or smoking. He withdrew from his friends except from those who used drugs with him, and stopped doing any work at school. The analysis tried to deal with his profound passive longings and his defenses against them. Marihuana, replacing his mother, alcohol, and the analyst, became much more important for him than understanding his feelings and his symptoms, and he finally gave up his treatment—no longer interested in working actively in his analysis. Instead, he sought to obtain immediate gratification through the drug.

Analytic Literature

There have been remarkably few psychoanalytic studies of drug-taking and drug addiction. In 1939 Crowley reviewed the "Psychoanalytic Literature on Drug Addiction and Alcoholism" and concluded that drug addiction was the stepchild of psychoanalytic theory. He stated that until 1926 "only the libidinal side of the problem" had been stressed (Freud, 1905; Abraham, 1908; Brill, 1922; Hiller, 1922; Sachs, 1923; H. Hartmann, 1925). After 1926 there appeared a few more extensive contributions attempting to evolve a more systematic psychoanalytic theory of addiction by taking into account the development of affect, ego, and defenses (Rado, 1926, 1933; Simmel, 1930, 1948; Glover, 1932; Fenichel, 1932; Gross, 1935).

Since 1939 even fewer psychoanalysts have been concerned specifically with addiction. There are some interesting case descriptions (Savitt, 1954; Meerloo, 1952; Chatterji, 1953, 1960; Mannheim, 1955; Chessick, 1960). All these authors emphasize orality, viewing the drug as a symbolic representation of the mother, or of mother's breast, or of mother's milk. Guarner (1966) and Rosenfeld (1960) point to similarities between drug addiction and manic-depressive mechanisms, but also stress, as does Savitt (1954), early disturbances

in the development of the ego, ego weakness, ego splitting, immaturity of the ego, as etiological factors contributing to drug addiction. Some authors, e.g., Bychowski (1952) and Meerloo (1952),
doubt that extramural intensive therapy, especially psychoanalysis,
can be employed in cases of addiction. Others seem to feel that the
success of therapy depends mainly on the amount of damage done
in early childhood and on the degree of maturity which the patient's
ego has reached (Savitt, 1954, 1963; Rosenfeld, 1960).

Lately, due to the enormous increase in drug-taking among
young people, more psychoanalysts have become interested in the
psychology of drug users and attempts are being made to distinguish,
also psychologically, between the drug users and the drug addicts
(e.g., W. A. Frosch, 1968; Esman, 1967).

Although Rado wrote on "The Psychoanalysis of Pharmacothymia" in 1933 and dealt only with adult narcotic addicts, I believe
that his paper contains some very important formulations applicable to many of the young nonnarcotic drug users whom we encounter in ever increasing numbers today. Rado underscores the fact
that there are many drugs, but there is only one drug taker: "Not
the toxic agent, but the impulse to use it makes an addict of a given
individual." The previous history of the addictive patient very often
reveals a state of depression. In addition, these patients show a great
intolerance to pain. Temporarily the drug changes the depression
into elation. The early omnipotent narcissism has not been slowly
transformed into normal ego growth; rather it has been severely
wounded and thereby disturbed normal adaptation. Through the
drug the early omnipotent narcissism becomes temporarily restored;
at the same time interest in reality is lost, inhibitions imposed by
reality disappear, and there is a striving to fulfill all unsatisfied impulses in fantasy. But these effects are only transitory—when the
drug effect wears off, the depression returns and the cyclic course
establishes itself again. Now the ego can maintain its self-regard only
by means of an artificial technique: the "realistic regime" is replaced
by a "pharmacothymic regime" which destroys the natural ego organization. This dangerous change leads to more and more ego
impoverishment and increasingly restricts the ego's freedom of action. With regard to object relations, Rado states that there are
crucial alterations in the sexual life of an addict. "After a transient

augmentation of genital libido, the [addicted] patient turns away from sexual activity and disregards more and more even his affectionate relationships . . . pharmacogenic pleasure . . . is autoerotic and modeled on infantile masturbation" (p. 11).

Some of the very important points which Rado makes in this paper seem to me to apply not only to adult drug addicts but also to many of the drug-taking adolescents whom I have discussed earlier. He stresses (1) their basic depressive character, early wounded narcissism (defects in ego development); (2) their intolerance for frustration and pain accompanied by the constant need to change a "low" mood into a "high" one (lack of satisfying early object relations); (3) the lack of affectionate and meaningful object relations which the adolescents attempt to overcome through the pseudocloseness and fusion with other drug takers during their common experience; (4) the artificial technique used to maintain self-regard and satisfaction; and the change from a "realistic" to a "pharmacothymic regime," which may lead to severely disturbed ego functions and to conflict with reality.

I believe we can see these psychologically very damaging effects in many of the young adolescents for whom drug-taking has become a way of life. They have changed from being drug users to drug addicts. They cannot tolerate frustration and tension; they do not want insight; they want the drug.

Among our group of drug-using adolescents were three boys whose early object relations were not severely disturbed and whose ego development was neither arrested nor retarded. They used drugs in defiance of their parents or therapists or out of "experimental curiosity" and were able to stop when they no longer needed this type of acting out.

There is, however, a middle group for whom easy availability of drugs can become very dangerous (four in our group). These are the youngsters who are seduced to maintain their self-regard through an artificial technique, as Rado calls it; they do not have to tolerate frustrations (or work hard in treatment to adapt to reality) once they have found such a simple way of avoiding displeasure. With the help of drugs they also avoid the active work needed to establish more mature object relations, a task which every adolescent has to face. They remain in a group of other drug users in a pseudoclose rela-

tionship, without much emotional commitment; their sexual gratifications are on the level of masturbation; therefore they are as often
homosexual as they are heterosexual. The more passive they were
to begin with, the greater is the danger of their being seduced to
this kind of gratification.

In this group the degree of the ego maturity of these adolescents
will determine whether they are able to tolerate the frustrations of a
treatment situation and will succeed in it.

BIBLIOGRAPHY

Abraham, K. (1908), The Psychological Relations Between Sexuality and Alcoholism.
  Selected Papers on Psycho-Analysis. London: Hogarth Press, 1927, pp. 80-89.
Blacker, K. H., Jones, R. T., Stone, G. C., & Pfefferbaum, D. (1968), Chronic Users of
  LSD: The "Acidheads." *Amer. J. Psychiat.,* 125:341-351.
Brill, A. A. (1922), Tobacco and the Individual. *Int. J. Psa.,* 3:430-444.
Bychowski, G. (1952), *Psychotherapy of Psychosis.* New York: Grune & Stratton.
Chatterji, N. N. (1953), Drug Addiction. *Samiksa,* 7:285-293.
—— (1963), Drug Addiction and Psychosis. *Samiksa,* 17:130-149.
Chessick, R. D. (1960), The 'Pharmacogenic Orgasm' in the Drug Addict. *Arch. Gen.
  Psychiat.,* 3:545-556.
Crowley, R. H. (1939), Psychoanalytic Literature on Drug Addiction and Alcoholism.
  Psa. Rev., 26:39-54.
Deutsch, H. (1967), *Selected Problems of Adolescence.* New York: International Uni-
  versities Press.
Esman, A. (1967), Drug Use by Adolescents: Some Valuative and Technical Implica-
  tions. *Psa. Forum,* 2:339-353.
Fenichel, O. (1932), *Outline of Clinical Psychoanalysis.* New York: Norton.
Freud, A. (1962), Assessment of Childhood Disturbances. *This Annual,* 17:149-158.
Freud, S. (1905), Three Essays on the Theory of Sexuality. *Standard Edition,* 7:125-243.
  London: Hogarth Press, 1953.
Frosch, W. A. (1968), Current Abuse Problems with Psychodysleptics (unpublished).
Glover, E. (1932), On the Aetiology of Drug-Addiction. *Int. J. Psa.,* 13:298-328.
Gross, A. (1935), The Psychic Effects of Toxic and Toxoid Substances. *Int. J. Psa.,*
  16:425-438.
Guarner, E. (1966), Psychodynamic Aspects of Drug Experience. *Brit. J. Med. Psychol.,*
  39:157-162.
Hartmann, H. (1925), Kokainismus und Homosexualität. *Z. Neurol. & Psychiat.,*
  95:79-94.
Hekimian, L. & Gershon, S. (1968), Characteristics of Drug Abusers Admitted to a
  Psychiatric Hospital. *J.A.M.A.,* 205(July 15):125-130.
Hiller, E. (1922), Some Remarks on Tobacco. *Int. J. Psa.,* 3:475-480.
Keeler, M. H. (1968), Motivation for Marihuana Use. *Amer. J. Psychiat.,* 125:386-390.
Konnor, D., ed. (1968), *Drug Addiction and Habituation: A Study of Drug Use, Control
  and the Pharmacist.* Detroit: Wayne State University Press.
Laufer, M. (1965), Assessment of Adolescent Disturbances. *This Annual,* 20:99-123.
McGlothlin, W. H. & West, L. J. (1968), The Marihuana Problem: An Overview. *Amer.
  J. Psychiat.,* 125:370-378.
Mannheim, J. (1955), Notes on a Case of Drug Addiction. *Int. J. Psa.,* 36:166-173.

Meerloo, J. A. M. (1952), Artificial Ecstasy. *J. Nerv. Ment. Dis.*, 115:246-266.

Munter, P. K. Abuse of Hallucinogenic Drugs: Some Observations of a College Psychiatrist (in preparation).

Rado, S. (1926), The Psychic Effects of Intoxicants. *Int. J. Psa.*, 7:396-413.

—— (1933), The Psychoanalysis of Pharmacothymia. *Psa. Quart.*, 2:1-23.

Rosenfeld, H. (1960), On Drug Addiction. *Int. J. Psa.*, 41:467-475.

Sachs, H. (1923), Zur Genese der Perversionen. *Int. Z. Psa.*, 9:172-182.

Savitt, R. A. (1954), Extramural Psychoanalytic Treatment of a Case of Narcotic Addiction. *J. Amer. Psa. Assn.*, 2:494-502.

—— (1963), Psychoanalytic Studies on Addiction: Ego Structure in Narcotic Addiction. *Psa. Quart.*, 32:43-57.

Simmel, E. (1930), Morbid Habits and Cravings. *Psa. Rev.*, 17:481.

—— (1948), Alcoholism and Addiction. *Psa. Quart.*, 17:6-31.

Weil, A. T., Zinberg, N. E., & Nelson, J. M. (1968), Clinical and Psychological Effects of Marihuana in Man. *Science*, 162:1234-1242.

Wieder, H. & Kaplan, E. H. (1969), Drug Use in Adolescents: Psychodynamic Meaning and Pharmacogenic Effect. *This Annual*, 24:

DRUG USE IN ADOLESCENTS

Psychodynamic Meaning and Pharmacogenic Effect

HERBERT WIEDER, M.D.

and

EUGENE H. KAPLAN, M.D. (Great Neck, N.Y.)

Despite wide interest in the drug problem, there are few generally accepted and well-founded conceptualizations available to orient our approach to it. Even the terminology, although hallowed by usage, is ambiguous and subject to distortion and misapplication. The prevailing sociological and pharmacological rubrics tend to isolate extremes from a continuum of attitudes and behavior toward drugs. More rigorous and consistent psychological hypotheses remain to be derived. To this end, we wish to draw attention to a relatively neglected aspect of the drug phenomenon, namely, the "drug of choice." Contrary to general opinion, we do not believe that drugs are chosen indiscriminately or are freely interchangeable. In fact, we place the phenomenon of choice of drug in the center of our formulations of why drugs are used at all. Although it appears that we generalize from a few case histories, our conclusions have evolved from extensive clinical experience with all types of drug users for many years.

We concur with Rado (1933) who states that the psychological investigation of drug addiction "begins with the recognition of the fact that not the toxic agent, but the impulse to use it, makes an addict" (p. 2). However, psychological data alone do not hold

Expanded version of paper presented at Fall Meeting of the American Psychoanalytic Association, 1968. Parts of this communication were read separately by the two authors at the New York Psychoanalytic Society, March 26, 1968. It is part of a larger, comprehensive essay on drugs and their use, which is in preparation.

Assistant Clinical Professors of Child Psychiatry, Albert Einstein College of Medicine.

the key to the riddle of drug use. From our experience, we conclude that specific drug preferences develop from a complex but internally consistent interaction of psychodynamic and pharmacological factors. Krystal and Raskin (1966) approach the same view in stating, "the pharmacogenic effect is of no less importance than the meaning of the act to the patient in terms of its symbolic wish fulfillment."

Any drug's influence is mediated through its psychodynamic meaning or "placebo effect," and, if it possesses them, pharmacological properties. Symbolic importance is attached not only to the *agent* itself, which may represent object or part object; or to the *act of using it,* which may be in the service of fulfilling wishes to control, attack or influence the object or self; but also *to the physiological concomitants,* which stimulate fantasies, or are secondarily incorporated into them—i.e., what we call the *pharmacogenic effect.* It represents diffuse, direct and indirect alterations in cellular physiology and biochemistry, whose ultimate psychic expression appears as a modification of the energy equilibrium of the personality structure or as cathectic shifts. It is the pharmacogenic effect which, we feel, has not been sufficiently studied.

Drugs may be used in a variety of ways—as a transient, occasional, recurrent or chronic phenomenon, they may be taken in secret or their use may be dramatically flaunted. The symptom of drug-taking, ranging from benign to malignant, occurs in patients belonging to all categories of psychiatric classifications. We believe that along the spectrum from health to illness, a basically adequate ego and structural development appreciably diminishes the need for sustained pharmacogenic effects. We further believe that a chronic need for specific pharmacogenic effects, or "craving," derives from developmental and structural deficits and distortions. These conditions are most clearly apparent in the borderline and psychotic personality organizations.

In this we are in agreement with Savitt (1963) who states that "the vicissitudes of early ego development and later ego maturation which facilitate fixation and encourage regression appear to play a dominant role in predisposing an individual to the development of the crippling morbid craving" (p. 56).

Our observations of the psychological changes induced by pharmacological agents have led us to draw some metapsychological inferences. These are energic and chemical substrate hypotheses, in which a key factor is the drug of choice acting as a psychodynamic-pharmacogenic "corrective" or "prosthesis."

The dictionary defines *drug* as both medicine and poison, the same antithetical polarity being found in the definition of *potion*. Many factors contribute to the development of the unconscious image and concept of *drug* and influence the conscious and lexigraphic concept.

Infantile sensations of relief and distress in the feeding situation coalesce as an image of a helping and hurting, loving and poisoning, magically endowed experience. Representations of "good" and "bad" objects evolve from oral ambivalence directed at food and objects. The earliest prototypes of "druglike" experiences probably are of milk, breast, and mother. In the argot of the addict, his supplier is often called "Mother" and his supplies "mood food." Transitional objects, through their magical relief-giving qualities, also contribute to the concept of "drug." And so do the various attempts made by parents to alleviate pain and discomfort brought on by illness. The image of the drug may be "good" or "bad," regardless of whether they used pharmaceuticals, caresses, food, laxatives or enemas. Severely or chronically ill children, such as diabetics and asthmatics, relate to their medications as to magic potions, especially during periods of remission.

Child-rearing practices affording either too much or too little relief have a deleterious effect on ego and superego development, tending to decrease tolerance to pain. Fairly tales, myths, and literature unrealistically confirm life's impressions and fantasy's truth. Ubiquitous childhood and adolescent fantasies expressing the wish for magic potions of diverse effects contribute to some eating disturbances and food fads. Parents who expose the child to their own indulgence in health foods, diets, pill taking or drinking—behaviors which originated in their own childhood—continue to exert an important influence and often subtly or actively encourage the child to identify with their habit.

Conscious fantasies about drugs are invariably present during times of illness, emotional distress, and developmental crises. The wish for instant, magic chemical influence on the brain or body is then ubiquitous.

We may safely postulate that everyone has both contributed and been exposed to an extensive "drug lore" which has powerfully influenced, by its pervasive unconscious and preconscious presence, the adolescent's later conscious attitudes concerning drugs and their use.

The psychoanalytic literature on the normal psychology and psychopathology of adolescence is extensive and no attempt will be made to survey it in its entirety. We focus only on those factors especially relevant to our topic. Blos (1962, 1967) and Anna Freud (1958) emphasize the recapitulation in adolescence of the economic and structural conditions of early childhood. Jacobson (1961) describes the turbulent psychic state associated with the process of disorganization and reorganization of psychic structure. In the matrix of anxiety, depression, and physical discomfort engendered by the adolescent process, the regressive reappearance of magical thinking reinvests the concept of drugs with the seductive promise of relief without the need for active mastery and adaptation.

Psychoanalysis of the individual adolescent adumbrates the multitudinous psychodynamic meanings of the symptom of drug use. Exposed to the appropriate drug, the one which fulfills his particular needs, the adolescent may experience temporary relief from distress and conflict. However, this is not a stable adaptation. The healthy adolescent eventually finds the sense of passive enslavement to the drug insufferable, and his progressive wish for development, active mastery, identity, and object relationship more urgent and satisfying than the drug's effect. Drug use will then be reduced to casual, intermittent employment of alcohol or marijuana, as in the manner of the adult. The individuals who either start drugs in early adolescence or who perpetuate conflict resolution with them have already manifested greater regressive disorganization in the course of the adolescent process because of structural deficits originating in early childhood. Intoxication at first offers them a temporary resolution, palliating through chemical alteration of psychic energy equilibria. With chronic use, the ego becomes more compliant to id demands, more passive when confronted by anxiety, and increasingly relies on the drug effect as a participant in its functioning.

Rapaport (1958) stated that: "The ego's autonomy may be defined in terms of ego activity, and impairment of autonomy in terms of ego passivity" (p. 741). He stressed that "the turning of passive experience into active performance is at the core of psychological structure development . . . [and] that the drive and/or stimulus versus structure balance expressed in these conceptions of activity and passivity is at the core of the problems of pathology" (p. 740). His models of passivity refer to nonautonomous ego states dominated and regulated by drive tension, while an autonomous ego actively executes drive discharge in keeping with its controls (p. 739). States of regression result in increased ego passivity vis-à-vis the drives.

Chronic drug use, which we believe always occurs as a consequence of ego pathology, serves in a circular fashion to add to this pathology through an induced but unconsciously sought ego regression.

The dominant conscious motive for drug use is not the seeking of "kicks," but the wish to produce pharmacologically a reduction in distress that the individual cannot achieve by his own psychic efforts. During early childhood, prior to the resolution of the oedipus complex and the formation of the superego, the still incomplete psychic structure requires an ongoing object relationship to maintain psychic homeostasis. The object compensates for the immaturity of the ego until its functions have developed. The adult borderline and psychotic personalities remain to a large extent dependent on their objects to supplement ego and superego functions (Jacobson, 1956, 1964). For many drug users, the drug serves that end. Some severely habituated users can safely become abstinent for long periods of time only in the confines of a regulated, protected milieu. This milieu replaces the drug as the homeostatic factor. Relapse, suicide, or psychotic episodes are the more usual sequelae to prolonged abstinence outside of the protective, anaclitic environment.

The desired subjective state, misleadingly called euphoria, varies from one user to another, while the intoxication produced in the individual user varies with the drug, the dose, the route of administration, the environmental setting, and the intrapsychic state of the user. We view the states of intoxication as chemically induced regressive ego states. Furthermore, we believe that different drugs induce different regressive states that resemble specific phases of early childhood development. The user harbors wishes or tendencies for a particular regressive conflict solution, which the pharmacology of a particular drug may facilitate; the repeated experiences of "satisfaction" establish preference for the specific drug.

LSD and related drugs apparently decrease anticathectic barriers between the psychic systems, producing a loss of ego integrity in varying degrees. Changes in body image and alterations in the cathexes of self and object representations and boundaries lead to subjective experiences of fusion and merger, depersonalization, hallucinations, delusional ideation, and other symptoms (Cole and Katz, 1964; Freedman, 1968; Jacobsen, 1963; Klee, 1963). Some people react with anxiety to those effects, while others seek to repeat them. The pharmacologic effect facilitates the fantasy fulfillment of wishes for union, reunion, and fusion with lost or yearned-for objects. The regressive ego state achieved is suggestive of the transitional period from autism to symbiosis. In this developmental context the LSD "trip" may represent either an attempt to achieve a sense of object relatedness by cracking the stimulus barrier or autistic shell, or an attempt to regain the autistic unity.

Mahler (1968) described the narcissistic regressive phenomenon as a characteristic adaptive pattern in the second half of the first year of life. After the child has established a specific tie to the mother, the memories of a previous state of oneness and closeness to a now absent mother are apparently hypercathected. This attempt to cope with the disorganizing quality of even brief absences is manifested by a diminution of motor activity, an underresponsiveness to external situations, and a reduction in perceptual intake, as if the child must shut out affective and perceptual claims from other sources during the mother's absence.

The state of opium intoxication, known as "being on the nod," is reminiscent of this narcissistic state. Opium and its alkaloid derivatives, as well as some synthetic narcotics, produce a state of quiet lethargy, of decreased involvement with external reality, and a feeling of blissful satiation conducive to hypercathecting fantasies of omnipotence, magical wish fulfillment, and self-sufficiency. A most dramatic effect of drive dampening, experienced subjectively as satiation, may be observed in the loss of libido and aggression and the appetites they serve (Nyswander, 1959; Wikler, 1953).

Amphetamines, methedrine, and cocaine seem to increase the awareness of drive feeling and impulse strength, and to diminish the awareness of fatigue (Kosman and Unna, 1968; Nash, 1962). These drugs also lead to an increase in the feeling of assertiveness, self-esteem, and frustration tolerance, and to a decrease in judgment and accuracy. Motoric restlessness contributes to an illusion of activity, which subserves denial of passivity. This intoxication is reminiscent of Mahler's description of the "practicing period." During the course of the separation-individuation phase, in the middle of the second year, there occurs a massive shift in cathexis from within the symbiotic orbit to the autonomous ego apparatuses. The freely walking toddler, seemingly at the height of his mood elation, appears to be at the peak point in his own magic omnipotence, although he is still to a considerable degree dependent on sharing his mother's powers.

We believe that the amphetamine intoxication and the practicing period are both characterized by a reinforcement of autonomous ego functions which aid in the neutralization of aggressive cathexes of self and object representations. The diminished danger of object loss in these analogous ego states facilitates "activity approach" in object-oriented behavior. Passive aims also appear to be counteracted by the real or illusory chemical increment in drive pressure. These effects complement each other in the regressive state. The paradoxical calming effect of amphetamine on the hyperactive child may be mediated through this mechanism (Conners et al., 1967).

Historically, when alcohol has been proscribed by religious law, marijuana or hashish replaces it. In low doses, alcohol and marijuana seem to have similar effects (McGlothlin and West, 1968; Pfeffer, 1958; Zwerling and Rosenbaum, 1959). Both seem to lessen defenses against drive and impulse discharge. Exteroperceptual and enteroperceptual acuity is accentuated; the subject becomes hyperactive and overtalkative, and is impressed with his profound thoughts and depth of feeling. He experiences changes in his time sense and body image, and may carry sexual and hostile impulses into action. In time, fatigue and sleep follow. With higher doses, hallucinations, excitement, and stupor occur. The younger adolescents experience the effect of alcohol as too diffuse and overwhelming; it raises their fears of losing control. They prefer the softer, more easily controlled effect of marijuana. The behavioral manifestations of both these drugs are a result of the ego and superego inhibitory functions being inactivated. The state of intoxication may resemble different developmental phases. A person with a healthier and more developed ego may be exposed casually to marijuana, as to alcohol, and not suffer disabling regressive consequences.

The infantile neurosis is characterized by regression of both the ego and the drives, causing increased ego compliance to id demands and a consequent diminution of internal conflict (Anna Freud, 1965). The drug user achieves such a state when he is intoxicated with the drug of his choice. Users become expert in knowing what substance will produce what effect. Changes in, or additions to, the preferred drug reflect psychodynamic changes which necessitate different pharmacogenic effects. The psychodynamic change may have been initiated by the previous pharmacogenic effect as well as other factors causing a modification of conflict. Our knowledge of the pharmacogenic effect of specific drugs can thus offer us additional insight into the specific type of conflict situation. Drugs that produce physical dependency add the complicating factor of initiating an artificial drive structure with its own rhythms and periodicity of need, akin to the hunger cycle. Early abstinence phenomena, through a secondary elaboration into fantasy, are experienced as overwhelming threats of destruction or abandonment, impelling a search for the relief-giving drugs.

The intoxicated states produced by other sedative, narcotic, antidepressant and antianxiety drugs will be considered in another communication. Their discussion would excessively lengthen this essay without changing the essence of our thesis. We restrict ourselves to those drugs preferred by the patients in the case reports that follow. We approach drug use as a symptom rather than as a unique clinical syndrome or entity, even in the extreme case of opium addiction, which is traditionally classified as an impulse disorder. In adolescence this symptom, like any other symptom, may be a sign of either a benign or a serious ego dysfunction which has its precursors in pre-adolescent development.

CLINICAL MATERIAL

Case 1: Marijuana

Apparently as an act of defiance against his parents, Dick at age seventeen took an LSD "trip." Although he experienced the characteristic LSD effect of ecstasy and unity with the universe and all things animate and inanimate, Dick did not seek to repeat it. His worried parents, decrying his association with drugs and a drug-using group, immediately sought treatment for him. Dick, highly creative and intelligent, accepted the recommendation for psychoanalysis.

The analyst was immediately cast as a stereotyped hypocritical, pseudoliberal parent. Dick's remarks that the analyst's attempts at clarification were "brainwashings" designed to change him to his mother's specifications foretold that the initial transference would dominantly carry the relationship to her. The mother treated him "like a case" by offering deprecatory, castrating criticisms of his behavior, which he felt were aimed at his masculinity. Against the fantasied attack of the analyst, as against the mother's demand for his submission, Dick could find only two alternatives—to "crack up" or "break away," both associated in his mind with dangerous consequences or hidden satisfactions. He baited his parents to throw him out and fantasied how their deaths would free him.

Dick himself was consistently mocking, sarcastic, and deprecatory, thereby demonstrating his attempt to reverse roles, turn passive into active, and identify with the aggressor. Confirmation of the interpretation that his behavior represented his defense against wishes to be submissive came when he subsequently requested hypnosis and confessed concern about his masculinity and worry over homosexuality. During the past year these worries had intensified, as his attitude to his father underwent a corresponding change: whereas he had previously idealized his father, Dick now felt pity and contempt for him. The transference intensification of his wish to be submissive quickened his need to repudiate it. To reassure himself that the analyst "could not change me," Dick resumed smoking marijuana after six months of abstinence. Consciously, Dick wanted to demonstrate his nonsubmission to the analyst and mother, but his defiant use of the drug also masked his desire to be loved and protected against the dangers of submission to passive wishes; moreover, it was designed to insure an overtly angry closeness.

Dick was soon complaining that nothing was wrong with him, and that he came to treatment only on his mother's insistence. When the analyst reminded Dick that he was in reality free to discontinue the analysis, Dick arrived at the next session "stoned" on marijuana. A school honor conferred that day filled him with forebodings of disaster. He stated that he really deserved punishment, to be "sterilized like an idiot" rather than to "get what I wanted." A series of dreams about sexual encounters with older women left no doubt that "getting what he wanted" stirred oedipal guilt.

It meant getting his way with mother, her sexual submission to him, with father castrated and unable to intervene. Active strivings, success, independence were for him filled with fantasy reprisals and dangers. The psychodynamic meaning of *taking the drug* could now be further understood as representing fulfillment of forbidden, dangerous impulses of the active oedipal constellation, while simultaneously producing a self-inflicted punishment. The incoordination and physical weakness experienced while he was "high" represented castration to him. Later in the analysis he revealed his underlying contempt for the ineffectual and uncoordinated childishness, the castration, of his associates. However, at this point the drug-taking and the crowd helped him feel consciously independent and masculine.

Dick then accused the analyst of planning to commit him to a hospital so that the analyst could get his way. Analysis of this transference fantasy involving the righteous but powerless son, punished by a sadistic, omnipotent father, revealed the underlying negative oedipal desires for a special, close relationship with the analyst-father. Dick knew of three drug-using youths whom the analyst had hospitalized. His own experience in treatment was so different that Dick felt special, which he apprehensively construed as foreboding gratification of passive wishes.

As his passive longings directed at both parents came more to light in the transference, his fear of his passivity increased. His wishes to be committed to a state hospital or cared for by a powerful parent became meaningful to him as derivatives of the wish for castration as the prerequisite for being loved. He now became fearful of his defiant actions, which represented both fulfillment and repudiation of his wishes.

The ensuing period of analytic work dealt with Dick's need to suffer sacrificially. At first Dick felt anxious, then as if relieved of a burden, and finally he developed a stronger, more conscious feeling of alliance with the analyst. Shortly thereafter, during a weekend, he took amphetamines, which he explained as a negating or denying response to his awareness that the analysis was really helping him. Dick feared uncritical agreement with the analyst as the transference derivative of the wish for castration. Silences and missed sessions became frequent until the homosexual conflict underlying the anxiety could be clarified.

Dick's mother, intrigued with the subject of male homosexuality, disparaged her husband as effeminate and Dick as physically unmasculine. Her ambivalent jokes that heterosexuality could be a professional disadvantage to Dick's artistic ambitions led him to believe that his mother would have preferred him to be a girl. He remembered that as a child he had always compared the advantages of being a girl or a boy, vacillating in fantasy between choosing one or the other. His identification with the strong aggressive mother was supplemented by his affectionate relationship with his older admired sister. Insofar as father seemed ' weak," and therefore castrated, he was for Dick a poor model of manliness; but insofar as Dick loved and admired him, father seemed homosexually threatening. Thus Dick's bisexual conflict was enhanced by the inappropriate indentificatory qualities of both parents.

As the analytic work progressed, significant developmental changes occurred. Dick's career choice became more stabilized, and although it was "in opposition" to his parents' wish, it was not made "to be oppositional." He realized one day, after turning down an offer of LSD, that he felt no "need" for drugs or the drug group. He was now critical of what he had formerly espoused and engaged in; and he recognized that what he really wanted to be—successful, independent, masculine—he now could be; that what he had been was the "negative."

Dick revealed that one of the motives behind his missing sessions was the establishment of a relationship with a new girl. This relationship was creative, dynamic, alive, and loving, and he feared that analysis might "invalidate" the changes he felt were occurring. Basically, he had to withdraw temporarily so that he could feel he was changing on his own.

His present girlfriend had urged him to give up drugs, but so had the girl before her. Dick concluded that he gave up the drugs in the context of the new and more profound relationship of which he had previously been incapable. The urge for drugs just disappeared. He was no longer ashamed of having used them, because he now felt he was a different person. The resolution of the infantile tie to the parents and the concomitant modifications of superego and ego ideal dispelled the sense of being "screwed up and involved" with his parents. Instead of experiencing dependent attachment, defiant hostility, and guilt, he could now oppose them without believing that opposition per se was wrong and, somewhat later, agree with them if their arguments appeared justified, without feeling diminished.

The homosexual doubts completely disappeared, as did the self-conscious concern over being mistaken for a homosexual. His self-confidence and creativity blossomed, and his need to idealize certain teachers progressively diminished. However, some of the old battles continued in the analysis, where Dick had to claim priority for insights. Nevertheless, the changed state of affairs, expressed in a dream of playing a duet with his teacher, signified his new ability to work closely with the analyst without fear of danger.

Psychodynamically, all drugs may be *symbolically equivalent,* but in a given patient, at a given time, they are not equally *symbolically effective.* Symbolic effectiveness necessitates that the pharmacogenic effect be consistent with the individual's overall desired conflict solution. Marijuana, which allowed Dick to feel free and exuberant, facilitated the satisfaction of conscious wishes to be assertive and independent. These wishes were usually inhibited by fear and guilt. Although passive trends needed to be warded off, he was in general oriented toward activity.

An individual may try many drugs until he finds one that relieves, satisfies, or pleases, by producing a yearned-for, but still unknown, total subjective effect. At the moment of discovery, for example, the future morphinist may say he feels "normal" for the first time, even though objectively he is nauseated, itchy, and lethargic. The marijuana initiate may say he no longer is "bored," but feels "loose and comfortable socially." When met by chance or design, the drug then is preferred. Previously conflicting libidinal and aggressive, ego, superego, and reality factors are all integrated into the effect of "satisfaction."

That Dick found and remained with marijuana and did not return to LSD or amphetamines is of crucial importance. Marijuana's pharmacogenic effect was consistent with his overall desired solution, and "drug use" itself stood for defiant action and independence. At different times, the drug symbolically represented phallus, breast, the incorporated object of the powerful mother, or the object over whom he exerted mastery and which on other occasions dominated him. Although the pharmacologic effects of marijuana and amphetamine potentiated their psychodynamic significance, this augmentation was not a primary prerequisite in Dick's case. Because he was basically equipped with an adequate ego and had developed fairly normally, Dick's need for sustained pharmacogenic effects was minimal. The effective curtailment of this factor by his intactness allows the psychodynamic significance of the drugs and their use to be demonstrated with greater clarity.

We contend that at the point of a heightened struggle with his dreaded feelings of passivity and while he was temporarily fearful of action, the change to amphetamine was motivated by the hope that his feelings of strength and activity would be enhanced. This transient drug choice was determined by and consistent with the altered inner struggle. Marijuana, LSD, or opium would have been inconsistent. Marijuana would have been too anxiety provoking by weakening defenses and facilitating the now feared actions. LSD would have led to fusion, an experience counter to his wishes for separateness, identity, and active reality-oriented satisfactions. Opium would have enhanced the feeling of satisfaction of the feared passive trends.

The analysis enabled Dick to detach himself from his parents, modify his superego and ego ideal in the direction of greater maturity, achieve a satisfactory ego identity, and establish a meaningful heterosexual relationship. With these achievements the negative identity of the "beat" drug user became superfluous and was discarded.

Case 2: Autopolypharmacy (Multiple Drug Choice)

Jay, a tall, articulate eighteen-year-old, was referred after he had been expelled from college for drug use. With rare exceptions during his nine months of thrice weekly vis-à-vis psychotherapy, Jay was continuously under the influence of various drugs. He smoked marijuana, preferably as hashish, throughout the day. LSD was used every two to three days in doses approaching 1000 mcgm, intravenously on occasion, for more than a hundred "trips." He also took STP, mescaline, DMT, and psilocybin. He used amphetamines, both orally and intravenously, in daily dosages of hundreds of milligrams, occasionally in combination with cocaine. Although he feared and avoided heroin for its dependence-producing quality, he enjoyed smoking opium occasionally, believing he would not become "dependent."

Jay spoke freely, and with obvious exhibitionistic intent to shock. He remembered his first "high" on marijuana at the age of sixteen as intensely gratifying and as relieving his chronic depression. "I had been looking at the world through dark glasses and now everything had a meaning. Pot gave me a vast playground right between my ears, a combination book, stereo system, prophet, and slide projector kaleidescope. . . . Drugs are instant mommy."

Initially, Jay did not object to treatment, but the frustration of his need for immediate satisfaction led to an intensification of conflict, laying bare his psychopathology. His extraordinary intolerance to stress and displeasure, his poorly controlled impulse discharge, his sporadically blurred distinction between self and object, and his delight in regression confirmed the impression of his borderline status.

Jay's disturbed functioning originated in disorganizing experiences of separations and object losses in early childhood, which led to regressive attempts at restitution and a related inability to cope with increments of drive energy. Following the death of their mother, when Jay was three and one half and his brother two years of age, the two children were exposed to a long, traumatizing series of foster homes. Essentially fatherless while boarding, they re-entered his life when he remarried and lost him again with his subsequent divorces. Jay would mockingly talk of "mommy number two," "three," and "four." "Mommy number three" was a screaming grimacing fury who terrorized him. In her frequent attacks of rage, she would dash her own small daughters against a wall, or drag the two brothers into the house by sinking her long fingernails into their gums. Hoping his father would protect him, Jay would climb a tree to await his return. The father, in the forlorn hope of decreasing his wife's vindictiveness, would side with her and punish Jay again.

A strong and protective closeness grew between Jay and his brother, and Jay would often interpose himself to spare the younger boy punishment. Together they would escape into a shared fantasy of a feces planet where social status was determined by the quality and quantity of excretory products. Repeated attacks by Earthlings were repulsed by fecal missiles. Sadomasochistic elements prevailed in their games in which the winner would inflict a predetermined pain. This agreed-upon and measured predictability represented an attempt to master the uncontrollable outbursts of "mommy number three."

After three years of violence and intimidation, the father obtained a divorce and established the first independent household with the boys. This lasted for six years until his last marriage to "mommy number four" when Jay was in high school. Jay grudgingly conceded the positive "motherly" quality of this woman, who "helped my father turn from masturbation to intercourse."

The loss of his mother at age three and the repeated subsequent losses, the sadistic behavior of the remaining parent and surrogates all contributed to Jay's immature level of object relationship, his anal sadomasochistic fixation, and heavily weighted his orientation to submission and passive aims. The increased instinctual pressures of revived oral and oedipal wishes in adolescence were augmented by the advent of "mommy number four." A flickering of the positive oedipal flame aroused old feelings of abandonment by women, and Jay regressed. The negative oedipal dangers and the rage at being abandoned by his father who formed an attachment to a new wife were implicit in Jay's reactive revengeful and jealous behavior to his father. Jay consciously wished to drive his father to suicide or to insanity.

Numerous dreams dealing with death, suicide, drugs, and memories of his dead mother reflected Jay's strongly felt, thinly disguised, symptomatically expressed wishes for reunion with the dead mother. These urgent yearnings motivated his impregnation of an older girl while he was at college. Going off to college had recapitulated the loss theme, as did brief absences of the analyst.

The conflictual situation of yearning for attachment to a woman contained on the one hand the danger of fusion with a dead object and of loss of a live one, and on the other the threat of castration, being devoured, or sadistically attacked for achieving his aims. Although he was afraid of the re-establishment of the mother-child relationship with new objects, his relationship to his brother, and to some extent that to his father, was a prototype of closeness that was more tolerable, despite the threat of homosexuality. In the transference, the use of marijuana allowed for closeness to the analyst, whom Jay wished to seduce to smoking, "turning him on." This recapitulated Jay's seducing his brother to smoke pot.

Drugs, the only objects Jay really desired, were preferable to masturbation, intercourse, and relationships: "You can take drugs when you want, but girls are a bother." He experienced intercourse as a primitive excretory function requiring a receptacle, felt extremely hostile to the girl afterward, and anxiously wished she would disappear. Amphetamines curbed his murderous rage and made him feel "in love" with the whole world without danger of closeness to anyone. Intoxication seemed to diminish aggression and its dangerous consequences, enabled him to have intercourse without the desire to hurt the girl, and allowed him to concentrate on her body and his own sensations. During a hashish and LSD orgy, Jay became transfixed in rapt, absorbed gazing at a girl's breast. He visually drank the breast in, experiencing merger with it. Jay's comment was: "Mind sex is better than body sex." Occasional fantasies of being a girl or homosexual could be tolerated without anxiety while intoxicated, whereas allusions to homosexuality while he was sober made it imperative to affirm his heterosexuality in repeated coitus.

LSD permitted the wishes for fusion with the dead mother to find satisfaction in the regressive illusion. However, he would also regularly sink his fingernails into his gums, repeating the childhood experiences with "mommy number three." In his jargon, he "grooved on the blood." Overt masochistic fantasies, in which he could be the sadistic object or the masochistic subject, were recurrently and gleefully experienced. Overwhelming battering assaults on his mind and body, designed to destroy his mind or self or object, were enacted through the use of drugs designed to "blow his mind."

If his only aim had been fusion with the dead mother and blissful reunion with her, he would have more actively sought an opiate. His conscious fear of the enslaving, dependency-producing quality of heroin reflected his fear of these wishes. With all his drugs, he avoided physical dependence; and to confirm his illusion of his active mastery over the object's leaving and returning, he would deliberately withdraw himself from each drug from time to time. One day he may stop opposing his wish for heroin, the drug most feared but most consistent with his wish for peaceful rest.

The regressive disorganizing effect of the chronic drug use became increasingly apparent, and Jay felt more and more the passive victim or object of the drug's activity. He complained that LSD and hashish were generating his ideas and that the amphetamines were doing his talking. To counteract the effects of LSD and hashish, he took increasingly larger doses of intravenously injected amphetamine in order to complete his college assignments.

Jay sought drug effects to reduce anxiety, curb aggression, enhance self-esteem, decrease depression, counter loneliness, facilitate action, express frustration, dissipate boredom, establish a sense of relationship. The drugs exerted their influence on each psychic system by carrying out the functions usually performed by the ego or the mother in the early years of life. Symbolically, drugs were truly "instant mommy," each drug representing the object he could control, from whom he could gain strength and power, whose loss could be predictably anticipated, and with whom reunion was assured.

Jay's psychic disorganization initially motivated the search for the magic potion which would produce relief of his distress. When drugs aggravated his pathology, he searched, with escalating urgency, for combinations of chemicals that would produce an equilibrium usually achieved through psychic conflict solutions. In the severely ill, resort to neurotic defenses alone may not be sufficient to resolve conflict. Drugs are the chemical aid to Jay's psychic homeostasis, and it is doubtful whether he ever will be able to live entirely without them.

His case illustrates the primary seeking of pharmacogenic effects, in contrast to Dick, where the psychodynamic element was primary. In both cases, however, the drug choices were governed by internally consistent psychodynamic-pharmacogenic reasons.

Case 3: Amphetamine

Miriam, a twenty-one-year-old student, has been a habitual drug user for seven years, with a definite preference for amphetamines for the past five. She took 40 to 60 mg. by mouth daily. Her symptom of drug-taking occurred in the matrix of a borderline psychotic reaction with paranoid and depressive features.

Miriam's weary and impatient mother, the youngest of three sisters, had married to escape the family's impoverished circumstances. Her chronic menometrorrhagia, beginning in late adolescence, eventually led to a hysterectomy when Miriam was seven years of age. Miriam had been aware, perhaps since that time, of her mother's excessive drinking habits and use of "pep" pills to maintain mood elevation. Overtly despising her husband, the mother was too dependent to act upon her frequent threats of divorce. Extremely ambivalent to Miriam, who complained of her mother's unpredictable mood changes, the mother openly resented her daughter's attachment to the father.

Miriam's father, an extremely shy, isolated, and inhibited man, was the frustrated, unhappy employee of his own vituperatively contemptuous father. He met his wife when she was his father's secretary, and often voiced the complaint that he lost his intellectual life following his marriage. He had had two severe depressive illnesses, the first during his wife's pregnancy with Miriam, and the second ten years later. His overinvolvement with Miriam, to whom he turned despairingly in retreat from his wife's abuse, had strong unconscious incestuous overtones.

Miriam's birth, three and a half years after the parents' marriage, had been "a thirty-six-hour ordeal which required two months of convalescence." Cared for by a nurse for the first three months, she was described as lively, healthy, smiling, and playful, but impatient at the very strict feeding schedule.

At fifteen months, severe functional diarrhea developed shortly after the parents returned from a three weeks' absence. At thirty months, Miriam would play by herself at the periphery of a group of children. Around that time, she was taken to a resort hotel, where she clung to her mother, refusing to leave the room except at mealtime. Miriam began to have a sleeping disturbance, especially when the mother was away for the evening. When the latter returned, Miriam would still be awake, silent, but unhappy.

At the age of four Miriam was hospitalized overnight for a tonsillectomy. Her mother did not think Miriam was apprehensive either before or after surgery. However, Miriam's thumb sucking brought on a hemorrhage of the tonsillectomy site, necessitating rehospitalization and cautery.

Miriam would become agitated during her mother's recurrent hospitalization for vaginal bleeding. When the mother became pregnant again, the family employed a housekeeper who remained with them until Miriam was five. The pattern of withdrawal to the periphery was noted in nursery school and kindergarten. She would sit quietly in class, sucking her thumb, apparently oblivious to her surroundings. Despite her shyness, she formed a friendship with a girl which lasted until she was twelve years old.

At the age of six, Miriam went to summer camp where she frequented the infirmary with somatic complaints. The alternation of extreme shyness with provocative restlessness was observed in school as well as in camp. In second grade, she began to manifest behavioral difficulties. Discipline at home was inconsistent, and she soon learned to manipulate her parents. Miriam would writhe on the floor in feigned agony when her father struck her, and cover her body with her mother's cosmetics, presenting herself to mother as bruised by father.

A psychiatrist, who began to treat her at age seven, diagnosed her as a "schizoid personality," unable to relate to more than one person, negativistic, albeit alert, bright, and inquisitive. This treatment ended twenty months later because of her opposition to it. She stopped her thumb sucking at age ten or eleven, but then kept her mouth covered to conceal her imagined "bad breath." At that time she also began habitually to play with a wisp of hair. Her only friend moved away when Miriam was twelve years old. Unable to befriend others, Miriam wrote letters to herself as if they came from friends.

On psychiatric advice, the parents placed Miriam in a residential school in the ninth grade. This led to striking improvement in her self-confidence and socialization. She did well academically and was elected to the National Honor Society. As she became involved with boys, her relationship with the housemother simultaneously took on homosexual overtones. At age fourteen, she first used terpin hydrate to counter apathy and bolster self-confidence; later she also tried phenobarbital, marijuana, and various tranquilizers.

Disappointed by rejections from prestige colleges and dreading the women's college where she was accepted, Miriam began to rely on her mother's dexedrine pills to combat her moods. As her depression deepened, she became unkempt and agitated. A week after her departure for college her parents refused her pleas to return home, and Miriam attempted suicide with terpin hydrate. The father denied the severity of her difficulties, rejecting the diagnosis of schizophrenia and prevailing in his insistence that she remain on campus. The freshman year was a frantic, drugged one.

Miriam medicated herself with amphetamines in increasing dosage, while receiving antidepressants from a psychiatrist. She became promiscuous in a search for "closeness." Typically, she did well academically, despite numerous infractions of the rules.

Home for the summer at age nineteen, Miriam flaunted her drug use and promiscuity, infuriating her mother by also excluding her from prolonged philosophical discussions with the father. Another psychiatrist found no gross evidence of thinking disorder or break with reality, but noted her semisomnolent state and vacillation between elation and depression. At the end of the summer, she was put in a closed hospital and withdrawn from all medication, with considerable improvement.

Miriam was resentful of her allegedly unjust incarceration, and after five months was transferred to a more open institution, where she showed some further improvement of the earlier more florid psychotic conditions, but soon resumed amphetamines and marijuana. Her involvement in groups was minimal and her only relationships were sexually promiscuous. After five months Miriam left against advice, having convinced her father of her wish to resume college studies near home. On her return home at the age of twenty and a half, she entered psychotherapy on a thrice weekly basis.

Miriam's early history is strongly suggestive of a regressive symbiotic reaction during her second and third year. Repeated experiences of frustration, deprivation, and separation in the relationship to a depressed and punitive mother were followed by the father's depression at the birth of her sister. Pervasive oral concerns and a damaged, chaotic sense of self remain central to her difficulties. Her capacity for consistent object relationship is vitiated by a tendency toward narcissistic withdrawal when her needs for symbiotic closeness are frustrated by the object. Angry, impulsive behavior often supervenes.

Amphetamine has been her drug of choice for over five years. Without the drug, she feels bored, lonely, empty, and shy; with amphetamine she feels self-confident, able to think and concentrate, and closer to people. Miriam rejects heroin: "I don't want to withdraw, to sit back and nod, or get away from feeling. . . . I take a drug to cope with life, to be productive, and get recognition. I'm a shy extrovert, and people come to me when I'm on dex because I look happy, I'm not up tight and my persecution complex is gone. I get inspired and enthusiastic, I can dream up and write term papers, I can think and concentrate."

Marijuana frightens her because of the unpredictability of its effect. It also heightens her self-consciousness and ideas of reference, and she has experienced hallucinations with it. Her fear of loss of control from smoking "pot" could be overcome only in the presence of a trusted male. "Ever-reliable" amphetamine, however, allows her to feel less dependent upon the object in the primitive and need-fulfilling mode, and consequently more capable of intimacy. DMT and hashish cause panic states, and she is terrified to try LSD lest she lose control.

It is fascinating to consider the similarities between the subjective effects of amphetamine and the psychic state of the toddler in the "practicing period" of the separation-individuation phase, the time when Miriam's psychopathology first became noticeable. Theoretically, the amphetamine effect may be conceptualized as curbing unneutralized aggression, resulting in a diminution of aggressive cathexis of the self representation. This diminution of aggressive cathexis would also diminish narcissistic vulnerability and enhance self-esteem. Decreased aggressive cathexis of object representations and diminished aggression against objects reduce the anxiety stemming from annihilation fantasies and projected aggression. Another effect of amphetamine—that of promoting the autonomous ego functions such as secondary process thinking, perception, and memory—might also stem from this postulated influence on aggression.

For the several months that Miriam remained drug-free, she was preoccupied with yearnings for amphetamine. Soon the pattern of drug dependence and promiscuity re-emerged and hospitalization became necessary once more.

Case 4: Alcohol

Alexa, a twenty-six-year-old unmarried college graduate, residing with her parents, has been drinking alcohol since age fifteen. The degree of her immaturity, manifest in an extremely low tolerance for frustration, anxiety, or other painful affects, her marked impulsivity, dependence on magical thinking, and terror of abandonment place her diagnostically in the borderline category.

Alexa feels split into two selves, a "good" observing, controlling Alexa opposite a "bad" impulsive wild Alexa (Kernberg, 1967). In moments of frustration when mounting anger could produce a temper tantrum, for example, in a traffic jam, the "good Alexa" could watch with detachment and control her temper through thinking, "This can't happen to me, only to 'bad Alexa.'" However, with greater frustration, e.g., in connection with the loss of a boyfriend whom she had alienated, "bad Alexa" would gain dominance and have a temper tantrum, which represented the attack on object and self.

When she began to drink, she first was aware that the "good Alexa" had disappeared and that she felt no opposition to her impulses. She felt strangely unconflicted and "intact," "not split." As her state of intoxication increased, she became maudlin and screamed out for "my baby" (an illegitimate pregnancy that had been terminated by an abortion). She also voiced wishes to "live among the animals," a statement that afforded some insight into her sober life interests. She was an expert equestrienne devoted to her horse, and an indefatigable nurse for her aged dog.

Violence inevitably erupted as she assaulted anyone near her with literal murderous intent. Sexual incidents were frequent. In these sexual and aggressive discharges she endangered herself as well as others. Eventually she became suffused with gratifying sensations of envelopment in a pillow of oblivion, and the sense of loneliness and depression dissolved. The representation of the oral triad and the fusion with the part object were unmistakable. The end point was stupor. After she awoke sober and amnesic, "good Alexa" amusedly listened to friends' accounts of her drunken behavior. Remorse or embarrassment were not in evidence, "for it happened to someone else, the bad Alexa."

The "hangover" was welcomed as a companion which, staying with her for a predictable time, would help orient her back toward reality concerns. Her description of the hangover headache as an "it" or "something" suggested that it functioned as a transitional phenomenon in facilitating her return from the regressive merger-fusion experience in the state of extreme intoxication, back to the imperfect separation-individuation state while she was sober. In mid-adolescence, approximately at the time when she began to drink, Alexa reverted to her former attachment to stuffed animals, which she took to bed when she was beset by nightmares or hypnagogic hallucinations of being murderously attacked by her mother.

Alexa talked about other drugs with depreciation and horror, stressing their unsatisfying qualities. She was terrified of LSD and never took it. The LSD intoxication which was repeatedly described to her resembled too closely an exaggeration of her own sober state with its split in self representation, tendencies toward depersonalization, and confusion of real and unreal. She rejected marijuana as insufficiently productive of the agitation and freedom "to act," which she found in the middle stages of her alcoholic intoxication. Her freedom to act was not the same as the marijuana user's freedom from control, but rather resulted from an elimination of part of the self. This led to a paradoxical sense of intactness, of "wholeness" which permitted conflict-free discharge. The desire for such discharge was a persistent theme. Opium was depreciated because it diminished action and activity. Being "on the nod" was not the "oblivion" which she achieved from alcohol. That which a better integrated woman experiences in coital orgasm in the context of a meaningful object relationship, Alexa could only approximate, solitarily, and in pathological intensity, in alcoholic intoxication. Other drugs might produce one or another regressive ego state, but not the desired, fluid sequential flow which began with the elimination of the split in self representation and ended with the undoing of separation-individuation, merger, and oblivion. Alexa's motto might well read: *"In vino unitas."*

Case 5: Alcohol

David, at fourteen years of age, entered analysis for symptoms related to an overidentification with his aggressive mother and fears stemming from his warded-off but desired active, independent, heterosexual goals. Witnessing his parents' sadomasochistic relationship, David experienced his father as helpless and unable to control the mother except through momentary threats. The mother's deprecating, insulting, hostile, and independent attitude to the father demeaned him in David's eyes. David hated his father's submission and feared for his own masculinity, for "if my father can't stand up to a woman, how can I?" He felt in awe of his mother's power and endangered by it. "If I'm to be loved by mother, I must be the way she wants me—like my sister, or herself, or a girl or woman. If I'm like my father who is kinder and more rational, and I do respect him, I'll get murdered!"

Defiance became David's means of fighting back, inviting punishment as his passive-masochistic expression of wishes to be loved, to be a man, and to retain some relationship with the parents. At times his overt behavior represented his alliance with his mother, an identification with the aggressor, in which he subordinated his love for his father. In this respect David felt guilty in relation to his father because David was then as disparaging as the mother. He wanted to please the father, but to do so exposed him to his mother's anger and "cutting tongue." "If I'm not with her, she feels I'm against her." At other times his behavior represented an identification with the "victim" (his father) and demonstrated an image of himself as "a weak man put down by women."

In the transference, his vacillation crystallized around the image of the analyst as "the strong man mother can't control or destroy." David's wish to become the analyst's son and thereby to insure his masculinity contained his wishes for a loving relationship with his father. His wish to show his love, affection, and identification with his father and analyst quickly intensified, simultaneously increasing his fear of his mother's fantasied retaliation, castration. This led to an obsessional state of tension and immobilization.

In this setting, he had a dream about "being in a bar, drinking, seducing women, spending money, and being real friendly with the bartender." Associating to the bartender, he mentioned his father as the social host at home, and the analyst as the "man of the bar" —like a judge who metes out justice. David recognized the fulfillment of his wishes for closeness to the father and analyst, and his desire to "become a man," but, he said, "I just can't do it alone. I need alcohol to give me courage!"

During the weekend, he went to his father's liquor chest, and got drunk. He became overly talkative, excited, and determined to confront his parents. He told his mother "off," and then told his father that he loved him and really wanted to be the kind of man his father expected. He kissed his father, and with a "contemptuous look at my mother," left the room and then passed out.

After he sobered up, he was aware of a variety of emotions. He felt guilty toward his mother because of his outburst and rejection of her; his taking father's possession, the liquor; and drinking, which also represented "being a man." He felt embarrassed by his declaration of love for his father. Yet, he also had a feeling of satisfaction because he was loved and nurtured: "They carried me to bed, called a doctor, and worried about me."

In spite of the guilt, remorse, and shame, he felt satisfaction at having accomplished his aim. However, the chaotic feeling of loss of control evoked strong anxiety: "I felt like a murderer with my outburst, and a sissy or homosexual for showing my love. I didn't even know all the time what I was doing, and if I did I couldn't control it. It was like being crazy, insane." He was relieved when he passed out into peaceful oblivion.

The fear of being out of control and overwhelmed by impulses in the drunken state outweighed the gratifications and made him resolve never to touch alcohol again. He adhered to this resolve for three years, until eighteen when drinking became legal.

However, two further exacerbations of his conflict during his sixteenth year induced him to turn to marijuana as a magical aid to its resolution. Marijuana was less disorganizing, left him in control, and gave him more satisfaction than alcohol. His guilt deterred him from continuing with it, and the psychodynamic significance of the use of the drug could be analyzed. At nineteen in college, he occasionally took marijuana as a magic means to overcome sexual inhibitions in his ongoing "battle to be a man."

Case 6: Alcohol

Psychodynamically akin to David, John at age sixteen resorted to alcohol to facilitate the discharge of drives held in check by excessive neurotic fear and guilt. His history differs from David's in that a delinquent tendency had been in evidence since age ten, when a brief episode of stealing, truancy, and fighting had occurred. His analysis, which started at age nineteen, revealed his "delinquency" as the symptomatic expression of aggression against his lawyer father, the self-incurred punishment for his guilt, and his passive wish to be loved. The tendency of this pattern to re-emerge in different forms characterized John's functioning. A brilliant student, he "dropped out" of college during a resurgence of his conflict, and this event led to his analysis.

His initial exposures to alcohol, at age sixteen, led to his stealing his father's car, then his brother's motorcycle, and speeding along highways endangering himself and others. On one occasion he completely undressed himself and stood by the side of a road waiting to get "picked up." His father's absences seemed to be the stimulus for his getting drunk. This came to light in the transference when weekends and holidays away from the analyst occasioned rage and retaliatory feelings toward the analyst.

Alcohol frightened John, however, because of the wildly agitated and disturbed behavior it produced. He echoed David in complaining: "I could have become a murderer, or homosexual, or killed myself, and I couldn't even remember what I had done!" As with David, these consequences outweighed the satisfactions of alcohol, and marijuana was substituted.

Both David and John were oriented to action in general, but feared the consequences. Alcohol diminished their inhibitions, restraints, and defenses to an excessive degree, and both youngsters preferred the similar but softer effect of marijuana. John's desperate attempts to "feel" and to achieve masculine goals eliminated opium as a drug of choice, while LSD would have been too disorganizing.

Case 7: Opium Addiction

Becoming increasingly apprehensive that he would be arrested for possession of narcotics, Gerald, at age twenty-one, sought treatment to control his addiction to heroin. This had been his drug of choice uninterruptedly since he was eighteen. One attempt at detoxification had failed about a year and a half prior to his seeking psychotherapeutic help.

The initial interviews were filled with accounts of his diverse "habits" and feeling of humiliation because he was unable to oppose any of his urges. Although he discoursed on his "erratic sleeping habits," "bad eating habits," and "poor work and study habits," he soon got to his "sexual habits." While he talked freely and interchangeably about his "drug habit" and "sexual habit," he seemed to be unaware of the link between them. He complained of a "masturbation habit," which filled him with feelings of disgust, and a humiliating inability to have intercourse. He would achieve orgasm only by means of "freakish" activities with the girl, by which he meant cunnilingus and fellatio, mutual masturbation, and mutual anal penetration. He related his failure to achieve a normal sexual adjustment to an experience at age fifteen when he had been unable to "perform for the girl I loved." At that time he sought marijuana, hoping it would help him overcome what he felt was shyness. In this he did not succeed. He did, however, at that time, indulge in mutual masturbation with a male friend. Those events both seemed to confirm and stimulate his ever-present conscious fears of and conflicts about homosexuality and heterosexuality.

Although he had always wished to become a musician, the thought of the years of study and practice necessary deterred him. In fact, working toward any future goal filled him with an overwhelming sense of frustration. As a young adolescent between eleven and fourteen years, he daydreamed excessively of possessing "big fancy cars with high-powered motors, flashy clothes, and rolls of money to attract women." These daydreams attempted to deny the reality of his feeling timid, asocial, and devoid of physical vigor and material resources that his father and ten-year-older brother possessed. He avoided physical contact sports as well as fights. He developed a "gift of gab" into a "gift of con" whereby he could "influence anyone I wanted to do what I wanted." After he started stealing to support his drug use, he coerced his comrades to do the "dirty work." At first he limited his stealing to the home, but soon branched out into the community.

Gerald related his "black sheep" development to a traumatic event at age three. At that time he scalded himself and incurred second and third degree burns on his arms and torso. Following months of immobilization, skin grafting, and convalescence, he retained a marked fear of being hurt or punished. He became very intolerant to pain and frequently complained about physical ills, which his mother immediately "medicated." Associations to this material left no doubt that he had experienced the reality events of that period as the punishment for and dangerous consequences of his active strivings. His retreat to the passive mode was perpetuated and encouraged by the satisfactions of his dependency needs. An overly punitive father realistically aggravated Gerald's neurotic fears of activity or competition.

Gerald was the youngest of three siblings. He experienced his older brother as a loving person, who sat with him when he was ill and who later was paternalistically protective. But he was also jealous of his brother and a five-year-older sister because "their intactness" reminded him of being "damaged and deprived." He recalled that during latency he had had temper tantrums in which he attacked his mother, hurt himself, and broke toys. During early adolescence he became gradually aware of his inability to compete with his father and brother; he saw himself in the position of "another woman" in the family, his needs being supplied by the "men."

He could talk about many aspects of his life, but merely mentioning his burn and scars brought on shame, embarrassment, fear, and guilt. "What would a girl think if she saw those, and my weak arm? She would be disgusted, want to vomit, and she would be scared to death. What an ugly sight! That's what I would think if I were the girl." His greatest pleasure would be to have a girl caress the scars. "It would be worse if I were a girl with scars, because I can't go near anyone who has them."

During middle adolescence, he could not decide whether to be "straight and conservative" or "offbeat, flashy, and drive cars." He often thought of suicide when confronted by his impotence and wished "I was a colored male and potent." He often wanted to carry a gun. "It gives me a feeling of power, makes people afraid of me. Gun is my symbol of maturity and power; every kid wants a gun." His actual body damage facilitated his identification with the "castrated," mother and sister. His physical weakness and fear of activity also contributed to the pervasive passive orientation which led to the development of masochistic traits.

Gerald's characteristic mode of defense was recourse to fantasy in which he magically reversed painful and humiliating reality. However, his intact reality testing intruded into his fantasy satisfactions. Heroin changed this experience: "When I was clean [preaddiction], my daydreams were short and always interrupted. With horse [heroin] it was movies all day long! . . . With my first joypop of horse, I felt normal for the first time in my life, and I knew this was it."

On heroin, Gerald would dream and fantasy that he possessed everything he wanted: cars, money, women, and potency. A feeling of contentment accompanied his awareness that he experienced neither yearnings for sexual activity nor anger at the thwarting world. "I'm not afraid of sex when I'm on; maybe if I don't have the desire I don't have to be afraid. Without drugs I have to do things and I'm not successful." Even his realistic activity was a living out of denial in fantasy, for as the con man who persuaded others to accept his falsehoods as truth, he momentarily realized his narcissistic omnipotence.

Gerald did not like marijuana, alcohol, or amphetamines: "because they made me mean, and I would get into fights or physical contacts that made me want to vomit. Anything I wanted, peace, normality, no desires, went on in the nod. It isn't real, I know, but it is real in my mind."

In the undrugged state, his awareness of reality, his fears and drive pressures enhanced his sense of castration, failure, and impotence. He could feel intact only while he was drugged. Wishes for potency in the form of houses, cars, money, and wishes for a beautiful body to attract females, for a penis to be a father or lover, for a gun to be male and competitive all found satisfaction in the drugged state. With opium, he recaptured the narcissistic bliss of intactness and closeness to the medicating mother (Niederland, 1965).

SUMMARY

In our formulations of the structure of the symptom of drug use, we emphasize that the choice of a specific drug derives from the mutual interaction of the psychodynamic meaning and pharmacogenic effect of the drug with the particular conflicts and defects in a person's psychic structure throughout his development. For this reason, drugs are not as indiscriminately chosen or as freely interchangeable as superficial observation might indicate. When changes in drug preferences occur, as they do, they indicate that internal psychodynamic changes have occurred.

The adolescent struggle with the biological upsurge of the drives and the regressive resurgence of archaic childhood fears and wishes temporarily threaten the loss of social adaptation, sublimations, rationality, and maturity. Therefore, the adolescent is particularly vulnerable to drugs holding out the promise of magic alleviation of his distress.

The drug user's reaction to the pharmacological properties of the drug—in terms of the degree and nature of the induced regressive experience sought—affords us insight into the extent and nature of his psychopathology. The chronic need for the pharmacogenic effect, subjectively experienced as craving, is a consequence of fixation or regression to pregenital levels of functioning. The more urgent the need for continuing pharmacogenic effects, the more severe is the pathology. Borderline and psychotic patients rely on drugs in this way to shore up and supply controls and gratifications which adequate structuralization provides unaided. Drugs act as an energic modifier and redistributor, and as a structural prosthesis.

The states of intoxication produced by different drugs have certain resemblances to specific developmental phases of early childhood. LSD states were compared with the autistic phase in the sense that LSD produces a toxic psychosis the phenomenology of which resembles "cracking the autistic shell." The dreamy lethargy, the blissful satiation, and the fantasies of omnipotence, experienced while "on the nod" with opiates, have similarities with the narcissistic regressive phenomenon of the symbiotic state. The effects of amphetamines are reminiscent of the "practicing period" of the separation-individuation phase.

Each drug in sufficient dosage will invariably and universally produce a specific state of intoxication, irrespective of individual psychopathology. However, the latter determines the person's reaction to these pharmacogenic effects. When an individual finds an agent that chemically facilitates his pre-existing preferential mode of conflict solution, it becomes his drug of choice. The drug induces a regressive state, but the drug taker supplies the regressive tendencies. The fixations and regressions that occurred prior to drug-taking and the unconscious wish to regress to a specific developmental level are among the determinants of drug choice.

These regressive tendencies are opposed by fears of loss of control and by progressive wishes for activity and mastery of both inner and outer worlds. Anxiety erupts when intoxication regressively transforms actively directed ego functions to passive ego experiences. Thus, both alcohol and marijuana in low dosages seem to lower the barrier against the discharge of drives and impulses. However, this effect of alcohol is experienced by the younger adolescents as releasing too much drive, leading to fears of loss of control. They prefer the shorter acting, less diffuse, and more controllable marijuana. The intoxications produced by alcohol and marijuana may be correlated with different developmental phases. The healthier adolescent who experiments with drugs will eventually reject his enslavement to drugs which conflicts sharply with his progressive wishes; he will then use alcohol or marijuana only casually and intermittently, in the manner of the healthier adult. Those who persist in taking drugs are persons who have suffered significant regressive disorganization and faulty structuralization in early childhood, that is, prior to taking drugs in adolescence. For this reason only the more disturbed individuals will seek the continued effects of opiates, amphetamines, or LSD. Only alcohol or marijuana can be employed casually without severe regressive consequences, although their continued, extensive use also reflects severe psychopathology.

430   H. WIEDER—E. H. KAPLAN

Physical dependency and abstinence phenomena add the complication of an artificial drive structure. Secondarily elaborated into fantasies threatening abandonment and destruction, these impulses renew the search for the drug.

Blos, P. (1962), *On Adolescence*. New York: Free Press of Glencoe.
—— (1967), The Second Individuation Process of Adolescence. *This Annual*, 22:162-186.
Cole, J. O. & Katz, M. M. (1964), The Psychotominetic Drugs. *J. Amer. Med. Assn.*, 187:758-761.
Conners, C. K., Eisenberg, L., & Barcai, A. (1967), Effect of Dextroamphetamine on Children. *Arch. Gen. Psychiat.*, 17:478-485.
Freedman, D. X. (1968), On the Use and Abuse of LSD. *Arch. Gen. Psychiat.*, 18:331-347.
Freud, A. (1958), Adolescence. *This Annual*, 13:255-278.
—— (1965), *Normality and Pathology in Childhood*, New York: International Universities Press.
Jacobsen, E. (1963), The Clinical Pharmacology of the Hallucinogens. *Clin. Pharmacol. Ther.*, 4:480-503.
Jacobson, E. (1956), Interaction between Psychotic Partners. In: *Neurotic Interaction in Marriage*, ed. V. W. Eisenstein, New York: Basic Books, pp. 125-134.
—— (1961), Adolescent Moods and the Remodeling of Psychic Structures in Adolescence. *This Annual*, 16:164-183.
—— (1964), *The Self and the Object World*. New York: International Universities Press.
Kernberg, O. (1967), Borderline Personality Organization. *J. Amer. Psa. Assn.*, 15:641-685.
Klee, G. D. (1963), *Arch. Gen. Psychiat.*, 8:461-474. Lysergic Acid Diethylamide (LSD-25) and Ego Functions.
Kosman, M. E. & Unna, K. R. (1968), Effects of Chronic Administration of the Amphetamines and Other Stimulants on Behavior. *Clin. Pharmacol. Ther.*, 9:240-254.
Krystal, H. & Raskin, H. A. (1966), Impaired Ego Function: A Primary Factor in Addiction. Read at the Annual Meeting, American Psychoanalytic Association.
Mahler, M. S. (1968), *On Human Symbiosis and the Vicissitudes of Individuation, Volume I: Infantile Psychosis*. New York: International Universities Press.
McGlothlin, W. H. & West, L. J. (1968), The Marijuana Problem: An Overview. *Amer. J. Psychiat.*, 125:370-378.
Nash, H. (1962), Psychologic Effects of Amphetamines and Barbiturates. *J. Nerv. Ment. Dis.*, 134:203-217.
Niederland, W. G. (1965), Narcissistic Ego Impairment in Patients with Early Physical Malformations. *This Annual*, 20:518-534.
Nyswander, M. (1959), Drug Addictions. In: *American Handbook of Psychiatry*, ed. S. Arieti, New York.: Basic Books, 1:614-622.
Pfeffer, A. Z. (1958), *Alcoholism*. New York: Grune & Stratton.
Rado, S. (1933), The Psychoanalysis of Pharmacothymia. *Psa. Quart.*, 2:1-23.
Rapaport, D. (1958), The Theory of Ego Autonomy. *The Collected Papers of David Rapaport*, ed. M. M. Gill, New York: Basic Books, 1967, pp. 722-744.

Savitt, R. A. (1963), Psychoanalytic Stuides on Addiction: Ego Structure in Narcotic Addiction. *Psa. Quart.*, 32:43-57.
Spiegel, L. A. (1958), Comments on the Psychoanalytic Psychology of Adolescence. *This Annual*, 13:296-308.
Wikler, A. (1953), *Opiate Addiction*. Springfield, Ill.: Thomas.
Zwerling, I. & Rosenbaum, M. (1959), Alcoholic Addiction and Personality. In: *American Handbook of Psychiatry*, ed. S. Arieti. New York: Basic Books, 1:623-644.

LOSS, RAGE, AND REPETITION

MARTHA WOLFENSTEIN, Ph.D. (New York)

I

In studying the reactions of children and adolescents to the death of a parent, we have found that mourning does not take place (Wolfenstein, 1966). Feelings of protracted grief are avoided, and the finality of the loss is denied. The representation of the lost parent remains intensely cathected and there are fantasies of his return. While such expectations persist, there is also an acknowledgment of the fact that the parent has died. These two trends, of acknowledgment and denial, coexist without being mutually confronted, constituting what Freud (1927) called a splitting of the ego. I shall try to show in what follows how this splitting may extend into the lives of such patients, impairing their reality testing in other relationships as well, and leading to repetitions of the loss which they are trying to deny.

Instead of grief, the most common reaction to the loss of a parent which we find in children and adolescents is rage. Bowlby (1961, 1963) has spoken of what he calls "protest" as the primary reaction to loss, and likened it to the screaming of the infant left alone, which serves to call the mother back to his side. We might suppose that the rage is directed at the parent who has abandoned the child, but the situation is more complex. There is a strong need to perpetuate a positive image of the lost parent, what Freud (1926) calls the hypercathexis of the lost object, as if thereby to preserve it from loss. What occurs is a decomposition of the ambivalence toward the lost parent, with the negative sector being diverted toward the sur-

---

This is a report from a research project on children's reactions to the death of a parent, which has been conducted with the collaboration of the Fellows in Child Psychiatry, in the Department of Psychiatry of the Albert Einstein College of Medicine.

viving parent and others in the child's environment. Often the bereaved child angrily wards off those who would help him. A rankling sense of having suffered an injustice may develop, with a vindictive need to prove how mistreated the child is. He may feel impelled to turn himself into a living and dying reproach. At the same time he may cherish the fantasy that his demonstrations of suffering must eventually force the lost parent to return and care for him.

In those in whom the loss of a parent in childhood or adolescence entails pathological consequences, we see an arrest in development at the point they had reached at the time of the parent's death. This has been observed by Fleming and Altschul (1963) in their studies of adult analytic patients who had lost a parent in childhood or adolescence. The arrest is observable particularly in the sector of object relations. It is as if the patient were still seeking and demanding that kind of relationship of which he was so abruptly and prematurely deprived. However, I should like to qualify this formulation and suggest that development is not only blocked, but there is also regression to earlier phases following loss. The threatened panic of being left unprovided for intensifies infantile demands for a need-gratifying object. The decomposition of ambivalence of which I have spoken also constitutes a regression, leaving the individual poorly equipped to deal with large amounts of unneutralized hostility.

There are also adaptive reactions to the loss of a parent in childhood, though they follow a different course than that of adult mourning. I shall illustrate these possibilities later in this paper.

II

The case of Mary, an adolescent girl whose father died when she was fourteen, exemplifies some of the common pathological consequences of the loss of a parent. It is a case in which we can see the inability to renounce the lost object, the persisting demand to be taken care of, the vindictive rage against the world at large, and the effort to force the lost parent to return by her sufferings. I shall also try to show that the loss in this case was particularly grievous because it was compounded with severe narcissistic injury. I would suppose that losses so compounded are in general the most difficult to recover from. This case shows the self-inflicted repetition of loss,

which appears to be an effort at undoing. In each repeated instance
there is an attempt to rewrite the tragedy with a happy ending. That
things yet again turn out badly to the shocked surprise of the patient
is related to the repeated scotomization of warning signals. The same
splitting of the ego instituted in response to the father's death applies in subsequent love relations. Forewarnings of disappointment
are noted and at the same time denied. The insistence that the
present unpromising affair must end in a happy union is a repetition
of the demand that the father must return.

Mary was nineteen when she came for treatment. She complained
of being depressed, having feelings of derealization; she felt unmo-
tivated to continue in college, and was leading a promiscuous life.
She also had such a penchant for precipitating herself into painful
predicaments that friends had repeatedly cautioned her and expos-
tulated with her about it. At our first meeting Mary said she wanted
to come for treatment once a week, and implied she expected to be
treated for nothing. When I told her that she should come at least
twice a week (later it was increased to three times) and that I would
charge a modest fee, she was dismayed. She said bitterly that she
supposed it was foolish to expect that there was some wonderful
therapist waiting to treat her in a clinic for nothing. They had more
worthy cases. She might just as well kill herself anyhow; it would be
the best solution all round. She added that since her mother was to
pay for her treatment, she would be further impoverishing her already poor mother. This would aggravate her guilt toward her
mother; so treatment would make her worse rather than better.
Thus she immediately directed toward the therapist her vindictive
reproachfulness, saying in effect: no one helps me, everyone treats
me badly, I expect nothing else from you.

While Mary felt embittered about the loss of her father, there
were many indications of the persisting demand for his return. In
the time following his death she had had the fantasy that there had
been some kind of doctors' plot, the family being told that the father
was dead to observe their reactions, and that after some time he
would return from where he was being kept in hiding. Later she had
fantasies of his returning and reproaching her for her promiscuous
life, and in her dreams he sometimes came back and attacked her.
Shortly after starting treatment she had commenced one of her over-

night affairs, which typically ended in quick disillusionment. On the second evening that she spent with the young man, they took marijuana, which she felt facilitated her telling him how disgusting she found him. When, nevertheless, he wanted to make love, she cried that he shouldn't touch her, she was just a little girl and she wanted her daddy.

A major motive for Mary's promiscuous way of life was to demonstrate what happened to a fatherless girl, or alternatively to force her father to return and take care of her. Shortly before her father's death, he had said that when she started going with boys, he would be very vigilant to see that nothing undesirable happened to her. But he had not lived to keep this promise. Mary's subsequent feckless behavior was calculated to show into what depths she must fall since she had no father to protect her. After a few months of treatment, during a brief absence of the therapist, Mary became pregnant by one of her overnight lovers. She obtained an illegal abortion. When she was coming out of the anaesthetic, she insisted that her father was coming to take her home.

During the first summer break in her treatment, Mary had what seemed to her unusually vivid memories of her childhood past. In half somnolent states she would see the view from the window of her former home, beautiful autumn trees in the distance, her father sitting somewhere close by, reading the newspaper. The atmosphere of her lost home and its surroundings was strongly evoked, with the sad, nostalgic feeling that she would never see it again. It seemed at the time that this might be the beginning of the process of mourning, of painful remembering and saying good-bye, and eventually becoming reconciled to her loss. But it was interrupted by an urgent impulse to live out a phase of life which had been curtailed by her father's death.

She had begun living with a man, several years her senior, who, like her father, was an artist. In this relationship she seemed to be resuming life from where she had left off when her father died. She experienced the throes of oedipal conflicts as they are revived in adolescence. Her young man had spoken of the girl he had had before her, and she became madly jealous of this rival. She had the impression that her predecessor had been devotedly domestic and a wonderful cook, and she mockingly referred to her as "mother nature." Mary would say pathetically that she could not cook or take care of the house as the other girl had done, since she had to go to school. Her jealousy became so tormenting that her lover tried to moderate it by telling her how unsatisfactory he had found the other girl. Mary now construed this relationship, which had preceded her arrival, as a very degrading one, and continued to reproach her lover for ever having had anything to do with such a low woman. (Mary had felt that she was much more on her father's level than her uneducated mother had been.) Alternating with her jealousy there was a feeling of deadly dullness, of being trapped in her life with this lover, who seemed much too old for her and who, she felt, treated her like a little girl. She frequently threatened to leave him, but then became overwhelmed with panic, with a sense of reliving what she had felt when her father died.

Next she began to have romantic dreams and daydreams about a fellow student with whom she had been friends for some time. While listening to music she thought of him amorously, and in her dreams walked hand in hand with him through flowering fields. She wished she could go out on dates with him and then have him bring her home to her older lover. It was as if she were trying to live out a phase of her life that had been missing, since her father had died before she had started going with boys. Typically for her, she cast the people in her life in roles from her fantasy. In this instance, neither of the young men would accept the role assigned. She was thus impelled to leave the daddy boyfriend to have an affair with the student boyfriend.

Once involved in a sexual relationship with this boy of whom she had thought so romantically, Mary began to feel increasingly contemptuous and disparaging toward him. Such feelings had also been prominent in her relation with her previous lover. What now came to the fore was her deep discontent with being a girl.

In our studies of children's reactions to the death of a parent, we have been occupied with sorting out multiple factors making for pathology in our patients. We have tried not to let our preoccupation with this one trauma lead us to ascribe one-sidedly all the disturbances we find to its impact. In Mary's case, when penis envy became the central theme, I felt for some time that she was dealing with problems unrelated to her father's death. However, I came to

see that these problems had become implicated with those deriving
from the loss of her father. Such a loss tends to be the more grievous
and insuperable as it reaffirms antecedent feelings of damage and
discourages hope of their ever being rectified. In this case object
loss was compounded with narcissistic injury, to which the patient
could not become reconciled (Jacobson, 1965).

Mary dramatized her wish to be a boy by constantly wearing
pants and sometimes a little boy cap. Her once long hair was now
cropped short, and she assured me that she looked just like a boy.
The artist with whom she had lived had possessed a very big motorcycle, which he had often allowed her to ride. After leaving him
she greatly regretted the loss of the motorcycle. For a while she continued to accompany her former lover to motorcycle races, and
boasted that the young men she met there treated her just like one
of the boys. She longed to have a motorcycle of her own. When she
received a student loan, she recklessly spent a sizable part of it to
buy a motorcycle. However, she found it vaguely disappointing. Apparently for this valuable piece of apparatus to have real worth it
had to be transferred to her from a man. I would reconstruct that
one of the fixation points in Mary's early development had been in
the phallic phase, at the point of hoping her father would bestow his
penis on her. The problem of undecided sexual identity would have
rearisen in early adolescence. Her father's death occurring then had
left her arrested at that point. As her preoccupation with motor-
cycles was waning, she had a dream in which a man took off his
penis, or she took it from him and attached it to herself. Subsequently Mary resumed a feminine decor, but was occupied with
things she had to add to herself in order to be beautiful, such as
false eyelashes and a hairpiece. Sometimes she stole from stores other
things which she felt she needed to be beautiful. This stealing was
overdetermined by her vindictive rage at being a deprived orphan.
But it also represented taking the penis. A stolen object, like the
motorcycle she got from a boyfriend, symbolized this better than
something she bought herself.

Mary repeatedly recalled the circumstances surrounding her
father's death. She spoke with intense indignation of how just after
her father died she had been deprived of something which should
rightly have been hers. Her father had had a large array of artist's

supplies, which she considered to be very valuable. Since she had shown artistic gifts, she could have used her father's equipment, and was sure he would have wanted her to have it. However, her older brother had summarily disposed of it, giving it to a friend of his who was an art student. Mary was still enraged at this injustice, and continued to protest about it to her mother, who turned a deaf ear to her complaints. Mary always spoke with strong disparagement of her brother, characterizing him as a stupid oaf, while she had been the clever, gifted child. Her father had bought a piano for her brother, who had never learned to play it. Mary had longed to play the piano, but did not dare to pre-empt it. Instead she had taken up the flute and learned to play it well. She had also been proficient at horseback riding, and her father had promised her a horse of her own if she advanced to where she could compete in shows. This was another promise that was not fulfilled. Thus we see a series of items of valuable equipment—piano, horse, artist's supplies, motorcycle— which Mary wanted to get from her father or some other man. The artist's supplies, the father's legacy, which she deserved, with which he would have wished to endow her, had been snatched away from her by her brother, just as he, the less worthy child, had been endowed with the penis. Mary's despair at her father's death was thus compounded with her despair at being a girl. The loss of her father was the more grievous as it meant also the loss of the penis which he might have given her.

At a later time, when she was involved with yet another boy, she was anticipating his leaving her, and said she wished at least to protect herself against being taken by surprise if this should happen. This led to the recollection of two traumas the impact of which was the more painful because they were sudden and unexpected. A year or two before her father died, he took her to a dentist who was to do orthodonture work on her teeth. She was only told immediately before the visit to the dentist's office that he was going to perform an operation, to cut out a piece of the gum between her two middle upper teeth in preparation to moving them. The operation had terrified and shocked her. The following trauma, which she associated with the operation, was that of her father's sudden death of a heart attack. The two traumas, recalled together, again confirm the connection between the father's death and loss of part of her own body.

Still later, under the influence of marijuana, she had a fantasy. Lying in a half somnolent state, she was looking at some lighted candles, and had the illusion that beyond them lay her father's coffin. She felt like reaching out toward it, to take something, to take his penis.

In her uncompleted development at the time of her father's death, this girl had been left still longing for a penis. In her fixed fantasy her father would have given it to her. His loss meant the discouragement of this hope as well, leaving her not only bereft but damaged, defective, and cheated of her due. The loss of a beloved person carried with it a grievous narcissistic injury, as if confirming that she had nothing, and was nothing. Her irreconcilable attitude toward the loss of her father was reinforced by her struggle against the sense of her own worthlessness.

Graduation from college and being forced to earn a living provoked increasingly violent rage in Mary. It was as if further proof were being forced on her that she had no father to provide for her. Meanwhile during her senior year she was much occupied with a vain quest for her "male counterpart." Manifestly she was seeking a young man with traits of mind and character exactly like her own (her low self-esteem alternating with the view that she was an exceptional being). But we could suppose that on a less conscious level she was looking for her lost father. As she failed to find the ideal man, and as she was confronted with the end of college, the loss of companionship of schoolmates, and the necessity of going to work, she became panicky and depressed. Once she started earning a living, she not only found her work onerous and degrading, but she began to rage increasingly at the injustices of the social system. The central injustice was that of the low and despised position of women. Her view of this was documented from experience and with many pseudointellectual arguments in which she construed human history through the ages as a continual exploitation of women. What incipient insight she seemed to have gained into her penis envy was lost, and she derided Freud as a Victorian who had believed woman's place was in the home. A chronic complaint was about the sexual overtures made to her on the street by Puerto Rican men and boys in the neighborhood where she lived. These Puerto Ricans, whom she contemptuously called "spics," thought every woman except the

Virgin Mary was just there to be used sexually. But this exemplified the pervasive attitude toward women in our society. She vowed that the next time a "spic" touched her, she would "kick him in the balls." This became a monotonously repeated leitmotiv. The dual complaint of having no father to provide for her and of not having been endowed with her father's equipment, the loss of the father and of the penis, seemed to rankle increasingly. It was her having to go to work which confirmed her orphaned state, but the focus of raging complaint was displaced to the injustice inflicted on women.

Mary repeatedly applied to her mother for financial help and was for the most part rebuffed. The mother, who had herself been brought up in circumstances of extreme poverty, seemed to suffer from chronic fears of destitution. She earned a modest living, and otherwise clung to a small "nest egg," left by the father, which she hoped would provide for her old age. Mary used to protest indignantly that her father would have wanted her to have some of his money. Both mother and daughter contended over it as if it were the last money in the world. Although both were able to earn a living, it was as if this money that came from father represented the sole source of provision. Their attitude expressed their inability to attach themselves to anyone else, their seeing the world as populated only by unlovable and unloving strangers. Mary eventually extracted from her mother a small amount, which seemed large to both of them, in order to start graduate studies. The money was soon exhausted, and the struggle over the "nest egg" was again resumed.

A tendency which has been observed in very young children, in reaction to separation, was also exemplified in Mary, namely, a shift away from object relations to an exaggerated evaluation of material things (Robertson, 1958; Heinecke and Westheimer, 1965). One of Mary's most cherished daydreams was of having charge accounts in expensive shops and being able to buy whatever she liked. When she was working she would constantly buy herself little presents to compensate for the hardship she was suffering. She was bitterly envious of the material things which others got from their parents. Her sense of being bereft assumed the form of desperate longing for clothes, travel, a luxurious home.

I turn now to the repetition of painful loss which was exemplified in Mary's relations with young men. Repeatedly she would in-

LOSS, RAGE, AND REPETITION 441

vest improbable hopes in an unpromising relation and then be overwhelmed with traumatic surprise when it turned out badly. She
would arrange a situation in which she would be pining for an
absent lover, but anticipating a future life in which they would be
always together. There would be signs of the lover's indecisiveness
and lack of commitment to her which she would be aware of. Yet
when the break came, it would affect her as a wholly unforeseen
fatality.

Following her graduation from college Mary began an affair with
a young man four years her junior. He was on the eve of going away
to college so that the beginning of the affair was under the shadow
of imminent separation. However, the plan was that in his second
year of college he would transfer to a school in the city, and they
would move into a new apartment together. Throughout the school
year the young man returned to spend weekends with Mary. But
there were times when he disappointed her and she waited in vain.
Then she felt as she had following her father's death. She would
look at an empty chair, where the beloved man had been wont to
sit, and experience feelings of unreality. She would hear a footstep
on the stairs, and think for a moment it must be he. The situation
of waiting for a beloved man to come back was repeated, but since
the lover was absent not dead, the hope of eventual reunion could
be better sustained. At the same time there were many indications
of how undecided the young man was about his future plans. For
instance, he allowed the deadline to pass for his application to the
college in the city where he was to enroll so that they could be together the following year. Mary began to anticipate that he would
not go through with their plan. It was then that she said that at least
she wanted to protect herself against surprise if she were going to be
disappointed. It was spring, the season following the anniversary of
her father's death, and she was painfully apprehensive that everything was going to be again as it had been in that unhappy time; she
would have to move, her money was running out, she would be
changing schools, and she would have to part from a beloved man.
Then her young man told her that he was too undecided, he could
not commit himself to living with her. Mary was thrown into
despair, said she had nothing to live for, and had thoughts of suicide.
When reminded of the signs she herself had noted of the uncertainty

of her young man's commitment to her plan for their future together, she said: "But I had counted on it totally."

We see here a dual attitude toward reality: there is a perception of the counterindications to the wished-for outcome and at the same time a blind insistence that the desired reunion must take place. Reality running counter to what is wished is superficially acknowledged, but on a deeper emotional level denied. In the pursuit of the unhappy love affair there is the same splitting of the ego as had been instituted in response to the father's death. The setting up of the predicament of pining for an absent lover, while cherishing the hope of eventual reunion, represented a repetition of the situation vis-à-vis her father, whose death she could not accept as something irreversible. To an immature individual the death of a parent deals an intolerable blow to the sense of omnipotence. In willfully precipitating a later situation which portends a similar loss, the individual is not aiming at a total repetition, but expects a last-minute reprieve. It appears that the same drama is being played again, but the earlier outcome has not been accepted, and there is the insistent hope that this time it will turn out differently. There may be repetitions whose motive lies beyond the pleasure principle. The kind of repetition which we are dealing with here, however, is not of that order. The underlying motive rather is one of undoing a past disaster, of recovering the injured sense of omnipotence, of coercing fate, rewriting the tragedy with a happy ending. That it does not turn out that way is due not to intent but to miscalculation. What was to have proved a rectification of the past becomes a repetition of the same misfortune because of the faulty relation to reality. The imperious clinging to infantile omnipotence leads to the underestimation of warning signs, which are perceived but disregarded. Thus, paradoxically, the denial that an unbearable loss could have taken place entails exposure to repeated losses.

The drive to repeat continued, with the insistence that the wished-for must take precedence over the probable. During the summer vacation the disappointing lover moved in with Mary, and in the fall I found that they were again planning to move to a new apartment together. At the same time she was half-aware of his becoming attracted to a younger girl. One night when he had made a flimsy excuse for going out, she followed him and found him walking hand in hand with the other girl. After making a violent scene, and then running distracted and weeping through the park, Mary arrived at a late hour on my doorstep, saying that she had to come or she would have killed herself. So twice within a brief space of time she was so traumatized by the defection of the same unreliable young man that she felt driven to suicide. We might say that when the improbable reunion with the surrogate figure proved unattainable, she felt impelled to rejoin her father in another way—by dying.

Since loss for her was so intimately associated with narcissistic injury, her lover's infidelity reduced Mary to feeling utterly worthless. She felt she was "a turd, a piece of pus." Committed as she was to trying to rectify distress by impulsive action, she now threw herself into a new affair. There was a young married man with whom she had been friendly, whose wife was away just at this time, when she confided to him all her unhappiness and they ended in each other's arms. She could understand how I might think that she had hastily contrived a new love triangle with herself as the winner rather than the loser. But this would be failing to recognize the unique mutual suitability that existed between herself and her new lover. While he loved his wife he found in Mary something very rare which his wife lacked. Mary had accomplished for the moment one of her reversals from being nothing to being something far above the common run of humanity. She spoke at this time of her fantasy of reaching the bottom-most point of suffering and then having the clouds open and Christ reach down his hands to her. (Mary had been religious in childhood, but had lost her faith in adolescence. The fantasy of salvation through suffering, however, still accorded with her emotional needs.) Her rescue by her new lover seemed a fulfillment of this fantasy. At the same time it appeared highly likely that she was exposing herself to yet another disappointment. In fact, the young man's wife returned and, after a few stolen meetings with Mary (who was again in the position of waiting and pining for the beloved man to come to her), he told her that he was too torn by this double life and left her. Mary said that this was the greatest loss of her life.

It was in this context of repeated disappointments that, after four years, Mary broke off her treatment. Besides the defection of the two young men, she had suffered yet another rebuff from her mother to one of her recurrent appeals for financial help. One and another friend had failed her. She was provocatively despairing and raging against the world at large, and became quarrelsome with me for not joining her in her indignation about the plight of women. Then abruptly she came in to announce that she had found a therapist who suited her better, a young instructor at her college, in whom she had confided, and who reminded her of her last lover. Evidently she was hoping to find a therapist who would more directly gratify her thwarted longings for love, while at the same time very likely courting yet another disappointment. But there were other factors involved; she had felt abandoned by everyone but her therapist, and she was impelled to turn passivity into activity by becoming the abandoner herself. Moreover, she was confirming the vindictive conviction which she had announced in her first session: having been mistreated by everyone, she had been impelled to prove that the therapist too could be of no help to her.

The loss of a parent while the individual is still immature inflicts a massive trauma from which it is very difficult to recover. The difficulty is the greater to the extent to which there have been failures or disturbances in development prior to the loss. I shall indicate briefly what some of these earlier factors were in Mary's case. She had had two brief hospitalizations before the age of four, which seemed to have shaken her trust in her mother's caring for her. Moreover, the mother had depressive tendencies, and would punish the child by long silences. The mother herself had had a very deprived childhood. When Mary asked her what toys she used to have as a child, the mother had said bitterly that she had had no toys. Mary had then looked at her own toys feeling guilty at possessing them, but perhaps also anxious whether mother did not begrudge them to her. The early separations, the mother's depressive withdrawals, the somber atmosphere of destitution of the mother's past contributed to anxious doubts about the reliability of needed supplies and a clinging to the need-gratifying phase of object relations. Her father's death then aggravated the already strong apprehension about not being provided for. A sense of helplessness and longing to be taken care of persisted into the time when she became able to earn a living. It was only in a playful and childlike way that Mary could assume the role of one able to provide. She had a cat whom she pampered and petted and about whose exceptional character and cleverness she often boasted. The cat (a castrated male) was a counterpart to herself. In her care of the cat she demonstrated how she would have wished to be treated by her parents, and created the illusion of a warm parent-child atmosphere in her otherwise lonely life.

The anxiety about losing her mother's love hindered Mary's oedipal development, since she did not dare to move too far away from her mother for fear of losing her altogether. While there were signs of oedipal striving, there was also an inconclusiveness and indecisiveness about sexual identity and object choice. Thus she approached adolescence with an unsure basis for building heterosexual relations. Mary and her brother had been on hostile and rivalrous terms, and she defended herself against her envy of him with the conviction that it was he who envied her for being the more gifted child. Doubtful of her mother's reliability as a need-gratifying object, Mary seemed to have turned to her father as the source of supplies. He was the one who could appreciate her (he was an artist and she was precociously artistic), and it was he to whom she looked to rectify the injustice in anatomical distribution between herself and her brother. These motives were condensed in the persistent overestimation of the artist's equipment which her father had left, which should have been hers, but which was taken from her by her brother.

It is interesting that Mary, who, at the time she came for treatment, was an impulse-ridden character, had had a classical compulsion neurosis in childhood. At about the age of eight, she went through a phase of continual hand-washing and tormented struggles to ward off bad thoughts. These symptoms set in shortly after her father had had a first heart attack. One of her obsessions was with stories then in the news about delinquent boys who had tortured tramps they found sleeping in the park. She felt obscurely implicated, and guilty that she could not stop thinking about these cruel acts committed by youths on older men. Another obsessive and guilty thought was: "How big are God's jockey shorts?" which may well have stood for both oedipal strivings and penis envy. She was fearful that her parents would go to hell because they used swearwords. It would seem that her father's dangerous illness had aggravated the conflict over her ambivalent feelings toward her parents, her death wishes, and her castrative impulses toward her father. The symptoms expressed the struggle to undo the bad wishes which she thought had caused the near-fatality. The obsessions betrayed the sadistic motives which later reappeared in her angry attitude toward men. The inclination to an obsessive-compulsive disorder further indicates the fixation on omnipotence of thoughts, which later impelled her to try to wrest reality to her wishes.

If we consider the sequence of childhood compulsion neurosis and adolescent impulse disorder, it would seem that the combined impact of puberty and the loss of the father shattered the earlier compulsive structure. Mary had been a conscientious and excellent student in school. Following her father's death her performance became erratic and her motivation to study dwindled. Gradually she drifted into a promiscuous sexual life, marked by upsets, more or less violent scenes, and disappointments. The deterioration of school performance is a recurrent (though by no means invariant) finding in cases of children who have lost a parent (Bonnard, 1961). In the absence of external superego support and with the loss of narcissistic supplies provided by parental praise and pride, the incentive for achievement is radically reduced. The surviving parent often, as in Mary's case, is so lost in incapacitating grief as to afford little support. In Mary, moreover, I believe that her compulsive scrupulousness and goodness were predicated on a quid-pro-quo contract with fate. The threat of death to her father (in the first heart attack) had induced the compulsion neurosis, with the implicit provision: If I am very good my father will not die. When later the father did die, nevertheless, it was as if the bargain with fate had been vitiated. Mary was dispensed from striving to control her impulses, since these efforts had not been rewarded. I have also mentioned the overdetermining motive to fall into degradation to demonstrate what becomes of a fatherless girl and to coerce her father's return.

III

Several other cases will be cited only briefly to show some of the same phenomena in children's reactions to the death of a parent: the persistent quest for the lost parent, rage rather than grief, the repetition of disappointments, and the vindictive determination to prove no one can help. I shall select from the cases that follow material which illustrates one or another of these recurrent themes.

Frank's father committed suicide when Frank was not quite four. The boy was brought for treatment at four and a half, with the complaints that he was enuretic and subject to temper tantrums. While Frank formed a positive attachment to the male psychiatrist, Dr. R., the sessions were marked by repeated tantrums, especially when it came time to stop. Each separation seemed, understandably, intolerable to this boy. His play was marked by the themes of people being put to sleep and reawakened, disappearing and reappearing, being endangered and rescued, dying and being restored to life. Members of a doll family were repeatedly precipitated into car crashs or drownings, but were then rescued, brought to the hospital and revived. Similarly, the therapist was put to sleep by magic potions or rays and then reawakened. When the therapist said that Frank might wish his father could be revived in the same way, Frank would say matter-of-factly that he knew his father was dead and then impatiently return to his play of restoring people to life.

At the end of the first year of treatment, Dr. R. was called away for army service, and Frank was transferred to another male psychiatrist, Dr. H., to whom he also became strongly attached. Since Dr. H. had succeeded to Dr. R's office, the setting and much of the equipment remained the same. However, Frank discovered that there was something missing, a little red car which had been there when Dr. R. was there. The quest for the little red car became a leitmotiv of the ensuing treatment. In almost every session, Frank expressed his longing for the little red car, searched for it yet again, and remained unreconciled to its disappearance. The significance of the car was in several ways overdetermined. The father's body had been found in a car; he had driven away from home to a deserted place where he had shot himself. At an earlier time, the father had injured himself seriously in a car accident, but had then been successfully restored. Frank had once helped his father to repaint the car and they had applied a first coat of red, rust-proof paint to parts where the paint had been scraped off. The missing toy car had had the special feature that when it crashed into some obstacle it went to pieces, but could then be put together again. Thus the associations to the little red car repeated the theme of destruction and restitution. But above all, the boy had displaced onto this small object which had disappeared the feelings he had for his lost doctor and for his lost father. The repetitive quest for the lost toy expressed his feeling of being unreconciled to the more grievous losses he had suffered.[1]

Karl, aged nine, was sent to the clinic by the school because he had stabbed another child in the hand with a scissors. This incident had followed on a sequence of increasingly aggressive outbursts. Karl's mother had died, after a long illness, eight months previously. Karl told his doctor that he had sometimes been angry before his mother died, but that he had been much angrier since. He wanted his mother to come back. If she did not come back, he would continue to stab people. He seemed to feel that his demonstration of the furious rage which the loss of his mother roused must force her return. One is again reminded of Bowlby's characterization of the prime reaction to loss as one of "protest" and his likening it to the raging cries of the abandoned infant which serve to recall the absent mother. Karl was not psychotic or deluded: he knew his mother was dead, but he could not accept this as an insuperable obstacle to his getting her back again. He resembled the intelligent ten-year-old boy, whose remark following his father's sudden death Freud (1900, p. 254n.) recorded: "I know father's dead, but what I can't understand is why he doesn't come home to supper." Karl's rage became moderated as he formed attachments to his therapist and other staff members of the hospital, where he was first an in-patient and subsequently came for day care. However, when his father's incapacity to provide for him led to the prospect of his being sent to a residential center, he again became very angry, began carrying a knife and threatening to stab people, and again demanded that his mother must come back. His rage at renewed deprivaiton was like that we observed in Mary when having to go to work intensified the distress of having no father to provide for her. In Karl's case the connection between the loss of the parent and the ensuing rage was particularly explicit.[2]

Edward's mother was suffering from incurable cancer when she brought him to the clinic. Edward was an eleven-year-old boy of

[1] Therapists: Dr. H. Rosenzweig and Dr. A. Heath.
[2] Therapist: Dr. G. Dabbs.

superior intelligence and high ambition, who showed signs of long-term difficulties with aggressive impulses. He had never got on well with other children, toward whom he tended to be contemptuous and supercilious. Facial tics gave evidence of repressed aggression breaking through, eluding voluntary control. Before his mother's last illness he had undergone repeated separations, as both parents had been periodically hospitalized. The rage he felt at these repeated abandonments he had had to subdue for fear of losing his parents altogether, but he displaced some of his anger toward others in the environment. In the course of a year's treatment, his woman therapist became a target for the boy's mounting rage. While the mother was still able to get around she repeatedly absented herself from home; subsequently she was hospitalized. Edward spoke of how, since his mother no longer accompanied him to the clinic, he could not go to the canteen to have hot chocolate after his sessions as they used to do. When the therapist offered to take Edward to the canteen, he haughtily refused. Similarly, with the snacks which the therapist provided, he was evidently torn between his longing for sweets and his unwillingness to accept anything from her. There was a strong repudiation of any possible, even partial, substitute for his mother. While his mother's condition worsened he was constantly anticipating her return from the hospital. When she died there was the usual absence of any manifest grief reaction. But the anger against the therapist became increasingly outspoken. He mocked and belittled her, and insisted more and more that she was no use to him. On the eve of his twelfth birthday, when his longing for his mother was intensified, he refused a birthday present from the therapist, and at this point broke off the treatment.[3]

This boy exemplifies the decomposition of ambivalence of which I have spoken. Edward did not confide expectations of his mother's return, of the sort which were so explicit in Karl's case. However, we may speculate that, far from decathecting the image of his mother, he was concentrating on her his strongest positive feelings, as if thereby to preserve her. The rage he felt at her abandonment of him was split off and diverted to others, notably the therapist. The reactions of this eleven-year-old boy are very similar to those of two-

[3] Therapist: Dr. A. Blum.

year-olds as described by Heinecke and Westheimer in *Brief Separations* (1965). I think particularly of the intensely negative reactions of these young children toward the researchers, who reminded them of their parents and yet were not the parents they so desperately sought. We could even liken this behavior to the stranger reaction of infants in the second half of the first year. Someone is there, and this evokes the longing for mother. But it is not mother, so the sense of her absence becomes unbearably acute. When we started our study of children who had lost a parent, we expected to find many variations with age. What has impressed us instead has been a pervasive regularity in the age range we explored, well into adolescence. We might say that reactions to a major loss throughout life precipitate us, at least for a time, back to a very infantile level. In his *In Memoriam*, Tennyson, grieving for his lost friend, wrote: "but what am I? / An infant crying in the night, / An infant crying for the light, / And with no language but a cry."

Diane started treatment when she was not quite fifteen, a month before her mother died. She had made a suicide attempt at the time that her mother was hospitalized with terminal cancer. Diane was exclusively attracted to other girls and women, seeking, as it seemed, to recapture an early mother-baby relationship. A younger sister had been born when she was two and a half, and she apparently had had the fantasy that it was her baby and mother's. This fantasy was repeated in relation to a beloved friend in high school, about whom she had the dream that they would live together and have a baby together. Diane had intense infatuations with actresses, who seemed to represent the phallic mother. She was particularly admiring of an actress who had been an ugly duckling, but who had surprised everyone when she got on the stage by showing how much she had to offer. Occasionally a young actress, not yet successful, would yield for a time to Diane's flattering devotion. With one of these ephemeral friends, Diane would spend days when she should have been in school, bringing her food from home or being fed by her in turn. At a restaurant the two of them jokingly told the waiter they were mother and daughter.

Diane experienced repeated disappointments in relation to the girls and women she pursued. In particular there was the high school friend, who was about to leave for college, while Diane with increasing desperation planned a future life together. As this friend became alarmed at the homosexual overtones of Diane's attachment, she tried to break off the relationship. Unable to renounce her friend, Diane provoked many times repeated rebuffs. After the friend had left for college, Diane pursued her there, made a scene in the college dormitory, and was thrown off the premises. She continued, however, to insist on her need to get this friend back, and to idealize their past relationship, which she saw as one of the most intimate mutual understanding. Her incredulity that her friend could have become disaffected represented a repetition of her feelings about her mother's death, which she had been unable to accept, as well as a revival of a much earlier sense of loss, when her mother had turned away from her to the new baby when she had been two and a half. As in the case of Mary, the repeated painful disappointments into which she precipitated herself were facilitated by the poor reality testing which had marked the reaction to the loss of the parent. The repetitions aimed at undoing an unbearable earlier disappointment, with the blind insistence: this time it must turn out differently.

In a self-destructive course, Diane made repeated suicide attempts, dropped out of school, and became increasingly addicted to drugs. As with Mary's efforts to force the return of her father, Diane's behavior could be construed as demonstrating what happens to a motherless girl and attempting to coerce the return of her mother to take care of her. There was also the motive of wanting to rejoin her mother in death. On the first anniversary of her mother's death, she threatened to commit suicide. Instead she turned up at the therapist's home at a late hour, the therapist having assured her that she could get in touch with him at any time. Unfortunately at the end of two years, the therapist had to leave to go into government service. From the time she knew he was leaving, Diane became increasingly erratic in her attendance at sessions. With her next therapist she continued to insist that she must get back the lost friend from high school days. This was the one thing that could help her. She flaunted her increasing addiction to drugs and disorganized life, mocked the therapist's concern for her, and dropped out of treatment. As in Mary's case, Diane, disappointed by so many, was impelled to turn passivity into activity and abandon the one person who was willing to stand by her, the therapist. Although we should not underestimate the impression of unreliability produced by the first therapist's leaving her, yet, with other unreliable people she had been impelled to blind and obstinate pursuit. She used the therapist as someone whom she in turn could disappoint, who would be left waiting for her in vain.[4]

IV

I now turn to children and adolescents who seem to have been able to react to the loss of a parent in more constructive ways. The first possibility is that in which there is a parent surrogate available to whom the child is able to transfer a large part of the positive feelings that were attached to the lost parent. Availability of such a satisfactory parent substitute is relatively rare in our culture in which the nuclear family, of two parents and their young children, is the mode. Evidently the best substitute for a lost parent is not a stranger who intrudes into the child's life following a loss, but someone he already knows and loves. It has been remarked that where there have been more extended family groups, there is greater possibility for such substitution, and the loss of a parent, though grievous, may not pose so insuperable a problem (Volkart and Michael, 1957). However, there are also inner factors which affect the readiness or unreadiness of a child to accept a parent substitute. There are great individual differences in the facility for forming new object ties or in the tenacity of clinging to old loves. Inner and outer circumstances must both be favorable if a successful substitution is to be made.

Recovery from the loss of a parent in childhood through the acceptance of an available surrogate is exemplified in the case of Walter, which I have cited in an earlier paper and will recapitulate briefly here. Walter was ten when his mother died. During her long terminal illness, both she and the boy were cared for by the maternal grandmother. This grandmother was already well known and well loved by the boy, and he increasingly turned to her for the care which his mother could no longer give him. After the mother's death, there were some angry upsets, of which the grandmother was very understanding. In addition, for a time Walter showed an in-

4 Therapists: Dr. C. Goodstein and Dr. I. Lunianski.

satiable hunger for food and sweets, but this gradually subsided. He continued to live with his grandmother, who functioned as a good mother substitute. Social and intellectual development proceeded without noticeable impairment, in contrast to the arrest observed in patients who have suffered a like loss. The process of recovery here differs, as I tried to show in my previous paper (1966), from that of adult mourning. There was no protracted absorption in the work of decathecting the lost object, which, in an adult mourner, we would expect to precede the formation of new ties. Rather there was a substitute object already present to whom feelings could be immediately transferred as they were being detached from the mother while she was dying and after her death. A child cannot tolerate the protracted painful remembering and giving up of a lost object that occur in adult mourning, a process during which it is not yet possible to seek or want a substitute. If a child is able to accomplish some decathexis of the lost parent (which our child patients seem unable to do), it is more likely to be in the presence of a suitable substitute who serves as a recipient for detached libido and source of satisfaction of needs, without delay or unassuaged yearning for someone no longer there.

A number of favorable circumstances combined in the case of Walter. The progressive loss of his mother which he experienced as she lay dying was continually compensated for by the devoted care of his grandmother. His readiness to transfer increasingly intense feelings to her was facilitated by the already existing attachment between them, which went back to his infancy. Moreover, this was a boy who from early years had shown an eager reaching out toward new people, rather than exclusive clingingness to the first objects. There was a facility here for shifting cathectic energy which, in the exigency of loss and replacement, was advantageous. Further, there were indications that, in the sector of object relations, he had advanced in his development beyond seeking exclusively gratification of his own needs. Some time before his mother's death (when she had had an operation and had just returned from the hospital) he showed a strong wish to be able to provide for her and to achieve independence. He elaborated a fantasy of what he would do if he were Superman: he would build a splendid mansion for his mother, where she could live in luxury, while he would fly around the world righting wrongs. There would always be a window open for his return, and meanwhile he would leave Supermouse to keep his mother company. Subsequently this wish to help materialized in action. In his adolescence, when his grandparents were ill, he assumed responsibility for doing the family marketing. Later on, as a young man, he showed a generous capacity to take care of his own children. As yet another factor affecting a favorable outcome, we may consider that the problem of rage, so acute in our child patients, was perhaps less prominent here. Walter's ambivalence toward his mother appeared to be only moderate; he was her only child. There may then have been less hostility which he had to divert toward others in the environment in order to preserve a good image of his mother.

A different way of adapting to the loss of a parent is one in which no substitute is found, but, by identifying in a constructive way with the lost parent, the child himself replaces the parent. This is exemplified in a young woman doctor, whose father died when she was ten. The father had been a doctor, and she recalled him in very ideal terms. He had been much beloved by his patients, who remembered him with gratitude years after his death. She herself had been a belligerent and unamenable schoolgirl, and her father had offered her a reward if she would bring home a better school report. She regretted in retrospect that when she did later achieve this, her father was no longer there to give her the reward. After his death she had, at her own request, gone to school away from home and had become an outstanding student. During this time she believed that if she were good enough, her father would return. She felt alienated from her mother, who spoke of the father's death as a *fait accompli*. Although her mother married again, she did not accept her stepfather as a replacement for her father, and was indignant that her younger brother changed his name to the stepfather's and would not perpetuate their father's name. When she was in high school, her mother made a disparaging remark about her grade in the one subject in which she was less than excellent. She then resolved that no more school reports should go to her mother and stepfather. To insure that the reports would be sent directly to her, she arranged to pay her own school fees. For this purpose she took on a heavy schedule of private tutoring. Eventually she went to medical school and became a doctor like her father.

We may contrast this career line with that of Mary, whose persisting demand to be taken care of impeded her forward development. The young woman doctor, from the time of her father's death, manifested a determined and precocious independence. She chose to go away to school. While still in high school she found work so that she would not have to depend on her mother and stepfather. She herself became the only substitute for her father. It was she who would get the now greatly improved school reports which he should have seen and rewarded her for. Instead of declining in her achievements, as so many of our patients do following the death of a parent, this girl made marked and continuing improvement. It would seem that a large amount of libido remained invested in the father while angry feelings were directed against mother and stepfather. But the father would seem to have been incorporated into the ego ideal and to have given an increased impetus to striving and achievement. By contrast, in Mary's case, the image of the father remained more that of a provider of supplies which she should have received but of which she was deprived after his death, notably in the instance of his artist's supplies. Without the external support of her father, Mary's childhood artistic ambitions wavered and eventually petered out. In relation to the fantasied return of the lost parent Mary and the young woman doctor exemplified opposite positions. The young woman doctor believed for some time following her father's death that if she was good enough, he would come back. Mary lived on the implicit assumption that if she suffered and floundered sufficiently, her father would have to return. For the doctor her father was a model for effort and achievement. In Mary's case the father remained a need-gratifying object.

An incipient tendency in the same direction of heightened ambition, as seen in the young woman doctor, appeared in the case of Edward. Edward, aged eleven when his mother died, angrily rejected any possible replacement for her. However, immediately following his mother's death, this bright and ambitious boy expressed an intensified aspiration to important accomplishments. In this he was not so directly identifying with the lost parent as did the young woman doctor, but rather we may suppose reinforcing his ego ideal by incorporating his mother's ambitions for him. On his last visit to his mother in the hospital he had been able to tell her that he had been promoted to a class for the intellectually gifted, to which he had long been looking forward, and his mother had expressed her pleasure and pride in him. Following her death, in his next therapeutic session, he rather surprisingly announced that he was just like Schliemann, the famous archaeologist. Did the therapist know, he asked, that Schliemann's mother had died when he was eleven? (The facts were slightly altered by the patient to achieve the identity he sought; in actuality Schliemann's mother had died when he was nine.) Continuing the analogy, Edward asserted that just as Schliemann had discovered unknown things in the earth, so he would discover new things in the skies, in the exploration of space. We may suppose that both Schliemann and this boy were motivated to seek for their lost mothers, whether in the earth or in heaven (cf. Niederland, 1965). Edward was no doubt being somewhat grandiose in comparing himself with Schliemann. Yet the hopes he expressed were in keeping with long-term plans he had had for scientific training. The striking circumstance was the feeling of reinforcement of strength rather than of being thrown back into helpless weakness by the loss of the parent. This is similar to what we saw in the young woman doctor, who showed a spurt of greater independence and much improved school performance following the death of her father. In such instances we may suppose that something of the power or aspiration for achievement of the parent's personality has been taken into the self.

We may ask why this solution to the loss of a parent does not seem to occur more often. Why is identification with the lost parent not more of a resource for further development? Probably the crucial factor here is the phase of development of object relations which has been achieved at the time of the parent's death. To the extent that the parent still serves predominantly as a need-gratifying object, the child feels helpless to assume the parent's role. We have then the persisting demand to be taken care of, as in the case of Mary. The image of the self and of the parent remain too disparate for identification to seem feasible. The relationship appears not one of likeness, but a complementary one, of the needy child and the parent as the source of supplies. In Mary's case, it is interesting that in childhood she had tried to emulate her father in artistic strivings.

Later she became discouraged and gave up this attempt. We may recall again that she did not get her father's artist's equipment. His death left her with a rankling sense not only of being unprovided for but personally defective. The hope to be like her father, too primitively implicated with the demand to have a penis bestowed on her, gradually dwindled. The one "creative" activity in which she persisted was in the service of her injured body narcissism, in making clothes for herself.

A further difficulty stands in the way of identification with a parent who has died. The image of the parent's illness and death may in its terrifying impressiveness blot out the image of the parent in his living and constructive aspects. There is then a fearful avoidance of identifying with the lost parent, which may alternate with suicidal ideas, that is, of becoming one with the parent by dying. We have seen this in the cases of Mary and Diane. Krupp (1965) has dealt with some of the exigencies of identification with a dead parent in adult patients. He noted fluctuations in assuming aspects of the parent as vital and competent or as diseased and moribund, depending on which sector of ambivalence toward the parent assumed the ascendancy.

V

The loss of a parent by death in childhood or adolescence is fraught with severe hazards to the development of the young person so bereaved. Mourning, as a painful but adaptive process of gradually decathecting the lost object, is not an available device until after adolescence has been passed through. As I tried to show in my previous paper (1966), adolescence is a kind of trial mourning. The adolescent, subject to the necessity of seeking a nonincestuous sexual object, is for the first time forced to undergo a radical decathexis of his first loves, the parents. The process in many ways resembles mourning (A. Freud, 1958; Jacobson, 1964). There are depressed moods and nostalgic feelings for a lost past. But there is also the gain of being able to invest freed libidinal energies in new love objects and new interests. Once this major transition has been achieved, it is as though a pattern has been established for decathecting a beloved object if the need arises, as when the individual is confronted with losses in later life. Having been initiated through the trial mourning of adolescence, he is then able to mourn.

We have found two possible substitutes for mourning in earlier stages of development, which are adaptive. One is that in which there is an available and acceptable parent substitute, to whom the child can transfer piecemeal the libido he gradually detaches from the lost parent. The process differs from that of mourning in the immediacy of transfer of the freed libido. The child cannot tolerate the painful hiatus between relationships which occurs typically in the adult mourner, as, for instance, in the time between being widowed and marrying again. The child must have the replacement already there before he can make an emotional move away from the lost object. Unfortunately, acceptable parent substitutes are not often available in our society. The best prospects of a child's making a successful transference of affections to such a substitute is if the substitute has been already a valued and trusted person in the child's life. There are also subjective conditions in the child which must be met. Among these we noted an antecedent facility for forming object relations and a relatively low level of ambivalence toward the parent who has died.

The other adaptive reaction to loss of a parent is that in which the child incorporates the lost parent into his ego ideal and gains an increased impetus to striving for achievement. This is a more narcissistic device than the preceding one. The child does not find or accept an external object as a replacement for the lost parent, but in his own person perpetuates the parent. Probably the condition for such a development is an antecedent strong mutual alliance of parent and child in the interests of the child's ambitions and accomplishments. In one of the instances I cited, a greatly beloved father had expressed strong wishes for his daughter to achieve in school, a behest which she later carried out in posthumous obedience. In the other instance, the son was already strongly committed to fulfilling his mother's ambitions for him at the time of her death. It is not yet entirely clear in which cases it is possible for a child to show such increased resolve for achievement following a parent's death, and in which cases there is the opposite effect, an outcome which seems to be more common. However, we have noted that in one case the child may make the secret compact with fate: if I am sufficiently good, my parent will return. In the other case there is an implicit attempt to coerce fate by the opposite means: if I demonstrate sufficient helplessness, my parent will have to come back and take care of me.

In the adverse reactions to the loss of a parent which we have observed in our child and adolescent patients, rage rather than grief is the dominant affect. The rage at being abandoned is diverted from the representation of the lost parent, which is hypercathected as though to guard it against being lost. The surviving parent, others in the environment, and the world at large become the targets of this rage. Particularly in adolescence this hostility is likely to assume the proportions of a comprehensive grievance and to be elaborated into an indictment of social injustice. The need to prove a case of having been mistreated is a hazard in the therapy of such patients. The sense of loss of a beloved and needed person may also be aggravated by associated feelings of narcissistic injury. This was exemplified in the case of the adolescent girl whose inability to renounce her dead father stemmed in part from her persisting hope that he would endow her with a penis. To acknowledge that her father was permanently lost to her also meant to accept being defective. The compounding of narcissistic injury with object loss makes it the more difficult to become reconciled to the loss.

For immature individuals the loss of a parent is also an intolerable injury to their fantasied omnipotence. I have attempted to interpret the repeated self-induced suffering of further losses as an unsuccessful effort to reassert this omnipotence. The young person remains unreconciled to something having happened that is so contrary to his wishes. He is impelled to recapitulate the painful circumstances in order this time to wrest from fate a different outcome. The implicit expectation is that this time the tragedy will be played with a happy ending. This effort at revision fails because of faulty reality testing. There is a dual attitude toward the unpromising circumstances into which such a patient may repeatedly precipitate himself. On the one hand danger signals are noted, on the other hand they are denied. This split between acknowledgment and denial is the same that characterized the attitude of the ego toward the loss of the parent. Superficial acceptance of the facts coexisted with the insistence on a deeper emotional level that the lost parent must still be recapturable. This split in the ego may then extend into subsequent relationships. In the case of Mary, unrealistic hopes were repeatedly revived in relations where at moments she could recognize signs that they were unpromising and uncertain. However, she was impelled again and again to precipitate herself into situations where she would be pining for an absent beloved man, while looking forward to their eventual reunion. This insistence on a happy outcome, despite circumstances which augured the opposite, expressed the need to undo the loss which she could not accept. The repetitions of disappointment and loss did not aim at this unhappy outcome but rather at a coercion of fate, an insistence that this time it must be different. As long as the ego remains split in regard to an unpalatable reality, as long as an infantile sense of omnipotence is maintained, there is a liability to this kind of repetition of loss.

BIBLIOGRAPHY

Bonnard, A. (1961), Truancy and Pilfering Associated with Bereavement. In: *Adolescents*, ed. S. Lorand & H. I. Schneer. New York: Hoeber, pp. 152-179.

Bowlby, J. (1961), Processes of Mourning. *Int. J. Psa.*, 42:317-340.

—— (1963), Pathological Mourning and Childhood Mourning. *J. Amer. Psa. Assn.*, 11:500-541.

Fleming, J. & Altschul, S. (1963), Activation of Mourning and Growth by Psycho-Analysis. *Int. J. Psa.*, 44:419-431.

Freud, A. (1958), Adolescence. *This Annual*, 13:255-278.

Freud, S. (1900), The Interpretation of Dreams. *Standard Edition*, 4 & 5. London: Hogarth Press, 1953.

—— (1926), Inhibitions, Symptoms and Anxiety. *Standard Edition*, 20:77-175. London: Hogarth Press, 1959.

—— (1927), Fetishism. *Standard Edition*, 21:149-157. London: Hogarth Press, 1961.

Heinicke, C. M. & Westheimer, I. (1965), *Brief Separations*. New York: International Universities Press.

Jacobson, E. (1964), *The Self and the Object World*. New York: International Universities Press.

—— (1965), The Return of the Lost Parent. In: *Drives, Affects, Behavior*, Vol. 2, ed. M. Schur. New York: International Universities Press, pp. 193-211.

Krupp, G. R. (1965), Identification as a Defence against Anxiety in Coping with Loss. *Int. J. Psa.*, 46:303-314.

Niederland, W. G. (1965), An Analytic Inquiry into the Life and Work of Heinrich Schliemann. In: *Drives, Affects, Behavior*, Vol. 2, ed. M. Schur. New York: International Universities Press, pp. 369-396.

Robertson, J. (1958), *Young Children in Hospitals*. New York: Basic Books.

Volkart, E. H. & Michael, S. T. (1957), Bereavement and Mental Health. In: *Death and Identity*, ed. R. Fulton. New York: Wiley, 1965, pp. 272-293.

Wolfenstein, M. (1966), How Is Mourning Possible? *This Annual*, 21:93-123.

APPLICATIONS OF ANALYSIS

ON THE FUNCTION OF CRIMINAL LAW
IN RIOT CONTROL

JOSEPH GOLDSTEIN, Ph.D., LL.B.

What can and should be the function of the *criminal law* in the control and regulation of riots? That is the question on which this essay will focus. It covers a relatively small, though complex, segment of a much larger problem in law—reaching the underlying causes of riots. That problem is of continuing concern to all agencies of decision in law—legislative, executive, and judicial. Any response therefore to the narrowly posed legislative question must ultimately be evaluated in the context of answers to such questions as: What are the underlying causes of riots? What are the functions of riots? How can riots be tolerated or prevented without sacrificing values fundamental to a democratic society? For purposes of long-range public and private planning in child care, education, employment, housing, technology, welfare, armed forces recruitment, and civil rights—to identify a few potentially relevant areas of decision —are there meaningful distinctions to be made between, for example, planned and spontaneous riots, between led and apparently leaderless riots, between riots with and without visible goals, or between riots *by* or *against* blacks, veterans, students, police, labor or any other group?

Walton Hale Hamilton Professor of Law, Science and Social Policy, Yale University.

This essay is an elaboration of a paper presented to a panel on "Applications of Psychoanalysis Beyond the Therapeutic," at the Fall Meeting of the American Psychoanalytic Association in New York, December, 1968; and of a paper presented to the students and faculty of the College of Old Westbury of the State University of New York, January, 1969. I am pleased to acknowledge the valuable editorial and research assistance of Max Gitter, Paul Friedman, and Jose de Lasa, students and former students at Yale Law School. I am also indebted to Joseph Goldsen, Sonja Goldstein, Seymour Lustman, Lottie and Richard Newman, William Pious, Roy Schafer, and to my students in the 1968 seminar on "Psychoanalysis and Law," for their critical suggestions.

Changing this quizzical stance somewhat, lawmakers might develop a series of questions starting with: What are the underlying causes of compassion, of affection, of generosity, of cooperation, and of love which have come to characterize the work and the feeling of a very significant, not always articulate, segment of each younger generation on its, hopefully nonviolent, way to power? All of these questions—questions to which much in psychoanalytic theory should prove relevant to decisionmakers in law[1]—present too wide a set of issues. In this essay the role and function of only the criminal law in its relationship to riots will be explored.

The criminal law is but a single piece in the mosaic of social controls which constitute our "average expectable environment." It is a last-resort community resource. With riots, as with most criminal conduct, government must rely on other means to reach underlying causes. Lawmakers must avoid the common error of attributing to the criminal process major responsibility for either the occurrence or the absence of riots. At best a law of crimes may reduce a fraction of the frustrations and pent-up forces that are so easily catalyzed into riot. Its maladministration may, however, contribute greatly to the exacerbation of such forces.

In deciding what the criminal law should provide for the purpose of deterring riots, the lawmaker must therefore focus on those characteristics of the event which require proscription and on those

---

[1] See, generally, *Report of National Advisory Commission on Civil Disorders* (1968) and the work of, for example, Erikson (1950), A. Freud (1949), Mitscherlich (1963), and Wangh (1964), which are directly relevant to the design of long-range programs for reaching some of the underlying causes of mob violence through, for example, legislation concerned with education, housing, employment, welfare, and technology.

On the law's potential for creating group safety valves through official holidays designed to release pent-up repressed feelings, to take another example outside the ambit of this essay, see Freud (1921): "In all renunciations and limitations imposed upon the ego a periodical infringement of the prohibition is the rule; this indeed is shown by the institution of festivals, which in origin are nothing less nor more than excesses provided by law and which owe their cheerful character to the release which they bring. The Saturnalia of the Romans and our modern carnival agree in this essential feature with the festivals of primitive people, which usually end in debaucheries of every kind and the transgression of what are at other times the most sacred commandments. But the ego ideal comprises the sum of all the limitations in which the ego has to acquiesce, and for that reason the abrogation of the ideal would necessarily be a magnificent festival for the ego, which might then once again feel satisfied with itself" (p. 105).

Similarly, Spiegel (1968) in his four-phase analysis of the riot process calls Phase 3 "The Roman Holiday."

means, within the narrow ambit of the law's authorized responses, which are most likely to reduce rather than exacerbate riotous conduct. Recognizing the limit and limitations of the criminal law he must focus, as does this essay, primarily on riots threatened and riots in being—that is on events at a point in time when the underlying causes which give rise to riots have already matured.

This analysis of the role the criminal law can and should play in riot deterrence will draw on traditional law as well as other sources, including psychoanalysis, which seem relevant. After a summary presentation of the traditional approach and after identifying the values in issue, which the drafters of a criminal code must clarify, this essay will place particular attention on what psychoanalysis might contribute to an examination of the problem.

The application of psychological knowledge to any sociolegal problem is highly complex. Although law and psychoanalysis converge in their concern for man, his mind, his behavior, and his environment, the two disciplines diverge in purpose, function, and the contexts in which some of their common concerns arise. Further, it must be recognized that the psychoanalytic theory of man as an individual may not be adequate to permit productive explorations of what may be even more complex than an individual— groups of human beings interacting in and with the legal process (see Goldstein, 1968).

With these caveats in mind about the twin dangers of attributing too much to the criminal law and of overstating the relevance of psychoanalysis to law, I turn to two questions which the promulgators of a criminal code would ask: First, since riot must involve conduct short of revolutionary activity already proscribed by the crimes of treason, insurrection, and mutiny, how is a riot to be distinguished, for criminal law purposes, from legally protected peaceful group conduct? Put another way, is there a need in a criminal code for a special substantive crime of "riot"? Second, whether or not there be such need, should such conventional crimes as assault, arson, or burglary committed during or in furtherance of a riot be subject to the same, greater, lesser, or somehow different sanctions from those authorized by statute for the same offense committed during more "normal" periods? Before turning to the second question, which will be analyzed in some detail, a brief conclusionary response to the first will be made in order to identify some of the socially shared values in issue and in order to define "riot" for criminal law purposes.

I

The never ending challenge to law in a democracy has always been to locate the line past which dissent and protest become intolerable burdens on a minimum need for order. The delegates to the Federal Convention, meeting in Philadelphia in 1787, were men who had rebelled against England and who were themselves plagued with the threat of the rebellion by Shay in Massachusetts. These men were acutely aware of the importance of order on the one hand, and of the value of protest and dissent on the other; the viability of the Union which they hoped to establish would depend on their ability to safeguard these values through law. Accordingly, the Constitution of the United States specifically provides that no law shall be made "abridging the freedom of speech, or of the press; or of the right of the people peaceably to assemble and to petition the Government for a redress of grievance." And the Supreme Court has "fashioned the principle that the constitutional guarantees of free speech and free press do not permit a State to forbid or proscribe advocacy of the use of force or of law violation except where such advocacy is directed to inciting or producing imminent lawless action and is likely to produce such action."[2] As the Walker Commission observed in its report on the 1968 Chicago convention riots:

> In principle, at least, most Americans acknowledge the right to dissent. And in principle, at least, most dissenters acknowledge the right of a city to protect its citizens and its property. But what happens when these undeniable rights are brought—deliberately by some—into conflict? [p. ii].

The criminal law is supposed to provide the answer. It writes in advance the scenario describing the circumstances under which the

---

[2] Brandenburg v. Ohio, 37 L W 4525 (U.S. Supreme Court, 1969). For attempts to enunciate the limits which the requirement of public order sets for the exercise of free speech generally, see Terminiello v. City of Chicago, 337 U.S. 1 (1949); Feiner v. New York, 340 U.S. 315 (1951); Kunz v. New York, 340 U.S. 290 (1951); Nietmotko v. Maryland, 340 U.S. 268 (1951).

government is authorized to arrest and impose other sanctions upon persons suspected or convicted of engaging in criminal conduct. In defining specific conduct as offensive, a criminal code thereby excludes from proscription—as is obvious once said—all other conduct and particularly all conduct protected by the Constitution.

The criminal law defines behavior of both the governed and the governors which is deemed intolerably disturbing to and destructive of widely shared community values. Harold Laski (1943) described the challenge to law in a way that is particularly relevant to the criminal process:

> Those who speak of restoring the rule of law forget that respect for law is the condition of its restoration. And respect for law is at least as much a function of what law does as of its formal source. Men break the law not out of an anarchistic hatred for law as such, but because certain ends they deem fundamental cannot be attained within the framework of an existing system of laws. To restore the rule of law means creating the psychological conditions which make men yield allegiance to the law. No limitations upon government can be maintained when society is so insecure that great numbers deny the validity of the very foundations upon which it is based [p. 15f.].

Thus the criminal law, in striving to keep our revolutions peaceful, must protect assembly and the free expression of unusual, even deviant, ideas and conduct so essential to the growth of a democratic society.

Riots, whether perceived from a historical, sociological, political or psychological vantage point, are often a form of protest, a dramatic reflection of dissatisfaction with either governmental or private institutions; riots are often an expression of undefined, but nonetheless real frustration and hostility, of the failure or apparent failure of society to provide certain groups of the population with adequate opportunities for hope, for fulfillment, and for equality of treatment.[3] As Freud (1921) noted:

[3] See, generally, *Report of the National Advisory Committee on Civil Disorders* (1968). Sauter and Hines (1968) highlight one of those frustrations: " 'The cat on Twelfth Street can look a hundred yards away and see another black cat living in an eight-room house with a 1967 Pontiac and a motorboat on Lake Michigan,' a Negro schoolteacher told a visitor to Detroit during the summer of 1967. 'For that matter, General Motors itself is only a few blocks away. I've seen kids from my school walk

[T]here grows up in . . . children a . . . group feeling. . . . The first demand made by this reaction-formation is for justice, for equal treatment for all. . . . If one cannot be the favourite oneself, at all events nobody else shall be the favourite [p. 120].

Since riots are in part a form of group communication, however chaotic and inarticulate, and since the Constitution and the criminal law are designed to protect speech and assembly, lawmakers must determine at what point lawful protest or assembly becomes illegal activity, a crime. Put another way, how is a riot to be distinguished from lawful demonstrations, from the exercise of liberties which require and deserve protection? There must be something more than protest, more than vague or precise expressions of discontent, to justify the imposition of criminal sanctions upon the participants or architects of group, crowd or mob behavior. That "something more" must be either:

(a) *violence*—the forceful exercise of power which results in injury to person or to property, or which seriously threatens such injury or damage; or

(b) *interference with the lawful pursuit of others*—unreasonable interference or serious threats of interference with lawful public or private activity, with constitutionally guaranteed rights or with lawful efforts to safeguard those pursuits and rights.

The essence of a riot, for purposes of the criminal law, then, is a large group of people, civilian or official, organized or not, with or without a leader, engaging over a generally relatively short span of time either in violent conduct, or in other coercive forms of intrusion on legitimate private or public activity.

Any justification for a separate substantive offense of "riot" in a criminal code would require a determination that the conventional body of criminal offenses, of proscribed conduct, in that code did not cover all forms of violent or coercive conduct which constitute the essence of a riot. An illustrative selection of offenses to

---

over to the showroom and sit down in a new model Cadillac, sort of snuggle their little rear ends into the soft leather, slide their hands over the slick plastic steering wheel, and say "Man, feel that." It's all so close, and yet it's all so far away, and the frustration just eats them up' " (p. 122). See also Dynes and Quarantelli (1968, p. 9).

be found in local, state, and federal codes suggests how wide and all-inclusive is the range of potentially riot-related conduct which is already proscribed: disorderly conduct, breach of the peace, obstruction of traffic, arson, criminal possession of explosives, criminal trespass, burglary, possession of burglar tools, theft, assault, possession of illegal weapons, traffic in unlawful weapons, denial of civil rights, reckless endangerment, creating a hazard, obstructing public officials, giving false alarms or information to authorities, destruction of evidence of a crime, manslaughter, homicide, treason, and finally, conspiracies or attempts to commit all of the above offenses.[4] Although most state codes do make special provision for riot, it is manifest that the arsenal of conventional offenses is sufficiently complete to enable officials to invoke the criminal process against all persons who make, threaten to make, or are trying to make a "riot" something more than peaceful protest or assembly.[5] Although this is far too brief an analysis of the question, I submit that there is neither need nor justification for a separate criminal offense of "riot" in local, state, or federal criminal codes.

II

There remains one characteristic of "riot"—a substantially large number of criminal offenses concentrated in a short span of time—which prompts asking the second question: Should a criminal code authorize different sanctions for an individual who commits or is suspected of committing a crime during or in furtherance of a riot than it does for an individual who commits or is suspected of committing the same offense during more "normal" periods?

Generally, the criminal law both proscribes behavior which is deemed intolerably disturbing to or destructive of community values and prescribes post- and preconviction sanctions which the state is authorized to impose upon persons convicted or suspected of engaging in prohibited conduct. Following a plea or verdict of guilty,

---

[4] See, e.g., *Michigan Revised Criminal Code* (Final Draft, 1967).
[5] *Report of the National Advisory Commission on Civil Disorders* (1968), pp. 288-291); and see *Model Penal Code* §250.1, Comment at pp. 4, 5, 19 (Tent. Draft No. 13, 1961). For common law construction of riot, see Perkins (1957, pp. 344-349).

the state deprives offenders of life, liberty, dignity, or property through convictions, fines, imprisonments, killings, and supervised releases, and thus seeks to punish, restrain, and rehabilitate them, a well as to deter others from engaging in proscribed activity. Before verdict, and despite the presumption of innocence which haloes every person, the state deprives the suspect of life, liberty, dignity, or property through the imposition of deadly force, search and seizure of persons and possessions, accusation, imprisonment, and bail, and thus seeks to facilitate the enforcement of the criminal law (Goldstein, 1960).[6]

The law has generally treated "riot" as an aggravating attendant circumstance justifying an increase in both pre- and postconviction sanctions. By permitting police officers physically to assault and even to kill individuals in the course of quelling a "riot" the common law authorized an increase in preconviction sanctions allowing the police to serve as judge, juror, and executioner prior to an orderly determination of guilt or innocence.[7] And the Civil Rights Act of 1968 paradoxically exempts police "engaged in suppressing a riot" from criminal liability for willfully and forcefully injuring or intimidating anyone exercising enumerated federally "protected" civil rights.[8] Thus while under present law "riot" serves as an aggravating factor which legitimizes and increases the preconviction sanctions to which a civilian participant may be subject, it simultaneously serves as a mitigating factor which relieves the police, the official participant, of liability for conduct otherwise criminal—i.e., for his

---

[6] Sanctions are imposed by the state presumably against, or at least without regard to, the wishes of the individual being deprived. Implicit in the word "sanction," as used in this essay, is involuntariness. In this context involuntariness is not treated as a psychological concept. Thus, for example, imprisonment is a sanction even if imposed on a person who commits a crime in order to be punished (Freud, 1916).

[7] "In the interpretation of [13 Hen. IV. c. 7] it has been held, that all persons, noblemen and others, except women, clergymen, persons decrepit, and infants under fifteen, are bound to attend the justices in suppressing a riot, upon pain of fine and imprisonment; and *that any battery, wounding, or killing the rioters, that may happen in suppressing the riot is justifiable* [p. 1 Hal. P.C. 495; 1 Hark. P.C. 161]. So that our ancient law, previous to the modern Riot Act, seems pretty well to have guarded against any violent breach of the public peace" (Blackstone, 1765, p. 155).

And see *Michigan Revised Criminal Code* §5510, comment at p. 426 (Final Draft, 1967). Michigan law also assigns to riot participants the liability for the death of one killed in trying to repress the riot. Mich. C.L. §750.527 (1948).

[8] 18 USC 245 (c) (1968).

failure to exercise the restraint that would be demanded of him in the "normal" course of his "law enforcement" duties.[9] Illustrative of postconviction sanctions which treat "riot" as an aggravating factor is to authorize increased sentences for offenders found guilty of a crime committed during a riot or, as Congress has done, to make such offenders ineligible for federal employment for a five-year period.[10]

Lawmakers have argued that "committed during the course of a riot" should be treated as an aggravating factor. There seem to be two reasons for this—retribution and deterrence. The retributive purpose often goes unacknowledged and becomes camouflaged by the label and language of deterrence. Increased sanctions for riot-related offenses would undoubtedly serve some as an outlet for the anger aroused against those who provoke with obscenities or who make life more difficult or more dangerous by engaging in criminal activity when protective public resources (police, firemen, prosecutors, defense counsel, and the courts) are overtaxed and at a disadvantage.

In theory, preconviction sanctions are not to serve a retributive function. The presumption of innocence means that there is no place for punishment prior to a finding of guilt. Preconviction sanctions are to be no more severe than is necessary to safeguard any individual from a direct threat to his life, as in self-defense, and to assure an opportunity for the criminal process to run its course until that

9 Even the traditional authority for the use of force, particularly lethal force by the police, may well be too great. Leary (1967, p. 2) states: "Though all American jurisdictions share the two basic assumptions that the police should be armed, and that their use of firearms should be limited, there are some significant differences with respect to precisely what the limitations should be. With respect to self-defense, there is little, if any, difference in principle, except, perhaps, with respect to a duty to retreat before using deadly force. But with respect to the use of deadly force to prevent the commission of crimes and to apprehend criminals, the differences are fundamental. The traditional rule with respect to prevention and apprehension was that the policeman could shoot, to kill, if he reasonably believed that the person at whom he shot was committing a felony or escaping from a felony. This is today the rule in most American jurisdictions. It is, I believe, overly broad."

10 5 USC 7313 (1968). For other proposals in the same spirit, see, e.g., Cong. Rec.: H. Res. 15067, 90th Cong., 2d Sess. §1302, 114 Cong. Rec. H7514 (1968) (to deny federal aid to students involved in university disturbances) and S. Res. 2183, 90th Cong., 1st Sess., §1 (1967) (to make any person convicted under either state or federal law of rioting or of a riot-connected crime permanently ineligible to receive any federal payment or assistance whatsoever).

innocence dissolves into guilt established beyond a reasonable doubt and in accord with due process.[11]

Increasing sanctions for retributive purposes following such a determination of guilt may, however, accord with the general purposes of most criminal codes and thus may be an appropriate response. But even for authorized vengeance there must be some collective point of diminishing returns—i.e., a point at which the sanction no longer serves its function. That assertion contains a prediction about the impact of an external event—the sanction—on conduct and thus moves this analysis away from an evaluation solely in terms of conflicts between the multiple purposes of a sanction and constitutionally protected values. Such speculations about the capacity of a sanction to fulfill its purpose—about the impact of external events on conduct—are, as psychoanalysis teaches, extremely risky and of doubtful validity. And since the analysis of whether sanctions for riot-related offenses should for deterrent purposes be different from sanctions for the same offense committed during "normal" periods will involve such predictions, it becomes important to repeat a caution on the application of psychoanalytic theory to law which is based on the findings of Freud (1920), Hartmann and Kris (1945), and Anna Freud (1965):

[T]he meaning of an actual experience [for example, being subjected to or imposing a specific sanction] in giving direction to a person's life rests . . . on countless internal and external variables. Not only may what appears to be a similar event have different significance for the same person depending upon his stage of development at the time of its occurrence, but it may also have different implications for different people at similar stages of development. Implicit in this observation is an insight of substantial significance to anyone seeking to evaluate the

11 Many police manuals contain exhortations reflecting this view. *The Richmond, Va., Bureau of Police Rules and Regulations* (1957), for example, provides "Advice to Policemen. . . . Whenever you deem it necessary to make an arrest, do it; but use no more force than is necessary to protect yourself and secure your prisoner"; *Portland, Me., Police Department Rules and Regulations* §1124.04 provides: "All officers should know that the prisoner has certain rights guaranteed him by the United States and Maine Constitutions. . . . He shall not be subject to more restraint than is necessary to hold or confine him. . . . *He is assumed to be innocent until pronounced guilty*" (my italics). This same rationale ought to apply to "riot" situations. And see Goldstein (1960, p. 549f.).

consequences of decisions in law. It points to a limitation frequently obscured in assumptions in empirical studies about the impact or likely impact of a statute, judgment, or administrative ruling. Unless such decisions are perceived as external events in the lives of many people—events which have different meanings for different people—statistical evidence of success may include, without recognizing a distinction, a number of people upon whom the decision had no impact; and, even more significant, it may include in the failure column a number upon whom the decision had a direct impact contrary to that sought —not just no impact.

For example, in evaluating a decision to impose a criminal sanction against a specific offender for purposes both of satisfying the punitive demands of the community and of deterring others from engaging in the offensive conduct, the student of law can or ought to assume that the decision may for some satisfy, for some exacerbate, and for some have nothing to do with punitive wishes, and may for some restrain, for some provoke, and for some have no impact on the urge to engage in the prohibited conduct. Recognition of the multiple consequences of every law-created event makes comprehensible both the never-ending search for multiple resolutions of what is perceived to be a single problem in law and the resultant need to find an ensemble of official and unofficial responses which on balance come closest to achieving the social control sought [Goldstein, 1968, p. 473f.].

A more significant and complex issue than retribution is whether more severe sanctions will on balance serve to reinforce or to undermine the criminal law's general deterrent impact.[12] Additional pre- and postconviction sanctions, it is often reasoned, will deter "potential offenders," civilian and police, by making them weigh the risk of being treated more harshly if convicted or discovered *against* the reduced risk of getting caught or convicted because law enforcement facilities are overtaxed. In other words, it is assumed that because of more severe sanctions "potential civilian and official offenders" caught up in a crowd will choose either consciously or unconsciously not to commit a crime or choose more "normal

[12] The word deterrence often carries with it two quite different meanings: individual prevention—the effect of a sanction on the individual being punished; and general prevention—the inhibiting effect of a sanction generally on the members of the community. In this essay, unless otherwise indicated, the concern is ultimately with general deterrence, as the phrase "on balance" in the text implies. See Andenaes (1966) for a discussion of the distinction.

periods" for their criminal activity, i.e., periods when a test of reality would reveal that the usual deterrent forces at work have not been weakened.

This assumption contains two concepts—"normal periods" and "choice"—which require examination. First, what is often forgotten in the righteous cries for a return "to law and order" which accompany official orders to "shoot to kill arsonists and shoot to maim looters" (Walker, 1968, p. viii) is that during "normal periods" law enforcement is and has always been selective, not full or total enforcement. Society has generally been unwilling to provide, for financial and other reasons, enough police, prosecutors, defense counsel, and judges to fully enforce, even within constitutional limits, the substantive law of crimes (Goldstein, 1960). To the extent that the breakdown, by riot, of an already overtaxed system of criminal law administration is a consequence itself to be deterred, an increase not of sanctions but of law enforcement manpower available during such critical periods offers the most direct and promising deterrent capability.[13] Greater numbers of men with specialized training in nonprovocative control should minimize consequences which otherwise would compound the progress of violence. By establishing emergency procedures for utilizing police, prosecutors, defense counsel, judges, supportive staff and facilities and by thus safeguarding the power of local and state authorities to determine priorities of enforcement, government can substantially reduce the

---

[13] See Janowitz (1968, pp. 20-28) and Leary (1968). For reports of efforts to increase law enforcement manpower, to improve police training, and to establish procedures for emergencies such as riots, see *New York Times*, Aug. 5, 1968, at 32, col. 4 (Report of the Mayor's Committee on the Administration of Justice Under Emergency Conditions [May 25, 1968]). See also Westley (1966): "Curiously, policemen show more wisdom when they face a violent crowd. Police assigned to a strike squad are taught to exercise phenomenal restraint, even to the extent of not reacting when they are spat upon. These specialists in crowd relations have learned to contain and to lead, rather than to restrain a crowd—a procedure which interrupts the antagonistic interaction and baffles the crowd. Policemen in Capitol cities have developed this to a fine art after great experience in meeting crowds determined to demonstrate, sometimes violently. The procedure which the police employ is to meet the group, describe to the group its rights, tell them the conditions under which they can exercise these rights, and provide police protection so that no one can deprive the crowd of its rights. . . . The effect of this tactic of facing the crowd and continuous talking seems to be to prevent the crowd from dehumanizing the policeman, thus freeing themselves for violence. As long as there is communication by voice, gesture, and eye, a human relationship can continue. But violence by the policeman breaks this compact, and the crowd feels free to become violent" (p. 123).

possibility of paralyzing the administration of justice. It can, with due regard to constitutional safeguards, maintain an external reality which continues to function at the "normal" level of deterrence, whatever that may be.[14]

Such contingency plans can also serve to reduce the likelihood of police panic and thus deter excesses of force. What Freud (1921) observed about the military would seem to apply as well to the police:

> [E]ach individual is bound by libidinal ties on the one hand to the leader . . . and on the other hand to the other members of the group . . . the essence of a group lies in the libidinal ties existing in it. . . . A panic arises if a group of that kind becomes disintegrated. Its characteristics are that none of the orders given by superiors are any longer listened to, and that each individual is only solicitous on his own account, and without any consideration for the rest. The mutual ties have ceased to exist, and a gigantic and senseless fear is set free . . . it is of the very essence of panic that it bears no relation to the danger that threatens, and often breaks out on the most trivial occasions [p. 95f.].

Evidence of police brutality, such as that characterized by Walker (1968) as "police riot," may bear this out and should prompt the development of emergency plans and training designed to reinforce or at least keep intact the libidinal ties essential to a disciplined professional police department. Without such plans, or in failing to carry out such plans, the consequent weakening of mutual ties within the department releases each for membership in a new, possibly, leaderless group—a mob in which as Freud (1921) observed "individual inhibitions fall away and all the cruel, brutal and destructive instincts, which lie dormant in individuals . . . , are stirred up to find free gratification" (p. 79).

Of course a "police riot" may be evidence not of panic but rather of strong libidinal ties between the members of a police department and their leaders whose orders they obediently follow. As Freud (1921) observed:

[14] See, generally, *Report of the National Advisory Commission on Civil Disorders* (1968). Also see, e.g., N.Y. Laws of 1968, chs. 1077 (S.5478-B), 1078 (S.5080-A), and 1079 (A.7172).

[E]verything that the object [the leader] does and asks for is right and blameless. Conscience has no application to anything that is done for the sake of the object; in the blindness of love remorselessness is carried to the pitch of crime. . . . *The object has been put in the place of the ego ideal* [p. 113].

Since both libidinal and aggressive forces are inherently neither "good" nor "bad" but underlie all behavior, the main question is how they are employed by the ego responding to external demands. Thus the very same strong libidinal ties between members of a police department and their leaders provide the greatest opportunity for restrained as well as excessive exercise of authority.

Law, particularly the administration of the criminal law in a democratic society, is, as both an ego and superego nutriment, to command respect for the dignity of each individual as a human being. It generally authorizes the use of lethal force only when life is endangered. Ramsey Clark, while Attorney General of the United States, reaffirmed the law's restriction on the exercise of police power: "An express mandate to the entire police complement to use the minimum force necessary to execute lawful orders, to refrain from use of excessive force must be understood by every officer.[15] Obscured then by the emotional freight carried by the cry for "law and order" in demands for increased sanctions against rioters is its real meaning which includes a mandate to the governors—the police, the judge, the prosecutors and legislators as well—for due process, for the orderly administration of justice at all times, whether normal or not.

The deterrence argument for increased sanctions rests on another concept, "choice." Generally the criminal law uses choice in terms of some undefined conscious exercise of free will which it calls voluntariness and *mens rea*. In so doing, it uses choice to mean control—self-control—which incorporates, in practice if not in theory, unconscious as well as conscious factors. While the following discussion responds primarily to an argument which seems to rest on choice, in a conscious sense, it will address itself to choice or control in terms of both the conscious and unconscious forces at work in each individual.

---

[15] *New York Times*, September 22, 1968, at E 7, col. 3.

What little is known about crowd psychology seems to suggest that excessive sanctions, particularly preconviction sanctions involving physical force, will, on balance and in the long run, increase the frequency or duration of the violence which characterizes riots. Indeed, any such "violence count" must include this very exercise of official force which society, through the criminal law, seeks to keep at a minimum.[16]

Existing psychological theories of the riot phenomenon reinforce doubts about the view that more severe sanctions will serve a deterrent function, and cast doubt on voluntariness and *mens rea*—both being fundamental requisites of all major crimes for which a rioter might be held criminally responsible.

In his now classic *Psychology of the Herd* (1895), Le Bon's major thesis about the crowds of the French Revolution was that once merged in a group, a law-abiding person seems temporarily to lose his critical and moral standards and thereby becomes prone to violence and capable of other unlawful activity. He observed, as do observers of the current scene:

[T]he individual forming part of a group acquires, solely from numerical considerations, a sentiment of invincible power which allows him to yield to instincts which, had he been alone, he would perforce have kept under restraint. He will be the less disposed to check himself, from the consideration that, a group being anonymous and in consequence irresponsible, the sentiment of responsibility which always controls individuals disappears entirely [as cited by Freud, 1921, p. 74].

In his *Group Psychology* (1921) Freud devotes much thought to the pioneering work of Le Bon and restates his observation in psychoanalytic terms: "For us it would be enough to say that in a group the individual is brought under conditions which allow him to throw off the repressions of his unconscious instinctual impulses" (p. 74). Why some people in a group regress to become a mob and

16 "[I]t is a fact that many of the recent riots in our urban centers had as one of their principal sparks a hostile reaction in the community to the use of a gun by a policeman. I am not passing judgment on the fairness or the unfairness of those reactions, nor am I suggesting that where force is clearly necessary a policeman must hold back for fear of causing such a reaction. But I do say that those incidents are one more reason why the community must know that the police policies and practices concerning firearms are fair and reasonable" (Leary, 1967, p. 2).

what releases the hostile and aggressive forces in some "reasonable men" and not in others and why and how such forces can sweep through a crowd is yet to be fully understood. It is as if the anonymity which an individual acquires in a crowd loosens, like alcohol, the ties between the inner checks which constitute conscience, and its many external nourishing forces (parents, friends, police, public opinion, etc.) which are a part of each man's reality—the "average expectable environment" (Hartmann, 1939). More specifically, to the extent that a riot constitutes a breakdown of law and its enforcement, external nutriments essential to the work of both *ego* and *superego* are weakened in their efforts to control hostile and aggressive *id* forces. The effect of this withdrawal of external nutriment is found in the often uninhibited conduct of soldiers and travelers abroad (Rapaport, 1958, p. 20). In a riot, however, there seems to be something more than withdrawal of the "usual" environment. There is the substitution of a new external nutriment—the crowd, which imposes new demands under rules of its own. In Freud's words:

> A group impresses the individual as being an unlimited power and an insurmountable peril. For the moment it replaces the whole of human society, which is the wielder of authority, whose punishments the individual fears, and for whose sake he has submitted to so many inhibitions. It is clearly perilous for him to put himself in opposition to it, and it will be safer to follow the example of those around him and perhaps even 'hunt with the pack.' In obedience to the new authority he may put his former 'conscience' out of action, and so surrender to the attraction of the increased pleasure that is certainly obtained from the removal of inhibitions [1921, p. 84f.].

Thus, for example, a civilian rioter facing a wide-open store full of goods can actually exclaim: "It would be a crime not to take something," or a police rioter can threaten news photographers with: "You take my picture tonight and I'm going to get you," or scream: "Get the fucking photographers and get the film" (Walker, 1968).

Related to the anonymity and breakdown of internal controls that may characterize membership in a crowd is what Bernard, Ottenberg, and Redl (1965) call "dehumanization—a composite psychological defense."[17] In its maladaptive form "dehumanization" allows a person to perceive others as if they lacked human attributes, to increase his emotional distance from them, and to experience conscious feelings of great fear and excessive hostility coupled with a blindness or denial of actual and generally foreseeable consequences of his conduct. A person stops identifying with other human beings, no longer seeing people outside his immediate group as essentially similar to himself. His relationships become stereotyped and rigid. His usual feelings of concern become anaesthetized, replaced by powerfully destructive forces within himself. The Nazis' capacity to perceive Jews as swine and to slaughter them by the millions is a dramatic illustration of this mechanism. Today, in the cities and on the campus, whites, as members of a subgroup, or white policemen, as members of an even more tightly bound subgroup, may cry: "Get the niggers"; reverse the color and the cry may be: "Get whitey"; integrate and hear the Yippies or the Hippies scream: "Police are pigs, kill the pigs." Such manifestations of the dehumanization mechanism which indiscriminately lumps individuals into groups labeled "nigger," "whitey," or "pig" are more likely to lead to excesses of force—to the release of aggression—in both directions than to the release of libidinal energy in the form of assistance, cooperation, and sympathy which would characterize mechanisms of "rehumanization."[18]

[17] Dehumanization also "serves important adaptive purposes in many life situations. . . . Certain occupations in particular require such selectively dehumanized behavior. These occupations . . . carry the extra risk of their requisite dehumanization becoming maladaptive if it is carried to an extreme or used inappropriately. Examples of these include law enforcement (police, judges, lawyers, prison officials); . . . Indeed, some degree of adaptive dehumanization seems to be a basic requirement for effective participation in any institutional process" (Bernard, Ottenberg and Redl, 1965, p. 67).

[18] "The current 'loose talk of shooting looters' is likely to cause guerrilla warfare between Negroes and whites in American cities, Attorney General Ramsey Clark said. . . . 'No civilized nation in history has sanctioned summarily shooting thieves caught in the commission of their crime,' he said. 'Will America be the first?' In a blunt speech to a group of state trial judges, Mr. Clark noted that nearly all the rioters and looters were Negroes and added: 'When order is restored, as it will be, we shall have to go on living together, black and white, forever on the same soil. Excessive force, inhumane action, a blood-letting can only lead to further division and further violence,' he said. 'A nation which permitted the lynching of more than 4,500 people, nearly all Negroes, between 1882 and 1930 can ill afford to engage in summary capital punishment without trial in our turbulent times,' he declared" (*New York Times*, p. 14, c. 1; August 16, 1968).
One of the most notorious incidents of alleged police brutality is the Algiers

Dehumanization is further reflected, more subtly and thus less visibly but no less insidiously, in the monumental indifference of city dwellers to their urban ghettoes and the widespread and long-standing violations of building safety and sanitation codes which inevitably take their toll in life, health, and human dignity. As Allen (1967) has observed:

> The departments of city government charged with the inspection of dwellings and the enforcement of building regulations are typically understaffed, lackadaisical, inefficient, and devoid of ingenuity, even when (as is often true) they are not literally corrupt or amenable to political pressures. . . . But many members of that same community reveal anything but indifference to the noise, inconvenience, and incidental law violations associated with demonstrations organized to protest the conditions of life in the slum tenements [p. 31].

And that indifference, both private and official, reasserts itself when those communities deny, without investigation, that excesses in police force took place during such demonstrations and fail to take disciplinary action against those police who engaged in criminal activity.

Sociological theory focuses on man's external, rather than internal, reality and provides an anatomy of the social setting and atmosphere which seems to foster and release those psychological forces which trigger riots. For one sociologist (Smelser, 1963) the six determinants of a riot are: (i) structural conduciveness—social conditions permissive of certain collective behavior, e.g., an atmosphere in which a large minority population perceives violence to be a possible means of expression as in urban ghettoes; (ii) structural strain—a conflict in the values or norms of two groups, e.g., inequality of opportunity for education, employment, and housing between, for example, blacks and whites; (iii) the growth and spread of a generalized belief—attributing certain characteristics to the

Motel Incident during the Detroit riot of 1967. Dehumanization may have been a crucial factor in the slaying by police of three Negroes during a search for snipers, thought to be operating from the motel. The incident is discussed by Hersey (1968) and Reis (1968). For an example of the dehumanization mechanism at work in the psychology of the Negro rather than the policeman, see *New York Times,* August 4, 1968 at 37 for an article entitled "Wounded Policeman Is Certain Ambushers Wanted 'Any 2 Cops.'" Also see Janowitz (1968).

source of the strain, e.g., visible manifestations of the dehumanization mechanism; (iv) a precipitating factor—an incident which is interpreted in terms of the generalized belief, e.g., perceiving a lawful arrest or an innocent remark in terms of the hostile belief;[19] (v) the mobilization of participants—someone or many assuming responsibility for spreading communication through the group (psychology of the crowd) about a real or imagined incident; and (vi) the operation of social control—to the extent that it is weakened or absent it becomes a determinant rather than a counterdeterminant, e.g., overtaxing the administration of justice.

The nature of the setting in which riots occur is eloquently set forth by Pope Paul in language freed of the vocabulary of both sociology and psychology:

> There are certainly situations whose injustice cries to heaven. When whole populations destitute of necessities live in a state of dependence barring them from all initiative and responsibility, and all opportunity to advance culturally and share in social and political life, recourse to violence, as a means to right these wrongs to human dignity, is a grave temptation.[20]

An appreciation of the psychology of a riot mob and its sociological determinants, though more descriptive than explanatory, leads to the conclusion that additional or more severe sanctions would on balance, and in the long run, weaken the general deterrent function of the criminal law. Individual "choice" control, essential to effective deterrence, is destroyed or substantially impaired when a person, police officer or civilian, loses his moral and critical faculties in or to a crowd or to its leader. Increased sentences, denial of an opportunity for government employment and, more particularly, authorization of lethal force or excessive force to apprehend looters or youthful protestors or anyone may be a temporary deterrent which affects some individuals but it can only

---

[19] Brown (1965, p. 733) cites Smelser (1963): "For instance, a racial incident between a Negro and a white may spark a race riot. But unless this incident occurs in the context of a structurally conducive atmosphere . . . and in an atmosphere of strain . . . the incident will pass without becoming a determinant in a racial outburst." Also see Spiegel (1968) and Janowitz (1968).

[20] Encyclical on the Development of People, *New York Times*, March 29, 1967, at p. 23, col. 8.

serve, in the long run, to increase structural strain and undo libidinal ties, allegiance if you will, to society at large. To further ali-
enate the alienated, to place the value of property over the value of
human life, or the value of official feelings hurt by verbal taunts and
obscenities over the value of an individual's physical integrity, can
only make highly explosive situations more explosive. As the then
Attorney General Clark observed:

> Of all violence police violence in excess of authority is the most
> dangerous. For who will protect the public when the police vio-
> late the law? . . . It is the duty of leadership and law enforce-
> ment to control violence, not cause it. To seek ways of relieving
> tension, not to look for a fight.[21]

In addition to countering the deterrence argument for increased
sanctions, our limited knowledge of the aberrant psychology of
crowds would undercut, at least for some participants, the very
basis of their criminal liability or pose an argument mitigating their
postconviction sanctions. Briefly (to develop this point in detail
would require another essay), the criminal law does not hold individuals responsible for involuntary conduct, coerced or automatized, or for offenses committed while insane, or for acts which are
unintended, that is for acts unaccompanied by the appropriate
degree of knowledge, purpose, intent *(mens rea)* on which the concept of "blameworthiness" is said to rest.[22] Being caught up in a
riot at the time of an offense might thus be perceived as evidence
casting doubt on an individual offender's voluntariness or *mens rea,*
requisites which are crucial to establishing guilt for all major offenses. Commission of an offense during the course of and as part
of a riot might also be perceived as evidence constituting an insanity "defense" or a provocation depriving a "reasonable man" of
his "capacity to conform his conduct to the requirements of the
law." Le Bon's description of the behavior of the unorganized
group—"like that of a wild beast, rather than like that of human
beings" (cited by Freud, 1921, p. 85)—recalls the early eighteenth-
century test of insanity which allowed the accused to be relieved
of criminal liability if he "does not know what he is doing, no more

21 *New York Times,* September 22, 1968, at E 7, col. 3.
22 Generally, see Donnelly, Goldstein, and Schwartz (1962, pp. 523-847).

than a wild beast."[23] Whether the contagion of lawlessness that sweeps through a crowd and turns it into a riot is explained in terms of "regression," "anonymity," "dehumanization," "withdrawal of external nutriments," or an exacerbating social setting,[24] an attorney for an "offender" might successfully develop a legal defense based on such concepts with relevant evidence, particularly from psychoanalytic observations, about a specific defendant or group of defendants. The observation is intended to forecast the use a defense attorney might make of material from the social psychology of mobs in developing an insanity defense or a direct challenge to *mens rea* or voluntariness. It does not, however, constitute an acceptance of the conceptual relevance of such concepts as insanity, *mens rea*, and voluntariness to the imposition of criminal sanctions or to the multiple functions of the criminal law.[25] Nor does the observation

[23] Earl Ferrer's case 19 How. St. Tr. 886 (1760), and see generally Durham v. United States, 214 F. 2d 862, 869 (1954).

[24] "Why not permit the defense of dwelling in a Negro ghetto? Such a defense would not be morally indefensible. Adverse social and subcultural background is statistically *more* criminogenic than is psychosis; like insanity, it also severely circumscribes the freedom of choice which a non-deterministic criminal law (all present criminal law systems) attributes to accused persons. True, a defense of social adversity would politically be intolerable; but that does not vitiate the analogy for my purposes. You argue that insanity destroys, undermines, diminishes man's capacity to reject what is wrong and to adhere to what is right. So does the ghetto—more so. But surely, you reply, I would not have us punish the sick. Indeed I would, if you insist on punishing the grossly deprived. To the extent that criminal sanctions serve punitive purposes, I fail to see the difference between these two defenses. To the extent that they serve rehabilitative, treatment, and curative purposes I fail to see the need for the difference" (Morris, 1968, p. 520).

[25] "[T]he insanity defense is not designed, as is the defense of self-defense, to define an exception to criminal liability, but rather to define for sanction an exception from among those who would be free of liability. It is as if the insanity defense were prompted by an affirmative answer to the silently posed question: 'Does *mens rea* or any essential element of an offense exclude from liability a group of persons whom the community wishes to restrain?' If the suggested relationship between *mens rea* and 'insanity' means that 'insanity' precludes proof beyond doubt of *mens rea*, then the 'defense' is designed to authorize the holding of persons who have committed no crime. So conceived, the problem really facing the criminal process has been how to obtain authority to sanction the 'insane' who would be excluded from liability by an overall application of the general principles of the criminal law.

"Furthermore, even if the relationship between insanity and '*mens rea*' is rejected, this same purpose re-emerges when we try to understand why the consequence of this defense, unlike other defenses, is restraint, not release. . . .

"The real problem which continues to face legislators, judges, jurors, and commentators is how to restrain persons who are somehow feared as both crazed and criminal. This oft-unconscious fear has precluded thinking about 'insanity' in terms of traditional principles of law, whether that 'insanity' is conceptualized as doubt-

mean that all group violence is the product of mob psychology. Such conduct may be not only the most adaptive but even the most just alternative to a repressive reality.

To sum up, recognition of the debilitating effect of the riot environment on a participant's internal restraints and of the claim of rioters that the rule of law has taken precedence over the rule of justice, does lead to the realization that a repressive reaction by lawmakers to riot-connected crimes, in the form of sanctions more severe than usual, will more likely serve as an invitation to regress and consequently more likely aggravate the problem which the criminal law seeks to alleviate. In other words, an undue emphasis on the retributive function of the criminal law with respect to riots would be counterproductive and would on balance defeat the more important function, deterrence (Allen, 1967, p. 120).

On the other hand, proof of "commission during the course of a riot" should not be given statutory recognition as a mitigating circumstance and thereby automatically relieve an accused of criminal liability. Understanding the effect of a riot on a participant's internal controls does not justify his criminal conduct, nor should it lead legislators (who too are not immune from panic) to withdraw or weaken existing external controls by excusing such offenders. An expectation of reduced sanctions may be perceived, in advance, as a toleration of violence and serve as an invitation to riot.[26] On balance, then, the argument that "riot" should generally (as opposed to individual cases in which, for example, a form of diminished responsibility is established) serve as a mitigating factor offsets the argument for treating it as an aggravating factor.

---

casting evidence or as an independent defense. Though unpleasant to acknowledge, the insanity defense is an expression of uneasiness, conscious or unconscious, either about the adequacy of such material elements of an offense as 'mens rea' and voluntariness' as bases for singling out those who ought to be held criminally responsible, or it is an expression of concern about the adequacy of civil commitment procedures to single out from among the 'not guilty by reason of insanity' those who are mentally ill and in need of restraint" (Goldstein and Katz, 1963, p. 8). And see Washington v. U.S. 380 F. 2d 444 (D.C. Cir. 1967).

26 "Punishment . . . involves risks. [I]t should be undertaken only after all efforts to persuade, patiently applied, have been exhausted. But the toleration of violence involves, I think, even greater risks, not only of present damage and injury but of erosion of the base of an ordered society. The point, I think, is not whether the aggressor should be halted and punished, but how; and it is here that moderation, consideration, and sympathetic understanding should play their part" (Fortas, 1968, p. 47).

Thus, too, police who, under color of law, use excessive force, ought not to be subjected to more severe sanctions than would be authorized for such crimes committed by them during more "normal" periods. But at the same time neither should policemen be relieved of criminal liability as they are by the Civil Rights Act of 1968.[27] Moreover, because abuse by a professionally trained force, when coupled with an inadequate opportunity for the redress of community grievances, real or imagined, may cause or exacerbate riots, the usual restraints on the police must be strictly enforced if the danger of riots is not to be enlarged. Some procedure must be found for preventing police offenders from finding shelter not only in statutory exemptions but also in local lethargy, the apparent incapacity of the local authorities to police the police through the criminal law to which they, like other members of the community, are subject.

In the final paragraph of his paper on "The Theory of Ego Autonomy" Rapaport (1958) recalls the old adage that "freedom is the acceptance of the restraints of law." That is true so long as those restraints are accepted in practice by the police as well as by the people, by the governors as well as by the governed. That is the meaning of law as a liberating force, that is the meaning of justice. "It is," as Bienenfeld (1947) observed, "the peculiar task of justice to reduce the exercise of power to the utmost possible limit, its social function is economy in the application of force" (p. 23). Therein, from society's vantage point, lies the law's real potential for channeling aggressive and libidinal forces into constructive work. To the extent then, that the criminal law has a role to play in riot control it is not to be found in a separate offense of "riot" or in treating "riot" as an aggravating or mitigating factor, but rather in holding police and civilians alike accountable for their violations of law.

Thus staying within the context of the questions posed and within the value, goals, and guides set by the Constitution, we see the very limited though significant role that the legislature may assign to the criminal law and the valuable though limited contribu-

[27] 18 U.S.C. 245 §c (1968).

tion psychoanalysis may make to a specific problem for decision in law.

BIBLIOGRAPHY

Allen, F. (1967), Civil Disobedience and the Legal Order. *Cin. Law Rev.*, 36:1-38.
Andenaes, J. (1966), The General Preventive Effects of Punishment. *Univ. Pa. Law Rev.*, 114:949-983.
Bernard, V., Ottenberg, P., & Redl, F. (1965), Dehumanization: A Composite Psychological Defense in Relation to Modern War. In: *Behavioral Science and Human Survival*, ed. M. Schwebel. Palo Alto: Science Behavior Books, pp. 64-82.
Bienenfeld, F. R. (1947), *Rediscovery of Justice*. London: George Allen & Unwin.
Blackstone, W. (1765), *Of Public Wrongs*. Boston: Beacon Press, 1962.
Brown, R. (1965), *Social Psychology*. New York: Free Press.
Donnelly, R. C., Goldstein, J., & Schwartz, R. D. (1962), *Criminal Law*. New York: Free Press.
Dynes, R. & Quarantelli, E. (1968), What Looting in Civil Disturbances Really Means. *Trans-Action*, 5:9-13.
Erikson, E. H. (1950), Growth and Crisis of the Healthy Personality. In: *Identity and the Life Cycle* [*Psychological Issues*, Monogr. 1]. New York: International Universities Press, 1959, pp. 50-100.
Fortas, A. (1968), *Concerning Dissent and Civil Disobedience*. New York: Signet.
Freud, A. (1936), *The Ego and the Mechanisms of Defense*. New York: International Universities Press, rev. ed., 1966.
—— (1949), Aggression in Relation to Emotional Development. *The Writings of Anna Freud*, 4:489-497. New York: International Universities Press, 1968.
—— (1965), *Normality and Pathology in Childhood*. New York: International Universities Press.
Freud, S. (1916), Criminals from a Sense of Guilt. *Standard Edition*, 14:332-336. London: Hogarth Press, 1957.
—— (1920), The Psychogenesis of a Case of Homosexuality in a Woman. *Standard Edition*, 18:145-172. London: Hogarth Press, 1955.
—— (1921), Group Psychology and the Analysis of the Ego. *Standard Edition*, 18:67-143. London: Hogarth Press, 1955.
Goldstein, J. (1960), Police Discretion Not to Invoke the Criminal Process: Low Visibility Decisions in the Administration of Justice. *Yale Law J.*, 69:543-594.
—— (1968), Psychoanalysis and Jurisprudence. *This Annual*, 23:459-479.
—— & Katz, J. (1963), Abolish the "Insanity Defense"—Why Not? *Yale Law J.*, 72:853-876.
Hartmann, H. (1939), *Ego Psychology and the Problem of Adaptation*. New York: International Universities Press, 1958.
—— & Kris, E. (1945), The Genetic Approach in Psychoanalysis. *This Annual*, 1:11-30.
Hersey, J. (1968), *Algiers Motel Incident*. New York: Bantam Books.
Janowitz, M. (1968), *Social Control of Escalated Riots*. Chicago: University of Chicago Center for Policy Study.
Laski, H. (1943), *Reflections on the Revolution of Our Time*. London: George Allen & Unwin.
Leary, H. R. (1967), *Law, Social Order and the Use of Deadly Force* (Press Release, March 21, 1967). New York: Police Department, Bureau of Public Information.
Le Bon, G. (1895), *The Crowd*. New York: Viking, 1960.
Mitscherlich, A. (1963), *Society Without the Father*. New York: Harcourt, Brace & World.

Morris, N. (1968), Psychiatry and the Dangerous Criminal. *South. Calif. Law Rev.*, 41:514-547.

Perkins, R. M. (1969), *Criminal Law*. Mineola: Foundation Press, 2nd ed.

Rapaport, D. (1958), The Theory of Ego Autonomy. *Bull. Menninger Clin.*, 22:13-20.

Reis, A. J. (1968), How Common Is Police Brutality? *Trans-Action*, 5(8):10-19.

Report of the National Advisory Commission on Civil Disorders (1968). Washington, D.C.: U.S. Government Printing Office.

Sauter, V. G. & Hines, B. (1968), *Nightmare in Detroit*. Chicago: Henry Regnery.

Smelser, M. J. (1963), *Theory of Collective Behavior*. New York: Free Press.

Spiegel, J. P. (1968), The Nature of the Riot Process. *Psychiat. Opin.*, 5(3):6-9.

Walker, D. (1968), *Rights in Conflict*. Washington, D.C.

Wangh, M. (1964), National Socialism and the Genocide of the Jews. *Int. J. Psa.* 45:386-395.

Westley, W. A. (1966), The Escalation of Violence through Legitimation. *Ann. Amer. Acad. Pol. & Soc. Sci.*, 364:120-126.

OBJECT LOSS, DREAMING, AND CREATIVITY

The Poetry of John Keats

JAMES W. HAMILTON, M.D. (New Haven)

> But if I was to report my own dreams, it inevitably followed that I should have to reveal to the public gaze more of the intimacies of my mental life than I liked, or than is normally necessary for any writer who is a man of science and not a poet.
>
> —FREUD (1900, p. xxiiif.)

This paper will deal with the poetry of John Keats in an attempt to gain some further understanding of the relationship between creative activity and intrapsychic functioning. Particular emphasis will be placed upon dreaming and the mourning process and upon recent clinical and research contributions concerning REM dreaming and children's responses to object loss. Pederson-Krag (1951a) has stressed that in choosing the career of a poet Keats was trying to master primarily oedipal conflicts, and in another paper (1951b) she traced the connection between a manifest dream of Keats and the composition of a particular sonnet. Barron (1963) viewed *Endymion* as a "quest for beauty" and an attempt to establish the beauty of the dream in order to gain relief from depressive symptomatology.

Formerly with the Department of Psychiatry, University of Cincinnati School of Medicine. At present with the Department of Psychiatry, Yale University School of Medicine.

Biographical Details

John Keats was born on October 31, 1795 in London, England, the first child of Thomas and Frances Keats.[1] His father was an innkeeper who had married his employer's daughter. Following John there were four other children, George, Thomas, Edward, and Frances, born in 1797, 1799, 1801, and 1803 respectively. Edward died in infancy, although there are no details as to the cause of his death. Keats's mother was a warm, affectionate person given to impulsive behavior, and John was felt to be her favorite, sharing with her the same temperament and having similar features. Always undersized for his age—his brother George was often taken as being older—he was described as having a vivid imagination and, as a small boy, once stood guard with an old toy sword outside his mother's door when she was ill, enforcing complete quiet and keeping others away. Another version of this story is that he used a real sword to hold his mother prisoner in their house. He showed a considerable talent for mimicry, one which he maintained all his life, and from three on would often respond to questions asked of him by rhyming the other person's last word.

At the age of seven he and his brother George were enrolled in a boarding school, Clarke's Academy, in Enfield, 12 miles from their home. On April 16, 1804, his father, of whom little is known, was killed. While riding at night on wet pavement, he fell from his horse and sustained a depressed skull fracture and massive concussion. His mother remarried two months later, a bank clerk named William Rawlings. However, she left him after a short time, thus forfeiting the inn and legal control of her children, and went to live in a common-law marriage with a man named Abraham in Enfield, where she drank heavily for several years. During her absence Keats and his siblings were cared for by their maternal grandparents, the Jennings. His grandmother was a kindly, considerate woman, and Keats grew to be quite fond of her. At this time, his behavior became markedly aggressive and rebellious; and he began to manifest extreme mood swings. He achieved a reputation as being

[1] All biographical data are taken from Ward (1963) and Gittings (1968).

the toughest fighter in his school and was described as one who "would fight anyone morning, noon, or night." He was well liked generally, but formed few friendships.

In March, 1805, his grandfather Jennings died; and in 1808 his Uncle Midgley, to whom he was close, succumbed to tuberculosis, leaving Keats the oldest surviving male member of his family at the age of thirteen. Shortly thereafter his mother returned home extremely ill with tuberculosis, her once remarkable beauty having faded considerably. In the London of the early nineteenth century, tuberculosis was responsible for 25 percent of deaths; the disease itself, considered to be hereditary, was not diagnosed clinically until the final irreversible stages, at which point it was called "consumption." Keats nursed his mother whenever he was home, preparing food, giving medicines, and sitting by her bedside for long hours reading aloud or just watching over her. She died in March, 1810, and Keats was overwhelmed with grief. Upon his return to school after her funeral, his belligerent behavior ceased; he became aloof and withdrawn, and his recurrent depressions became more intense. He began to read copiously, especially in the areas of history, mythology, and astronomy, and was seldom seen without a book. He became preoccupied with his own health to a hypochondriacal degree and began to entertain the choice of medicine as a career. He was much impressed with the *Aeneid*, which he attempted to translate completely in his final year, and established a friendship with Cowden Clarke, the headmaster's son who was eight years older, but who shared enthusiastically his interest in books and music.

In order to qualify as a surgeon Keats began in 1811 an apprenticeship with Thomas Hammond who was practicing in the town of Edmonton, and who had attended both Keats's mother and his grandfather in their terminal illnesses. The field of medicine in England at that time was split among three principal groups—the physicians who were trained in the universities and constituted an elite minority; the surgeons who after serving their apprenticeship spent one year in a London hospital and then wrote a series of exams to qualify for their certificate; and the apothecaries. The latter two would be the equivalent of today's general practitioner. With Hammond, Keats began to study anatomy, physiology, and pharmacology, to assist in the surgery, and to accompany his preceptor on house-calls. He continued to experience severe depressions which he referred to as his "blue devils," and remained very much alone. He made no new friendships and was described by his brother George as "nervous" and "morbid" during this period. He was extremely shy with girls and was involved with them only in overidealized fantasies. He continued to read a great deal, finished his translation of the *Aeneid*; took long walks frequently; and began to develop an inner sense of beauty, spending many hours lying in the fields staring upward at the clouds and the stars.

He became attracted to poetry at the age of eighteen when Cowden Clarke introduced him to Spenser's *Epithalamion* and the *Faerie Queene*, both of which contain elaborate descriptions of beautiful women. He wrote his first poem shortly thereafter and began reading the *Examiner*, a radical publication edited by Leigh Hunt, who was imprisoned in 1813 for two years after having slandered the Prince Regent.

In December, 1814, Keats lost his maternal grandmother and again failed to mourn, although he did compose a sonnet in her memory which implied that she would attain heavenly immortality. With her death, his brothers and sister went to live with Richard Abbey, a London merchant whom Mrs. Jennings had appointed as guardian to her grandchildren shortly after her daughter's death, while Keats remained in Edmonton. The only escape from his depressions which became more marked seemed to be through reading and writing poetry. When Hunt was released from prison in 1815, Keats wrote a sonnet in celebration of the event, and, in October of that year, having completed his apprenticeship, he went to London and the United Hospitals where he began work in the dissection rooms. He soon won a coveted position as dresser to William Lucas, a surgeon at Guy's Hospital, which meant, in addition to his regular studies, long hours in the operating theater with Lucas whose skill as a surgeon both diagnostically and technically left much to be desired. At first, Keats was a keen student, but, in the spring of 1816, he began to miss classes for weeks at a stretch and to concentrate on poetry. It was then that he decided to become a poet, stating to a friend that poetry was "the only thing worthy of superior minds." In his dress he began to emulate Byron, wearing a sailor's jacket and trousers and letting his hair grow long. In May, his first published poem "O Solitude" appeared in the *Examiner*.

After qualifying for his Apothecary's license in July, 1816, he took a vacation along the Kentish coast with his brother Tom, devoting most of his time to writing poetry and wandering along the seashore. Upon his return to London in the fall he was introduced to Leigh Hunt by Cowden Clarke, and made a very favorable impression which resulted in his becoming a member of a group of young artists—musicians, painters, sculptors, writers, and poets, including Shelley—who met regularly at Hunt's home to discuss the issues of the day. These exchanges were to serve as a considerable inspiration for Keats as he struggled to become a poet in his own right and Hunt himself was to become one of his staunchest supporters. In October, he discovered George Chapman's translation of Homer, again through his friend Clarke, and was so overpowered that he wrote the famous sonnet describing his reactions next day.

In February of the following year, he failed to take his surgical exams in keeping with his growing disillusionment with medicine, and shortly thereafter made a total commitment to poetry. In response to a friendly challenge from Shelley, he started working on *Endymion* in which he was to be absorbed for the next year, and which was to constitute one quarter of his poetic output. Before he had finished this poem, Keats made a pilgrimage to Stratford to visit the birthplace of Shakespeare, who was becoming his ideal as a poet.

No sooner had he completed *Endymion* when he was confronted in December, 1817 with the fact that his brother, Tom, had tuberculosis. Keats initially responded to this news by reconsidering the possibility of practicing medicine. However, when Tom showed some improvement, he quickly dismissed this idea. In June, 1818, his brother George and his bride emigrated to America and Keats left on a walking tour of Northern England, Scotland, and Ireland with his friend Charles Brown, during which he visited the grave of Robert Burns, whose poetry he admired greatly. Upon his return to London in August, he spent much time nursing Tom. He began writing *Hyperion*, his second major work; and met Fanny Brawne for the first time. It is worth noting that three of the most important women in his life, his mother, sister, and Miss Brawne, all had the same first name. On December 1, Tom died and Keats, unable to express any grief, became severely depressed. His relationship with Fanny Brawne began to develop along platonic lines, with Keats overidealizing her and finding it difficult to tolerate any lasting, genuine intimacy. During this time he experienced much financial hardship as his brother George underwent some business reverses in America and needed to borrow extra money from him.

In February of the following year, still struggling with his "blue devils," Keats briefly thought again of forsaking poetry and going to Edinburgh to complete his medical training. However, he soon resumed his writing, and the period from January to November, 1819, during which he was gaining critical acceptance as a poet and throughout which he drew heavily upon Burton's *Anatomy of Melancholy,* constitutes one of his most productive phases. In addition to *Hyperion,* it encompasses such works as *The Eve of St. Agnes, The Eve of Saint Mark,* and the famous odes "On Indolence," "On Melancholy," "On a Grecian Urn," "To a Nightingale," and "To Psyche." Gittings (1968) refers to this time as "the greatest year of living growth of any English poet." Despite the fact that he had developed "the deep-seated conviction that no woman could ever love him for himself," he became secretly engaged to Fanny Brawne on October 20, 1819. In February, 1820 he developed hemoptysis; and, in September, his health failing rapidly, he set sail for Italy with his friend, the painter Joseph Severn, in order to avoid the rigors of the English winter. He died of tuberculosis in Rome on February 23, 1821, and at autopsy both lungs were found to be completely destroyed by the disease process.

While such a brief biographical sketch hardly does justice to the richness and the intensity of Keats's life, it does indicate that the chronic depression from which he suffered was based upon early, profound, and repeated object losses. Beginning with the death of his brother Edward when Keats was six, there followed the deaths of his father when he was eight, his grandfather Jennings when he was nine, his Uncle Midgley at thirteen, his mother at fourteen, his maternal grandmother at nineteen, and finally his brother Tom, when he was twenty-three. In addition, six months before Tom's death, his brother George was virtually lost when he left for America, as can be seen in the tone of the letters which the brothers exchanged afterward. In a letter to Fanny Brawne, Keats once declared, "I have never known any unalloy'd Happiness for many days together: the death or sickness of some one has always spoilt my hours" (L. 134).[2]

Psychodynamic Aspects of Childhood Bereavement

There is considerable clinical material available concerning the difficulties which the young child faces in mourning a dead parent. Bowlby (1960, 1961a, 1961b, 1963) emphasized the inability to renounce the loss and the persistent demand on a more or less conscious level for the object's return. Jacobson (1965) described the fantasy of someday finding the lost parent. Robert Furman (1964), however, feels that children can mourn; but in order to do so they must have a concept of death and have achieved the level of object constancy. In a study of forty-two children and adolescents who had lost a parent through death, Wolfenstein (1966) reports:

> As our observations accumulated we were increasingly struck by the fact that mourning as described by Freud did not occur. Sad feelings were curtailed; there was little weeping. Immersion in the activities of everyday life continued. There was no withdrawal into preoccupation with thoughts of the lost parent. Gradually the fact emerged that overtly or covertly the child was denying the finality of the loss. The painful process of decathexis of the lost parent was put off, with the more or less conscious expectation of his return. Where depressed moods emerged, especially in adolescence, they were isolated from thoughts of the death of the parent, to which reality testing was not yet applied. Thus we gained the definite impression that the representation of the lost object was not decathected, indeed that it became invested with an intensified cathexis [p. 96f.].

She also stresses the child's idealization of and transitory identifications with the lost parent as a means of coping with ambivalence, and that denial may persist along with an appropriate conscious awareness of what has happened. In considering developmental preconditions which make successful mourning possible she states:

2 All letters by Keats are quoted from the collection edited by M. B. Forman (1931).

The hypothesis which I wish to propose is this: not only does adolescence resemble mourning, it constitutes the necessary precondition for being later able to mourn. The painful and gradual decathexis of the beloved parents which the adolescent is forced to perform serves as an initiation into how to mourn. The individual who has passed through this decisive experience has learned how to give up a major love object. In circumstances of later loss he is able to recapitulate the process [p. 112f.].

In Keats's case, the death of his father was compounded by the fact that his mother virtually abandoned him and his siblings almost immediately following the death of her husband to marry William Rawlings. With her subsequent divorce, she gave up legal control of her children and disappeared from their lives for several years to live with another man. Her behavior, particularly her dependence upon alcohol, would indicate that she was having much difficulty working through the loss within a year of both her husband and her father. One would expect that any rage Keats felt toward his father for leaving him would be intensified because of the simultaneous loss of his mother, and that these feelings in turn could be displaced easily onto peers as seen in his truculent behavior at school. Being considered her favorite, it would not have been possible for Keats to account for his mother's action without sacrificing much of his own self-esteem—he once remarked to a friend that he "had no mother." Keats never talked about his childhood in later life and disliked to have his birthday celebrated. The fact that he was born on Hallowe'en with its symbolic connotation of the return of the souls of the dead would contribute further to this reluctance (Sterba, 1948). When his mother did return home with tuberculosis in 1809, he seemed to be utilizing a good deal of reaction formation in taking care of her, and with her death was unable to get beyond the first stage of mourning, that of introjection (Fenichel, 1945). By becoming a prolific reader—he was hardly ever without a book, literally devouring them—he attempted to sustain an incorporative relationship with his mother (Strachey, 1930), and his interest in astronomy and mythology could be interpreted as a means of trying to recover her directly in a concrete, symbolic fashion.

Because of the intensity of Keats's ambivalence toward his

mother, once the internalization had occurred, much of his aggression was directed inward with the result that he relinquished his role as tough guy among his peers, became hypochondriacal, began to give thought to a career in medicine, and became a mother or caretaker to his siblings (Wolfenstein, 1966). He was attracted to and made his own translation of the wanderings of Aeneas with its theme of the constant search for a paradise on earth. Having begun his medical apprenticeship he remained aloof, depressed, and became more and more involved with nature. Searching the sky constantly, as he did, is a means of trying to retrieve the lost mother as clouds themselves can be a symbolic representation of the breast and one often sees faces outlined in various cloud formations (Almansi, 1961). Furthermore, smaller clouds will dissolve into wisps before fading completely into the blue background, recalling the fusion of infant with mother at the breast, and clouds themselves are mentioned frequently in Keats's works.

It was at this period of his life that Keats became interested in poetry through his friendship with Cowden Clarke and that he started to write his own poems. Later when he began his year at Guy's, it would seem that he was experiencing considerable difficulty coming to terms with the death of his patients, especially those due to tuberculosis, and with his own aggressive impulses, thus straining his use of reaction formation and overidentification with patients. His medical career ended finally after he underwent a brief period of depersonalization while performing surgery, which Ward (1963) describes as follows:

> One day at the hospital as he was opening a man's temporal artery, he found himself overwhelmed by the thought of the disaster that would result from a possible slip of his lancet. With a great effort he went on and performed the ligation neatly but all the while he seemed to be standing outside himself and watching his own dexterity with disbelief. The conflict between the cool scientific detachment required of a surgeon and the sensibility and warmth of feeling instinctive to him as a poet had reached its crisis. When he lay down his instruments at the end he realized he could never operate again [p. 102].

Here Keats appears to be struggling with the return of repressed feelings associated with the death of his father from a head injury.

In giving up medicine, he vowed that he would kill himself if he did not succeed as a poet.

Dream Research and Some Metapsychological Aspects of Dreaming

I would like now to deal with the principle thesis of this paper which is: that poetry represented for Keats an attempt to work through the mourning process and that dreaming was integrally related to his creative output. First, some comments related to recent findings in REM dream research. Summarizing the work that has been done in the field, Whitman (1963) states:

A reasonable hypothesis, derived from a number of lines of inquiry, would be that the dream supplies a small amount of visual (oral) gratification derived from the early phenomena of nursing. The major function of the dream—the preserving of sleep—would be accomplished by providing a small quantity of oral satisfaction which enables the person once more to return to deeper sleep, a cycle which goes on four or five times a night. Gifford [1960] has drawn on the original work of Kleitman [1960] to show that at three months, the number of night feedings goes down exactly at the moment that the mean hours of sleep per night goes up. It therefore seems logical to assume that it is at this moment that the dream takes over the function of an unconscious wish-fulfilling hallucinatory experience which enables the infant to continue sleeping. A noteworthy parallel observation is that the number of dreams of a night roughly is equivalent to the usual number of breast feedings of an infant [p. 769f.].

Thus the ever-recurring wish for a primary breast experience becomes the prototype of hallucinatory wish fulfillment in all subsequent dream life. Though the wishes of life become progressively more complex and subtle, this remains as the deepest substrate occasionally to be revealed in regressive experiences during the course of analysis or other intense psychological vicissitudes. The dream may be conceptualized as a minute oral experience which maintains sleep by not only discharging drive cathexis but offering a certain amount of oral gratification. This is completely compatible with Freud's basic postulate that the dream has a sleep-protecting function [p. 771].

Other clinical studies have shown that individuals deprived of
REM dreamtime for two to fifteen days will develop an increased
appetite and oral intake (Whitman et al., 1967).

Garma (1966) emphasized the traumatic, rather than wish-fulfill-
ment, genesis of dreams, a classic example of which occurs when
the ego has been threatened by a devastating, traumatic event. The
dreaming in this instance is an attempt to gain mastery over the
original threat through repetition and, if unsuccessful, results in
the development of a definite neurosis, with the depth of regression
being conditioned by the magnitude of the threat and the ego's defensive resources at the time. Object loss, especially of the mother or
other nurturing persons, may be considered an overwhelming
trauma, and I would postulate that the mourner, in so utilizing
dreams, is attempting to cope primarily with separation anxiety and
the loss of the object by regressing to an early primitive state of incorporative fusion with the mother, represented by the maternal
breast, the dream, as mentioned previously, having served the sleeping infant as a hallucinatory substitute for the breast (Krupp, 1962).

However, in the case of the preadolescent child, the mourning of
a parent or other significant person becomes much more difficult
because of the immaturity of the ego and the child's extreme dependence upon the parent, particularly the mother. As Wolfenstein
(1966) has stated, the end point becomes a hypercathexis of the in-
trojected object and incomplete mourning or melancholia. Another
reason for this outcome is the fear which the young child has that if
intense grief is expressed, it will become interminable.

THE POETRY OF KEATS—ORALITY AND DEPRESSION

I shall try to demonstrate by direct reference to Keats's poems
and letters that the above mechanisms were most important sources
of creative inspiration for Keats and that the writing of poetry was
an attempt to externalize the dream, to decathect the introject, and
thereby to restore the lost object.[3]

The first poem "Fill For Me" was written early in his career
and will be quoted in its entirety:

[3] All excerpts are from *The Poetical Works of John Keats,* ed. H. W. Garrod
(1939).

Fill for me a brimming bowl
And let me in it drown my soul:
But put therein some drug, designed
To Banish Women from my mind:
For I want not the stream inspiring
That fills the mind with fond desiring,
But I want as deep a draught
As e'er from Lethe's wave was quaff'd;
From my despairing heart to charm
The Image of the fairest form
That e'er my reveling eyes beheld,
That e'er my wandering fancy spell'd,

In vain! away I cannot chace
The melting softness of that face,
The beaminess of those bright eyes,
That breast—earth's only Paradise.
My sight will never more be blest;
For all I see has lost its zest:
Nor with delight can I explore
The Classic page, or Muse's lore.

Had she but known how beat my heart,
And with one smile reliev'd its smart,
I should have felt a sweet relief,
I should have felt 'the joy of grief.'
Yet as a Tuscan mid the snow
Of Lapland thinks on sweet Arno,
Even so for ever shall she be
The Halo of my Memory.

From this poem, one gets the definite impression of pronounced loss, and of the equation of breast and face as described by Almansi (1960). The hypercathexis of the lost object is unmistakable and contributes to a failure to work through the loss. The following passage is the last two stanzas of "Woman."

Light feet, dark violet eyes, and parted hair;
  Soft dimpled hands, white neck, and creamy breast,
  Are things on which the dazzled senses rest
Till the fond, fixed eyes forget they stare.
From such fine pictures, heavens! I cannot dare
  To turn my admiration, though unpossess'd

They be of what is worthy,—though not drest
In lovely modesty, and virtues rare.
Yet these I leave as thoughtless as a lark;
    These lures I straight forget—e'en ere I dine,
Or thrice my palate moisten: but when I mark
    Such charms with mild intelligence shine,
My ear is open like a greedy shark,
    To catch the tunings of a voice divine.

Ah! who can e'er forget so fair a being?
    Who can forget her half retiring sweets?
    God! she is like a milk-white lamb that bleats
For man's protection. Surely the All-seeing,
Who joys to see us with his gifts agreeing,
    Will never give him pinions, who intreats
    Such innocence to ruin—who vilely cheats
A dove-like bosom. In truth there is no freeing
One's thoughts from such a beauty; when I hear
    A lay that once I saw her hand awake,
Her form seems floating palpable, and near;
    Had I e'er seen her from an arbour take
A dewy flower, oft would that hand appear,
    And o'er my eyes the trembling moisture shake.

Again one senses the loss, the vivid breast imagery, and the hyper-cathexis, "In truth there is no freeing one's thoughts from such a beauty." The next examples will also describe the effect of object loss.

            . . . there too should be
The frequent chequer of a youngling tree,
That with a score of light green brethren shoots
From the quaint mossiness of aged roots:
Round which is heard a spring-head of clear waters
Babbling so wildly of its lovely daughters
The spreading blue-bells: it may haply mourn
That such fair clusters should be rudely torn
From their fresh beds, and scattered thoughtlessly
By infant hands, left on the path to die.

This is an excerpt from "I Stood Tip-Toe . . ." and presents an idyllic natural setting which is suddenly shattered when the small flowers are carelessly picked and "left on the path to die." The same feelings are expressed in these lines from "To Charles Cowden Clarke":

> . . . small good it were
> To take him to a desert rude, and bare,
> Who had on Baiae's shore reclin'd at ease,
> While Tasso's page was floating in a breeze
> That gave soft music from Armida's bowers,
> Mingled with fragrance from her rarest flowers:
> Small good to one who had by Mulla's stream
> Fondled the maidens with the breasts of cream;

The following is taken from "To J. H. Reynolds, Esq.," written at the time his brother Tom was dying.

> O that our dreamings all of sleep or wake
> Would all their colours from the Sunset take:
> From something of material sublime,
> Rather than shadow our own Soul's daytime
> In the dark void of Night. For in the world
> We justle—but my flag is not unfurl'd
> On the Admiral staff—and to philosophize
> I dare not yet!—Oh never will the prize,
> High reason, and the love of good and ill
> By my award. Things cannot to the will
> Be settled, but they tease us out of thought.
> Or is it that Imagination brought
> Beyond its proper bound, yet still confined,—
> Lost in a sort of Purgatory blind,
> Cannot refer to any standard law
> Of either earth or heaven?—It is a flaw
> In happiness to see beyond our bourn—
> It forces us in Summer skies to mourn:
> It spoils the singing of the Nightingale.
> Dear Reynolds, I have a mysterious tale
> And cannot speak it. The first page I read
> Upon a Lampit Rock of green sea weed
> Among the breakers—'Twas a quiet Eve;
> The rocks were silent—the wide sea did weave
> An untumultuous fringe of silver foam
> Along the flat brown sand. I was at home,
> And should have been most happy—but I saw
> Too far into the sea; where every maw

The greater on the less feeds evermore:—
But I saw too distinct into the core
Of an eternal fierce destruction,
And so from Happiness I far was gone.
Still am I sick of it: and though today
I've gathered young spring-leaves, and flowers gay
Of Periwinkle and wild strawberry,
Still do I that most fierce destruction see,
The Shark at savage prey—the hawk at pounce,
The gentle Robin, like a pard or ounce,
Ravening a worm—Away ye horrid moods,
Moods of one's mind! You know I hate them well,
You know I'd sooner be a clapping bell
To some Katschatkan missionary church,
Than with these horrid moods be left in lurch—
                              [lines 67-109].

Here one feels the imminent loss, the helplessness of Keats—it will be recalled that he thought briefly of resuming his medical career at that time—the rage in response to the frustration, along with a good deal of primitive, oral aggressive imagery. Certainly, Tom's pending death, resulting from tuberculosis, had reawakened feelings associated with the loss of his mother and uncle from the same illness.

"To Sleep"

O soft embalmer of the still midnight,
    Shutting, with careful fingers and benign,
Our gloom-pleas'd eyes, embower'd from the light,
    Enshaded in forgetfulness divine;
O soothest Sleep! if so it please thee, close,
    In midst of this thine hymn, my willing eyes,
Or wait the amen, ere thy poppy throws
    Around my bed its lulling charities;
Then save me, or the passed day will shine
Upon my pillow, breeding many woes;
    Save me from curious conscience, that still lords
Its strength for darkness, burrowing like a mole;
    Turn the key deftly in the oiled wards.
And seal the hushed casket of my soul.

This sonnet well describes Keats's ambivalence and guilt in relation to the multiple losses he experienced. Next is another sonnet, one of Keats's last works, written to Fanny Brawne and reflecting intense oral dependent strivings in the form of a relentless demand for total, unwavering love and care.

> I cry your mercy—pity—love!—aye, love!
>   Merciful love that tantalises not,
> One-thoughted, never-wandering, guileless love,
>   Unmask'd, and being seen—without a blot!
> O! let me have thee whole,—all—all—be mine!
>   That shape, that fairness, that sweet minor zest
> Of love, your kiss,—those hands, those eyes divine,
>   That warm, white, lucent, million-pleasured breast,—
> Yourself—your soul—in pity give me all,
>   Withhold no atom's atom or I die,
> Or living on perhaps, your wretched thrall,
>   Forget, in the mist of idle misery,
> Life's purposes,—the palate of my mind
> Losing its gust, and my ambition blind!

The very last poem Keats ever wrote conveys a sense of frustration, rage toward the frustrating object, in this instance, Miss Brawne, and attempts to awaken in her the same guilt for not saving his life which Keats himself lived with in regard to his various losses and which was previously dealt with in "To Sleep."

> This living hand, now warm and capable
> Of earnest grasping, would, if it were cold
> And in the icy silence of the tomb,
> So haunt thy days and chill thy dreaming nights
> That thou wouldst wish thine own heart dry of blood
> So in my veins red life might stream again,
> And thou be conscience-calm'd—see here it is—
> I hold it towards you.

To summarize, the previous examples reflect the problems of object loss, unresolved dependent strivings and chronic depression, and their dynamic interrelatedness.

The following excerpts will deal with the phenomena of internalization, sleep, and dreaming. Internalization as used here was defined by Schafer (1968) as "all those processes by which the subject transforms real or imagined regulatory interactions with his environment, and real or imagined characteristics of his environment, into inner regulations and characteristics" (p. 9).

"Ode to Psyche"

> Yes, I will be thy priest, and build a fane
>   In some untrodden region of my mind,
> Where branched thoughts, new grown with pleasant pain,
>   Instead of pines shall murmur in the wind:
> Far, far around shall those dark-cluster'd trees
>   Fledge the wild-ridged mountains steep by steep;
> And there by zephyrs, streams, and birds, and bees,
>   The moss-lain Dryads shall be lull'd to sleep;
> And in the midst of this wide quietness
> A rosy sanctuary will I dress
> With the wreath'd trellis of a working brain,
>   With buds, and bells, and stars without a name,
> With all the gardener Fancy e'er could feign,
>   Who breeding flowers, will never breed the same:
> And there shall be for thee all soft delight
>   That shadowy thought can win,
> A bright torch, and a casement ope at night,
>   To let the warm Love in!

The second is an exchange between Apollo and the goddess Mnemosyne taken from *Hyperion* (Book III, lines 59-91):

> 'Goddess! I have beheld those eyes before,
> 'And their eternal calm, and all that face,
> 'Or I have dream'd.'—'Yes,' said the supreme shape,
> 'Thou hast dream'd of me; and awaking up
> 'Didst find a lyre all golden by thy side,
> 'Whose strings touch'd by thy fingers, all the vast
> 'Unwearied ear of the whole universe
> 'Listen'd in pain and pleasure at the birth
> 'Of such new tuneful wonder. Is't not strange
> 'That thou shouldst weep, so gifted? Tell me, youth,
> 'What sorrow thou canst feel; for I am sad
> 'When thou dost shed a tear: explain thy griefs
> 'To one who in this lonely isle hath been
> 'The watcher of thy sleep and hours of life,
> 'From the young day when first thy infant hand
> 'Pluck'd witless the weak flowers, till thine arm
> 'Could bend that bow heroic to all times.

'Show thy heart's secret to an ancient Power
'Who hath forsaken old and sacred thrones
'For prophecies of thee, and for the sake
'Of loveliness new born.'—Apollo then,
With sudden scrutiny and gloomless eyes,
Thus answer'd, while his white melodious throat
Throbb'd with the syllables.—'Mnemosyne!
'Thy name is on my tongue, I know not how;
'Why should I tell thee what thou so well seest?
'Why should I strive to show what from thy lips
'Would come no mystery? For me, dark, dark,
'And painful vile oblivion seals my eyes:
'I strive to search wherefore I am so sad,
'Until a melancholy numbs my limbs;
'And then upon the grass I sit, and moan,
'Like one who once had wings.'

The third is taken from *Sleep and Poetry:*

> What, but thee, Sleep? Soft closer of our eyes!
> Low murmurer of tender lullabies!
> Light hoverer around our happy pillows!
> Wreather of poppy buds, and weeping willows!
> Silent entangler of a beauty's tresses!

The fourth: "Bright Star":

> Bright star! would I were steadfast as thou art—
>   ᷣNot in lone splendour hung aloft the night
> And watching, with eternal lids apart,
>   Like nature's patient, sleepless Eremite,
> The moving waters at their priestlike task
>   Of pure ablution round earth's human shores,
> Or gazing on the new soft fallen mask
>   Of snow upon the mountains and the moors—
> No—yet still steadfast, still unchangeable,
>   Pillow'd upon my fair love's ripening breast,
> To feel for ever its soft fall and swell,
>   Awake for ever in a sweet unrest,
> Still, still to hear her tender-taken breath,
> And so live ever—or else swoon to death.

In the above lines, Keats describes his search for the lost mother
whom he has incorporated, "Yes, I will be thy priest, and build a

fane in some untrodden region of my mind," and with whom he attempts to reunite in his dreams. Sleep is referred to as the "Silent entangler of a beauty's tresses," and is related to nursing at the breast: "Pillowed upon my fair love's ripening breast." In a letter to Benjamin Bailey in 1818, Keats wrote: "When I was a Schoolboy I thought a fair Woman a pure Goddess, my mind was a soft nest in which some one of them slept, though she knew it not—I have no right to expect more than their reality" (L. 79). In *Endymion,* the Goddess of the Moon, Cynthia, with whom Endymion has fallen in love, appears three times to him in his dreams—from the sky, from a well, and in a cave. At one point in the poem, after Endymion renounces temporarily his love for Cynthia, there occurs the following passage: "I have clung to nothing, lov'd a nothing, nothing seen or felt but a great dream! O, I have been presumptuous against love . . ." (Book IV, lines 636-639).

The Eve of St. Agnes, which was based on the superstition that a maiden would see her future husband in a dream if she fasted on St. Agnes Eve, supports the theoretical assumption that oral deprivation can lead to hallucinated wish fulfillment:

> They told her how, upon St. Agnes' Eve,
> Young virgins might have visions of delight,
> And soft adorings from their loves receive
> Upon the honey'd middle of the night,
> If ceremonies due they did aright;
> As, supperless to bed they must retire,
> And couch supine their beauties, lilly white;
> Nor look behind, nor sideways, but require
> Of Heaven with upward eyes for all that they desire.

The same causal relationship is seen in the sonnet "The Day is Gone":

> The day is gone, and all its sweets are gone!
>   Sweet voice, sweet lips, soft hand, and softer breast,
> Warm breath, light whisper, tender semi-tone,
>   Bright eyes, accomplish'd shape, and lang'rous waist!
> Faded the flower and all its budded charms,
>   Faded the sight of beauty from my eyes,
> Faded the shape of beauty from my arms,
>   Faded the voice, warmth, whiteness, paradise—

Vanish'd unseasonably at shut of eve,
  When the dusk holiday—or holinight
Of fragrant-curtain'd love begins to weave
  The woof of darkness thick, for hid delight;
But, as I've read love's missal through to-day,
He'll let me sleep, seeing I fast and pray.

Owing to the crucial, adaptive significance that dreaming had for Keats, his sense of reality and his reality testing were at times rather tenuous. The following passages reflect his uncertainty as to what was dream and what reality:

From "Ode to a Nightingale"

Forlorn! the very word is like a bell
  To toll me back from thee to my sole self!
Adieu! the fancy cannot cheat so well
  As she is fam'd to do, deceiving elf.
Adieu! Adieu! thy plaintive anthem fades
  Past the near meadows, over the still stream,
    Up the hill-side; and now 'tis buried deep
      In the next valley-glades:
  Was it a vision, or a waking dream?
    Fled is that music:—Do I wake or sleep?"

From "Ode to Psyche"

O Goddess! hear these tuneless numbers, wrung
  By sweet enforcement and remembrance dear,
And pardon that thy secrets should be sung
  Even into thine own soft-conched ear:
Surely I dreamt to-day, or did I see
  The winged Psyche with awaken'd eyes?

From *Lamia*

It was no dream; or say a dream it was,
Real are the dreams of Gods, and smoothly pass
Their pleasures in a long immortal dream
           [Part I, lines 126-129].

"On Death"

Can death be sleep, when life is but a dream,
 And scenes of bliss pass as a phantom by?
The transient pleasures as a vision seem,
 And yet we think the greatest pain's to die.

How strange it is that man on earth should roam,
 And lead a life of woe, but not forsake
His rugged path; nor dare he view alone
 His future doom which is but to awake.

Waking, of course, implies separation from the figures in his dream.

THE DREAM AND THE POEM

I would now like to explore the specific relationship between dreaming and poetic creativity. Regarding poetry, Kris (1953) wrote:

> The multiple meaning constitutes richness; the dichotomy between appropriate ambiguity and hidden precision, the latter more stringent as the lines flow into the stanza, becomes an important criterion in the study of poetic language. There are poets who are masters of multidimensional vagueness, without leading finally into the growing precision; there are others, whose lines differ from ordinary verbal communication only by meter, rhythm and setting, by the "music of poetry"—but do hardly use the very complexity of meaning. All this seems to have become more understandable to us through our experience with contemporary poetry: here complexity of words tends to be maximized, multiple meanings abound, and uncertainty of interpretation tends to prevail. There can be little doubt that in this the modern poet is more than accidentally akin to the dreamer; also the phenomenon is not limited to any one artistic medium [p. 343].

About his own creative processes, Stephen Spender, the poet (1962), writes:

> Sometimes, when I lie in a state of half-waking, half-sleeping, I am conscious of a stream of words which seem to pass through my mind, without their having a meaning, but they have a sound, a sound of passion, or a sound recalling poetry that I know. Again sometimes when I am writing, the music of the

words I am trying to shape takes me far beyond the words, I am aware of a rhythm, a dance, a fury, which is at yet empty of words.'

In the opening lines of *The Fall of Hyperion* which is subtitled "A Dream," Keats wrote:

> Fanatics have their dreams, wherewith they weave
> A paradise for a sect; the savage too
> From forth the loftiest fashion of his sleep
> Guesses at Heaven: pity these have not
> Trac'd upon vellum or wild indian leaf
> The shadows of melodious utterance.
> But bare of laurel they live, dream and die;
> For Poesy alone can tell her dreams,
> With the fine spell of words alone can save
> Imagination from the sable charm
> And dumb enchantment. Who alive can say,
> 'Thou art no Poet—may'st not tell thy dreams'?
> Since every man whose soul is not a clod
> Hath visions, and would speak, if he had Lov'd
> And been well nurtured in his mother tongue
> Whether the dream now purposed to rehearse
> Be Poet's or Fanatic's will be known
> When this warm scribe my hand is in the grave.

The following lines are from "I Stood Tip-Toe . . ."

> Closer of lovely eyes to lovely dreams,
> Lover of loneliness, and wandering,
> Of upcast eye, and tender pondering!
> Thee must I praise above all other glories
> That smile us on to tell delightful stories.
> For what has made the sage or poet write
> But the fair paradise of Nature's light?

Keats wrote *Sleep and Poetry* after he had spent an evening visiting with Leigh Hunt who invited him to stay overnight. He was given a bed in Hunt's study, but was unable to sleep at all as his mind was flooded with vivid imagery beginning with scenes from a painting of Poussin's "Empire of Flora," which portays a mythological scene of nymphs and lovers in a garden with Apollo flying overhead in his golden chariot. Keats was in an almost hypomanic state and Ward (1963) describes him thus: "As he lay on his narrow bed between sleep and waking, line followed on line with the miraculous ease of dream and when the light began to glimmer at the window he could not believe morning had come so soon. He rose up full of the energy of a man with a task which he is eager to start." Two quotations from that poem are pertinent; the first is:

> . . . and the shade
> Keeping a silence round a sleeping maid;
> And many a verse from so strange influence
> That we must ever wonder how, and whence
> It came [lines 67-71].

and

> . . . yet I must not forget
> Sleep, quiet with his poppy coronet:
> For what there may be worthy in these rhymes
> I partly owe to him—[lines 347-350].

"On First Looking Into Chapman's Homer," was composed under much the same circumstances as *Sleep and Poetry*. Keats and Cowden Clarke had remained up all night reading Chapman's translation of Homer, a most exciting discovery for Keats. He was ecstatic throughout and keenly aware "of a sonnet beating in his head" (Ward, 1963) which he wrote out completely while walking home at dawn.

> Much have I travell'd in the realms of gold,
>   And many goodly states and kingdoms seen;
>   Round many western islands have I been
> Which bards in fealty to Apollo hold.
> Oft of one wide expanse had I been told
>   That deep-brow'd Homer ruled as his demesne;
>   Yet did I never breathe its pure serene
> Till I heard Chapman speak out loud and bold:
> Then felt I like some watcher of the skies
>   When a new planet swims into his ken;
> Or like stout Cortez when with eagle eyes
>   He star'd at the Pacific—and all his men
> Look'd at each other with a wild surmise—
>   Silent, upon a peak in Darien.

As an aside, one must wonder why Keats made the slip of attributing the discovery of the Pacific Ocean to Cortés rather than Balboa. The sea occupies a central position in many of his poems as a symbolic representation of his mother, while the line "Silent, upon a peak in Darien" recalls an image of the breast. When Keats himself first saw Lake Windander he was so affected that he wrote to his brother Tom, "the two views we have had of it are of the most noble tenderness—they can never fade away—they make one forget the divisions of life; age, youth, poverty, and riches; and refine one's sensual vision into a sort of north star which can never cease to be open lidded and stedfast over the wonders of the great Power" (L. 71). It is therefore understandable that Keats would feel considerable ambivalence toward a man who had actually discovered one of the largest bodies of water in the world.

Before composing the "Ode on a Grecian Urn," Keats wrote a letter to his brother George and his sister-in-law Georgiana:

> This morning I am in a sort of temper indolent and supremely careless: I long after a stanza or two of Thompson's Castle of indolence. My passions are all asleep from my having slumbered till nearly eleven and weakened the animal fibre all over me to a delightful sensation about three degrees on this side of faintness —if I had teeth of pearl and the breath of lillies I should call it langour—but as I am [n.:]—Especially as I have a black eye.—I must call it Laziness. In this state of effeminacy the fibres of the brain are relaxed in common with the rest of the body, and to such a happy degree that pleasure has no show of enticement and pain no unbearable frown. Neither Poetry, nor Ambition, nor Love have any alertness of countenance as they pass by me: they seem rather like three figures on a Greek vase—a Man and two women whom no one but myself could distinguish in their disguisement. This is the only happiness; and is a rare instance of advantage in the body overpowering the Mind. I have this moment received a note from Haslam in which he expects the death of his Father—who has been for some time in a state of insensibility—his mother bears up he says very well—I shall go to town[4] tomorrow to see him. This is the world—thus we cannot expect to give way many hours to pleasure—Circumstances are like Clouds continually gathering and bursting—While we are

[4] While most of Keats's spelling errors have been reproduced from the originals, those requiring lengthy explanations have been corrected.

laughing the seed of some trouble is put into the wide arable
land of events—while we are laughing it sprouts it grows and
suddenly bears a poison fruit which we must pluck—Even so
we have leisure to reason on the misfortunes of our friends; our
own touch us too nearly for words. Very few men have ever
arrived at a complete disinterestedness of Mind: very few have
been influenced by a pure desire of the benefit of others—in
the greater part of the Benefactors to Humanity some meretri-
cious motive has sullied their greatness—some melodramatic
scenery has fa(s)cinated them—From the manner in which I feel
Haslam's misfortune I perceive how far I am from any humble
standard of disinterestedness—Yet this feeling ought to be carried to its highest pitch as there is no fear of its ever injuring
Society—which it would do I fear pushed to an extremity—For
in wild nature the Hawk would loose his Breakfast of Robins
and the Robin his of Worms—the Lion must starve as well as the
swallow. The greater part of Men make their way with the same
instinctiveness, the same unwandering eye from their purposes,
the same animal eagerness as the Hawk. The Hawk wants a
Mate, so does the Man—look at them both they set about it and
procure on(e) in the same manner. They want both a nest and
they both set about one in the same manner—they get their
food in the same manner—The nobel animal Man for his amusement smokes his pipe—the Hawk balances about the Clouds—
that is the only difference of their leisures. This it is that makes
the Amusement of Life—to a speculative Mind. I go among the
Fields and catch a glimpse of a Stoat or a fieldmouse peeping
out of the withered grass—the creature hath a purpose and its
eyes are bright with it. I go amongst the buildings of a city and
I see a Man hurrying along—to what? the Creature has a purpose and his eyes are bright with it. But then, as Wordsworth
says, "We have all one human heart"—there is an ellectric fire in
human nature tending to purify—so that among these human
creature(s) there is continu(a)lly some birth of new heroism.
The pity is that we must wonder at it: as we should at finding a
pearl in rubbish. I have no doubt that thousands of people
never heard of have had hearts comp(l)etely disinterested: I can
remember but two—Socrates and Jesus—their Histories evince
it. What I heard a little time ago, Taylor observe with respect
to Socrates may be said of Jesus—That he was so great a man
that though he transmitted no writing of his own to posterity,
we have his Mind and his sayings and his greatness handed to
us by others. It is to be lamented that the history of the latter
was written and revised by Men interested in the pious frauds of

Religion. Yet through all this I see his splendour. Even here though I myself am pursuing the same instinctive course as the veriest human animal you can think of—I am however young writing at random—straining at particles of light in the midst of a great darkness—without knowing the bearing of any one assertion of any one opinion. Yet may I not in this be free from sin? May there not be superior beings amused with any graceful, though instinctive attitude my mind m(a)y fall into, as I am entertained with the alertness of a Stoat or the anxiety of a Deer? Though a quarrel in the Streets is a thing to be hated, the energies displayed in it are fine; the commonest Man shows a grace in his quarrel—By a superior being our reasoning(s) may take the same tone—though erroneous they may be fine—This is the very thing in which consists poetry; and if so it is not so fine a thing as philosophy—For the same reason that an eagle is not so fine a thing as a truth—Give me this credit—Do you not think I strive—to know myself? Give me this credit—and you will not think that on my own accou(n)t I repeat Milton's lines

> "How charming is divine Philosophy
> Not harsh and crabbed as dull fools suppose
> But musical as is Apollo's lute"—

No—no(t) for myself—feeling grateful as I do to have got into a state of mind to relish them properly—Nothing ever becomes real till it is experienced—Even a Proverb is no proverb to you till your Life has illustrated it. I am ever affraid that your anxiety for me will lead you to fear for the violence of my temperament continually smothered down: for that reason I did not intend to have sent you the following sonnet—but look over the two last pages and ask yourselves whether I have not that in me which will well bear the buffets of the world. It will be the best comment on my sonnet; it will show you that it was written with no Agony but that of ignorance; with no thirst of any thing but Knowledge when pushed to the point though the first steps to it were throug(h) my human passions—they went away, and I wrote with my Mind—and perhaps I must confess a little bit of my heart—

> Why did I laugh tonight? No voice will tell:
> No God no Demon of severe response
> Deigns to reply from heaven or from Hell.—
> Then to my human heart I turn at once—
> Heart! thou and I are here sad and alone;
> Say, wherefore did I laugh? O mortal pain!

O Darkness! Darkness! ever must I moan
  To question Heaven and Hell and Heart in vain!
Why did I laugh? I know this being's lease
  My fancy to its utmost blisses spreads:
Yet could I on this very midnight cease
  And the world's gaudy ensigns see in shreds.
Verse, fame and Beauty are intense indeed
But Death intenser—Death is Life's high mead."

I went to bed, and enjoyed an uninterrupted Sleep—Sane I
went to bed and sane I arose (L. 123).

As Keats describes his thoughts in this letter one must be curious
as to whether the vase could represent the dream screen which
Lewin (1946) feels is derived from the breast. Pursuing his free
associations Keats goes on to talk of the death of a friend's father;
about clouds "continually gathering and bursting"; about the difficulty of facing one's own misfortunes: "our own touch us too nearly
for words"; and about oral dependent and cannibalistic imagery
expressed in terms of animal behavior. He quotes Wordsworth and
then states "that among these human creatures there is continually
some birth of new heroism," and wonders about the purity of his
own writings and whether they will be not only immortal but undis-
torted through the years. He seems to be concerned here about the
amount of aggressive as compared with libidinal energy that is
utilized in the writing of his poetry, "I am however young writing
at random—straining at particles of light in the midst of a great
darkness—without knowing the bearing of any one assertion of any
one opinion. Yet may I not in this be free from sin?" and later
"I am ever affraid that your anxiety for me will lead you to fear
for the violence of my temperament continually smothered down:
for that reason I did not intend to have sent you the following
sonnet." Then comes the sonnet and the concluding statement about
sleep.

The poetry of Samuel Taylor Coleridge shows a close relationship between dreaming and creative activity, with unresolved oral
strivings being very much a part of Coleridge's characterological
structure. In "The Rime of the Ancient Mariner," after the mariner
repents the killing of the albatross, he falls asleep and dreams of

being fed at the breast. In his later life, Coleridge became addicted to opium, and claimed that "Kubla Khan" had been dreamed in its entirety during an opium sleep (Beres, 1961; Marcovitz, 1964).

The following clinical material is pertinent. A young, depressed, alcoholic man, who was being treated in intensive psychotherapy, brought a poem to one of his hours which he had dreamed the previous night. His mother had been extremely overprotective and seductive in her relationship with him and one of his earliest memories consisted of lying in bed with her at the age of four or five and masturbating her to climax. In the above hour after presenting the poem to his therapist he went on to talk about the frustrations of his marriage, of his wife's infidelity, of his promiscuous search for a better woman, and how independent he was of his mother. However, in the poem, he stated:

> My thoughts change to all the things that once I have had
> Now is when I really become sad.

And in the last lines he declared:

> O, how I wish I could grab all the bright things
> And push out all the sad.[5]

Prince (1914) has described in detail the creative responses of a subject who had written a poem "automatically" which was derived from a dream or series of dreams.

THE POEM AND THE LOST OBJECT

Segal (1952) feels "that all creation is really a re-creation of a once loved and once whole, but now lost and ruined object, a ruined internal world and self." The next selections attempt to establish that for Keats the poem represented an attempt at restoration or restitution of the lost object. The first is from "I Stood Tip-Toe . . ."

> The breezes were ethereal, and pure,
> And crept through half closed lattices to cure
> The languid sick; it cool'd their fever'd sleep,

[5] I am indebeted to Dr. Salvatore Tuzzo for the above material.

And soothed them into slumbers full and deep.
Soon they awoke clear eyed: nor burnt with thirsting,
Not with hot fingers, nor with temples bursting:
And springing up, they met the wond'ring sight
Of their dear friends, nigh foolish with delight;
Who feel their arms, and breasts, and kiss and stare,
And on their placid foreheads part the hair.
Young men, and maidens at each other gaz'd
With hands held back, and motionless, amaz'd
To see the brightness in each other's eyes;
And so they stood, fill'd with a sweet surprise,
Until their tongues were loos'd in poesy.
Therefore no lover did of anguish die:
But the soft numbers, in that moment spoken,
Made silken ties, that never may be broken.
Cynthia! I cannot tell the greater blisses,
That follow'd thine, and thy dear shepherd's kisses:
Was there a Poet born?—but now no more,
My wand'ring spirit must no further soar.—[lines 221-242].

The following passages are from *Sleep and Poetry* (lines 96-212, 267-268, 288-293).

O for ten years, that I may overwhelm
Myself in poesy; so I may do the deed
That my own soul has to itself decreed.
Then will I pass the countries that I see
In long perspective, and continually
Taste their pure fountains. First the realm I'll pass
Of Flora, and old Pan: sleep in the grass,
Feed upon apples red, and strawberries,
And choose each pleasure that my fancy sees;
Catch the white-handed nymphs in shady places,
To woo sweet kisses from averted faces,—
Play with their fingers, touch their shoulders white
Into a pretty shrinking with a bite
As hard as lips can make it: till agreed,
A lovely tale of human life we'll read.
And one will teach a tame dove how it best
May fan the cool air gently o'er my rest;
Another, bending o'er her nimble tread,
Will set a green robe floating round her head,
And still will dance with ever varied ease,
Smiling upon the flowers and the trees:

Another will entice me on, and on
Through almond blossoms and rich cinnamon;
Till in the bosom of a leafy world
We rest in silence, like two gems upcurl'd
In the recesses of a pearly shell.

And they shall be accounted poet kings
Who simply tell the most heart-easing things.

. . . though no great minist'ring reason sorts
Out the dark mysteries of human souls
To clear conceiving: yet there ever rolls
A vast idea before me, and I glean
Therefrom my liberty; thence too I've seen
The end and aim of Poesy.

From *The Fall of Hyperion*

. . . Art thou not of the dreamer tribe?
The poet and the dreamer are distinct,
Diverse, sheer opposite, antipodes.
The one pours out a balm upon the world,
The other vexes it [Canto I, lines 198-202].

In the Preface to *Endymion,* Keats declared:

Knowing within myself the manner in which this Poem has been produced, it is not without a feeling of regret that I make it public.

What manner I mean, will be quite clear to the reader, who must soon perceive great inexperience, immaturity, and every error denoting a feverish attempt, rather than a deed accomplished. The two first books, and indeed the two last, I feel sensible are not of such completion as to warrant their passing the press; nor should they if I thought a year's castigation would do them any good;—it will not: the foundations are too sandy. It is just that this youngster should die away: a sad thought for me, if I had not some hope that while it is dwindling I may be plotting, and fitting myself for verses fit to live.

This may be speaking too presumptuously, and may deserve a punishment: but no feeling man will be forward to inflict it: he will leave me alone, with the conviction that there is not a fiercer hell than the failure in a great object. This is not written with the least atom of purpose to forestall criticisms of course, but from the desire I have to conciliate men who are competent

to look, and who do look with a zealous eye, to the honour of
English literature.

The imagination of a boy is healthy, and the mature imagination of a man is healthy; but there is a space of life between, in
which the soul is in a ferment, the character undecided, the way
of life uncertain, the ambition thick-sighted: thence proceeds
mawkishness, and all the thousand bitters which those men I
speak of must necessarily taste in going over the following pages.

I hope I have not in too late a day touched the beautiful
mythology of Greece, and dulled its brightness: for I wish to try
once more, before I bid it farewell.

In various letters Keats has dealt with the same theme:

What the imagination seizes as Beauty must be truth—whether
it existed before or not—for I have the same Idea of all our
Passions as of Love they are all in their sublime, creative of
essential Beauty. In a Word, you may know my favorite Speculation by my first Book and the little song I sent in my last—which
is a representation from the fancy of the probable mode of operating in these Matters. The Imagination may be compared to
Adam's dream—he awoke and found it truth. I am the more
zealous in this affair, because I have never yet been able to perceive how any thing can be known for truth by consequitive
reasoning—and yet it must be. Can it be that even the greatest
Philosopher ever arrived at his goal without putting aside
numerous objections. However it may be, O for a Life of Sensations rather than of Thoughts! It is 'a Vision in the form of
Youth' a Shadow of reality to come—and this consideration has
further convinced me for it has come as auxiliary to another
favorite Speculation of mine, that we shall enjoy ourselves here
after by having what we called happiness on Earth repeated in a
finer tone and so repeated. And yet such a fate can only befall
those who delight in Sensation rather than hunger as you do
after Truth. Adam's dream will do here and seems to be a conviction that Imagination and its empyreal reflection is the same as
human Life and its Spiritual repetition. But as I was saying—the
simple imaginative Mind may have its rewards in the repeti(ti)on
of its own silent Working coming continually on the Spirit with
a fine Suddenness—to compare great things with small—have
you never by being Surprised with an old Melody—in a delicious
place—by a delicious voice, fe(l)t over again your very Speculations and Surmises at the time it first operated on your Soul—
do you not remember forming to yourself the singer's face more

beautiful than it was possible and yet with the elevation of the Moment you did not think so—even then you were mounted on the Wings of Imagination so high—that the Protrotype must be here after—that delicious face you will see [L. 31].

I never was in love—yet the voice and the shape of a Woman has haunted me these two days—at such a time when the relief, the feverous relief of Poetry seems a much less crime—This morning Poetry has conquered—I have relapsed into those abstractions which are my only life—I feel escaped from a new strange and threatening sorrow.—and I am thankful for it.— There is an awful warmth about my heart like a load of Immortality [L. 87].

I am convinced more and more every day that (excepting the human friend Philosopher) a fine writer is the most genuine Being in the World. Shakespeare the paradise Lost every day become greater wonders to me. I look upon fine Phrases like a Lover [L. 142].

As can be seen, Keats went to great lengths to develop a concept of beauty which, among other things, would allow him to deal with the abstraction rather than the person in an attempt to cope with the threat of loss, thus rendering immortality more certain. This struggle is best expressed in the opening lines of *Endymion:*

A thing of beauty is a joy for ever:
Its loveliness increases; it will never
Pass into nothingness; but still will keep
A bower quiet for us, and a sleep
Full of sweet dreams, and health, and quiet breathing.

And in the closing lines of "Ode on a Grecian Urn," he wrote:

'Beauty is truth, truth beauty',—That is all
Ye know on earth, and all ye need to know.

Through sleep and dreaming Keats was able to regress and to fuse with the lost object, the introject, which upon awakening he must abandon (Krupp, 1962). An attempt to compensate for this separation is made by externalizing the dream in the writing of poetry (Barron, 1963). However, Keats was seldom satisfied with his poems and indeed wrote a savage criticism of *Endymion,* as his brother, Tom, was dying. At this time, he declared, "I am sometimes so very sceptical as to think Poetry itself a mere Jack-a-Lantern to amuse whoever may chance to be struck with its brilliance" (L. 53). Here the problem becomes one of failure to re-create in actuality, to make total restitution of the lost object and to submit to a temporary loss or partial decathexis of the introject after completing a given work, which places him in a position of having to reincorporate and continually to try and gain further mastery, to work through the problem via his writing. This in turn accounts for such a prolific output in such a short time span. In a letter to John Reynolds he once stated:

> The difference of high Sensations with and without knowledge appears to me this—in the latter case we are falling continually ten thousand fathoms deep and being blown up again without wings and with all (the) horror of a bare shouldered creature— in the former case, our shoulders are fledge, and we go thro' the same air and space without fear. This is running one's rigs on the score of abstracted benefit—when we come to human Life and the affections it is impossible (to know) how a parallel of breast and head can be drawn—(you will forgive me for thus privately treading out (of) my depth, and take it for treading as schoolboys tread the water)—It is impossible to know how far Knowledge will console us for the death of a friend and the ill "that flesh is heir to" [L. 64].

And in the poem "On Sitting Down to Read King Lear Once Again" he wrote:

> O golden tongued Romance, with serene lute!
>   Fair plumed Syren, Queen of far-away!
>   Leave melodizing on this wintry day,
> Shut up thine olden pages, and be mute:
> Adieu! for, once again, the fierce dispute
>   Betwixt damnation and impassion'd clay
>   Must I burn through: once more humbly assay
> The bitter-sweet of this Shakespearian fruit:
> Chief Poet! and ye clouds of Albion,
>   Begetters of our deep eternal theme!
> When through the old oak Forest I am gone,
>   Let me not wander in a barren dream,
> But, when I am consumed in the fire
> Give me new Phoenix wings to fly at my desire.

THE QUEST FOR IDENTITY

To put it another way, the conflict over fusion and separation-individuation was a crucial one for Keats, with its implications of ill-defined ego boundaries, and difficulties in distinguishing dream from reality. He used the term "identity" a great deal, at times almost in Erikson's (1956) sense of the word. In a letter to John Reynolds, Keats wrote:

I compare human life to a large Mansion of Many Apartments, two of which I can only describe, the doors of the rest being as yet shut upon me. The first we step into we call the infant or thoughtless Chamber, in which we remain as long as we do not think—We remain there a long while, and notwithstanding the doors of the second Chamber remain wide open, showing a bright appearance, we care not to hasten to it; but are at length imperceptibly impelled by the awakening of this thinking principle within us—we no sooner get into the second Chamber, which I shall call the Chamber of Maiden-Thought, than we become intoxicated with the light and the atmosphere, we see nothing but pleasant wonders, and think of delaying there for ever in delight: However among the effects this breathing is father of is that tremendous one of sharpening one's vision into the heart and nature of Man—of convincing one's nerves that the world is full of Misery and Heartbreak, Pain, Sickness and oppression—whereby this Chamber of Maiden Thought becomes gradually darken'd and at the same time on all sides of it many doors are set open—but all dark—all leading to dark passages—We see not the balance of good and evil. We are in a Mist. *We* are now in that state—We feel the "burden of the Mystery" [L. 64].

Here he describes the passive, dependent position of intrauterine and early infant development and the uncertainty related to separation from the mother, "We are in a Mist."

Similar feelings are expressed in still other letters:

As to the poetical Character itself (I mean that sort of which, if I am any thing, I am a Member; that sort distinguished from the wordsworthian or egotistical sublime; which is a thing per se and stands alone) it is not itself—it has no self—it is every thing and nothing—It has no character—it enjoys light and shade; it lives in gusto, be it foul or fair, high or low, rich or poor, mean or elevated—It has as much delight in conceiving an Iago as an Imogen. What shocks the virtuous philosopher, delights the camelion Poet. It does no harm from its relish of the dark side of things any more than from its taste for the bright one; because they both end in speculation. A Poet is the most unpoetical of any thing in existence; because he has no Identity —he is continually in for—and filling some other Body—The Sun, the Moon, the Sea and Men and Women who are creatures of impulse are poetical and have about them an unchangeable attribute—the poet has none; no identity—he is certainly the most unpoetical of all God's Creatures. If then he has no self, and if I am a Poet, where is the Wonder that I should say I would write no more? Might I not at that very instant have been cogitating on the Characters of Saturn and Ops? It is a wretched thing to confess; but is a very fact that not one word I ever utter can be taken for granted as an opinion growing out of my identical nature—how can it, when I have no nature? When I am in a room with People if I ever am free from speculating on creations of my own brain, then not myself goes home to myself: but the identity of every one in the room begins so to press upon me that I am in a very little time an(ni)hilated—not only among Men; it would be the same in a Nursery of children: I know not whether I make myself wholly understood: I hope enough so to let you see that no dependence is to be placed on what I said that day.

In the second place I will speak of my views, and of the life I purpose to myself. I am ambitious of doing the world some good: if I should be spared that may be the work of maturer years—in the interval I will assay to reach to as high a summit in Poetry as the nerve bestowed upon me will suffer. The faint conceptions I have of Poems to come brings the blood frequently into my forehead. All I hope is that I may not lose all interest in human affairs—that the solitary indifference I feel for applause even from the finest Spirits, will not blunt any acuteness of vision I may have. I do not think it will—I feel assured I should write from the mere yearning and fondness I have for the Beautiful even if my night's labours should be burnt every morning, and no eye ever shine upon them. But even now I am perhaps not speaking from myself: but from some character in whose soul I now live. I am sure however, that this next sentence is from myself. I feel your anxiety, good opinion and friendliness in the highest degree [L. 93].

Do you not see how necessary a World of Pains and troubles

is to school an Intelligence and make it a Soul? A Place where the heart must feel and suffer in a thousand diverse ways. Not merely is the Heart a Hornbook, It is the Minds Bible, it is the Minds experience, it is the teat from which the Mind or intelligence sucks its identity" [L. 123].

In *Hyperion* Keats writes:

'. . . I am gone
'Away from my own bosom: I have left
'My strong identity, my real self [Book I, lines 122-124].

As Keats's literary career developed, particularly as he became critically accepted and began to make ego-syntonic identifications with Byron, Milton, Shakespeare, and Burns, his own sense of self-identity became more firmly consolidated and he was able partially to work through the mourning process. However, this task was tragically interrupted in February, 1820 when he became aware that he had tuberculosis and that his own death was imminent.

There is a strong suggestion of regressive fusion in his Epitaph "Here lies one whose name was writ in water," plus the fact that he requested that his name not be inscribed on his tombstone. At the time when Keats read Chapman's Homer with Cowden Clarke, he shouted with delight when he came upon the last line in the passage describing the shipwrecked Ulysses struggling to get ashore,

. . . both knees falt'ring, both
His strong hands hanging down, and all with froth
His cheeks and nostrils flowing, voice and breath
Spent to all use, and down he sank to death
The sea had soak'd his heart through.

As mentioned previously, the sea as a maternal symbol appeared frequently in Keats's poems (Ward, 1963). Clinical experience has shown that depression does render one more vulnerable to such illnesses as tuberculosis—George Keats himself died in 1841 of tuberculosis which manifested itself only after he had become depressed following a business failure which threatened him with bankruptcy. It is interesting to note the interrelationship of early object loss, depression, a love of the sea and travel, respiratory infections, and creative writing in the lives of Conrad, Maugham, O'Neill, and Thomas Wolfe (Meyer, 1964; Pfeiffer, 1952; Weissman, 1957; Nowell, 1960).

While he displayed a strong wish for intimacy with a woman throughout his life, Keats was at the same time fearful of the implications of such a relationship, and found it very difficult to develop a basic trust in such situations. In a letter to Benjamin Bailey he wrote: "When among men I have no evil thoughts, no malice, no spleen—I feel free to speak or to be silent—I can listen and from every one I can learn—My hands are in my pockets I am free from all suspicion and comfortable. When I am among Women I have evil thoughts, malice spleen—I cannot speak or be silent— I am full of Suspicions and therefore listen to nothing—I am in a hurry to be gone—You must be charitable and put all this perversity to my being disappointed since Boyhood" (L. 79). Barron (1963) has postulated that female inconstancy "may well be a spur of central significance to artistic creativity."

DREAMING AND CREATIVITY

The role of dreams in certain areas of creativity other than literature has been an integral and well-established one. Kekulé conceived of the Benzene ring after having had a dream wherein atoms turned to snakes which formed a ring by swallowing each other's tails (De Becker, 1968). Einstein formulated the theory of relativity after he visualized $E = MC^2$ in a dream (Lindon, 1966). Descartes felt dream material was crucial to his scientific thinking, although there is some question as to whether his dreams preceded or followed his discoveries (Schönberger, 1939; Lewin, 1958). Otto Loewi (1960) came upon the proof of the role of acetylcholine in the chemical mediation of nerve impulses in a dream, which he forgot upon awakening in the morning, but fortunately repeated the next night with total recall. In attempting to discover the theory of Fuchsian groups and functions, the French mathematician Poincaré (1913) had pored over the problem for fifteen days trying to prove that no such functions existed. He then experienced a sleepless night during which "ideas rose in crowds; I felt them collide until pairs interlocked, so to speak, making a stable construction." The next day as he boarded a bus, the solution came to him when he put his foot on the first step. Giovacchini (1966) has reported a case where dreams taken in the context of transference played an important part in scientific creativity. Paul Marco, a contemporary sculptor, claims that "most of the ideas for statues to make come to me in the middle of the night. That is when fantasies are running best" (Folsom, 1966). Within the field of literature, Robert Louis Stevenson attributed his inspiration to the "Little People or Brownies" who appeared in his dreams and presented complete tales to him (Kanzer, 1951). Eugene O'Neill, who experienced considerable early maternal deprivation, would dream entire scenes of his plays (Weissman, 1957). Many of the poems of Conrad Aiken and several of his short stories, most notably, "Bring! Bring!" and "Mr. Arcularis," were derived from dreams (personal communication) and Aiken, like Keats, lost both parents during childhood (Aiken, 1952).

In attempting to link object loss, dreaming, and creativity, no personal example is more significant than that of Freud. In the preface to the second edition (1908) of *The Interpretation of Dreams* (1900) he wrote: "For this book has a further subjective significance for me personally—a significance which I only grasped after I had completed it. It was, I found, a portion of my own self-analysis, my reaction to my father's death—that is to say, to the most important event, the most poignant loss, of a man's life. Having discovered that this was so, I felt unable to obliterate the traces of the experience." Both Freud and Keats were prolific letter writers and Freud's correspondence with Fliess (1950) was a crucial part of his self-analysis.

Dreams do not lend themselves readily to secondary process forms of expression or elaboration and are easily repressed or forgotten. Schachtel (1959) feels that the forgetting of dreams is a result of the incompatibility of primary and secondary processes. Both the dream and the poem have a manifest and latent content, and the ambiguity and multiple imagery of the former may be more readily conveyed by the latter than by other forms of creative expression. I have described the case of an adolescent girl who used poetry in an attempt to resolve a conflict in sexual identity (1968). The patient had written a particular poem which on the manifest level compared the automobile unfavorably with the horse. However, the latent content revealed that she was contrasting the horse, which represented unattainable phallic strivings, with her debased, feminine self representation, "auto" being used as a switchboard to denote both "car" and "self." Muratori (1774), an eighteenth-century scholar, once composed a Latin poem, a pentameter, in a dream and felt afterward that it could not have been written during waking hours other than by using extremely complicated metric technique.

In a recent attempt to correlate visual imagery with cognitive organization, Horowitz (1967) offers some interesting hypotheses:

> Freud and Rapaport have described a hypothetical state of infantile hallucination as one of the earliest forms of mentation. In this inferred state the infant experiences increasing hunger tension, and recalls the mnemic impression associated with previous satiation of such needs with hallucinatory vividness. Such hallucinations are not yet subject to reality testing and provide sufficient partial gratification to temporarily reduce the pressures of internal need stimuli and enhance the ability to tolerate delay.
>
> Following this, as the infant gains in sensory discrimination and motility, hallucinations are thought to be inhibited as the infant learns to differentiate what is real from what is only internal mental activity. During this preverbal stage of development, cognition proceeds in terms of memories of sensory impressions. Even later, when word representations have been achieved, gaps in conceptual ability are probably expressed cognitively in the form of imagery.
>
> Thinking in imagery and particularly thinking pictorially would, therefore, be regarded as an earlier cognitive system than thinking in word representations. In later life it would reemerge under certain circumstances, e.g., dreams and fantasy thinking, be preserved as a cognitive style in certain persons, but generally be suppressed in favor of thinking in word representations.
>
> The very fact of its reemergence and the occasional simultaneous occurrence of thought moving temporally in both word and picture "tracks" suggests, however, that it is retained as a definable system. That is, instead of viewing thought as a unitary process using different kinds of "bits" or monads we would regard it as a process that can activate or suppress multiple cognitive systems, each with its own characteristics and utility.
>
> Each system, also, would have its own circuitry or physiologic substrate and various neurophysiologic states might alter the propensities of usage of the various systems. This would be similar operationally to motor reflexes: primitive muscle reflexes reappear after cerebral trauma alters inhibition and affects opera-

tion of later and more elaborate systems. Just as differing persons vary in their style of perception, individuals also vary in their "style of consciousness"—and this would have to do with variations in the patterns of usage of various cognitive systems [p. 945].

Further Metapsychological Considerations Regarding the Creative Process

Before closing, I would like to add some comments about Keats's small stature, which may have been a determinant of his creativity. Throughout his life, Keats was acutely aware of and sensitive about his lack of height; Niederland (1967) has shown clinically that physical malformations, among which he includes shortness, lead to specific ego defects, the narcissistic repair of which may be attempted in the creative act.

Greenacre's contributions (1963) about the childhood of the artist and the collective alternates are extremely relevant. She states:

The readiness for contact with, and the capacity for using, the collective alternates tend then to permit a less decisive closing of the successive libidinal phases of early childhood than might otherwise be true. One result of this intrinsic state of affairs may be a diminished firmness of the barrier between primary-process and secondary-process thinking and imagery, a condition which seems characteristic of gifted individuals.

It is a psychoanalytic truism that poets and other artists know well and travel readily the high road to the Unconscious. They seem naturally to know and to use the language of dreams. What the analyst must work patiently to decipher with his patient, the artist knows and expresses. Yet paradoxically he is often unaware that he knows, at least in personal ways, what he may have expressed with beautiful conciseness in universal or collective terms. If we think of the creative product being achieved in part through "a regression in the service of the ego"—to use the concept of Ernst Kris—we may well ask whether the tenuous character of the barrier between primary- and secondary-process thinking does not make regression extraordinarily easy in the creatively gifted person, and whether, indeed, he does not have so ready an access to primary-process thought, imagery, and relationships that his use of them is not truly a regression in the sense in which we ordinarily think of it. It seems rather that primary-process thought remains vitally present in the creative person, and is carried throughout life as part of the collective object relationships which do not have always to be sweepingly sacrificed to the personal. This continued access to states of early childhood may be the basis of the *innocence* of the artist, and his ability frequently to utilize the direct vision of the child [p. 15ff.].

In attempting to define the essential attributes of the creative person, Keats observed that "several things dovetailed in my mind, and at once it struck me what quality went to form a Man of Achievement especially in Literature and which Shakespeare possessed so enormously—I mean *Negative Capability,* that is when a man is capable of being in uncertainties, Mysteries, doubts, without any irritable reaching after fact and reason" (L. 32).

Expanding upon Greenacre's formulations, Weissman (1968) writes:

Put figuratively but schematically, the artist-to-be infant equipped with more than usual sensorial sensitivity had more intensely cathected an imagined (hallucinated) breast than he had ever cathected the real breast. To the advent of an increasing sense of reality he brings his established state of intense attachment to hallucinated objects and their representations. In adult life, he retains his relative indifference to real objects. It is this more unusual capacity to hypercathect imaginary objects which early in life characterizes the future creative person. . . . A stronger influence for the increased cathexis of hallucinated objects is derived from the given individual's greater than usual sensorial sensitivity to stimuli from objects." In his opinion, creative elaboration is predominantly in the service of the ego ideal and he concludes that "the creative state may be viewed as a transient hallucinatory or delusional psychosis without ego regression but reinforced and maintained by the coordinated activities of the dissociative and integrative functions of the ego."

Summary

The poetry of John Keats has been examined to determine if there is a meaningful connection between the early and repeated losses of essential people in his life, his failure to mourn adequately, and his creative output. It is a basic postulate of this paper that object loss leads to a regressive fusion with the lost object and that the dream becomes an integral part of this process having originally been utilized by the infant to cope with the loss of direct oral gratification from the mother during sleep. Recent developments in ego psychology have demonstrated that the working through of adolescent conflicts is essential before one can come to terms with the death of significant persons, especially parents. When his choice of medicine as a career became too conflictual, Keats resorted to poetry in an attempt to complete the mourning process and to make restitution for the lost object, most importantly his mother, by externalizing his dreams in the form of poems. Because of the intense ambivalence and hypercathexis of the introject, this method was only partially successful and, having to be repeated over and over again, led to one of the richest, most profuse creative efforts in all of literature.

In closing, the following remarks by Mircea Eliade (1967) seem appropriate:

All poetry is an effort to recreate the language; in other words, to abolish current language, that of every day, and to invent a new, private, and personal speech, in the last analysis secret. But poetic creation, like linguistic creation implies the abolition of time—of the history concentrated in language—and tends toward the recovery of the paradisiac, primordial situations; of the days when one could create spontaneously, when the past did not exist because there was no consciousness of time, no memory of temporal duration. It is said moreover in our own days that for a great poet the past does not exist: the poet discovers the world as though he were present at the cosmogenic moment, contemporaneous with the first day of the Creation. From a certain point of view we may say that every poet is remaking the world for he is trying to see it as if there were no Time and no History.

BIBLIOGRAPHY

Aiken, C. (1952), *Ushant.* Cleveland: Meridian.
Almansi, R. J. (1960), The Face-Breast Equation. *J. Amer. Psa. Assn.,* 8:43-70.
—— (1961), Cloud Fantasies. *J. Hillside Hosp.,* 10:143-153.
Barron, D. B. (1963), Endymion: The Quest for Beauty. *Amer. Imago,* 20:27-47.
Beres, D. (1961), A Dream, a Vision, and a Poem: A Psycho-Analytic Study of the Origins of the Rime of the Ancient Mariner. *Int. J. Psa.,* 32:97-116.

Bowlby, J. (1960), Grief and Mourning in Early Infancy and Childhood. *This Annual*, 15:9-52.
—— (1961a), Processes of Mourning. *Int. J. Psa.*, 42:317-340.
—— (1961b), Childhood Mourning and Its Implications for Psychiatry. *Amer. J. Psychiat.*, 118:481-498.
—— (1963), Pathological Mourning and Childhood Mourning. *J. Amer. Psa. Assn.*, 11:500-541.
DeBecker, R. (1968), *The Understanding of Dreams*. New York: Hawthorn, p. 84.
Eliade, M. (1967), *Myths, Dreams and Mysteries*. New York: Harper & Row.
Erikson, E. H. (1956), The Problem of Ego Identity. *J. Amer. Psa. Assn.*, 4:56-121.
Fenichel, O. (1945), *The Psychoanalytic Theory of Neurosis*. New York: Norton, p. 394.
Folsom, M. (1966), Junk Becomes Sculptor's Quarry. *New York Times*, March 5.
Forman, M. B., ed. (1931), *The Letters of John Keats*. London: Oxford University Press, 4th ed., 1952.
Freud, S. (1900), The Interpretation of Dreams. *Standard Edition*, 4 & 5. London: Hogarth Press, 1953.
—— (1950), *The Origins of Psychoanalysis: Letters, Drafts and Notes to Wilhelm Fliess (1887-1902)*. New York: Basic Books, 1954.
Furman, R. A. (1964), Death and the Young Child. *This Annual*, 19:321-333.
Garma, A. (1966), *The Psychoanalysis of Dreams*. New York: Delta.
Garrod, H. W. (1939), *The Poetical Works of John Keats*. London: Oxford University Press, 2nd ed., 1958.
Gifford, S. (1960), Sleep, Time and the Early Ego. *J. Amer. Psa. Assn.*, 8:5-42.
Giovacchini, P. (1966), Dreams and the Creative Process. *Brit. J. Med. Psychol.*, 39:105-115.
Gittings, R. (1968), *John Keats*. Boston: Atlantic-Little, Brown.
Greenacre, P. (1963), *The Quest for the Father*. New York. International Universities Press.
Hamilton, J. W. (1968), Gender Rejection as a Reaction to Early Sexual Trauma and Its Partial Expression in Verse. *Brit. J. Med. Psychol.*, 41:405-410.
Horowitz, M. (1967), Visual Imagery and Cognitive Organization. *Amer. J. Psychiat.*, 123:938-946.
Jacobson, E. (1965), The Return of the Lost Parent. In: *Drives, Affects, Behavior*, Vol 2, ed. M. Schur. New York: International Universities Press, pp. 193-211.
Kanzer, M. (1951), The Self-Analytic Literature of Robert Louis Stevenson. In: *Psychoanalysis and Culture*, ed. G. B. Wilbur & W. Muensterberger. New York: International Universities Press, pp. 425-435.
Kleitman, N. (1960), The Nature of Dreaming. In: CIBA Foundation Symposium, *The Nature of Sleep*. Boston: Little, Brown.
Kris, E. (1953), Psychoanalysis and the Study of Creative Imagination. *Bull. N.Y. Acad. Med.*, 29:334-351.
Krupp, G. R. (1962), The Bereavement Reaction: A Special Case of Separation Anxiety. *The Psychoanalytic Study of Society*, 2:42-74. New York: International Universities Press.
Lewin, B. D. (1946), Sleep, the Mouth and the Dream Screen. *Psa. Quart.*, 15:419-443.
—— (1958), *Dreams and the Uses of Regression*. New York: International Universities Press.
Lindon, J. (1966), On Freud's Concept of Dream Action. *Psa. Forum*, 1:32-43.
Loewi, O. (1960), An Autobiographic Sketch. *Perspectives in Biology and Medicine*, 4:3-25.
Marcovitz, E. (1964), Bemoaning the Lost Dream: Coleridge's 'Kubla Khan' and Addiction. *Int. J. Psa.*, 45:411-425.

Meyer, B. C. (1964), Psychoanalytic Studies on Joseph Conrad. *J. Amer. Psa. Assn.,* 12:32-58, 357-391, 562-586, 802-825.

Muratori, L. A. (1774), *Della Forza della Fantasia Amana.* Naples: Langiacomo.

Niederland, W. G. (1967), Clinical Aspects of Creativity. *Amer. Imago,* 24:6-34.

Nowell, E. (1960), *Thomas Wolfe.* New York: Doubleday.

Pederson-Krag, G. (1951a), "O Poesy! For Thee I Hold My Pen." In: *Psychoanalysis and Culture,* ed. G. B. Wilbur & W. Muensterberger. New York: International Universities Press, pp. 436-452.

—— (1951b), The Genesis of a Sonnet. *Psychoanalysis and the Social Sciences,* 3:263-276. New York: International Universities Press.

Pfeiffer, K. G. (1952), *W. Somerset Maugham: A Candid Portrait.* New York: Norton.

Poincaré, H. (1913), Mathematical Creation. In: *Foundations of Science.* Lancaster: Science Press, 1946, pp. 383-394.

Prince, M. (1914), *The Unconscious.* New York: Macmillan.

Schachtel, E. G. (1959), *Metamorphosis.* New York: Basic Books.

Schafer, R. (1968), *Aspects of Internalization.* New York: International Universities Press.

Schönberger, S. (1939), A Dream of Descartes: Reflections on the Unconscious Determinants of the Sciences. *Int. J. Psa.,* 20:43-57.

Segal, H. (1952), A Psycho-Analytical Approach to Aesthetics. *Int. J. Psa.,* 33:196-207.

Spender, S. (1962), *The Making of a Poem.* New York: Norton.

Sterba, R. F. (1948), On Hallowe'en. *Amer. Imago,* 5:213-224.

Strachey, J. (1930), Some Unconscious Factors in Reading. *Int. J. Psa.,* 11:322-331.

Ward, A. (1963), *John Keats: The Making of a Poet.* New York: Viking.

Weissman, P. (1957), Conscious and Unconscious Autobiographical Dramas of Eugene O'Neill. *J. Amer. Psa. Assn.,* 5:432-460.

—— (1968), On Creative Fantasies and Beyond the Reality Principle. Presented at the Annual Meeting of the American Psychoanalytic Association, Boston.

Whitman, R. M. (1963), Remembering and Forgetting Dreams in Psychoanalysis. *J. Amer. Psa. Assn.,* 11:752-774.

—— et al. (1967), The Physiology, Psychology and Utilization of Dreams. *Amer. J. Psychiat.,* 124:287-302.

Wolfenstein, M. (1966), How Is Mourning Possible? *This Annual,* 21:93-123.

CONTENTS OF VOLUMES I–XXIII

CROCKER, D.
The Study of a Problem of Aggression (1955) *10*:300–335

DANN, S., *see* FREUD & DANN (1951)
DAUNTON, E., *see* SANDLER, DAUNTON, &
SCHNURMANN (1957)
DAVISON, C., *see* E. KRIS (1954)
DAWES, L. G., *see* LINDEMANN & DAWES (1952)
DE SAUSSURE, R.
J. B. Felix Descuret (1946) 2:417–424
DEMAREST, E. W. & WINESTINE, M. C.
The Initial Phase of Concomitant Treatment of Twins (1955) *10*:336–352
DESPERT, J. L.
Dreams in Children of Preschool Age (1949) *3/4*:141–180
DWYER, T. F., *see* BIBRING, DWYER, HUNTINGTON,
& VALENSTEIN (1961)

EDWARDS, M.
Libidinal Phases in the Analytic Treatment of a Preschool
Child (1967) 22:199–215
EISSLER, K. R.
Ego-psychological Implications of the Psychoanalytic Treat-
ment of Delinquents (1950) *5*:97–121
Notes upon the Emotionality of a Schizophrenic Patient and
Its Relation to Problems of Technique (1953) *8*:199–251
An Unusual Function of an Amnesia (1955) *10*:75–82
Notes on Problems of Technique in the Psychoanalytic Treat-
ment of Adolescents: With Some Remarks on Perversions
(1958) *13*:223–254
On Isolation (1959) *14*:29–60
Notes on the Environment of a Genius (1959) *14*:267–313
On the Metapsychology of the Preconscious: A Tentative Con-
tribution to Psychoanalytic Morphology (1962) *17*:9–41
Notes on the Psychoanalytic Concept of Cure (1963) *18*:424–463
A Note on Trauma, Dream, Anxiety, and Schizophrenia (1966) *21*:17–50
The Relation of Explaining and Understanding in Psycho-
analysis: Demonstrated by One Aspect of Freud's Approach
to Literature (1968) *23*:141–177
EISSLER, R. S.
Riots: Observations in a Home for Delinquent Girls (1949) *3/4*:449–460
EKSTEIN, R.
Puppet Play of a Psychotic Adolescent Girl in the Psychothera-
peutic Process (1965) *20*:441–480
———— & FRIEDMAN, S.
Object Constancy and Psychotic Reconstruction (1967) 22:357–374
———— & WALLERSTEIN, J.
Observations on the Psychology of Borderline and Psychotic
Children: Report from a Current Psychotherapy Research
Project at Southard School (1954) *9*:344–369

WALLACH, H. D.
Termination of Treatment as a Loss (1961)   *16*:538–548
WALLERSTEIN, J., *see* EKSTEIN & WALLERSTEIN (1954, 1956), EKSTEIN, WALLERSTEIN, & MANDELBAUM (1959)
WALLERSTEIN, R., *see* RAMZY & WALLERSTEIN (1958)
WANGH, M.
The "Evocation of a Proxy": A Psychological Maneuver, Its Use as a Defense, Its Purposes and Genesis (1962)   *17*:451–469
WEIL, A. P.
Certain Severe Disturbances of Ego Development in Childhood (1953)   *8*:271–287
Some Evidences of Deviational Development in Infancy and Early Childhood (1956)   *11*:292–299
See also ALPERT, NEUBAUER, & WEIL (1956)
WEILAND, I. H. & RUDNIK, R.
Considerations of the Development and Treatment of Autistic Childhood Psychosis (1961)   *16*:549–563
WEISSMAN, P.
The Childhood and Legacy of Stanislavski (1957)   *12*:399–417
Shaw's Childhood and *Pygmalion* (1958)   *13*:541–561
WERMER, H. & LEVIN, S.
Masturbation Fantasies: Their Changes with Growth and Development (1967)   *22*:315–328
WHIPPLE, B., *see* JESSNER, LAMONT, LONG, ROLLINS, WHIPPLE, & PRENTICE (1955)
WIEDER, H.
Intellectuality: Aspects of Its Development from the Analysis of a Precocious Four-and-a-half-year-old Boy (1966)   *21*:294–323
WILKIN, L. C., *see* JACKSON, KLATSKIN, & WILKIN (1952)
WILLER, M. L., *see* COOLIDGE, TESSMAN, WALDFOGEL, & WILLER (1962)
WILLS, D. M.
Some Observations on Blind Nursery School Children's Understanding of Their World (1965)   *20*:344–364
WINESTINE, M. C., *see* DEMAREST & WINESTINE (1955)
WINNICOTT, D. W., *see* STEVENSON (1954)
WOLF, K. M.
Evacuation of Children in Wartime: A Survey of the Literature with Bibliography (1945)   *1*:389–404
Edouard Pichon: *Le Développement de l'Enfant et de l'Adolescent* (1945)   *1*:417–423
See also SPITZ & WOLF (1946, 1949)
WOLFENSTEIN, M.
Some Variants in Moral Training of Children (1950)   *5*:310–328
A Phase in the Development of Children's Sense of Humor (1951)   *6*:336–350
Children's Understanding of Jokes (1953)   *8*:162–173
Mad Laughter in a Six-year-old Boy (1955)   *10*:381–394